The Law of Evidence
in Ireland

Second Edition

To Alan, for being there, and Mum and Dad, always.

The Law of Evidence in Ireland

Second Edition

by

Caroline Fennell

BCL (NUI), LLM (Osgoode), PhD (Wales), BL
Professor of Law, University College Cork
Consultant on the Law of Evidence with the Law Society of Ireland
Examiner in Evidence, Entrance Exam, Hon. Society of the King's Inns

LexisNexis™
Butterworths

Members of the LexisNexis Group worldwide:

Ireland	Lexis Nexis, DUBLIN
Argentina	LexisNexis Argentina, BUENOS AIRES
Australia	LexisNexis Butterworths, CHATSWOOD, New South Wales
Austria	LexisNexis Verlag ARD Orac GmbH & Co KG, VIENNA
Canada	LexisNexis Butterworths, MARKHAM, Ontario
Chile	LexisNexis Chile Ltda, SANTIAGO DE CHILE
Czech Republic	Nakladatelství Orac sro, PRAGUE
France	Editions du Juris-Classeur SA, PARIS
Germany	LexisNexis, Deutschland GmbH, FRANKFURT, MUNSTER
Hong Kong	LexisNexis Butterworths, HONG KONG
Hungary	HVG-Orac, BUDAPEST
India	LexisNexis Butterworths, NEW DELHI
Italy	Giuffrè Editore, MILAN
Malaysia	Malayan Law Journal Sdn Bhd, KUALA LUMPUR
New Zealand	LexisNexis Butterworths, WELLINGTON
Poland	Wydawnictwo Prawnicze LexisNexis, WARSAW
Singapore	LexisNexis Butterworths, SINGAPORE
South Africa	LexisNexis Butterworths, DURBAN
Switzerland	Stämpfli Verlag AG, BERNE
United Kingdom	LexisNexis UK, a Division of Reed Elsevier (UK) Ltd, Halsbury House, 35 Chancery Lane, LONDON, WC2A 1EL, and 4 Hill Street, EDINBURGH EH2 3JZ
USA	LexisNexis, DAYTON, Ohio

© Butterworths Ireland Ltd (2003)

A CIP Catalogue record for this book is available from the British Library.

First edition 1992

ISBN 1 85475 8365

ISBN 1-85475-836-5

9 781854 758361 >

Typeset by Marlex Editorial Services Ltd, Dublin
Printed and bound by Hobbs the Printers Ltd, Totton, Hampshire
Visit us at our website: http//www.lexisnexis.ie

Preface

A feature of this text is the inclusion of that part of evidentiary law which might often be ignored – the 'extraordinary' or 'temporary' – not because it fails to impact on citizens, because patently it does, but because its aberrational quality is thought to exclude it from any normative consideration. To include such exceptional provision in a review of the rules of evidence, therefore, may be seen as an exercise in excessive overcompensation. It is, however, my belief that such a focus reveals something fundamental about the nature of our justice system. In Ireland exceptional provision for terrorism has preceded further subsequent nomination of other such necessities in the field of drugs/organised crime and sexual offences. All of these accused are uniformly and similarly despised, the public and 'community' acquiescence ensured by media response to 'moral panics' and 'crises'. The demonisation of such accused is effective in facilitating diminution of said accused's rights, as identification with community and victim secures an effective counter-balancing of rights in favour of the state in the nominated areas. This pattern is also reflected in transnational co-operation in criminal law, perhaps at its zenith in Europe, with similar criminality being targeted, and equal diminution of traditional rights, most recently manifest in the European Award Warrant which will come into force in January 2004.

Ireland and Europe share constitutional commitments to rights, which yet seem to have left this flow of procedural change unabated. Moreover, in sanctioning such change in context, the judiciary has instigated the inevitable progression of 'extraordinary' powers to the generality of criminal law. This is evident not only in the proliferation of exceptions, seen to facilitate a government law and order agenda, but more disquietingly in the field of rights analysis, where judicial sensitivity to state need and accommodation of change, means mutation of what is already guaranteed. Hence exceptional provision in the criminal process literally becomes the norm to effect a 'recalibration of the scales of justice'. Sequential extraordinary or exceptional provision, has resulted in a re-identification of standpoints in the criminal process, to the detriment of constructions of *'fairness'* to the accused. The alienation of community from accused initiates a process of rights abrogation, which is ultimately not restricted to some, but ironically, meted out to all. Democratically, these changes ignore the fact that, as Tyler has advised in his book *Why People Obey the Law,* that "[c]itizens seem to care a great deal about issues of fairness…Within the realm of fairness, procedural fairness seems the key issue, especially in judgments of legitimacy."[1]

Finally, however, it must be stated that the inclusion of exceptional provision in the narrative of the ordinary in this text, demonstrates not just that extent to which that extraordinary has become the norm; nor the degree to which its methodology is based on an alienation between community/public interest (us) and accused (them), but manifests a refusal on my own part to 'live within the lines', which Lacey describes thus:

> 'The draw consists in law's promise of order, of security and of identity for those who are both eligible for and willing to accept membership of its community – those who know where to draw the line. Its hidden face is its power to silence and exclude those who insist on reading between its lines or who live on the wrong side of the tracks, while effecting the discursive alchemy of nonetheless including them in the universal reach of legal subjectivity.'[2]

As ever, I am grateful to University College Cork's law students, in particular, for their indulgence of that view, and for their insightful companionship in examining the rules of evidence, reading between the lines, and exploring that particular brand of contradiction and exception, so very much a feature of the Irish law of evidence.

Caroline Fennell

August 2003

---

[1]   TR Tyler *Why Do People Obey the Law* (1990) Yale University Press, New Haven & London, p 81.

[2]   N Lacey *Unspeakable subjects – Feminist essays in legal and social theory* Hart Oxford (1998), p 125

Contents

Chapter 4   Illegally Obtained Evidence

Chapter 5   Witness System: Competence and Compellability

Chapter 6   Witness System: Corroboration

Chapter 7   Opinion Evidence

Chapter 8   Privilege

Chapter 9   The Rule Against Hearsay

Chapter 10 Similar Fact Evidence

Chapter 11 Cross-Examination of the Accused

Chapter 12 Estoppel

Chapter 13 Discovery

Table of Cases

D

E

R

Table of Statutes

Constitution of Ireland

United Kingdom

Introduction

'There was a moment when I didn't have the answer, and then there was a moment when I did. I can't say I did anything to make this happen. I didn't work anything out. I kept picking up pieces of the puzzle, I kept turning them this way and that, and all of a sudden I had the whole puzzle, with one piece after another locking effortlessly and infallibly into place. They were so obvious I felt as though I were discovering something I had known all along'.

Block *When the Sacred Ginmill Closes* (1986)

This text is divided into two: a general part and a specific part. The general part forms a foundation for subsequent review of the individual rules which comprise in the main the rules of evidence operating in Ireland. The purpose of the general part is twofold: to elevate the rules of evidence from a rather dry limited enunciation of their precepts into a context which illustrates their strength and power; and secondly, to imbue in the reader a sense of their history and possible future. More than any other area, that of adjectival law – in cutting across and through the substantive areas of law and in structuring fact finding and adjudications therein – tells us much about and is itself much informed by human nature. Fact finding, decision making, distillation of assumption, are what lie at the heart of the rules of evidence. Their development, growth and application is inevitably influenced by our views of others and of ourselves. It is culturally and traditionally contingent in a manner that is somewhat underappreciated.

The law of evidence has the power to influence our maintenance of values — in the intersection of human and individual rights for instance — and facilitate our response to crisis events. Very often it fails us only if we do not appreciate how it is very much comprised of parts of a whole and that some of its parts cannot be tinkered with in isolation, as it is a product of, and reflective of, the type of society – and justice – we offer now and in the future. Part 1 attempts to remind us of that context in reviewing the whole of the system, not simply its constituent parts.

Part 2, while examining the detail of those parts, remains conscious of the rules underlying the rationale.

Part One
General Part

Chapter 1

Rules of Evidence: Fact Finding, Determinations and Application

The role of popular culture

[1.01] Cultural nuances dictate how we assess the information before us. Courts have always been sensitive to that fact. The rules of evidence contain many examples of this and indeed in the past have been characterised as rooted in the need to control the jury. Of course cultural nuances change over time and if fossilised in law certain rules relating to fact determination or credibility can be found then to contain the vestiges of another age, ill-suited to the current climate.

[1.02] Corroboration rules provide a good example of this. In several jurisdictions these have been subject to change both as to the need for a warning at all (Canada in the case of accomplices) and its required application in certain cases (Ireland in relation to sexual offence victims and children). Wigmore's suggestion that every sexual offence complainant should be subjected to psychiatric examination before being allowed to testify seems extraordinary to-day as do those general assumptions regarding the veracity of women in rape cases or the supposed hierarchy of trustworthiness between different types of sex offence victims.[1] Nonetheless a continuing theme is the distillation of assumptions regarding veracity into law, there then being brought to bear on assessments of credibility and fact-finding, either on the basis of preventing dangerous assumptions by jurors, or in order to mitigate societal or cultural norms regarding certain offences or victims. Once solidified, they become part of legal culture, and can be correspondingly difficult to uproot, even in face of legislative reform.

[1.03] One avenue of pursuit is whether any particular bias or thread is to be found throughout these rules, or if indeed such a theme varies over time to introduce newer rules and eliminate others? A single or deeper pattern to the ways in which such evidentiary rules develop would have very different implications for inquiry than if they were the product of the vagaries of popular, and hence legislative and judicial sentiment, at the time – or a reaction to them.

---

[1] See further: Fennell, C 'Differential Treatment of Sexual Complaints by the Law of Evidence: A Case for Reform?' [1987] V51 XXII Irish Jurist 228.

[1.04] It is appropriate to locate the rules of evidence in the context of their application: the adjudicative process. As Jonakait[2] reminds us:

'Evidence law is only a small part of the much larger fact-determination system ...We need to be scholars of the fact-determination, not just of evidence. The accurate determination of facts is crucial to justice, and we need to explore all the possibilities that can affect that accuracy.'

Even more profoundly Nicolson[3] states:

'Adjudicative decisions are not, however, only about "what happened". They do not only rule on factual truth; they actually purvey truth. In a banal sense every decision is itself a truth in the sense that its outcome creates a truth for the parties: guilty/not guilty, responsible/not responsible, etc. Decisions and trials may also communicate a number of truths of a more overtly moral and political nature.'

It is that communication between trial and culture or society – and a corresponding one from society back to trial – that lies at the heart of an exploration of evidentiary rules.

The trial

[1.05] The adjunctive process which is the trial involves the roles of judges, jurors, and investigators (police) in (re)constructing the 'law story'. Hence legal adjudication within the criminal process carries within it the elements of individual or situational bias, inequity of bargaining power, inevitable error due to human fallibility and forensic inaccuracy, in the context of what is evidently the most powerfully symbolic and symptomatic procedure or event in the hegemony of the state. Nonetheless the system is demonstrably vulnerable to prevailing shifts in public opinion as to what factors or features of that system are the most valuable, or essential, to the manner in which we do justice.

[1.06] Language is, of course, a major consideration here, not only in terms of setting the tenor or context for change, but also more centrally and continually in the criminal process itself. Goodrich comments that:

'... irrespective of the aura of rationality and of specialism that surrounds legal hearings, they are best depicted not in terms of the law's own image, that of impartiality and the inexorable necessity of the application of pre-existent rules of statute and precedent, but rather in terms of the uneven exchange that characterises the flawed dialogue or 'distorted communication' of the most

---

2   Jonakait 'Making the Law of Factual Determinations Matter More' [1992] 25 Loyola of Los Angeles LR 673.
3   Nicolson and Donald 'Truth, Reason and Justice: Epistemology and Politics in Evidence Discourse' [1994] MLR 726.

contemporary bureaucratic discourses. What underpins and prolongs the unilateral monologue of most legal auditoria is not the exquisite precision of scientific expression but simple *political expedience and the linguistic manifestation of the vested interest of economically and sexually dominant social groups*[4]' [Emphasis added]

In this context, the jury is of course the most obvious conduit for the transference of popular nuance.

The role of the jury

[1.07]

'It is commonly suggested that lawyers use stories to organise evidence, but the actual presentation of evidence in trials does not conform easily to a coherent normative structure. Juries too will construct stories from the evidence and will test the plausibility of such stories by reference to common sense generalisations'.[5]

Two interesting factors identified by Jackson and Doran and relevant to our focus here are first, that the prevalent view among counsel that sexual cases are particularly difficult to defend before juries, and second that one of the reasons for having juries is their ability to channel 'community values' into the decision making process[6].

Arguing for the necessity of both judge and jury in fact finding, they conclude:

'In the absence of any perfect line of communication to "how it happened", triers of fact must play a part in bringing their own experiences, their own "evidence", to bear on the case.'[7]

[1.08] The use of a jury has, of course, been a major factor in the development of the rules of evidence. Garcia[8] advises closer scrutiny of the jury:

'The rules of evidence are a child of the jury system, yet we seldom focus on the issues of jury composition and jury selection in evidence courses. We should. We can. Selection strategies depend heavily on the particulars of a specific case, such as the nature of the charge, what the evidence shows, who the witnesses are, who

---

[4] Goodrich *Languages of Law – From Logics of Memory to Nomadic Masks*, Weidenfeld & Nicolson London (1990) pp 185–186.

[5] Jackson and Doran 'Judge and Jury: Towards a New Division of Labour in Criminal Trials' [1997] MLR 759 at 763.

[6] Jackson and Doran 'Judge and Jury: Towards a New Division of Labour in Criminal Trials' [1997] MLR 759 at 764-766.

[7] Jackson and Doran 'Judge and Jury: Towards a New Division of Labour in Criminal Trials' [1997] MLR 759 at 766.

[8] Garcia 'Rape, Lies and Videotape' [1992]25, Loyola of Los Angeles LR 711 at 736.

the defendant is, who the lawyers are, and who else is in the jury pool. It is not enough to read about empirical studies in the abstract. We should think about these issues in the context of a particular case.'

[1.09] The Rodney King trial[9] in the United States threw up the issue of jury selection of the jury, the locale of the trial being a central concern particularly with regard to race. A commentary in the Harvard Law Review argues for race to be made a consideration in the judge's determination of alternative venues. Although change of venue is a relative rarity, such a decision, it is suggested, would have an important symbolic value:

'Our society does not perfectly reflect the idea of a melting pot, and today more closely resembles a 'salad bowl'. Different geographical areas can produce widely different jury pools, with different experiences, different cultural knowledge, different sympathies and different beliefs. [It is important] to recognise that a change of venue can sometimes lead to a trial being held in a locale that differs markedly from the original community, and that such an outcome effects a deviation from principled notions at the heart of community involvement in the criminal process. The question, then, is not if we should explicitly recognise race in choosing a new venue. For if we are to remain true to the goals of impartial juries and community participation, the question is really how can we ignore it?'[10]

Jury composition issues in our own jurisdiction might include those situations where travellers may be tried by an all settled jury.

[1.10] Jackson and Doran[11] invoke the Diplock Court system to make the case that the roles of the judge and jury in the criminal justice system are not as simplistic or obvious as one might think. Moreover on the demerit side, both can suffer from a lack of diversity and a facility for prejudice. The Runciman Commission in England looked at the jury by means of a Jury Questionnaire[12]. What is remarkable is the extent to which jurors declared themselves satisfied with their ability to comprehend the material presented and the points of law. Such confidence in the ability of the jury is not, by contrast, found among those interviewed by the *Observer*,[13] amongst them leading barristers and criminologists who doubted the jury's ability and representativeness, which

---

[9]   *Powell v Superior Court* 283 Cal Rptr 777.

[10] 'Out of the Frying Pan or into the Fire? Race and Choice of Venue After Rodney King'. (1993) Vol 106 Harv LR 705 at 722.

[11] J Jackson and S Doran, 'Judge and Jury: Towards a New Division of Labour in Criminal Trials' (1997) 60 Modern LR 759.

[12] Zander and Henderson *The Royal Commission on Criminal Justice Crown Court Study Reseach Study No 19* (HMSO, 1993) London.

[13] The Observer, 20 October 1994.

ensured that certainly in fraud trials defendants were not tried by their peers. Jackson and Doran do make the suggestion that just as jurors may be skilled on credibility issues (what might be called 'gut instinct'), Judges may have the edge in emotionally charged cases (eg sexual offences), where the legal scales on the eyes of lawyers helps stop the high beam of politics and media discourses. Defence lawyers in these cases might well like the option of non-jury trial.

[1.11] The non-representativeness of juries is not a unique example of lack of diversity in law. The technique of storytelling has been invoked by some to challenge the orthodoxy and exclusion in law. The power of the law story is examined by Green et al:[14]

> 'A power of the law story is that it can translate other stories, including the stories of experts in other fields like psychiatry, paediatrics, criminology. The "law story" may therefore carry more weight than many other stories, not because it is intrinsically more valuable but rather because it has a special power, traditionally seen as the power to command backed by the supreme force of the state. Minow amongst others points out: "When judges interpret text somebody loses his freedom, his property, his children, even his life." However, law is not just a power to command. It can also be seen as the power to exclude, for the law sets its own boundaries, establishes what is to lie at the core and what beyond its margins.'

Later they comment:

> 'Thus law restricts, confines and places into hierarchy those who may speak the discourse, the texts of the discourse and the settings where legal discourse takes place. This power of exclusion may indirectly render invisible individuals and even whole communities, for the law places at its liberal centre the equal, disembodied individual and thereby robs human beings of much of themselves – sex, colour, religion, class, age ...'[15]

The role of the police

[1.12] The police themselves in the pre-trial process have impacted upon what is presented to (and further (mis)interpreted by) the courts, leading to miscarriage of justice. Zuckerman[16] comments:

> 'It is widely believed that the case presented by the police to the prosecutor and, through him to the court, consists purely of facts. Nothing could be further from the truth. The police case does not contain just raw objective facts. The police

---

[14] Green, K, Lim, H, Roche, J 'The Indeterminate Province: Storytelling in Legal Theory and Legal Education' (1994) 28 *Law Teacher* 138 at 148.

[15] Green, K, Lim, H, Roche J 'The Indeterminate Province: Storytelling in Legal Theory and Legal Education', (1994) 28 *Law Teacher* 138 at 142.

[16] Zuckerman 'Reducing Miscarriage of Justice' [1993] 44 NILQ 3 at 4.

construct and present an entire picture of reality which is interlaced with evaluative conclusions (such as the description of the conduct to fit a particular legal definition), with evidence created by the police in their interaction with the suspect (the confession), and is shaped by numerous decisions, mostly unrecorded and sometimes even unconscious, to pursue certain leads or hypotheses and drop others, to ask certain questions rather than others, and to look in some places but not in others.'

Reconstructing the law story

[1.13] Particular contexts can also influence the way in which decision making within the criminal legal process evolves and is undertaken. An interesting commentary in this regard is made by Patton, in so far as the implications of earlier decision making in child abuse scenarios can affect the later determinations in a way which remains unappreciated by the judiciary at the earlier stage. Patton notes the various ways in which the decision making process has been altered to attend to the micro-concerns in different contexts, and compares that unfavourably with the composite whole:

'Compare this series of separately rational evidentiary and procedural rulings to individual body parts waiting to be transplanted. Independently each appears normal, but when combined they create a horrible Frankensteinian creature. The resulting body of law does not at all resemble anything remotely similar to traditional notions of fairness.'[17]

[1.14] Patton's thesis is that we must pay attention to the multiplicity of hearings now emerging from any core issue, and consider the extent to which the variety of decision-making processes we now create therein merge:

'Since the number of fact patterns triggering multiple hearings in different courts is increasing, we must begin to develop new procedures and evidentiary theories to assure cumulative accuracy and fairness in all proceedings ... [E]vidence law still must play a vital role because a court's rulings can dramatically affect the strategy and results of subsequent jury trials based upon the identical facts.'

This is particularly important given the tendency recently to legislate for particular issues, to accommodate certain concerns, without an eye on the composite whole.

[1.15] This is not without direct relevance to the application, for example, in the Irish jurisdiction of the presumption of innocence in the context of applications for prohibition on the basis pre-trial publicity or delay. In *P O'C v DPP*[18] there

---

[17] Patton 'Evolution in Child Abuse Litigation: The Theoretical Void Where Evidentiary and Procedural Worlds Collide' [1992] 25 Loyola of Los Angeles LR 1009 at 1019.

[18] *P O'C v DPP* [2000] 3 IR 87. See ch 6 on corroboration.

were differences between Supreme Court Justices Murray and Denham regarding same. Denham J would not apply the presumption of innocence whereas Murray J was of the view that it was a fundamental right of the citizen.

[1.16] It is also important to appreciate the limitations of the effects of change when introduced – the notion that law can act, for example, as a vigorous feminist instrument. Althouse[19] debunks the rape shield rules making the point that at the level of interpretation and application a rule's purpose can be skewed:

> 'One cannot simply rely on the promise of the rule because a judge or jury that does not share the goals and beliefs embodied in the rule can drastically undercut its effect.'[20]

Generous interpretation of exceptions to the rape shield rules, particularly when coupled with expansive definitions of constitutional rights, Althouse contends, can substantially influence the impact of the rule:

> 'Thus if the judge thinks the evidence of past sexual behaviour has strong probative value, it becomes more likely that the right to confront the witness or the process right to present evidence will require its admission.'[21]

Althouse continues:

> 'Rape shield rules cannot simply outlaw this kind of decision-making. Nevertheless, they convey a strong message to judges that many persons who have considered the relevance of past sexual behaviour have reached the conclusion embodied in the rape shield rule. Knowing this, a judge may become more likely to agree and assign the evidence low probative value and consequently reject the constitutional claim. On the other hand, a judge still maintain independent doubt about that conclusion, particularly if he or she sees the statute as a mere political move, dismissive of the rights of the criminally accused and intended to appease a powerful group or to make a show of crime control. If so, the judge can interpret either the rule's exceptions or the defendant's constitutional rights to minimize the effect of its general ban on the use of evidence of sexual behaviour.'[22]

The point that is made by Althouse is of general significance: 'The way people think about the evidence they hear is more important than any rule.'[23]

---

[19] Althouse 'Thelma and Louise and the Law: Do Rape Shield Rules Matter?' [1992] 25 Loyola of Los Angeles LR 757.

[20] [1992] 25 Loyola of Los Angeles LR 757 at 764.

[21] [1992] 25 Loyola of Los Angeles LR 757 at 765.

[22] [1992] 25 Loyola of Los Angeles LR 757 765, 766.

[23] [1992] 25 Loyola of Los Angeles LR 757 at 768.

[1.17] Althouse finally poses the question as to whether the rape shield matters. She sees its importance as lying in its value as a 'cultural phenomenon'. It matters in her view as a film or a famous rape case might:

'It is a cultural phenomenon that shapes the minds of the judges and juries who decide the outcomes of trials. The rule represents an attempt to control the information a jury will hear and to rein in their tendencies to decide rape cases by judging the victim, but it cannot in one grand gesture change those tendencies. Judges who resist the conclusions that underlie the rule can find their way out from underneath even its strictly worded prescriptions. Juries who do not share the mindset of the rule's legislators can, even when the rule is used to bar evidence, find whatever way they can to judge the victim and not the defendant.'[24]

Althouse places faith, however, in the power of such a rule to influence judges and juries because of the weight of expertise and political opinion behind it. This process she acknowledges is '... disconcertingly slow and uncertain, particularly compared with the impressive (but deceptive) speed and clarity of a new rule.' However, she concludes that '[i]f their minds genuinely undergo this change, then the rule will finally have its intended effect.'

Media

[1.18] Much has been made of the interpretive role of judge or jury, or indeed legislator, yet the subtext of the crime debate is often ignored. Those who are involved in the decision making in the criminal process, most particularly the jury, are interpreting the tales told to them in accordance with a background and criteria imbued with popular images and the interpretations of the *media*. In this sense adjudication by one's peers also includes popular wisdom as to the nature and gravity of particular types of harm, as well as the credibility of particular victims, accused and witnesses. There is the symbiotic relation of fact, faction, fiction and the interconnectedness of *media tales* of real life, crime fiction and the audience response in home or trial.

[1.19] Sparks writing on television and the drama of crime comments:[25]

'The fictional narration of thematics of crime and law enforcement stands in a more oblique relation to the immediacy of current concerns than do news, documentary and polemic. This does not mean that they are any the less fundamental, however, only that the effort of translation between their manifest appearance and the underlying principles of their operation is more complicated and less clear-cut, and that it is unwise to foreclose the range of meanings which

---

[24] [1992] 25 Loyola of Los Angeles LR 757 at 772.
[25] R Sparks *Television and the Drama of Crime* (1992) Open University.

they may be taken to carry ... It may thus be that the expectation of narrative resolution in fiction frames the expectations which are brought to the reporting of real events. Equally, it may be that the audience turns to crime fiction precisely in consolation for the messy inconclusiveness of their process of justice in the world and its obdurate failure to conform to morally or aesthetically satisfying patterns.'

[1.20] In the Irish context, O'Mahony[26] points to the role of the media in distorting the discourse about crime in Ireland, given that the role of programmes such as 'Crimeline' is doubly powerful in such a small and media saturated country. Kerrigan and Shaw in an article on crime and the media suggested that:

'The real problem of crime, the real evidence of its origins and causes and of measures which have a chance of relieving the problem, are all buried and distorted by vested interests for whom crime is a useful phenomenon.'[27]

[1.21] Box[28] takes a cynical, if not sinister, view of the role of the public fear of crime much touted by media and politicians:

'It appears that public opinion is the last refuge for the politically bankrupt. Justifications which use an imaginary public opinion to support them usually have something to hide. At this instance it is not too hard to discover. In both the USA and the UK the recession has produced a growing number of economically marginalised people amongst whom ethnic minorities are over represented. While it would be impossible for a government to justify "law and order" policies as attempts to defuse the threat posed by these "problem populations", it is easier to announce that public opinion demands that something be done now about the growing crime problem. The media can be safely left to fill in the script and provide the characters. In this unfolding drama, equations are easily made between unemployment, black and crime, thus justifying increased policing against the unemployed and the blacks as well as the imposition of stiffer sentences and the building of more prisons. But in making this response, government spokespersons hammer home the "crime" part of the equation and leave other state officials quietly to get on dealing with the other parts – the unemployed and the blacks.'[29]

[1.22] Chomsky is equally cynical and critical of the role of the media in contemporary politics:[30]

---

[26] P O'Mahony *Crime and Punishment in Ireland* (1993) Round Hall Press.
[27] Kerrigan and Shaw 'Crime Hysteria' (1985) *Magill* 18 April.
[28] S Box *Recession Crime and Punishment* (1987), Macmillan.
[29] S Box *Recession Crime and Punishment* (1987), Macmillan p 124.
[30] N Chomsky *Media Control, Open Fire Anthology* (1993) p 270.

'The compelling moral principle is that the mass of the public are just too stupid to understand things. If they try to participate in managing their own affairs, they're just going to cause trouble. Therefore it would be immoral and improper to permit them to do this ... So we need something to tame the bewildered herd, and that something in this new revolution in the art of democracy: the manufacture of consent. The political class and decision makers have to provide some tolerable sense of reality, although they also have to instill the proper beliefs.'

Chomsky later comments:[31] 'Propaganda is to a democracy what the bludgeon is to a totalitarian state.' In the Irish context (coinciding with the reportage on the 'drugs crisis') Farrel Corcoran, writing in the *Irish Times*, drew some broad concerns for the Irish situation from looking at the Italian media. Making the point that all media are (sic) about the making of public meanings, Corcoran comments:[32]

'The media intimately affect our thoughts and actions because they have the power to decide what is important in the public sphere, to set the agenda, to light up certain events and keep others in darkness. They have the power to define the world in a particular way, to establish a partial (maybe even a bespoke) point of view as universal common sense, not to be questioned.

They may not tell us what to think but they control the crucial information with which we make up our minds about the world, influencing what we think about and what we think with.

This is not to say that people are in any simple way manipulated by the dominant voices structured into media texts. People do negotiate meaning and use for their own purposes the cultural materials made available to them by the media.

But it would be as mistaken to believe that reader interpretations are entirely random as it would be to believe that cultural texts are never used for manipulative purposes, just because the mechanisms and effects of ideological power are not immediately available to experience.

The notion of power is therefore crucial to any analysis of the press.'

[1.23] A useful analogy can be found in the realm of feminist critique of law. Susan Edwards in *Sex & Gender in the Legal Process*[33] draws on Lacan to make the point that at least in part, pornography precedes sexual relations and so communicates, largely to men, a particular meaning for sexual relations underpinned by the conflation of sex and violence and pleasure.

---

[31] Chomsky *Media Control, Open Fire Anthology* (1993) p 272.
[32] Corcoran, Irish Times, 26 July 1995.
[33] Edwards *Sex and Gender in the Legal Process* (1996) Blackstone Press.

[1.24] By similar means the media in its presentation of a criminal event or identity of a perpetrator of a particular crime fashions amongst its audience a particular identity for criminals and a knee-jerk response to that class. Hence priests (eg Father Brendan Smyth), nuns (Sr Xavier, Goldenbridge), rape victims (Lavinia Kerwick) bear a particular hallmark and evoke a ready response. Such news is literally 'worthy' to the papers – it sells, is plentiful, is cheap and it creates a prurience amongst the public which can be readily satiated by vast column inches of great detail on the latest trial with salacious overtones. Victims are so freed to go public (eg Kerwick) and we the public justify our intimate knowledge of their lives by reference to its horror. The Lavinia Kerwick incident arose out of her dissatisfaction with a suspended sentence handed down to William Conry (her former boyfriend), on 15 July 1992 on his pleading guilty to having raped her. Lavinia Kerwick became the first Irish rape victim to go public on the issue, thereby waiving her anonymity. The ensuing public debate centered on matters related to the trial and sentencing of sexual offenders generally.[34] The cycle is complete and intractable: the story is horrific so we publicise and justify reading it and in turn are horrified. The 'public interest' then is largely constructed by the media who lend further legitimacy to the subject – whether it be crime or pornography – its growing ubiquity thus bringing crime/pornography into mainstream popular culture. Since the public define crime or harm, that has consequences then for the framing of legislation. It is therefore no longer appropriate or possible to consider either crime or prostitution in isolation from the institutions which support it.

[1.25] Edwards[35] points out that in the 1990s a new approach opened up to constructing violence and abuse. Her claim is that in the wake of sexual liberalism, the comments made by the courts indicates that what otherwise would have been in the domain of the violent is now considered part of the sexual. Criminal issues are arguably similarly circumscribed.

[1.26] The problem lies in media influences and the 'schooling' of the public response. Consider the difficulty of establishing a case for the defence that has cultural meaning or significance in relation to battered women who kill, where, as Edwards remarks,[36] 'the nagging husband does not have the same cultural meaning', yet 'when building up the case for the defence the scene constructed must be one capable of convincing a jury of the congruence between social and legal accounts.'[37]

---

[34] See further: Kate Shanahan *Crimes Worse than Death* Attic Press, Dublin, 1992.
[35] Edwards *Sex and Gender in the Legal Process* (1996) Blackstone Press, ch 8.
[36] Edwards *Sex and Gender in the Legal Process* (1996) pp 398-399.
[37] Edwards *Sex and Gender in the Legal Process* (1996) p 400.

Changing societal needs

[1.27] In the same manner whereby the upswing in the number of sexual abuse/ offence cases leads to a belief in witnesses, which increases the number of successful prosecutions, the upsurge in organised crime leads to the use of devices such as the Witness Protection programme (WPP) and greater reliance on accomplice evidence. Miscarriages of justice can also lead to a change in attitude to confessions and an apparent greater concern for justice.

[1.28] In *The People v Ward*,[38] for example, rejection and disbelief of the police and confession at trial, combined with belief of the accomplice, and refusal to 'upgrade' that doubt regarding accomplices in the case of WPP participants – hence strengthening the credibility of 'ordinary' accomplices.

[1.29] Similar difficulties surely now exist for the defence of certain accuseds – the innocent paedophile priest, or the innocent date rapist? Ramsey's maxim[39] claims that:

'... where there is a prolonged and persistent dispute ..., it is often the case that the disputants ... are really in agreement about an assumption, hypothesis, premise, fundamental to their argument, which is false. They share a common but false premise[40]

... the truth lies not in one of the two disputed views but in some third possibility which has not yet been thought of, which we can only discover by rejecting something assumed as obvious by both the disputants. Both the disputed theories make an important assumption which to my mind, has only to be questioned to be doubted.'[41]

Both parties in a criminal trial currently assume an operative principle in the presumption of innocence and the burden of proof resting on the state. What if, at least in certain cases, that were a false premise?

[1.30] Foucault's discourse analysis allows us to identify and recognise the power of language and certain voices to distort a discussion:

'Truth is not outside power or lacking in power ... Each society has its regime of truth, its "general politics" of truth: that is the types of discourse which it accepts and makes function as true; the mechanisms and instances which enable one to distinguish true and false statements, the means by which each is sanctioned; the

---

[38] In *The People v Ward* (27 November 1998, unreported), SCC (Barr J).

[39] Invoked by Russel Christopher in the context of the Dadson principle in self defence. 'Unknowing justification and the logical Necessity of the Dadson Principle in Self Defence' (1995) Oxford J of Legal Studies, Vol 15, No 2.

[40] 'Unknowing justification and the logical Necessity of the Dadson Principle in Self Defence' (1995) Oxford J of Legal Studies, Vol 15, No 2, 240.

[41] Ramsey *Foundations of Mathematics* (1931) pp 115-116.

techniques and procedures accorded value in the acquisition of truth; the status of those who are charged with saying what counts as true[42].'

[1.31] An extreme example of loss of meaning between reportage and what is actually happening is provided by the 'Dutchy' Holland trial.[43] Patrick 'Dutchy' Holland was convicted before the Special Criminal Court of possession for purposes of supply of a controlled drug (cannabis). He was convicted and appealed, succeeding only in having his sentence reduced from 20 to 12 years. In this case, an ostensible drugs trial for cannabis possession was reported and interpreted in the context of the Veronica Guerin murder, and although commented on as 'unfortunate' on appeal, at trial virtually no one found that strange. It is interesting to reflect on the meaning of that event for the status of truth within Irish society. White's comments[44] are apposite:

'It is not in general surprising for any of us to miss the reality and force of language, for as we lead our ordinary lives we normally look right through our languages and our habits of thought. They are in fact what we see with.[45]

But what is said does matter, and it matters in the law. The law is in fact a complex texture of things said, of relations established with and through language[46]

Such horrors as lynching are part of power, of course; but power is most complete when resort to physical violence is unnecessary. And even power that seems physical in form is dependent upon power of a consensual and linguistic kind: I can call out the police to fire bullets at you only if the police agree to be called out by me, and for these purposes. This power is created through persuasion, it is textual, not physical, in nature.[47]

A discipline based on these assumptions ... [that language is a machine/that texts can depict the real world, etc] ... erases the whole world of people talking to each other in the hope of being understood, the whole dimension of meaning that is created whenever we speak, which I have called constitutive: who we are and become in our talking with each other. This is not only a central question for literature: it is a central concern of the law as well, for the law is not simply an instrument for achieving a certain distribution of items in the world, but a way of creating and sustaining a political and ethical community[48].'

---

[42] Foucault *Power/Knowledge; Selected Interviews and Other Writings 1922-1977*, Gordon (ed) (1980) p 131, translated by Gordon et al (1980), p 131.

[43] *The People v Holland* (15 June 2002) CCA Barrington J.

[44] JB White, Book Review of *Posner's Law and Literature* [1989] Harv LR 2014.

[45] [1989] Harv LR 2014 at 2036.

[46] [1989] Harv LR 2014 at 2044.

[47] JB White, Book Review of *Posner's Law and Literature* [1989] Harv LR 2014, at 2045.

[48] [1989] Harv LR 2014 at 2047.

[1.32] Undoubtedly we face uncomfortable challenges here. Sherwin[49] provides a sharp insight into our reason for collusion or blindness here, as well as a mark to its import:

> '... [L]aw's demand for truth and justice can clash with the modern mind's demand for closure and certainty. When truth defies certainty and becomes complex, justice requires difficult decisions on the basis of that doubt.'[50]

Conclusion

[1.33] Within the Irish context, the existence of the non-jury Special Criminal Court is pivotal to the application of the rules of evidence in certain cases and to general perspectives on their value. It exemplifies the artificiality of fact finding as being divisible from legal application – what Zuckerman calls the cosmetic application of rules of evidence. The trial of Paul Ward provides a good example of judicial self warning of the dangers of accomplice evidence – and reliance on same – as well as scepticism regarding confession evidence and on that occasion its (symbolic) rejection.

[1.34] Prosecutorial bias is evident in the rejection of the confession, yet securing of conviction, alongside criticism of police behaviour. Who knows the effect the excluded confession had on the judges as triers of fact and law? Certainly refusal to countenance the WPP witnesses as anything 'more' than mere accomplices secured the double effect of strengthening accomplice evidence generally and of sanctioning the WPP. The conclusion of the Court on appeal in *Ward* that the trial Court was 'confused' does not augur well for professional as opposed to lay fact-finders. In this regard the Hederman Report's majority recommendations that the non-jury Court be retained will have major implications for the Irish criminal justice system.

[1.35] Another crucial issue is whether there is any continuing justification for corroboration-type rules – do they alert fact-finders to hidden prejudice which may skew their findings – or merely reinforce outmoded beliefs and so result in judgments not just out of synch with 'reality' but dangerous and duplicitous in what they represent?

[1.36] Is Hardiman J right to counsel caution in face of historic sex abuse claims and is McGuinness J correct in identification of a parallel response equally reprehensible to that previously applicable to sex abuse victims, now affecting

---

[49] Sherwin, 'Law Frames: Historical Truth and Narrative Necessity in a Criminal Case' [1994] 47 Stan LR 39.

[50] [1994] 47 Stan LR 39 at 41.

the accused?[51] Has the construction of fairness in sexual offences resulted in the accused's presumption of innocence being usurped by a presumption of guilt?

[1.37] In truth is it better to rely on the unexpressed biases and prejudices in all fact-finders to cancel each other's effect rather than attempt to counterbalance them with legislative attempts at collective wisdom representing only the distillation of another bias, inevitably to fall prey to an equal (and equally misinformed) counterreaction as society will inevitably have moved on? Is fact-finding so central to our system of justice and so obtuse that we have to constrain it on occasion? If so, should those occasions be greater, or do we remain confined within the boundaries identified by another era, their 'bete noir': sex offenders, children, accomplices?

[1.38] To refuse to address this may leave others subject to judicial discretion on an individual basis, or community feeling, manifest through the jury on occasion when they feel so moved: most likely by non identification with the victim or accused – prostitute, drug dealer, paedophile, rapist – those currently furthest from us and so 'other'.

Is it right that our criminal process should be nakedly vulnerable to current emotion or, on the contrary, victim to the grip of an earlier age?

[1.39] Taking the current culture into account can one argue for a pro-accused approach in dealing with that which the 'story' of a criminal trial is written against? Any crime that is currently the subject of a perceived 'crisis' or 'witch-hunt', whose perpetrators are thus distanced from all fact-finders – jury, judge, legislator, and public requires an adjustment in terms of credibility as we cannot recognise their 'story'. It literally makes no sense or does not ring true to us, in as equal measure as the opposing tale does. It is here that we need to be very afraid if we do not hinder their accusers. This may undoubtedly be uncomfortable for us as a society collectively and individually, as we do not like these people and are not 'like' them, yet to use the criminal process to draw that distinction is not just wrong – it is a travesty and a perversion of justice. It is to those whom we regard as perverse that we owe most or we pervert not only the course of justice, but by definition, ourselves. In the long term we also benefit by guarding against the inevitable back-lash – the 'Oleanna' effect:

> 'The symbolic trial is viewed as a signifier within the dominant legal culture: it is a forum that projects authoritative messages through language and legal form about identity and social relationships in a struggle between the antagonistic world views of the defence and the prosecution.'[52]

---

[51] Hardiman J in *PO'C v DPP* [2000] 3 IR 87 at 120–121; McGuiness J in *PC v DPP* [1999] 2 IR 25 at 43.

[52] Bumiller, 'Fallen Angels: The Representation of Violence Against Women in Legal Culture' [1990] 18 International Journal of the Sociology of Law 125 at 126.

[1.40] In adjudging whether European precedents are purely symbolic, and whether Article 6 of the European Convention on Human Rights, when incorporated technically will offer any more protection than its domestic incarnations for those who are seen as abhorrent – the victims of current witch-hunts and collective wisdom – one must consider precedents such as *Forbes*,[53] *Brown v Stott*[54] *and Kebilene*[55] where *Murray*[56] is consistently preferred to *Saunders*.[57] Occasional rights vindications do appear, but they are either drowned in the rush of certainty and belief – or worse, invoked merely to reassure as to the prevailing and overarching nature of justice. It is human nature to want to be on the side of the angels but there must be a recognition amongst those of us concerned with criminal law that that is a moveable feast and that for criminal lawyers, it is with the devils we ride.

[1.41] The rules of evidence are very often criticised as being the product of another climate or age. Perhaps however it is *precisely* when they reflect another climate and not the certainties or tenor of our own culture and values, that they are of most worth, and indeed necessary to effect a counterbalance to our prejudices as fact-finders and law makers. Currently, that may be to operate in favour of tilting the balance – for the accused – if that is to remain or be sustained as our criminal justice system's bias.

---

[53] *R v Forbes* (2001) AC 473.
[54] *Brown v Stott* [2001] 2 All ER 97, [2003] IA C 681.
[55] *R v DPP ex p Kebilene* 28/10/99 (2001) 2 AC 326.
[56] (1996) 22 EHRR 29.
[57] (1997) 23 EHRR 313.

Chapter 2

Crime and Crisis in Ireland

'Poets, philosophers and other creative thinkers are not, however, the only representatives of the Irish mind. The characteristics of this mind have also found negative expression. For example, the logic of ambivalence, the ability to have "two thinks at a time" can equally manifest itself in our own particular brand of "double-think", our peculiar relish for moral equivocation and evasiveness, for having it both ways: Tadgh an da thaobh. No culture, Irish or otherwise, is above critical approach...the need to discriminate between positive and negative, authentic and inauthentic, expressions of mind.'

The Irish Mind: exploring intellectual traditions Kearney (ed), (1985) p 14.

Crime and justice

[2.01] 'Crime' and 'justice' are traditional concepts. This begs many questions and may cloak an assumed and unwarranted familiarity with their meaning and purpose. Previously, debate centred on what was criminal[1]. A more critical or central question nowadays, however, is perhaps, what is justice, or more specifically, criminal justice in the Irish criminal system? As seen in chapter 1, Dahl[2] would suggest, for instance, that a 'fair trial' would be one that A would choose in the knowledge that he was to be tried. The traditional concept of justice or fairness that has grown up in Ireland has a constitutional base. Recently the Irish criminal justice system has undergone much change in procedure.[3] Lip service at least is paid to concepts such as 'interests of justice' or 'fairness to accused' in the context of change, but the question is whether their traditional meaning persists in light of these changes.

---

[1] Eg, should drugs be decriminalised or certain victimless crimes removed from the criminal code? Resonances of that debate continue in Ireland, in the context of the legalisation of cannabis. See Murphy *Rethinking the War on Drugs* (1996).

[2] Dahl *Democracy and its Critics* (1989) Yale University Press.

[3] The Criminal Evidence Act 1992, for example, allowed testimony to be given by certain witnesses by live television link, and questions to be put to that witness through an intermediary, provided such is required by 'the interests of justice' (s 14(2)). A video recording can similarly be admitted as evidence in chief, provided it is 'in the interests of justice' (s 16(2)(a)), and the Court is specifically directed in considering this to have regard to any risk of 'unfairness to the accused'.

[2.02] The victim's role has come more to the fore in the Irish criminal justice system as a result of some of these recent changes[4]. Other changes such as the bail amendment to the Constitution or the detention provision for seven days under the drug trafficking legislation focus on the accused, and might be said to constitute a 'narrowing down' of his rights. Of course a focus on victims' rights need not necessarily result in a narrowing of the accused's rights. There are other avenues such as a victims' charter to improve services for and treatment of victims[5]. The current concept of the 'victim' is, moreover, circumscribed in its definition. It is not taken to include the families of those accused[6], nor those accused who find themselves victims of miscarriages of justice[7]. While acknowledging that no system may be accurate and so strives to be fair, it is important to remember that we do a double disservice to the community if we fail to adhere to the standard of convicting the guilty and not convicting the innocent.

[2.03] The centrality of certain principles to our criminal justice system may change and other principles replace them. What is important is that these principles of 'political morality,'[8] either get replaced or renewed, not just sidelined and forgotten. The latter risks change occurring in a vacuum, where it is considered legitimate merely because of the *process* that brought it about. A Discussion Paper issued by the Irish Department of Justice entitled *Tackling Crime*[9] for example, comes uncomfortably close to endorsing such a limited concept of 'legitimacy' without any reference to principle, when, regarding the mood for reducing rights, it comments: 'It is perfectly understandable that the mood should be thus and perfectly *legitimate* that the balance should be

---

[4] The Criminal Justice Act 1993 makes provision for victim impact statements to be introduced at sentencing, and empowers the Court to award compensation to the victim.

[5] See, eg, publication by the Department of Justice, Equality and Law Reform *Victim's Charter and Guide to the Criminal Justice System* (1999).

[6] Rynn 'Working with Perpetrators: What are the Issues?' in *Safety for Women Conference*, (1993), Government of Ireland, Dublin, p 49 at 52.

[7] Irish miscarriage of justice cases include such as the Tallaght Two (*People v Meleady & Grogan* [1995] 2 IR 517, (4 March 1997), SC); Vincent O'Connell (*People v Connell* [1995] 1 IR 245, (16 October 1997), SC) and Peter Pringle (*People v Pringle* [1995] 2 IR 547, (4 March 1997), SC. The Martin Committee Report (*Report of Committee to Enquire Into Certain Aspects of Criminal Procedure* (1990)) and the subsequent Criminal Procedure Act 1993, which introduced a process for review of such miscarriages can be said to identify two injustices: one innocent convicted, a guilty person not.
    In *DPP v Lynch* [1982] IR 64, for example, there were two victims – both Vera Cullen, the homicide victim, and Lynch, the victim of the miscarriage of justice.

[8] AAS Zuckerman, *Principles of Criminal Evidence* (1989) Clarendon Press, Oxford.

[9] Discussion Paper, Department of Justice, May 1997, *Tackling Crime* (1997) Government of Ireland, ch 8, p 57.

constantly reviewed' [emphasis added][10]. The report offers a qualification that the change in the balance of legal rights 'proceed with caution and following public debate in which the case for change has been demonstrated, and not on the basis of hastily devised responses to events'[11], yet surely the important issue here is the quality of that debate and the very necessary reference to principle. Legislative debates on recent criminal procedural changes in Ireland have evidenced an absence of any such acknowledgement or reassessment of principle[12].

[2.04] By contrast with the legislative field, the Irish courts seem to at least struggle with principle in the context of criminal cases. Judicial statements evidence a relative prioritising of interests, principles, and rights, and carve out a notion of exceptions to general principle where appropriate. There is no evidence of this happening in legislative or policy terms. More worrying, however, is evidence that in some areas judicial imprimatur of change is itself contributing to the 'normalisation' process. In other words 'extraordinary' changes to our criminal process become over time, and with judicial sanction, sanitised and acceptable within the 'ordinary' regime. Instances of this include the Irish Supreme Court decision in *DPP v Quilligan*,[13] sanctioning the use of emergency powers of detention under the Offences Against the State Act 1939, s 30, in relation to 'ordinary' offences; and in *DPP v Kavanagh*, approving the use of the non-jury Special Criminal Court (established under Part V of the Offences Against the State Act 1939) in relation to 'non-subversive' related crimes[14].

[2.05] Recognition that a system of criminal justice needs constant reassessment and change, might have been seen as manifesting in the establishment of the Irish National Crime Forum in February 1998[15]. The brief of the Forum was to

---

[10] Discussion Paper Department of Justice May 1997, *Tackling Crime* (1997) Government of Ireland, para 8.38.

[11] Discussion Paper Department of Justice May 1997, *Tackling Crime* (1997) Government of Ireland.

[12] A failure to address the issue of subversive crime in *'Tackling Crime'* is even more significant. In that discussion paper the existence of particular provision with regard to subversive crime, and the significance of the resource implications, are acknowledged, but neither is engaged with (paras 5.23-5.25). This both ignores and obscures the very heavy influence 'terrorist legislation' has had in criminal procedure reform methodology in the Irish jurisdiction.

[13] *People (DPP) v Quilligan* [1986] IR 495, [1987] ILRM 600.

[14] *Kavanagh v Government of Ireland, DPP, AG* [1996] 1 IR 321.

[15] *Report of the National Crime Forum* (1998) Government of Ireland. There was a strong case for a fulsome discussion cognisant and encompassing of all the issues relating to crime — comfortable or not — and conscious of the visibility and significance of the criminal law in our society. Such a discussion had indeed been anticipated by the earlier *Tackling Crime* document, which had also promised the establishment of a Crime Council.

canvass comment, assessments and suggestions on crime and crime-related issues from the general public, and from national and international experts. In the Chairman's Foreword to the *Crime Forum Report* there is an acknowledgment of change in the context in which the Irish criminal justice system operates:

'Old values are challenged. Individualism has caused traditional restraints to be weakened. We are witnessing the emergence of a drug culture and the growth of organised crime.'[16]

Recognising that outrages such as the Omagh bombing and the killing of Veronica Guerin require a response, the Chairman refers, instead, to the restraints on Government in his response:

'The constitutional constraints are ever present and even though the State must be in a position to defend itself in such situations, legislative reactions must always be measured, proportionate and constitutionally permitted.'[17]

Those limitations are then instanced:

'Ireland can be classified as a liberal democracy with a written constitution. It is in the tradition of a liberal democracy that its criminal justice system is to be defined ...The presumption of innocence, the right to silence and the right to a jury trial, to mention but a few, are some of the features inherited from this [common law] tradition ... Bunreacht na hÉireann ... provides the defining context within which our criminal legal system must operate.'[18]

[2.06] Interestingly, the Chairman identifies the fundamental provisions of the Constitution as providing a check on legislative attempts to regulate or suppress certain activities. The reinforcement of those principles by international measures guaranteeing human rights is also noted. Moreover, reference is made to the presence of ' a natural tension between governments which promote "law and order" politics ... and the judiciary who, by and large, champion the individual's liberty, and who seem in these matters to prefer a policy of minimum intrusion'.[19]

[2.07] The second defining feature of the Irish criminal justice system, identified by the Chairman, is the political unrest as a result of the situation in Northern Ireland. The existence of two systems of criminal justice is remarked upon, as is the inherent danger of normalisation whereby '[i]f exceptional measures are required, they should clearly be seen to be unusual and irregular

---

[16] *Report of the National Crime Forum* (1998) Government of Ireland, p 9.

[17] *Report of the National Crime Forum* (1998) Government of Ireland, p 11.

[18] *Report of the National Crime Forum* (1998) Government of Ireland, p 11-12. Bunreacht na hÉireann is the Constitution of Ireland (1937).

[19] *Report of the National Crime Forum* (1998) Government of Ireland, p 14.

and they should not be allowed to stretch out beyond their intended sphere of application, or translate into permanent status when the temporary crisis is past'.[20]

[2.08] Significantly these are Chairman's comments, separate from the body of the *Crime Forum Report* itself, and contained in a Foreword specified to be personal[21]. While the Forum process was undoubtedly useful, a quintessentially democratic exercise, and one which served to debunk some myths regarding the public mood, it is ultimately not normative in nature or effect.[22] Neither are the Chairman's views, while reflective of the liberal democratic paradigm to which our system *should* belong, necessarily constitutive of it. Mere reference to and endorsement of such values does not ensure their currency and relevance. The question remains as to our continuing alliance to such an ideal in light of the recent (and some not so recent) legislative events. Viewed from an angle where the exceptions become the rule, our position may have become quite different.

Constitutional constraints

[2.09] Since concepts of fairness and justice in Ireland have been identified as having a constitutional base, it is perhaps appropriate to introduce the outlines of traditional criminal justice in Ireland in terms of these parameters. On paper, the backdrop to the criminal trial is a Constitution with an explicit guarantee that 'no person shall be tried on any criminal charge save in due course of law'[23]. This has been variously interpreted to include: in accordance with fair procedures in the pre-trial process, expeditiously, with access to a lawyer, the

---

[20] *Report of the National Crime Forum* (1998) Government of Ireland, p 18.

[21] *Report of the National Crime Forum* (1998) Government of Ireland, p 10. The Chairman categorises the Forum Report as 'a series of reflections', presenting the citizens' views on crime and crime-related matters (at p 18). The most surprising result of this, as he notes, was the absence of any significant demands from the public for dramatic reactions to crime from the authorities, (at p 10).

[22] In the context of the Runciman Commission (*Royal Commission on Criminal Justice Report* Cm 2263), Walker has commented that the 'absence of principled argument was a wasted opportunity for civic education'. Furthermore he noted that '... the publication of the Report coincided with the advent of a period of attempted populist repression by the Home Office which found the Report to be suitably malleable for its purposes to achieve its own agenda without having to snub the Commission.' (Walker 'The Commodity of Justice in States of Emergency' (1999) 50 NILQ 164).

Despite the considerable civic involvement in the work of the Crime Forum in Ireland, which received oral and written submissions from individuals and community groups, that Report may prove equally ineffectual in terms of influence, given the subsequent contrast between public demands and government legislative response. The public quietude with regard to harsher crime control measures, and the Chairman's invocation of value and principle, may not have proven any more impervious to subsequent government interpretative measures.

[23] Article 38.1, Bunreacht na hÉireann (Constitution of Ireland).

absence of oppression in interrogation, and fundamental fairness in the execution of search warrants; and at trial, the presumption of innocence, the right to counsel, the opportunity to cross-examine, and the opportunity to have access to information. Some constitutional rights are, of course, qualified. There is, for example, an explicit Constitutional guarantee under Article 38 of the 1937 Constitution of the right to trial by jury on any criminal charge[24] with provision for exception in three circumstances:

1.   minor offences which may be tried by a court of summary jurisdiction

2.   military offences alleged to have been committed by persons while subject to military law may be tried by military tribunals

3.   circumstances where special courts may be established

[2.10] With regard to the establishment of Special Courts, Article 38.3 states:

'(1) Special courts may be established by law for the trial of offences in cases where it may be determined in accordance with such law that the ordinary courts are inadequate to secure the effective administration of justice and the preservation of public peace and order.

(2) The constitution, powers, jurisdiction and procedure of such special courts shall be prescribed by law.'

[2.11] The Irish State can declare a state of emergency to the effect that the ordinary courts are inadequate to secure the effective administration of justice, and the preservation of public peace and order, thereby invoking the Offences against the State Act 1939, Part V, and so operate the non-jury Special Criminal Court. A resolution of national emergency was passed by the Oireachtas on 3 September 1939, and was terminated on 1 September 1976 and replaced by a similar declaration based on the strife in Northern Ireland.[25]

[2.12] Writing in 1974 on the rationale for the provision of special courts, Mary Robinson[26] commented:

'It is a precondition to the establishment of special courts that the ordinary courts are found to be inadequate. In other words, their establishment testifies to the existence of extraordinary circumstances in the State during a particular period. It is vital to maintain a strict scrutiny of such circumstances – which justify departing from the norm – to analyse the way in which special courts can be introduced to cope with such circumstances, and to keep under constant review the day to day functioning of these special courts.'

---

[24]   Article 38.5 'Save in the case of the trial of offences under section 2, section 3 or section 4 of this Article no person shall be tried on any criminal charge without a jury.'

[25]   See further Kelly *The Irish Constitution* Hogan and Whyte (eds) (3rd edn, 1994), pp 238-239.

[26]   Robinson *The Special Criminal Court* (1974), p 5.

[2.13] Given the difficulty in estimating exactly how much of our criminal business goes to the Special Criminal Court, it is hard to substantiate but – given its high profile in Irish criminal cases – easy to make the argument that it compromises the strength of our right to trial by jury. Gearty and Kimble in the context of the Northern Irish non-jury Diplock Courts make the point that:

'[t]he integrity of the criminal justice system that has developed in England and Wales depends to a large degree on the combination of judge and jury. Removing either one from the other seriously affects the balance and integrity of the system'.[27]

[2.14] Undoubtedly the access of the State to a non-jury court in relation to drugs and organised crime in the aftermath of the resolution of the Northern Ireland conflict, ensures it has a future. The Hederman Committee Review of the Offences Against the State Act and related matters conducted by virtue of the Government's commitment under the Good Friday Agreement, in its terms of reference, specifically referred to inter alia 'the threat posed by international terrorism and organised crime.'[28]

---

[27] Gearty and Kimble *Terrorism and the Rule of Law: A Report into the Laws Relating to Political Violence in Great Britain and Northern Ireland* (1995) p 53-54. Gearty and Kimble identify the principal reason for assigning to a jury the determination of guilt the need to secure public confidence in the criminal process. This is precisely because there is no external check for accuracy of verdicts. The three features of jury participation which engender confidence are:

'... first through the jury twelve citizens have a direct effect on how a law operates in a particular set of circumstances. Secondly it is through the jury that contemporary standards of justice and morality are imported into the system. Thirdly apparently "perverse verdicts" can provide a direct impetus to change "unjust" laws or alternatively they can act as a way through which ordinary people are empowered to condemn oppressive behaviour generally. The latter point highlights the fact that producing results that satisfy prosecuting authorities or the police or government ministers is not a feature of the jury system.' (At p 55).

[28] The Committee to review the Offences Against the State Acts 1939-1998 and related matters under the Chairmanship of Hederman J was established to review the Offences Against the State Acts and mandated by the 'Good Friday Agreement' 10 April 1998 which required that the Irish government initiate a wide ranging review with a view to both reform and dispensing with those elements no longer required as circumstances permit. It had the following terms of reference:

'The Committee is requested to examine all aspects of the Offences Against the State Acts 1939-98, taking into account:

(a) the view of the participants to the Multi-Party negotiations that the development of a peaceful environment on the basis of the Agreement they reached on 10 April 1998, can and should mean a normalisation of security arrangements and practices;

(b) the threat posed by international terrorism and organised crime, and

[2.15] In the Irish context, the existence of an 'emergency' or extraordinary regime outside constitutional parameters in the context of the Special Criminal Court has been facilitated by the folk devil of terrorism. This emergency measure has facilitated the existence of differential, exceptional or 'non-constitutional' treatment for certain offenders. Moreover, as Cohen would suggest, the phenomenon would appear to be ongoing as the demonisation of drugs and organised crime may ensure a future currency for this exceptional provision, and its persistence even in light of elimination or resolution of its originating raison d'être. This dissonance at the heart of the Irish criminal justice system in terms of departure from overt constitutional values is not insignificant in assessing its adherence to principle.

Judicial concept of 'fair' procedure

[2.16] Judicial commentary in Ireland with regard to constitutional constraint and fair procedure might indicate that the Irish judiciary have a strong sense of fair procedure. They have not been reluctant to invoke an over-arching and constitutionally grounded concept of fairness or justice in order to avoid or amend the strictures of rules of procedure or evidence. In the decision of the Court of Criminal Appeal in *DPP v T*,[29] for example, which secured the competence of a spouse to testify in the context of charges of sexual abuse by a father of his child, Walsh J declared that the common law rule impeding such testimony was contrary to and negated by the Constitution as '... the administration of justice itself requires the public has a right to every man's evidence'.[30]

---

[28] (contd)

    (c) Ireland's obligations under international law;

And to report to the Minister for Justice Equality and Law Reform as soon as practicable with recommendations for reform.' (1999) Irish Times, 23 July.

The Committee produced an interim and final report: Interim Report, *The Special Criminal Court* (June 2001); Final Report: *Report of the Committee to Review the Offences Against the State Act 1939-1998 and Related Matters* Government Publications, Dublin, May 2002.

[29] *DPP v T* (27 July 1988, unreported) CCA, judgment of Court delivered by Walsh J (Record No 106/86)

[30] *DPP v T* (27 July 1988, unreported), CCA, p 42. He also declared:

'The exercise of the judicial power carried with it the power to compel the attendance of witnesses, the production of evidence and, *a fortiori*, the answering of questions by the witnesses. This is the ultimate safeguard of justice in the State, whether it be in pursuit of the guilty or vindication of the innocent.' (At p 43).

In relation to the common law rule that one spouse may not give evidence against the other in a criminal prosecution he stated:

'Insofar as that may be based upon the view that it would tend to rupture family relationships it must be set against the public interest in the vindication of the innocent who have been subjected to injustice.' (At p 43).

[2.17] In *Mapp v Gilhooley*[31], a decision concerned with the necessity of swearing a child in a civil case, Finlay CJ stated that it was a fundamental principle of common law in criminal or civil trials that *viva voce* [oral] evidence must be given on oath or affirmation. In a similar vein, Hederman J, in *McGrail*[32] abandoned the previous common law rule inhibiting accused persons from attacking prosecution witnesses stating that '...the principles of fair procedure must apply. A procedure which inhibits the accused from challenging the veracity of the evidence against him at the risk of having his own previous character put in evidence is not a fair procedure'.

[2.18] O'Higgins CJ in *State (Healy) v Donoghue*[33] stated that:

'... the concept of justice, which is specifically referred to in the preamble [to the Constitution] in relation to the freedom and dignity of the individual, appears again in the provision of Article 34 which deals with the Courts. It is justice which ... must import not only fairness, and fair procedures, but also regard to the dignity of the individual.'

[2.19] In contrast to the aforementioned co-existence of a non-jury court in Ireland with a constitutional guarantee of jury trial, is the attitude of courts to the jury. The fact finding role of a jury at trial, in terms of its centrality to the process, is endorsed by the view that appellate courts should be slow to interfere, as that finding is made on the basis of physically seeing and hearing witnesses, and not simply receiving their testimony in documentary form. McCarthy J, for example, in *DPP v Egan*[34] pointed out that:

'[i]n reading the record of the evidence, the appellate Court cannot assess the credibility of witnesses nor the cogency of evidence of primary facts, or of inference of fact which are dependent upon the credibility of a witness or witnesses.'

[2.20] *DPP v Kehoe*[35] was concerned with the role of the jury, and their potential over-shadowing by an expert. In this case the expert had testified that the accused, who was mounting a defence of provocation, did not have the intent to kill and was telling the truth. O'Flaherty J delivering the judgment of the court stated:

---

[31] *Mapp v Gilhooley* [1991] 2 IR 253.
[32] *DPP v McGrail* [1990] 2 IR 38 at 51.
[33] *State (Healy) v Donoghue* [1976] IR 325 at 348.
[34] *DPP v Egan* (30 May 1990, unreported), SC (McCarthy J), p 9, [1990] ILRM 780 per McCarthy J quoting Griffin J delivering judgment of Criminal Court of Appeal in *People (DPP) v Mulligan* (1982) Frewen 16 at 20-23.
[35] *DPP v Kehoe* (6 November 1991, ex temp), CCA (O'Flaherty J).

'These are clearly matters four square within the jury's function and a witness no more than the trial judge or anyone else is not entitled to trespass on what is the jury's function.'[36]

Ó Dálaigh J, in similar vein, commented in the case of *Melling v O'Mathgamhna and AG* 'The safeguard of trial by jury is against an improbable but not-to-be-overlooked future; and it is for this reason the Constitution enshrines it.'[37]

In *DPP v O'Shea*[38], O'Higgins CJ said of a criminal trial that:

'... the outstanding and truly distinguishing feature of such a trial, and the one that puts it apart from any other form of judicial investigation, is that the guilt or innocence of the accused and the determination of relevant facts are exclusively functions of the jury and not of the judge.'

Henchy J in *DPP v O'Shea* expressed the view that the prosecution had no right of appeal from an acquittal by a jury for reasons which he describes as being '... part of the price that has to be paid for the independent verdicts of lay people sitting as jurors and applying community standards.'[39]

In a defence of the perverse verdict, Henchy J continued:

'Both judges and legislators have accepted that while a jury properly instructed by the trial judge have no right to bring in a verdict for the accused which is against the evidence, yet they have a power to do so; and that the risks inherent in any efforts at controlling the exercise of that power would not be warranted. The use of the power to err in favour of the accused is left to the consciences of the jurors. In any event, what may seem to judges to be a perverse verdict of acquittal

---

[36] A later comment is interesting for its endorsement – and faith – in jurors' roles, rather than that of the trial judge. O'Flaherty J may be said to be placing a brake on the judicial role in this area: 'Increasingly, it is the experience in this jurisdiction as in other jurisdictions that a trial judge abstains from offering any view of the evidence, good bad or indifferent. That is not to say that trial judges are not entitled to offer a view but more and more trial judges consider that *juries are best left to see evidence through a glass clearly rather than to have it either magnified or diminished by the judge's intervention.'* [emphasis added] at p 20.
This is particularly significant in a jurisdiction where judicial charges to the jury on matters of law are largely unbridled and a matter of judicial discretion. This latter can be exercised very powerfully, without ever overstepping the mark, and matters of inflection, tone of voice and intonation, cannot be derived from transcripts. In the United States, by contrast, instruction by the trial judge to the jury is taken from a composite code mandating in a very pragmatic way the central role of the jury, and the limited input from the bench.

[37] *Melling v O'Mathgamhna* [1962] IR 1 at 39.

[38] *DPP v O'Shea* [1982] IR 384 at 402.

[39] *DPP v O'Shea* [1982] IR 384 at 438. Interesting in light of the provision for prosecution appeal against leniency of sentence in the Criminal Justice Act 1993.

may represent the layman's rejection of a particular law as being unacceptable. So it is that such verdicts have often led to reform of the criminal law.'[40]

[2.21] One of the strongest statements to date on the overall philosophy behind constitutional 'due process' in the Irish criminal justice system, and the role of procedure, remains that of the Supreme Court in *Kenny*.[41] In a pragmatic sense the effect was considerable, as it led to the jettisoning of 'real' evidence in the form of drugs found on the accused's premises, and invalidated a procedure for the obtaining of warrants used by the gardaí for over thirty years, on the basis of which thousands of warrants had been issued, and searches carried out.

[2.22] The Irish Supreme Court also specifically referred to the American Supreme Court decision of *US v Leon*[42] which introduced the 'good faith' exception to the *Miranda* ruling, and, in the view of some, mortally wounded the American exclusionary rule, in its sanitizing of any police (mis)behaviour carried out in 'good faith'. While a previous line of decisions by the Irish courts had similarly seemed to allow for a good faith or 'green Garda' exception to the exclusionary rule (particularly in confession cases[43]), these were now subsumed by the Supreme Court decision in *Kenny*, where a firm protectionist stance was taken. Finlay CJ, delivering the majority judgment, noted the precedent adopted by him and McCarthy J in *Healy*[44], the 'absolute protection test' for evidence obtained by reason of breach of a detained person's constitutional right of access to a lawyer. As between two alternate rules or principles governing the exclusion of evidence obtained as a result of the invasion of personal rights of citizens, the court has, according to Finlay CJ, an obligation to choose the principle which is likely to provide stronger and more effective defence and vindication of that right. That leads to the absolute protection rule of exclusion, which he acknowledges places a limitation on the capacity of courts to arrive at truth and so administer justice. Nonetheless the position of Finlay CJ, and ultimately of the Supreme Court in *Kenny*, is that:

> '[t]he detection of crime and the conviction of guilty persons, no matter how important they may be in relation to the ordering of society, cannot…outweigh the unambiguously expressed constitutional obligation 'as far as practicable to defend and vindicate the personal rights of the citizen.'[45]

---

[40] *DPP v O'Shea* [1982] IR 384 at 438.
[41] *DPP v Kenny* [1990] ILRM 569, [1990] IR 110.
[42] *US v Leon* (1983) 468 US 897.
[43] See *DPP v Madden* [1977] IR 336.
[44] *DPP v Healy* [1990] ILRM 313.
[45] *PP v Kenny* [1990] IR 110 at 134 (Finlay CJ).

[2.23] A further statement as to the bias of the Irish criminal justice system is found in the endorsement by the Supreme Court in *Davis*[46] of the statement of Carroll CJ in *Youman v The Commonwealth of Kentucky*[47]:

> 'It is much better that a guilty individual should escape punishment than that a court of justice should put aside a vital fundamental principle of the law in order to secure his conviction. In the exercise of their great powers, courts have no higher duty to perform than those involving the protection of the citizen in the civil rights guaranteed to him by the Constitution, and if at any time the protection of those rights should delay, or even defeat, the ends of justice in the particular case, it is better for the public good that this should happen than that a great constitutional mandate should be nullified'.

[2.24] Challenges to that protectionist stance have emerged, not least in the context of terrorism. *O'Leary v AG*[48] concerned the conviction of O'Leary, in the Special Criminal Court, for membership of an unlawful organisation contrary to s 21 of the Offences Against the State Act 1939 (as amended), and possession of incriminating documents contrary to s 12 of that Act. Section 24 of the 1939 Act provides that proof of possession of incriminating documents shall, without more, unless the contrary is proven, be evidence that such person was a member of the organisation at the time of the charge. O'Leary claimed this infringed the constitutional right to a trial in due course of law and, in particular, the presumption of innocence by placing on the accused the burden of disproving his guilt.

In the High Court, Costello J found the presumption of innocence, part of the common law prior to 1937, to have been for so long a postulate of every criminal trial, that a criminal trial held otherwise was prima facie not held in due course of law. Costello J confirmed that the Constitution conferred on every accused in every criminal trial a constitutionally protected right to the presumption of innocence, but went on to state that in certain circumstances the Oireachtas can restrict the exercise of such a right, which is not absolute. The Supreme Court confirmed his decision on appeal. O'Flaherty J declared that:

---

[46] *DPP v Davis* [1993] 2 IR 1 at 15 (Finlay CJ) previously cited with approval in *People v O'Brien* [1965] IR 142 and *People v Madden* [1977] IR 336).

In *DPP v Davis* the Supreme Court also considered both the guarantee in Article 38.1 of the Constitution that 'no person shall be tried on any criminal charge save in due course of law' and that by virtue of Article 38.5 that 'no person shall be tried on any criminal charge without a jury'. In this case where the trial judge had unduly interfered with the jury's function by instructing them to bring in a verdict of murder, the Supreme Court allowed the appeal emphasising a series of decisions underscoring the importance of the role of the jury and judgment of one's peers.

[47] *Youman v The Commonwealth of Kentucky* 189 Ky 152.

[48] *O'Leary v AG* [1991] ILRM 454 (Costello J).

'...the presumption of innocence in a criminal trial is implicit in the requirement of Article 38.1 of the Constitution that no person shall be tried on any criminal charge save in due course of law...'[49]

With regard to s 24 of the 1939 Act, O'Flaherty J stated that the opinion of the Court was that it permitted no more than that:

'... if an incriminating document is proved to be in the possession of a person ... that shall, without more, be evidence until the contrary is proved that such possession is to amount to evidence only ; it is not to be taken as proof and so, the probative value ... might be shaken in many ways ... there is no mention about the burden of proof changing, much less that the presumption of innocence is to be set to one side at any stage.'[50]

He later stated his view that it was the evidentiary burden of proof which has shifted. (The latter belies the fact that the evidentiary burden had always been regarded as of tactical or pragmatic effect. By contrast here the accused has to 'shake' the evidence, or face conviction.) Despite trenchant acknowledgement at both High and Supreme Court levels that the presumption of innocence is inherent in Article 38, the section was 'saved'. Such an apparent 'strong rights' stance in face of accommodation of exceptional provision represents a janus-like approach prescient of decisions to come.

[2.25] Recent adjustment to procedure in Ireland in response to perceived crisis 'events' includes the invocation of the civil process in the context of organised crime to secure forfeiture of the 'proceeds of crime', absent a trial or conviction. In this regard it is worth remembering the response of the Irish judiciary to a challenge to the fairness of proceedings in the context of the Beef Tribunal which latter was enquiring into the sales of beef from Ireland into the European Community.[51] A challenge was made to Tribunal procedures by Goodman (one of the factory owners engaged in selling beef), whereby it was contended that the proceedings were unconstitutional, in not according due process or fair procedure by adhering to all of the rules of evidence in its proceedings. The challenge was ultimately unsuccessful but the Supreme Court acknowledged that the constitutional right to fair procedure did require adherence to many of the rules of evidence, and incorporated notions like cross-examination, the right to confront, etc. McCarthy J stated that common law rights were subsumed by the Constitutional guarantee of fundamental rights:

---

[49] *O'Leary v AG* [1995] 1 IR 254 at 263 (O'Flaherty J).

[50] *O'Leary v AG* [1995] 1 IR 254 at 265.

[51] In brief, the allegation was that Goodman International engaged in questionable practices in the processing of beef in Ireland thus defrauding both Government and the EC. It was a tribunal of inquiry, not a court, though headed by the President of the High Court with the power to call witnesses.

'The prescripts of natural justice – to hear the other side and not to be a judge in one's own cause, have, themselves, been subsumed by the constitutional right to fair procedures.' [52]

[2.26] Finlay CJ rejected the submission made, but accepted the proposition that a guarantee of fair procedure is a part of Article 40.3 and made some interesting comments about criminal trials and Article 38:

'The essential ingredient of a trial of a criminal offence in our law, which is indivisible from any other ingredient, is that it is heard before a court or judge which has got the power to punish in the event of a verdict of guilty. It is of the essence of a trial on a criminal charge or a trial on a criminal offence that the proceedings are accusatorial, involving a prosecutor and an accused, and that the sole purpose and object of the verdict, be it one of acquittal or conviction, is to form the basis for either a discharge of the accused from the jeopardy in which he stood, in the case of an acquittal, or for his punishment for the crime which he has committed, in the case of a conviction.' [53]

[2.27] Hederman J, also took the opportunity to address the suitability of the process here (a tribunal hearing), quoting from a dissenting judgment of Murphy J in the High Court of Australia, as follows:

'The trial and finding of guilt of political opponents and dissenters in such a way is a valuable instrument in the hands of governments who have little regard for human rights. Experience in many countries shows that persons may be effectively destroyed by this process. The fact that punishment by fine or imprisonment does not automatically follow may be of no importance; indeed a government can demonstrate its magnanimity by not proceeding to prosecute in the ordinary way. If a government chooses not to prosecute, the fact that the finding is not binding on any court is of little comfort to the person found guilty; there is no legal proceeding which he can institute to establish his innocence. If he is prosecuted, the investigation and findings may have created ineradicable prejudice. This latter possibility is not abstract or remote from the case. We were informed that the public conduct of these proceedings was intended to have a "cleansing effect".' [54]

---

[52] *Goodman International v Judge Hamilton, Ireland and the Attorney General* [1992] 2 IR 542 at 609 (McCarthy J).

[53] *Goodman International v Judge Hamilton, Ireland and the Attorney General* [1992] 2 IR 542 at 588 (Finlay CJ).

[54] *Goodman International v Judge Hamilton, Ireland and the Attorney General* [1992] 2 IR 542 at 599-600 (Hederman J) referring to dissent of Murphy J in High Court in Australia in *Victoria v Australian Building Construction Employees and Builders' Labourers Federation* (1982) 152 CLR 25. That case involved the appointment of a Royal Commissioner to inquire into the activities of a trade union. The organisation challenged the validity of the appointment claiming the Commission would be in contempt of court and interfere with the course of justice.

Hederman J's comments are prescient with regard to the use of the civil process in order to avoid the strictures of the criminal regime, in particular procedural rights of the accused, to the detriment of the individual, and consequent advantage to the State of the appearance of action.

[2.28] If then there is evident a consciousness of principle on the part of the Irish judiciary, seen to have been elucidated in terms of the criminal process and constitutional parameters, the question arises as to how that is affected by the co-existence and tolerance of an emergency regime? If the latter does not conform to prior judicial assertion of standard, that may render the extraordinary regime constitutionally invalid. Alternately if the constitutional structure is capable of accommodation of such exception, does that render the Constitution a façade, in the manner suggested by Nicolson:

> 'It is possible that the cathedral of legal process is fronted by a façade of contested cases in the higher courts, in which, at least from a distance, the values of liberal justice are seen to operate. However behind this façade stretches the vast majority of cases in which these values are significantly absent. Nevertheless, because these liberal claims are seen to be fulfilled with sufficient (but by no means universal) frequency, and because the liberal façade is so overwhelmingly visible in legal discourse and contemporary culture, the system somehow coheres, despite the gaps between liberal rhetoric and sociological 'reality'. This greater visibility – through textbooks, academic journals, the media, films etc – detracts attention from day to day business of the courts and creates the impression of a legal system which impartially seeks truth, protects the weak, gives ordinary citizen his or her day in court and even allows for an element of democracy through the jury system. As in many areas of modern Western law, we thus see a highly visible ideology of justice and rights grafted onto an older more authoritarian system of power and control.'[55]

Exploration of this tension through the medium of case law concerning judicial consideration of compatibility and constitutionality of the extraordinary regime may indicate the true nature of the system.

Normalisation: the beginnings

[2.29] To gain a perspective on the Irish judiciary's approach to matters of fair procedure in the criminal process, it is useful to focus on the conceptual confusion that arose in relation to arrest and detention, an area of the criminal process to experience change directly as a result of special provision for arrest of 'terrorists' under s 30 of the Offences Against the State Act 1939. In considering its treatment in the courts, one may gain an insight into the manner in which

---

[55] D Nicolson, 'Trust, reason and justice: Epistemology and Politics in Evidence Discourse' [1994] 57 MLR 726 at 743.

change was introduced in a particular context, and accommodated by the Irish Courts in terms of principle and constitutional parameters. It is worthwhile, therefore, examining the case law surrounding 'ordinary' arrest, arrest under s 30 of the Offences Against the State Act 1939, and arrest leading up to the introduction of s 4 of the Criminal Justice Act 1984, which may be seen to represent the commencement of normalisation with the introduction of an emergency-type measure into the ordinary or normal criminal justice system.

[2.30] Section 30 of the Offences Against the State Act 1939 provides for a period of detention consequent on arrest of 24 hours, with a further possible 24 hour period being authorised by a garda officer of a certain rank.[56] Section 4 of the Criminal Justice Act 1984 provides for a period of detention subsequent to arrest of six hours with a further possible extension of six hours. The relevant constitutional provisio,n Article 40.4.1° of Bunreacht na hÉireann guarantees that: 'No citizen shall be deprived of his personal liberty save in accordance with law.'

Arrest

[2.31] At common law the arrest process is the only means whereby Irish law envisages a legitimate deprivation of liberty. Its function is to ensure the presence of an accused at trial. Strict rules were traditionally laid down with regard to powers of arrest: who can exercise them and on what grounds[57]. Further, arrest as a process was seen as being part of the pre-trial process whereby an accused was put on a path leading irrevocably to judicial scrutiny. An arrest originally, indeed, was seen as indicative of the culmination of the investigative process. When a person was arrested, it was a signal that the State's case against him had been established to their satisfaction and now merely awaited airing in a court of law. Over the years, however, the concept of arrest has become more nebulous. Courts have distinguished between 'lawful' and 'unlawful' arrests and between the former concepts and that of 'detention'. In addition, the function of arrest had been metamorphosed somewhat, in that arrest became viewed by many as forming not part of the process by which an accused is brought to trial, but rather as part of the investigative process of which, heretofore, arrest was the end result. Because of this conceptual confusion, the function of an arrest became uncertain, and within this uncertainty, grew away from its original raison d'être. Instances of this

---

[56] In 1976 the passage of the Emergency Powers Act created a temporary substitution for s 30 of the 1939 Act, a power to detain for up to seven days. (s 3). This Act, which was implemented as part of a response to the assassination in Dublin of the British Ambassador Sir Christopher Ewart-Biggs, went out of operation after one year and the declaration of emergency, which lent it constitutional validity, has now been revoked.

[57] See Ryan and Magee *The Irish Criminal Process* Mercier, Cork (1980) pp 95-99.

confusion can be seen in the statement of Griffin J in *The People v Shaw*[58], viz, 'I do not think it is correct to state without qualification that no person may be arrested with or without a warrant for the purpose of interrogation or securing evidence from that person', by contrast with Walsh J's view in that case that arrest was 'simply a process of ensuring the attendance at Court of the person so arrested'.[59]

[2.32] The judiciary initially might be seen to have aimed to vindicate the rights of the individual in the face of State infringement on liberty. This led to judgments such as that of the *People v Christopher Lynch*[60] where the Supreme Court effectively abolished the police tactic of 'inviting someone to the police station to help them with their inquiries' thereby taking advantage of the latter's misconception of his obligation to comply with their request and so remain and answer their questions. The police, in turn, developed a hostile attitude to what they regarded as the 'over-watchfulness' of the judiciary. They began to resent judgments such as *People v Lynch* which outmanoeuvred their efforts to take advantage of the 'grey areas' in the arrest process. At the time Garda Commissioner McLaughlin commented:

> '...for a while we surmounted this problem of being unable to detain a suspect by inviting him to come voluntarily to the Garda station to be interviewed. For many years suspects who had in this fashion come voluntarily to Garda stations were interviewed, unless they expressed a desire to leave the station.'[61]:

[2.33] Far from regarding the arrest process as the culmination of the investigative function, it seemed that the Irish police (gardaí) regarded it as the very vehicle by which they could solve crimes. This view is supported by the finding of the O'Briain Committee,[62] that '... 80% of serious crimes, in respect of which convictions are obtained, are solved by confessions ie as the end product of questioning sessions.'[63]

[2.34] A contrasting judicial view of the role and function of the process of arrest, was given emphatically by Hanna J, in *Dunne v Clinton*[64]:

---

[58] *People v Shaw* [1982] IR 1 at 55.
[59] *People v Shaw* [1982] IR 1 at 29.
[60] *People v Christopher Lynch* [1981] ILRM 389.
[61] McLaughlin 'Legal Constraints in Criminal Investigation' (1981) XVI Ir Jur (ns) 217 at 210-211.
[62] Committee to recommend certain safeguards for persons in custody and for members of an Garda Síochána. Report (1978) Prl 7158.
[63] O'Briain Committee Report (1978) Prl 7158 at para 38.
[64] *Dunne v Clinton* [1930] IR 366 at 372.

'In law there can be no half-way house between the liberty of the subject, unfettered by restraint, and an arrest ... But the practice has grown up of "detention" as distinct from arrest. It is, in effect, keeping a suspect in custody...without making any definite charge against him and with the intimation in some form of words or gesture that he is under restraint and will not be allowed to leave. As in my opinion, there could be no such thing as notional liberty, this so called detention amounts to arrest, and the suspect has in law been arrested and in custody during the period of his detention.'[65]

[2.35] In decisions in the context of 'ordinary' powers of arrest, the individual's right to liberty seemed to be trenchantly defended. Protection in relation to the initial stages was provided by the courts on the occasion of trial of the charge, if they felt the arrest to have been unlawful, the detention to have been insufficiently justified, or the rights of the accused insufficiently protected. The tactic of excluding evidence against an accused, if obtained in breach of his constitutional rights (leading to automatic exclusion in all but 'extraordinary excusing circumstances'), or otherwise illegally obtained (leading to a discretion to exclude), was developed by the judiciary in the hallmark cases of *People v O'Brien, People v Shaw* and *People v Lynch*.[66]

---

[65] The requirement to bring a person under arrest before a court within a reasonable time, if someone was arrested on a warrant, existed by virtue of s 15 of the Criminal Justice Act 1951. In *AG v Burke* [1955] IR 30 that Davitt J said that in the case of an arrest without a warrant the common law rules applied; ie, the person arrested must be brought before a court within a reasonable time. The question arises, of course, as to what constitutes a 'reasonable time' in the view of the Irish judiciary. In *Dunne v Clinton* [1930] IR 366 at 374-375, it was stated:

'No hard and fast rule can be laid down to cover every case. It must depend on many circumstances, such as the time and place of the arrest, the number of the accused, whether a Peace Commissioner is easily available, and such other matters as may be relevant.'

In *The People v Shaw* [1980] IR 1 Costello J accepted the propositions set forth by the English Court in *John Lewis & Co Ltd v Timm* [1952] AC 676 at 691, where Lord Porter stated:

'The question throughout should be: has the arrestor brought the arrested person to a place where his alleged offence can be dealt with as speedily as is reasonably possible? But all the circumstances in the case must be taken into consideration in deciding whether this requirement is complied with. A direct route and rapid progress are no doubt matters for consideration, but they are not the only matters.

Those who arrest must be persuaded of the guilt of the accused, they cannot bolster up their assurances or the strength of their case by seeking further evidence and detaining the arrested man meanwhile or taking him to some spot where they may or may not find further evidence ... Whether there is evidence that the steps taken were unreasonable or the delay too great is a matter for the Judge.'

[66] *People v O'Brien* [1965] IR 142; *People v Shaw* [1982] IR 1; *People v Lynch* [1982] IR 64.

[2.36] The court in *People v O'Brien*[67] provided the basic format for safeguarding the individual right to liberty, (although the case itself concerned an issue of search and seizure concerning a defective warrant) viz, illegality gives to the trial judge the discretion to exclude the evidence obtained as a result of same, while evidence obtained as the result of a deliberate and conscious breach of an individual's constitutional rights, must be excluded. In *People v Shaw*[68] the Supreme Court, counter-balanced the constitutional right to liberty of the accused – a right that prima facie would seem to have been infringed – with the girl's constitutional right to life which right also had been infringed. The court in *Shaw* acknowledged the deliberate violation of constitutional rights by the gardaí, yet excused it because of the existence of 'extraordinary excusing circumstances'. In this case, breach of the individual's constitutionally guaranteed right to liberty was deemed sanctioned, albeit the said breach being deliberate and conscious, by the prevailing right to life of the accused's suspected victim[69].

[2.37] In *People v Lynch*[70], where the accused was held for questioning without any lawful arrest having been made, and 'grilled' for 22 hours, Walsh J stated:

> 'If a person is asked to come to a Garda station and he goes voluntarily ... When he is subjected to interrogation of a nature which would suggest he may well be a suspect in the case or questioned or interrogated in circumstances which reasonably would give rise to that inference, he should be informed that he is free to leave at any time unless and until he is arrested.'[71]

---

[67] *People v O'Brien* [1965] IR 142.

[68] *People v Shaw* [1982] IR 1. Mr Shaw was arrested at 11.30 pm on 26 September 1976 at Salthill. He was not given any reason for the arrest, ergo it was an unlawful arrest. At 12.10 am the 'unlawfulness' was 'cured' when Shaw was told of the correct reason for the effecting of his arrest. In the normal course of events he would then have been brought before Galway District Court on the morning of 27 September 1976. Yet in fact, he was detained throughout 27 September and 28 September. The Supreme Court held that, prima facie, the detention of Shaw after 10.30 am on 27 September was unlawful. However, the gardaí pointed out that the reason for so detaining Shaw, was the fact that he and another man were charged with the abduction of two girls, and there remained the possibility that one or other or both of the girls might still be alive.

[69] Though Griffin J in *Shaw* attempted to restrict the *O'Brien* rationale to instances of real evidence only, such a suggestion was later castigated by O'Higgins CJ in *People v Lynch*, where the *O'Brien* criteria were confirmed to justify the exclusion of confessions made by the accused while detained in breach of his constitutional rights.

[70] *People v Lynch* [1982] IR 64.

[71] *People v Lynch* [1982] IR 64 at 85 (followed in the *People v Coffey* (6 March 1981, unreported), HC and *DPP v Herron* (27 October 1981, unreported), HC. Similarly in *People v O'Loughlin* [1979] IR 312 because an investigating Garda stated in court that, although not arrested while in the barracks, if he had attempted to leave, O'Loughlin would have been arrested, the court determined the deprivation of liberty to have been unlawful.

It can be seen, therefore, that the situation of an accused in the aftermath of an arrest and prior to the fulfillment of the obligation to bring him before a court was somewhat uncertain, but characterised by judicial pronouncements on the importance of vindicating the accused's rights in that trial process.

Extraordinary arrest

[2.38] The measure of discretion given to the police, and as such the dilution of the protection of the individual, was greater, however, in the case of the individual dealt with under extraordinary legislation introduced in relation to terrorism. As seen, s 30(3) of the Offences Against the State Act 1939 provided for a possible 48 hour period of detention consequent on arrest. After said period of detention, of course, the normal rule comes into operation, and the individual must be charged before a court (though the court is the Special Criminal Court), and offered the right to bail etc. It is interesting to assess the performance of the Irish judiciary in relation to vindication of rights in the context of such extraordinary powers.

[2.39] In the *People v Madden*[72], a case where the arrestee (Madden) was indeed held under s 30(3) of the Offences Against the State Act 1939, a question arose as to the requirement of bringing the arrestee before the court within the time allotted. Madden had been detained longer than is allowed under s 30(3), allegedly for the purpose of giving a statement which he commenced within the time period allowed, yet finished after the said period had elapsed. It was held by the Court of Criminal Appeal that his statement was inadmissible in evidence as having been obtained when the accused was unlawfully in custody. O'Higgins CJ in his judgment stated:

> 'This lack of regard for and failure to vindicate, the defendant's constitutional right to liberty may not have induced or brought about the making of this statement, but it was the dominating circumstance surrounding its making. In the view of this Court this fact cannot be ignored ...'[73]

[2.40] In the judgment of O'Higgins CJ in *People v Madden*, the loyalty of the judiciary to their constitutional mandate and to the fundamental adversarial nature of the criminal justice seems readily apparent. The judgment, it might be thought, would reassure all civil libertarians, who might quail at the thought of emergency powers being introduced into the realm of the ordinary criminal law. If the judiciary will protect the rights of the subversive, it would seem certain that the ordinary accused will have his rights safeguarded. An alternative interpretation could, however, be that while such a regime as that prevailing

---

[72] *People v Madden* [1977] IR 336.
[73] *People v Madden* [1977] IR 336 at 347-8.

under the Offences Against the State Act 1939, in regard to extensive powers of detention, exists *outside* the rationale of our normal criminal justice system, its use may well be carefully monitored, and yet abuses seen as a temporary aberration in our criminal justice system, and not symptomatic of a basically illegitimate system of justice.

[2.41] Very grave dangers may arise, however, when such powers are no longer 'extraordinary', but have been integrated into the normal criminal process. They may cease to receive special consideration and monitoring. That integration may take many forms: the sanctioning of the use of extraordinary powers in ordinary situations; the introduction of similar provisions in the ordinary regime; or the desensitisation of legislature, judiciary and people to such powers, implicit, and indeed essential, to any such move.

[2.42] *DPP v Kelly*[74] was a case concerning the appeal of the accused against a conviction based on the sole evidence of a number of verbal statements and one comprehensive written statement made while in police custody. The appellant had been arrested pursuant to s 30 of the Offences Against the State Act 1939, and thereafter moved to several garda stations in succession. It was held by the Supreme Court that as long as the duration of the detention was within the permitted period and for the purpose of removal to or in a place complying with the subsection, it was permitted, and plurality of such places or of removals thereto did not contravene the sub-section[75].

[2.43] A certain retrenchment can perhaps be observed in the attitude of the judiciary in this case. In regard to the right to counsel, this phenomenon may be more evident. At the time of trial, an accused has a recognised right to legal counsel free of charge (if indigent) and a consequent right to be informed of that right. In *State (Healy) v Donoghue*[76] the right to legal representation at trial had been recognised as inherent in an accused person caught in the Irish criminal process, with, of necessity, a corresponding right to be informed of it.

[2.44] In the *People v Madden*[77] it was held, however, that in the pre-trial period, an accused's right to counsel is not infringed by the failure to inform him of it[78]. It could be said that the Court in *Madden* retreated from the very strong position taken in *State (Healy) v Donoghue* in regard to the right to counsel in the case of an accused before a court, to a correspondingly much weakened guarantee, in the pre-trial scenario.

---

[74] *DPP v Kelly* [1983] ILRM 271.
[75] *DPP v Kelly* [1983] ILRM 271 at 275.
[76] *State (Healy) v Donoghue* [1976] IR 325.
[77] *People v Madden* [1977] IR 336.
[78] *People v Madden* [1977] IR 336 at 355-356 (O'Higgins CJ).

[2.45] *Madden* and a subsequent decision, *Farrell*[79], were cases in which a retrenchment from the general right to counsel of an accused, particularly in relation to individuals caught in the pre-trial process, was effected. It may be significant that they also involved the use of the extraordinary pre-trial holding powers under the Offences Against the State Act. Such extraordinary powers are not traditionally part of the ordinary common law and so it may well be questioned why, in regard to an ordinary accused, (who is or should be placed under arrest only for the purpose of bringing him before a Court of trial), a right to counsel should only be recognized as inherent in the accused at the trial. To distinguish between such an accused's position before and after appearance at trial seems incongruous as, unlike an individual caught in the throes of extraordinary powers, his/her position will not materially have changed (or should not) in the intervening period.

[2.46] The *State (Healy) v Donoghue*[80] did not involve an exercise of an extraordinary pre-trial detention power and so presented the court with an ideal opportunity to vindicate the rights of an accused, by ensuring him of the right to legal counsel at the trial and, equally importantly, of his right to be informed of such right. Why the courts saw fit to retreat from this position in the case of the pre-trial process is difficult to understand. The court in *Madden* did not deny the right of such an accused to legal representation but it effectively emasculated such a right by not imposing any obligation on the police officers in charge of the case to inform the individual of such right. Perhaps the courts were motivated by considerations related to extraordinary offenders; yet this was not clearly enunciated. Arguably, it is the extraordinary accused who needs greater protection at this pre-trial stage. Behind the rationale of the extraordinary powers, invoked for his detention, lies the philosophy that his arrest is not just 'a step in the criminal process', but is rather a vital and rather large part of the investigative process, if not the entirety, as a large number of cases do not reach a court of trial at all[81].

Whether or not one accepts the latter suggestion, it would seem that a legal system which tolerates two coexistent regimes for 'terrorist' and non-'terrorist' offenders, with very different (indeed even contradictory) legitimising philosophies underlying both, risks the distinction between the two being obliterated to the disadvantage of both. In essence this is what may have happened in the *State (Healy) v Donoghue, Madden* and *Farrell*.

---

[79] *DPP v Farrell* [1978] IR 13 at 20.

[80] *State (Healy) v Donoghue* [1976] IR 325.

[81] O'Mahony *Criminal Chaos: Seven Crises in Criminal Justice* Round Hall, Dublin (1996), p 33 notes that '[b]etween 1975 and 1985, 14,000 people were arrested under section 30, but only 500 of these were charged and less than 300 were eventually convicted under the Act.'

[2.47] It may be that the Irish judiciary, sanguine in the face of exceptional powers, or desensitised to the necessity for vigilance in the maintenance of strict borders around their operation, is one careless of its constitutional mandate, or at least vulnerable to complicity in the accommodation of those powers within the 'normal' regime. It will be interesting to reflect on the origins and development of this tendency, when the judiciary are later faced directly with questions concerning accommodation of the use of s 30 of the 1939 Act and the Special Criminal Court with the 'extraordinary' regime, as well as those validating the constitutionality of 'emergency' type powers in the ordinary criminal process.

Crisis discourse and decision-making in the Irish criminal process

[2.48] A recurrent theme in the Irish criminal justice system, might be seen to be the facility to the State of a sustained and ever renewable 'politics of the last atrocity', which until recently, has been seen to be single focused, short-lived and only dangerous in terms of 'leakage' or 'normalisation' in the criminal process. A more sophisticated analysis has to take account of on-going 'crises' within the State, addressed through the medium of the criminal justice system, which go beyond the direct threat to the State's existence posed by the 'terrorist' or political offender. That analysis would focus also on threats posed more immediately personally to individual citizens. The occasions of these 'crises', together with their implications for the nature of the State and more particularly, its criminal justice system, include the immediately obvious one of 'terrorism' or direct violence related to the overthrow of the State; but also the abuse of drugs and organised crime[82]. The international and financial dimension to the drugs underworld gives a dimension to that problem, which is of national and international concern - and posits an occasion for consensus and change in a virtually unparalleled unanimity regarding 'good' and evil.

[2.49] In the aftermath of happenings in Britain such as Bulger, Dunblane and Philip Lawrence, Downes and Morgan[83] document the change from a broadly bipartisan to a sharply contested politics of law and order, noting there was little

---

[82] This can also be said of sexual abuse, which is less obviously related to a danger to the State, but is disruptive of gender roles, identity and family, each of great import to the State. In relation to sexual offences the changes in criminal procedure include facilitation of live television link and video testimony by witnesses, under the Criminal Evidence Act 1992, which facility was recently extended to intimidated or vulnerable witnesses intimidation by the Criminal Justice Act 1999. The Sexual Offences Act 2001 has also recently provided for limited separate legal representation for rape victims.

[83] Downes and Morgan 'Dumping the "Hostages to Fortune"'? The Politics of Law and Order in Post-War Britain' in *The Oxford Handbook of Criminology* Maguire Morgan Reiner (eds (2nd edn, 1997) p 87.

parliamentary scrutiny or debate of change[84], while the 'politics of law and order in the post-war period have been shaped by the nature of responses to the continuous rise in rates of recorded crime and to the unforseen explosion of politically inspired terrorism and illicit drug trafficking.'[85]

[2.50] That comment could with equal measure be made of Ireland. A plethora of legislative moves has greeted each of the designated crises. The Offences Against the State Act 1939 was invoked in the 1970s in response to Northern Ireland related subversive activity. The Drug Trafficking Act 1996, the Constitutional Bail Amendment, and the establishment of the Criminal Assets Bureau were in response to drugs in the 1990s. More recently, the Omagh bombing[86] led to the introduction of further extended powers of detention relating to terrorism under the Offences Against the State (Amendment) Act 1998[87].

[2.51] Prior to the change in the law relating to bail, under the Supreme Court decision in *O'Callaghan*[88], bail could only be refused on limited grounds. It would subsequently seem as if the change was indeed symbolic, as the urgency in relation to the introduction of extended grounds for refusal could not be said to be reflected in the delay with regard to their eventual enactment and implementation. Of course the point may well be that the appearance is what is important, not the effect. Alldridge makes this point in the context of the field of sexual tourism, and exceptions to the territoriality provisions, where the explanation as to why no prosecution had been brought might be '...that the legislation ... was not enacted for any effect it might have, but...is purely symbolic'[89]. This notion of legislation being implemented as part of a political

---

[84] Downes and Morgan 'Dumping the "hostages to fortune"'? The Politics of Law and Order in Post-War Britain'' in *The Oxford Handbook of Criminology* Maguire Morgan Reiner (eds), (2nd edn, 1997) p 120.

[85] Downes and Morgan 'Dumping the "hostages to fortune"'? The Politics of Law and Order in Post-War Britain'' in *The Oxford Handbook of Criminology* Maguire Morgan Reiner (eds), (2nd edn, 1997) p 128.

[86] The bombing of Omagh town on 15 August 1998. Twenty eight people were killed and the incident was interpreted as a direct attack on the peace process which had been endorsed through the ballot box, North and South. Two weeks later the Offences against the State Bill 1998 was introduced providing for inferences from silence (s 2), and amendment of s 30 of the Offences Against the State Act 1939, allowed for further detention of 24 hours.

[87] Offences Against the State (Amendment) Act 1998, s 10, authorises an officer not below the rank of superintendent to apply to a District Court for a warrant authorising the detention of a person detained under s 30 for a further period not exceeding 24 hours, if he or she has reasonable grounds for believing that such further detention is necessary for the proper investigation of the offence concerned.

[88] *DPP v O'Callaghan* [1966] IR 501.

[89] Allridge 'Sex Offenders Act 1997 – Territoriality Provisions' [1997] Crim LR 655 at 658.

public relations exercise may be seen to be pervasive. Celia Wells has identified the core of assumptions and beliefs underlying the debate on criminal law in the context of stalking as '…that 'violence' is on the increase; that 'something must be done'; and that law, as a vehicle of social change, is the neutral instrument with which to achieve results.'[90]

[2.52] It is important to examine the *cumulative* effect of the changes to the Irish criminal justice system. Each of the recent changes in its particular context merits some attention in order to ascertain the implications for the entirety of criminal justice. An examination of the impetus and background to the introduction of each of these measures, and their subsequent judicial reception, or judicial vindication of rights in those targeted areas, should facilitate an understanding not just of their import for criminal justice and accused's rights, but also for the sustainability of a judicial mandate to uphold rights in the criminal justice system. In the context of a regime with an historic and ongoing toleration of differential treatment of certain accused, it may be especially important to gauge the overall effect of differential treatment(s) and the impact of such exceptions on the overall system.

'Terrorism'

[2.53] Section 30 of the Offences Against the State Act 1939 provided for 48 hour detention after arrest in the context of a regime where the ordinary criminal process did not conceive an arrest as anything other than a mechanism for bringing the accused before a court. The difficulty with this piece of legislation, however, was that it had been introduced for, and was presumed to be, confined to 'terrorist' offences. Hence its use in relation to ordinary crime was perceived as problematic. Indeed this was the origin of the demand for s 4 of the Criminal Justice Act 1984.

Section 4 of the Criminal Justice Act 1984 was introduced as part of a package to combat a contemporary crisis of 'joy riding' in Dublin and other inner-city areas in the country. There was, at the time, widespread concern with regard to civil liberties implications of the proposed powers of detention, and as a result certain safeguards were put in place by the then Minister for Justice. These comprised a provision in the Act itself, s 1 sub-s 2, that certain of its provisions, notably those relating powers of detention, would not come into operation until such time as regulations regarding the treatment of persons in Garda custody were introduced and a Garda Complaints Board was established. The 'Regulations regarding the treatment of persons in Garda custody' were introduced[91] and comprised, in the main, of provisions relating to the appointment of a custody officer (not the person instigating the arrest), the

---

90 Wells 'Stalking: The Criminal Law Response' [1997] Crim LR 463 at 464.

91 SI 119/1987. See Appendix A.

keeping of a custody record of the individual's detention, limitations on powers of interrogation and the number of persons present during same, etc. Under that 1984 Act's regime there was then at least the appearance of a modicum of protection for the accused[92].

It is somewhat ironic that following the introduction of the Criminal Justice Act 1984 and its powers of detention in relation to 'ordinary' crime under s 4, the Irish Supreme Court in *DPP v Quilligan*[93] confirmed the lawfulness of the use of s 30 of the 1939 Act in relation to non-subversive crime. Nevertheless, the 1984 Act continued to be the main vehicle for powers of detention after arrest in the case of ordinary 'non-subversive' related activities of individuals.[94]

[2.54] The change in relation to the function of arrest, and the general facilitation of interrogation subsequent to arrest, can be identified as the

---

[92] Prior to 1984 there had been decisions like *Pringle* and *Lynch (People (DPP) v Pringle* (22 May 1981, unreported) CCA (O'Higgins CJ); *People (DPP) v Lynch* [1982] IR 64) where the s 30 of the 1939 Act powers were used. *People (DPP) v Pringle* involved the interrogation of *Pringle* arrested under s 30, for lengthy periods over 43 hours, and the involvement of his girlfriend by the gardaí bringing her to the station and interrogating her while he was in custody (cf *Ward*). Nonetheless, he was convicted solely on the basis of a confession. Due to the subsequent discovery of non-disclosure of forensic evidence to the defence, *Pringle* was later processed as a miscarriage of justice case. *(People (DPP) v Pringle* [1995] 2 IR 547). *People (DPP) v Lynch* is perhaps the least well-known of the miscarriage of justice cases, as the individual did not pursue any such claim. Here a conviction was based on a confession obtained under interrogation of 22 hours duration, and was later revealed in the Supreme Court to be contrary to factual evidence which supported Lynch's account.

Subsequent to 1984, despite the safeguards introduced to allay civil liberties concerns, in decisions like *People (DPP) v Connell* [1995] 2 IR 244, interrogation was revealed to be conducted in breach of all directions regarding length and conduct of investigations. Connell had been arrested under s 30 of the Offences Against the State Act 1939, interrogated in breach of the 1987 Custody Regulations and denied access to his solicitor. His conviction of murder on the basis of an inculpatory statement was quashed. In *People (DPP) v Meleady & Grogan* [1995] 2 IR 517, relating to the conviction of two young men from Tallaght (to be known as the *Tallaght Two* case) on the basis, primarily, of the visual identification evidence of the car owner who clung to the hood as they escaped, it later emerged as a result of a TV investigation that forensic evidence of a fingerprint which would have substantiated the boys' account was not revealed by the prosecution.

It was in recognition, perhaps of these miscarriages of justice, as much as their more highly publicised counterparts in England, that the provision found in the Criminal Procedure Act 1993 s10, requiring corroboration of confession evidence was introduced, which provides 'where at the trial of a person evidence is given of a confession made by that person and that evidence is not corroborated, the Judge shall advise the jury to have due regard to the absence of corroboration.'

[93] *DPP v Quilligan* [1987] ILRM 600.

[94] In similar vein, the use of the Special Criminal Court, established under Part V of the Offences Against the State Act 1939 and operating as a non-jury court despite the explicit guarantee to trial by jury under the Constitution, was accommodated out with the terrorist context, and in relation to non-subversive cases by the Supreme Court in *Kavanagh*.

beginning of the process of normalisation in Ireland. The focus of this work is not on the manner of that particular accommodation – other than to note its occurrence – so much as the ongoing effects of the existence of an 'extraordinary' regime within the jurisdiction, and in particular the more recent manifestations of exception. This has broadened beyond terrorism itself, but the purchase of terrorism is still effective and its usefulness to the State not spent. This is evidenced by the augmentation of the powers of detention under s 30 by the Offences Against the State (Amendment) Act 1998 which allows for an additional 24-hour period of detention (72 hours in total).

This change was introduced in direct response to the Omagh bombing[95]. The Minister was reported as describing the provisions as 'draconian'. The Government statement in its response to Omagh, left open the option of internment, and in relation to measures which were introduced, stated '(t)he primary consideration in considering any case for amendment of the criminal law is to maximise its efficiency in tackling the activities of criminals.'[96] Several cabinet members, it was reported, were in fact in favour of the use of internment[97]. It was argued at the time (although not a generally held view) that such re-introduction of internment would be more honest than

'... further attempts to undermine the fundamental principles of our criminal justice system with the attendant risks of police brutality, forced confessions, miscarriages of justice, unacceptably long detention periods, abolition of the right to silence, the perversion of the rules of evidence and ultimately the discrediting of the legal system itself.'[98]

This legislation was due to lapse on 30 June 2000. Significantly, on the occasion of its renewal for a further year, the Minister reported to the Dáil that not a single prosecution had been brought under the Act and that the only provisions used were those relating to the extension of detention. This was used in 29 instances, none leading to a charge. Despite reference in the debates to the view of the Garda Commissioner that those responsible for Omagh were unlikely now to be discovered, the continuance of the legislation was approved for a further year.[99]

---

[95] The Offences Against the State Act 1998 also introduced new offences of directing an unlawful organisation (s 6), possession of articles for purposes connected with certain offences (explosives, firearms) (s 7), unlawful collection of information (s 8), and training persons in the making or use of firearms (s 12).

[96] (1998) Irish Times, 20 August.

[97] (1998) Sunday Business Post, 23 August, p 1.

[98] Hogan 'Internment preferable to Laws that Fail the Tests' (1998) Irish Times, 19 August, p 14.

[99] The Minister expressly referred to garda advice as to the necessity for continuance of the legislation, and the desire to maintain the existing regime pending the Hederman review which would address the overall Offences against the State Acts regime, Dáil Debates Official Report 20-06-00. In accordance with the requirements of the 1998 Act, s 18(3) the Minister has to lay a report before the Dáil on the use of the legislation.

Since then the legislation has been renewed annually. There could hardly be greater evidence of the symbolic nature of such legislation in terms of effectiveness, or of State appetite for continuance and extension beyond its remit.

[2.55] Under the Offences Against the State Act regime, an infringement on the right to silence existed by virtue of s 52 of the Offences Against the State Act 1939. The right to silence was nonetheless found to be constitutionally guaranteed under Article 38.1 in *Heaney v McGuinness*[100], by Costello J, who classified s 52 as a proportional infringement of that right of the accused. Such provision with regard to inferences from silence is now mirrored by ss 18 and 19 of the Criminal Justice Act 1984 (the constitutionality of which was upheld in *Rock v Ireland*[101]), and s 7 of the Criminal Justice (Drug Trafficking) Act 1996. The right to silence has been further eroded by the 1998 Act, ss 2 and 5 which allow inferences to be drawn from the failure of an accused to mention facts later relied on in his defence, while s 9 of the 1998 Act makes it an offence for a person to stay silent without a reasonable excuse, when he has information he knows or believes may be of assistance to the gardaí.

Drugs

[2.56] The legacy of the 'terrorist regime' was evident when the Minister for Justice, Nora Owen, TD,[102] pledged in 1995 in relation to 'major initiatives' termed the 'New Government Measures to Combat Drugs', that the government would 'wage an all out fight against the drugs scourge' which she described as 'a threat to the very fabric of our society'. The Minister stated that these were tough measures but described drug trafficking as 'a form of modern day

---

[100] *Heaney v McGuinness* [1994] 3 IR 593.

[101] *Rock v Ireland* [1998] 2 ILRM 35.

[102] The Minister for Justice, Nora Owen TD, in the press statement issued by Government Information Services on 19 July 1995. It is instructive to note that initially the locus of change here was the criminal justice system generally, and not the drugs problem simpliciter. The Criminal Justice Bill 1994, which might be seen as the precursor of what is now the Criminal Justice (Drug Trafficking) Act 1996, was introduced as a Private Members Bill by Progressive Democrat TDs Liz O'Donnell and Michael McDowell. It proposed to increase existing infringements on an accused's right to silence (thus building on initial incursions introduced by the Criminal Justice Act 1984), amend the law in relation to bail, and bring about a radical shift in emphasis from traditional criminal procedure in so far as the accused could be called upon to testify by the prosecution and might be interrogated in the District Court. Although this was a measure emanating from a small political party with a perceived right-wing orientation, it is illustrative of the level of cross-party support and indeed pressure for a 'law and order' approach.

terrorism' (sic) which attacks the very core of our society[103]. The press statement issued declared that the measures proposed an enhancement of Garda powers, though this must be *proportionate* at all times. The Minister concluded by stating:

> 'We must be prepared to wage the fight on the educational, health and law enforcement sides for as long as it takes. We are confronted by ruthless people who are destroying whole *communities* all over the world. We must face them down' [Emphasis added].[104]

[2.57] The Criminal Justice Act 1984 was to be the vehicle for the introduction of these extended powers of detentions subsequent to arrest. This was not a novel function for that particular piece of legislation, which as seen in 1984 introduced the first power of detention after arrest in relation to 'ordinary' crime. Although the Criminal Justice (Drug Trafficking) Bill 1996, when ultimately introduced, contained a power of arrest and detention in its own right, and not an amendment of s 4 of the 1984 Act, the initial connection is interesting, not least for the historical connection with the 'terrorist' power under s 30, which might be said to have honed police powers of investigation by

---

[103] The use of 'war-like' terminology in this area continues as a theme: *The First Annual Report of the Department of Justice, Equality and Law Reform* (1997), p 7, comments that the State agencies are 'in the *battle against crime*'; and the press release issued by the Department of Justice, Equality and Law Reform on the launch of the *First Report of the Expert Group on Probation and Welfare Services* by the Minister for Justice John O'Donoghue, states: 'We are *winning the war* against crime, crime levels are down.' http://www.irgov.ie/justice/Press%20releases/Press.htm.

[104] *First Report of the Expert Group on Probation and Welfare Services.* At that stage, the key measures to combat drugs were to include: inter-agency co-operation, and increased powers to include the amendment of the Criminal Justice Act 1984 so as to allow the gardaí, on the certification of a Chief Superintendent, to detain a person suspected of drug trafficking for a period of 24 hours initially and, if necessary, for a further period up to a maximum of an additional 72 hours if satisfied that this is necessary and, upon further request, may permit a final extension to the detention period for up to a maximum of a further 48 hours, if satisfied that this is necessary. There was also to be extension of responsibility for the issue of search warrants in drug trafficking cases to a Garda superintendent; new structures; and demand reduction/education measures.

It is an indication of the overall tenor of the response and its perception, that on 22 November 1995, the Irish Times in a report in relation to the new Drugs Bill, mentioned simply the tough measures which were to be introduced to combat drug trafficking and which were said to have been given priority by the government. The measures mentioned were the increased powers of detention for gardaí, which would mean that suspects could be detained for up to seven days, a judge having to authorise detention after 48 hours. There was also mention of the Garda Superintendent's power to issue search warrants under the Bill, and that the Naval Officers were also to be given new powers of search and seizure and arrest under orders made under the Criminal Justice Act 1994. There was no mention of the alternative measures to combat the drugs problem, simply the law enforcement ones.

interrogation in Ireland, but also because of the particular crisis or context in which the 1984 Act was itself introduced.

[2.58] The process of change and normalisation can be seen to culminate in the drugs context with the introduction of further and extensive powers of detention, search and confiscation of assets, by virtue of the so-called 'crime-package'.[105] The measures introduced included the following: increased powers of detention – up to seven days – together with garda power to issue search warrants in certain circumstances provided for under the Criminal Justice Drug Trafficking Act 1996; broad powers of search under the Criminal Assets Bureau Act 1996 (s 14), which established the Bureau, and allowed for issuance of search warrants by certain of its officers; and provision for the issuance of production orders, and increased powers relating to the proceeds of crime, enabling confiscation of proceeds of crime independent of conviction introduced under the Proceeds of Crime Act 1996 (this was to lead to constitutional challenge – see *Gilligan*). The Disclosure of Information for Taxation and Other Purposes Act 1996 also amended and extended an earlier Disclosure of Information for Taxation and Other Purposes Act 1996 to allow for wider use of information obtained under money-laundering provisions of that Act.

[2.59] The drugs scenario also saw the birth of the State's first Witness Protection Programme. The Witness Protection Programme was established by the Government in November 1997[106] to be administered entirely by the Garda Síochána. Announcing the scheme, the Minister for Justice, Mr O'Donoghue, said, 'the new breed of ruthless and well-organised criminals, particularly in drugs and money-laundering showed the need for new measures'. Issues surrounding criminal convictions on the ground of the uncorroborated evidence of accomplices have subsequently arisen in the cases of *Holland, Ward* and *Meehan*. It is also true to say that the spectre of the *supergrass* phenomenon in the context of terrorism in Northern Ireland, hangs over these cases, and is reinforced by the fact that these cases take place in the non-jury Special Criminal Court. The legal issues arising are central to the heart of pre-trial and trial justice and include those of access to a lawyer, recording of interviews, treatment during detention, admissibility of statements and accomplice evidence[107]. The manner of their resolution raises the question of interrelation

---

[105] The legislation in relation to drugs and organised crime, referred to as the 'Crime Package', was introduced in the aftermath of the Veronica Guerin murder and guillotined through on a recall of the Dáil. It met with a stultifying cross-party consensus.

[106] See (1997) Irish Times, 7 November.

[107] In terms of consistency or coherence in the non-jury court it is interesting to note that in the recent *Meehan* case (July 1999), Charles Bowden one of several state witness protection programme witnesses whose testimony formed the State's case against Meehan, and whose testimony alone had been the basis of Ward's earlier conviction was found to be entirely incredible.

between legislative change and judicial monitoring of criminal justice principles, together with the ongoing implications of exceptional provisions and their ring-fencing. The accommodation of exceptional provision and its implication for overall principle can be usefully pursued through the language of these judgments and their conclusions.

[2.60] Section 2 of the Criminal Justice (Drug Trafficking) Act 1996 provides for powers of detention of the order of 6 hours followed by a further period (directed by a garda not below the rank of Chief Superintendent) of 18 hours if he has reasonable grounds for believing that such further detention is necessary for the proper investigation of the offence concerned. He can then further sanction a period of 24 hours on the same basis. At this point application can be made by an officer not below the rank of Chief Superintendent, to a Circuit Court or District Court judge for a warrant authorising detention of the person detained for a further period of 72 hours if he has reasonable grounds for believing that such further investigation is necessary for the proper investigation of the offence concerned. This may be authorised if the judge is satisfied that such further detention is necessary and that the investigation is being conducted diligently and expeditiously. A further period of 48 hours can again be authorised on application to a judge if the officer has reasonable grounds for believing such is necessary for the proper investigation of the offence concerned and the investigation is being conducted diligently and expeditiously. In total a person can be detained for a maximum period of 168 hours (one week) under the terms of the Act. The reason for the judicial intervention after 48 hours, was to ensure compliance with the European Convention of Human Rights, found to mandate same in the context of the *Brogan* case relating to the Prevention of Terrorism Act in the United Kingdom.

[2.61] Section 8 of the Drug Trafficking Act 1996 provides for the issuance of search warrants by a member of the Garda Síochána not below the rank of Superintendent under s 26 of the 1977 Act where he is satisfied:

(a)   that the warrant is necessary for the proper investigation of the suspected drug trafficking offence, and

(b)   that circumstances of urgency giving rise to the need for the immediate issue of the search warrant would render it impracticable to apply to a District Court judge or Peace Commissioner.

[2.62] The Criminal Assets Bureau was given similarly broad powers to issue search warrant (under s 14 of the Criminal Assets Bureau Act 1996), and was equipped with powers to seize assets suspected of being the proceeds of crime. The powers to issue warrants without judicial intervention is unusual, precedented only in the Offences Against the State context, and in stark contrast to a series of higher Irish court decisions underscoring the importance of the judicial role in the issuance of search warrants and their invalidity in the case of rubberstamping police suspicions (*DPP v Kenny,* and *DPP v Yamanoha*[108]).

[2.63] The Proceeds of Crime Act 1996, ss 2 and 3 permits the High Court to make orders preventing someone from dealing with specified property worth not less than £10,000 (€12,697.38). It must be shown that the property represents the proceeds of crime (the civil standard applying). When the order is made the respondent then bears the onus of proof to establish the property is not the 'proceeds of crime' in order to have the court discharge or vary the order. Once an order has been in place for seven years, the High Court can make a disposal order transferring all rights in the property to the Minister for Finance. The concept 'proceeds of crime' is defined very broadly in s 1 of the 1996 Act as 'any property obtained or received at any time (before or after the passing of the Act) by or as a result of or in connection with, the commission of an offence'. This Act had a precursor in the Disclosure of Information for Taxation and Other Purposes Act 1996, but augments previous powers included in the 1994 piece of legislation, in so far as a conviction is not now required as the basis for forfeiture, and a burden of disclosure is placed on a greater number of professionals.

[2.64] The Criminal Justice Act 1999, signed into law on 26 May 1999, contains further provisions particularly targeted at the area of drugs. Part 2 of the 1999 Act, which came immediately into effect, creates a new offence of possession of drugs with intent to supply with a value of £10,000 (€12,697.38) or more, with a minimum mandatory 10 year sentence, signifying, according to Minister O'Donoghue, that '... there is no room for complacency, the Act is further evidence of the Government's zero tolerance approach to crime'.[109]

[2.65] Part 6 of the 1999 Act also came into operation immediately and contains provisions dealing with the intimidation of witnesses. The provisions (similar to those in operation for victims of sexual offences under the Criminal Justice (Evidence) Act 1992), allow intimidated or vulnerable witnesses to give evidence by video-link and provide further evidence of the facility for expansion of exceptional provisions. A new statutory offence of intimidation of witnesses, jurors etc, with a penalty of up to ten years is created, as well as a new offence with a penalty of up to five years, of attempting to track down witnesses who have been relocated under the Witness Protection Scheme[110].

---

[108] *DPP v Kenny* [1990] ILRM 569; *DPP v Yamanoha* [1994] 1 IR 565.

[109] Http://www.irlgov.ie/justice/Press%20Releases/Press-99/pr-2605a.htm.

[110] Provision is also included in the Act to abolish preliminary examinations, and facilitate automatic asset inquiries in drug trafficking cases, but these do not come into effect immediately.

The Bail Amendment to the Constitution

[2.66] The background to the Constitutional amendment on bail was the announcement in September 1995 of an increase in crime rates in Dublin of 8%. The immediate response of the Fianna Fáil spokesperson on justice, John O'Donoghue, was to urge Nora Owen, the then Minister for Justice, to urgently bring forward what she had already proposed: a referendum which would allow refusal of bail if the gardaí and the judge thought the individual was likely to commit crime while on bail[111].

[2.67] Article 40.4.1° of the Constitution provides that no one shall be deprived of liberty save in accordance with law. Under Irish law, prior to the Sixteenth Amendment to the Constitution[112], there were only two grounds on which a person could be refused bail:

(a) the likelihood that the accused will not turn up for trial,

(b) the likelihood that he will interfere with witnesses or evidence.

[2.68] That these were the only grounds on which bail could be refused was stated by the Supreme Court in *O'Callaghan*[113] and confirmed by the Supreme Court in *Ryan v DPP*[114]. The Sixteenth Amendment would widen the grounds for refusal considerably. It would provide that someone charged with a serious offence could be refused bail where it was reasonably considered necessary to prevent the commission of a serious offence – serious offences included those meriting five years-imprisonment or more, thereby including most criminal offences. The criteria or matters to be taken into account by the court in deciding whether to grant bail to an accused charged with one of these offences are the following:

---

[111] See Editorial 'Bail reform: Expediency Before Principle' (1995) 13 (10) ILT223. In the event, the killing of Veronica Guerin also had an input, as that journalist was also on record as wanting a change in the bail laws.

[112] The Sixteenth Amendment stated: 'Provision may be made by law for the refusal of bail by a court to a person charged with a serious offence where it is reasonably considered necessary to prevent the commission of a serious offence by that person.' This was an 'enabling' provision in the Constitution to be followed by a separate Bill indicating the terms on which bail could be refused. The amendment was passed and the implementing legislation, the Bail Act 1997, enacted in May 1997.

At the time of writing, the provisions have not yet been brought into effect, although at the Fianna Fáil Ard Fheis, 3 March 2000, the Minister announced that the Act would be brought in effect in its entirety on 15 May 2000. http://www.irlgov.ie/justice/Press%20Releases/Press-2000/pr-0303.htm. In the Irish Times (2000) 4 May, Jim Cusack, security correspondent, reported that the Minister was to implement new restrictions on the right to bail that month.

[113] *People (Attorney General) v O'Callaghan* [1966] IR 501.

[114] *Ryan v DPP* [1989] IR 399.

— the nature and degree of seriousness of the offence charged and the potential penalty;

— the nature and degree of seriousness of the offence apprehended and the potential penalty;

— the conviction of the accused in respect of an offence committed while on bail on a previous occasion;

— any previous conviction of the accused;

— any other offence in respect of which the accused is charged and awaiting trial;

— the nature and strength of the evidence in support of the charge; and

— whether the accused has a substance addiction.

Should an accused be refused bail, and where the trial has not commenced within four months, the court could order his release if satisfied that the 'interests of justice' require it. Once again it was left to the judiciary to finesse that equation.

[2.69] Finlay CJ in *Ryan* had stated the proper methods of preventing crime were the long-established combination of police surveillance, speedy trial and deterrent sentences. As an example of the latter he instanced s 11 of the Criminal Justice Act 1984 which provides for consecutive sentences for offences committed while on bail. Since its introduction the latter had been somewhat stymied as the courts had taken the opportunity to suspend that sentence, by looking at the proportionality of the totality of the sentence in relation to the crime. The Law Reform Commission[115] had earlier been asked by the Government to examine the law on bail (but not make recommendations) and had put forward alternative strategies such as an offence of breaching bail conditions, attaching a good behaviour condition to bail, estreatment of bail if the accused commits a further offence, as well as reduction of delay, and implementation of s 11.

[2.70] With regard to the argument that under current conditions, criminals on bail could reoffend with impunity and be unlikely to receive greater sentences, the Commission had commented that:

> '…this argument…prescribes stronger medicine than is warranted by the disease. If Judges do not punish offenders adequately for bail offences, it may be argued that the appropriate solution is that they should so punish them, not that offenders be preventatively detained to prevent these offences.'[116]

---

[115] *Report on An Examination of the Law on Bail* (LRC 50-1995). The Commission was asked in February 1994 to undertake examination of and conduct research in relation to the law on bail but was not asked to formulate and submit proposals for reform.

[116] *Report on An Examination of the Law on Bail* (LRC 50-1995), p 166.

[2.71] The Constitutional Review Group in its report[117] had pointed out that Article 5 of the European Convention on Human Rights provides for an exhaustive enumeration of the categories of deprivation of liberty. It noted these correspond broadly with the categories of detention authorised by Irish law, except in two respects: Irish legislation provides for internment and, in some cases, the Convention permits preventive detention[118]. The Constitutional Review Group noted that pre-trial preventative detention expressly contemplated by Article 5(1) had been held to be inconsistent with the provisions of the Constitution in *O'Callaghan* and *Ryan*. It noted that a switch to an Article 5(1)(c) type provision 'would result in a lessening of the general protection of the right to individual liberty in the circumstances'[119] and recommended no change.

[2.72] Prior to the amendment campaign, therefore, neither the Constitutional Review Group nor the Law Reform Commission (albeit that the latter had not been asked for a recommendation) evidenced a need for a change in the law. Pre-amendment judicial statements with regard to bail give an insight into judicial views on its position within our system, and so helped assess the effect of the proposed change.

[2.73] In *O'Callaghan*[120] Ó Dálaigh CJ stated in response to the argument that there should be such further grounds for refusal of bail:

> 'The reasoning underlying this submission, is in my opinion, a denial of the whole basis of our system of law. It transcends respect for the requirement that a man shall be considered innocent until he is found guilty and seeks to punish him in respect of offences neither completed nor attempted. I say "punish" for deprivation of liberty must be considered a punishment unless it can be required to ensure that an accused person will stand his trial when called upon.'[121]

---

[117] *Report of the Constitution Review Group* (1996).

[118] The power of internment they note is conferred by the Offences Against the State (Amendment) Act 1940, which came into law following reference to the Supreme Court by the President as to its constitutionality (an almost identical provision had been struck down by Gavan Duffy J in *State (Burke) v Lennon* [1940] IR 136 the year before). It was deemed constitutional and, on one view, remains unassailable by virtue of the provisions of Article 34.3.3° of the Constitution. Some doubt is expressed in the Constitutional Review Group's Report as to the decision, as it is a decision of the old Supreme Court (see further Report, p 282). However, an Article 15 derogation could 'save' such internment, as happened when Ireland reintroduced internment in 1957, which event was reviewed by the Court of Human Rights in the *Lawless* case. (*Lawless v Ireland* (1961) 1 EHRR 15.)

[119] *Lawless v Ireland* (1961) 1 EHRR 15 at 283.

[120] *The People (AG) v O'Callaghan* [1966] IR 501.

[121] *The People (AG) v O'Callaghan* [1966] IR 501 at 508-509.

[2.74] Walsh J also emphasised that the sole purpose of bail was to secure the attendance of the accused at his trial, as '...[t]he presumption of innocence is a very real thing and is not simply a procedural rule taking effect only at the trial.'[122] Walsh J emphatically rejected the likelihood of committing further offences as a reason for refusing bail, which he saw as '... a form of preventative justice which has no place in our legal system ...'.

[2.75] In *Ryan v DPP*[123], upholding the decision in *O'Callaghan*, Finlay CJ (Walsh, Griffin and Hederman JJ agreeing) stated that an intention to commit a crime is not itself a crime unless furthered by overt acts or converted by agreement with others into a conspiracy:

> 'The criminalising of mere intention has been usually a badge of an oppressive or unjust system. The proper method of preventing crime are long-established combination of police surveillance, speedy trial and deterrent sentences. Section 11...constitutes a good example of such a deterrent'[124]

McCarthy J stated that if a person were to be denied his liberty because of a well-founded suspicion, there was:

> ...'no logical reason why any other citizen, not so charged, might not be detained upon a similar contention supported by similarly impressive evidence. The pointing finger of accusation, not of crime done, but of crime feared, would become the test. Such appears to me to be far from a balancing of constitutional rights; it is a recalibration of the scales of justice.'[125]

It would seem that the judiciary espoused trenchantly the cause of individual rights, seeing the limited grounds for restriction of bail as fundamental to the Irish system of criminal justice.

[2.76] By contrast, in terms of the construction of the 'public voice' on the matter of the bail amendment, government speech and lobbyist voices in the run up to the referendum, placed the option before the people of whether they chose protection of the accused's rights in face of, or as opposed to, the community's need to prevent crime[126]. As a result of the Supreme Court judgment in

---

[122] *The People (AG) v O'Callaghan* [1966] IR 501 at 513.

[123] *Ryan v DPP* [1989] IR 399.

[124] *Ryan v DPP* [1989] IR 399 at 407.

[125] *Ryan v DPP* [1989] IR 399 at 410.

[126] One representative of the victims association stated the case thus: 'Victims of crime will see the introduction of the bail amendment as an acknowledgement of their plight. It will also represent a hopeful sign that after years of marginalisation, the rights of crime victims are moving towards the centre-stage. (Keaveney, 'Victims of Crime also have Right to Justice' (1996) Irish Times, 20 November.) The Irish Times in its editorial of 14 October 1996 recognised the 'right to bail' had been one of the fundamental freedoms of this jurisdiction over the last 30 years, but stated that concerns about same must be 'set against public unease about crime and criminality'.

McKenna[127] in November 1995, it was unconstitutional for the government to spend public monies in a referendum advocating a particular result. An ad hoc Commission on Referendum Information was therefore established for the purposes of informing the public, and, took out advertisements in national newspapers, advocating the cases for and against the amendment[128].

[2.77] In favour of the amendment, under the heading 'The Amendment will give Greater Protection to the Public', it was stated: 'There is…a public demand for changes in criminal law and procedure and the Amendment will help to restore the balance between the rights of victims and the rights of those charged with crime.' The opposition of accused and victim is neatly effected. A later statement that '[t]he proposal is a carefully balanced and reasonable measure under which it will be necessary for the court to be satisfied of the risk to society posed by an accused person before bail is refused' made the further opposition between society and accused clear[129].

---

[126] (contd) By contrast, the Irish Commission for Justice and Peace (a commission of the Irish Catholic Bishops Conference) calling for a 'no' vote, tailored their argument to try to persuade victims by making reference to the lack of prison spaces available ('The Bail Referendum: Adequacy and Costs of Proposed Additional Prison Accommodation' statement issued on 26 November 1996). In similar vein the Irish Council for Civil Liberties *Position Paper on the Forthcoming Bail Referendum* (1996), pointed out that the Law Reform Commission had found that despite the powers of the English courts to remove from circulation persons who might re-offend on bail, the percentage of offences committed by persons on bail for both 1992 and 1993 was at 9%, lower than its English equivalent.

[127] *In the matter of Bunreacht na hEireann: Patricia McKenna v An Taoiseach and Others* [1995] 2 IR 10.

[128] *Referendum on a Proposal to Amend the Constitution in relation to Bail* published in the Provincial papers 18-22 November 1996; national Daily and evening papers on 21 November 1996; Foinse (in Irish only), Sunday Independent, Sunday Business Post, Sunday Tribune and Sunday World on 24 November 1996. The Minister for the Environment, Mr Brendan Howlin TD, requested the Chairman of the Bar Council to nominate two Senior Counsel, one of whom, Mr Sean Ryan, prepared the statement of the case in favour of the proposed constitutional amendment, and the other, Mr Edward Comyn, the case against.

[129] It is then declared that 'The Amendment complies with international Standards and makes Common Sense' and the statement concludes:

'The question is not an ideological one but is basically a matter of common sense. The proposal does not dictate that bail will be refused in any particular case. It just gives the court the capacity to refuse it if the accused is likely to commit serious crime while awaiting trial. The State has an obligation to protect people against individuals who persistently re-offend while on bail.'

Once again the identification is made between State and people, and their opposition with the individual underscored. The appeal to common sense and denial of ideology would seem both duplicitous and worrisome.

[2.78] The statement of the case against the Amendment commenced with the heading: 'The Amendment will Breach a Fundamental Principle of Justice.' This was followed by the statement: 'Every person is presumed innocent until, after a valid trial, such person is found guilty. This simple statement, so well known to everybody, is a fundamental principle of justice both constitutional and natural.' The right is clearly stated here as an individual right, which is not related directly to the public as important in their terms.

[2.79] Under the next heading, 'The Crucial Importance of Bail', the section commenced: 'Fundamental principles of liberty are involved in the law of bail. The right to bail is that right which every accused has to personal liberty until his/her trial.' Once again, the right is that of the accused, not related to the public or society. The remainder of the argument set out the consequences if the amendment was passed – solely in terms of repercussions for the accused and prison places – and stated the amendment to be unnecessary. No public or community dimension to the (individual) right was acknowledged. Moreover, quiescent in the case made in favour of the Amendment, is the assumption that the current charges were validly laid – hence as Kieselbach points out, '[p]redicating detention on the basis of this assumed validity is inconsistent with the presumption of innocence ... charges [are] turned into evidence that the accused [is] guilty or would soon be guilty of something else.'[130]

[2.80] It would seem to be clear from the enunciation of the case for and against the amendment in relation to bail, that the construction of a division between the individual (accused) and society (victim) in this context completely overwhelms and dominates the arguments, such that the public, on reading same, perceive its interests as on one side rather than the other. This implicit sacrifice of individual rights for the greater good involves, according to Von Hirsh:

> '...cost-benefit thinking [which] is wholly inappropriate here. If a system of preventative incarceration is known systematically to generate mistaken confinements, then it is unacceptable in absolute terms because it violates the obligation of society to do individual justice. Such a system cannot be justified by arguing that its aggregate social benefits exceed the aggregate amount of injustice done to mistakenly confined individuals.'[131]

[2.81] It was not all that surprising that the amendment passed on November 28, 1996. Given the urgency with which the amendment was presented, it is insightful, however, that the implementing legislation, the Bail Act 1997, was

---

[130] Kieselbach 'Pre-trial Criminal Procedure and Preventative Detention and the Presumption of Innocence' (1989) 31 Crim LQ 168.

[131] Von Hirsh 'Prediction of Criminal Conduct and Preventive Confinement of Convicted Persons' (1972) 21 Buffalo LR 717 at 740.

not enacted until May 1997, and the provisions were not brought fully into effect until May 2000[132]. Despite that fact, the first reported use of the Bail Act 1997 was in October 1999, when it was reported as having been invoked to refuse bail in the case of individuals caught at a 'Real IRA' training camp where gardaí had discovered guns and ammunition[133]. O'Higgins J, presiding in the Special Criminal Court, was reported to have refused bail on the grounds that the accused would not have turned up for their trial and that he believed they would commit further offences if granted bail. The former is in fact the original pre-amendment basis for refusal of bail which was effective here solely, as the amendment could not have been invoked, not having been brought into law. Yet the interpretation of what had occurred in the public context – and indeed judicially referenced – was the essence of what had been passed through the amendment, even though the latter was merely of appearance and not of substantive effect. There could hardly be better manifestation of the symbolic role of the amendment or legislation. In terms of the ostensible use of the new power, the case was moreover a 'terrorist' one connected with a recent atrocity, always suitable for invocation of extraordinary measures.

Proposals for further extension of exceptional provision

[2.82] On the occasion of each of these legislative changes, whether introduced in the context of drugs, or terrorism, the language of the 'media', politicians and protagonist representatives, is similar. The unanimity can be chilling. The suggestion that exceptional provision, once introduced, will find a host of new justifications for its continued presence – outside its originating rationale – is further supported by the expansion of the ambit of many of these provisions, envisaged by the Report of the Expert Group on Criminal Law, 25 November

---

[132] At the Fianna Fail Ard Fheis on the 3 March 2000, the Minister announced that the Act would be brought into effect in its entirety on 15 May 2000. The Minister's speech made the point that the 'Government's unprecedented prison building programme where over 1,200 additional prison spaces have to date been provided' made it possible for him to bring this 'key anti-crime measure' into force. 'O'Donoghue Announces Bail Act to Come into Force on 15 May next' (2000) Press Release 3 March http://www.irlgov.ie/justice/Press%20Releases/Press-2000/pr-0303.htm. The Minister for Justice signed the commencement order to implement the Bail Referendum on 4 May 2000. See 'Minister warned over bail law' Catherine Cleary, (2000) Sunday Tribune, 2 July, p 4.

[133] (1999) Irish Times, 28 October 'Bail for Seven Men on Meath arms charges is refused under 1977 (sic) Act'. Detective Chief Superintendent Walsh said the seven were members of the 'Real IRA', which was responsible for the Omagh bombing and dedicated to bringing down the peace process in Northern Ireland. Chief Superintendent Walsh was reported as having invoked the provisions in the Bail Act to refuse bail where the gardai believe an accused might commit further offences if granted bail.

1998[134]. One such recommendation of the Group was that in all circumstances of immediate urgency, a garda, not below the rank of superintendent, be able to issue a search warrant (which would expire after 24 hours). This mirrors previous provision under the Offences Against the State Act 1939[135], subsequently followed in the Criminal Justice (Drug Trafficking) Act 1996.

[2.83] The Expert Group also concluded that the 12 hour period of detention consequent on arrest under the Criminal Justice Act 1984 is 'inadequate for the proper investigation of murder, rape or other serious offences', and recommended a provision similar to s 30 of the Offences Against the State Act 1939 for specified serious offences to include murder, manslaughter, kidnapping, false imprisonment and rape.

[2.84] With regard to the right to silence, the Group's recommendation was that the provisions of the Criminal Justice (Drug Trafficking) Act 1996, relating to the right to silence, be extended to all serious offences. (It noted that this had already been done in relation to a number of Offences in the Offences Against the State (Amendment) Act 1998.) Where a defendant relied on a fact in his defence which he could reasonably have been expected to mention on being questioned, such adverse inferences as may appear proper may be drawn from a failure to mention it (this could corroborate other evidence but not suffice for a conviction)[136].

[2.85] The Group stated it was conscious of:

---

[134] *Report of the Expert Group on Criminal Law Department of Justice* 25 November 1998, http://www.irlgov.ie/justice/Press%20 Releases/Press-98/pr-2511.htm. At the time of writing the implementation of these recommendations is under consideration at the Department of Justice, Equality and Law Reform and the Criminal Justice (Garda Powers) Bill at an advanced stage of preparation, to be published at the end of 2003: http/www.justice.ie/PressRelease 4 July 2003.

[135] Offences Against the State Act 1939, s 29, permits a member of the Garda Síochána not below the rank of Superintendent to issue a 'search order' to search any place if there is reasonable ground for supposing an offence under that Act has been, or is about to be committed.

[136] Htpp:/www.irlgov.ie/justice/Press%20Releases/Press-98/pr-2511.htm.
Although not particularly related to a given exceptional provision under consideration here as related to emergency provisions, but rather part of the generalised trend towards 'law and order' powers, it is interesting to note with regard to search warrants the Group recommended that the Criminal Justice (Miscellaneous Provisions) Act 1997, s 10 — which provides for the issuance of a warrant by a District Court Judge authorising a garda to search a place for evidence of certain offences, and which currently applies only to a limited number of serious offences (indictable offences involving death or serious injury, false imprisonment, rape and certain other sexual offences) — be extended to all criminal offences punishable by five years imprisonment or more. Other recommendations of the group relate seizure of evidence, power to arrest, crime scene preservation, (ie parades, fingerprinting and forensic evidence) and station bail.

'the need to balance additional powers with appropriate safeguards. They had been careful to include in their proposals any specific safeguards which they thought necessary and to that extent their proposals, individually and in their totality, were designed to respect the critical balance between the rights of the individual and the common good.'[137]

In this regard it recommended video-taping of interviews in garda custody or the right of a suspect to have a solicitor present during questioning.[138]

[2.86] With regard to the operation of non-jury trial in Ireland, which as noted as implications in particular for the effective operation of rules of evidence predicated on the division of friction between arbiter of fact (jury) and law (judge) the future of the Special Criminal Court would seem secure. The Hederman Committee, in reviewing the continued operation of the non-jury court, sanctioned the centralising of the non jury court in the criminal justice system proper. The majority of that Committee found justification for its continued maintenance, even in the absence of a 'terrorist' threat.[139] Despite assurances that the current Minister for Justice, Michael McDowell, is on record as wanting to maintain jury trial as much as possible, and specifically not

---

[137] Htpp:/www.irlgov.ie/justice/Press20 Releases/Press-98/pr-2511.htm.

[138] It is notable that on 4 August 1999 the Minister announced Government approval to introduce a nation-wide scheme of electronic recording of Garda questioning of detained persons. Http://www.irlgov.ie/justice/Speeches/Speeches-99/sp-0408a.htm.
This followed the recommendations of a Committee chaired by Esmond Smyth J which had been monitoring and evaluating a pilot scheme of both audio and audio/video recording of Garda questioning of detainees in selected Garda stations for a number of years. The Smyth Committee recommended only one exception to recording — where it is considered absolutely necessary by the Garda Síochána to obtain confidential information in life-threatening situations. The scheme is to be introduced over 12-18 months, and will operate in accordance with existing regulations, ie, the Criminal Justice Act 1984 (Electronic Recording of Interviews) Regulations 1997. The time lag indicated by the year of the Act is significant, as is the very different context into which the regulations now become operative.

[139] See para 7.9 et seq. The Committee's final report endorses that view (with the minority of Professors Walsh, Binchy and Judge Hederman dissenting). Regarding the issue as to whether the ordinary courts are capable of dealing with organised crime, according to the Committee's Interim Report: "Recent experience has shown that juries have been made to feel distinctly uncomfortable in dealing with certain cases involving organised crime". Hederman, para 7.4. They refer to *DPP v Special Criminal Court* [1999] 1 IR 60, where Carney J alluded to their ability to maintain a 'wall of silence' by resort to any means, including murder. There is also reference to 'instances' (not specified) where 'attempts have been made to tamper with juries in high-profile criminal trials in ordinary courts.' Hederman, para 7.7. Referencing in the reasoning process by the majority to Carney J in *Ward*; and Charleton & McDermott 'Constitutional Aspects of Non-Jury Courts' (2000) 6 Bar Rev 106 (Part 1); 142 (Part II) (at para 7.5), facilitates a decision-making process here which reflects a consensus regarding the challenge posed to the ordinary courts by organised crime.

introducing non-jury trial in fraud cases, it would seem the Irish Special Criminal Court is not so 'special', despite the disappearance of its originating rationale.[140]

[2.87] As can be seen the progression is readily apparent whereby provision tailored exceptionally for a particular context gradually extends its ambit to include others. The prototype was provision under the Offences Against the State Act 1939, particularly s 30, targeted against terrorism, but the precedent has expanded to incorporate other forms of exceptional provision with distinct rationales for their introduction. Having regard to the fragility of judicial resilience in face of normalisation of such provision in the context of powers of arrest and detention, it may later prove useful to scrutinise their pronouncement in relation to direct questions as to the accommodation of such 'emergency' provisions within the constitutional process and their approach to 'newer' manifestations of difference.

---

[140] Coulter, 'Minister with a mission to push through reform of the system' (2002) Irish Times, July 13, p 8. Minister McDowell was also quoted as stating in a radio interview on RTE radio on 30 June 2002, that he did not believe in deviating from jury trial, 'except where it is absolutely necessary', and that the protection for juries should be strengthened where necessary went on to state that the non-jury Special Criminal Court should 'remain for the time being because there is a very significant subversive threat still in existence in this state, and anybody who thinks that they have gone away, you know, is very mistaken.' 'McDowell Disturbed that Tribunal is Needed to Investigate Donegal Gardaí' by Nuala Haughey (2002) Irish Times 1 July, p 6.
This interview occurred in the aftermath of statements by a retiring judge, Mr Justice Robert Barr, who had presided over the Special Criminal Court for 15 years. On retirement he made the point that he was not asked for his opinion by the Committee and argued that Government should consult the judiciary before making a decision. He pointed to the US where even Mafia leaders are convicted by juries who can be anonymous or located in a different place. He also raised the possibility of non-jury trials in particular cases, for the benefit of the accused, instancing the hypothetical case of a person charged with a vicious sexual assault of a child that ends in murder where a huge public outcry ensues. A jury may, because of the passions surrounding the case, decide to ignore any element of doubt. 'Court awaits Committee's judgment' John Breslin (2002) Irish Examiner 1 July 2002, p 17.

Part Two
The Rules of Evidence

Chapter 3

Basic Concepts of the Law of Evidence

'Beauty is truth, truth is beauty, – that is all ye know on earth, and all ye need to know.'

John Keats *Ode on a Grecian Urn*

Terminology

[3.01] A brief account of the terminology used in relation to the categorisation of evidence produced at trial is as follows:

The *factum probandum* or *fact in issue* or *principal fact,* refers to questions such as: Did A knock B down?; Did X rape Y? The *factum probans* or *evidentiary fact* or *fact relevant to the issue* is that from which the jury may infer the existence of the *factum probandum*. This is sometimes referred to as 'circumstantial evidence' and could include, for example, the statement of a witness at the trial for the murder of X, that he saw X carrying a blood-stained knife at the door of the house where X's friend was mortally wounded. It could also comprise evidence of habit or habitual behaviour as, for example, in the facts of *Joy v Phillip Mills & Co Ltd*[1], where in the context of the death of a stable boy from the kick of a horse giving rise to a workman's compensation claim, evidence was allowed in as to the boy's habit of teasing the horse.

[3.02] Evidence is classified or categorized in a number of ways, aside from its relation with the question at issue in the proceedings. Such categories include the following which will be met later.

Categories of evidence

Direct evidence

[3.03] Direct evidence is the statement by a witness of facts that the witness has perceived through his own senses. For example if he sees a car hitting X, that constitutes direct evidence of the *factum probandum*. If he sees X at the side of the road in the aftermath of such an incident, that is direct evidence of the *factum probans*.

---

[1]   *Joy v Phillip Mills & Co Ltd* [1916] 1 KB 849.

Real evidence

[3.04] Real evidence can take a variety of forms. It can prove the fact in issue or a relevant fact by, for example, the presentation of a gun, the alleged murder weapon. It can comprise evidence of the view of the site of the incident giving rise to the case. It can amount to evidence of a physical characteristic: for example, a rupture may imply a man is not guilty of a charge of rape. Real evidence may also constitute simply the demeanour of a witness.

Documentary evidence

[3.05] Documentary evidence can form circumstantial evidence – for example, to prove motive – or could constitute testimonial evidence ie say something about the fact in issue, through, for example, a confession. Documentary evidence itself may be a piece of real evidence, as, for example, where the issue is one as to the existence of a physical document.

Functions of judge and jury: arbiter of fact and law

[3.06] All questions of law are for the judge to decide. The trial judge is the sole arbiter of questions of law. Arguments on points of law are always heard in the absence of the jury (where relevant). The judge determines the issue of law, and the jury accepts the judge's evaluation of law. The jury in turn, is then the arbiter of fact. Where there is not a jury, the judge has both distinct functions: arbiter of fact and arbiter of law.

Receivability of evidence

[3.07] The question as to what evidence – to use Montrose's[2] term – is 'receivable' in a court of law, should perhaps at this juncture be addressed, as it is related to the running of the trial. In the first place only relevant evidence is receivable ie evidence relevant to the *factum probandum or factum probans.* Secondly the evidence must be admissible in accordance with the rules of evidence. This leads us to the situation where evidence (like a confession, for example) could be very relevant yet not admissible. It is this factor which draws the fundamental distinction between scientific and legal investigation. There is also, however, the added refinement of the concept of relevance known as 'materiality'. This is not the question of whether the evidence is adequately related to the facts sought to be established (relevance); but whether those facts are adequately related to the case made by the party. An example may serve to illustrate the point: X is accused of murdering Y. Witness A saw X running from Y's house brandishing a knife. Witness B knew Y was of a religious persuasion

---

[2]   Montrose 'Basic Concepts of the Law of Evidence' (1954) 70 LQR 689.

forbidding violence in all circumstances. At the trial X pleads self-defence. The only issue at trial becomes self-defence. Hence the material evidence is only that of witness B.

[3.08] This introduces a further concept into this already terminologically overcrowded area of the law – that is, evidence which is 'receivable'. Receivable evidence is that which is relevant, admissible and material. It is important to keep clear the borderline between these concepts (something, as will be seen, the judiciary do not always achieve). Thayer[3] puts it thus: 'No evidence is receivable unless it is relevant' (the negative averment) and 'all evidence that is relevant is receivable unless excluded by a rule of admissibility' (the positive). In other words, only the concept of admissibility was ignored and all relevant evidence deemed receivable.

Stephens[4] gives a very good definition of relevance:

> 'The word "relevant" means that any two facts are so related to each other that according to the common course of events one, either taken by itself or in connection with other facts proves or renders probable the past, present or future existence or non-existence of the other.'

This concept of relevance, then, is one of fact; that of admissibility, one of law.

Distinctions: relevance/admissibility

[3.09] The extent to which these distinctions are blurred or mistaken is illustrated by a comparison of two decisions of the Irish Court of Criminal Appeal. The first is that of *The People v Patrick O'Neill*[5], which involved a charge of manslaughter resulting from a motor car accident. The facts presented were as follows: the defendant had spent about an hour in the pub on the evening of the accident, and there consumed a shandy and two glasses of ale. There was evidence that he was sober when he left at around 8.50pm. The accident occurred at 9.50pm. The trial judge admitted the evidence as to the consumption of alcohol by the accused, but charged the jury to the effect that the prosecution disclaimed any suggestion that the accused was adversely affected by drink, and that the evidence was given for the purpose of tracing the accused's movements. The accused was found guilty and sentenced to 12 months' imprisonment. The accused appealed to the Court of Criminal Appeal. There it was held that the evidence as to the alcoholic drink taken by the accused prior to the accident, should have been excluded on the ground that such evidence was irrelevant to the issues at trial. Kenny J[6] commented as follows:

---

3 Thayer *Preliminary Treatise on Evidence and the Common Law* (1898) pp 264-6.
4 Stephens *A Digest of the Law of Evidence* (1936).
5 *The People v Patrick O'Neill* [1964] Ir Jur 1.
6 [1964] Ir Jur 1 at 4.

'As the prosecution were not making the case that the accused's driving was affected by alcoholic drink, this evidence was wholly irrelevant to any of the issues in the trial. The argument that it was admissible because it was given for the purpose of tracing the movements of the accused before the accident assumes the very matter which the argument attempts to establish, that is, the relevance of those movements to any of the issues in the trial. As the evidence was not relevant it should not have been given.'

[3.10] A similar factual situation led to consideration of the same issue in *People v Laurence Moore*[7]. In that case, a youth of 16 years was charged with dangerous driving causing death, contrary to the road traffic legislation. Unsworn statements by him made reference to visits to public houses and the consumption of three pints of stout. These were admitted in evidence, notwithstanding counsel's objections. In his charge to the jury, the trial judge read the statements without comment. After submission by the accused's counsel, the jury were recalled and told by the trial judge that the prosecution had not suggested that drink had anything to do with the case and there was no question of the accused being drunk. They should leave the matter of drink out of consideration. The accused was convicted. On application for leave to appeal to the Court of Criminal Appeal, Davitt P reasoned that:

'Where a person has during a period of time which is material, consumed a significant quantity of alcoholic drink it will therefore tend to render his driving unsafe. The evidence that he has consumed such a quantity during such a period is therefore in our opinion of probative value on a charge of dangerous driving and therefore relevant and admissible in law. To this end we venture respectfully to differ from the principles enunciated in *O'Neill's* case.'[8]

He continued:

'We agree ... that he (the trial judge) should exercise his discretion to exclude evidence as to drink taken by a driver where he is satisfied that its probative value is outweighed by its prejudicial effect, that is, in our opinion, where the amount of drink is insignificant either as to the amount or time of consumption.'

[3.11] The importance of clarity of concepts is evident. There are two stages. Firstly the determination of relevance; then that of admissibility (one criteria of adjudication of the latter, being that of balancing prejudicial effect against probative value). As can be seen from a comparison of the above case law the delineation of same is not without consequence in substance.

---

[7] *People v Laurence Moore* [1964] Ir Jur 6.
[8] [1964] Ir Jur 6 at 12.

Trial judge's discretion to exclude relevant evidence

[3.12] In *People (AG) v O'Neill*[9] Kenny J had confirmed what has long been recognised as a general principle, that of a trial judge's general discretion to exclude relevant evidence when its probable value is small but its prejudicial effect considerable. Although this principle has been overshadowed in this jurisdiction by constitutional parameters regarding fair trial (see chapter 4 on Illegally Obtained Evidence), it is important to remember this particular judicial discretion to exclude relevant evidence which is core to the jury's function in any criminal trial. It was reaffirmed by Geoghegan J in *People (DPP) v Meleady (No 3)*[10].

> 'It is well established that, although there is no authority to permit a criminal court to admit, as a matter of discretion, evidence which is inadmissible under an exclusionary rule of law, the converse is not the case. A judge, as part of his inherent power, has an overriding duty in every case to ensure that the accused receives a fair trial and always has a discretion to exclude otherwise admissible prosecution evidence if, in his opinion, its prejudicial effect on the minds of the jury outweighs its true probative value.'

A vindication of the role of the trial judge in determining all issues of admissibility is found in *Blanchfield v Harnett*.[11] Here proceedings had been brought by the applicant by way of judicial review seeking certiorari to quash the respondent District Judge's order under the Bankers Books Evidence Act 1879.

The respondent argued the purpose of the application was to render the evidence obtained under the orders inadmissible at the criminal trial. It was held that whether or not the evidence could be admitted is a determination solely for the discretion of the trial judge. All questions relevant to the determination of such items were held to rest with the trial judge, as otherwise, trials would be suspended for lengthy periods while such issues were litigated in other courts. The desirability of such continuity had also been referred to by O'Flaherty J in *DPP v Special Criminal Court*.[12]

Determination of the ultimate issue

[3.13] One issue which merits attention at this stage, although it will arise and be dealt with more fully later (in the context of opinion evidence), is the extent to which evidence presented can come close to determining the fact in issue, which is more properly the prerogative of the jury; or indeed questions of law, the

---

9   *People (AG) v. O'Neill* [1964] Ir Jur Rep 1.
10   *People (DPP) v Meleady (No 3)* [2001] 4 IR 16 at 31, Geoghegan J.
11   *Blanchfield v Harnett* [2001] 1 ILRM 193.
12   *DPP v Special Criminal Court* [1999] 1 IR 60.

province of the trial judge. Particularly with the increase in specialisation of knowledge in the scientific arena, this can pose some considerable difficulty.

[3.14] An early instance of this is provided by the decision in *Maher v AG*[13], which examined the Road Traffic Act 1968 that stated that 'conclusive evidence' of same would be given in the form of blood alcohol concentration a certificate tendered in the prescribed fashion.

In the Supreme Court, Fitzgerald CJ commented that the Constitution, which allocates the administration of justice to the courts and judges, necessarily reserves to them the determination of all essential ingredients of any offence charged against the accused person. Such a statutory provision as here encapsulated in this case, would purport to remove such determination and so constitute an invalid infringement of judicial power. Further proof of a tolerance of expert testimony coming close to determining the fact in issue, is provided by a number of earlier English decisions faced with the phenomenon of the increased use of specialists in courts. The courts' approach led to a legal culture tolerant (if not sanguine) in the face of same, and the development of a burgeoning industry of 'expert' advices without which lawyers dare not present a case, and within which realm they were frequently peculiarly ill-equipped to challenge evidence prejudicial to their client.

[3.15] In *Lowery v R*[14], the evidence of a psychologist was tendered on behalf of one of the two accused to establish that one of the accused's version of the facts was more probable than that put forward by the other accused. The Privy Council sanctioned the admissibility of same. By contrast, in *R v Turner*[15], Lawton LJ made reference to the decision in *Lowery* and stated that:

> 'We do not consider that it [*Lowery*] is authority for the proposition that in all cases psychologists and psychiatrists can be called to prove the probability of the accused's veracity. If any such rule was applied in our courts, trial by psychiatrists would be likely to take the place of trial by jury and magistrates.'

[3.16] In another jurisdiction faced with a similar issue, the Supreme Court of Canada stated in *R v Lupien*[16] that although expert psychiatric testimony was not admissible to show the absence of requisite intent on the part of an accused to commit the crime charged, it would be admissible to show his lack of capacity to form that intent.

---

[13] *Maher v AG* [1973] IR 140. The section in question was s 44 of the Road Traffic Act 1968.
[14] *Lowery v R* [1974] AC 85.
[15] *R v Turner* [1975] QB 834.
[16] *R v Lupien* [1970] SCR 263.

[3.17] The decision in *DPP v A & BC Chewing Gum Ltd*[17] came close to the position of usurping the function of the jury as determinants of the fact in issue. In the context of a charge of obscenity against the defendants in relation to a series of graphically violent 'war cards' issued with their product, expert testimony of a child psychiatrist was admitted to show the likely effect of these allegedly obscene articles upon children. The expert testified as to whether they were likely to 'corrupt or deprave', the latter constituting the legal test for obscenity.

[3.18] Before exploring further the issue as to the relative functions of judge and jury and the pivotal nature of the role of the witness (not particularly the expert witness), it is timely to consider both the issue as to the onus of proof and its location, together with the extent of that obligation. These notions are referred to respectively as the 'burden of proof' and the 'standard of proof'.

Burden of proof

[3.19] The phrase 'burden of proof' is traditionally regarded as having two distinct aspects or meanings:

    (1)   the legal burden of proof; and

    (2)   the evidential burden of proof.

The first of these, the legal burden of proof, is more typically what we regard as being the burden of proof proper, ie the obligation to persuade. It is what Wigmore termed 'the risk of non-persuasion' and the House of Lords in *DPP v Morgan*[18] called 'the probative burden'.

[3.20] The legal burden of proof may be differently placed in respect of different issues arising in the same case. If a person bears the legal burden of proof in respect of a particular issue or disputed question of fact (fact in issue), that implies that if there is not adduced what the law regards as an adequate preponderance of probative materials in favour of that issue being decided in favour of that party, it must as a matter of law be decided against him. In plainer terms, if the requisite standard of proof is not reached by the party bearing the legal burden, he loses.

Shifting the burden of proof

[3.21] A legal burden, once placed, cannot be shifted by the mere production of evidence by the other party to the proceedings. On the other hand, as the initial placement of the burden of proof is determined by a rule of law, so it may shift

---

[17] *DPP v A & BC Chewing Gum Ltd* [1968] 1 QB 159.
[18] *DPP v Morgan* [1976] AC 182.

as a result of the coming into operation of some other legal rule such as a compelling although rebuttable presumption of law.

[3.22] On a more pragmatic level, there may come a point in the course of a trial when the legal burden upon an issue seems, in the light of the evidence so far adduced, to have been satisfied. In such circumstances there is a real sense in which considerations of prudence or good tactics – but not of law – impose an obligation upon the opponent. He is then sometimes said to bear a tactical burden of proof or, as it is sometimes put, that the legal burden of proof has tactically shifted to him.

Evidential burden of proof

[3.23] The evidential burden of proof is an obligation to raise an issue, or to make out a prima facie case and so to get the issue past the trial judge and before the trier of fact. To describe the evidential burden as a burden of proof therefore, is something of a misnomer. Similarly to the legal burden, the evidential burden relates to a particular issue and may therefore be differently placed in respect of the different issues which may arise in a case.

[3.24] The evidential burden is discharged by evidence sufficient to warrant but not necessarily to require an affirmative finding by a reasonable jury. If the evidence is sufficient, the issue must be put before the jury. Whereas it is for the jury or trier of fact to determine whether a legal burden has been satisfied, discharge of an evidential burden is the exclusive concern of the judge. Illustrative of a situation where a direction was given by the trial judge (though, as it transpired, incorrectly) is *DPP v O'Reilly*[19]. The defendant was charged with aggravated burglary. The District Justice found inter alia that the only incriminating evidence against the defendant was contained in a cautioned statement. No evidence was tendered to show or suggest that the defendant was at or near the post office in question at any material time or to show or suggest that he had used a firearm at any material time.

[3.25] The learned District Justice, of the opinion that the State must prove the accused's physical presence on the premises, in the absence of evidence that the defendant had entered the premises, dismissed the case at the close of prosecution evidence. In the High Court on a case stated, Egan J asserted, however, that the District Justice was wrong in holding it was an essential ingredient of the charge that there should be proof the defendant was physically present at or about the premises where the offence was committed. However, although incorrectly applied here, as the District Judge was wrong in law, this case does demonstrate the power of the burden of proof.

---

[19] *DPP v O'Reilly* [1991] 1 IR 77.

Who bears the burden of proof?

[3.26] Case law precedent, or the construction of a statute, determines on which party to the proceedings the burden of proof lies. It is sometimes said that the legal burden rests upon he who affirms rather than he who denies, yet this is an uncertain guide. Carter[20] contends that the legal and evidential burdens often reflect the way in which a relevant rule of substantive law is formulated - for example proof of what is described as a defence will often rest upon the defendant, and especially in civil cases, may project the policies underlying that particular rule. Criminal cases certainly, as Carter[21] acknowledges, call for more general considerations. For instance, whereas at common law, the evidential burden in respect of a defence in a criminal trial may lie upon the accused, the legal burden in respect of all issues except insanity lies upon the prosecution. Allowance must be made, however, for the instance where statutes may, by means of a 'reverse onus clause', expressly place the legal burden in respect of a particular issue upon the accused.

[3.27] Civil cases do not allow for such general statements. The nineteenth century case of *Amos v Hughes*[22] held that the burden of proof of the issue is upon the party who would be unsuccessful in the case if no evidence at all were given, and such party has the right to begin. In *Joseph Constantine Steamship Line Ltd v Imperial Smelting Corp Ltd,*[23] the House of Lords held that the burden of proof lies upon the party who affirms and not upon the party who denies. This rule applies to a plaintiff who asserts an exception to the defence pleaded.

Res ipsa loquitur

[3.28] The doctrine of *res ipsa loquitur* merits a mention, as it may be considered to bear upon the incidence of the legal or evidential burden of proof in civil cases. Mostly, the doctrine is regarded as affecting the burden by the operation of a presumption.[24]

---

[20] Carter *Cases and Statutes on Evidence* (1981).

[21] Carter *Cases and Statutes on Evidence* (1981).

[22] *Amos v Hughes* (1835) 1 Mood & R 464.

[23] *Joseph Constantine Steamship Line Lid v Imperial Smelting Corp Ltd* [1942] AC 154.

[24] The doctrine of *res ipsa loquitur* was given expression by Erle CJ in *Scott v The London Dock Co* (1865) 3 H & C 596 at 601, viz:

'Where the thing is shown to be under the management of the defendant or his servants, and the accident is such as in the ordinary course of things does not happen if those who have the management use proper care, it affords reasonable evidence, in the absence of explanation by the defendants, that the accident arose from want of care'.

[3.29] In *Hanrahan v Merck Sharp & Dohme (Ireland) Ltd,*[25] where it was alleged that the escape of noxious gases caused damage to the plaintiff farmer's dairy herd, it was held that the plaintiff had failed to adduce prima facie evidence that the escape of malodorous fumes from the defendant's premises was the cause of deterioration in the condition of the plaintiff's herd and pastures. It was also held, that the cause of the alleged damage was not a matter peculiarly within the knowledge of the defendant so as to transfer to the defendant the onus of proving that the damage had not been caused by the defendant's activities.[26] Henchy J's somewhat controversial restatement of the doctrine in the Supreme Court, involves the notion that the defendant's superior knowledge of how the tort was caused, would render it 'palpably unfair' to require the plaintiff to prove something 'peculiarly within the range of the defendant's capacity of proof'.

[3.30] Other cases involving application of the said doctrine of *res ipsa loquitur* include the 'supermarket negligence' actions. In *Mullen v Quinnsworth*[27], the Supreme Court found inter alia that the maxim *res ipsa loquitur* applies to a claim of negligence asserted by the plaintiff in the context of a spillage of oil on the defendant's supermarket floor, which caused her to fall and sustain damage. This doctrine had the effect of shifting the onus of proof onto the defendants to show that they had taken all reasonable care.

[3.31] Similarly in *O'Reilly v Lavelle*[28], the doctrine of *res ipsa loquitur* was applied in the context of liability for animals. Section 2(1) of the Animals Act 1985 provides that those rules of the common law relating to liability for negligence which exclude or restrict liability in respect of an animal straying on the highway are abolished. The plaintiff was driving on the highway after dark, when his car came into collision with a fresian calf. The plaintiff sought to rely on the doctrine of *res ipsa loquitur* which he had not specifically pleaded. The action was dismissed by the Circuit Court, as the plaintiff had not sufficiently discharged the burden of proof. On appeal to the High Court, Johnson J[29] referred to the statements of the law by Griffin J in *Mullen v Quinnsworth Ltd*[30], where he adopted the principle of Erle CJ in *Scott v London and St Catherine's Docks Co*, viz:[31]

---

[25] *Hanrahan v Merck Sharp & Dohme (Ireland) Ltd* [1988] ILRM 629.

[26] See 'Peculiar knowledge principle' at para **[3.67]** et seq.

[27] *Mullen v Quinnsworth Ltd* [1990] 1 IR 59.

[28] *O'Reilly v Lavelle* [1990] 2 IR 372.

[29] [1990] 2 IR 372 at 373.

[30] *Mullen v Quinnsworth Ltd* [1990] 1 IR 59 at 62.

[31] *Scott v London and St Catherine's Docks Co* (1865) 3 H & CS 96 at 601.

'There must be reasonable evidence of negligence. But where the thing is shown to have been under the management of the defendant or his servants, and the accident is such as in the ordinary course of things does not happen if those who have the management use proper care, it affords reasonable evidence, in the absence of explanation by the defendants, that the accident arose from want of care.'

[3.32] Griffin J also commented that the doctrine does not have to be pleaded before a plaintiff can rely on it. If the facts pleaded and the facts proved show that the doctrine is applicable to the case, this is sufficient. On application of the facts before him, Johnson J concluded that cattle properly managed should not wander on the road, and therefore the burden of proof in this case shifted to the defendant to show that he took reasonable care of his animals. 'I believe that there is no matter more appropriate for the application of the doctrine of *res ipsa loquitur* than cattle wandering on the highway'. On the balance of probabilities, he found the defendant failed to discharge the onus of proof.

[3.33] In *Murray v Miller*[32] Judge McMahon imposed liability on the basis of s 2 of the Animals Act 1985 in a situation where a traffic accident occurred when the defendant's cow jumped out in front of the plaintiff's car. The judge provided a useful summary of the case law in this area:

'[T]he effect of this statutory provision is that reasonable care must now be taken to ensure that animals do not stray onto the highway and cause damage thereon. This normally translates into an obligation to ensure that the land is stock proofed and that the fencing is sufficient to prevent animals from breaking out. Moreover, in relation to proof, the case law indicates that the onus of proof, that the land was properly fenced, is now on the landowner or the owner of the animal who seeks to evade liability. In *O'Reilly v Lavelle* [1990] 2 IR 372 and again in *O'Shea v Anhold and Horse Holiday Farm Ltd* (Supreme Court, 23 October 1996) the courts in this jurisdiction have clearly accepted that the principle of *res ipsa loquitur* applies to these situations. Accordingly, in cases such as the present, to escape liability, the first and second defendants must provide the evidence to show that they took reasonable care in the management of the land to ensure that the fencing was secure. [T]he first and second defendants ... tendered no significant evidence in this regard, and on this ground, I have little hesitation in holding them liable for the damage which their straying animal caused to the plaintiff.'

Although the majority of *res ipsa loquitur* cases proceed on the basis of the 'classic formulation', in *Scott v London & St Catherine's Docks Company*,[33]

---

[32] *Murray v Miller* (14 November 2001) Circuit Court, Roscommon, 2001 (Judge B McMahon).
[33] See *Lindsay v Western Health Board* [1993] 2 IR 147; and *Merriman v Greenhills Foods Ltd* [1997] ILRM 46.

Hanrahan's grounding of the doctrine in 'unfairness' still has influence, as can be seen from the decision of *Rothwell v Motor Insurers Bureau of Ireland*.[34] Here, the plaintiff's vehicle had skidded on a patch of oil on the road, left by an unknown driver of a truck or lorry on which the fuel tank was ill-fitting. The plaintiff argued it was a case where *res ipsa loquitur* applied. McCracken J did not agree because there might circumstances in which a spillage occurred without any fault on the part of the driver. Although McCracken J. preferred the reasoning of *Hanrahan*, he disagreed on the facts:

'It appears to me that the judgment in *Hanrahan* requires not merely that a matter in respect of which the onus is to shift is within the exclusive knowledge of the defendant, but also that it is "peculiarly within the range of the defendant's capacity of proof." That is not the position here ... neither party could go further: the matter was not within the knowledge, exclusive or otherwise, of either of them.'

However he did find for the plaintiff without recourse to the doctrine, on the basis it would be contrary to the purpose of the Motor Insurers Bureau of Ireland agreement that a plaintiff would have a burden of proof (that the driver could have no defence) he would not have had, if the identity of the driver were known.

Despite developments in other jurisdictions (eg Canada)[35] regarding it as no more than circumstantial evidence establishing a sufficient case to go to the jury, the Irish courts do seem to take the view that once the doctrine applies, the question then arises as to what the defendant must do to avoid liability.[36]

Criminal cases: the 'golden thread'

[3.34] The 'golden thread' running through our law is that enunciated in *Woolmington v DPP*[37] by the House of Lords and specifically approved and adopted in Ireland in *The People (AG) v Byrne*,[38] to the effect that as a general rule in a criminal case, it is always the duty of the prosecution to prove the guilt of the accused beyond a reasonable doubt.

[3.35] In *Woolmington*, having fully considered the authorities to date, Viscount Sankey stated as follows:

'If at any period of a trial it was permissible for the judge to rule that the prosecution had established its case and that the onus was shifted on the prisoner

---

[34] *Rothwell v Motor Insurers Bureau of Ireland* (6 July 2001) High Court, McCracken J at para 20.

[35] *Fontaine v British Columbia (Official Administrator)* [1998] 1 SC 424.

[36] See further McMahon & Binchy, *Law of Torts* (3rd edn, 2000) para 9.11 et seq.

[37] *Woolmington v DPP* [1935] AC 462 at 467 per Avory J and at 475 per Sankey LC.

[38] *The People (AG) v Byrne* [1974] IR 1 at 5 per Kenny J.

to prove that he was not guilty and that unless he discharged that onus the prosecution was entitled to succeed, it would be enabling the judge in such a case to say that the jury must in law find the prisoner guilty and so make the judge decide the case and not the jury, which is not the common law.'[39]

[3.36] He then enunciated the rule which is reiterated to this day:

'Throughout the web of the English Criminal Law one golden thread is always to be seen, that is the duty of the prosecution to prove the prisoner's guilt, subject to what I have already said as to the defence of insanity and subject also to any statutory exception. If, at the end of and on the whole of the case, there is a reasonable doubt, created by the evidence given by either the prosecution or the prisoner, as to whether the prisoner killed the deceased with a malicious intention, the prosecution has not made out the case and the prisoner is entitled to an acquittal. No matter what the charge or where the trial the principle that the prosecution must prove the guilt of the prisoner is part of the common law of England and no attempt to whittle it down can be entertained.'[40]

[3.37] In *People (DPP) v Kiely*[41], one of the grounds of appeal was that the trial judge, in his charge to the jury, had not specifically stated that there were two versions of events and the jury should adopt the accused's version unless the prosecution version had been proven beyond reasonable doubt.

Reliance was placed on *People v Byrne*[42], where Kenny J had stated that 'the jury should be told ... that when two views ... are possible on the evidence, they should adopt that which is favourable to the accused.'

McGuinness J held that it was the trial judge's charge as a whole that is important. Hence, although it would have been preferable if he had included an explanation of the benefit of the doubt as per Kenny J.'s judgment in *Byrne*, what was important was that he had emphasised the concept of the presumption of innocence and proof beyond a reasonable doubt and she was satisfied the jury had been properly instructed as to the burden and standard of proof here.

[3.38] In *People (DPP) v C*[43] the applicant appealed on the basis that the trial judge failed to charge the jury correctly in relation to the conflict between the evidence given by the Complainant in Chief and her evidence under cross-examination. Murray J held that the trial judge had not erred in failing to direct the jury to accept the version more favourable to the applicant. He was of the view that to direct the jury to rely on one version rather than another was to usurp its function, and here the jury had been properly directed, that where a

---

[39] *Woolmington v DPP* [1935] AC 462 at 480.
[40] *Woolmington v DPP* [1935] AC 462 at 481 per Viscount Sankey.
[41] *People (DPP) v Kiely* (21 March 2001) Court of Criminal Appeal, McGuinness J.
[42] *People v Byrne* [1974] IR 1 at 9.
[43] *People (DPP) v C* [2001] 3 IR 345.

conflict arose, they should accept the version most favourable to the accused, when the other version had been proved beyond a reasonable doubt.

Exceptions to the rule in Woolmington

[3.39] There are, of course, exceptions to that general principle laid down in *Woolmington*. As enunciated in the case itself, there may well be specific statutory exceptions – occasions when the burden of proof is placed on an accused person in relation to a given issue by virtue of an express provision in the relevant statute. There is also, the well-established exception at common law: that of the defence of insanity. As confirmed in *R v McNaughten*[44] by the House of Lords, the legal burden of establishing the common law defence of insanity rests upon the accused. The relevant standard of proof in this, as on any occasion, indeed, when the burden of proof rests on the accused in a criminal case, is proof on the balance of probabilities. It is important to distinguish these occasions from situations in which the accused may bear only the evidential burden of proof – as in the case of the defence of 'sane-automatism', where the accused bears an obligation to adduce some evidence in relation to same, sufficient to raise that defence, or get the issue placed before the jury (*Bratty v AG for Northern Ireland*).[45]

[3.40] The validity of statutory exceptions to the golden rule was questioned in the Irish context in the case of *O'Leary v AG*.[46] That case concerned the conviction of O'Leary in the Special Criminal Court of membership of an unlawful organisation contrary to s 21 of the Offences against the State Act 1939 (as amended), and possession of incriminating documents contrary to s 12 of that Act. Section 24 of the 1939 Act provides that proof of possession of incriminating documents shall, unless the contrary is proven, be evidence that such person was a member of the organisation at the time of the charge. O'Leary claimed this infringed the constitutional right to a trial in due course of law, and, in particular, the presumption of innocence, by placing on the accused the burden of disproving his guilt. In the High Court, Costello J founds the presumption of innocence, part of the common law prior to 1937, to have been for so long a postulate of every criminal trial, that a criminal trial held otherwise is prima facie not held in due course of law:

> 'The Constitution, of course, contains no express reference to the presumption but it does provide in Article 38 that no person shall be tried on any criminal charge save in due course of law. It seems to me that it has been for so long a fundamental postulate of every criminal trial in this country that the accused was

---

44 *R v McNaughten* (1843) 10 Cl & F 200.
45 *Bratty v AG for Northern Ireland* [1963] AC 386.
46 *O'Leary v AG* [1991] 2 ILRM 454 at 459 per Costello J. Also [1993] 1 IR 102 at 107.

presumed to be innocent of the offence with which he was charged that a criminal trial held otherwise than in accordance with this presumption would, prima facie, be one which was not held in due course of law. It would follow that puma facie any statute which permitted such a trial so to be held would be unconstitutional.'[47]

Costello J confirmed that the Constitution confers on every accused in every criminal trial a constitutionally protected right to the presumption of innocence, but went on to state that in certain circumstances the Oireachtas can restrict the exercise of such a right which is not absolute. The Supreme Court confirmed his decision on appeal, O'Flaherty J declaring that '... the presumption of innocence in a criminal trial is implicit in the requirement of Article 38, s 1 of the Constitution that no person shall be tried on any criminal charge save in due course of law...'[48]

[3.41] With regard to s 24 of the 1939 Act, O'Flaherty J stated that the section permitted no more than:

> 'if an incriminating document is proved to be in the possession of a person ... that shall, without more, be evidence until the contrary is proved that such possession is to amount to evidence only; it is not to be taken as proof and so, the probative value...might be shaken in many ways ... there is no mention about the burden of proof changing, much less that the presumption of innocence is to be set to one side at any stage'.[49]

[3.42] He later stated that it was the evidentiary burden of proof which had shifted. (This belies the fact that the evidentiary burden has always been regarded as of tactical or pragmatic effect. By contrast, here the accused has to 'shake' the evidence or face conviction.) Despite trenchant acknowledgment at both High and Supreme Court level that the presumption of innocence was inherent in Article 38, the section was 'saved'. Such an apparent 'strong rights' stance in face of accommodation of exceptional provision represents a janus-like approach, prescient of decisions to come.

Support for the notion that the burden of proof when placed on the accused will be considered by the Irish courts to be an evidential burden is found in *Hardy v Ireland*[50], where it was held that the effect of s 4(1) of the Explosive Substances Act 1883 was to shift a persuasive burden of proof onto the accused requiring him only to raise a doubt of substance in relation to the prosecution case.

---

[47] *O'Leary v AG* (1991) 2 ILRM 454 at 459.
[48] *O'Leary v AG* [1995] 1 IR 254 at 263.
[49] *O'Leary v AG* [1995] 1 IR 254 at 265.
[50] *Hardy v Ireland* [1994] 2 IR 550.

[3.43] Similarly, in *DPP v Byrne*[51], in the context of the presumption of intention to drive in s 50(8) of the Road Traffic Act 1961, as inserted by s 11 of the Road Traffic Act 1964, the court did not take the view that that section placed a legal burden on the defendant to prove he did not have the intention to drive. Rather, the assumption appeared to be that the defendant bore an evidential burden, to raise a reasonable doubt in the jury's mind.

Reverse onus provisions and the right to silence

[3.44] Several pieces of Irish legislation now provide for inferences from silence or constitute withholding information as a criminal offence.

[3.45] The Criminal Justice Act 1984, s 18, provides for inferences from failure or refusal to account for objects/marks, etc:

'(1) Where—

(a) a person is arrested without warrant by a member of the Garda Síochána, and there is—

(i) on his person, or

(ii) in or on his clothing or footwear, or

(iii) otherwise in his possession, or

(iv) in any place in which he is at the time of his arrest

any object, substance or mark, or there is any mark on any such object, and the member reasonably believes that the presence of the object, substance or mark may be attributable to the participation of the person arrested in the commission of the offence in respect of which he was arrested, and

(b) the member informs the person arrested that he so believes, and requests him to account for the presence of the object, substance or mark, and

(c) the person fails or refuses to do so,

then if, in any proceedings against the person for the offence, evidence of the said matters is given, the court, in determining whether to send forward the accused for trial or whether there is a case to answer and the court (or, subject to the judge's directions, the jury) in determining whether the accused is guilty of the offence charged (or of any other offence of which he could lawfully be convicted on that charge) may draw such inferences from the failure or refusal as appear proper; and the failure or refusal may, on the basis of such inferences, be treated as, or as capable of amounting to, corroboration of any other evidence in relation to which the failure or refusal is material, but a person shall not be convicted of an offence solely on an inference drawn from such failure or refusal.'

---

[51] *DPP v Byrne* (6 December 2001) Supreme Court, Murray J.

[3.46] The Criminal Justice Act 1984, s 19, provides for inferences from an accused's failure to account for presence at a particular place:

'(1) Where—

(a)   a person arrested without warrant by a member of the Garda Síochána was found by him at a particular place at or about the time the offence in respect of which he was arrested is alleged to have been committed, and

(b)   the member reasonably believes that the presence of the person at that place and at that time may be attributable to his participation in the commission of the offence, and

(c)   the member informs the person that he so believes, and requests him to account for such presence, and

(d)   the person fails or refuses to do so,

then if, in any proceedings against the person for the offence, evidence of the said matters is given, the court, in determining whether to send forward the accused for trial or whether there is a case to answer and the court (or, subject to the judge's directions, the jury) in determining whether the accused is guilty of the offence charged (or of any other offence of which he could lawfully be convicted on that charge) may draw such inferences from the failure or refusal as appear proper; and the failure or refusal may, on the basis of such inferences, be treated as, or as capable of amounting to, corroboration of any evidence in relation to which the failure or refusal is material, but a person shall not be convicted of an offence solely on an inference drawn from such failure or refusal.

(2) References in subsection (1) to evidence shall, in relation to the preliminary examination of a charge, be taken to include a statement of the evidence to be given by a witness at the trial.

(3) Subsection (1) shall not have effect unless the accused was told in ordinary language by the member of the Garda Síochána when making the request mentioned in subsection (1) (c) what the effect of the failure or refusal might be.

(4) Nothing in this section shall be taken to preclude the drawing of any inference from the failure or refusal of a person to account for his presence which could properly be drawn apart from this section.

(5) This section shall not apply in relation to a failure or refusal if the failure or refusal occurred before the commencement of this section.'

The constitutionality of the Criminal Justice Act 1984, ss 18 and 19 was upheld in *Rock v Ireland*.[52]

[3.47] The Criminal Justice (Drug Trafficking) Act 1996, s 7, provides for inferences from failure to mention particular facts:

---

[52]   *Rock v Ireland* [1998] 2 ILRM 35.

'(1) Where in any proceedings against a person for a drug trafficking offence evidence is given that the accused—

(a)   at any time before he or she was charged with the offence, on being questioned by:

    (i)   a member of the Garda Síochána, or

    (ii)   pursuant to regulations made under section 6, an officer of customs and excise, within the meaning of that section,

endeavouring to ascertain whether an offence had been committed, or by whom, or

(b)   when being charged with the offence or informed by—

    (i)   a member of the Garda Síochána, or

    (ii)   pursuant to the said regulations, a said officer of customs and excise, that he or she might be prosecuted for it,

failed to mention any fact relied on in his or her defence in those proceedings being a fact which in the circumstances existing at the time he or she could reasonably have been expected to mention when so questioned, charged or informed, as the case may be, then the court, in determining whether to send forward the accused for trial or whether there is a case to answer and the court (or, subject to the judge's directions, the jury) in determining whether the accused is guilty of the offence charged (or of any other offence of which he or she could lawfully be convicted on that charge) may draw such inferences from the failure as appear proper; and the failure may, on the basis of such inferences, be treated as, or as capable of amounting to, corroboration of any evidence in relation to which the failure is material, but a person shall not be convicted of an offence solely on an inference drawn from such failure.

(2) Subsection (1) shall not have effect unless the accused was told in ordinary language when being questioned, charged or informed, as the case may be, what the effect of such failure might be.

(3) Nothing in this section shall, in any proceedings—

(a)   prejudice the admissibility in evidence of the silence or other reaction of the accused in the face of anything said in his or her presence relating to the conduct in respect of which he or she is charged, in so far as evidence thereof would be admissible apart from this section, or

(b)   be taken to preclude the drawing of any inference from the silence or other reaction of the accused which could properly be drawn apart from this section.

(4) This section shall not apply in relation to a failure to mention a fact if the failure occurred before the commencement of this section.'

[3.48] The Offences Against the State (Amendment) Act 1998, s 2, provides that in relation to membership of an unlawful organisation, inferences may be drawn from failure to answer any question:

'(1) Where in any proceedings against a person for an offence under section 21 of the Act of 1939 evidence is given that the accused at any time before he or she was charged with the offence, on being questioned by a member of the Garda Síochána in relation to the offence, failed to answer any question material to the investigation of the offence, then the court in determining whether to send forward the accused for trial or whether there is a case to answer and the court (or subject to the judge's directions, the jury) in determining whether the accused is guilty of the offence may draw such inferences from the failure as appear proper; and the failure may, on the basis of such inferences, be treated as, or as capable of amounting to, corroboration of any evidence in relation to the offence, but a person shall not be convicted of the offence solely on an inference drawn from such a failure.

(2) Subsection (1) shall not have effect unless the accused was told in ordinary language when being questioned what the effect of such a failure might be.

(3) Nothing in this section shall, in any proceedings—

(a)   prejudice the admissibility in evidence of the silence or other reaction of the accused in the face of anything said in his or her presence relating to the conduct in respect of which he or she is charged, in so far as evidence thereof would be admissible apart from this section, or

(b)   be taken to preclude the drawing of any inference from the silence or other reaction of the accused which could be properly drawn apart from this section.

(4) In this section—

(a)   references to any question material to the investigation include references to any question requesting the accused to give a full account of his or her movements, actions, activities or associations during any specified period,

(b)   references to a failure to answer include references to the giving of an answer that is false or misleading and references to the silence or other reaction of the accused shall be construed accordingly.

(5) This section shall not apply in relation to failure to answer a question if the failure occurred before the passing of this Act.'

[3.49] The Offences Against the State (Amendment) Act 1998, s 5, provides for inferences to be drawn from failure to mention particular facts:

'(1) This section applies to—

(a)   an offence under the Acts,

(b)   an offence that is for the time being a scheduled offence for the purposes of Part V of the Act of 1939,

(c)   an offence arising out of the same set of facts as an offence referred to in paragraph (a) or (b),

being an offence for which a person of full age and capacity and not previously convicted may, under or by virtue of any enactment, be punished by imprisonment for a term of 5 years or by a more severe penalty.

(2) Where in any proceedings against a person for an offence to which this section applies evidence is given that the accused—

(a)   at any time before he or she was charged with the offence, on being questioned by a member of the Garda Síochána in relation to the offence, or

(b)   when being charged with the offence or informed by a member of the Garda Síochána that he or she might be prosecuted for it,

failed to mention any fact relied on in his or her defence in those proceedings, being a fact which in the circumstances existing at the time he or she could reasonably have been expected to mention when so questioned, charged or informed, as the case may be, then the court, in determining whether to send forward the accused for trial or whether there is a case to answer and the court (or, subject to the judge's directions, the jury) in determining whether the accused is guilty of the offence charged (or of any other offence of which he or she could lawfully be convicted on that charge) may draw such inferences from the failure as appear proper; and the failure may, on the basis of such inferences, be treated as, or as capable of amounting to, corroboration of any evidence in relation to which the failure is material, but a person shall not be convicted of an offence solely on an inference drawn from such a failure.

(3) Subsection (2) shall not have effect unless the accused was told in ordinary language when being questioned, charged or informed, as the case may be, what the effect of such a failure might be.

(4) Nothing in this section shall, in any proceedings-

(a)   prejudice the admissibility in evidence of the silence or other reaction of the accused in the face of anything said in his or her presence relating to the conduct in respect of which he or she is charged, in so far as evidence thereof would be admissible apart from this section, or

(b)   be taken to preclude the drawing of any inference from the silence or other reaction of the accused which could properly be drawn apart from this section.

(5) This section shall not apply in relation to a failure to mention a fact if the failure occurred before the passing of this Act.'

[3.50] With regard to inferences from silence there is under consideration for implementation in the Criminal Justice (Garda Powers) Bill currently being prepared a proposal to allow for a general inferences from silence provision with regard to offences meriting 10 or more years imprisonment.

[3.51] By contrast, with the proliferation and extension of 'reverse onus' provisions, the Supreme Court in *DPP v Finnerty*[53] reversed a conviction for rape and ordered a retrial on the basis of the trial judge's allowance of an inference to be drawn from the accused's silence in the aftermath of an arrest under s 4 of the Criminal Justice Act 1984. There was no statutory provision allowing the drawing of an inference in this case. The court emphasised that the right to silence was constitutionally guaranteed, and hence any abridgement, such as allowing inference to be drawn, must be expressly legislated for and such provision proportionate to the objectives of that legislation. Hence no cross-examination by the prosecution, or inferences from silence during a s 4 detention, should have been allowed.

This decision serves as a reminder of the general position still extant here, that inferences from silence need to be specifically provided for; but also illustrates, perhaps, the penetration of judicial culture by legislative intent.

[3.52] Outside the criminal law field 'proper' there are also provisions infringing upon the right to silence which are relevant to placement of the burden of proof. *National Irish Bank Ltd and in the matter of the Companies Act 1990*[54] concerned such a provision in the Companies Act 1990, Part II, which provided a mechanism for the investigation of companies by inspectors under the Act who had power to compel answers and production of documents from all officers and agents of a company under investigation.

[3.53] Two inspectors were appointed pursuant to s 8(1) of the 1990 Act to investigate and report on, inter alia, the improper charging of interest, the improper charging of fees and the improper removal of funds from customer accounts between 1988 and 1998. The inspectors sought guidance from the High Court as to whether persons from whom such evidence was sought were entitled to refuse on the grounds that such might incriminate them, and as to whether the procedure proposed by the inspectors was consistent with the requirements of natural and constitutional justice.

[3.54] The High Court held that the right to silence could be abrogated expressly or impliedly by statute. A proportionality test would determine whether that restriction was greater than necessary to enable the state to fulfil its obligations

---

[53] *DPP v Finnerty* [1999] 4 IR 364.
[54] *National Irish Bank Ltd and in the matter of the Companies Act 1990* [1999] 3 IR 145.

under the Constitution. Section 10 of the 1990 Act the High Court held was constitutional, in so far as the abrogation on the right to silence was no greater than necessary to enable the State to fulfil its constitutional obligations. The Supreme Court agreed that the powers given to the inspectors under s 10 were no greater than the 'public interest' required. They held that what was objectionable under Article 38 of the Constitution was compelling a person to confess and then convicting that person on the basis of that confession. As any confession obtained by inspectors would not be admissible at a subsequent criminal trial, unless the trial judge was satisfied it was voluntary, they found no difficulty with upholding the validity of these provisions.

[3.55] That decision illustrates the phenomenon of a second evidentiary rule (here regarding the admissibility of confessions) being introduced to justify/ excuse the modification or abrogation of another.

[3.56] Statutory provisions which are of a different nature in that they criminalise silence are also relevant here, as they abrogate, almost entirely, the task of the prosecution. The Offences Against the State (Amendment) Act 1998 contains such provision in s 9 which provides that:

'(1) A person shall be guilty of an offence if he or she has information which he or she knows or believes might be of material assistance in –

(a) preventing the commission by any other person of a serious offence, or

(b) securing the apprehension, prosecution or conviction of any other person for a serious offence,

and fails without reasonable excuse to disclose that information as soon as it is practicable to a member of the Garda Síochána.

(2) A person guilty of an offence under this section shall be liable on conviction on indictment to a fine or imprisonment for a term not exceeding five years or both.

(3) In this section 'serious offence' has the same meaning as it has in section 8.'

[3.57] The Offences Against the State Act 1939, s 52, sets down a requirement to give full account of movements:

'(1) Whenever a person is detained in custody under the provisions in that behalf contained in Part IV of this Act, any member of the Garda Síochána may demand of such person, at any time while he is so detained, a full account of such person's movements and actions during any specified period and all information in his possession in relation to the commission or intended commission by another person of any offence under any section or subsection of this Act or any scheduled offence.

(2) If any person, of whom any such account or information as is mentioned in the foregoing subsection of this section is demanded under that subsection by a member of the Garda Síochána, fails or refuses to give to such member such account or any such information or gives to such member any account or information which is false or misleading, he shall be guilty of an offence under this section and shall be liable on summary conviction thereof to imprisonment for a term not exceeding six months.'

[3.58] The constitutionality of this type of provision and the latter in particular was considered initially by the High and Supreme Courts in Ireland and ultimately by the European Court of Human Rights in *Heaney & McGuinness v Ireland*.[55] In *Heaney & McGuinness v Ireland* it was argued that s 52 of the Offences Against the State Act 1939 was in violation, inter alia, of Article 38 of the Constitution, and Articles 6, 8 and 10 of the European Convention.

[3.59] The factual context of that case concerned an explosion at an RUC checkpoint in Derry where five British soldiers and one civilian were killed. An hour and a half later the Irish police noted a light in a house four miles from the scene. They obtained a warrant to search and found an assortment of gloves, balaclavas, caps, etc. The men in the house (numbering seven), including the owner and the applicant were arrested and detained under the Offences Against the State Act 1939, s 30. It was thought that the bombing was carried out by the IRA and the applicants were suspected of membership and involvement in the bombing. Both were cautioned and questioned (s 52 was read to them) and the two refused to answer questions. On 25 October 1990, the two were brought to the Special Criminal Court in Dublin and charged with membership contrary to s 21, and failure to give an account of movements contrary to s 52.

[3.60] In the High Court[56] the plaintiff claimed s 52 infringed a right to silence guaranteed by Articles 38.1 and 40.3; the guarantee of equality under Article 40.1; a right to adversarial trial under Article 38.1 and the presumption of innocence under Article 38.1.

In the High Court, Costello J gave a perspective on the concept of justice envisaged by Article 38.1:

'It is an article ... [which has] ... been constructed as a constitutional guarantee that criminal trials will be conducted in accordance with basic concepts of justice. Those basic principles may be of ancient origin and part of the long established principles of the common law, or they may be of more recent origin and widely accepted in other jurisdictions and recognised in international conventions as a basic requirement of fair trial. Thus, the principle that an

---

[55] *Heaney & McGuinness v Ireland* [1994] 3 IR 593 (HC) (Costello J), [1996] 1 IR 580 (SC), (2001) 33 EHRR 12 at 264, 21 December 2000.
[56] [1994] 3 IR 593 at 605.

accused is entitled to the presumption of innocence, that an accused cannot be tried for an offence unknown to the law, or charged a second time with the same offence, the principle that an accused must know the case he has to meet and that evidence illegally obtained will generally speaking be inadmissible at his trial, are all principles which are so basic to the concept of a fair trial that they obtain constitutional protection from this Article. Furthermore the Irish courts have developed a concept that there are basic rules of procedure which must be followed in order to ensure that an accused is accorded a fair trial and these basic rules must be followed if constitutional invalidity is to be avoided.'[57]

Costello J did accept, however, that there could be restrictions on the right to fair trial which in this case, in applying the proportionality test he accepted were proportionate to the objective (investigation and punishment of serious subversive crime).

[3.61] On appeal, the Supreme Court agreed with that conclusion but chose to focus on the freedom of expression clause in the Constitution rather than Article 38. Significantly, this weakens the right by classifying it with weaker 'collective' rights. There is also an interesting contrast drawn (see judgment of O'Flaherty J at p 586) between those 'totally innocent of any wrongdoing' and others who might avail of the right.

[3.62] The European Court of Human Rights recalled[58] that it was part of its established case law that '... the right invoked by the applicants, the right to silence and the right not to incriminate oneself, are generally recognised international standards which lie at the heart of the notion of a fair procedure under Article 6.'[59] The Court accepted that the rights to silence and not to incriminate oneself guaranteed by Article 6.1 are not absolute rights. The Court noted further that, although there were protections available to the applicants (as noted by the High Court),

> '[t]he application of section 52 of the 1939 Act in an entirely lawful manner and in circumstances which conformed with all of the safeguards referred to above, could not change the choice presented by section 52 of the 1939 Act: either the information requested was provided by the applicants or they faced potentially six months' imprisonment.'[60]

Accordingly the Court found that the 'degree of compulsion' imposed on the applicants by s 52 destroyed the very essence of their privilege against self-incrimination and their right to remain silent.[61]

---

[57] [1994] 3 IR 593 at 605-606.

[58] *Heaney & McGuinness v Ireland* 21 December 2000 (ECHR), para 40, (2001) 33 EHRR 12.

[59] 21 December 2000 (ECHR), (2001) 33 EHRR 12, para 40.

[60] 21 December 2000 (ECHR), (2001) 33 EHRR 12, para 51.

[61] 21 December 2000 (ECHR), (2001) 33 EHRR 12, para 55.

[3.63] In terms of the case put forward by the State as to the need for such provisions, the European Court held that the security and public order concerns of the government could not justify such a provision '...which extinguishes the very essence of the applicants' rights to silence and against self-incrimination guaranteed by Article 6.1 of the Convention' (at para 58). Hence the Court found a violation of the applicants' right to silence under Article 6.1 and presumption of innocence under Article 6.2.[62]

[3.64] Judgment was given by the European Court of Human Rights on the same day in a second case concerning the same issue. In *Quinn v Ireland*,[63] the facts related to the investigation of a robbery of a post office van in Adare, Co Limerick, another in the course of which one garda was killed and one wounded. The applicant was one of those arrested, under s 30 of the Offences Against the State Act 1939, on suspicion of being a member of the IRA contrary to s 21. He was questioned on eight occasions during the two 24-hour periods, and on three occasions saw his solicitor. He was cautioned in relation to s 52. He was eventually charged and convicted under that provision for refusing to give an account of his movements. The decision here of the ECHR was to the same effect as that in *Heaney & McGuinness*.

Imposition of a legal burden on the accused – compatibility with the European Convention on Human Rights

[3.65] In *Regina v Lambert*[64] the House of Lords had the opportunity to address issues regarding the compatibility of reverse onus provision with the European Convention, hence indicating the possible future of provisions which have become increasingly common in Ireland. The appellant here was convicted of possession of a controlled drug, cocaine, contrary to s 5 of the Misuse of Drugs Act 1971. He relied on s 28(3)(b)(i) of the 1971 Act, that he did not believe or suspect or have reason to suspect that the bag contained such a controlled drug. The judge directed the jury that the prosecution only had to prove he had possession, and that the bag had a controlled drug. He had to prove on the balance of probabilities that he did not know the bag contained a controlled drug. Hence he bore the legal burden of proof with regard to that.

[3.66] The appellant contended, on appeal to the House of Lords, that this latter violated Article 6 of the Convention rights, as set out in the Schedule to the Human Rights Act 1998. The majority of the House of Lords proceeded on the basis that it was possible to read that section as imposing an evidential, not a

---

[62] 21 December 2000 (ECHR), (2001) 33 EHRR 12, para 59.
[63] 21 December 2000 (ECHR) Appl No 36887/97 (decided same day as *Heaney & McGuinness*).
[64] *Regina v Lambert* UKHL 37 (5 July 2001), [2002] 2 AC 545.

legal burden on the appellant, and so ensured its compatibility with the Convention rights. With regard to the general issue of placing a legal burden on the accused, the House of Lords did comment that the section in imposing a legal burden was 'a disproportionate reaction to perceived difficulties facing the prosecution in drugs cases'.[65]

'Peculiar knowledge principle'

[3.67] Quite apart from the case of insanity and statutory provisions, the existence of a third exception to the *Woolmington* principle has been a matter of some controversy. The English Court of Appeal, in *R v Edwards*[66], held that if on its true construction an enactment prohibits the doing of an act, save in specified circumstances, the defendant must (by way of exception to the fundamental rules of the criminal law that the Crown must establish every element of the offence charged) prove the existence of the specified circumstances. This rule, moreover, the court in *Edwards* emphasised, does not depend upon his possession of peculiar knowledge, enabling him to prove the positive of a negative averment.

[3.68] The reason for this latter statement on the part of the Court of Appeal may have been related to the attempt to establish an exception to the general rule under the rubric and within the confines of 'peculiar knowledge'. Irish case law certainly, had proven itself amenable to such a development and it is worth examining some earlier Irish decisions in that regard.

[3.69] In *Minister for Industry and Commerce v Steele*,[67] the defendant was prosecuted under the Emergency Powers (Pork Sausages & Sausage Meat) (Maximum Prices) Order 1943, which established certain requirements as to the meat content of sausages. Evidence was given at the hearing which showed that it was not possible to prove by analysis or any other scientific method what percentage of the meat content of the sausages was pork. On appeal against conviction in the Circuit Court it was contended on the appellant's behalf, that no evidence had been adduced that what he had offered for sale were 'pork sausages' within the meaning of the Act. Hence the onus of proof, which lay on the prosecution, had not been discharged.

[3.70] A case was stated to the Supreme Court, where O'Byrne J (referring to *Taylor on Evidence*) held that an exception to the general rule as to the onus of proof existed, where the subject matter of the allegation lies peculiarly within the knowledge of one of the parties and that the party must prove it, whether it be of

---

[65] Per Lord Steyn at para 41.
[66] *R v Edwards* [1975] QB 27.
[67] *Minister for Industry and Commerce v Steele* [1952] IR 301.

an affirmative or a negative character, and even though there be a presumption of law in his favour. It was held that as the matter here was clearly peculiarly within the knowledge of the defendant, the burden of proof lay on him.

[3.71] In contrast is the decision of the Supreme Court in *McGowan v Carville*,[68] where on a charge of driving a motor van without a licence, the onus of proving that the defendant had no licence was held to rest on the prosecutor, the possession or the contrary of such a licence not being a matter peculiarly within the knowledge of the defendant.

[3.72] In the High Court, Murnaghan J took the view that in order for peculiar knowledge to bring about a shift in the legal burden of proof, the prosecution would at the very least have to establish a prima facie case. The Supreme Court affirmed this view, pointing out, that if on the facts, the defendant had been stopped and asked to produce a driving licence by the garda, but failed to do so then or at a reasonable period thereafter, given the knowledge possessed by the parties, the burden of proof would shift to the defendant to show he had a licence. Since no evidence had been here produced by the complainant as to whether the defendant did in fact subsequently produce his licence, the onus of proof had not shifted and so remained with him.

[3.73] In *Attorney General v Shorten*,[69] the defendant had made a declaration on 6 May 1958, that his motor car had not been used by him or with his consent since 31 December 1957. He was charged with making such a statement, knowing it to be false and misleading. The prosecution gave evidence that the car was seen on the road, but the driver had not been identified. The District Justice stated that as the user of the car had been proved by the prosecution, the onus was thrown on the defendant, as owner of the car, to prove that the vehicle had not been used by him, or with his knowledge or consent.

[3.74] On appeal, Davitt P, on taking into account all the circumstances (including the fact that the owner did not guard his car 24 hours a day), was not prepared to hold that the District Justice was entitled to find the burden of proof had shifted to the defendant. Davitt P's comment at one point in his judgment[70] is interesting:

> 'I confess that I do not feel at all happy about the application in criminal cases of what I have referred to ... the "peculiar knowledge" principle ... I found it very hard to regard resorting to the "peculiar knowledge" principle even in its modified form or to any similar principle as other then attempts to whittle down the presumption of innocence.'

---

[68] *McGowan v Carville* [1960] IR 330.
[69] *Attorney General v Shorten* [1961] IR 304.
[70] [1961] IR 304 at 309.

[3.75] Davitt P distinguished this case from *McGowan* in that here there was no statutory provision involved; and hence deciding the issue by reference to common law principles, insisted the prosecution prove the case beyond all reasonable doubt.

[3.76] A rather different conclusion was reached by Davitt P in *Bridgen v Dowd*[71], where the defendants were charged with carrying merchandise in a lorry without holding a merchandise licence. The complainant had only observed the carrying within an exempted area, but contended that once it was established the lorry had been carrying merchandise, and that the defendants owned the lorry and did not hold a merchandise licence, the onus then shifted to the defendants to show the merchandise had been carried on the occasion in question, exclusively within an exempted area. The District Justice dismissed the complaint but stated a case to the High Court.

[3.77] Davitt P felt, in light of *McGowan*, it was clear that in a prosecution for the offence of carrying goods without a merchandise licence, the onus of proving that the defendant has no such licence rests initially upon the prosecution:

> 'Once, however, it has been established that the defendant has no merchandise licence and that he has carried the merchandise by road in a mechanically propelled vehicle then if he is to escape liability, he must in my opinion bring himself within one of the exceptions which has the effect of relieving him of liability'.

[3.78] It seems here, as in *McGowan*, that once the prima facie case is established against the defendant, the peculiar knowledge principle comes into operation to shift the burden of proof. This approach would seem to herald some support for the notion that what shifts to the defendant is in fact an evidential burden, which if not then discharged by the defendant, leads to the legal burden having been satisfied by the plaintiff.

[3.79] Although this approach is contrary to Lawton LJ's suggestion in *Edwards* that it is the legal burden which moves, and there is some Irish judicial support for that view, academic opinion, in the main, has resisted a movement towards further development of exceptions to *Woolmington's* basic precept.

[3.80] Zuckerman,[72] most persuasively perhaps, feels this to be at best historically dubious, and moreover, to involve a departure from the placement of the burden of proof in criminal cases on the prosecution, in the context of very

---

[71] *Bridgett v Dowd* [1961] IR 313.
[72] AAS Zuckerman *The Principles of Criminal Evidence* (1989) Clarendon Press, Oxford.

minor offences where very little evidence is required to discharge the burden of proof.

Standard of proof

[3.81] Phrases such as 'standard of proof' and 'quantum of proof' refer to the size of the legal burden of proof. The trier of fact decides whether the probative force of evidence presented to discharge the legal burden on a particular issue, outweighs the evidence presented to show the contrary.

[3.82] In jury trials the trial judge bears the responsibility to direct the jury as to the nature of that quantum or standard. The common law knows two standards of proof, civil cases requiring that of proof on the balance of probabilities and criminal cases requiring proof beyond reasonable doubt. The latter, higher standard, owes its rationale to the bias in our criminal justice system towards risking a guilty person's acquittal, rather than that an innocent be convicted. An important aspect to this general standard is that when the legal burden is placed on an accused, in a criminal case, it is the civil standard which applies.

[3.83] The difficulty with such a system that allows standards of proof – as opposed to the scientific empiricism of something having been proven or not – is as to when that standard has been reached. Any delineation or adjudication of that point may vary with the subjectivity of the individual concerned. For that reason, the judiciary have from time to time attempted to express what the particular standards translate into. Denning LJ is probably most notable for his effort to grapple with this difficulty in *Miller v Minister for Pensions*,[73] where he stated, in relation to the criminal standard, that:

> 'Proof beyond reasonable doubt does not mean proof beyond the shadow of doubt. The law would fail to protect the community if it admitted fanciful possibilities to deflect the course of justice. If the evidence is so strong against a man as to leave only a remote possibility in his favour which can be dismissed with the sentence "of course it is possible but not in the least probable" the case is proved beyond reasonable doubt, but nothing short of that will suffice.'

[3.84] In relation to the civil standard Denning LJ commented that:

> 'If at the end of the case the evidence turns the scale definitely one way or the other, the tribunal must decide accordingly, but if the evidence is so evenly balanced that the tribunal is unable to come to a determinate conclusion one way or the other, then the man must be given the benefit of the doubt ... It must carry a reasonable degree of probability but not so high as in a criminal case ... If a tribunal can say "we think it more probable than not", the burden is discharged but if the probabilities are equal it is not.'

---

[73] *Miller v Minister for Pensions* [1947] 2 All ER 372.

[3.85] In the Irish context, Kenny J in *People v Byrne*[74] commented in the Court of Criminal Appeal:

'In this case the trial judge used the words "satisfied" and "to your satisfaction" on many occassions when explaining the onus of proof. He then said that "being satisfied" means the same thing as "beyond a reasonable doubt". This is not correct because one may be satisfied of something and still have a reasonable doubt.'

Kenny J's enunciation of the correct charge to a jury in a criminal case was as follows:

'The correct charge to a jury is that they must be satisfied beyond reasonable doubt of the guilt of the accused, and it is helpful if that degree of proof is contrasted with that in a civil case. It is also essential, however, that the jury should be told that the accused is entitled to the benefit of the doubt, and that when two views on any part of the case are possible on the evidence they should adopt that which is favourable to the accused unless the state has established the other beyond reasonable doubt.'

[3.86] It may be said that it is easier to establish what does not amount to an adequate explanation of the standard than what does: the comment of Megaw LJ in *R v Gray*[75] *was* to the effect that the description of 'reasonable doubt' as the sort of doubt which might affect you in the conduct of your everyday affairs, might suggest too low a standard to the jury. If the trial judge had referred to the sort of doubt which might affect the mind of a person in the conduct of important affairs, there could, however, he reasoned, be no proper criticism.

[3.87] The difficulties in giving further expression to an already abstract and vague criterion of proof or adjudication are obvious. Perhaps given the longevity of the provisions, and our familiarity as lawyers and lay-persons with them, it is best to leave the phrases as they are, albeit subject to the vagaries of subjective interpretation, rather than encouraging what amounts to no more than further articulation of particular aspects of those subjective approaches.

[3.88] In this regard it is difficult to disagree with the statement of the English Court of Appeal in *R v Ching*[76]:

'We point out and emphasize that if judges stopped trying to define that which is almost impossible to define there would be fewer appeals. We hope there will not be any more for some considerable time.'

---

[74] *People v Byrne* [1974] IR 1.
[75] *R v Gray* [1974] 58 Cr App Rep 177.
[76] *R v Ching* (1976) 63 Cr App Rep 7 at p 11.

[3.89] An endorsement of a trial judge's direction with regard to standard of proof was given in *People (DPP) v Kiely*.[77] The trial judge, in his direction to the jury, explained the difference between the civil and criminal standards of proof as follows:

> 'You will have a decision to make and an important decision and you will have to weigh it up. I must refer you to that, during your whole life, you are making decision after decision and they are in various categories. There is one category of decision which I will call of a passing or trivial nature. Will I go to the cinema tonight? Will I buy a lottery ticket? Will I look at the Late Late Show? ... All these things are little decisions that we make. They are not life changing decisions ... There is another kind of decision which is much more fundamental which we all again make. Are we going to get married or if we are already married are we going to leave our marriage partner and go with someone else? Are we going to sell our house in the rising property market? ... They are all decisions which we all have to make from time to time, not very often but we have to make them, but you make those decisions in a much more fundamental and careful way than the kind of decisions that you are going to watch the Late Late Show or you are going to buy a lottery ticket. They are totally different kinds of decisions. Now the civil standard of proof that I spoke about, the traffic case, injury at work, that kind of thing, you can equate that to the trivial kind of decision and the much more serious decision is equated with the criminal case, so, the difference between the trivial decision and the serious decision gives you some idea of the difference between the civil standards of proof which is lower and the criminal standard of proof which is much higher. I do not think I can explain it much better than that to you. It is very serious and you have to be satisfied beyond reasonable doubt, that it not mathematical doubt, but beyond reasonable doubt.'

McGuinness J held that there could be no criticism of his direction which she regarded as abundantly clear and comprehensive.

Tribunals; other contexts

[3.90] Occasions when the strict application of the general rule as to the standards of proof and their effect may well be departed from, are provided by tribunal proceedings, and less obviously perhaps by instances on the civil side, when particular circumstances seem to warrant greater caution in reaching a determination on an issue. In other words the basic civil standard will never have to be less than satisfied; but may occasionally be augmented. Firstly, in the case of tribunals, rules of evidence may well be relaxed or not adhered to. No general provisions exist with regard to same; and (judicial) discretion as to satisfaction on the issues concerned is the standard mooted. It is interesting to note as an

---

[77] *People (DPP) v Kiely* (21 March 2001), CCA, McGuinness J.

example of this, the statement of Lynch J in the *Report of Kerry Babies Tribunal* to the effect:

'With one exception ... the Tribunal finds facts only if the Tribunal is satisfied of such facts as a matter of *substantial probability.* This is a degree of proof in excess of the mere balance of probabilities and short of proof beyond reasonable doubt.'

[3.91] Furthermore, in the Goodman Tribunal, the standard adopted by Hamilton J was that of proof beyond reasonable doubt. It would seem that the civil standard is the benchmark, which on occasion may be raised for reasons of pragmatism or policy. Under the Residential Institutions Redress Act 2002, s 7[78], entitled 'Entitlement of Award', concerning the burden of proof, the standard of proof required is a lower one than that required by the civil standard – ie, 'establishes to the satisfaction of the Board'.

This may be seen in the context of certain civil actions requiring higher standard of proof because of their wider implications for others, whether directly concerned in the action or not.

[3.92] In *Leahy v Corboy*[79], in a situation where a legatee named in the will of a testator, who had also drafted a codicil to that will which increased the said legatee's bequest, Budd J, in the Supreme Court review of the case law (including *Fulton v Andrews*[80]), found the rules to be twofold:

'(1)   The *onus probands* lies upon the party propounding a will and he must satisfy the conscience of the court that the instrument so propounded is the last will of a free and capable testator; and

(2)   if a party writes or prepares a will under which he takes a benefit that is a circumstance that ought generally to excite the suspicion of the court and calls upon it to be vigilant and jealous in examining the evidence in support of the instrument in favour of which it ought not to pronounce unless the suspicion is removed, and it is judicially satisfied that the paper as propounded does express the true will of the deceased.'

[3.93] The Supreme Court referred to *Windle v Nye*[81], where Viscount Simonds stated that if a person who prepared a will for the testator takes a benefit under it, that fact creates a suspicion that must be removed by the person propounding the will. In all cases the court must be vigilant and jealous. The degree of suspicion will vary with the circumstances of the case. On the facts in this

---

[78]   Residental Institution Redress Bill first presented in the Dáil on 12 June 2001, and passed on 28 March 2002. Section 7 was originally s 6 of the Bill.

[79]   *Leahy v Corboy* [1969] IR 148.

[80]   *Fulton v Andrews* (1875) LR 7 HL.

[81]   *Windle v Nye* [1959] 1 WLR 284.

particular case, the Supreme Court felt the heavy burden of proof had not been satisfied.

[3.94] Similarly in the case of *In the Matter of the Succession Act 1965, s 117 and in the Estate of IAC deceased; C and F v WC & TC*,[82] which concerned a challenge to the will of the deceased testatrix, who at the date of her death had been a widow with four surviving children. The plaintiff daughters of the deceased testatrix brought an application under s 117 of the Succession Act 1965, claiming that their mother had failed in her moral duty to make proper provision for them under the will according to her means. The High Court had upheld that claim. Finlay CJ in the Supreme Court, adopted the statement of general principles with regard to s 117 of Kenny J in *Re GM deceased: FM & TAM*[83], but added the following qualification:

> 'I am satisfied that the phrase contained in s 117(i) "failed in his moral duty to make proper provision for the child in accordance with his means" places a relatively high onus of proof on an applicant for relief under the section. It is not apparently sufficient from these terms in the section to establish that the provision made for a child was not as great as it might have been, or that compared with generous bequests of other children or beneficiaries in the will, it appears ungenerous. The court should not, I consider, make an order under the section merely because it would on the facts proved have formed different testamentary dispositions. A positive failure in moral duty must be established.'

[3.95] A further decision concerning wills and the standard of proof requisite is that of *Re Glynn (decd).*[84] The case provides an interesting insight into judicial assessment (and divergence) on the quantum of proof, at trial, based on credibility of witnesses, and on appeal. The Succession Act 1965, s 77, requires that to be valid a will shall be made by a person who 'is of sound disposing mind', a legislative adoption of a judicial term requiring that the testator should know and approve the contents of the will and, at the time of execution of the will, be of sound mind, memory and understanding. The issue arose here in the context of a will made by William Glynn, the instructions of which were given to a priest in the presence of a layperson prior to 5 October 1981, on which date the testator suffered a massive stroke. On 20 October, in the presence of those two same individuals, the purported execution of the will took place. Medical evidence was given to the effect that on that date it was practically impossible to communicate with the testator, and 'it may well be the case with this patient that he didn't understand what was being said to him'.[85] The two witnesses

---

[82]   *In the Matter of the Succession Act 1965, s 117 and in the Estate of IAC deceased; C and F v WC & TC* [1989] ILRM 815.

[83]   *Re G M deceased: FM & TAM* 106 ILTR 82 at 87.

[84]   *Re Glynn* [1990] 2 IR 326.

[85]   [1990] 2 IR 326 at 328 (McCarthy J).

considered William Glynn knew what was going on and was capable of making a will.

[3.96] The President of the High Court, Hamilton P admitted the will to probate. He noted that:

> 'Normally the legal presumption is in favour of the will of a deceased and in favour of the capacity of a testator to dispose of his property and to rebut this presumption, the clearest and most satisfactory evidence is necessary. However in a case like this when a person suffers a stroke which may affect his capacity, the onus shifts and lies on the party propounding the will. Having regard to the nature of the stroke suffered by the deceased and the disability resulting therefrom, there is a heavy onus on the defendant in this case to establish that on 20th October 1981, the deceased had the mental capacity to make a testamentary disposition of his property, that he had a sound disposing mind, that he was capable of comprehending the extent of his property, the nature of the claims of his sister, the plaintiff herein, and that he was disposing of his property.'[86]

[3.97] He was satisfied that the two witnesses, Fr Donoghue and Mr Carter, had no interest in the disposition and their sole concern was to give effect to the testator's wishes as stated to them on a number of occasions. On appeal to the Supreme Court, that decision was upheld, Walsh J dissenting. Walsh J pointed out that although there was ample evidence to show that the document was in accordance with instructions given prior to the stroke: 'The question which arises for decision is whether at the time of the purported execution of the will the testator was of sound disposing mind'. Hamilton P had found that he was, on the basis of the evidence of Fr Donoghue and Mr Carter. However, Walsh J considered that to be the opinion of both of these gentlemen, but that opinion did not establish that the sick man knew what he was doing.

[3.98] Walsh J adopted the judgment in *Leahy v Corboy*[87] that nothing but firm medical evidence could suffice to discharge the onus of proving him to have been a capable testator. In that case, he pointed out the testator was a man who except during bouts of illness, had a reasonable degree of understanding although some difficulty in communicating. In the present case, the entire basis of the finding that the deceased had the necessary understanding was based on an interpretation of his smiles and nods. No code of communication had been established to indicate he knew or approved the contents of what he was doing. Walsh J stated it was not the integrity or veracity of the witnesses which was in issue, but the correctness of their assessment of what was essentially a medical problem. In light of the medical evidence in this case, he felt it could not be

---

[86] [1990] 2 IR 326 at 330 (Hamilton J).
[87] *Leahy v Corboy* [1969] IR 148 at 167.

proved that at the time of execution of the will the deceased was of sound, disposing mind.

[3.99] McCarthy J (Hederman J concurring) gave the majority judgment, however, and admitted the will to probate. He stated that:

'The learned President, who accepted the honesty and truthfulness of all of the witnesses, held that William did know what he was doing on 20 October 1981. This holding is an inference of secondary fact to be derived from the primary facts as found by the President who heard the witnesses ...'

[3.100] Reference had been made to *Parker v Felgate*[88] as authority for the proposition that, although a person may no longer have the capacity to go over the whole transaction, if he can say that, having settled the business with a solicitor, he relies upon his having embodied the instructions in words, and accepts the paper as embodying it, that is sufficient. Similar authorities include *Re Wallace: Solicitor for the Duchy of Cornwall and Batten*[89], where the document was executed without being read over to the testator; and *Perera v Perera*[90], wherein McCarthy J considered that Lord Mcnaughton expressed a common sense and good public policy approach if a person has given instructions to a solicitor to make a will and the solicitor prepares it in accordance with same, all that is necessary for it to be a good will if executed, is that the testator can accept the document put before him as embodying those instructions. McCarthy J further stated that:

'A duly attested will carries a presumption of due execution and testamentary capacity. That presumption was displaced because of the circumstances of the will in the instant case ... It is a fundamental matter of public policy that a testator's wishes should be carried out, however, at times, bizarre, eccentric or whimsical they may appear to be. One man's whimsy is another man's logic.

... The nub is William's capacity as of 20 October. If on that date he had been required to give instructions for the making of any sort of testamentary document, even as simple a one as the one in question, it may be that the validity of its execution may be challenged. That is not what he was doing, he was confirming instructions already given ... there was ample evidence before the President that the testator fully appreciated what was going on and that the terms of the document upon which he placed his mark fully represented what he wanted done with regard to his property. Admittedly the conclusion of the learned President is expressed as being that Fr Donoghue and Mr Carter had the opportunity to and did satisfy themselves as to this circumstance. That was not the issue, their opinion or conclusion is immaterial. It is a necessary inference,

---

[88] *Parker v Felgate* (1883) 8 PD 171.
[89] *Re Wallace: Solicitor for the Duchy of Cornwall and Batten* [1952] 2 TLR 925.
[90] *Perera v Perera* [1901] AC 304.

however, that the learned President came to the same conclusion and that consequently the will should stand.'

[3.101] A case again illustrating an increased standard of proof, in a civil case where serious repercussions followed from the determination, is that of *Preston-Jones v Preston-Jones*[91] which involved a husband petitioning for divorce on grounds of adultery. The husband had been absent from the UK from 17 August 1945 to 9 February 1946. On 13 August 1946 his wife gave birth to a normal child. The House of Lords accepted that in such cases, the standard of proof required by a petitioner in the case of an allegation of adultery was the criminal standard of proof beyond all reasonable doubt. This was so because of the gravity of the interests of the State and those of the child, as the effect of a *decree nisi* would be to bastardise the child.

[3.102] On the facts, as the husband had proven the child to have been born 360 days after he last had the opportunity of intercourse with his wife; and that the birth was a normal one, the court taking judicial notice of the normal period of gestation (9 months or 270 days) held as follows (per Lord McDermott):

> 'I do not think it open to doubt that a time must come when, with the period far in excess of the normal, the Court may properly regard its length as proving the wife's adultery beyond reasonable doubt and decree accordingly.'

(Of course this decision raises issues as to where one draws the line: here it was 360 days. Ultimately, there was an acceptance by most of the judges that proof of an abnormal period of gestation threw an evidentiary burden on the wife in this instance).

[3.103] In *Lyons v Lyons*[92], the standard applicable in relation to proof of adultery was deemed more stringent than is required of a plaintiff in other civil actions, but less stringent than beyond reasonable doubt. Cruelty has been adjudged to require proof on the balance of probabilities by the person alleging it (*O'Reardon v O'Reardon*[93]), the standard requisite being less than that in the context of the presumption of legitimacy and the policy considerations mooted earlier. In the context of an application for nullity on the grounds of 'incapacity to form a caring marital relationship' in *RT v VP (orse VT)*,[94] Lardner J in dismissing the petition applied the standard of proof as expressed by Kenny J in *S v S*, ie, 'that the petitioner has to establish his or her case to a degree of probability or as Lord Birkenhead expressed it "must remove all serious doubt".'

---

[91] *Preston-Jones v Preston-Jones* [1951] AC 391.
[92] *Lyons v Lyons* [1950] N1 181.
[93] *O'Reardon v O'Reardon* (February 1975, unreported) HC.
[94] *RT v VP (orse V T)* [1990] 1 IR 545.

[3.104] A further variation on the 'standard of proof' on the civil side was considered in *Murphy v Green*[95]. Section 260 of the Mental Treatment Act 1945 requires the leave of the High Court as a precondition to the institution of proceedings under the Act. The High Court shall not give such leave unless there are 'substantial grounds' for contending that the person against whom the proceedings are to be brought acted in bad faith or without reasonable care. The interpretation of the section had come before the Supreme Court in *O'Dowd v North Western Health Board*.[96] O'Higgins CJ in that case was of the opinion that the section required something approaching a prima facie case. Griffin J felt the section put the onus of proof squarely on the person seeking to bring the action and the use of the word 'satisfied' indicated that the Oireachtas had in mind a somewhat higher standard of proof than that which a plaintiff must ordinarily discharge in a civil case. He referred to a statement by Denning LJ in *Richardson v London County Council*[97] with regard to the same words in the English Act '... there must be solid grounds for thinking that there was want of reasonable care or bad faith'. Parker LJ had stated: 'It is, I think, at the opposite end of the scale ... to a flimsy ground. It is something short of certainty, but something considerably more than bare suspicion'. Henchy J in *O'Dowd*[98] was of the opinion that '... the adjective "substantial" should be given ... a connotation of weight or solidity'.

[3.105] Finlay CJ in *Murphy v Green*[99] commented that it is reasonable to require a precondition of leave of the court, in the context of the Mental Treatment Act 1945, although it limits constitutional access to the courts. In that case, Finlay CJ stated that a prima facie standard would appear to be more consistent with the situation where a court is asked to adjudicate upon the state of the case at the conclusion of evidence adduced on behalf of a plaintiff and before a defendant has been given an opportunity to refute. To establish facts to the satisfaction of the court he was not satisfied that the intending plaintiff must prove them beyond a probability:

> 'I am satisfied that the use of the phrase "substantial grounds" in this context ... would mean something more than probable or prima facie grounds. However, it is not necessary for the court to try and conclude at the end of the s 260 application, whether the plaintiff is, as a matter of probability, likely to succeed in his action'.

---

[95] *Murphy v Green* [1990] 2 IR 566.

[96] *O'Dowd v North Western Health Board* [1983] ILRM 186.

[97] *Richardson v London County Council* [1957] 1 WLR 751.

[98] [1983] ILRM 186 at 198.

[99] *Murphy v Green* [1990] 2 IR 566 at 572.

[3.106] Griffin J having regard to the decision in *Re R Ltd*[100], that restrictions on the general provision in Article 34 for the administration of justice should be strictly construed, changed his position in *Murphy v Green*, feeling that in *Dowd* he imposed a standard which was too high. He concluded that what is required by s 260 of the 1945 Act is that the applicant establishes as a matter of probability, that there are substantial grounds for the contention that the defendant acted without reasonable care.

[3.107] O'Flaherty J stated:

> 'But even if the plaintiff established that he had a stateable case, that is not enough ... The test is not that he can contend (or assert) that he has substantial grounds but that the "substantial grounds" which will help him prove his case ultimately do exist in fact. I would equate "substantial grounds" with potentially credible evidence ... It is not necessary that the evidence should be so compelling as to make it certain (because that is to set too high a standard) that he will establish his case but the evidence must be there and must be demonstrated to be there to a credible extent before he should be permitted to bring his proceedings.'

[3.108] An example of a case in which the burden having been placed on the accused was not satisfied (ie, the requisite (civil) standard was not reached) is *DPP (Garda Malachy Crowley) v Michael Connors*.[101] The case, stated by Hubert Wine DJ, was as to whether he was correct in dismissing a charge against the defendant on the grounds that s 22(3) of the Road Traffic (Amendment) Act 1978, requiring the Medical Bureau to forward a copy of the relevant certificate of analysis to the defendant (provider of the specimen), was not complied with.

[3.109] Lavan J adopted and applied the decision of Gannon J in *DPP v Ronnie Walsh*.[102] In that case, it was submitted the defendant should not be convicted since he had not received a copy of the certificate of blood alcohol level from the Medical Bureau of Road Safety. It had been returned 'not collected'. Gannon J construed s 22(3) of the 1978 Act firstly in terms of its ordinary meaning, resolving any ambiguity by considering other provisions of the Road Traffic Acts insofar as they related to the matter. Gannon J went on to state that (per Lavan J):

> 'whether the statutory requirements in relation to the taking of a sample or specimen and in relation to the analysis thereof, and in relation to the results of such analysis, have been complied with are matters of proof which, but for

---

[100] *Re R Ltd* [1989] IR 176.

[101] *DPP (Garda Malachy Crowley) v Michael Connors* (10 May 1990, unreported) HC, (per Lavan J).

[102] *DPP v Ronnie Walsh* [1985] ILRM 243.

s 21(4) and s 23(2) of the 1978 Act, would have to be undertaken by the prosecution.'

He then pointed out that s 21(4) of the 1978 Act provides for the presumption, unless the contrary be shown, that the subsections in relation to the requirement for the taking of specimens and sending them to the Bureau, have been complied with. Section 23(2) of the 1978 Act provides that a certificate expressed to have been issued under s 22 shall, until the contrary is shown, be sufficient evidence of the facts certified to in it – and unless the contrary is shown – be sufficient evidence of compliance by the Bureau with requirements of the Act. Gannon J went on to state (per Lavan J) that these provisions:

'... are in relief of the onus of proof which, because of the presumption of innocence in favour of an accused person, would otherwise be borne by the prosecution. It does not affect in any way the nature or performance of the functions of the Bureau. It does have the effect of casting upon the accused person the onus of establishing either from evidence adduced by the prosecution or the evidence given or called by him that there was a failure by the Bureau of compliance with the statutory requirements relating to its functions. Because this onus is then cast upon an accused person and having regard to the procedures prescribed in s 16(5) and s 21 it seems to me that an accused person, who has not received delivery from the Bureau of the copy certificate cannot rely on that fact alone as showing the contrary for the purposes of avoiding the effect of s 23(2).'

For these reasons, Lavan J held that the determination of the District Justice in this case in dismissing the case, was deemed not correct in law.

[3.110] In essence, therefore, while general standards of proof apply and a consensus exists as to their application, content and effect (although not necessarily as to the elucidation of same), variation in the spectrum of proof possible on the criminal side is limited to the occasion when an accused is fixed with the burden or onus of proof and liable to reach the civil standard, while on the civil side, greater variety might accrue, although rarely reaching below the base standard, augmentation rather occurring in light of the 'gravity and public importance of the issues ... concerned'.[103]

---

[103] Per Lord McDermott in *Preston v Preston* [1951] AC 391.

Chapter 4

Illegally Obtained Evidence

'I'm telling you... Joxer ... th' whole worl's ... in a terr....ible state o' ... chassis!'

Sean O'Casey *Juno and the Peacock* (1980) MacMillan, p 73 (Boyle, Act III)

Introduction

[4.01] Perennial issues highlighting problems central to the criminal justice system include the process of bringing an accused before a court and the attitude of the court to the pre-trial criminal procedure. The rules of evidence very often represent that attitude. Problems also arise with regard to the concept of admissibility (particularly on policy grounds) and resolution of that most 'contentious' political issue in the context of the criminal trial. It is that resolution which this chapter considers.

[4.02] Consideration thereof necessarily invokes questions as to the kind of criminal justice system we choose to operate within our jurisdiction, and the particular philosophical underpinning or rationale to which it claims adherence. The criminal justice system involves the most intimate confrontation between the individual and the State in our society, and rests on the 'cutting edge of the abuse of power'. Hence the treatment of the individual caught within it, should be symptomatic or characteristic of the nature of that system.

[4.03] Our criminal justice system adheres to the trial model of an adversarial system: what Frank called the 'fight theory of justice'[1]. This operates on the premise that:

> '... [T]he best way for a court to discover the facts in a suit is to have each side strive as hard as it can, in a keenly partisan spirit, to bring to the court's attention, the evidence favourable to that side.'

In the criminal context, the protagonists are the State, and the individual accused. The operative presumption adopted in the context of that criminal inquiry, is one of 'innocent until proven guilty'. It is for the State to prove beyond all reasonable doubt, that the accused is guilty of the offence alleged. Moreover, the bias of the system is such that it is allegedly preferred that nine guilty men go free, rather than one innocent be convicted. In the context of

---

[1] Jerome Frank *Courts on Trial: Myth and Reality in American Justice* (Princeton, New Jersey) p 89.

determining the issue of guilt, the court does not have regard to all evidence relevant to the issue before it. This is due most immediately to application of the rules of evidence; the concepts of relevance and admissibility; and ultimately to the fact, that, for various policy reasons over the years, the courts have found it possible to admit, or to rely on, certain types of evidence less frequently than others. Various interests and value judgments come into play, in delineating the distinction between relevance and admissibility. One of these – the consideration of this chapter – relates to the desire that in the obtaining of evidence by agents of the State, pre-trial criminal procedures be observed. Hence, with varying degrees of strictness, the courts decline to admit what is termed 'illegally obtained evidence', ie, evidence obtained in breach of procedure. Yet these procedures bear no small relationship to the fundamental bias of our system and the interest it claims to serve.

[4.04] The balancing of interests involved includes a recognition that the interest of the public in combating crime must be counterbalanced, by the need to secure the fair trial of an accused, the public interest in vindication of constitutional rights, and the operation of the rule of law. Overall, the system is characterised as 'due process' rather than 'crime control'. The 'due process' model, purports to safeguard in the criminal context, those individual rights guaranteed to citizens in liberal democracies, and to centre on the extent to which State incursion on the individual is permissible.

Historical perspective: the criminal trial

[4.05] It is perhaps appropriate in considering the concept of inadmissibility on policy grounds in the criminal trial, to view the matter in perspective, in order to adjudge its current role. In the context of the trial itself, the safeguarding of an accused's rights had early recognition. In eighteenth century England, for example, the criminal law was characterised by a harsh regime, culminating very often in the death sentence. 'The most recent account suggests that the number of capital statutes grew from 50 to over 200 between the years 1688 and 1820. Almost all of them concerned offences against property'.[2]

[4.06] Against this background, the criminal trial became encrusted with a fair measure of procedural safeguards, to which strict adherence was then held. The credibility of the structure was thus ensured. As Douglas Hay commented:

> '"Justice" was an evocative word in the eighteenth century, and with good reason. The constitutional struggles of the seventeenth century had helped to establish

---

[2]   Douglas Hay 'Property, Authority and the Criminal Law' in *Albion's Fatal Tree: Crime and Society in Eighteenth Century England*, (Eds: Hay, Linebaugh, Rule, Thompson and Winslow) (1975) Pantheon, New York.

the principles of the rule of law: that offences should be fixed, not indeterminate; that rules of evidence should be carefully observed; that the law should be administered by a bench that was both learned and honest ... Equally important were the strict procedural rules which were enforced in the high courts and at assizes, especially in capital cases. Moreover, most penal statutes were interpreted by the judges in an extremely narrow and formalistic fashion. In part this was based on seventeenth-century practice, but as more capital statutes were passed in the eighteenth century the bench reacted with an increasingly narrow interpretation ... If a name or date was incorrect, or if the accused was described as a "farmer" rather than the approved term "yeoman", the prosecution could fail ... These formalisms in the criminal law seemed ridiculous to contemporary critics, and to many later historians. Their argument was (and is) that the criminal law, to be effective, must be known and determinate, instead of capricious and obscure. Prosecutors resented the waste of their time and money lost on a technicality, thieves were said to mock courts which allowed them to escape through so many verbal loopholes. But it seems likely that the mass of Englishmen drew other conclusions from the practice. The punctilious attention to forms, the dispassionate and legalistic exchanges between counsel and the judge, argued that those administering and using the laws submitted to its rule ...'[3]

Hay's ultimate thesis is that this absurd formalism was part of the strength of the law as an ideology, which later he alleges was class-based. Eighteenth century formalism is thus revealed by Hay as instrumental in the oppression of the working classes.

[4.07] Twentieth century formalism, or adherence to procedure, in the criminal justice context, has ostensibly a different function: limitation of State incursion on the individual. The ideology is that of the criminal justice regime adhering to the aforementioned 'due process' model.

[4.08] The historical perspective illustrates the beginnings of the precedent of a criminal justice system encrusted with procedure. The current rationale of such procedure is now that of regulating State power and the apparent inequality between citizens and the State, in the context of a criminal trial. Yet the criminal justice system had its origins in a very harsh regime: one where the accused was not competent, for some considerable time, as a witness in his own trial. Even when competent, he invariably came from the poorer sectors of society, was badly educated, and so ill-equipped to put forward a defence or, in the absence of a legal aid scheme, to afford legal representation. If conviction ensued (as was,

---

[3]   Douglas Hay 'Property, Authority and the Criminal Law' in *Albion's Fatal Tree: Crime and Society in Eighteenth Century England*, (eds: Hay, Linebaugh, Rule, Thompson and Winslow) (1975) Pantheon, New York, p 32.

therefore, almost inevitable), very many of the offences merited the death penalty.

[4.09] It can be argued that current conditions require a different system of criminal justice: one whose procedures do not so jealously guard the rights of the accused. In a democracy, however, any such debate should be an open and full one, mindful of the constitutional guarantees to citizens, and conscious of the need to develop a structure with an inherent logic; a system of checks and balances to ensure overall equity to the citizens caught within it. This is what liberal democracy guarantees, after all.

[4.10] Recent events may suggest, however, that in the context of the Irish criminal justice system, change has occurred in the absence of debate; and under the guise of adjustments of no substantive effect. Such adjustment or mutation can be observed in the context of recent pronouncements by the Irish courts on the issue of the admissibility of illegally or unconstitutionally obtained evidence.

[4.11] Prior to examining this, however, it is useful to set out the current parameters on police use of powers of incursion on the liberty and or freedoms of the individual citizen. These can usefully be termed powers of search and seizure, as in this context one is talking of the admissibility of evidence obtained by force in an unlawful or invalid search, rather than a process of interrogation which results in confession-type evidence. Although the latter similarly involves a constitutional dimension, it is further complicated by the requirement of 'voluntariness' and will be considered separately together with police powers of arrest and detention and the regulation thereof.

Search and seizure

[4.12] Consent of the person concerned can of course be lawful justification for a search by a police officer. Statutory authority may provide a power of search (eg Misuse of Drugs Act 1977, s 26(3), which permits persons to be searched). In *O'Callaghan v Ireland*[4] such a statutory power, short of arrest under s 23 of the Misuse of Drugs Act 1977 (as amended by s 12 of the Misuse of Drugs Act 1984), was upheld under a constitutional challenge.

[4.13] The Supreme Court held such persons did have all rights accruing on arrest – a decision which seems to indicate a possible implied statutory power or common law power short of arrest is *DPP v Fagan*.[5] Carney J held that the Garda Síochána had both an implied statutory power under the Road Traffic Acts and a common law power to operate random road traffic checks involving

---

[4]   *O'Callaghan v Ireland* [1994] 1 IR 555.
[5]   *DPP v Fagan* [1993] 2 IR 95.

the stopping of vehicles, even where the gardaí did not suspect the drivers of any criminal offence. The Supreme Court confirmed on appeal (Denham J dissenting) that such a power existed at common law.

[4.14] On arrest, a person can be searched for the protection of the arresting officer. His immediate environment may also be searched (*Dillon v O'Brien & Davis*[6]). In *Jennings v Quinn*,[7] O'Keeffe J outlined in the High Court the parameters of police powers of search and seizure of material in the aftermath of a lawful arrest, police can take:

(1)   evidence in support of the crime charged on which the arrest is made;

(2)   evidence in support of any crime charged or then in contemplation against the person; and

(3)   evidence reasonably believed to be stolen property or to be property unlawfully in possession of that person.

[4.15] This can be contrasted wtih *Jeffrey v Black*[8] where Mr Black was arrested because he stole a sandwich from a pub. Before being brought to the police station and charged, however, the police officers brought him to his home where they found cannabis. The evidence on the charge of possession of cannabis was deemed inadmissible.

Search warrants

[4.16] Search warrants are probably the most common justification for search and seizure. Traditionally, search warrants were very specific and limited exceptions made to the historical important principle of the common law that 'a man's home is his castle'. In *Leach v Money*[9], the concept of a general warrant was rejected, as the courts had a horror of the 'general ransack', and in *Entick v Carrington*[10] the concept of a warrant issued on grounds of 'state necessity' was rejected. In general, a search warrant was 'spent' when used once, and could not be used again. However, many warrants are now exceptionally and specifically provided to 'live' for a specified time. An early example of such an exception is the Misuse of Drugs Act 1977, s 26(2) which allows for the execution of a warrant 'at any time or times within one month from the date of issue of the warrant'.

---

[6]   *Dillon v O'Brien & Davis* (1897) 20 LR Ir 300.
[7]   *Jennings v Quinn* [1968] IR 305 at 309.
[8]   *Jeffrey v Black* (1978) 1 All ER 555.
[9]   *Leach v Money* (1765) 19 St Jr 1001.
[10]   *Entick v Campion* (1795) 2 Wils 275.

[4.17] With regard to the use of a premises for the purposes of prostitution and living on the earnings of prostitution s 10(2) of the Criminal Law (Sexual Offences) Act 1993 also provides that a District Court can issue a warrant authorising a search of such premises 'at any time or times within one month from the date of issue of the warrant'.

[4.18] Recent legislative changes to the provisions regarding the issue of search warrants include changes to their traditional specificity (ie warrants are now more broad sweeping in terms of the powers they confer), their longevity and their issuance in that provision is made for avoidance of the judicial imprimatur in granting a warrant (ie, in circumstances of urgency or necessity they can be issued by gardaí of a certain rank). In that case they generally do not 'live' for as long, but the notion of independent (ie judicial) scrutiny of the justification for such search is lost.

[4.19] It is worth examining some of the more recent provisions with regard to changes in powers of search under warrant, in terms of the powers granted to the police and agencies such as CAB in order to note the areas where such powers of search and seizure have increased. The manner in which broad sweeping powers of search have moved from such limited areas of concern, to gradually (as those areas increase) overwhelm the whole, is remarkable, and typical of a piecemeal approach, which facilitates change incrementally, without the need to address therefore the implications for the whole of the system. The latter relate to privacy, property rights, self-incrimination and the role of the court in civil liberties.

The gradual diminishing in importance of the role of the judiciary as a 'brake' on police action is also perhaps a product of State anxiety to avoid the implications of arguments which led to the loss of evidence at trial (inadmissibility) because of the fragility of the judicial role – as witnessed in *Kenny*, etc.

Avoidance of the Peace Commissioners/judges as reviewers of 'police suspicion' in an effort to circumvent defence attacks on same, the loss however is that of the only independent review of the police action in this most highly charged area.

Warrants regarding the commission of serious offences

[4.20] The Criminal Justice (Miscellaneous Provisions) Act 1997, s 10 provides for warrants regarding the commission of serious offences as follows:

'(1) A judge of the District Court, on hearing evidence on oath given by a member not below the rank of inspector, may, if he or she is satisfied that there are reasonable grounds for suspecting that evidence of, or relating to the commission of:

(a) an indictable offence involving the death of or serious bodily injury to any person,

(b) an offence of false imprisonment,

(c) an offence of rape, or

(d) an offence under an enactment set out in the First Schedule to this Act, is to be found in any place, issue a warrant for the search of that place and any persons found at that place.

(2) A warrant under this section shall be expressed to and shall operate to authorised member accompanied by any other member to enter within one week of the date of issuing of the warrant (if necessary by the use of reasonable force), the place named on the warrant, and to search it and any persons found at that place and seize anything found at that place or anything found in the possession of a person present at that place at the time of the search, which the said member reasonably believes to be evidence of or relating to an offence referred to in subsection (1).

(3) A member acting under the authority of a warrant under this section may—

(a) require any person present at the place where the search is carried out to give to the member his or her name and address, and

(b) arrest otherwise than on foot of a warrant any person:

    (i) who obstructs or attempts to obstruct that member in the carrying out of his or her duties,

    (ii) who fails to comply with a requirement under paragraph, or

    (iii) who gives a name or address which the member has reasonable cause for believing is false or misleading.

(4) A person who obstructs or attempts to obstruct a member acting under the authority of a warrant under this section, who fails to comply with a requirement under paragraph (a) subsection (3) or who gives a false name or address to a member shall be guilty of an offence and shall be liable on summary conviction to a fine not exceeding £1,500 or to imprisonment for a period not exceeding 6 months, or to both:

(a) The power to issue a warrant under this section is in addition to and not in substitution for any other power to issue a warrant for the search of any place or person.

(b) In this section Commission in relation to an offence, includes an attempt to commit such offence; and 'place' includes a dwelling.'

Although this provision might retain the judicial role in its issuance, because of the broad number of offences covered for the purposes of the search; the provision to allow search of those on the premises, and the requirements imposed with regard to giving of information and the criminal consequences of such failure, it is very far removed in nature from more limited traditional warrants.

Warrants for entry for the purposes of arrest

[4.21] The Criminal Law Act 1997, s 6 provides for warrants for entry for purpose of arrest as follows:

> '(1) For the purpose of arresting a person on foot of a warrant of arrest or an order of committal, a member of the Garda Síochána may enter (if need be, by use of reasonable force) and search any premises (including a dwelling) where the person is or where the member, with reasonable cause, suspects that person to be, and such warrant or order may be executed in accordance with section 5.
>
> (2) For the purpose of arresting a person without a warrant for an arrestable offence a member of the Garda Síochána may enter (if need be, by use of reasonable force) and search any premises (including a dwelling) where that person is or where the member 'with reasonable cause' suspects that person to be, and where the premises is a dwelling the member shall not, unless acting with the consent of an occupier of the dwelling or other person who appears to the member to be in charge of the dwelling, enter that dwelling unless—
>
> (a) he or she or another such member has observed the person within or entering the dwelling, or
>
> (b) he or she, with reasonable cause, suspects that before a warrant of arrest could be obtained the person will either abscond for the purpose of avoiding justice or will obstruct the course of justice, or
>
> (c) he or she, with reasonable cause, suspects that before a warrant of arrest could be obtained the person would commit an arrestable offence, or
>
> (d) the person ordinarily resides at that dwelling.
>
> (3) Without prejudice to any express amendment or repeal made by this Act, this section shall not affect the operation of any enactment or rule of law relating to powers of search or powers of arrest.'

This warrant, in allowing for a power of entry effectively in 'hot pursuit' is remarkable by contrast with traditional jurisprudence. Its origin is also notable in that it was introduced in direct response to *Freeman v DPP*[11] where constitutionally of such an entry was deemed prohibited.

Warrants for Criminal Assets Bureau in relation to proceeds of crime

[4.22] The Criminal Assets Bureau Act 1996, s 14 provides for its power of search as follows:

---

[11] *Freeman v DPP* [1996] 3 IR 565.

'(1) A judge of the District Court, on hearing evidence on oath given by a bureau officer who is a member of the Garda Síochána, may, if he or she is satisfied that there are reasonable grounds for suspecting that evidence of or relating to assets or proceeds deriving from criminal activities, or to their identity or whereabouts, is to be found in any place, Issue a warrant for the search of that place and any person found at that place.

(2) A bureau officer who is a member of the Garda Síochána not below the rank of superintendent may, subject to subsection (3), if he or she is satisfied that there are reasonable grounds for suspecting that evidence of or relating to assets proceeds deriving from criminal activities, or to their identity or whereabouts is to be found in any place, issue a warrant for the search of that place and any person found at that place.

(3) A bureau officer who is a member of the Garda Síochána not below the rank of superintendent shall not issue a search warrant under this section unless he or she is satisfied that circumstances giving rise to the need for the immediate issue of the search warrant would render it impracticable to apply to a judge of the District Court under this section for a search warrant.

(4) Subject to subsection (5), a warrant under this section shall be expressed to and shall operate to authorise a named bureau officer who is a member of the Garda Síochána, accompanied by such other persons as the bureau officer thinks necessary, to enter, within one week of the date of issuing of the warrant (if necessary by the use of reasonable force), the place named in the warrant, and to search it and any person found at that place and seize and retain any material found at that place, or any material found in the possession of a person found present at that place at the time of the search, which the officer believes to be evidence of or relating to assets or proceeds deriving from criminal activities, or to their identity or whereabouts.

(5) Notwithstanding subsection (4), a search warrant issued under subsection (3) shall cease to have effect after a period of 24 hours has elapsed from the time of the issue of the warrant.

(6) A bureau officer who is a member of the Garda Síochána acting under the authority of a warrant under this section may—

(a)   require any person present at the place where the search is carried out to give to the officer the person's name and address, and

(b)   arrest without warrant any person who:

(i)   obstructs or attempts to obstruct that officer or any person accompanying that officer in the carrying out of his or her duties,

(ii) fails to comply with a requirement under paragraph (a), or

(iii) gives a name or address which the officer has reasonable cause for believing is false or misleading.

(7) A person who obstructs or attempts to obstruct a person acting under the authority of a warrant under this section, who fails to comply with a requirement under subsection (6)(a) or who gives a false or misleading name or address to a bureau officer who is a member of the Garda Síochána, shall be guilty of an offence and shall be liable on summary conviction to a fine not exceeding £1,500, or to imprisonment for a period not exceeding 6 months, or to both.

(8) The power to issue a warrant under this section is in addition to and not in substitution for any other power to issue a warrant for the search of any place or person.

(9) In this section "place" includes a dwelling.'

The CAB warrant was specifically drawn up to facilitate its officers with the widest powers of search and seizure. In addition to the judicial power, there is a garda power to issue a warrant, and accompanying wide-ranging powers in relation to those on the premises in question.

Warrants for the purposes of drug trafficking

[4.23] The Criminal Justice (Drug Trafficking) Act 1996, s 8 provides for the issuing of search warrants by a member of the Garda Síochána not below the rank of superintendent under s 26 of the 1977 Act, where he is satisfied:

(a)   that the warrant is necessary for the proper investigation of the suspected drug trafficking offence and

(b)   that circumstances of urgency giving rise to the need for the immediate issue of the search warrant would render it impractical to apply to a District Court Judge or Peace Commissioner.

This demonstrates the avoidance, once more, of judicial review of garda suspicion/opinion before necessary issuance of a warrant.

Judicial approach – historical and comparative

[4.24] The proliferation of specific and more extensive provision in relation to warrants for particular offences, targeting certain areas of crime or facilitating bodies such as the Criminal Assets Bureau, will undoubtedly continue. As rules relating to admissibility of evidence, and in particular illegally obtained evidence, focus on abuse or breach of procedure, the increasing complexity and variety of procedures renders this a more complicated task. Scrutiny of the grounds for issuance of a warrant, by reviewing the role of the peace commissioner or judge, may now in many cases be obviated by the role of the issuing garda officer. Implications of such changes for the role of the reviewing courts will only then emerge. To gain an insight into potential development here, an historical and comparative perspective on the possible divergent views of the courts is useful.

Approach of the English courts

[4.25] Traditional judicial approach in England could be seen as epitomised in the statement 'It matters not how you get it, if you steal it even, it would be admissible in evidence'.[12] A change of approach, with regard to the admissibility of illegally obtained evidence, was then introduced in that jurisdiction and found in the Police and Criminal Evidence Act 1984, s 78, which provides:

> 'In any proceedings the Court may refuse to allow evidence on which the prosecution proposes to rely to be given if it appears to the Court that, having regard to all the circumstances, including the circumstances in which the evidence was obtained, the admission of the evidence would have such an adverse effect on the fairness of the proceedings, that the Court ought not to admit it.'

[4.26] In *R v Mason* the Court of Appeal commented that although the Court's role was not to discipline the police, the 'hood winking' of the client and his solicitor in this case (by informing them falsely that the police had forensic evidence implicating the accused), necessitated exclusion of the evidence thereby obtained. The basis for exclusion in *Mason* was that provision in the Police and Criminal Evidence Act 1984 (s 78) which was said to encapsulate the English courts' previous discretion at common law. The advent of the Human Rights Act 1998 has meant an impact, as noted by Ashworth, mainly felt in criminal procedure and evidence.[13] However, the English courts have followed the House of Lords' interpretation of *Khan v UK*,[14] that the obtaining of evidence by violation of another Convention right does not render a trial unfair under Article 6, and that it is always a question of judicial discretion under s 78.

Approach of the United States courts

[4.27] The exclusionary rule in relation to illegally obtained evidence in the United States was developed initially in *Boyd v US*[15] in relation to forfeiture proceedings. *Weeks v US*[16] extended the doctrine to federal criminal trials, and *Mapp v Ohio*[17] to State Criminal trials. Furthermore, the doctrine of the 'fruit of the poisoned tree' in the United States, operated to exclude evidence obtained indirectly in consequence of a constitutional violation. The rationale for the exclusionary rule was based firmly in the notion of deterrence of unacceptable violation of constitutional rights by the police:

---

[12] Crompton J in *R v Leatham* (1861) 8 Cox CC 498 at 503.
[13] Ashworth A 'Criminal Proceedings after the Human Rights Act: the First Year' [2001] *Criminal Law Review* 855.
[14] *Khan v UK* (2000) Crim LR 684.
[15] *Boyd v US* (1866) 116 US 616.
[16] *Weeks v US* (1914) 332 US 383.
[17] *Mapp v Ohio* (1961) 367 US 643.

'Only by exclusion can we impress upon the zealous prosecutor that violation of the constitution will do him no good. And only when that point is driven home can the prosecutor be expected to emphasise the importance of observing constitutional demands in his instructions to the police'.[18]

The United States Supreme Court became less enamoured of the exclusionary rule, however, and in a number of decisions, has somewhat reduced its monolithic effect. For example, if the Court determined that the rationale of the rule – deterrence – will not be effected in a given case, the evidence will be admitted, notwithstanding the breach of constitutional rights involved.

[4.28] This was the situation in *US v Leon*[19] where the warrant was invalid but the officers acted in good faith. Exclusion of the evidence obtained thereunder, would not have any deterrence effect, hence a 'good faith' exception was carved out to the exclusionary rule.

Approach of the Irish courts

[4.29] The yardstick by which the Irish courts determine admissibility of illegally obtained evidence is *The People (AG) v O'Brien*[20]. The search warrant used in *The People (AG) v O'Brien* contained an error in relation to the name of the street. The search was deemed illegal – so incorporating a discretion on the part of the trial judge to admit or exclude the evidence. A distinction was drawn by the court between 'mere illegality' which could facilitate admissibility, and a breach of constitutional rights which would exclude evidence.

[4.30] The Supreme Court held that evidence obtained in 'deliberate and conscious' breach of constitutional rights, was inadmissible, save in 'extraordinary excusing circumstances'. Although Kingsmill-Moore J was reluctant to define the latter, Walsh J was of the opinion that they would include circumstances such as the imminent destruction of vital evidence, or the need to rescue a victim in peril. He also placed in the excusable category, evidence obtained by a search incidental to and contemporaneous with a lawful arrest, although made without a valid search warrant. If a breach involved a mere illegality, the trial judge had a discretion as to whether to exclude the evidence. The considerations then to be invoked, per Kingsmill-Moore J, were as follows:

'Was the illegal action intentional or unintentional, and if unintentional was it the result of an ad hoc decision or does it represent a settled or deliberate policy? Was it illegality of a trivial and technical nature or was it a serious invasion of important rights, the recurrence of which would involve a real danger to

---

[18] Murphy J (dissenting) in *Wolfe v Colorado* (1949) 338 US 25 at 41.
[19] *US v Leon* (1983) 468 US 879.
[20] *People v O'Brien* [1965] IR 142.

necessary freedom? Were circumstances of urgency or emergency which provide some excuse for the action?[21]'

[4.31] In the *People v Shaw*,[22] Griffin J suggested that the *O'Brien* ratio was confined to real evidence. In *People v Christopher Lynch*, Higgins CJ, however, castigated this suggestion and reasserted that, in fact the *O'Brien* ratio covered both real and confession evidence.[23]

[4.32] In *Trimbole v Govemor of Mountjoy Prison*[24] the applicant was arrested at 2 pm on 25 October 1984 under s 30 of the Offences Against the State Act 1939. On 26 October an additional 24 hours detention was sanctioned. At 3 pm on 26 October, an application was made to the High Court. Egan J was satisfied no genuine suspicion could have been formed by gardaí regarding possession of firearms/ammunition. An order for release was granted. A short while later, the applicant was arrested on foot of provisional warrant under s 27 of the Extradition Act 1965. On 26 October 1984 the Government made an order applying the Extradition Act 1965 to Australia as and from then. The applicant was brought before the District Court and remanded in custody. On 21 November 1984 the Minister made order for extradition. Egan J added:[25]

> 'the only rational explanation for the s 30 arrest on 25th October 1984 was to ensure that the applicant would be available for arrest and detention when Part II of the 1965 Act would apply to the Commonwealth of Australia. There was a gross misuse of s 30 which amounted to a conscious and deliberate violation of constitutional rights. There were no extraordinary excusing circumstances.'

[4.33] Finlay CJ (Henchy, Griffin, Hederman JJ concurring):[26]

> 'I am satisfied that from those decisions (*State (Quinn) v Ryan* [1965] IR 70; *People (AG) v O'Brien* [1965] IR 342; *People v Madden* [1977] IR 336; *People v Lynch* [1982] IR 64) certain principles can be deduced. They are:
>
> The Courts have not only an inherent jurisdiction but a positive duty:
>
> (i)   To protect persons against the invasion of their constitutional rights.
>
> (ii)   If invasion has occurred, to restore as far as possible the person so damaged to the position in which he would be if his rights had not been invaded; and
>
> (iii)   To ensure as far as possible that persons acting on behalf of the Executive who consciously and deliberately violate the constitutional right of citizens

---

[21] *People v O'Brien* [1965] IR 142 at 160.
[22] [1982] IR 1 at 59–60.
[23] *People v Lynch* [1982] IR 64 at 77–78. Also at [1981] ILRM 389 at 395.
[24] *Robert Trimbole v Govemor of Mountjoy Prison* [1985] ILRM 465.
[25] [1985] ILRM 465 at 479.
[26] [1985] ILRM 465 at 484.

do not for themselves or their superiors obtain the planned results of that invasion

... I am satisfied that this principle of our law is of wider application than merely to either the question of the admissibility of evidence or to the question of the punishment of persons for contempt of Court by unconstitutional action.'

[4.34] In the context of the Irish courts' approach to illegally obtained evidence, an increased willingness to admit evidence under the *O'Brien* formula is evident on occasion, which leads to a certain inconsistency among the decisions. Some decisions are particularly interesting in this regard.

[4.35] *DPP v Lawless*[27] involved a conviction under the Misuse of Drugs Act 1977. Police went to flats in Dublin with a warrant under the said Act, and using the necessary force entered. The applicant was in the lavatory, where the noise of flushing was heard. Detectives found a quantity of heroin in the manhole. The warrant was deemed defective. It was held that as the warrant was defective, the entry and search of premises was unlawful. However, as the accused was not a tenant of the flat, no breach of his constitutional rights occurred. But even if there had been a breach of constitutional rights, the court held that it was not a conscious and deliberate violation. There was no evidence of deliberate deceit or illegality, no policy to disregard the provisions of the Constitution or conduct searches without a warrant (per *O'Brien*). Even if it was a deliberate and conscious violation, however, there were 'extraordinary excusing circumstances' – the need to prevent the imminent destruction of vital evidence. It can be seen that on any possible construction of the facts, the evidence goes in. This demonstrates the flexibility of the formula laid down in *O'Brien*.

[4.36] In *DPP v McMahon, McMeel and Wright*[28] the owners of a licenced premises were charged and convicted of offences against the Gaming and Lotteries Act 1956. The gardaí had made observations leading to evidence of the offences, without having identified themselves as guards or having a search warrant. It was held that the gardaí on entering premises were outside the implied invitation of the owner of the premises. Therefore, in law, they were trespassers. Yet entering, as a trespasser, the public portion of a licenced premises, which is open for trade, does not, the court held, constitute any invasion or infringement of the constitutional rights of the owner. Thus, it was a question of the admissibility of illegally obtained evidence, which according to the majority judgment of Kingsmill-Moore J in *AG v O'Brien*, is dependent on the court's discretion. Therefore, in balancing the public interest that the crime should be detected, against the undesirability of using improper methods,

---

[27] *DPP v Lawless* (28 November 1985, unreported) per Keane, McCarthy, O'Hanlon JJ.
[28] *DPP v McMahon, McMeel and Wright* [1987] ILRM 86.

particular importance was attached to the fact that the gardaí, in entering the public houses to view the machines, were trespassers only; they were not involved in any criminal or opproprious conduct, and that the offence of permitting gaming on licensed premises might be considered as one with grave social consequences. The definition of the breach here as a mere illegability by the Court was crucial, and facilitated the subsequent admissibility of the evidence in accordance with the court's discretion. The view taken of the gravity of the offences involved was ultimately vital in determining admissibility.

[4.37] In *DPP v Gaffney*[29] the accused's failure to stop at a garda checkpoint resulted in a car chase to his home. Gardaí called on the accused to stop, he refused and entered the house. On two occasions, the accused's brother refused the gardaí entry; and on the second of these he was arrested. The question arose as to whether the accused's response to a knock, 'Yes, in here', constituted an invitation to the gardaí to enter. It was held that in view of the fact the gardaí had twice been expressly refused entry and that there had been no express invitation, an invitation cannot be presumed simply because there was no refusal. Hence the gardaí were trespassers and their entry was in violation of Article 40.5 (inviolability of the dwelling); and the arrest of the accused was deemed unlawful.

[4.38] In *DPP v McCreesh*[30] a similar factual situation arose but this time the accused was arrested on the driveway leading into his house. Nonetheless, the Court held the same constitutional protection applied, and being without authority, the garda invasion of the property tainted the evidence obtained after the arrest. The careful attitude of the courts towards the right of householders in these cases contrasts sharply with the approach to tenants in *Lawless* and publicans in *McMahon*. The seriousness with which the relevant offences were viewed in both these cases (drugs, gaming) may also have been a factor, although drink-driving is certainly now viewed as a grave offence. The legislation did, however, respond to amend the law in accordance with the lacunae identified by the court in *Gaffney* and *McCreesh*. This situation has now been the subject of attention in the Road Traffic Act 1994. Sections 10 and 11 provide for a power on the part of the gardaí to arrest without warrant in relation to 'drink-driving' offences. Section 39 provides for a power to enter a dwelling in relation to 'hit and run' offences. (Section 106(3)(a) also gives a power to arrest without warrant in relation to same). A power to enter the cutelage of a dwelling is also provided for in this section. This applies to 'drink-driving' offences, as does the power to enter a hospital to obtain a specimen. The burden

---

[29] *DPP v Gaffney* [1987] IR 173.
[30] *DPP v McCreesh* [1992] 2IR 239.

of proof with regard to consumption of alcohol, after an incident (the so-called 'hip-flask' defence) is placed on the accused under s 20 of the 1994 Act, as is that regarding a defence to a refusal to permit the taking of specimen of blood or breath (s 23).

[4.39] In *DPP v Forbes*[31] the Supreme Court held that there is an implied permission on the part of every householder with regard to entry onto the forecourt of the premises. This may be rebutted but was not here – therefore, the arrest of the defendant for drunk-driving on a third party's property (driveway of a private house) was valid.

[4.40] The high water mark in terms of an exclusionary approach by the Irish courts is probably found in *Kenny*. In *People (DPP) v Mark Kenny*[32] garda surveillance of a flat in Rathmines, Dublin, led to a telephone request to obtain a search warrant under s 26(1) of the Misuse of Drugs Act 1977. The standard form used to obtain the warrant did not give the issuing Peace Commissioner facts sufficient to satisfy him as to the presence of reasonable grounds for suspicion. The gardaí used the warrant to obtain entry to the flat in question, where they found a quantity of controlled drugs, for which the accused took responsibility. The accused was convicted and sentenced to five years imprisonment. The Court of Criminal Appeal certified a point of law of exceptional public importance for the Supreme Court viz, whether the forceable entry of the accused's home by the gardaí on foot of an invalid search warrant constituted a deliberate and conscious violation of the accused's constitutional rights such as to render any evidence obtained thereby inadmissible at the trial of the accused. The Supreme Court held that the warrant was invalid and so breached Article 40.5 of the Constitution. Further, the breach was deliberate and conscious, as it was immaterial whether the person carrying out the breach was aware it was illegal, or it amounted to a breach of constitutional rights. There were no extraordinary excusing circumstances. Hence, the evidence was inadmissible at the trial. *Kenny* specifically refused to follow the 'good fault' exception endorsed by the United States Supreme Court in *Leon*[33] and so the absolute protectionist principle (not a deterrence one) was endorsed as the rationale for exclusion under Irish law.

[4.41] *DPP v Yamanoha*[34] followed *Kenny* where a warrant was issued in relation to a hotel room under s 26 Misuse of Drugs Act 1977 (as amended by s 13 of the Misuse of Drugs Act 1984). The warrant was challenged on the basis that the

---

[31] *DPP v Forbes* [1994] 2 IR 542.

[32] *People (DPP) v Mark Kenny* [1990] ILRM 569.

[33] *US v Leon* (1983) 468 US 897.

[34] *DPP v Yamanoha* [1994] 1 IR 565.

information on oath was confined to reciting the Detective Sergeant's reasonable grounds were not sufficient. The DPP contended that oral evidence was given as well. However, as that was unsworn, the warrant was deemed invalid and the evidence excluded.

[4.42] In *DPP v Dunne*,[35] a warrant under s 26 of the 1997 Act was again deemed invalid, as the words 'is on the premises' were deleted from it. Carney J held that if the inviolability of the dwelling is to be set aside by a printed form, it should be clear.

Given the due process approach of the Supreme Court in *Kenny*, subsequent decisions can be reviewed with a view to ascertaining if that is a necessary function of the *O'Brien* formula, or merely illustrative of its malleability. From the latter perspective, all manner of decisions and applications to facts facilitate exclusion and inclusion, and so demonstrate its elasticity.

[4.43] In *People (DPP) v Balfe*,[36] s 42(1) of the Larceny Act 1916 provided the basis for the issue of a search warrant. Here, the address on the information was incorrect, the date of the larceny was incorrect, and the name 'Eddie Balfe' was incorrect. The Criminal Court of Appeal held the defect was similar to and fell within *O'Brien* rather than *Kenny*, and that the evidence seized, therefore, was properly admitted.

[4.44] In *DPP v Owens*[37] the Supreme Court endorsed the focus on the importance of the role of the Peace Commissioner, which had been evident in *Kenny*. The intermediary role played by the Peace Commissioner, ensuring that Garda suspicion is not merely 'rubber-stamped' for issuance of a warrant, is a guarantee of a safeguard for individual rights which is preventative, being prior to rights invasion, rather than curative, at trial.

The facts in *Owens* concerned a situation where gardaí acting on information received that robbery proceeds might be at a particular premises in Dublin, obtained a warrant to search that premises from a Peace Commissioner. The gardaí went to the premises, where the door was opened by the accused, and conducted a search but found nothing incriminating.

Nonetheless, on the basis of confidential information received, they believed Owens was responsible for the robbery and arrested him, brought him to Ballymun Garda Station where he was detained under s 4 of the Criminal Justice Act 1984 and where he made an incriminating statement consisting of the principal evidence against him. The defence challenged the validity of the search

---

[35] *DPP v Dunne*, [1994] 2 IR 537.
[36] *People (DPP) v Balfe* [1998] 4 IR 50.
[37] *DPP v Owens* [1999] IESC 107.

warrant, arguing the entry was therefore illegal, the arrest and detention invalid and the evidence consequently inadmissible.

At the date of issuance of the warrant, the Peace Commissioner was 85-years-old, and at the date of the trial was too ill to go to court to explain his state of mind at the time he issued the warrant. The trial judge felt bound by *People (DPP) v Byrne*[38] to hold that the Peace Commissioner's signature was not sufficient to establish the validity of the warrant and that the Peace Commissioner must be present in person to prove his state of mind and to be available for cross-examination by the defence.

People (DPP) v Byrne[39] concerned the extension of the detention of the accused under s 30 of the Offences Against the State Act 1939 by a Chief Superintendent who was no longer alive at the date of trial, hence the evidence being adduced as to his state of mind when directing the extension period. The Supreme Court upheld the trial judge's determination that an overriding statement made during that extended period was therefore inadmissible.

In *Owens*, similarly the Supreme Court held to the same effect, ie, that a search warrant is a document which may affect constitutional rights and does not speak for itself in a criminal trial. As seen in the review of provisions regarding warrants, the recent phenomenon whereby warrants can increasingly (at least in certain circumstances) be issued by the gardaí themselves, obviates to some extent many of the difficulties – and safeguards – provided by that additional layer of supervision and proof. There remain, however, occasional reminders of judicial scrutiny of powers of search.

[4.45] *Hanahoe v Hussey*[40] involved a situation where although a discovery order could have been made under s 63 of the Criminal Justice Act 1994, s 64(1) of the Criminal Justice Act 1994 also made provision for a search warrant. On evidence presented with regard to the danger of the targeted individual interfering with the ability of the solicitors firm concerned to comply with a discovery order, a search warrant was granted in relation to the applicant solicitors' premises under s 64(1), rather than said discovery order. The media were present at the execution of the warrant. On application for certiorari, the issue came to the High Court where it was held that any intrusion on the personal rights of citizens and the inviolability of the dwelling must be closely scrutinised and justified. The District Justice must be satisfied as to the need for issuance of a warrant (and not just rely on garda averment), while the publicity attending the search warrant would not in itself invalidate the warrant, there was a duty of care on the part of the gardaí to the citizen about such information

---

[38] *People (DPP) v Byrne* [1989] ILRM 613.
[39] *People (DPP) v Byrne* [1989] ILRM 613.
[40] *Hanahoe v Hussey* [1998] 3 IR 69.

becoming public. The Court noted that the provisions under the Criminal Justice Act 1994 (a precursor of the Criminal Assets Bureau provisions) greatly extended the power to grant search warrants. Whereas hitherto persons subject to search warrants were essentially suspects, it contemplated the obtaining of documentation from wholly innocent third parties, which was 'a new and serious invasion of constitutional rights including the invasion of privacy and possibly the invasion of confidential relationships'.[41]

The Court awarded damages here due to the resultant 'media circus' which had caused the applicant's harm.

[4.46] In terms of subsequent provisions extending provision with regard to search warrants, Kinlen J's comment is worthy of note:[42]

> 'The primary concern of the judge ... must be so far as is practicable, to protect the rights of the citizen. We live in an era of fantastic and intrusive invasions of privacy. The State, the media and the many electronic devices have combined in a growing and worrying assertion that the invasion is allowable because of the battle against crime and corruption and also based on the alleged 'public's right to know'. These invasions are increasing but the courts must be the restraining arm to protect privacy and only allow invasion into privacy where on balance it can be justified.'

[4.47] In *DPP v Michael Delaney*[43] Sergeant M and nine gardaí were at the scene of a disturbance where a crowd was threatening to burn down a flat. The appellants had barricaded themselves in and were armed. Two women claimed there were children in the flat. The sergeant felt he had a right to enter for the safety of the children and the interests of the persons in the flat, because of the mob. In the High Court, Morris J said entry was justified if (1) there was the implied consent of the owner; (2) to protect the constitutional right to life of those in the flat. The Supreme Court held that, provided the sergeant acted bona fide in the belief he should enter the dwelling to safeguard life and limb, there was no breach of the Constitution.

[4.48] *Freeman v DPP*[44] concerned s 41 of the Larceny Act 1916 which provides that any person committing an offence under the act may be apprehended without warrant. Two gardaí received information that the appellant and two other men were seen unloading goods from a van into the appellant's house. There was a van outside the house and three men, including the appellant, at the porch. They saw the gardaí and ran into the house. The gardaí pursued using the

---

[41] *Hanahoe v Hussey* [1998] 3 IR 65 at 94.
[42] *Hanahoe v Hussey* [1998] 3 IR 65 at 96.
[43] *DPP v Michael Delaney* [1997] 3 IR 453.
[44] *Freeman v DPP* [1996] 3 IR 565.

key in the door. There were cigarettes, spirits, etc in the room. The appellant ran out of the house onto the street where he was arrested under s 41. Subsequent to the arrest, a search warrant was obtained. A number of shoes were shown to have been in contact with the surface in the shop from where the goods in the van were stolen. A challenge was made to the arrest and admissibility of the evidence. In the High Court, Carney J held that the appellant's presence in a public place was induced by the unconstitutional entry into the dwelling, and hence the arrest was invalid. The exclusionary rule, he stated, did not as a corollary entitle the State to breach constitutional rights in extraordinary excusing circumstances – it was to protect the rights of citizens including the inviolability of the dwelling. In the circumstances, however, it was held that the appellant was *in flagrante delicto* and the dwelling was being used in the commission of an offence. The trial judge could therefore exercise discretion to admit evidence obtained as a result of an illegal entry and unlawful arrest under extraordinary excusing circumstances (per *Lawless*). In any event there was deemed to be ample evidence grounding the search warrant independent of the unconstitutional entry.

[4.49] Although in *Freeman* the evidence was admitted due to extraordinary excusing circumstances, in the aftermath of this decision there was the introduction of s 6 of the Criminal Law Act 1997, which made provision for just such 'hot pursuit' entries for the purpose of arrest in *every* case not just where there are such extraordinary excusing circumstances.

The introduction of this legislative provision shows the interface between legislative facilitation of greater police powers in this area, running alongside judicial vindication of due process rights.

It can be also said to demonstrate another application of the particular (exception) to the general process ie, that which was first allowed in one exceptional circumstance becomes the norm.

[4.50] In *People v McCann*[45], the defendant had been convicted of the murder of his wife and foster child at their family home. They had died in a deliberate arson attack. It was argued that the forensic evidence gathered by the prosecution from the burnt-out dwelling, without McCann's consent, was a breach of his constitutional rights. It was also argued that his arrest in the private residential area of his business premises (a pub) was not consented to, and hence unlawful. The Criminal Court of Appeal held that the gardaí had a duty to investigate. McCann had made extensive representations to them about the ongoing investigation, which therefore implied consent. It was also queried if a burnt-out house was 'a dwelling' for these purposes, and in any event, whether

---

[45] *People v McCann* [1998] 4 IR 397.

there were extraordinary excusing circumstances, (ie, the need to preserve vital evidence). With regard to the locale of the arrest, the court held that there was no forcible entry and an implied invitation.

[4.51] In *Simple v Revenue Commissioners*[46] the Supreme Court (Keane CJ, Barrington J) held that, given the draconian nature of the powers concerned – in this case, under the Customs legislation – a warrant could not be regarded as valid when it carries on its face a statement that it had been issued on a basis not in fact authorised by statute (ie that, the custom's officer not the District Justice was satisfied of the evidence of 'reasonable grounds'). Barron J (dissenting) held the warrant was merely ineffective not invalid.

'Fruit of the poisoned tree'

[4.52] In *People (DPP) v O'Donnell*[47] the defendant was travelling in a van and was stopped by gardaí who recognised him as a suspected IRA member. At the request of gardaí, the defendant stepped out of the van and was told he was to be searched under s 30 of the 1939 Act. The gardaí found a walkie-talkie in his right-hand-pocket. The gardaí attempted to search his left-hand-pocket and the defendant resisted. The gardaí cautioned him, and arrested him under s 30 on suspicion of membership. The defendant gave them a parcel containing explosives from his left-hand-pocket. It was submitted on appeal that although gardaí informed the applicant that he was suspected of being a member of an illegal organisation before they searched his pocket, failure to do so before searching his right-hand-pocket tainted everything subsequently. The Court of Criminal Appeal affirmed the conviction holding that evidence following a deliberate and conscious breach was only excluded if obtained as a result of that breach and if a causative link existed between the breach and obtaining evidence. Even if it were conceded that the search of a right-hand-pocket was unlawful, there was no casual connections between that search and later search of a pocket containing explosives.

Conclusion

[4.53] Admissibility of illegally obtained evidence, in the context of the use or abuse of the pre-trial process, has been the subject of changing judicial attitude in the United States (formerly exclusionary, now a more inclusionary approach); Britain (formerly inclusionary now rather more exclusionary), and in the Irish courts. In Ireland, the *O'Brien* formula, although still the applicable criterion to

---

[46] *Simple v Revenue Commissioners* [2000] 2 IR 243.
[47] *People (DPP) v O'Donnell* [1995] 3 IR 551.

determine admissibility, has been seen to demonstrate a facility for inclusion or exclusion of evidence.

Given the recent proliferation of more extensive powers of intrusion, it may be that the Court will become more vigilant (Kinlen J in *Hanahoe*) in terms of scrutiny of these powers. However, that is in a context where with increasing avoidance of independent review of garda suspicion, the scope for judicial scrutiny is narrowed. It may also emerge that the facility for accommodation is so great in the original *O'Brien* yardstick of judgment, that only the appearance of rights vindication will be maintained.

Chapter 5

Witness System: Competence and Compellability

'Cross-examination is an adversarial war of words, sequences, and ideas, a war in which capability to finesse reality through talk represents the ultimate weapon of domination. When considering the reproduction of rape as a criminal social fact, I am looking at how a woman's experience of violation is transformed into routine consensual sex through the organization of courtroom linguistic practice, and not at how that violation is subjectively experienced through the meanings and intentions of individual victims, rapists, or administrators of justice. In very tacit and taken for granted fashion, language categorizes, objectives, and legitimates our interpretations about social reality, sustaining some versions while disqualifying others, and conceals the hierarchical arrangements and sexual differences between men and women. Language is a system of power for those who control it, and, in the context of the rape trial, talking power transforms the subjective violation of the victim, the victim's experience of sexual terror, into an objectivity: namely, consensual sex ...

Because of procedural and evidentiary strictures in court, blame work is conducted inferentially through powerful procedures of talk and sense-making practices. But access to these procedures is not equally distributed across social position. Attorneys and victims possess differential access to the procedures of talk. The defense attorney possesses the linguistic and sequential capital to make his/her account "count" relative to the victim. Attorneys control the topic, the syntactic form of questions, and the sequential resources with which to manipulate words, utterances, and turns as microtechniques of disciplinary power. When interlaced and synchronised with patriarchal ideology – ideas about sexual access and practice – these power mechanisms generate the accusatory sense of what happened during the rape incident; they thereby reproduce the constraining and enabling facticity - facts constructed locally in context - of both rape and the legal order.'

Gregory M Matoesian *Reproducing Rape: Domination through Talk in the Courtroom* (1993)

Competence and compellability

[5.01] Given the centrality of testimonial evidence to our system of legal adjudication, it is appropriate to examine together both the manner in which such testimony is elicited from a witness, and the criteria by reference to which a witness ability to testify is adjudged.

Process of elicitation of testimony

Examination-in-chief

[5.02] Assuming a witness to be both competent and compellable, the procedure by which testimony is elicited from that witness is as follows. The witness is firstly sworn in. That witness then gives testimony by means of the process of examination by counsel for that party on whose behalf the witness is being called. Examination-in-chief is the means whereby the witness tells whatever relevant evidence he has to proffer. It is not as simple as a witness merely telling the story as he saw it. In the course of eliciting the information from the witness, counsel may not ask leading questions of his own witness. There are, however, exceptions to this situation:

(1) non-contentious issues;

(2) in order to identify persons, or things in court; and

(3) in relation to hostile witnesses.

Cross-examination

[5.03] Cross-examination, is then carried out by counsel for the other side. It is therefore a much less regulated procedure, and has been described as 'the most effective weapon yet devised to test truth'. In the course of such cross-examination, counsel can ask any leading questions. However, if the question is deemed to be a collateral question, the witness's answer to such a question is final. There are exceptions to this in relation to a defendant's previous convictions (the Criminal Justice Procedure Act 1866, s 6), and the question of bias (for example, the witness's relation to the accused).

[5.04] With regard to the finality of collateral questions, it is interesting to note a decision of the Court of Criminal Appeal (*DPP v Patrick Barr*[1]) endorsing same, in refusing to allow an appeal against convictions of indecent assault and buggery based on the discovery of evidence which could have been put to the complainant in cross-examination. The evidence concerned involved the familiarity of the complainant with the Phoenix Park, and in particular the scene of the crime. The court on viewing the transcript as a whole doubted if there had, in fact, been any inconsistency on the part of the complainant, and in any event felt pursuance of the issue would have been to seek to contradict a witness on a collateral fact:

'It seems to the Court that there is a sound general rule, based on the desirability of avoiding a multiplicity of issues, that the answers given by a witness to questions put to him in cross-examination concerning collateral facts must be

---

[1] *DPP v Patrick Barr* (2 March 1992, unreported) CCA, *ex temp* (O'Flaherty J).

treated as final. They may or may not be accepted by the jury, but the cross-examiner must take them for better or worse and cannot contradict them by other evidence.'

[5.05] The strength of the entitlement and basis for cross-examination, and its centrality to our process of legal adjudication, is illustrated by the decision of *O'Brien v DJ Ruane and Attorney General*[2]. The applicant here was arrested under s 21 of the Road Traffic (Amendment) Act 1978, which provides that it shall be presumed, until the contrary is proven, that the statutory procedure has been complied with. The applicant's solicitor cross-examined the prosecuting garda sergeant in regard to compliance with s 21. Objection by the prosecution to the effect that such a general question was not permissible having regard to sub-4, was upheld by the District Justice.

[5.06] Lynch J in the High Court, however, held that although the cross-examination was a 'fishing cross-examination', in the sense that the solicitor for the applicant was not in a position to show any particular non-compliance with s 21 unless something should be elicited in the course of same, it was allowable. Lynch J was of the opinion that:

'It seems to me ... that the defending solicitor is entitled to enquire in a general way as to what happened to his client from the time he was brought to the Garda Station in relation to the taking of specimens and the treatment of such specimens in order to see whether compliance with s 21 was observed. I think he may do this in a general way ...

... Of course on the other hand the District Justice must be entitled to control cross-examination and keep it within reasonable bounds. If, for example, the general sort of cross-examination seemed to go on repetitively, the District Justice, would clearly be entitled to say: that's enough of that. You have made your point. But he must allow some reasonable general enquiry as to what procedures were in fact done and followed in the Garda station so that the defending solicitor, even in the absence of any specific allegation of a contravention of the requirements of s 21, may ensure that these requirements were complied with.'[3]

Re-examination

[5.07] The third process of eliciting information is called re-examination. This again is carried out by the party tendering that witness. Re-examination is not, however a second chance at examination-in-chief. It must be strictly confined to matters which have arisen in the course of cross-examination. For this reason counsel may or may not opt in given cases for re-examination. In the same

---

[2]   *O'Brien v DJ Ruane and Attorney General* [1989] ILRM 732.

[3]   [1989] ILRM 732 at 734.

manner, a facility for the other party to opt for a reply, with similar restrictions, may or may not be exercised.

Hostile witnesses

[5.08] A distinction should be drawn between unfavourable witnesses, and hostile witnesses. An unfavourable witness is one who is called to prove a particular fact, and fails to do so. A hostile witness, on the other hand, is one not desirous of telling the truth at the instance of the party who called him. While the general rule is that a party cannot impeach his own witness, this rule applies in relation to unfavourable witnesses, but not in relation to those deemed to be hostile. The trial judge decides if a witness can be treated as hostile (*The People (AG) v Hannigan*[4]). In making his determination, the trial judge considers the following: the witnesses demeanour, the terms of any inconsistent statement made by that witness and the circumstances in which it was made. The decision is taken in the absence of the jury. Should the witness be declared hostile, the examination-in-chief then takes on the format of cross-examination. The witness may be asked leading questions, challenged as to his means of knowledge, and asked if on another occasion he had made a statement which differed materially from, or contradicted, the one made in the witness box. This latter statement, however, does not, due to the operation of the rule against hearsay,[5] constitute evidence of any facts referred to in that statement, but only constitutes evidence going to that witnesses's credibility (*People (AG) v Taylor*).[6]

Calling of witnesses

[5.09] In general, a party is free to call any witnesses, provided that once called they are confined to evidence which is relevant and admissible. Their ability to provide such is generally not determined in advance. However, there may be circumstances where a judge may query the purpose of calling a witness, and so refuse to permit that witness to be called if satisfied that he has no relevant evidence to offer.

[5.10] In *Herron v Haughton*[7], the appellant was prosecuted for failure to have a tax disc displayed and to wear a seatbelt. Her defence alleged a campaign of harassment by the gardaí. She wished to call the prosecuting solicitor, and when asked why by the District Judge, explained that he was a party to the conspiracy. The District Justice refused to allow her to call that witness as he regarded the allegation irrelevant to the proceedings. Geoghegan J in the Supreme Court took

---

[4] *The People (AG) v Hannigan* [1941] IR 252.
[5] See chapter 9.
[6] *People (AG) v Taylor* [1974] IR 97.
[7] *Herron v Haughton* (19 May 2000, unreported) SC.

the view that it was perfectly in order for a trial judge to refuse a witness to be called for frivolous or irrelevant reasons and that the obligation to ensure a fair trial obliges him to probe the purpose for which a witness is called.

Elicitation of testimony

[5.11] At common law a general rule existed that if a person was capable of giving testimony, that person had a duty to do so, and was often compellable to give same. Evidence is usually taken on oath from a witness. The oath may take any form the witness wishes and unsworn evidence is also allowed, particularly in the case of children.

[5.12] Witnesses are examined-in-chief by the party calling them, during which they may not be asked leading questions; then cross-examined by the other side (who can ask leading questions); then re-examined on issues arising in the course of the latter. In *O'Brien v DJ Ruane and AG*[8], a 'fishing cross-examination' by the accused's solicitor was allowed in respect of procedure under the Road Traffic (Amendment) Act 1978, s 21, despite presumption in the statute of compliance with same.

Competence of witnesses

Physical disability

[5.13] If persons with a physical disability are capable of giving evidence by whatever means, it will be treated as admissible.

Mental disability

[5.14] The judge must be satisfied that persons of defective intellect can understand the nature of the oath.

Children's evidence

[5.15] The Criminal Evidence Act 1992, s 27 provides that in any criminal proceedings the evidence of a person under 14 years of age may be received otherwise than on oath or affirmation if the Court is satisfied that he is capable of giving an intelligible account of events which are relevant to those proceedings:

> (1) Notwithstanding any enactment, in any criminal proceedings the evidence of a person under 14 years of age may be received otherwise than on oath or affirmation if the court is satisfied that he is capable of giving an intelligible account of events which are relevant to those proceedings.

---

[8] [1989] ILRM 732.

(2) If any person whose evidence is received as aforesaid makes a statement material in the proceedings concerned which he knows to be false or does not believe to be true, he shall be guilty of an offence and on conviction shall be liable to be dealt with as if he had been guilty of perjury.

(3) Subsection (1) shall apply to a person with mental handicap who has reached the age of 14 years as it applies to a person under that age.

[5.16] The 1992 Act changes the manner of receipt of children's evidence by introducing live television link and video testimony. These are similar to changes made in England, on the basis of the *Pigot Committee Report*[9], and here follow on recommendations of the Law Reform Commission[10]. The reasoning behind the changes relating to reception of childrens' testimony are elucidated by the Law Reform Commission in its consultation paper, *Child Sexual Abuse* (1989). In the consultation paper the reasons for that change were elucidated as follows:

'... The relief of trauma to the child, is the Commission's paramount objective in making provisional recommendations for reform in this Paper. In making our recommendations, however, we must ensure that the defendant is not asked to pay too high a price for the attainment of that objective. If, for example, the defendant is to lose his right to cross-examine, it is vital that there be great confidence in the reliability of the evidence in question ... While in this Paper we are not treating child witnesses as inherently unreliable, we nevertheless place great store firstly on the court's assessing their competence before they can give evidence and secondly on the defendant's right to cross-examine.

Confrontation and cross-examination are indelible characteristics of the adversarial system as normally operated. The quest is for immediacy tempered with accuracy. The law leans against the second-hand as stale and potentially unreliable. But the use of modern technology asks searching questions of the traditional system and can be accommodated to the advantage of the system. The law must provide for the keeping of records on computer chip or micro-film. In turn, these records should prove much more accurate and reliable than records compiled by hand, which compilation has subsequently to be recalled in evidence.

Modern TV and video technology raise serious questions as to the desirability of the Rule against Hearsay. A video recording not only preserves the ipsissima of the questions and answers, the pauses and the vocal inflexions, but also the facial expressions and body languages of the witness being recorded. The availability of closed circuit television can take a witness out of an oppressive atmosphere

---

9 Pigot, Thomas, *Report of the Advisory Group on Video-Recorded Evidence* London: HMSO 1990, Great Britain Home Office.

10 The Law Reform Commission *Consultation Paper on Child Sexual Abuse* August 1989. Ireland, *Report on Child Sexual Abuse* Dublin, 1990.

while preserving the immediacy of a trial and can even provide for the "live" participation in a trial of a witness in another jurisdiction or continent. In fact the use of a live video-link cannot truly be regarded as tendering an out-of-court statement except to the extent that the witness is not physically present.'[11]

[**5.17**] The facility for live television link (s 13), video testimony (ss 15, 16) and evidence through an intermediary (s 14) in certain criminal proceedings is also found in Part III of the Criminal Evidence Act 1992 and is quite radical in departing from oral testimony being given by witnesses in the presence of the accused, subject to the sanction of the oath and cross-examination. However, the provisions themselves mandate (s 14) that the Court operate same on the basis of the 'interests of justice', and s 16(2)(b), in the context of video recording, specifically states that the Court should have regard to all the circumstances, including any risk that its admission will result in unfairness to the accused.

[**5.18**] The constitutionality of this provision was upheld in *Donnelly v AG*.[12] The impugned provisions were those which facilitated the elicitation or giving of testimony by sexual offence victims, particularly children, but at the trial judge's discretion also vulnerable witnesses in such cases,[13] by means of a live video link. The plaintiff claimed that it interfered with his right to a fair trial. It was argued the plaintiff had a constitutional right physically to confront his accused in open court, and that the presumption of trauma created for child witnesses testifying in such circumstances placed an unconstitutional and unfair burden of proof on an accused who would have to prove the child capable of testifying in open court. The constitutional provisions referred to were Articles 38.1, 38.5, 40.3, and 40.1.[14]

[**5.19**] Costello J in the High Court dismissed the applicant's claim, adjudging inter alia that the general view of what was fair and proper in relation to criminal trials was always the subject of change and development.[15] In the Supreme

---

[11] *Law Reform Commission Consultation Paper Child Sexual Abuse* (1989) p 144-146.

[12] *Donnelly v AG* [1998] 1 IR 321.

[13] Part 3 of the Act applies to sexual offences and offences involving violence or the threat of violence to a person (s 12). This facility has recently been extended to apply in relation to witnesses subject to intimidation, particularly in the context of organised crime. See Criminal Justice Act 1999, s 39.

[14] Costello J noted how the procedure operated as documented previously by the Court in *White v Ireland* [1995] 2 LR 268. The trial judge is required to assume the young witness will be traumatised (this had not been part of the plaintiff's submission) and that he was asked to determine the conclusion in *White* was wrong.
It is interesting that Costello J makes reference to context and, in particular, to Law Reform Commission documentation and Reports.

[15] *White v Ireland* [1995] 2 LR 268 at 332. Significantly, he specifically alludes to the 'growing concern for the victims of crime ... most particularly ... the victims of sexual assault'. He notes that the impugned provision had been preceded by *A Law Reform Consultation Paper and Report*, which recommended its introduction.

Court, Hamilton CJ noted[16] that it was well established in our constitutional jurisprudence that an accused person's right to a fair trial was '... one of the most fundamental constitutional rights accorded to persons and that in so far as it is possible or desirable to construct a hierarchy of constitutional rights it is a superior right.'[17]

[5.20] Hamilton CJ then went on to say that '[t]he general view of what is fair and proper in relation to criminal trials has always been the subject of change and development. Rules of evidence and rules of procedure gradually evolved as notions of fairness developed.'[18] Relating these concepts to the question before him in *Donnelly,* Hamilton CJ noted that an essential ingredient in the concept of fair procedures was that an accused person should have the opportunity to 'hear and test by examination the evidence offered by or on behalf of his accuser'. The plaintiff in these proceedings submitted that this right to test by examination the evidence offered against him, to be effective, and to give him the opportunity to defend himself adequately, necessarily implied and required that the witness should give evidence in his presence and that the witness, when giving evidence, should physically confront him. In *White v Ireland* the High Court had held that the right to 'eye-ball to eye-ball' did not exist.[19]

[5.21] Having reviewed the United States case law[20], Hamilton CJ noted that although the confrontation clause was clear and specific, it did not give to criminal defendants the absolute right to a face-to-face meeting with witnesses against them:

---

[16] *Donnelly v Ireland* [1998] 1 IR 321 at 348-349.

[17] He notes in particular statements regarding the importance of the guarantee of basic fairness in the Constitution in *Re Haughey* [1971] IR 217 at 264 and *State (Healy) v Donaghue* [1976] IR 325 at 335 -336 and *Donnelly v Ireland* [1998] 1 IR 321 at 348-349 per Hamilton CJ.

[18] *White v Ireland* [1995] 2 IR 268 at 350 quoted by Hamilton CJ in *Donnelly* at p 349.

[19] *White v Ireland* [1995] 2 LR 268.

[20] Hamilton CJ referred to the judgments in two cases decided by the Supreme Court of the United States of *America Coy v Iowa* (1987) 487 US 1012 and *Maryland v Craig* (1989) 497 US 836, but comments that these cases turned upon differently worded constitutional statutory provisions to those under examination in the present case. Nevertheless, they contained certain discussions of principle which he finds useful. He refers to the Sixth Amendment of the American Constitution and notes:

'No such provision exists in the Irish Constitution and an accused person's rights are determined not by any specific provision of the Constitution but by the requirements of due process and fair procedures. All the rights, other than the right "to be confronted with the witnesses against him" set forth in the sixth amendment, have been established by this Court's constitutional jurisprudence as being necessary ingredients in and required by the concepts of "due process" and "fair procedures".' (at p 351).

'[T]he Constitution of Ireland, 1937, contains no specific right such as that guaranteed in the confrontation clause, [but] the central concern of the requirements of due process and fair procedures is the same, that is to ensure the fairness of the trial of an accused person. This undoubtedly involves the rigorous testing by cross-examination of the evidence against him or her.'[21]

[5.22] The logic of Hamilton CJ's reasoning is from what the impugned provisions do not do in order to insulate them:

'The impugned provisions of the Act of 1992 do not restrict in any way the rights of an accused person as established by the constitutional jurisprudence of this Court ... What they do permit in the case of proceedings for the offences set forth in s 12 of the Act of 1992 is the giving of evidence by persons under 17 years (unless the court sees good reason to the contrary) and by any other person, with the leave of the court, through a live television link. It is accepted that the reason for the procedure permitted by s 13 of the Act of 1992 was that it is generally accepted that young persons under the age of 17 are likely to be traumatised by the experience of giving evidence in court and that its purpose is to minimise such trauma.'[22]

[5.23] Hamilton CJ concluded that therefore:

'... the assessment of such credibility does not require that the witness should be required to give evidence in the physical presence of the accused person and that the requirements of fair procedures are adequately fulfilled by requiring that the witness give evidence on oath and be subjected to cross-examination and that the judge and jury have ample opportunity to observe the demeanour of the witness while giving evidence and being subjected to cross-examination. In this way, an accused person's right to a fair trial is adequately protected and vindicated.

Such right does not include the right in all circumstances to require that the evidence be given in his physical presence and consequently there is no such constitutional right.'[23]

[5.24] Hamilton CJ's circular reasoning is resonant of that found to exist in the legislature's enactments in this area, typified in the qualification (as here) that the provision be invoked 'in the interests of justice' or without detriment to

---

[20] (contd) The Sixth Amendment provides as follows:

'in all criminal prosecutions, the accused shall enjoy the right to a speedy and public trial, by an impartial jury of the State and district wherein the crime shall have been committed, which district shall have been previously ascertained by law, and to be informed of the nature and cause of the accusation; to be confronted with the witnesses against him; to have compulsory process for obtaining witnesses in his favour, and to have the Assistance of Counsel for his defence.'

[21] *Donnelly v Ireland* [1998] 1 IR 321 at 356-357.

[22] *Donnelly v Ireland* [1998] 1 IR 321 at 356-357.

[23] *Donnelly v Ireland* [1998] 1 IR 321 at 357.

'fairness to the accused'. This perspective gives the view that the existence of this provision quiescent in the legislation (arguably precisely because there is such a problem with the relevant change) is invoked and relied upon by the judiciary, thereby copperfastening the lack of a correlation or relationship between what was changed and what is now fair. There could hardly be a greater irony: the legislation is 'saved' because the judiciary need not invoke it where it would be unfair to do so – hence it is potentially unfair. Hamilton CJ's reasoning along these contradictory lines is as follows:[24]

> 'The accused person's right to a fair trial is further protected by the fact that it is open to the court not to permit the giving of evidence by a young person through a live television link if the accused person establishes that "there is good reason to the contrary" and that the leave of the court is required before any other person may give evidence in this manner. A judge considering either of these issues will be obliged to have regard to the accused person's right to a fair trial.'

[5.25] The reasoning is familiar from earlier terrorist cases – the individual's rights are underscored and their importance emphasised, but the limited nature of the provision impugned (indicated by what it does not do) is invoked to save it. The linkage is a familiar one: moving from what the provision does not do, through what safeguards do exist, here augmented with the 'goodness' of the victim (as opposed to simply the need or safety of the State) which is set in opposition to the individual accused, all to the same effect.

[5.26] Over-familiarity or perhaps cynicism with regard to the State and State entities may mean it no longer has as much purchase as hitherto, so the invocation of the victim poses a nice substitute to bolster State power, supposedly in the interests of the victim, who may prove in fact be merely another pawn in the 'law and order' momentum.

[5.27] The Criminal Evidence Act 1992 mechanism for elicitation of the testimony of children is as follows: Evidence can be given through live television link (s 21), through an intermediary (s 22) and provision is made for the admissibility of hearsay evidence when the court considers the child unable to give evidence by reason of age or that it would not be in the interests of the welfare of the child (s 23(1)(a) & (b)).

Such will not be admitted however if not in the 'interests of justice' (s 23(2)(a)) or where it would result in 'unfairness to any of the parties' (s 23(2)(b)). Oath or affirmation is not necessary for child witnesses where the child is under 14 years of age and the court is satisfied the child 'is capable of giving an intelligible account of events' (s 28).

---

[24] *Donnelly v Ireland* [1998] 1 IR 321 at 357.

The 1992 Act's provision for the reception of childrens' evidence in criminal cases was extended to civil cases under the rubric of the Childrens Act 1997. Part III of that Act applies to civil proceedings before any court concerning the welfare of a child, and civil proceedings concerning the welfare of a person who has a mental disability such that s/he is not able to live independently.

[5.28] This particular 'exceptional' provision once introduced (Criminal Evidence Act 1992) and sanctioned (*Donnelly*) became normalised as the facility to give evidence through a live television link granted to children and other vulnerable witnesses was extended by Criminal Justice Act 1999, s 39, to a person other than the accused with leave of the court (s 39(1)). Under s 39(2) the court order granted leave if 'satisfied that the person is likely to be in fear or subject to intimidation in giving evidence otherwise'.

Defendant's spouse as a witness

[5.29] There existed a general rule at common law that a spouse was not competent as a witness for the prosecution at a criminal trial. The rule extended to the joint trial situation, so that even if the evidence of a spouse was only against the co-accused, the spouse was not permitted to testify. The rationale of the rule lay in the public policy of upholding marriage. Inroads were made into this rule both at common law, and by statute.

[5.30] This area of law has now been substantially amended by the Criminal Evidence Act 1992. Part IV of that Act provides for the competence of the spouse of an accused as a prosecution witness in any criminal proceedings (s 21). The spouse of an accused is also rendered compellable as a prosecution witness in certain instances. Section 22 of the 1992 Act provides that the spouse of an accused shall be compellable as a prosecution witness in the case of a violent or sexual offence against the spouse, a child of the spouse or accused or any person who at the material time was under 17 years of age, or any sexual offence against a child of the spouse or accused or person under 17 years, or an attempt or conspiracy to commit either.

[5.31] This change in the law with regard to spousal competence and compellability was preceded, and mandated to some degree, by the Irish Court of Criminal Appeal in *DPP v T*[25], where the Court found reason in the Constitution's protection of the family (Article 41), together with its vindication of personal rights (Article 40.3) – and in particular those rights of individual family members – to render a spouse competent in cases where personal violence had been perpetrated upon a member of that family by the other spouse.

---

[25] *DPP v T* (27 July 1998, unreported) CAA.

[5.32] In this situation, where the mother of a Downs Syndrome child was not rendered competent by statutory exception, in the case of a charge of incest against the child's father (now separated from his wife), Walsh J deemed the spouse to be rendered both competent and compellable.

[5.33] Section 23 of the Criminal Evidence Act 1992 provides for the compellability of a spouse or former spouse of an accused to give evidence at the insistence of the accused (in so far as they may be charged in the same proceedings (s 25)). Section 24 provides for compellability to give evidence at the insistence of a co-accused in the same circumstances providing for compellability as a prosecution witness.

The accused as a prosecution witness

[5.34] The accused is not competent as a prosecution witness, with the exception of the Public Nuisance Act 1887. When there is more than one defendant, they cannot give evidence against one another. However, by means of various technical devices the prosecution can get around this prohibition:

(1)   If no evidence is offered against an accused and he is acquitted the defence of *autre fois acquit* operates as a bar against possible subsequent prosecution and the individual concerned is free to testify against the other accused.

(2)   The prosecution can *nolle prosequi* the charges preferred against an accused, which protects the accused de facto from the possibility of a trial on the same charges again. The accused is once more free to testify against others.

(3)   If the accuseds are not tried together and one pleads guilty and is sentenced, the latter is then free to give evidence against others.

(4)   When the accused has been found guilty and sentenced he may give evidence against other(s).

Diplomats and prosecution witnesses

[5.35] Under the Geneva Convention and the Diplomatic Relations Immunity Act 1962, a diplomat cannot be compelled to give evidence. This provision is also extended to cover his/her family, provided they are not nationals of the deciding state, this rule also applies to mission members in Ireland. The Diplomatic Relations and Immunities (Amendment) Act 1976, s 1 provides that the government may by order extend immunity to international bodies, persons etc under an international agreement to which the State or the Government is or intends to become a party.

Chapter 6

Witness System: Corroboration

Definition of corroborative evidence

[6.01] The major question when considering a corroboration requirement is as to what kind of evidence is corroborative or satisfies the said requirement. The authority here is *R v Baskerville*, where Reading LCJ defined corroboration as:

> 'independent testimony which affects the accused by connecting or tending to connect him with the crime. In other words it must be evidence which implicates him, that is, which confirms in some material particular not only the evidence that the crime has been committed, but also that the prisoner committed it'.

[6.02] In *People (Attorney General) v Williams*[1], Sullivan CJ formulated corroborative evidence as 'independent evidence of material circumstances tending to implicate the accused in the commission of the crime with which he was charged'. A straightforward example of the application of this definition is found in *R v Gregg*[2] in the context of a charge of rape. The fact that the victim here was found to be suffering from a particular type of venereal disease soon after the offence, and that the accused at the time of the offence suffered from that particular venereal disease, constituted corroboration.[3]

[6.03] An important qualification here is the fact that a witness cannot corroborate herself. So, for example, a witness cannot corroborate herself by an early complaint in a rape case.[4] Yet, if the danger that is being averted by the requirement is one of fabrication, would logic not seem to dictate that the jury be permitted to take account of anything indicating that the story is not fabricated?

[6.04] In *R v Redpath*[5], the distressed condition of the victim was deemed capable of constituting corroboration, although its probative worth was greater if

---

[1] *People (AG) v Williams* [1940] IR 195 at 200, confirmed in *People (AG) v Trayers* [1956] IR 110 at 114.

[2] *R v Gregg* (1934) 24 Cr App Rep 13.

[3] The presence of the venereal disease would, of course, only constitute corroboration of the act of intercourse, the subject matter of the alleged offence. The development of DNA fingerprinting has considerable significance for this area of the law. See also Fennell, 'Genetic Fingerprinting for Sexual Offences' (1988) Irish Medical Times 18 and Fennell, 'DNA Profiling, Hidden Agendas' (1991) 1 Irish Journal of Criminal Law 34.

[4] *R v Christie* [1914] AC 557.

[5] *R v Redpath* (1962) 46 Cr App Rep 319.

it was witnessed by an independent witness. Similarly, in *R v Zielinski*[6], the evidence of the victim's son as to the distressed condition of the victim a few minutes after the appellant left, was held to constitute corroborative evidence.

[6.05] Where difficulty readily arises in this area is in relation to the trial judge's direction as to the finding of corroborative evidence. The present position is one in the context of sexual offence complaints, for example, which allows the avenue of defence to the accused, whereby admission of all actions up to the act of the intercourse itself undermines the potential corroborative value of evidence of a struggle (torn clothing, etc). This is because the accused, by alleging last-minute consent on the part of the victim, can force corroboration as to the issue of consent itself. Hence, evidence of an earlier struggle, which would have had corroborative value had the defence put forward been one of alibi or a denial of the act of intercourse, is of no avail.

[6.06] Selective defence tactics can, therefore, manipulate the corroboration requirement to render the prosecution's task extremely and artificially difficult. In turn, this further complicates the roles of the judge and jury at trial, and creates a fertile source of appeals. In *People (DPP) v Patrick Collins*[7] the applicant had been convicted of one offence of unlawful sexual intercourse contrary to s 1(1) of the Criminal Law (Amendment) Act 1935. The details of that offence were that he met with the complainant outside her school in his car, and they drove to his house where the alleged sexual intercourse took place in his bedroom. The trial judge had given a corroboration warning to the jury and then commented on the evidence to the effect, as counsel for the applicant alleged, that the description of the windows and curtains in the bedroom given by the complainant, if accepted, amounted to corroboration of her story. The Court of Criminal Appeal held that this was the direction given and that the trial judge was wrong in conveying to the jury that the complainant's evidence regarding the windows and curtains was capable of constituting corroboration, citing the *Baskerville*[8] definition that the evidence 'must be independent testimony to connect (the accused) with the crime.'

Doctrine of recent complaint

[6.07] The 'doctrine of recent complaint' does allow for the introduction of evidence of a complaint made by the victim of a sexual offence in the aftermath of the incident. The evidence may not amount to corroboration, yet does go to the issue of the witness' credibility.

---

6 *R v Zielinski* (1950) 34 Cr App Rep 193.
7 *People (DPP) v Patrick Collins* (22 April, 2002), CCA (Murray, Barr, Kinlen JJ).
8 *R v Baskerville* [1916] 2 KB 658 at 667 per Reading LCJ.

[6.08] In *DPP v Brophy*[9], the accused had been convicted of the indecent assault of a fourteen year old schoolgirl, and appealed inter alia on the grounds that the trial judge had erred in law in refusing an application to have the jury discharged following the giving of inadmissible evidence of complaint.

[6.09] The facts, in brief, concerned allegations of an incident of indecent assault occurring at the home of the accused on 28 December 1989. The complainant had later informed her father and some friends of the incident, but had not informed her mother or others immediately after the alleged incident. The prosecution accepted that since the complaint had not been made at the first opportunity, they should not give the terms, but only the fact of complaint.

The Court of Criminal Appeal had to consider then, whether evidence of the fact of the making of a complaint was admissible in circumstances, where it was conceded, the complaint was not made at the first opportunity which reasonably presented itself. Considering the history of admissibility of complaints in sexual cases, O'Flaherty J noted it was only the *fact* of complaint that was admissible, until in *R v Lillymar*[10], the court extended admissibility of a complaint to its terms. O'Flaherty J continued:

> 'It seems to the court therefore, that either evidence of a complaint having been made, is admissible, or it is not. If it is admissible, then, subject to the discretion of the trial judge to prevent unnecessary prejudicial repetition, the terms of the complaint are also admissible ... there seems no room for half measures in regard to this; either the fact of a complaint is admissible or it is not.'

[6.10] O'Flaherty J then summarised the law on the topic of admissibility of complaints:

'(a) Complaints may only be proved in criminal prosecutions for a sexual offence.

(b) The complaint must have been made as speedily as could reasonably be expected and in a voluntary fashion, not as a result of any inducements or exhortations. Once evidence of the making of a complaint is admissible then particulars of the complaint may also be proved.

(c) It should always be made clear to the jury that such evidence is not evidence of the facts on which the complaint is based but to show that the victim's conduct in so complaining was consistent with her testimony.

(d) While there is mention in one of the older cases, *R v Osborne*[11] of a complaint being corroborative of the complainant's credibility, this does not mean that such a complaint amounts to corroboration of her testimony

---

[9] *DPP v Brophy* [1992] ILRM 709.

[10] *R v Lillyman* [1896] 2 QB 167.

[11] *R v Osborne* [1905] 1 KB 551.

in the legal sense of that term but as pointing to the consistency of her testimony. Corroboration in the strict sense involves independent evidence, that is evidence other than the complainant's evidence.

(e) The law on complaints should not be confused with what takes place once the police institute their inquiries. That is a separate matter. A complaint made to the police may, as such, be admissible or not under the guidelines set out above but just because a complaint is not made at the first opportunity to the police does not, of course, inhibit their inquires. Indeed a complaint to the police may be made by someone other than the injured party.'

O'Flaherty J noted that in this case the prosecution had conceded the complaint was not made as speedily as possible: 'since the prosecution was clearly of the view that the terms of the complaint were not admissible the fact of the complaint should not have been admitted either'.

[6.11] In this case, in fact, the Court of Criminal Appeal went further, interfering with the trial judge's decision not to order a discharge of the jury in light of the admission of the evidence. Per O'Flaherty J:

'The judge ruled that he would not discharge the jury, and, in the ordinary way, the discharging of a jury in any trial must be a very extreme remedy but we are of the opinion that in this case where the prosecution depended on the uncorroborated evidence of the complainant, the requirement that a balance had to be kept to preserve fairness in the trial – since the evidence was so minimal – required that the jury should have been discharged when this evidence got in'.

[6.12] This and the earlier cases may be examples of what *Pattenden*[12] asserts is the greater willingness on the part of appeal courts to interfere with even the exercise of a trial judge's discretion, even if that latter is not what she terms an 'overt' discretion (ie, is in fact dictated by rules or criteria, however vague, and so constitutes a question of admissibility – of law – readily interfered with on appeal). In *People (DPP) v Synott*[13], Finlay CJ, relying on *Brophy*, held that a complaint made after a year by a child was not admissible. More recently, however, a series of cases have made it clear that delay (in terms of complaint and prosecution) will not necessarily lead to prohibition of evidence in the case of historic sex abuse claims (see eg *G v DPP*[14]).

[6.13] In *People (DPP) v Gavin*[15] there was an inconsistency between the complaint's own evidence at the trial and the garda evidence of the complainant.

---

[12] R Pattenden *Judicial Discretion and Criminal Litigation* (2nd edn, 1990) (Clarendon) pp 6–7.
[13] *People (DPP) v Synott* (29 May 1992, unreported), CCA.
[14] *G v DPP* [1994] 1 IR 374.
[15] *People (DPP) v Gavin* [2000] 4 IR 557.

In the complaint it was stated that the complainant awoke to discover the appellant in his bed, with his hand on the complainant's groin. This was not stated in the complainant's evidence. According to McGuinness J, it is clear from *Brophy* that the purpose of allowing the evidence of complaint is to demonstrate the consistency of the complainant. Here the complaint met the criterion of being voluntary and made at an early stage, but not that of being consistent with the complainant's evidence at trial and so should not have been admitted. It should, in any event, have been made clear by the trial judge that the complaint does not amount to corroboration.

[6.14] In *People (DPP) v Jethi*[16] inconsistencies between complaint and evidence were characterised by the court as minor in nature, and as on the central issue of consent, they were clear and consistent, the complaint was admissible.

Corroboration required as a matter of law

[6.15] The Treason Act 1939, ss 14 and 22, states that corroboration is required as a matter of law in regard to the charge of perpetrating the act of treason or aiding, abetting or harbouring the perpetrator of same.

[6.16] The Road Traffic Act 1961, s 105, states that corroboration is required as a matter of law in regard to offences involving the proof of speed at which a person was driving under the Road Traffic Act. Section 105(a) states that: 'the uncorrobrated evidence of one witness stating his opinion as to that speed shall not be accepted as proof of that speed'. Paragraph (b) of that section goes on to allow evidence of speed to be established *prima facie* by a watch or electronic or other apparatus. Section 44 of the Road Traffic Act 1994 extended that to photographic apparatus.

Section 105 was considered in *People (DPP) v Connaughton*[17], where the applicant had been convicted of dangerous driving causing serious bodily harm. The appeal on the basis of section 105 objected to the admissibility of the evidence of a number of witnesses who gave evidence that the applicant had been driving at speed.

It was held, however, that the section was not relevant, as their evidence was confined to a general impression of speed, and no witness has testified as to an enumerated speed of the applicant.

[6.17] The above are the instances when corroboration is required as a matter of law because of statutory provisions. There is one instance when corroboration is

---

[16] *People (DPP) v Jethi* (7 February 2000, ex tempore) CCA (Barrington J).

[17] *People (DPP) v Connaughton* (5 April 2001), CCA.

required as a matter of law at common law that is the crime of perjury. (In other words, no one can be convicted of perjury without some kind of corroborative evidence being produced by the prosecution).

Corroboration required as a matter of practice

[6.18] This category has been the subject of much change. Whereas previously all evidence which required corroboration as a matter of practice or at least a warning to the jury, met with that requirement on every occasion such evidence was presented, reform of this area of the law has meant that certain categories (sexual offence/children) have been removed from this category, to the extent that the requirement to give such a warning now constitutes a discretion on the part of the trial judge. Justification for caution in respect of these witnesses varies, from the characteristics of the witnesses to the nature of the offence charged. The latter comprises sexual offence victims' evidence, for example, while evidence which requires corroboration as a matter of practice, because of the characteristics of the witness, is accomplice evidence.

Accomplices

[6.19] The first category of witnesses, where corroboration is required as a matter of practice, or at least a warning to the jury is required as a matter of practice, is that of accomplice evidence. The definition of accomplices for the purpose of the rule, is that of the House of Lords in *Davies v DPP*[18], where Simonds LC stated:

> 'There is in the authorities no formal definition of the term accomplice ... On the cases it would appear that the following persons if called as witnesses for the prosecution, have been treated as falling within the category:

> (1) persons who are *participis criminis* in respect of the actual crime charged, whether as principals or accessories before or after the fact (in felonies) or persons committing, procuring or aiding and abetting (in the case of misdemeanour). This is surely the natural and primary meaning of the term 'accomplice'. But in two cases persons falling strictly outside the ambit of this category have, in particular decisions, been held to be accomplices for the purpose of the rule: viz:

> (2) Receivers have been held to be accomplices of the thieves from whom they receive goods on the trial of the latter for larceny ...

> (3) When X has been charged with a specific offence on a particular occasion and evidence is admissible and has been admitted, of his having committed crimes of this identical type on other occasions as proving system and intent and negativing accident in such cases the court has held that in

---

[18] *Davies v DPP* [1954] AC 378.

relation to such other offences, if evidence of them were given by parties to them the evidence of such other parties should not be left to the jury without a warning that it is dangerous to accept it without corroboration ...'

[6.20] The House of Lords in *Davies* (although on the facts held the failure to give the warning as insignificant, on the basis that there was no evidence that the witness was a participant) also said the requirement, in relation to the warning, was a rule of practice akin to a rule of law.

[6.21] It is important to remember that evidence given by a witness who has already been convicted remains accomplice evidence (*Davies*). The test is not whether the witness is subject to conviction at the time of testifying but whether he has become liable to prosecution as a result of the events in issue. Even if the witness is acquitted, he may be an accomplice, as the acquittal may have been wrong. In *Davies* the witness had been acquitted of murder but he was not an accomplice because there was little evidence against him and the Crown had offered none.

[6.22] Schools of thought vary in relation to the ambit of the definition of 'accomplice' in this context. In the *King*[19] case, the appellant had been convicted of living on the immoral earnings of a prostitute. It was contended that the latter's evidence was accomplice evidence and that there should have been a warning in relation to same. The Lord Chief Justice commented that there was no evidence that she was an accomplice; and seemed to indicate that if someone were not charged or implicated in relation to the charge before the court, that person was not an accomplice for the purposes of the rule.

[6.23] This narrow approach was criticised in *McNee v Kay*[20], where School J recommended a wider definition of accomplice. The true principle, he stated, was that a person was an accomplice who was chargeable in relation to the same offence as those in the charge preferred against the accused; and would be, if convicted, liable to such punishment as might tempt him to lie or fabricate in regard to the accused, and, secondly, if not doing it for the accused, could well be testifying to deflect prosecution from himself.

[6.24] The focus of this approach, then, is essentially that of the interest the accomplice has in giving this evidence, which, after all, forms part of the rationale of the corroboration requirement in this context, in the first place.

In the Irish context, it has been held that a 'police spy' who participates in the entrapment of the criminal (the accused) is in law not an accomplice. Thus, a distinction is drawn between someone who acts as 'agent provocateur' and an accomplice (*Dental Board v O'Callaghan*)[21].

---

[19] *King* (1914) 10 Cr App Rep 117.
[20] *McNee v Kay* (1953) VLR 520.

[6.25] In *AG v Linehan*[22], the Irish courts considered, but did not feel it necessary to lay down a definition of accomplice. The facts involved a woman who had been charged with the murder of her granddaughter's illegitimate child. The case against her depended on the granddaughter's evidence, the latter having been tried and acquitted. The granddaughter's evidence was uncorroborated and showed she could have been involved. The court felt a warning should have been given in those circumstances, but felt a narrow and precise definition of accomplice should be avoided. The court did indicate that a principal or accessory to a crime would be an accomplice for the purposes of the rule, and the warning should apply.

[6.26] The Court of Criminal Appeal, in *People (DPP) v Murtagh*[23], held that in a prosecution for the offence of subornation of perjury, the perjurer is a accomplice of the suborner, and the trial judge must warn the jury that, although they may convict on the evidence of an accomplice, it is dangerous to do so unless it is corroborated. Likewise, in a prosecution for an offence of attempting to pervert the course of justice by inciting another person to make a false statement to the gardaí, that other person, by allowing himself to be incited, is an accomplice to the accused's crime and the same warning must be given.

[6.27] The Irish approach to the warning, would seem to be one where the format of same can vary from case to case. The degree of gravity and complicity may vary; and in as much as complicity will vary, so will the strength of the warning.

[6.28] One issue that has led to some difficulty is, who decides when the witness is an accomplice? *Cross*[24] postulates that there are three potential situations here. Firstly, that where there is no evidence that the witness is an accomplice – hence no warning is necessary. Secondly, the English authorities have indicated that the matter may have to be left to a jury with a warning to the effect that if they think a witness is an accomplice they should be cautious before convicting. Thirdly, it has been stated that in some cases the trial judge will direct a particular witness is an accomplice because of the weight of the evidence preferred.

[6.29] In *People (AG) v Carney*[25], the defendants were jointly charged with shopbreaking and receiving stolen goods. They were convicted on a charge of receiving. During the trial, the trial judge left the question to the jury as to

---

[21] *Dental Board v O'Callaghan* [1969] IR 181.

[22] *AG v Linehan* [1929] IR 19.

[23] *People (DPP) v Murtagh* [1990] 1 IR 339.

[24] *Cross on Evidence* (Butterworths 7th edn 1990) at pp 219-222.

[25] *People (AG) v Carney* [1955] IR 324.

whether the witness against them was an accomplice or not. The Supreme Court felt that it was not proper to leave to the jury the issue as to whether the witness was an accomplice. The nature of the warning to the jury should not have been dependent on whether the witness was an accomplice or not, but should have been absolute and unconditional.

[6.30] O'Byrne J for the majority, based his view on a reasonable view of the evidence. The witness was an accomplice within the meaning of *Linehan*, being involved in the crime either as a principal or accessory. The majority were satisfied that in the circumstances, the trial judge should not have left the issue to the jury, but given an absolute and unconditional warning. Dixon J dissented, holding that it was for the jury to decide if the witness was an accomplice. While the trial judge should have put the view more forcibly as to who was an accomplice, the issue was for the jury to decide. Once so directed, it was for the jury to determine if the individual was an accomplice.

[6.31] An example of an instance of corroboration in relation to accomplices, is that in *R v Cramp*[26], where the silence of the accused, when a reply was to be expected, was held to corroborate the testimony of a girl whose miscarriage was alleged to have been attempted by the accused. The silence of the accused was in response to the girls father's statement, 'I have here those things you gave my daughter to produce abortion'.

[6.32] An important rule in the context of accomplice evidence, is the rule against mutual corroboration. One accomplice cannot corroborate another (*R v Gay*[27], confirming the earlier decision to that effect in *R v Noakes*[28]).
This rule has since been disapproved of in the context of children in *DPP v Hester*[29]. In *DPP v Kilbourne*[30], a case which involved two groups of young boys, against which the accused had allegedly perpetrated assaults in 1970 and 1971. The court felt that, while children within each group could not corroborate each other, members of one group could corroborate members of the other group. To this extent, therefore, that 'third' category of witnesses considered to be accomplices, could corroborate each other.

[6.33] In *Kilbourne's* case, Halisham LJ stated that:

> '[The rule against mutual corroboration] ... applies to those in the first and second of Lord Simond LC's categories and to many other cases where witnesses are not or may not be accomplices. It does not necessarily apply to all witnesses

---

[26] *R v Cramp* (1880) 5 QB 307.
[27] *R v Gay* (1909) 2 CR App Rep 327.
[28] *R v Noakes* (1832).
[29] *DPP v Hester* [1973] AC 297.
[30] *DPP v Kilbourne* [1973] AC 728.

in the same case who may deserve to be categorised as "accomplice". In particular it does not necessarily apply to accomplices of Lord Simond LC's third class where they give independent evidence of separate incidents, and where the circumstances are such as to exclude the danger of a jointly fabricated story'.

[6.34] The abolition of the rule against mutual corroboration, has been proposed by the English Criminal Law Reform Committee[31], yet thus far is still extant. There may well be greater justification for the rule's continuance in the context of accomplices than in that of children, because the factors making it dangerous to rely on the evidence of both types of witnesses are different. Whereas accomplices may tend to tell the same lie, ie, one against the accused; there is no reason to suppose that children's imaginations should lead to the same untruth.

[6.35] Quite often, if a witness is tendered who qualifies to be considered as an accomplice, that witness may have struck a deal guaranteeing immunity from prosecution with the authorities. In England, it is only the Crown which has such authority; in Ireland that the DPP should give an offer of immunity, not the police. Should the latter make such an offer, it would probably amount to an 'inducement'.

[6.36] In the New Zealand case of *R v Weightman*[32], the witness was given such immunity from prosecution in return for his testimony. He was deemed an accomplice, and it was suggested that in addition to the normal warning, the jury should be told he was escaping prosecution because of his testimony.

[6.37] The supergrass phenomenon in Northern Ireland led to the issue of accomplice evidence being the subject of scrutiny by Tony Gifford QC, who conducted an investigation under the auspices of the Cobden Trust in 1984. The terms of reference of the inquiry were as follows:

'i.   Whether and in what circumstances the interests of justice can be served by the uncorroborated evidence of accomplices in criminal trials in the United Kingdom.

ii.   What particular considerations arise from the use of such evidence in non-jury trials in Northern Ireland.

iii. What consequences may the keeping of such accomplices and their families in protective custody have for their interests and the interests of justice generally.'[33]

---

[31] English Criminal Law Revision Committee Eleventh Report *Evidence (General)* (1972) Cm 4991 paras 186-188.

[32] *R v Weightman* [1978] 1 NZLR 79.

[33] Anthony Maurice Gifford, Baron: *Supergrasses: the use of accomplice evidence in Northern Ireland* Cobden Trust (1984).

[6.38] Gifford QC concluded from his survey, that the use of supergrass evidence can lead and has led to the telling of lies, and to the conviction of the innocent. He felt the use of supergrasses in Northern Ireland had discredited the judicial institutions, and in the context of Northern Ireland recommended the abolition of the Diplock Court system, the restoration of the jury and the warning of the latter by the trial judge of the dangers involved. Should the latter system continue, however, Gifford recommended that there should be no further grant of immunity from prosecution to those who have been repeatedly involved in serious terrorist crimes[34]; and secondly the uncorroborated evidence of a supergrass should not be accepted as a valid basis for convicting a defendant in a non-jury court. Gifford felt defendants should no longer be convicted on uncorroborated supergrass evidence; that prosecutions should not in such cases be initiated by the DPP; trial judges should adopt the criterion that it is highly dangerous and wrong to convict on the uncorroborated evidence of a supergrass and that the Court of Appeal should, when faced with that uncorroborated evidence, examine very carefully whether the convictions which have been recommended are safe and satisfactory[35]. His final recommendation was that Parliament should legislate to provide safeguards for the Diplock system by a simple measure which provides that in a Diplock Court there must, as a matter of law, be corroboration of the evidence of an accomplice.

[6.39] What is interesting about Gifford's report, is the extent to which he distinguishes supergrass evidence from accomplice evidence in general, and in that context justifies a stronger corroboration requirement in relation to that species of accomplice. What the report does not address is the issue of the rationale of the corroboration requirement in relation to accomplices, generally, in the first place.

[6.40] In *R v Turner*[36] Lawton LJ addressed the issue of the corroboration requirement in the context of a witness testifying against the perpetrators of a bank robbery, which offence he himself was involved in. The evidence of the witness had been secured, by virtue of a deal granting immunity to the witness for those crimes, given by the DPP. Lawton LJ addressed the historical issue of the corroboration requirement in relation to accomplices, first rejecting the contention on the part of the defence, that such witnesses were not competent in such circumstances. Lawton LJ commented that there could be no doubt at common law that an accomplice who gave evidence for the Crown in the expectation of getting a pardon for doing so, was a competent witness. The nineteenth century contribution to this topic, he noted, was to introduce a rule of

---

[34] Gifford, Cobden Trust (1984), para 98 at p 35.
[35] Gifford, Cobden Trust (1984), paras 100-102 at p 36.
[36] *R v Turner* (1975) Vol 61 Cr App Rep 67.

practice that judges should warn juries of the dangers of convicting on the uncorroborated evidence of accomplices. In this century that practice became a rule of law.

[6.41] In relation to whether the trial judge should exercise his discretion to exclude such testimony, Lawton LJ stated that:

'If the inducement is very powerful, the judge may decide *(*to exercise his discretion; but when doing so he must take into consideration all factors, including those affecting the public. It is in the interests of the public that criminals should be brought to justice; and the more serious the crimes the greater is the need for justice to be done. Employing Queen's evidence to accomplish this end is distasteful and has been distasteful for at least 300 years to judges, lawyers and members of the public. It is, however, no part of our function to add to the weight of ethical condemnation or to dissipate it. We are concerned to decide what the law is and whether the judge should, as a matter of discretion, have excluded Smalls' evidence, and whether, having admitted it, he gave the jury an adequate warning about acting on it.'[37]

[6.42] Lawton LJ did continue to consider the witness's (Small's) position in this case when he gave evidence, and noted that all charges preferred against him had already been terminated at that stage. There was no real likelihood of his being prosecuted if he refused to give evidence. These facts would have justified the judge in refusing to exercise his discretion to exclude Small's evidence had he been so requested.

Lawton LJ further found that there was no question but that the judge had given adequate direction to the jury as to the danger of Small's evidence and the need for corroboration. He concluded:

'Further, if the jury found Small's to be a credible witness, as they did, and there was independent evidence supporting him we can find no reason for adjudging that verdict based on his evidence were unsafe or unsatisfactory'.

However, Lawton LJ then issued the following caution:

'Undertakings of immunity from prosecution may have to be given in the public interest. They should never be given by the police. The Director should give them most sparingly; and in cases involving grave crimes it would be prudent of him to consult the law officers before making any promises. In saying what we have, we should not be taken as doubting the well-established practice of calling accomplices on behalf of the Crown who have been charged in the same indictment as the accused and who have pleaded guilty'.

[6.43] Whereas the requirement was mandatory if an accomplice gave evidence for the prosecution, it was discretionary if on his own behalf *(R v Bagley)*[38]. In

---

[37] (1975) 61 Cr App Rep 67 at 79.
[38] *R v Bagley* [1980] Crim LR 572, CA.

Muff[39], the Court of Appeal held that in deciding whether to give the warning, the judge must weigh the difficulties of achieving a fair trial of the defendant who has given evidence implicating another defendant, against the risk that the trial of a person implicated by that evidence will not be fair unless a warning is given.

[6.44] In England, parliament abolished the warning requirement for children in s 34(2) of the Criminal Justice Act 1988, and for accomplices and complainants in s 32(1) of the Criminal Justice (Public Order) Act 1994.

[6.45] In Ireland it is notable that the Criminal Law (Rape) (Amendment) Act 1990 and the Criminal Evidence Act 1992 amended the corroboration requirement in relation to sexual offences complainants and children – but not accomplices.

[6.46] In *People (DPP) v Hogan*[40], with regard to the necessity of giving a warning in relation to the dangers attendant on the evidence of an accomplice, the Court emphasised that the purpose of pointing to the need for corroboration was not to confirm the accomplice's account but to find whether it implicates the accused in the crime with which he is charged.

[6.47] In *DPP v Ward*[41], *DPP v Holland*[42] and *DPP v Meehan*[43], the use of accomplice evidence through the medium of the State's Witness Protection Programme was sanctioned. The Special Criminal Court refused to accept that any particular warning was required in relation to such participants, apart from the standard warning in relation to accomplices.

[6.48] An additional requirement of corroboration has now been introduced in relation to confession evidence, which would seem fit into this category. Section 10 of the Criminal Procedure Act 1993 provides:

> '(1) Where at a trial of a person on indictment evidence is given of a confession made by that person and that evidence is not corroborated, the judge shall advise the jury to have due regard to the absence of corroboration.
>
> (2) It shall not be necessary for a judge to use any particular form of words under this section.'

The main distinguishing feature of this second category of instances requiring corroboration or a warning to the jury as a matter of practice, as opposed to the earlier category requiring corroboration as a matter of law, is that in the former

---

[39] *Muff* (2 November 1979, unreported), CA.
[40] *People (DPP) v Hogan* (21 January 1994, unreported), CCA.
[41] *DPP v Ward* (23 October 1998, unreported), HC.
[42] *DPP v Holland* (15 June 1998, unreported), HC.
[43] *DPP v Meehan* (29 July 1999, unreported), HC.

instance the jury has a right to convict despite the absence of corroborative evidence.

Visual identification evidence

[6.49] The third category of evidence, (or extension of the second), requiring corroboration to any degree, is one most recently developed by the judiciary – that of visual identification evidence. It merits separate consideration, in that it represents the most recent addition to this catalogue of evidence demanding corroboration, and requires it to a separate and different extent to those considered hitherto.

Rationale

[6.50] Perhaps the least contentious of those categories of evidence requiring corroboration to some degree, are those cases involving visual identification evidence. The rationale for the requirement in this instance is expressed variously in the dangers of defective memory; inadequate opportunity for recognition (the witness may only have had a fleeting glimpse of the individual in question); that a witness may have been overly influenced by tendered photographs or identikits; that the witness may err in relation to outsiders ('they all look alike to me' syndrome); and the likelihood of stubborn pride, in that the witness once committed to identifying the accused may be loath to reconsider. Finally, the usual way of overcoming risk in the context of testimonial error (that of cross-examination) is not all that effective in this context, an identification being either wrong or right, and not all that susceptible to that 'great legal engine for the discovery of truth'.

The requirement

[6.51] The formulation of the corroboration requirement in relation to visual identification evidence, occurred in the Supreme Court of Ireland in the decision of *People v Casey (No 2)*[44]. Casey had been convicted of assault and sentenced to four years penal servitude. In the Court of Criminal Appeal, Casey challenged the veracity of the visual identification by witnesses to whom he was not previously known. One witness was a boy of eleven years; the other had caught a momentary view in the light of the headlamps of a car. On a point of law of public importance, the issue went to the Supreme Court. Kingsmill-Moore J delivering judgment, held that there should be a general warning given, in all cases wholly or substantially dependent on visual identification evidence. He then formulated the direction that the trial judge should give the jury in such cases, as follows:

---

[44] *People v Casey (No 2)* [1963] IR 33.

'We are of opinion that juries ... may not be fully aware of the dangers involved in visual identification nor of the considerable number of cases in which such identification has been proved to be erroneous; and also that they may be inclined to attribute too much probative effect to the test of an identification parade. In our opinion it is desirable that in all cases, where the verdict depends substantially on the correctness of an identification, their attention should be called in general terms to the fact that in a number of instances such identification has proved erroneous, to the possibilities of mistake in the case before them and to the necessity of caution. Nor do we think that such warning should be confined to cases where the identification is that of only one witness. Experience has shown that mistakes can occur where two or more witnesses have made positive identifications ...'[45]

[6.52] The Irish courts were quite progressive in delineating such a requirement in relation to visual identification evidence. It was certainly true that such evidence had been found to be faulty on a number of occasions in the past, and had led to several (some quite notorious) false convictions. Indeed the Criminal Law Revision Committee in England, in its *Eleventh Report*[46], regarded mistaken identification as by far the greatest cause of actual or possible wrong convictions. The English courts, however, showed an initial reluctance to impose such a requirement in these cases. In *Arthurs v AG for Northern Ireland*[47], a case involving the identification by an RUC constable of the accused – at night and in the midst of a riot, hardly a situation conducive to a clear appraisal of identity – the House of Lords refused to impose such a requirement. They felt it undesirable to lay down that a general warning must be given where the case against the defendant depends wholly or substantially on identification evidence.

[6.53] In the subsequent decision of *R v Turnbull*[48], however, the English courts relented, and laid down quite elaborate guidelines as to the manner in which they would approach the matter of visual identity and recognition in the future. Widgery LCJ initially set out and adopted the *Casey* requirement, viz, where the case against the accused depends wholly or substantially on eye-witness identification, which is alleged to be mistaken, the judge should warn the jury of the special need for caution. The Court continued, that not only should the judge give the simple warning, but also the reasons for the warning should be explained to the jury. Widgery LCJ felt it should be pointed out that it is possible that a witness who sounds convincing, has in fact made a mistake. The trial judge should direct the jury to examine the circumstances of the case in a minute fashion. There is also a duty on the prosecution if there is a material discrepancy

---

[45] [1963] IR 33 at 38.
[46] Criminal Law Revision Committee Cmnd 4991 Eleventh Report *Evidence* (1972) at para 196.
[47] *Arthurs v AG for Northern Ireland* (1971) 55 Cr App Rep 161.
[48] *R v Turnbull* [1977] QB 224.

between the description given by a witness shortly after first sight of the culprit, and the actual appearance of the accused, to furnish same to the accused. Likewise, if the accused asks for a description, he should be given it.

[6.54] The guidelines further indicate that the trial judge should remind the jury of any specific weaknesses in the prosecution evidence. Where the identification evidence is good, and a warning as to caution is given, then the trial judge can leave the jury to act. Where the identification evidence is of a poor quality, the trial judge should withdraw the case from the jury and direct an acquittal unless there is evidence supporting the identification. This supporting evidence would take the form of corroboration, or any other evidence which supports the identification evidence. The trial judge should always point to evidence which does, and evidence which does not, corroborate identification evidence. Finally it was emphasised that the absence of the accused from the witness box is not evidence of anything, although the jury may take into account the fact that the identification has not been contradicted. The setting up of a false alibi, or telling lies, is not of itself proof that the accused was where the identifying witness says he was. Failure to follow these guidelines, the House concluded, is likely to result in a conviction being quashed.

[6.55] The Irish Court of Criminal Appeal in the decision of *People v Strafford*[49], held that the warning in this context, extended to cases of recognition (where the witness was previously acquainted with the appearance of the accused), and cited the guidelines laid down in the *Turnbull* decision. A recent decision of the Privy Council in *Scott v R*[50] confirms the necessity of a direction by the trial judge on the issue of identification evidence.

[6.56] The decisions in *Casey* and *Turnbull* lay down general principles, the application and relevance of which will depend on the particular facts of any given case.

[6.57] In the *People v Wallace*[51] the Irish Court of Criminal Appeal emphasised that if there are a number of counts on an indictment, and visual identification is an issue at trial; it is the duty of the trial judge to comment upon the visual identification, and draw the jury's attention to those courts to which it relates.

[6.58] The strength of the warning, similarly, will vary with the facts. In *The People v Fagan*[52], the accused had been convicted of the robbery of a garage attendant. The robbery had been carried out by two men, one of whom was

---

[49] *People v Strafford* [1983] IR 165.
[50] *Scott v R* [1989] 2 All ER 305.
[51] *People v Wallace* (22 November 1982, unreported) CCA.
[52] *The People v Fagan* (13 May 1974, unreported) CCA.

masked. The attendant was brought to the District Court by the gardaí, and informed that he would there see the person who carried out the robbery. In these circumstances the attendant identified the accused. The trial judge gave a warning to the jury, in accordance with *Casey*. The Court of Criminal Appeal found that, having regard to the circumstances of the case, a much stronger warning should have been given.

[6.59] With regard to the manner in which the police obtain visual identification evidence, it is interesting to note that in the *People v Mill*[53], it was stated that the gardaí can go around with a number of photos and show them to the victim of the crime for the purpose of identifying the culprit. The prosecution cannot, however, introduce these at trial; and they can only go into evidence, if they are referred to in cross-examination.

[6.60] With regard to the conduct of identification parades, a recent decision of the Court of Criminal Appeal is instructive. In *The People (DPP) v Patrick O'Reilly*[54], that Court laid down parameters with regard to the necessity for, and the conduct of, such parades. The applicant had been convicted of larceny and sentenced to four years penal servitude. He applied for leave to appeal the conviction and sentence. Identification evidence was given by a woman aged 81 years, whose description of the perpetrator was as 'a stout butt or a fair haired man' with 'a most notorious, and awful face'. The gardaí had brought that witness to the main street in Edgeworthstown (at or near the courthouse), to ascertain if she could identify anyone. She identified the applicant. The defence argued that evidence of identification should not have been admitted in the absence of a satisfactory explanation as to why a formal identification parade was not held; that fairness directs that no convenient short-cuts be taken by the State in obtaining evidence if it affects a defendant's ability to test the evidence adduced by the prosecution; and that there were valuable safeguards which applied to the holding of formal identification parades, and one should be held unless there was a good reason for not doing so. The case was further complicated by the fact that photographs of the applicant were shown to the injured party, prior to the identification. The defence also contended that the *Casey* warning should not have been given in a stereotyped manner, but applied to the particular facts of the case.

[6.61] O'Flaherty J delivering the judgment of the Court noted that the investigating garda had stated that in 23 years in the force he had never held an identification parade; and, in fact, felt that an informal identification was fairer to the accused because of the difficulty in picking someone out on a street with

---

[53] *People v Mill* [1957] IR 106.
[54] *The People (DPP) v Patrick O'Reilly* [1990] 2 IR 415.

any number of other around. In relation to the latter, O'Flaherty J noted that the garda was yet unable to give any description of any person on the street that morning. The Court noted that in *People (AG) v Peter Fagan*[55], the fact that the applicant was not living at home and so not always readily available for holding an identification parade, was deemed a less than satisfactory explanation, for failure to hold same.

[6.62] In *People (AG) v Martin*[56], O'Flaherty J noted, the Supreme Court had stated there was no rule of law or practice that required visual identification to be by means of an identification parade: each case must be considered on its facts. The Supreme Court had there acknowledged that other types of identification might in certain circumstances be fairer, and more dependable, than a formal identification parade, which, because of its surroundings, atmosphere, range of choice and limited opportunity for observation, might be less than satisfactory in achieving a reliable identification. The acceptability of such an alternative method would depend on the circumstances of the case.

[6.63] The reason given in this case for the failure to hold a parade, was that it might be 'more beneficial' to the defendant not to hold one. While accepting that it was right that those involved in the prosecution should be scrupulous in looking to the rights of the accused, O'Flaherty J nonetheless felt the decision as to what is most beneficial for an accused in the preparation and conduct of his defence, must be primarily a matter for the accused and his legal advisor.

[6.64] O'Flaherty J acknowledged that there would be circumstances where – for reasons of the singular appearance of the accused, the witness' previous acquaintance with him or the uncooperative attitude of the suspect – the holding of an identification parade might be impossible or redundant (although a warning would still be given per *Casey*). This case, however, he reasoned, was clearly one where the Court would require the holding of an identification parade. Such formal parades were an important filter for both prosecution and defence, and enabled the accused (and his legal advisor) to object to its composition if it were perceived to be unfair. Similarly, the court of trial would have the benefit of the description of same. By contrast, in the case of an informal identification, the accused had no input; was unlikely to be even aware of its happening, and might, therefore, be seriously inhibited in challenging its fairness at trial.

The Court emphasised that the result of the identification in the parade was not however conclusive, and confirmed the application of the *Casey* warning to same.

---

[55] *People (AG) v Peter Fagan* 1 Frewen 375.

[56] *People (AG) v Martin* [1956] IR 22.

[6.65] Counsel for the applicant pointed out that the way in which such identification parades were held was in no doubt: assemble eight or nine people similar in age, height, appearance, dress, and walk of life to the suspect; supervised by an independent garda (ie not involved in case); full details being kept of the descriptions of those in the parade; the witness not having an opportunity to see the suspect in advance of the parade.

O'Flaherty J further commented:

> 'This is not intended to be an exhaustive list for such parades and on occasion, the way in which an identification parade has been held has itself been subject to criticism (see eg *People (AG) v Michael O'Driscoll)*'.[57]

[6.66] Of interest is the concern expressed by the Court at the fact that photographs (including one of the accused) were shown to the injured party prior to her visit to Edgeworthstown. This further substantiated the Court's fears that this was an identification obtained in unusual and doubtful circumstances, which rendered the conviction unsafe. Indeed the Court felt the trial judge's ruling should have been sought on the admissibility of the identification obtained in such frail circumstances.

[6.67] With regard to the appeal on the ground of the trial judge's failure to adequately warn the jury in accordance with *Casey* of the danger of acting on uncorroborated visual identification evidence, the Court acknowledged the danger that the direction might be treated as a 'stereotyped formula'. While the Court felt that the trial judge here had complied fully with the first part of the direction and went on to deal with the particular circumstances in which the injured party observed the accused man; he should have given firmer guidance to the jury as regards the particular infirmities that affected this case: viz, the fact that the lady was elderly, in a state of shock, suffered a good deal of pain from an arthritic condition and had only a short period in which to observe the perpetrators. Further, the trial judge should have highlighted the deficiencies to the jury in the actual identification that was made at Edgeworthstown.

[6.68] O'Flaherty J pointed out that this was a case that required the holding of an identification parade. An important distinction between an informal and formal identification is that in the latter, the accused has full knowledge of its composition and may object if it is perceived to be unfair. The Court has a detailed account of same. However, the *Casey* warning is still required. The Court also pointed to the fact that here the witness was shown photographs (including one of the accused) prior to her visit to Edgeworthstown. This added weight to the Court's concern and indicated that the trial judges' ruling should have been sought on the admissibility of the identification evidence obtained in

---

[57] *People (AG) v Michael O'Driscoll* 1 Frewen 351.

such frail circumstances. Thirdly the Supreme Court emphasised that the *Casey* warning should not be treated as a 'stereotyped' formula. In this case, the trial judges' direction should have been much more specific as regards the danger of acting on the evidence of Mrs Farrell. The only difference between this and *Fagan's* case was that the witness in the latter was shaken under cross-examination. Mrs Farrell was made of sterner stuff.

> 'However, it is central to the need to give warnings in cases of visual identification that people young and old, tend to be certain. If they are not certain their evidence will fall to the ground anyway. No matter how certain a witness appears to be, the requirement laid down in *Casey* ... remains' (per O'Flaherty J).

[6.69] This confirmation on the part of the Irish courts of the inherently fallible nature of visual identification evidence; the necessity for caution in relation to same, and the confirmation of the *Casey* warning is significant. It is in contrast with other perceived judicial rejection or abolition of the corroboration requirement (witness decisions such as *R v Spencer*[58], *R v Bagshaw*[59], *R v Chance*[60] etc). The reason for the strength of judicial support for the warning in relation to cases substantially dependent on visual identification evidence)[61], may lie in the availability of empirical evidence substantiating such a requirement. This, coupled with the difficulty of countering this type of evidence by cross-examination (see O'Flaherty J's comment with regard to the certainty of witnesses) may explain the judicial desire to maintain this requirement, and indeed avoid the 'ritualistic incantation' of a stereotyped formula.

[6.70] Of additional interest for the Irish law of criminal procedure is O'Flaherty J's recognition in *O'Reilly* of the inherently adversarial nature of the process; the conflict of interest between prosecution and defence; and the requirement of 'fairness' to the accused in the pre-trial process – an element of which may well be the holding of a formal identification parade. (This follows the concept of 'fairness' per *Healy* as including a right to counsel).

[6.71] In contrast with the decision in *O'Reilly*, is the subsequent Court of Criminal Appeal decision in *People (DPP) v Dermot O'Callaghan*[62], where the characteristics of the identifying witness strengthened the case. This case concerned charges of robbery and larceny arising out of an armed hold-up of a bank in Dublin. It was contended that the evidence was inadequate to support a

---

[58] *R v Spencer* [1985] 1 All ER 673.
[59] *R v Bagshaw* [1984] 1 WLR 477.
[60] *R v Chance* [1988] QB 932.
[61] See also the Privy Council decision in *R v Scott* [1983] IR 165.
[62] *People (DPP) v Dermot O'Callaghan* (30 July 1990, unreported), CCA (per O'Hanlon J).

conviction, particularly in relation to the purported identification of the applicant, and that the trial judge had insufficiently warned the jury in relation to same.

[6.72] The witness called to give evidence of identification was a security officer. He had the robber in sight for a few seconds prior to being made lie on the floor. A video recorder had recorded the incident, and on seeing it twice, it occurred to the witness that the man was one of two men who had aroused his suspicions two days before the robbery. On looking at the video of that earlier day, he claimed to be able to identify the applicant. The jury saw both videos. The applicant had been in disguise on the day of the robbery.

[6.73] The trial judge had refused an application to withdraw the case from the jury. O'Hanlon J upheld that decision. He pointed out that this witness was not:

'a mere casual passer-by, but a security officer who had worked in the bank for over a year prior to the robbery ...,'

If such a witness in such circumstances gives positive evidence on which he is not shaken on cross-examination ... it appears to this Court that it was proper to leave to the jury to decide whether they were convinced as to the truthfulness and reliability of his evidence'. (Of course warning must be given)

[6.74] Given the fact that identification evidence is perhaps the least contentious area of the law with regard to corroboration, and in light of the recent endorsement by the judiciary of the necessity for caution in regard for same, it is perhaps curious s 17 of the Criminal Evidence Act 1992 proposes that in the case of a person accused of a sexual offence, or offence involving violence or the threat of violence, where the victim is under 17 years of age, and the identifying witness is the victim or other person under that age, it shall be presumed, until the contrary is proven, that the person so identified, is the accused (s 17(1)).

[6.75] In *People v Duff*[63], the optimum method of visual identification was noted to be by means of an identification parade.

In *DPP v Cooney*[64], the Supreme Court held, however, that while dock identifications were undesirable and unsatisfactory, they may be admitted by the trial judge with a specific warning to the jury of acting on same. This was confirmed in *DPP v Brian Meehan*[65], where the dock identifications had the added weakness of being provided by an accomplice, and the non-jury court involving the judges warning themselves as arbiters of fact.

---

[63] *People v Duff* [1995] 3 IR 296.
[64] *DPP v Cooney* [1997] 3 IR 205.
[65] *DPP v Brian Meehan* (29 July 1999, unreported), SCC.

Discretion to give warning

Sexual offences

[6.76] Whereas, formerly, the evidence of a complainant in a 'sexual offence' action was deemed to require corroboration as a matter of practice or at least a warning to the jury as to the dangers of acting on such evidence, since the passing of the Criminal Law (Rape) (Amendment) Act 1990, this position has been altered.

[6.77] Under s 7 of the Criminal Law (Rape) (Amendment) Act 1990, the trial judge in such a case has a discretion as to whether to give such a warning or not. The warning remains the traditional one in relation to sexual complainants, although no particular form of words need be utilised. The extent to which this judicial discretion to issue the warning in relation to sexual complainants, would be exercised, would of course determine the effectiveness of this mechanism of reform.

[6.78] It seemed as though the resurgence of the warning in practice through the exercise of judicial discretion was realised by the Court of Criminal Appeal judgment in *People (DPP) v Molloy*[66], where Flood J criticised the failure of the trial judge to give a warning, as was 'prudent practice' in a sexual offence case. However, in *People (DPP) v JEM*[67], Denham J refers to the English decision of *R v Makanjoula*[68] with approval. There, the English Court of Appeal had trenchantly rejected the notion that the warning had any continued existence in the aftermath of s 32(1) of the Criminal Justice (Public Order) Act 1994 which removed mandatory corroboration warning for accomplices and sexual offence victims. Although s 7 of the 1990 Act did not contain the same wording, Denham J stated that the legal principle underpinning the two statutes was similar. She endorsed the following principles laid down in that case:

'(1) Section 32(1) abrogated the requirement to give a corroboration direction in respect of an alleged accomplice or a complainant of a sexual offence simply because a witness falls into one of those categories.

(2) It is a matter for the judge's discretion what, if any, warning he considers appropriate in respect of such a witness, as indeed in respect of any other witness in whatever type of case. Whether he chooses to give a warning and in what terms will depend on the circumstances of the case, the issues raised and the content and quality of the witnesses' evidence.

---

[66] *People (DPP) v Molloy* (28 July 1995) CCA.
[67] *People (DPP) v JEM* [2001] 4 IR 385.
[68] *R v Makanjoula* [1995] 3 All ER 730.

(3) In some cases, it may be appropriate for the judge to warn the jury to exercise caution before acting upon the unsupported evidence of a witness. This will not be so simply because the witness is the complainant of a sexual offence nor will it necessarily be so because a witness is alleged to be an accomplice. There may be an evidential basis for suggesting that the evidence of the witness may be unreliable. An evidential basis does not include mere suggestions by cross-examining counsel.

(4) If any question arises as to whether the judge should give a special warning in respect of a witness, it is desirable that the question be resolved by discussion with counsel in the absence of the jury before final speeches.

(5) Where the judge does decide to give some warning in respect of a witness, it will be appropriate to do so as part of the judge's review of the evidence and his comments as to how the jury should evaluate it rather than as a set piece legal direction.

(6) Where some warning is required, it will be for the judge to decide the strengths and terms of the warning. It does not have to be invested with the whole florid regime of the old corroboration rules.

(7) ... Attempts to re-impose the straightjacket of the old corroboration rules are strongly to be deprecated.''[69]

[6.79] In *People (DPP) v C*[70] an appeal against conviction on a charge of rape on the basis of the trial judge's failure to give a corroboration warning failed, the Court of Criminal Appeal emphasising that it was no longer a rule of law or practice that a jury be warned of the danger of convicting on the uncorroborated evidence of a complainant in a sexual offence trial by reason of the nature of the offence. Murray J was satisfied that it had not been demonstrated to the Court that there was any ground on which the trial judge could be said to have exercised his discretion improperly in this case.

Children's evidence

[6.80] The requirement that children's evidence be corroborated was abolished by s 28 of the Criminal Evidence Act 1992. It was replaced by a judicial discretion to give such a warning, and no particular form of words is necessary to do so. Section 28 provides:

'(1) The requirement in section 30 of the Children Act, 1908, of corroboration of unsworn evidence of a child given under that section is hereby abolished.

(2)(a) Any requirement that at a trial on indictment the jury be given a warning by the judge about convicting the accused on the uncorroborated evidence

---

[69] *People (DPP) v JEM* [2001] 4 IR 385 at 401–402. The final 8th principle with regard to interference with a trial judge's discretion was not endorsed by Denham J.

[70] *People (DPP) v C* [2001] 3 IR 345.

of a child is also hereby abolished in relation to cases where such a warning is required by reason only that the evidence is the evidence of a child and it shall be for the judge to decide, in his discretion, having regard to all the evidence given, whether the jury should be given the warning.

(b)   If a judge decides, in his discretion, to give such a warning as aforesaid, it shall not be necessary to use any particular form of words to do so.

(3) Unsworn evidence received by virtue of section 27 may corroborate evidence (sworn or unsworn) given by any other person.'

[6.81] The Criminal Evidence Act 1992 weakened the corroboration rule in relation to sexual offences, giving the judiciary a discretion as to whether to give such a warning to the: jury. The application of the said corroboration rule in relation to accomplices remains at full strength, but would seem to be somewhat cosmetic in effect, as evidenced by the *Holland*[71] and *Ward*[72] cases. Moreover, the application of the rules of evidence in the Special Criminal Court suffers from the artificiality of judges instructing themselves to be cautious of accomplice evidence, for example, or to ignore evidence as in the case of excluded confessions (eg *Ward*).

They haven't gone away, you know...

[6.82] Much has been made of the influence of rules of evidence in a popular cultural sense arising from the popular mood, perhaps, to solidify into rule, or gradually permeating existent rules in the aftermath of legislative change, thus heralding the birth and effectiveness of assumptions regarding credibility. Such changes can enter the legal culture rather slowly, in terms of influencing fact-determination. Once integrated, however, they may be correspondingly difficult to uproot. Ironically, Althouse's point[73] with regard to the difficulty of effecting a legislative change prior to a cultural one, can be made by reference to the Irish position on corroboration – ie after its removal or weakening it continues to emerges as a player in the courts' adjudication. *DPP v Finnerty*[74] is a case in point. The factual scenario was that of a sexual offence: the alleged rape of a student after a disco. The defendant claimed they had met after the disco and that the intercourse was consensual. At trial, a corroboration warning was given by the trial judge. On appeal it was commented that 'No criticism has been, or could be, made of those aspects of his charge'.[75]

---

[71] *DPP v Holland* (15 June 1998, unreported), HC.

[72] *DPP v Ward* (23 October 1998, unreported), HC.

[73] Althouse, Ann 'Thelma and Louise and the Law: Do Rape Shield Rules Matter?' [1992] Loyola of Los Angeles LR 757 at 772.

[74] *DPP v Finnerty* [1999] 4 IR 364.

[75] [1999] 4 IR 364 at 372-373 (per Keane J).

[6.83] *Finnerty* illustrates how a once crystallised perspective on credibility prevails, even through legislative change, because of judicial adherence to its original precepts[76]. However, even when that transition is complete, a case can be found being made for its re-emergence. The re-emergence of rules of evidence encapsulating scepticism and caution may not in this context seem unjustifiable or indeed unwelcome. This is despite the fact that their origins may be dubious, or the rumours of their demise been greatly exaggerated. There are signs of disenchantment with 'received wisdom' and actions of verity on the part of the victim. Ironically this manifested itself in a renewed argument for the re-introduction of corroboration in Ireland, in face of its comparatively recent legislative reform.

[6.84] In *P O'C v DPP*[77], where an order of prohibition on ground of delay was granted, the applicant was charged with five counts of indecently assaulting PK at dates unknown from 1 January 1982 to 31 December 1983. The applicant was a violin teacher, and the incidents allegedly took place in a music room, a significant factor being the existence of a facility to lock same, something that was difficult for the applicant to obtain evidence of after the delay – grounds for prohibition. Of specific interest in terms of the rules of evidence, and the impact or influence of popular culture, is the judgment of Hardiman J. He refers to the fact that corroboration requirement in sexual cases was abolished by s 7 of the Rape Amendment Act 1990 and the Criminal Evidence Act 1992, s 27, and comments:

'It may well be that these pieces of legislation were enacted before the prosecution of very old offences became routine as it now is. Cases which will be tried more than ten years after the offences are alleged to have been committed are very common, and a twenty to twenty five year interval is by no means uncommon. My personal experience extends to a case proposed to be prosecuted more than forty-six years after the alleged offences and one has heard of an interval of more than fifty-two years. These, even the shorter periods, are remarkable lengths of time. They appear to me of themselves, and independently of the Director's reliance on possible unspecified "directions" of a trial judge, to require serious consideration of what can or should be said to a jury in these cases. At present, one cannot be sure that any direction or warning will be given

---

[76] Birch, 'Corroboration: Goodbye to All That?' [1995] Crim LR 524. In earlier consideration of reform of the corroboration requirement by s 32(1) of the Criminal Justice (Public Order) Act 1994, Birch had expressed an appreciation of the value of *Beck* [1982] 1 WLR 461, which creates a witness specific obligation, arising only if material to suggest a particular witness's evidence may be tainted by improper motive. Those changes which have extended the accommodation of vulnerable witnesses so that it is a concept now beyond that of women and children do not avoid those particular criticisms of inflexibility and complexity.

[77] *P O'C v DPP* [2000] 3 IR 87.

... A plausible and sympathetic witness is not necessarily telling the truth, nor a furtive and cowed one lying. The very pressures of litigation of this sort, so deeply personal and perhaps central to a Complainant's self worth on the one hand and so threatening of prolonged imprisonment, life long stigmatistion and financial and familial catastrophe on the other, in themselves have the potential drastically to alter the witnesses' presentation and effect. To permit such prosecutions, in the absence of any scope for corroboration or contradiction after one, two or more decades is, to say the least to venture into unchartered territory where the normal forensic safeguards are gravely attenuated. The process of the trial itself may be a life altering event for one or both parties and their families, and rarely for the better. In these circumstances it appears to me that there is in each case a point at which a trial in those circumstances "puts justice to the hazard" so that the issue of guilt or innocence is "beyond the risk of fair litigations".'[78]

Hardiman J clearly makes a case for the 'reclaiming' of corroboration in this context.

[6.85] Subsequently, vindication of that stance is given in *JL v DPP*[79] by McGuinness J, who says Hardiman J's experiences accord with her own in the Central Criminal Court.[80] There is also, in that case, vindication of the presumption of innocence, Keane J concluding:

'Given the presumption of innocence to which, at this stage of the inquiry, the applicant is entitled, I am satisfied that he has discharged the onus ... that there is a real and serious risk of an unfair trial.'[81]

McGuinness J also states:

'I do not accept, however, that the presumption of innocence plays no part in the decision which must be made by the court in this case ... While for the purposes of looking at the reasons for a complainant's delay in reporting a sexual assault to the gardaí an assumption as to the truth of her allegations may be made, when the court subsequently considers whether there is a real risk of an unfair trial it is a trial based on the presumption of innocence that is in question. By this approach

---

[78] *PO'C v DPP* 6 July 2000 at 20-21 (per Hardiman J).

[79] *JL v DPP* [2000] 3 IR 122. The applicant here was charged with three counts of rape, indecent assault and buggery of J O'R (female) on a date unknown between 1 June 1979 and 30 September 1980. The High Court had dismissed an application to restrain the trial because of delay, leading to the Supreme Court appeal. There was evidence (uncontradicted) of psychologist presented. Keane J identifies two special features not typically present in cases of alleged child abuse: complaint was about one incident only; (2) as in *P O'C v DPP* the applicant claims inability to construct a defence through passage of time (ie that he was no longer living in a caravan at time of offence).

[80] [2000] 3 IR 122 at 133 (McGuinness J).

[81] [2000] 3 IR 122 at 126-127 (Keane J).

the court will hold the balance between a situation in which it would be impossible to try any accused of sexual offences against children where delay in reporting had occurred, and the equally undesirable situation where all persons accused of sexual offences against children would have to face trial no matter how long the time was which had elapsed since the alleged offence and no matter how great was the danger of an unfair trial.'

[6.86] *DPP v Robert Gentlemen*[82] was a case involving a number of counts of indecent assault in relation to a young boy, alleged to have been the pupil of the accused teacher, where 22 years had elapsed since the alleged offending conduct had taken place. There was no corroboration of the applicant's allegation, which the court noted to be frequently a feature of these cases. The trial judge had exercised his discretion to give a warning (under s 7 of the Criminal Law (Rape) (Amendment) Act 1990). Once exercised, Keane CJ points out that the appellate court is entitled to consider whether, in all the circumstances, he gave the appropriate warning.

[6.87] The Court of Criminal Appeal commented that this was obviously a case where a trial judge would give a warning for three reasons: (i) the absence of corroboration of the applicant's story; (ii) that 22 years had elapsed; and (iii) that no act or complaint was made at the time.

[6.88] The Court (Keane CJ) found the warning not to have been adequate, specifically because it did not indicate to the jury why the law considers it dangerous to convict, that it is one person's word against another, and it had not been explained that this is not some formalistic requirement but a 'real and important requirement based on the experience of the courts that must be exercised'.[83]

[6.89] The Irish courts, therefore, have turned full circle: the exception carved out to the principle of expeditious justice, invoking assumptions of credibility and proof to the detriment of the accused's fair trial rights, and the presumption of innocence, turning to the judicial rejection of received wisdom and vindication of fair trial rights for the accused.

---

82 *DPP v Robert Gentlemen* (25 February 2002, unreported), CCA.
83 *DPP v Robert Gentlemen* (25 February 2002, unreported), CCA at 2 (Keane CJ at 7).

Chapter 7

Opinion Evidence

'Pansy was really a blank page, a pure white surface, successfully kept so; she had neither art, nor guile, nor temper, nor talent – only two or three small exquisite instincts: for knowing a friend, for avoiding a mistake, for taking care of an old toy or a new frock.'

Henry James *The Portrait of a Lady* (London 1972), p 315.

Introduction

[7.01] The rule of evidence in relation to the admissibility of evidence of opinion on the part of a witness is yet another exclusionary rule. The general rule is that which provides that witnesses must speak only to the facts which they have observed, and not of the inferences which they have drawn from such facts. In particular, the justification for this particular exclusionary rule lies in the fact that for a witness to draw conclusions and form opinions in regard to proved facts would constitute a usurpation of the function of the jury as trier of fact.

[7.02] Exceptions to the general rule do exist, however, and not unusually in this branch of the law, they are often more powerful in effect, than the rule itself. The exceptions are twofold:

(1)   'Expert' witnesses can give opinion evidence. The motivation for calling such witnesses is, of course, to benefit from the expertise of their opinion, and they are generally stated to be permitted to opine on matters of 'science and art'.

(2)   Secondly, non-expert witnesses may, in certain circumstances, give what might be regarded as opinion evidence. This type of evidence is mostly received because it would be virtually impossible for the witness to confine himself to the observed facts, and so leave the inference to the jury. Examples of this occurring include testimony that the accused had been drinking, the identification of a person's belongings and handwriting, the speed of a vehicle; the age of a person and the state of the weather.

For example, in *R v German*[1], the accused was charged with dangerous driving and driving while intoxicated, and a lay person was allowed to testify with regard to same.

---

[1]   *R v German* [1947] 4 DLR 68.

Expert evidence

Qualification

[7.03] In order to qualify for consideration as an expert witness capable of giving opinion evidence, it was not traditionally required that the expertise take a professional format. In *R v Silverlock*[2] a solicitor with 'a bit of an interest in handwriting' was allowed to testify. However, as specialisation has increased, and designation of expertise status perhaps became correspondingly more elusive, witnesses tendered must be shown to have acquired more than just a 'little knowledge' before coming within this category.

[7.04] In the Canadian case of *R v Kusmack*[3], for instance, the accused was charged with murder. His defence was that the victim had a knife when he grabbed her, hence the killing was an accident. A doctor's testimony to the effect that the wounds on her hands were sustained while defending herself was not allowed on the basis that that doctor was not an expert on wounds or forensic medicine.

[7.05] In regard to handwriting evidence, another Canadian case (*Pitre v R*[4]) held it necessary to prove that there was regular correspondence with the witness, ie the witness must have been acquainted with the person's handwriting if not with the writer.

[7.06] In *Poynton v Poynton*,[5] Madden J differentiated in the case of evidence in regard to the medical incapacity of a testator between that of a lay or non-medical person (here, such witnesses being the testator's brother-in-law and a clergyman) and that of a doctor. A similar distinction was drawn by Walsh J (dissenting) in the Supreme Court decision of *Glynn*,[6] with regard to evidence peertaining to whether at the time of execution of a will, the deceased was of sound mind.

[7.07] In general, the modern rule can be said to be that the opinions of skilled witnesses are admissible when the person who is giving the opinion has a particular expertise or experience in the relevant area, which is based on a special study or his day-to-day experience.

The burden of proof with regard to such expertise on the part of a witness rests with the person tendering such witness in evidence. In adducing evidence by an expert witness certain principles must be observed. The witness gives evidence

---

2   *R v Silverlock* [1894] 2 QB 766.
3   *R v Kusmack* (1955).
4   *Pitre v R* (1933) SCR 69.
5   *Poynton v Poynton* (1903) 37 ILTR 54.
6   *Re Glynn (decd); Glynn v Glynn* [1990] 2 IR 326 at 335.

under oath, during examination-in-chief having first established his credentials, on which he may, if the other side does not object, be led. He can then be cross-examined by the other side. A prosecution for perjury may ensue if he gives evidence of an opinion he did not *bona fide* hold.

[7.08] Developments in society, and the increasing specialisation of knowledge, has meant an increase in the tendering of expertise in the course of any litigation. The burgeoning use of expertise has spawned candidates – in the form of expert witnesses – for both sides. It is unusual to see even the more mundane 'running-down' action without experts of various hues – engineers, medical consultants, etc – ranged on both sides. This poses some difficulties for the role of the adjudicators in the process (the judge as to admissibility; the jury as to credibility) and a challenge to counsel on cross-examination.

[7.09] In relation to the issue of whether jurors are capable, or indeed entitled, to choose between conflicting experts on an issue which, by definition they are not themselves fully competent, the Australian High Court has recently vindicated the role of the jury in this context and their entitlement to so choose. In *Velveski v The Queen*[7], on the trial of the applicant for the murder of his wife and their children, where medical and pathological evidence had been tendered with regard to whether wounds were self-inflicted or not, the High Court held that the fact that there was conflicting evidence did not mean the case should be withdrawn from the jury:

> 'Juries are frequently called upon to resolve conflicts between experts. They have done so from the inception of jury trials. Expert evidence does not, as a matter of law, fall into two categories: difficult and sophisticated expert evidence giving rise to conflicts which a jury may not and should not be allowed to resolve; and simple and unsophisticated expert evidence which they can. Nor is it the law, that simply because there is a conflict in respect of difficult and sophisticated expert evidence, even with respect to an important, indeed critical matter, its resolution should for that reason alone be regarded by the appellate court as having been beyond the capacity of the jury to resolve.'[8]

[7.10] In terms of accessibility and comprehension of expert evidence, improvement with regard to complex fraud trials, for example, is provided by the Criminal Justice (Theft and Fraud) Offences Act 2001, s 57 of which provides that in trials on indictment under that Act, transcripts of the whole or any of the evidence including documentation from accountants explaining transactions, may be given to the jury.

---

[7]   *Velveski v The Queen* [2002] 76 ALJR 402.
[8]   Per Gummow and Callinan JJ (2002) 76 ALJR 402 at 433.

[7.11] In relation to the issue of when such expertise is admissible or desirable, Zuckerman[9] states that a judge determining if expert opinion should be accepted on a certain matter, must consider the state of public opinion on the point.

'If the community has come to defer to professional standards on the matters in question, the courts will normally follow suit. Medical evidence is admissible on matters of health because we accept the authority of the medical profession in this regard.'

[7.12] The theory as to the purpose or effect of the expert evidence when so admitted is interesting. In *Davie v Edinburgh Magistrates*,[10] Cooper LJ put the classical theory as follows:

'[T]heir duty is to furnish the judge or jury with the necessary scientific criteria for testing the accuracy of their conclusions, so as to enable the judge *or* jury to form their own independent judgment by the application of these criteria to the facts proved in evidence.'

Of course, the extent to which this theory is effective in practice, is muted by the presentation by the other party to the action of completely contrary opinion evidence, leaving the jury to choose between them.

[7.13] Taylor stated that:

'It is often quite surprising to see with what facility, and to what an extent their views [of experts] can be made to correspond with the wishes or the interests of the parties who call them. They do not, indeed, wilfully misrepresent what they think but their judgments become so warped by their regarding the subject in one point of view, that even when conscientiously disposed they are incapable of forming independent opinion.'[11]

[7.14] In the United States, the test for admissibility of an expertise was the general acceptance of that technique or science within the scientific community, the so-called '*Frye* test' laid down in *Frye v US*.[12] In *Daubert v Merrell Dow Pharmaceuticals*[13], the US Supreme Court rejected that standard in favour of the court ensuring that the expert's testimony both rests on a reliable foundation and is relevant to the task at hand. This would involve consideration of:

1. Whether the theory or technique can be (and has been) tested;

2. Whether it has been subjected to peer review and publication;

3. Its known or potential error rate;

---

[9] Zuckerman *The Principles of Criminal Evidence* Clarendon Law Series (1989) p 67.
[10] *Davie v Edinburgh Magistrates* (1953) SC 34.
[11] Taylor *Treatise on the Law of Evidence* (12th edn, 1931) p 59.
[12] *Frye v US* 54 App DC 46, 47, 293 F 1013,1014.
[13] *Daubert v Merrell Dow Pharmaceuticals* 509 US 579.

4.   Existence and maintenance of standards controlling its operation;

5.   Whether it has attracted widespread acceptance within a relevant scientific community.

[7.15] In 1999 the US Supreme Court in *Kumho Tire Co Ltd et al v Carmichael*[14] held that *Daubert's* requirement of reliability not only applied to scientific experts, but to all experts. Under *Daubert* and *Kumho* the opinion of the expert must be based on reliable methodology or analysis and not subjective belief or unsupported speculation. Reliability of expert testimony is as important as the relevance of the expert testimony.

[7.16] Expert testimony, in theory, is called to assist the jury in their adjudication. In practice, the jury must choose between varying expert opinions on matters on which they have been deemed to require expert assistance. What criteria do they then use to make their choice. Often it is the personality and presentation of the particular experts – hence, the search for witnesses skilled in the presentation of their expertise. The significance of an opportunity to rebut an expert's opinion was raised to some degree in the case of *DPP v Ian Smith*.[15] It was argued here inter alia that the evidence of the handwriting expert called by the prosecution differed at the hearing from the book of evidence, to the prejudice of the accused, yet did not allow then for the accused to get his own expert witness to put forward the opposite point of view. In the circumstances, the Court felt it did not involve a real danger of wrong conviction.

[7.17] Related to the importance of expert witnesses, is the issue as to the determination of the 'ultimate issue' at trial. The theory of adjudication is such that it is for the jury or arbiter of fact to determine. Thus, the opinion of a witness, if given, is not the final word on any issue that is the prerogative of the arbiter of fact in that case. So, for example, if expert testimony has been tendered on identical characteristics of fingerprints, it is for the jury to decide, on examination of the evidence, if they are indeed identical. In other words, they may choose to act on the evidence before them, but the expert witnesses' testimony is not conclusive. They must themselves be satisfied. We saw where difficulties arise with regard to the effect of that particular choice, given a conflict of expert opinion.

[7.18] The statement is not without complete effect, however, because if the subject is one upon which the jury is capable of forming an opinion without the aid of an expert, expert evidence is not admissible. For example, if the defence of insanity is not raised, but the defence seeks to adduce evidence in the form of

---

[14]   *Kumho Tire Co Ltd et al v Carmichael* 119 SC 1167 (1999).
[15]   *DPP v Ian Smith* (5 November 1990, unreported) CCA (Finlay CJ, *ex temp*).

expert testimony as to the likely state of mind of the accused at the time of the incident, that is inadmissible as evidence of *mens rea* which is a matter entirely for the jury and within their competence. In *R v Chard*[16] Rossville LJ held that in the absence of an insanity defence, it was simply a matter for the jury on the evidence presented whether in fact the requisite *mens rea* was present. In *R v Turner*[17], the trial judge rejected expert psychiatric evidence as to the likelihood of the accused being provoked by his girlfriend's admission of infidelity, this evidence had been tendered to support a defence of provocation to murder. This ruling was upheld on appeal. Lawton LJ explained the rationale for rejection as follows:

> 'If on the proven facts a judge or jury can form their own conclusions without [expert] help, then the opinion of an expert is unnecessary. In such a case if it is given dressed up in scientific jargon it may make judgment more difficult. The fact that an expert witness has impressive scientific qualifications does not by that fact alone make his opinion on matters of human nature and behaviour within the limits of normality any more helpful than that of the jurors themselves; but there is a danger that they may think it does'.

[7.19] The reluctance of the courts to admit evidence of an expert on a matter which the jury or lay person is considered competent is understandable; not only for the purpose of vindicating the role and function of the jury, but also that of upholding the rationale of legal adjudication by lawyers and lay persons – not experts. Should experts be deemed capable of giving definitive opinion conclusive of certain issues in a trial, the dawn of 'trial by psychiatrist' or 'trial by scientist' would not be very far away; yet we may not yet be ready to concede that position without justification. For this reason, expert testimony or opinion evidence as to the ultimate issue has not been allowed. Some inroads have, on occasion, been made on this rule, but may be indicative of the time-period in which the decisions were made, where courts were not yet overly familiar and so did not remain underwhelmed by the tendering of expertise.

[7.20] In *DPP v A & BC Chewing Gum Ltd,*[18] on a charge of obscenity against the defendant manufacturers who had provided a range of graphically violent war picture cards to distribute with their produce, evidence of child psychiatrists was allowable as to whether that material was likely to corrupt and deprave (this being the legal test or criteria for obscenity).

Similarly, in *Lowery v R,*[19] the trial judge was adjudged to have correctly admitted evidence of a psychiatrist on behalf of one of the accused, to the effect

---

[16] *R v Chard* (1972) 57 Cr App Rep 268.
[17] *R v Turner* [1975] 1 All ER 70.
[18] *DPP v A & BC Chewing Gum Ltd* [1968] 1 QB 159.
[19] *Lowery v R* [1974] AC 85.

that one of the two accused persons was more likely than the other to have committed the crime in question.

[7.21] By contrast, in the case of *R v Anderson & Neville,*[20] on the trial of the magazine 'Oz', for obscenity, a witness for the defence testified to show that the article in question was not obscene, as it did not have a tendency to corrupt and deprave. Widgery J excluded the evidence on the ground that whether '... an article is obscene or not is a question exclusively for the jury, and expert evidence should not be admitted as to whether it is obscene or not. The courts must relate the facts of the case to the standard'.

[7.22] An awareness of the potential for the usurpation of the role of the jury by the presentation of expert testimony and a vindication of the former's role in that light is evident in the judgment of the Court of Criminal Appeal in *DPP v Paul Kehoe.*[21] This was an application for leave to appeal brought by the applicant who was convicted of murder in the Central Criminal Court. The appeal centred on the issue of the evidence of Dr Behan, called to buttress the only defence put forward by the accused – that of provocation. Dr Behan had not been called to establish a defence of insanity or mental illness or any form of derangement that might have occurred by the accused's use of drugs or alcohol. O'Flaherty J, delivering the judgment of the Court, commented that:

> 'While the evidence of a psychiatrist is, undoubtedly, relevant and admissible in such circumstances, as it will be if the defence of diminished responsibility or such is given recognition in our law it is clear to the Court that Dr Behan could not in this case give any relevant, admissible evidence in relation to the state of mind, the temperament and those other matters that are referred to in *MacEoin's* case, that the accused could not do himself.
>
> There is no doubt that Dr Behan was attempting to articulate in a fuller way what the accused has stated, rather briefly, viz his annoyance and upset but on which he based his defence of provocation.
>
> The Court is of the opinion that the accused's defence was properly to be considered by the jury without such elaboration and that, further, in the course of his evidence it is clear that Dr Behan overstepped the mark in saying that he believed the accused did not have an intention to kill and that the accused was telling the truth. These are clearly matters four-square within the jury's function and a witness no more than the trial judge or anyone else is not entitled to trespass on what is the jury's function.'

[7.23] O'Flaherty J noted that this had been recently emphasised by the Supreme Court in *The People (DPP) v Egan*[22] and concluded, therefore:

---

[20] *R v Anderson & Neville* [1971] 3 All ER 1152.
[21] *DPP v Paul Kehoe* (6 November 1991, unreported) CCA (*ex temp* O'Flaherty J).
[22] *The People (DPP) v Egan* [1990] ILRM 780.

'So, it appears to the Court, that the correct approach, where there is any doubt in the matter, is for the defence to canvass the view of the trial judge in the first instance as to whether psychiatric evidence is properly admissible, because the view of Court is that this was not a case for the admission of psychiatric evidence, and it would appear to be, as far as criminal cases are concerned, properly to be confined to the matters already mentioned, such as the defence of insanity or the like.'

O'Flaherty J noted that the issue was considered by the English Court of Appeal in *R v Turner*[23], where the evidence of a psychiatrist was tendered in support of a provocation defence put forward by an accused on the basis of his girlfriend's alleging her relations with other men. The court there took the view that these matters were well within ordinary human experience, and the capabilities of the jury. The law in Ireland, stated O'Flaherty J, is the same.

[7.24] The *Turner* rule has been reconsidered in Australia in *Murphy v Queen*:[24]

'In *R v Turner* Lawton LJ expressed the basis upon which expert evidence is received in terms about which there can be no quarrel: "An expert's opinion is admissible to furnish the court with scientific information which is likely to be outside the experience and knowledge of a judge or jury. "Later Lawton LJ added some remarks which may not be so unquestionable: "Jurors do not need psychiatrists to tell them how ordinary folk who are not suffering from any mental illness are likely to react to the stresses and strains of life." There are difficulties with such a statement. To begin with, it assumes that "ordinary" or "normal" has some clearly understood meaning and, as a corollary, that the distinction between normal and abnormal is well recognised. Further, it assumes that the common sense of jurors is an adequate guide to the conduct of people who are "normal" even though they may suffer from some relevant disability. And it assumes that the experience of psychiatrists (or, as in the present case, psychologists) extends only to those who are "abnormal." None of these assumptions will stand close scrutiny.'

[7.25] In *DPP v Kehoe*[25] that very same issue was addressed by the Irish courts. The facts of the case involved the accused's killing of PH, his former best friend, who now had a relationship with the mother of the accused's child. The defence to the charge of murder was provocation. O'Flaherty J delivering the judgment of the Court of Criminal Appeal, found that the expert witness here was not called to establish a defence of insanity or any form of mental illness or derangement that might have occurred by the accused's use of drugs and alcohol in regard to which it appeared he had become dependent.[26] He could not,

---

[23] *R v Turner* [1975] QB 834.
[24] *Murphy v Queen* (1988-89) 167 CLR 94 at 110.
[25] *DPP v Kehoe* [1992] ILRM 481.
[26] *DPP v Kehoe* [1992] ILRM 481 at 484.

according to the court, give any relevant admissible evidence in relation to state of mind, temperament, etc, that the accused himself could not do. However, according to the court:[27]

'... he attempted to do so, and his approach ... was to say that he had a great deal of experience of people who had been through emotional upset, people who had become involved with drink and drugs, and so forth, and that, therefore, he was in a strong position to give a clinical pronouncement on the reality of the defence that the accused man was putting forward.'

[7.26] In this case the court held that the accused's defence was properly to be considered by the jury without such elaboration.[28] They also held that Dr Behan overstepped the mark in saying he believed the accused did not have an intention to kill and that the accused was telling the truth:

'These are matters four-square within the jury's function and a witness no more than the trial judge or anyone else is not entitled to trespass on what is the jury's function.'[29]

The case is significant in restricting the evidence of an expert to matters without the jury's function – *mens rea*, credibility, etc – and also restricting the admissibility of opinion evidence in relation to mental or emotional disturbance short of an insanity defence, very much in line with *Turner* and distinct from the decision in the Australian case of *Murphy*.

[7.27] The English courts since *Turner* have allowed expert testimony where the evidence would be beyond the normal experience of the jury. In *R v Toner*[30], evidence that a mild hypoglycaemic attack could have negatived specific intent required for a charge of grevious bodily harm was allowed. In *R v Ward*[31] the Court of Appeal allowed psychiatric or psychological testimony that the defendant, while not suffering from a mental illness was suffering from a personality disorder so serious as to be described as a mental disorder, if such evidence demonstrated the unreliability of the defendant's confession.

[7.28] With regard to designation as an expert and receipt of opinion evidence it is significant that the designation of expert status and receipt of opinion is facilitated in the context of drugs/organised crime with the ease one has come to expect in such contexts, whatever strict application of the rules of evidence might have been thought to imply. In *People (DPP) v John Gilligan*,[32] John

---

27 *DPP v Kehoe* [1992] ILRM 481 at 484.
28 *DPP v Kehoe* [1992] ILRM 481 at 484.
29 *DPP v Kehoe* [1992] ILRM 481 at 485.
30 *R v Toner* 93 Cr App R 382.
31 *R v Ward* 96 Cr App R 1.
32 *People (DPP) v John Gilligan* (22 March 2002, unreported), SCC.

Gilligan having been convicted of drug trafficking offences, the Special Criminal Court under s 4 of the Criminal Justice Act 1994, as amended by s 25 of the Criminal Justice Act 1999, had to determine whether he had benefitted from the drug trafficking. The court had to determine the cost, amount, expenses, consideration received and profit in the activities. Assistant Commissioner Tony Hickey was regarded by the court:

'as a person with considerable experience in the field of investigating illicit drug trafficking and, in light of that experience, was in the view of the court a person with a wealth of knowledge of all aspects of illicit drug trafficking.'[33]

The court concluded that he was therefore:

'a person who is well qualified to express a credible opinion or belief on the subject; so much so, that the Court is entitled to regard such opinion and belief as admissible evidence for the purpose of supplying the Court with information which is outside the range and knowledge of the Court.'[34]

[7.29] In *People (DPP) v Fox*[35], evidence of a handwriting expert was put forward by the prosecution to establish that it was the accused's signature which appeared on a passport application form alleged to have been a forgery. The Court quoted from and adopted the principles laid down in *Dowie v Edinburgh Corporation*[36] with reference to the role of the expert:

'Their duty is to furnish the judge or jury with the necessary scientific criteria for testing the accuracy of their conclusions so as to enable the judge or jury to form their own independent judgment by the application of these criteria to the facts proved in evidence. Scientific evidence if intelligible, convincing and tested becomes a factor and often an important factor for consideration, along with the whole other evidence in the case. But the decision is for the judge or jury. In particular the bare *ipso dixit* of a scientist, however eminent, upon the issue in controversy will normally carry little weight for it cannot be tested by cross-examination or independently appraised and the parties have invoked the decision of the judicial tribunal and not an oracular pronouncement by an expert.'

In this case, the court noted that the evidence presented was not backed by any scientific criteria enabling the accuracy of its conclusions to be tested. Normally, various aspects of writing similarities and dissimilarities would be testified to which would have enabled testing by the defence. The expert witness also relied solely on lower case writing and gave no explanation for same. Hence the expert evidence was rejected by the Court.

---

[33] *People (DPP) v John Gilligan* (22 March 2002, unreported), SCC.
[34] *People (DPP) v John Gilligan* (22 March 2002, unreported), SCC.
[35] *People (DPP) v Fox* (23 January 2002, unreported) SCC.
[36] *Dowie v Edinburgh Corporation* [1953] SLT 54.

Defence access to evidence and the duty to preserve evidence

[7.30] With regard to access to material on which to conduct tests and testify, the Irish courts have seen such as being a prerequisite to fair procedure. In *Murphy v DPP*[37], where a fingerprint expert for the defence wished to examine the car in which the alleged offences were carried out, the fact that the car had been disposed of and was now unavailable, was held to amount to a breach of fair procedure.

[7.31] In *Mitchell v DPP*[38] it was held that there was no duty to retain all CCTV recordings, although there will be cases where the Gardaí are obliged to inform the defence of the existence of video evidence, and of any intention to destroy it. In *Braddish v DPP*[39] Hardiman J noted:

> 'It is the duty of the gardaí, arising from their unique investigative role, to seek out and preserve all evidence having a bearing or potential bearing on the issue of guilt or innocence. This is so whether the prosecution proposes to rely on the evidence or not, and regardless of whether it assists the case the prosecution is advancing of not.'

[7.32] In *Dunne v DPP*[40] the only evidence against the appellant on a charge of robbery of a filling station was an alleged signed admission. The prosecution was unable to produce any tapes to the defence when requested, although a number of video cameras covered the station. The High Court had taken the view that it was more likely than not that the gardaí had been given the tapes by the station, but refused relief on the basis of the delay from the date of the offence (January 1998) and the defence's request for them (January 1999). Hardiman J delivered the majority judgment of the Supreme Court, emphasising the duty of the gardaí not simply to preserve evidence, but to seek it out. Hardiman J emphasised that the test applied is whether or not there is a real risk that the applicant will not receive a fair trial. This is a lower standard than the English test of establishing that the defendant cannot receive a fair trial, a standard he characterised as one extraordinarily favourable to the prosecution, and one which involves the English courts looking for bad faith on the part of the authorities. This is not the case in Ireland, and once again fairness is invoked here:

> 'The "real risk" of an unfair trial ... does not necessarily involve blaming any person. The main focus in these applications should be on the *fairness* of the intended trial without the missing evidence, and not on whose fault it is that the

[37] *Murphy v DPP* [1989] ILRM 71.
[38] *Mitchell v DPP* [2000] 2 ILRM 396.
[39] *Braddish v DPP* [2002] 1 ILRM 151 at 157.
[40] *Dunne v DPP* (25 April 2002, unreported) SC.

evidence is missing and what degree of that fault may be. The latter factors, however, are not always relevant.' [Emphasis added].[41]

McGuinness J agreed with Hardiman J as follows:

'Where a court would be asked to prohibit a trial on the grounds that there was an alleged failure to seek out evidence, it would have to be shown that any such evidence would be clearly relevant, that there was at least a strong possibility that the evidence was available, and that it would in reality have a bearing on the guilt or innocence of the accused person. It would also be necessary to demonstrate that its absence created a real risk of an unfair trial.'[42]

[7.33] Fennelly J, in a strong dissenting judgment, took the view that the State's evidence had not been challenged by the applicant who bore the burden of proof, with regard to the authorities possession of the video evidence. In *Robert Dunne v DPP*[43] Fennelly J pointed out that unlike *Braddish*, here it had not been established the video evidence had actually been in the possesion of the gardaí and refused the order of prohibition. In *Swaine v DPP*[44] it was held the prosecution's duty not to hold back material evidence helpful to a defendant may vary with the seriousness of the offence.

Intoxication

[7.34] An area, where a good deal of controversy has arisen, both as to the question of the admissibility of the evidence of a non-expert witness on the issue, and as to the impact of such testimony, if admitted, on the ultimate issue at trial, is that of evidence as to the existence, degree and effect of intoxication. Specifically in the context of charges of driving while intoxicated and the inability to drive while intoxicated, the admissibility of garda evidence (which latter is treated as non-expert testimony for the purpose of the rule) as to drunkenness and capability to drive has arisen. This was facilitated by the original charge under the Road Traffic Act 1961, where the standard was adjudged in terms of incapacity as opposed to intoxication concentration. Incapacity was acknowledged to vary with the person (*AG v Ryan*[45]), and thus many difficulties resulted in the adjudication of same (see the comment by Pierse to the effect that convictions are up to 65 per cent greater since the introduction of scientific tests in the area).[46] However, the incapacity standard may still well be utilised in the event of a refusal to give a sample; and is of

---

[41] (25 April 2002, unreported), Supreme Court at 27.
[42] (25 April 2002, unreported), Supreme Court at 3.
[43] *Robert Dunne v DPP* (25 April 2002), SC Fennelly J.
[44] *Swaine v DPP* (26 April 2002), SC.
[45] *AG v Ryan* [1975] IR 367.
[46] Pierse *Road Traffic Law in the Republic of Ireland* (1st edn, 1989).

considerable jurisprudential worth in terms of differing views expressed as to the value of opinion evidence.

[7.35] The definitive position under Irish law as to the admissibility of non-expert opinion evidence on (a) drunkenness and (b) incapacity to drive, within the context of a charge of intoxicated driving under s 49 of the 1961 Act (using the said 'incapacity test', ie, whether the defendant was under the influence of an intoxicant to such an extent as to be incapable of having proper control of the vehicle)[47], is set out in *AG (Ruddy) v Kenny*.[48] The prosecution here tendered the evidence of a Garda witness, to the effect that, in his opinion, the defendant 'was drunk and incapable of driving the vehicle'.

[7.36] In the High Court, Davitt P stated:

> 'Drunkenness, unfortunately, is a condition which is not so exceptional or so much outside the experience of the ordinary individual, that it should require an expert to diagnose it. In my opinion a Garda witness may give evidence of his opinion as to whether a person is drunk or not.'

In relation to the second question – whether a non-expert may express his opinion as to whether a defendant is drunk to such an extent as to be incapable of exercising proper control over a mechanically-propelled vehicle – Davitt P continued:

> 'It seems to me that if it is admissible for an ordinary witness to express his opinion as to whether a defendant is drunk or not, it should be admissible for him to express an opinion as to how drunk he was.'

[7.37] On appeal to the Supreme Court, the majority endorsed Davitt P's position that non-expert opinion evidence was admissible on both issues. In terms of both determination of the ultimate issue at trial (incapacity due to intoxication) and the subjectivity involved in the criteria, the decision is assailable. In this regard Kingsmill-Moore J's dissent in the Supreme Court is noteworthy:

> 'It is a long-standing rule of our law of evidence that, with certain exceptions, a witness may not express an opinion as to a fact in issue. Ideally in the theory of our law, a witness may testify only to the existence of fact which he has observed with one or more of his own five senses. It is for the tribunal of fact – judge or jury as the case may be – to draw inferences of fact, form opinions and come to conclusions. The witness, as far as possible, puts the judge and jury in the position of having been present at the place and time when the fact deposed occurred and having been able to make the observations. The witness may be lying, his powers of observation may be deficient, his ability to express clearly

---

[47] Pierse *Road Traffic Law in the Republic of Ireland* (1st edn, 1989) s 4.9.1 at p 182.
[48] *AG (Ruddy) v Kenny* (1960) 94 ILTR 185.

what he observed may be inadequate, his memory may be faulty. These are inescapable hazards. But it is possible to avoid the further hazards of prejudice, faulty reasoning and inadequate knowledge which would be introduced if a witness were allowed to have his opinion and the tribunal of fact were allowed to act upon it.'

[7.38] In addition to placing the issue in the context of the role of a witness (testimonial) and that of the arbiter of fact (determinative) in the legal process, Kingsmill-Moore J reminds us of the vagaries of the term concerned. He points out that admitting evidence of opinion that a person was drunk is grounded on the vagueness of that term which can incorporate anything from 'stone cold sober' to 'dead drunk'. All is dependent on what that particular witness understands as drunkenness. Kingsmill-Moore J similarly objects to the admission of a further expression of opinion as to whether the defendant is incapable of driving a motor vehicle. Opinion evidence by a non-expert, he regards as being 'either obtiose or dangerous', particularly when the expression of opinion is as to the exact question at issue. He concludes:

'I am of the opinion that the interests of justice can be adequately served by getting a witness to describe the appearance, movements, demeanour, actions and words of a person whose condition is in question and leaving it to the District Justice to draw his own conclusions'.

[7.39] Other jurisdictions have grappled with these same issues in a similar context and it is interesting to consider and contrast their views. The English courts considered the question in *R v Davies*.[49] In relation to the same dual issue considered in *Kenny*, Parker LJ held that opinion evidence as to whether the defendant was drunk was admissible and opinion evidence as to the defendant's capability to drive inadmissible.

[7.40] In *Sherrard v Jacob*,[50] the Northern Ireland Court of Appeal held opinion evidence as to the issue of drunkenness admissible. On the issue of capability to drive, Curran and McVeigh JJ held opinion evidence on the issue inadmissible while McDermott LCJ would have deemed opinion evidence on both issues admissible. His dissenting judgment is again interesting for a perspective on the matter which takes issue with the artificiality of so restricting opinion evidence – a logic perhaps not dissimilar to that favoured by the Irish courts in *Kenny*. McDermott LCJ stated:

'I can find no good reason for allowing the non-expert witness to give his opinion of the driver's observable condition, and then denying him the right to state an

---

[49] *R v Davies* [1962] 3 All ER 97.
[50] *Sherrard v Jacob* [1975] NI 151.

opinion on the consequences of that observed opinion, as far as driving is concerned.'

[7.41] The logic of this 'all or nothing' approach is persuasive, but could just as easily be used to argue the contrary position, ie, that favoured by Kingsmill Moore J – non-admissibility on both issues.

[7.42] Howsoever that might be, the position is now a well-established one that the opinion of a non-expert is admissible on both these issues; and given the supersedence of proof of intoxication by reference to a certificate of alcohol concentration is such cases, is not likely to be reviewed. However, the question of a non-expert's opinion has arisen as seen in *DPP v Richard Kenny*,[51] where a doctor (albeit an expert, although not perhaps on this issue), was tendered to give evidence as to the accused's observable condition.

The accused was arrested under s 49(6) of the Road Traffic Act 1961. On arrival at the garda station he consented to a sample of blood being taken by a designated registered medical practitioner. No analysis was ever made of that sample. Subsequently, he was charged with the offence of being intoxicated to such an extent as to be incapable of having proper control of his vehicle, contrary to s 49(1)(4)(a) of the Road Traffic Act 1961 as amended.

[7.43] At the hearing the issue centred on whether the medical practitioner concerned could give evidence as to his observation of the accused, and his opinion as to his fitness to drive. The case stated concerned the same issue, viz, whether a right to privacy existed such as that he should have been cautioned as to the tendering of such evidence. It was submitted that, notwithstanding his lawful arrest, the accused was entitled to his privacy in the sense that persons, including the doctor, could not be brought into his company for the purpose of observing his behaviour. Barron J noted that in *Sullivan v Robinson*[52] Davitt P dealt with the need to caution suspects in circumstances akin to the present case, and felt these similar to situations of confession or admission in so far as the same principles apply. Per Barron J:

'That ... suggests that the evidence of the condition of an accused should not be given by a doctor called on behalf of the gardaí unless such accused had consented to be examined or tested. There is not however anything in the passage which suggests that evidence cannot be given as to the condition of the accused by those who were lawfully required to deal with him or has otherwise observed him lawfully.'

[7.44] Here the accused had consented to a sample of his blood being taken by the doctor. Barron J felt it was perfectly permissible for the doctor to give

---

[51] *DPP v Richard Kenny* (8 March 1990, unreported) HC (Barron J).
[52] *Sullivan v Robinson* [1954] IR 161.

evidence of his observation of the accused incidental to the taking of that sample. Many of the authorities cited on behalf of the applicant dealt with cases where evidence was obtained while the accused was in unlawful detention. These cases he felt had no bearing on the present case. The two questions raised were thus answered as follows:

(1) The accused does have a right to privacy while in custody.

(2) This right of privacy is not breached by observation of the accused by persons who are lawfully required to deal with him while in custody. Whether it would be breached by observation of the accused by persons in any other category and if so in what circumstances, does not arise for decision.

Although perhaps in the broader context of opinion evidence, those opinions of experts may prove in future to be more controversial than non-experts, issue can still arise (as in the case of drunkenness and capability to drive) as to the admissibility of such testimony.

[7.45] The mandatory nature of garda opinion in the context of road traffic offences arose in *DPP v Pascal Lynch*[53]. Here the respondent was prosecuted under s 13 of the Road Traffic (Amendment) Act 1978 for failure to permit a designated medical practitioner to take a specimen of his blood or providing for same a specimen of urine. The respondent was acquitted and a case stated to High Court. The facts were that Garda Fitzgerald on 10 October 1989 stopped a motor vehicle driven by the respondent, formed an opinion that the latter was incapable of driving and arrested him and brought him to the Bridewell. The respondent was later introduced to a registered medical practitioner, and was requested to permit the doctor to take from him a sample of his blood or provide him with sample of urine but refused.

[7.46] Counsel for the respondent submitted that the charge should be dismissed for want of evidence validating the arrest, to the effect that the garda, when making the arrest, had formed the opinion that the respondent was committing or had committed an offence under the Road Traffic Acts. The appellant conceding that no positive evidence to this effect had been given, and that such was a necessary link in the chain of proof to lead to a conviction, submitted there was a clear inference that the garda had formed the necessary opinion. The appellant relied on the Supreme Court decision of *DPP v O'Connor*[54] in particular. However, the circumstances in that case were of a very extreme nature, involving the driving of a bus in a very dangerous manner etc. That judgment should not be read, according to O'Hanlon J:

---

[53] *DPP v Pascal Lynch* (7 November 1990, unreported) HC (O'Hanlon J).

[54] *DPP v O'Connor* [1985] ILRM 333.

'[as] a statement that in every case where a Garda informs a person who is being arrested that he is being arrested under the provisions of s 49(6) of the Road Traffic Act 1961 (as amended by the Road Traffic (Amendment) Act 1978) there is a necessary inference to be drawn he has concurrently formed the opinion that the person who is placed under arrest is committing or has committed an offence under s 49'.

The rule in *Hollington v Hewthorn*

[7.47] Before considering further the implications of greater reliance on expert testimony amidst increasing concern as to its probity, mention should be made of the existence of a particular rule in the context of the Irish law on opinion evidence, which has been statutorily removed in our neighouring jurisdictions of Northern Ireland and England. The rule is that laid down in the case of *Hollington v Hewthorn*.[55] It provides that a judicial finding is inadmissible as evidence of the facts found in relation to different proceedings. For example, if D runs his car up on a footpath and hits someone and is subsequently charged and convicted of careless driving, the rule provides that in a subsequent civil action for personal injuries, arising out of that same incident, the plaintiff will not be able to introduce evidence of such conviction as proof of the defendant's negligence. This is because that finding is regarded as judicial opinion on the matter. It is otherwise, of course, if the defendant in the initial charge pleaded guilty. In that event, evidence of his plea (analogous to a confession) would be admitted. It is evidence of the judicial finding on the facts that is excluded by the rule. Of course, in practice, the rule may well be more honoured in the breach than the observance and has been removed in other jurisdictions where it fell into disrepute. In any event, it is mitigated in effect because of the practical factors dictating the plaintiff's keeping a 'watching brief' on the prior criminal action which, if successful, will indicate the relative ease with which the lower civil standard of proof will be met if the criminal standard has already been attained. In England the rule in *Hollington v Hewthorn* was overruled by the Civil Evidence Act 1968, ss 11–13 in regard to civil cases, the Police and Evidence Act 1984, ss 74 and 75 making similar provision for criminal cases. In *Kelly v Ireland*,[56] O'Hanlon J in the High Court left open the question of whether *Hollington v Hewthorn* was good law in Ireland.

Expert evidence: personal injuries actions

[7.48] There is a long-established practice in personal injury actions of examination of a plaintiff by a medical specialist on behalf of the defence,

---

[55] *Hollington v Hewthorn* [1943] 1 KB 587.
[56] *Kelly v Ireland* [1986] ILRM 318 at 327.

traditionally in the presence of the plaintiff's expert. The practice of joint examination gave way, however, to examination of injured plaintiffs on their own by defence specialists. This led to a situation where complications, not readily discernible from particulars furnished to the defence (which right has emerged on a joint examination) would arise at trial. Section 45 of the Courts and Court Officers Act 1995 attempted to address that difficulty in so far as it provided that notwithstanding any rule of privilege pertaining to legal advice, attaching to such documents any such report from an expert intended to be called to give evidence of a medical opinion in relation to an issue in the case could be ordered to be disclosed by the court.

The objective was to shorten the length of personal injury trials and to reduce costs. Under the Rules of the Superior Courts (No 6) (Disclosure of Reports and Statements) 1998,[57] new rules introduced in October 1998 further clarified the situation to ensure that actions covered included any claim for charges for personal injuries however caused and reports included a report from any expert including doctors, engineers, scientists, etc.

The difficulty experts – particularly medical experts – faced in these contexts is whether potentially prejudicial information should be included. This of course is a product of difficulties adhering to perceptions of their role (as advocate when it would not be included or 'independent' expert (when it should).[58]

Expert opinion: controversy

[7.49] Throughout the law of evidence are found examples of judicial scepticism with regard to the probity of certain types of evidence: either because of the intrinsic nature of the evidence or the manner in which it was obtained. For this reason, rules have been developed to mark judicial wariness in the admissibility for example, of confession evidence, and the consequent development of the requirement of voluntariness. By contrast, forensic evidence, particularly, was regarded as being of that species of expert testimony which was objective, rational, scientific, immutable and reliable.

[7.50] Hence the judiciary, with what may appear to have been unseemly haste, rushed to rely on same, and defence counsel, faced with a species of knowledge of which they did not even have the rudiments to begin querying, accepted it at face value and threw in the metaphorical towel. This was a particularly insidious development given the absence of independent forensic laboratory testing facilities in this country. Gradually, however, question marks began to appear

---

[57] (SI 391/1998). Although the Rules came into force on 14 October 1998, they apply to proceedings begun on or after 1 September 1997.

[58] See Barr, J 'Expert Evidence – A few Personal Observations and Implications of Recent Statutory Development' Bar Review, Jan/Feb 1999 at 186.

over the actual probity of the glass shards found in the accused's clothing, or the carpet fibres on his shoes. Although they did match those of the house in which the crime was perpetrated, the apparent potency weakened when it was discovered that such materials enter this country in very large quantities, and their distribution is such that carpet fibres in Ballymun are as similar as to those in Killorglin, as the glass strands in Galway are as alike as to those in Meath.

[7.51] Difficulty also pertains as to the safeguarding of procedure observance in the obtaining of forensic results. Witness the controversy as to the concentration of test material used, and the ultimate probity of its results, in the light of scientific developments in the *'Birmingham Six'* case. The use of the 'Griess test' on the defendants to give a positive result was interpreted by the Home Office scientists (Dr Skuse in particular) to give a 99% certainty that the men had been in recent contact with high explosives. In fact, the 'Griess test' was subsequently discovered to react positively with nitrocellulose, an everyday substance also found on veneers and present on the railway seats and playing cards with which the men had been in contact. Quite apart, then, from difficulties with regard to the adherence to procedure in the carrying out of the test in that case, a changing scientific consensus as to its merit or probative worth was evident. This, in relation to what the trial judge termed 'the clearest and most overwhelming evidence I have ever heard'.

[7.52] Difficulties in challenging confession evidence have been recently ameliorated by the development of techniques enabling linguistic analysis of words allegedly spoken by defendants (the 'Morten test' of linguistic analysis used in the *'Armagh Four'* case); and electro-static document analysis (ESDA) (used to challenge the contemporaneity of police notes in the *'Birmingham Six'*[59] case). Further potential for challenging the veracity of personal injury claims (particularly back pain), is now provided by isokinetic machines (currently available in Dublin's Blackrock Clinic, not used yet in Ireland). All such developments raise concerns surrounding the implications of forensic/expert testimony for legal proceedings particularly severe in criminal jury adjudication.[60]

DNA evidence

[7.53] The difficulty is, of course, a cultural one: a clash between the scientific world accustomed to 'black holes' and 'scientific revolutions'[61] – and the legal

---

[59] See further Jackson *One Word against Another, the Effect of ESDA Evidence* (1991) Vol 7 Ir Crim LJ 18; Bob Woffinden *Miscarriages of Justice* Hodder and Stoughton (1989).

[60] See further (1992) Sunday Tribune, 2 February 'Spinal Trap For Courts' at p 4.

[61] Thomas Kuhn *Structure of Scientific Revolutions* (1990).

one where such qualified certainties are not sufficient. A manifestation of this clash and the difficulties lawyers must face in coming to terms with same, is evident from the current controversy with regard to DNA (genetic fingerprint) evidence – its probity and the obtaining of same.

[7.54] Moreover, the context in which this concern had developed, highlights the difficulties of funding the expertise for mounting such challenges (particularly important for the defence). Indeed the extent to which the Irish legislature currently appears overwilling to facilitate the obtaining of genetic fingerprinting evidence and its subsequent admissibility in criminal trials – without adequate procedural safeguards or defence access to independent forensics, and in the light of growing scientific unease as to its probity – is worrying. Lawyers and legislators alike, must become aware that science is no more immutable than human nature; human fallibility has an input at the procedural level of the application of 'the test' and the test itself may be less probative empirically than originally mooted.

[7.55] DNA provides a perfect example of this clash of legal and scientific culture. Based on the discovery that we each have a genetic fingerprint which is individual and so identifiable to us, DNA fingerprint evidence was initially tendered in immigration claims based on blood relationships and in paternity suits. (See for example, *JPD v MG*,[62] where a wife sought an order pursuant to s 38 of the Status of Children Act 1987, to the effect that both children and husband and wife should submit to DNA tests. The context was one where the plaintiff husband was seeking sole custody of the children, the defendant wife alleging they were not in fact his.) Gradually it found its way into criminal trials – offering particular potential in the context of sexual offences, where traces of blood or semen could link one person to a particular incident.

[7.56] One of the first criminal trials in the United Kingdom to illustrate the potential of this evidence, both in terms of exoneration and implication, was that of *R v Pitchfork*[63], where Pitchfork was both discovered and convicted of murder, rape and indecent assault on the basis of his DNA fingerprints, and a 17 year-old youth, initially arrested and charged for the offence, exonerated. Yet, quiescent in that case was an indication of the potential for a miscarriage of justice inherent in this type of forensic testimony. Pitchfork had initially evaded capture, on the basis of the substitution of a sample from a friend, for his own. This fact served as an early indicator of the importance of procedure and effective monitoring of the manner in which samples are obtained and tested. These difficulties may be compounded, of course, where in a criminal case (unlike an

---

[62] *JPD v MG* [1991] ILRM 212.

[63] *R v Pitchfork* (1998) The Guardian, 23 January.

immigration or paternity case) there may only be a very small sample available, which may be damaged or have deteriorated to some degree.

[7.57] All of these variable considerations and facts which impact upon this type of evidence came to light in the American context where leading scientists first warned of the dangers inherent in an unqualified acceptance by the legal world of the products of science. The result is an interesting insight into a cultural clash which results when two particular fields of knowledge, having different perspectives, attempt to fashion an alliance which is not cognisant of the implications of an unquestioning acceptance of the premises of the other. The history of this clash between scientific discovery and legal adjudication is valuable for the insight it gives into the potential for injustice, should law follow too readily at the heels of 'cutting edge' science.

[7.58] In the June 1989 issue of the journal *Nature*, Dr Eric S Lander, in an article entitled 'DNA Fingerprinting on Trial'[64], described the pitfalls in the forensic use of the technique of DNA fingerprinting. Central to the difficulty was that DNA, like most other evidence, requires interpretation. 'Interpretation' of data is inevitably influenced by a difference in perspective between legal and scientific investigation. The journal's editor commented that:

'Both pretend to discover truth, science by continually narrowing the range of allowable dispute, the law by its supposition that the judicial process can conjure truth from whatever data are available. Courts are not content with declaration that defendants are, say, 60% guilty, nor should they be ...'

[7.59] Dr Lander pointed out that DNA fingerprint evidence, since first introduced in a trial in Florida in 1988, has been used in more than 80 criminal trials in the United States. Trial judges, he suggests:

'... have raced to admit DNA fingerprinting as evidence on the grounds that the methods are "generally accepted in the scientific community", citing the application of RFLP's in DNA diagnostics and accepting claims that false positives are virtually impossible.'

Dr Lander took issue with the courts' enthusiasm:

'With due respect, the courts have been too hasty. Although DNA fingerprinting clearly offers tremendous potential as a forensic tool, the rush has obscured two critical points: first, DNA fingerprinting is far more technically demanding than DNA diagnostics; and second, the scientific community has not yet agreed on standards that ensure the reliability of the evidence.'

[7.60] Dr Lander pointed out that DNA fingerprinting results were being introduced into US criminal courts without adequate safeguards: 'Not only are

---

[64]   Eric S Lander *DNA Fingerprinting on Trial* (1989) 339, Nature 501-505.

mixing experiments and internal controls often omitted, but some laboratories use no objective standards whatsoever for declaring a match'. Lander's rather disturbing conclusion, then, is that the scientific community has failed to attain rigorous standards to which courts, attorneys and forensic testing laboratories can look for guidance – with the result that some of the conclusions presented to the courts are quite unreliable. This danger was graphically illustrated by reference to one particular murder trial in New York.

The Castro *case*

[7.61] On 5 February 1987 Vilma Ponce and her two year-old daughter were stabbed to death in their Bronx apartment. The police, acting on a tip-off, interviewed Jose Castro, a local handyman. A small bloodstain on Castro's watch was sent for analysis. It is here that the difficulties arose. Dr Lander discusses the procedure used by the laboratory concerned (Lifecodes), and takes issue with it, in so far as it was not sufficiently cognisant of the importance of procedure, and the dangerous implications of not adequately monitoring comparison in this context. Lifecodes issued a report to the District Attorney stating that the DNA patterns on the watch and of the mother matched, and reporting the frequency of the pattern to be about 1 in 100,000,000 in the Hispanic population. The report indicated no difficulties or ambiguities, yet according to Dr Lander, there was several. For example, with regard to comparison of DNA bands found on the watch and in the mother Dr Lander comments that:

'The tendency to use lane-to-lane comparison to distinguish between bands and artifacts is perfectly natural; such comparison can be quite helpful in certain experiments. However, in my opinion, it is inappropriate in DNA fingerprinting analysis of unknown samples – as one runs the risk of discounting precisely those differences that would exonerate an innocent defendant. Forensic laboratories should be required to use objective criteria for identifying the bands in each lane, and to use experiments to rule out proposed artifacts.'

[7.62] According to Dr Lander, when a result is reported to have an error rate of 1 in 100,000,000, it seems essential that the underlying data are not left as a matter of subjective opinion. Under the objective matching rule in this case, the bands were poor matches – yet a match was declared. Dr Lander concludes that there had been a significant misunderstanding about the matching rule Lifecodes had been using. In any event, he feels visual matching is inappropriate in DNA fingerprinting, in as much as:

(1)   many alleles have very similar sizes;

(2)   the accuracy of the measurement process is reported to be known; and

(3)   without an objective definition of a match, there is no meaningful way
to determine the probability that a declared match might have arisen
by chance.

[7.63] Further difficulties arose with regard to the control of DNA in that case,
of which no precise record had been kept. Moreover, the small quantity of DNA
on the watch, was clearly degraded, and as nearly 90% of alleles in the Hispanic
population lie above 10.25 kb, one could not be sure whether the sample was a
homozygous for a 10.25kb, as contended, or a heterozygote with a higher band
undetected due to degradation.

[7.64] Further difficulties also included the fact that whatever matching rule is
used to declare a forensic match, should also be used for counting the matches
occurring in the population database; yet in fact, Lifecodes did not use the same
matching rule. In addition, to justify applying the classical formulas of
population genetics in the *Castro* case, the Hispanic population must be in the
Hardy-Weinberg equilibrium. In fact, it is not.[65] Quite apart from the
significance of the *Castro* case, in terms of Dr Lander's analysis of the
procedure used by the laboratory for the DNA matching process, the case itself
is significant in terms of the manner of discovery of the inadequacies of the
process.

[7.65] In the *Castro* case, the prosecution witness, whose testimony was
intended to provide the court with a primer on DNA analysis, became concerned
about the evidence tendered and organised a joint scientific meeting of experts
from either side to review that evidence. The result was a statement by the
experts to the effect that 'the DNA data in the case are not scientifically reliable
enough to support the assertion that the samples ... do or do not match'. The
prosecution nevertheless persisted with the case, in the course of which, former
prosecution witnesses now testified for the defence.

[7.66] Although ultimately a vindication of expert credibility or ethics in this
context, the case may be seen to illustrate the inability of lawyers alone to raise a
doubt sufficient to pierce the veil of scientific immutability. Lawyers, without
scientific knowledge and co-operation, have difficulty contending with such
testimony. Dr Lander instances a death penalty case where a Lifecodes scientist
testified to the effect that the process was a very simple one 'Either it matches or

---

[65]   Eric S Lander *DNA Fingerprinting on Trial* (1989) 339, Nature, p 504. The classical test for
Hardy-Weinberg equilibrium is based on the principle that the rate of homozygosity in a
population containing distinct sub-groups will be higher than would be expected under the
assumption of random mating. This is not without considerable significance in the context of
the Irish population.

it doesn't. It's like if you walk into the parking lot and see two Fords parked next to each other.'[66]

The statement is patently misleading, as DNA discrepancies are not necessarily visible to the eye, but lawyers must themselves become aware, and make the court aware, of that fact. Some degree of tenacity may well be called for, as in the case of *New York v Neysmith*[67]. The accused hired Lifecodes to compare his blood with the allegedly incriminating semen samples, and challenged their initial reaction that the blood may not have been his own, which led to their second contention that a further sample had a different source, to the third submission, which resulted in their admission that an error had occurred. Neysmith had almost lost his liberty as a result of the error.

[7.67] Significantly, DNA evidence has been most recently invoked in the United States in aid of indigent defendants who are on death row in an attempt to prove their innocence. This is as a result of the Innocence Project run by Barry Scheck and Peter Neufeld at the Benjamin N Cardozo Law School, New York, which reportedly has exonerated 131 prisoners serving long sentences following DNA testing.[68]

[7.68] Meanwhile, in terms of the use of DNA evidence by the prosecution, controversies have continued to emerge – for instance, with regard to the reliability of the methodology used to correct for 'band shifting'. This refers to the fact that samples from the same person will not run at exactly the same speed every time. The buffer, gel and salt solution used in testing are all manufactured and can vary minutely between batches – hence the lanes into which samples are poured can have varied imperfections. The result is called band shift: the banding of two different samples containing the same DNA may not line up exactly – close but not exact. This returns us to differences in acceptability of proof and implications of innocence, with science having a different mandate from law.[69] DNA evidence has already been used in serious crimes in Ireland including those of murder and rape.

---

[66] *Georgia v Caldwell* (1987) per Lander, p 505.

[67] (1987) Lander, p 505.

[68] Law Society Gazette, Vol 100 No 01 at p 13, 'Morton's Musings'. See also www.innocenceproject.org.

[69] See, for example, the adoption of *Daubert v Merrell Dew* (US Supreme Court 1993), standard by Louisiana Supreme Court in *State v Foret* (Louisiana SC 1993), to determine the procedure used by Lifecodes, the laboratory, to correct for band-shifting is not a reliable methodology and inadmissible.

See further, *New Law Journal* 7 February 1997 Butterworths Vol 147 No. 677 at p 187 *NLJ Expert Witness Supplement* 'Band Shift in DNA Evidence' by Brian McConnell.

[7.69] In an early article on the issue in the British context, Andrew Hall[70] expressed concern that, although not per se posing a threat to civil liberties, 'the uniqueness of the procedure ... may hold unique dangers in the absence of a critical approach by both lawyers and forensic scientists'. Hall elucidated the fear that the process should become '... a black box into which the scientific evidence is placed at one end and the verdict in a criminal case is produced at the other'. Hall rightly pointed out that it is the very complexity of the science involved in DNA analysis which may pose difficulties. Lawyers and juries may well not understand it and become overwhelmed by it. The evidence is unlike fingerprint evidence, in so far as accuracy depends on extremely precise measurement of the distance DNA fragments have travelled in the gel, and as seen, minute discrepancies between DNA fingerprint bands not necessarily visible to the eye, may wholly undermine positive identification. In *Doheny*[71] Phillips LJ emphasised in an important judgment on DNA evidence, that the expert witness should not express a view on the probability of the defendant's guilt, given the DNA match. That is for the jury to decide.

[7.70] One further difficulty is a practical one involving current access to alternative testing facilities, given the absence of such laboratories in Ireland. The requisite control may therefore be more apparent than real. The dangers of inadequate testing or regulation of procedure will not be revealed if evident, and a failure to provide adequate safeguards will risk the conviction of, or failure to exonerate, the innocent and perhaps aid the acquittal of the guilty[72].

[7.71] These issues need to be addressed by the Irish legislature. Unfortunately, in the haste to provide adequate powers for the gardaí to obtain samples to use in the detection and prosecution of crime, the Irish legislature would seem to have lost sight of the context – both forensic and legal. Despite advances in forensic science and DNA testing in particular, the point should not be lost that there is a different culture in operation in both these contexts, and as the *Castro* case still validity demonstrates, usurpation of the one by the other diminishes both.

---

[70] *Andrew Hall* (1990) NJ 203.
[71] *Doheny* [1997] 1 Cr App R 396, CA.
[72] See further comments of Hall, p 204 viz:

> 'Another unique feature of the technique is the virtual monopoly over testing procedures. The *Jeffreys* testing system is subject to patent, and so far as the writer is able to discover, only the police scientific laboratories and Cellmark Diagnostics, a private company, are able to apply the procedure in the United Kingdom ... since the same procedures are used by the police forensic laboratories and by Cellmark, if laboratory techniques are less than perfect, or if the underlying science is flawed, there may simply be a replication of the same inaccurate result. Where a scientific process is unregulated and the procedure is essentially a 'trade secret'- what protection is there in this vitally important area.'

Criminal Justice (Forensic Evidence) Act 1990

[7.72] Since the introduction of the Criminal Justice (Forensic Evidence) Act 1990, it has been apparent that the Irish legislature, and public favour the implementation of provisions securing the facility for use of genetic fingerprinting information in the criminal process. The 1990 Act, as passed, provides that the powers conferred on the Garda Síochána to obtain such information are without prejudice to any other powers exercisable by them. Such other powers would include all relevant garda common law and statutory powers. Particularly noteworthy, perhaps, are those related to 'ordinary' fingerprinting, and those found under the Status of Children Act 1987. Our most recent provision has been in the context of an arrest under s 4 of the Criminal Justice Act 1984, in relation to which, regulations provide that fingerprints, palm prints or photographs shall not be taken of, or swabs or samples taken from, a person in custody except with his written consent.[73]

[7.73] In the context of arrests not under the Criminal Justice Act 1984, provision is made by the Regulations as to the Measuring and Photographing of Prisoners 1955.[74] These permit an untried person to have fingerprints taken if he has been informed of his right to object, but does not do so. Without his consent, he may nevertheless be fingerprinted with the Minister's authority or upon approval of an application of a garda (not below the rank of Inspector) to a Justice of the District Court, or in Dublin by a Commissioner or Deputy Commissioner.

[7.74] Authority in relation to those detained under s 30 of the Offences Against the State Act 1939 is provided by s 7(1) of the Criminal Law (Jurisdiction) Act 1976, which allows fingerprinting and explosive tests (hair and skin swabs, also) to be carried out. Relevant in this context is the Status of Children Act 1987, Part VII which makes provision for the use of blood tests as evidence in questions of parentage arising in civil proceedings. Section 37 of the 1987 Act defines 'blood tests' as any test carried out with the object of ascertaining inheritable characteristics. According to the explanatory memorandum this includes such tests as serological analysis, enzyme analysis, tissue typing and DNA profiling.

[7.75] Under s 38 of the 1990 Act, a court, either of its own motion or on an application by any party to the proceedings, can give a direction for the use of blood tests for the purpose of assisting the court to determine parentage.
Section 39 of that Act provides that a blood sample should not be taken from that person, except with his consent. However, the court may draw such

---

[73] Regulations with regard to the treatment of persons in Garda custody, SI 119/1987, s 18. (See Appendix A).
[74] Regulations as to the Measuring and Photographing of Prisoners (SI 114/1955).

inferences, if any, from the failure to consent, as appear proper in the circumstances (s 38(1)). Interestingly, s 43 provides for penalties for personation of blood tests.

[7.76] In accordance with the regime under the 1990 Act, it is that period consequent on arrest which is most significant. This is because the bench-mark as to when an individual can become the subject of such a test is under s 2 of the Act when that person is 'in custody' under s 30 of the Offences Against the State Act 1939, or s 4 of the Criminal Justice Act 1984. Presumably that means any time during the period following the arrest, right up to appearance in court – potentially 48 hours or 20 hours respectively. (The maximum potential period of detention under s 30 is two 24 hour periods. Section 4 of the 1984 Act allows for two periods of 6 hours, but because of an inability to count the hours between 12 and 8 am the potential maximum is 20 hours). Difficulties inherent in the concept of 'custody' arise: the position of an individual 'helping the police with their inquiries' (presumably, if voluntary not in custody, if in *People (DPP) v O'Loughlin's*[75] situation a valid subject for the test) an individual deemed not to be voluntarily helping the police with their inquiries, a Garda witness declared that he would have arrested the accused if he had attempted to leave); that of an individual unlawfully arrested (whether 'cured' or not, *People v Walsh*[76] allowed for the concept of 'curing' of an unlawful period of arrest – where individual has not been told of the reason for same); and that of an individual held longer than the permitted period (*People v Madden*[77]). Failure to observe strictly the temporal limitations of the s 30 detention provisions in a situation where the accused commenced making a confession statement shortly before the expiry of same and was detained further to facilitate its completion, led to the court constituting same a breach of rights.

[7.77] Presumably, all of the jurisprudence to date on that issue, exercised in the context of other forms of evidence (eg testimony or real evidence (*People (DPP) v Kenny*))[78], should apply with at least as much vigour here. Counter arguments based on the immutability or reliability of DNA data could not be sustained in light of *Kenny.*

[7.78] Samples which can be taken under the 1990 Act are divided in terms of those requiring consent on the part of the person concerned, and those which do not. Section 4(b) of the 1990 Act provides that the appropriate consent must be given in writing in relation to the following samples:

---

[75] *People (DPP) v O'Loughlin* [1975] IR 85.
[76] *People v Walsh* [1980] IR 294.
[77] *People v Madden* [1977] IR 336.
[78] *People (DPP) v Kenny* [1990] ILRM 569.

(a)   blood;

(b)   pubic hair;

(c)   urine;

(d)   saliva;

(e)   a swab from a body orifice or a genital region;

(f)   a dental impression.

The other samples allowed, provided for by the Act – viz, hair other than pubic hair, a nail, any material found under a nail, a footprint or similar impression of any part of the person's body other than a part of his hand or mouth – do not require consent.

[7.79] This method of distinguishing between those samples – the taking of which does or does not require consent – merits criticism on two grounds. Firstly, the exhaustive listing of all samples to be taken under the auspices of the 1990 Act is questionable, in terms of the ongoing development of this science to facilitate testing of less obvious material for a DNA profile (there are already indications that hair samples, for example, may be sufficient)[79]. DNA profiling, therefore, might be feasible under other garda powers which the Act does not prejudice, but would then be without even these limited safeguards foreseen by the Act.

[7.80] Secondly, the list method is a non-principled basis for distinction, and in similar fashion to the categorical approach of the English Act ('intimate' and 'non-intimate'), facilitates all too readily a modification of that number requiring consent. (Sections 62-63 of the Police and Criminal Evidence Act 1984 permit taking of 'intimate' and 'non-intimate' samples. Section 65 defines an 'intimate' sample as: 'a sample of blood, semen or any other tissue, fluid, urine, saliva or pubic hair, or a swab taken from a person's body orifice'. A 'non-intimate' sample means: '(a) a sample of hair other than pubic hair; (b) a sample taken from a nail or under a nail; (c) a swab taken from any part of a person's body other than a body orifice; (d) a footprint or similar impression of any part of a person's body other than a part of his hand'.) In this regard, witness the recategorisation in Northern Ireland of mouth (or buccal) swabs as 'non-intimate'.[80] Under the Criminal Justice Bill 2000 (proposed to implement the Expert Group recommendations of 25 November 1998), saliva was reportedly to be classified as a non-intimate sample and gardaí to be able to use reasonable force to obtain non-intimate samples like saliva.[81]

---

[79]   Lawrence Connors (1989) Irish Times, 17 June referred to by Walter & Cram 'DNA Profiling and Police Powers' (1990) Crim LR at pp 479, 487.

[80]   Article 53 of the Police and Criminal Evidence (Northern Ireland) Order 1989. Cf Walter and Cram 'DNA Profiling & Police Powers' (1990) Crim LR 479 at 486.

[81]   'Sweeping Powers for Gardaí in War against Crime', Irish Examiner, 18 February 2000.

[7.81] There is a requirement under the 1990 Act that the garda officer with the requisite authorisation (who cannot be below the rank of Superintendent (s 2(5)(a) of the 1990 Act) has 'reasonable grounds' for suspecting the involvement of the person from whom the sample is to be taken. Whether – given that the individual is already 'in custody' in relation to that crime – these would ever be found to be absent is questionable), and unlike the analogous prerequisite in warrant procedures for entry onto private property, there is no provision for an outside (judicial) review of same. In general, as seen warrant procedures require the swearing of an information before an independent third party – usually someone with a judicial standing.

[7.82] A further requirement is that there must be a belief that the sample will tend to confirm or disprove the involvement of the person (s 2(5)(b) of the 1990 Act). Since this does not require conclusiveness from the test result, the aim of the section is not clear.

[7.83] Provision is also made under s 2(b) of the 1990 Act for informing the individual of the nature of the offence, the authorisation been given, and that the results may be given in evidence. Although the provision does include a caution of sorts, it is as remiss as the equivalent English provision in failing to provide a requirement relating to legal advice or prior judicial authorisation (s 62(2) of the Police and Criminal Evidence Act 1984). Section 2(8) of the 1990 Act requires that certain samples be taken by a medical practitioner: blood, pubic hair, swabs from body orifices or genital regions.

[7.84] In the event of a refusal of consent by an individual to the provision of a sample where consent is required, the 1990 Act provides at s 3, that such inferences 'as appear proper' may be drawn from such refusal by the court, and although such refusal may not in itself lead to a conviction of an offence, it can amount to evidence corroborative of any evidence in relation to which the refusal is material.

[7.85] Once the sample has been taken and the matter analysed and the result recorded, a major issue arises as to the use of that information – apart from its presentation in court in relation to the given charge. Section 4 of the 1990 Act provides for the destruction of samples and records (in this latter regard it is more comprehensive than its English counterpart, s 64 of the Police and Criminal Evidence Act 1984) in the case of acquittals, non-prosecutions or non-continuance of charges against an accused. A claw-back provision allows for the Director of Public Prosecutions to make application that there is 'good reason' why such records or samples should not be destroyed, and so gain an order for their retention (s 4(5) of the 1990 Act).

[7.86] No guidelines are issued in relation as to how this power might be exercised. As well as raising broader issues as to the maintenance of State DNA data banks, spectres of area and regional testing in the aftermath of a crime, and compulsory testing of citizens – on a more basic level of concern, this raises the issue of what is being stored in the cases of those individuals who have been convicted or when there constitutes a 'good ' reason to maintain data.

[7.87] A cursory glance at the 1990 Act's provisions then, indicates its shortcomings. Issues are not only inadequately provided for – they have not been addressed. Yet the implications for the pre-trial procedure of our criminal law are considerable. Perhaps undue haste on the part of our legislators to introduce these provisions leaves now to lawyers at the next stage of the process, the task of challenging the result. However, as seen, it requires fiscal and temporal resources beyond those of the average defence lawyer to take issue with same. Moreover, it demands a degree of tenacity, as the clients (particularly if recidivists) may be indigent, and all too anxious to accept the offer of a guilty plea in face of apparently conclusive evidence.

[7.88] The scientific and legal communities have both expressed concern about the safeguards, procedures and adequate testing facilities. Issues of adequate resources scientific and financial, to deal with the introduction of this evidence into the criminal justice system have to be addressed before such garda powers should be invoked. If the legal system is to maintain any credibility in this area – in terms of guarantees of 'due process' to those individuals caught within it or trial in accordance with presumptions of innocence and adequate redress, – all concentration of effort from a legislative point of view should not be at the level of garda powers to obtain substances (with a fair degree of encroachment on individual rights), which is often all of no particular use unless admissible. Courts and lawyers, with the aid of the scientific community, must stringently guard against the too ready admissibility of the evidence obtained, unless adequately and rigorously tested in accordance with scientific consensus and procedure. Defence counsel must have a real opportunity to test same.

[7.89] If such provision is not made prior to the availability and enforcement of those powers, the criminal justice system will have been reduced to the imprimatur of the police station regime, and criminal justice moved correspondingly back. To this extent, the 'DNA controversy' may foreshadow a lot of things to come and constitute, in microcosm, the true forensic battlefield for further criminal trials. Quite apart from challenging the dynamics of science itself, Irish lawyers will find that in the most mundane and 'uncontroversial occasions', they must grapple with the increasingly evident 'expert'.

[7.90] Dr James Donovan, the former head of the State Forensic Laboratory in Ireland, finds the requirement under Irish law to get the written consent of a suspect for an intimate sample, 'incongruous ... when a DNA profile on a bodily sample can eliminate a suspect or be used to prosecute successfully'.[82] He points out that in Britain, buccal cell swabs from inside the mouth and hair roots can be taken without consent. He further criticises the fact that in Ireland, as samples have to be destroyed after six months if no charge is brought, it is not possible for a database of DNA profiles to be built.

[7.91] Of course the difficulties remain in relation to DNA, as enumerated by Redmayne.[83] Doubts about the significance of matching a DNA profile can arise at the stage of the procedures used by the lab to prepare the DNA profile and declare a match (samples may be confused or mislabelled, or as in *R v Deen*[84] there may be a dispute regarding the number of bands matching); in the statistical techniques used to determine a match probability (population genetics – certain racial groups may have a very low rate of genetic variation); and in the combination of match probability with prior odds (the jury may have earlier information, for example, that an eyewitness said it was a Greek – this would be different from proving he just came from the same city of 3 million). Of course there is an additional difficulty where that it is likely the accused and the perpetrator come form the same population subgroup.

[7.92] The *Auld Report* in England has made recommendations including that the various expert witness organisations concentrate their work in one body which will set standards for forensic scientists. *Auld* also recommends that experts' overriding duty be to the court; courts to have the power to control the admissibility of expert evidence; courts to have the power to authorise expenditure on expert's fees in publicly defended cases; experts to meet before trial and identify the extent to which they agree and disagree; courts to have the power to order experts to meet to discuss areas of disagreement and to prepare a joint report thereon. However, courts are not to be empowered to appoint or select experts.[85]

[7.93] One area where 'expertise' has recently proliferated is that of historic sex abuse cases. In such instances, in order to explain the element of delay in a manner which complies with the recognition of an exception to expeditious trial

---

[82] Donovan, James 'The Obtaining, Examining, Analysis and Retaining of Forensic Samples in Criminal Investigation' (2001) Medico Legal Journal of Ireland.

[83] M Redmayne 'Doubts and Burdens: DNA Evidence, Probability and the Courts' [1995] Crim LR 464.

[84] *R v Deen* (1994) Times, 10 January.

[85] Lord Justice Auld *Review of the Criminal Courts of England and Wales* (2001).

in such cases, expert evidence is tendered as to the normal reaction of someone subjected to such abuse. Typically the same experts have been tendered in very many cases and questions have been raised by the courts as to their 'expertise', the reliability (and recognition) of the science involved in certain cases and their methodology. Criticism of the expert witness testimony is a feature of these cases, with Hardiman J in *JO'C v DPP*[86] finding the nature of the examination by the psychologist to have been 'gravely inadequate'.[87] Expert witnesses in both the presentation of evidence, and recognition of their area of research or expertise, have met with sharply differing judicial views of their testimony (see, for example, the contrasting views of McGuinness J and Denham J in *PC v DPP*[88]). In *NC v DPP*[89], the actual unavailability of the hypnotist under whose ministrations the complainant had revived her memory of events forming the basis of the complaint (which also triggering the other complaints made by her sister), where the trial would have taken place 40 years and 10 months after the first alleged assault, led Hardiman J, in granting the application to restrain prosecution, to point out that there was therefore no effective test or control of the mechanism of alleged recovery, rendering this a situation 'fraught with the risk of unfairness'.

Practical pointers in relation to the examination of the expert witness

Examination-in-chief

[7.94] In establishing the 'expertise' of a tendered witness, the onus of proof is on counsel calling the witness to establish his status on the basis of qualification or day-to-day experience in the area. A witness should be encouraged not to be shy or unforthcoming in the elucidation of same. In this regard, see, for example, the decision of O'Hanlon J in *DPP v Eamonn O'Donoghue*.[90] This case constituted an appeal by way of a case stated against the decision of District Justice Windle to dismiss a charge brought against the respondent for failure to permit a designated registered medical practitioner to take from him a specimen of his blood (or provide a specimen of urine for same), contrary to s 13(3) of the Road Traffic (Amendment) Act 1978. The evidence had shown that the doctor had been introduced by the sergeant in charge as 'the designated registered medical practitioner', that that doctor had been asked in the District Court the rhetorical question, 'I think you are a registered medical practitioner?' to which he replied 'I am'. The next question was: 'Were you designated by the Gardaí on

---

[86] *JO'C v DPP* [2000] 3 IR 478.

[87] [2000] 3 IR 478 at 527.

[88] *PC v DPP* [1999] 2 IR 25.

[89] *NC v DPP* (5 July 2001) SC at p 18 (Hardiman J).

[90] *DPP v Eamonn O'Donoghue* (15 February 1979, unreported) HC.

the night in question?', to which he replied, 'I was'. The District Justice took the view that this failed to elicit confirmation of a necessary fact for the purposes of the prosecution, ie, that the doctor was at the time, he attended the station a registered medical practitioner. All that had been established was that he was introduced as such by the sergeant, and that on the day the matter came before the District Court he confirmed that as of that time he was a registered medical practitioner.

[7.95] O'Hanlon J notes that *Martin v Quinn*[91] involved confirmation by the Supreme Court that it was necessary to prove that the person for whom the defendant had failed to provide a specimen of his urine, was a registered medical practitioner. The Supreme Court also held that the testimony of that person that he was such a practitioner at the relevant time was prima facie evidence of that fact and, unless rebutted, would support a conviction. O'Hanlon J commented that this latter finding constituted an acceptance of some relaxation of the application of the 'best evidence' rule, which would otherwise give rise to the intolerable burden of having to produce formal proof of qualifications held by professional witnesses on every occasion when they were called on to give evidence. An appropriate form of prima facie evidence must still be furnished, however, and O'Hanlon J did not consider that the prosecution could ask for the rule of evidence to be further relaxed when it could be satisfied by the simple expedient of the registered medical practitioner testifying as to his status as same 'at the material time'. As the necessary formal evidence was not given in this case, the appeal was dismissed.

Cross-examination

[7.96] There are three basic options with regard to the manner in which an expert witness can be cross-examined:

(i) putting questions to the expert which place a different interpretation on the facts upon which the expert has based his opinion and eliciting, if possible, answers which show that the different interpretation of the facts – an interpretation which is favourable to the cross-examiner's case – is reasonable;

(ii) challenging the expert witness's opinion by confronting him with authoritative works, or even his own writings, which cast doubt on the correctness of his opinion;

(iii) establishing that the expert witness formed his opinion without taking into consideration facts which have either been established, or which

---

[91] *Martin v Quinn* [1980] IR 244.

the cross-examiner hopes to establish and which modify, or should modify the expert's opinion.

In such manner, and by reference to the most appropriate and suitable tactic on the occasion, the lawyer can vindicate his client's interests and participate in the process of maintaining the province of legal adjudication.

Chapter 8

Privilege

'All animals are equal but some animals are more equal than others.'

George Orwell *Animal Farm* (1989) Penguin p 90.

Introduction

[8.01] The area of the law of evidence relating to privilege is divided into that which is called private privilege, and that which has been called, in turn, Crown privilege, State privilege, and more recently, public privilege. State or public privilege, having had its origins in a very limited attachment to matters of State security or defence (the design of submarines, or warships or the like), has been broadened to take account of instances of confidentiality which should not become public because of the greater usefulness of the relationship involved to the public. In a sense, what results is a balancing act by the courts, taking into account the damage that would be done to the relationship involved, and the public good, against that of the good that would be done in terms of the administration of justice, should the information be revealed. Private privilege, has a much more absolute if limited effect.

[8.02] Private privilege attaches to certain relationships, which have been specifically fostered by the courts, and where a witness can choose on the basis of that relationship to refuse to reveal certain information. That this category of privilege is limited is not surprising, for the recognition of private privilege attaching to these relationships, inevitably cuts down on the amount of relevant information before a court of law, which correspondingly reduces that court's ability to engage in the effective administration of justice. Although there may well come a day when State or public privilege will subsume the area of private privilege, those who are party to a private privilege will jealously guard the independence it gives in terms of non-scrutiny by the court of the reasonableness of the decision to raise that private privilege.

Private privilege

[8.03] Privilege, according to Heydon[1], relates to an instance when one is not obliged to answer particular questions or produce particular documents. It is

---

[1]   Heydon *Evidence – Cases and Materials* (2nd edn, 1984, Butterworths, London).

important to distinguish between privilege in this context and competence. In relation to competence, the incapacity of the witness is complete, and prevents that particular witness from testifying at all. Private privilege, on the other hand, may well be waived by its possessor. When a witness raises a privilege in a criminal trial, he is relying on a legal right to withhold certain information which would otherwise be relevant and admissible. The State is obviously reluctant to grant such privileges, as they exclude relevant and probative evidence which might enable justice to be done between the parties to the litigation. However, private privilege has been held to attach or to arise in the following situations. This means that individuals in these situations may choose to raise a privilege and so refuse to answer particular questions or produce particular documents. Equally, however, they may well decide to waive the particular privilege. In either event, it is existent.

[8.04] Privilege arises in the following situations:

(1) Privilege against self-incrimination.

This is a privilege which allows a witness to refuse to answer incriminating questions in criminal and civil cases.

(2) Marital privilege.

This relates to the disclosure of communications made to a spouse by the other spouse during the marriage.

(3) Lawyer/client privilege or legal professional privilege.

If a lawyer, this privilege allows the lawyer as a witness to refuse to disclose communications made to him by his client without the client's consent, and if a client, allows the client to refuse to disclose communications made to him by his lawyer.

(4) 'Without prejudice' communications.

In civil proceedings, disclosing 'without prejudice' communications made to a witness without the consent of the parties to the communication.

Legal professional privilege

[8.05] The rationale or reasoning behind the existence of legal professional privilege is that of encouraging the client to put all facts before the lawyer, not just the ones which favour his position. Yet this is undeniably another obstacle to the truth, and further proof that the law is not a scientific investigation for the discovery of truth. Indeed, Bentham[2] objected to the privilege, on the ground

---

[2] Bentham, *A Rationale of Judicial Evidence* (1827) Book IX, Pt IV, c 5.

that if a man was guilty, there should be nothing to betray; and that abolition of the privilege would lead to tighter professional standards amongst lawyers as it would remove any power to hide an accused's guilt. Yet in modern conditions, skilful cross-examination may be used to mitigate any possible harm such privilege might cause, and it is arguably necessary for the successful perusal of a lawyer/client relationship.

[8.06] This privilege was recognised in *Wheeler v Le Marchant*[3], where Jessel MR stated that the protection was of a very limited nature, and restricted to the obtaining of the assistance of lawyers, as regards the conduct of litigation or the right to property. It has never gone beyond the obtaining of legal advice and assistance; and all things reasonably necessary in the shape of communication to the legal advisers are protected from production or discovery in order that that legal advice may be obtained safely and sufficiently.

[8.07] There are two basic aspects to legal professional privilege:

    (1)   Lawyer/client communications; and

    (2)   Communications with third parties.

These two categories are examined in turn.

Lawyer/client communications

[8.08] Communications between a lawyer and client may not be given in evidence without the consent of the client. In order to attract this legal professional privilege, however, the communication must occur in the course of a professional legal relationship. Thus, a conversation with a lawyer in the course of a social event, or in relation to non-professional business, would not be covered by the privilege. The authority which suggests that the legal professional privilege in this instance belongs to the client is the decision in *Minter v Priest*[4], where it was held that the client can waive or not waive the privilege as he sees fit.

[8.09] It has similarly been held that the privilege here does not extend to third parties. In the case of *Schneider v Leigh*[5], which involved an action for personal injuries, a claim of privilege was made by Dr Leigh in relation to a medical report which he had compiled on the plaintiff's injuries. In the context of the personal injury action, the defendant company would have had legal professional privilege with regard to that letter. However, the action involved here was one where the plaintiff alleged that he was defamed in the communication sent by Dr Leigh to that company. The plaintiff therefore sued

---

3   *Wheeler v Le Marchant* (1881) 17 Ch D 675.
4   *Minter v Priest* [1930] AC 588.
5   *Schneider v Leigh* [1955] 2 All ER 173.

Dr Leigh, and the issue arose as to whether Dr Leigh could claim that legal professional privilege. The court held that no legal professional privilege attached to Dr Leigh here. (Although under the substantive law of defamation, it might have been possible for Dr Leigh to have taken refuge in the defence of qualified privilege, ie, that of a person making a statement with a genuine reason for so doing. Another possible defence might have been that of justification).

[8.10] Legal professional privilege attaches only to confidential communications. It is not applied, therefore, to a letter which is written, for example, on a client's instruction. Such an instance arose in the decision of *Bord na gCon v Murphy*[6]. In this case Bord na gCon wrote to Murphy accusing him of being in breach of the Greyhound Industry Act 1958. Subsequently, Murphy was convicted of offences under that Act, and he appealed. On appeal, Bord na gCon wished to put in evidence against Murphy a letter which related to the offence, and which was written by Murphy's solicitor in reply to the Bord's initial communication to Murphy. The High Court refused to allow that document to go in because Murphy had not given permission to it being tendered in evidence. The Supreme Court held, however, that correspondence between Murphy's solicitor and Bord na gCon was inadmissible in evidence because it constituted hearsay, and not because of the privilege. The Court did say that the correspondence and the statement were not confidential, and therefore would not in any event be inadmissible on grounds of legal professional privilege.

[8.11] In *R v Crown Court ex p Baines & Baines*[7], it was held inter alia that conveyancing documents are not privileged, as they do not come within the meaning of the giving of advice, consisting as they do of the records of the financing of the purchase of a house.

[8.12] One qualification on the ambit of legal professional privilege in relation to solicitor and client is that it does not extend to communications made in furtherance of a criminal offence. These are excluded from the rubric of the privilege, as had been held in a line of authority, including the decision in *R v Cox & Railton*[8]. The communication must be shown to be preparatory to a crime and not merely be a warning. In *Butler v Board of Trade*[9], an unsolicited letter from a lawyer to a client advising him that certain conduct would be likely to lead to his being prosecuted, was held to constitute a mere warning and so not to come under the decision in *Cox & Railton*. In the Irish context, the court in

---

[6] *Bord na gCon v Murphy* [1970] IR 301.
[7] *R v Crown Court ex p Baines & Baines* [1987] 3 All ER 1025.
[8] *R v Cox & Railton* (1884) 14 QBD 153.
[9] *Butler v Board of Trade* [1970] 3 All ER 593.

People (AG) v Coleman[10], held that the document in question was an attempt to procure the subornation of witnesses, and therefore, even if it had reached the solicitor in question as intended, it would not be a privileged communication since it contemplated and suggested the commission of a crime.

[8.13] The question of the ambit of the privilege in terms of various types of communications on different issues which pass between lawyers and clients, arose in *Smurfit Paribas Bank Ltd v CAB Export Finance Ltd*[11]. The issue here was taken whether the defendant's claim to legal professional privilege in respect of communications passing between it and its solicitors, was carried in law. The facts concerned a dispute between the plaintiff and defendant, with regard to the defendant's floating charge. Following an order for discovery, the defendant claimed privilege in relation to correspondence between it and the solicitor then acting for it in relation to the charge.

The documents in question did not request or contain legal advice about the transaction, but held reference to instructions regarding the drafting of documentation necessary to the transaction. In the High Court these documents were deemed not privileged (Costello J), on the grounds that they did not request or contain legal advice and contained no information that could be regarded as confidential. Reliance was placed on *Smith-Bird v Blower*[12], in which a letter written to the solicitors by the defendant, in answer to an inquiry as to whether he had agreed to sell the property in question, was deemed not privileged. In the Supreme Court, Finlay CJ[13] identified the relevant policy issue as being:

> '... the requirement of the superior interest of the common good in the proper conduct of litigation which justified the immunity of communications from discovery insofar as they were made for the purpose of litigation as being the desirability in that goal of the correct and efficient trial of actions by the courts.'

[8.14] Finlay CJ referred to *Minter v Priest*[14], which gives support to the notion that the extent of the privilege is outside that of actual or contemplated litigation. He commented that some cases appear to support a contention that it is sufficient if legal assistance, other than advice, only were sought. However, Finlay CJ noted that the ultimate decision as to the existence of a privilege, lies with the courts[15]. Finlay CJ further noted that:

> 'The existence of a privilege or exemption from disclosure for communications made between a person and his lawyer clearly constitutes a potential restriction

---

[10] *People (Attorney General) v Coleman* [1945] IR 237.
[11] *Smurfit Paribas Bank Ltd v CAB Export Finance Ltd* [1990] ILRM 588.
[12] *Smith-Bird v Blower* [1939] 2 All ER 406.
[13] *Smurfit Paribas Bank Ltd v CAB Export Finance Ltd* [1990] ILRM 588 at 593.
[14] *Minter v Priest* [1930] AC 588.
[15] As per *Murphy v Dublin Corporation* [1972] IR 215.

and diminution of the full disclosure both prior to and during the course of legal proceedings which in the interests of the common good is desirable for the purpose of ascertaining the truth and rendering justice. Such privilege should, therefore, in my view, only be granted by the courts in instances which have been identified as securing an objective which in the public interest in the proper conduct of the administration of justice can be said to outweigh the disadvantage arising from the restriction of disclosure of all the facts.'[16]

[8.15] Hence, where a communication is made to a lawyer for the purpose of obtaining from such a lawyer legal advice, whether at the initiation of the client or the lawyer, Finlay CJ was satisfied that it should in general be privileged, or exempt from disclosure, except with the consent of the client. Similar considerations, he found, do not apply to communications made to a lawyer for the purpose of obtaining his legal assistance, other than advice. He continued:

'There are many tasks carried out by a lawyer for his client, and properly within the legal sphere, other than the giving of advice, which could not be said to contain any real relationship with the area of potential litigation. For such communications there does not appear to me to be any sufficient public interest or feature of the common good to be secured or protected which could justify an exemption from disclosure.'

[8.16] Finlay CJ thus affirmed the trial judge's decision. McCarthy J's judgment is to the same effect:

'In the instant case, the fundamental issue arises from the contrasting demands – candour by the client to his solicitor and the public interest in the true resolution of litigation. In my view communication of fact leading to the drafting of legal documents and requests for the preparation of such, albeit made to a solicitor unless and until the same results in the provision of legal advice, is not privileged from disclosure.'[17]

The decision in *Smurfit* was followed in *Miley v Flood*[18] which extracted the principle that a communication only attracts privilege if it seeks or contains legal advice and that the communication of any other information is not privileged. Therefore, it was held that the identity of a client is not privileged, as it is a 'mere collateral fact'.

[8.17] In *Buckley v Incorporated Law Society*[19], correspondence between the complainants and the respondent society regarding the alleged misconduct of a

---

[16] *Smurfit Paribas Bank Ltd v CAB Export Finance Ltd* [1990] ILRM 588 at 594.
[17] *Smurfit Paribas Bank Ltd v CAB Export Finance Ltd* [1990] ILRM 588 at 597 (McCarthy J).
[18] *Miley v Flood* [2001] ILRM 489.
[19] *Buckley v Incorporated Law Society* [1994] 2 IR 44.

solicitor was held not to be privileged because the complainants were not consulting the Law Society as a legal adviser.

In *Buckley v Bough*[20] the plaintiff was claiming damages from the defendant for medical negligence. After an order for discovery, the defendant claimed legal professional privilege over a number of documents. It was challenged as the documents concerned a hearing of the Fitness to Practice Committee under the Medical Practitioners Act 1978.

Morris J held that the documentation consisting of correspondence between the defendant's solicitors was not communicating legal advice to the defendant so as to attract legal privilege. Should there have been any privilege attaching on the basis of the patient-medical practitioner relationship, it was, in any event, being waived by the patient.

[8.18] If the issue of privilege is involved in a criminal trial when the accused is trying to exculpate himself, the courts will probably not allow legal professional privilege to attach in relation to exculpatory evidence. This is because the importance of the relationship which has led to the recognition of a privilege, in this instance, could not override the importance of not convicting an innocent person.

[8.19] In *R v Barton*[21], the defendant worked in a solicitor's office. He was charged with fraudulent conversion in the course of his employment with that firm of solicitors. A solicitor who was a partner in the firm said that certain documents could not be produced at trial because they were privileged. The accused wanted them produced in an effort to exculpate himself. Caulfield J stated that working on the rules of natural justice, no privilege could attach here. He commented 'the law will not allow a solicitor or anyone else to screen from the jury information which if disclosed might enable a man to establish his innocence'. (In that instance the judge relied on the rules of natural justice, in particular the AAP rule, yet in Ireland, one could arguably rely on the even stronger rule of constitutional justice.)

[8.20] In *R v Ataou*[22], the accused's solicitor discovered during the trial that he was in possession of a statement by a former client, now testifying against the accused, which was inconsistent with that testimony and favourable to the accused. The court gave permission for use of the statement in cross-examination, but surprisingly criticised the solicitor. Arguably again, the basis for admissibility in Ireland would be greater, and that criticism less.

---

[20] *Buckley v Bough* (2 July 2001), HC, Morris P.
[21] *R v Barton* [1972] 2 All ER 1192.
[22] *R v Ataou* [1988] 2 All ER 321.

[8.21] In *Ataou*, the Court of Appeal emphasised that, in the joint trial situation, where the privilege belongs to one of the defendants, and the information, if revealed, would exonerate him and cause harm to the other party, the trial judge must balance the conflicting interests of the defendants. The defendant seeking to introduce the privileged information must show, on the balance of probabilities, that his legitimate interest in seeking to breach the privilege outweighs the co-defendant's in its maintenance.

Communications with third parties

[8.22] The second aspect to the legal professional privilege rule relates to communication between clients and third parties or between legal advisers and third parties, which are made for the purpose of pending or contemplated litigation. 'Pending litigation' refers to a situation when some legal proceeding has been issued in relation to the issue. For example, where parties have either issued civil bills or plenary summons in the High Court. 'Contemplated litigation' is a rather more difficult concept; it is clear that there has to be a definite proposal of litigation, not a mere anticipation of it.

[8.23] Earlier Irish case law includes the decision in *Kerry County Council v Liverpool Salvage Association*[23], where, because no litigation was then in contemplation, the claim of privilege failed; and *Rushbrooke v O'Sullivan*[24], where documents prepared with a view to ascertaining whether litigation should be initiated at some future time (but not with a view to actual or threatened litigation) were not privileged.

[8.24] In the case of *Alfred Crompton Amusement Machines v Commissioners of Customs & Excise*[25], documents were received in relation to same. However, these documents concerned the market value of a number of one-armed bandit machines. It was held therefore that they were not entitled to legal professional privilege as their only purpose was to permit the assessment of purchase tax, and not to assist in litigation.

Dominant purpose

[8.25] A similar incident occurred in the decision of the House of Lords in *Waugh v British Railways Board*[26]. The facts of this case were that the plaintiff's husband, who was employed by the defendant Board, received injuries in a collision between locomotives and died. The practice of the Board when such an

---

[23] *Kerry County Council v Liverpool Salvage Association* (1903) 38 ILTR 7.
[24] *Rushbrooke v O'Sullivan* [1926] IR 500.
[25] *Alfred Crompton Amusement Machines v Commissioners of Customs & Excise* [1973] 2 All ER 1169.
[26] *Waugh v British Railways Board* [1980] AC 521.

accident occurred was that on the day of the accident a brief report was made to a railway inspectorate. Soon after, a joint internal report (joint inquiry report) was prepared, including statements of witnesses, and that was also sent to the inspectorate. The inspectorate then made a report for the Department of Environment. The heading of the joint inquiry report said that it had to be sent to the Board's solicitor so it could advise the Board. The question arose as to whether the joint inquiry report was then privileged. Lord Wilberforce commented as follows:

> '... unless the purpose of submission to the legal advisor in view of litigation is at least the dominant purpose for which the relevant document was prepared the reasons which require privilege to be extended to it can not apply.'

Yet that is not to go so far as to require litigation to be the sole purpose of the communication.

[8.26] In a similar vein, Lord Edmond Davies reasoned as follows. He would deny a claim to privilege when the litigation was merely one of several purposes of equal or similar importance intended to be served by the material sought to be withheld from disclosure, and *a fortiori* where it was merely a minor purpose. However, similarly, he would not go so far as to require litigation to be the sole purpose of the document:

> 'But in so much as the only basis of the claim to privilege in such cases as the present one is that the material in question was brought into existence for use in legal proceedings, it is surely right to insist that, before the claim is conceded or upheld, such a purpose must be shown to have played a paramount part.'

[8.27] This 'dominant' purpose as to the test of privilege from disclosure in such circumstances has been endorsed in Ireland in *Silver Hill Duckling Ltd v Minister for Agriculture*[27] and in *Davis v St Michael's House*[28]. In *Silver Hill Duckling Ltd v Minister for Agriculture*[29], the defendants were claiming damages for loss of a flock of ducks who had to be destroyed following an influenza outbreak. The defendant claimed privilege on the ground that certain documents had come into being in contemplation of and for the purpose of advising the Minister in relation to the plaintiff's claim. O'Hanlon J was of the view that as it was apparent that the disparity between the two parties in terms of the amount of compensation to be claimed would have to be resolved by litigation, litigation could be regarded as apprehended and the documentation privileged.

---

[27] *Silver Hill Duckling Ltd v Minister for Agriculture* [1987] IR 289.
[28] *Davis v St Michael's House* (25 November 1993, unreported) HC (Lynch J).
[29] [1987] IR 289.

[8.28] In *PJ Carrigan Ltd v Norwich Union Fire Society Ltd*[30], the defendants on being notified by the plaintiffs of a claim in relation to a fire, commissioned a report from loss adjusters, as they viewed the claim with suspicion. O'Hanlon J took the view that they were contemplating, even at that stage, the possibility of repudiating liability under the policy, and so the report had been obtained in apprehension of litigation. The purpose is determined objectively. In a Court of Appeal decision in *Guinness Peat Properties v Fitzroy*[31], it was held that a letter written by a firm of architects to their professional indemnity insurers, notifying the insurers of a possible claim against the architects, was privileged because the dominant purpose of the letter was to enable the insurers to obtain legal advice or to conduct litigation which was then in prospect. Accordingly the architects were granted an injunction prohibiting the plaintiffs, to whom the letter had inadvertently been disclosed, from using the letter in an action against the architects. The Court of Appeal took an objective view of the evidence as a whole ie looking at the reality of the situation, in terms of the reason why the letter was brought into existence – being that of the insurers' interest in seeing that such claims were defended. In those circumstances it was felt the letter owed its genus to the dominant purpose that it should be used for the purpose of obtaining legal advice and any ensuing litigation. Per Lord Slade:

> '... I accept that the dominant purpose of the letter was to be viewed objectively on the evidence, particularly by reference to the intention of the Insurers who produced its genesis.... I accept that so viewed, the dominant purpose was to produce a letter of notification which would be used in order to obtain legal advice or to conduct or aid in the conduct of litigation which was at the time of its production in reasonable prospect.'[32]

[8.29] Consideration of the purpose of a communication in the context of legal professional privilege and its attachment occurred in the Irish case of *Bula Ltd v Crowley*[33]. As often occurs, the challenge to the claim of privilege in this case was in the context of affidavits of discovery submitted by Ulster Investment Bank Ltd and Allied Irish Investment Bank Ltd. The plaintiff's challenge to one group arose solely from the use of the word 'purposes' as distinct from 'purpose'. The plaintiff alleged that the privilege extended only to those documents which came into existence for the purpose of obtaining legal advice. They asserted that once documents are created for two different purposes, one of which would attract privilege and the other not, then it must be asserted and if necessary established, that the dominant purpose was the one attracting privilege

---

[30] *PJ Carrigan Ltd v Norwich Union Fire Society Ltd* [1987] IR 618.
[31] *Guinness Peat Properties v Fitzroy* [1987] 2 All ER 716.
[32] New Law Journal, 15 May 1987 at p 453.
[33] *Bula Ltd v Crowley* [1990] ILRM 756.

before such a claim can succeed. (*Silver Hill Duckling Ltd v Minister for Agriculture*[34] and *Tromso Sparebank v Beirne*[35] relied on).

[8.30] Per Murphy J:

'... it seems to me that the principle is material only where it appears that a document or documents came into existence for a duality of reasons one of which would attract the privilege and the other not. In the present case ... in effect the defendant has sworn that *all* the purposes for which the documents in question were brought into existence were privileged and accordingly it would be neither necessary nor appropriate to assert that there was a particular dominant purpose.'

[8.31] A second attack was made on certain categories of alleged privilege on the basis that communications between the banks with each other or with any of the other defendants are not privileged as such and would only be privileged on the same basis as communications with a third party, ie only if they were made at the express or implied suggestion of the legal advisers to one or other of the parties for the purpose of obtaining legal advice and for the purpose of litigation existing or in contemplation of the time[36]. Per Murphy J:

'Of and insofar as the communications consist of legal advice there can be no doubt whatever but that they are privileged in the hands of the client on whose behalf they are obtained. Equally well it seems to me that the same advice is privileged in the hands of a third party who shares a common interest in the litigation with the client whether or not the third party is joined in the proceedings' (see *Buttes Gas & Oil Co v Hammer*).[37]

[8.32] The privilege attaches to 'communications'. Communications in this sense are those which are communicated orally or in writing. Thus, to postulate a hypothetical situation, should a woman stab her husband, and go to her solicitor, a statement such as 'I stabbed him', would constitute a communication which would be privileged. However, should that woman be carrying a knife dripping with blood, the solicitor may well be asked about her demeanour, as no privilege attaches to the instance of the blood and the knife, as these are not communications but information available to anyone.

[8.33] The privilege may also be lost by waiver, and a party may well choose to waive a privilege in relation to particular evidence. However, a party cannot be over selective in terms of waiver. A party cannot tender only part of a document, as this may result in disclosure of parts merely favourable to that party. The whole of the document must lose its privilege.[38]

---

[34] *Silver Hill Duckling Ltd v Minister for Agriculture* [1987] ILRM 516.
[35] *Tromso Sparebank v Beirne* [1989] ILRM 257.
[36] *Hamilton v Nott* (1873) LR 16.
[37] *Buttes Gas & Oil Co v Hammer* [1981] QB 223.
[38] *Great Atlantic Insurance Co v Home Insurance Co* [1981] 2 All ER 485.

[8.34] The privilege arises even where someone mistakenly believes a person to be a lawyer, whether that mistake is innocent or the result of deceit[39].

Loss of the privilege

[8.35] The qualification on the doctrine of legal professional privilege, and one that is somewhat questionable in its roots, yet presents an undeniable instance when the privilege may be lost, relates to instances when third parties may gain access to information which is prima facie privileged.

[8.36] In the case of *R v Tompkins*[40], the appellant was charged inter alia with handling goods which included a stereo identified by a Mr Evans as having special characteristics – to wit, a loose button. The appellant denied that a button had ever been loose on the stereo, and was then confronted with a note which he had written to his counsel saying that he had glued the button back on with air-fix glue. Prosecuting counsel had found the said note on the floor of the courtroom. In the absence of the jury, the document was ruled inadmissible. However, counsel for the prosecution asked questions based on its contents, ie had the appellant glued the button back on. He said he had. An appeal was launched on the basis of the use of the information obtained in breach of an alleged privilege between counsel and client, this being contrary to natural justice. Lord Ormrod noted that the argument of how the document came into the possession of the prosecution had not been pursued. He then commented:

> 'Privilege in this context relates only to the production of a document; it does not determine its admissibility in evidence. The note, though clearly privileged from production was admissible in evidence once it was in the possession of the prosecution.'

He referred to *Butler v Board of Trade*[41], where this point was made – ie once the privileged document is in the hands of the party who wishes to use it (and who is not party to the privilege), the question of privilege disappears and the question becomes one of admissibility and it is admissible even though it was obtained in breach of confidence. This line of authority goes back, it was alleged, to the decision in *Calcraft v Guest*[42].

Mistaken disclosure

[8.37] The general principle in relation to mistakenly disclosed documents has been said to have been laid down by the case of *Re Briamore Manufacturing Ltd (in liq)*[43], where in proceedings to set aside an alleged fraudulent preference the

---

[39] *Fauerheerd v London General Omnibus Co Ltd* [1918] 2 KB 1565.
[40] *R v Tompkins* (1977) 67 Cr App Rep 18B.
[41] *Butler v Board of Trade* [1971] Ch 680.
[42] *Calcraft v Guest* [1898] 1 QB 759.
[43] *Re Briamore Manufacturing Ltd (in liq)* [1986] 3 All ER 132.

liquidator's solicitor made a mistake in his list of documents for discovery, including documents for which privilege could have been claimed, and which should have been included in the list of documents which he objected to produce. The respondent's solicitor was shown copies of the privileged documents, read them and made notes of their contents and a photocopy of at least one of them. Although the liquidator's solicitor informed the respondent the following day, the respondent's solicitor nevertheless made a formal request for copies of the privileged documents. The Registrar refused to order delivery of copies of the privileged documents. The respondent appealed. It was held that it was too late for the liquidator to correct the mistake in the list, and consequently, the respondent was entitled to the copies sought. The appeal would therefore be allowed on production of the documents ordered.

[8.38] In a subsequent decision of *English and American Insurance Co Ltd v Herbert Smith & Co*[44], it was held in a situation where a bundle of papers given by counsel to his clerk for return to his instructing solicitors, were mistakenly delivered to counsel's chambers for the first defendant, that the plaintiffs were entitled to their order that the defendants deliver up the papers concerned, and that they be restrained from using them until after judgment in the action. The court recognised the obvious difficulties in reconciling decisions in this area, some concentrating on the right of the client to maintain his entitlement to confidentiality and enforce against anybody holding privileged documents, others upholding the rule that evidence which is relevant should be admitted, however obtained. The position, the court decided, was dependent on whether proceedings are taken before the document is tendered in evidence or not. On the face of it, that decision was conclusive in that particular case. There was no dispute that the documents were legally professionally privileged and there was no dispute that Messrs Herbert Smith had obtained information from them. In those circumstances, the relief should be granted. However, certain arguments were put by counsel which should be mentioned. Firstly, that the present case was one where receipt of the confidential information by Messrs Herbert Smith was entirely innocent. The court was not, however, satisfied that the receipt of the information was so entirely innocent. The second argument was that application of the *Calcraft v Guest* principle – namely that if when you get to trial you still have a document and you tender it, evidence of that document is admissible, notwithstanding that it may have been improperly obtained – would result in the information being used in this instance. The Court, however, felt bound by the previous decisions of *Ashburton v Pape*[45] and *Goddard v Nationwide Building Society*[46], insofar as relief should be granted to the

---

[44] *English and American Insurance Co Ltd v Herbert Smith & Co* [1988] FSR 232.
[45] *Ashburton v Pape* [1913] 2 Ch 469.
[46] *Goddard v Nationwide Building Society* [1987] QB 670.

plaintiff. It is interesting to note that following on this conclusion the court commented:

'I confess that this is a result which gives me some satisfaction. Legal professional privilege is an important safeguard of a man's legal rights. It is the basis on which he and his advisers are free to speak as to matters in issue in litigation and otherwise without fear that it will subsequently be used against him. In my judgment it is most undesirable if the security which is the basis of that freedom is to be prejudiced by mischances which are of everyday occurrence leading to documents which have escaped being used by the other side' (per Sir Nicholas Brown Wilkinson VC).

[8.39] A similar vindication of legal professional privilege is found in the decision of Hoffman J in *Chandler v Church*[47]. In this particular case, discovery of documents which were prima facie protected by legal professional privilege was sought on the grounds that privilege did not attach to a communication between a client and his legal adviser which was intended to facilitate the commission of a crime or fraud. It was held, however, that the fact the defendant might be using his solicitors to put forward a bogus defence, did not outweigh the fact that the plaintiffs were seeking, for the purpose of making good their charge of fraud, disclosure of what the defendant had told his solicitors to enable them to defend him against that charge, and accordingly discovery was refused. It is interesting to note the comments of Hoffman J:

'This submission seems to me to raise a point of considerable importance. It suggests that if the plaintiffs can induce prima facie evidence that the defendant is mounting a bogus defence, with or without the assistance of manufactured documents, he can penetrate professional privilege and require production of the opposing solicitor's notes, letters, instruction to counsel and so forth. I find this a startling proposition. All the cases which have been cited to me concerned the disclosure of legal advice taken in connection with a particular transaction which was alleged in subsequent civil or criminal proceedings to have been criminal or fraudulent. None involved an allegation of fraud in the conduct of the proceedings themselves.'

[8.40] Finally in *Guinness Peat Properties v Fitzroy*, it was further noted by the Court of Appeal that the relevant principles in relation to loss of legal privilege in such circumstances were as follows:

'(1) Where solicitors for one party to litigation have on discovery mistakenly included a document for which they could properly have claimed privilege in a list of documents without claiming privilege, the court will ordinarily permit them to amend the list ... at any time before inspection of the document has taken place.

---

47 *Chandler v Church* [1987] NL I 451.

(2) However, once in such circumstances that the other party has inspected the document in pursuance of the rights conferred on him ... the general rule is that it is too late for a party who seeks to claim privilege to attempt to correct the mistake by applying for injunctive relief. Subject to what is said in (3) below the *Briamore* decision is good law.

(3) If, however, in such a case the other party or his solicitor either:

(a)   has procured inspection of the relevant document by fraud, or

(b)   on inspection realises that he has been permitted to see the document only by reason of an obvious mistake, the court has the power to intervene for the protection of the mistaken party by the grant of an injunction in exercise of the equitable jurisdiction illustrated by the *Ashburton, Goddard & Herbert Smith* cases.

Further in my view it should ordinarily intervene in such circumstances unless the case is one where the injunction can properly be refused on the general principles affecting the grant of a discretionary remedy, for example on the ground of inordinate delay ...'[48]

[8.41] The Irish courts have considered loss of the privilege by disclosure in the context of *Bula Ltd v Crowley*[49], where the plaintiffs contended inter alia that as legal advice is disseminated within (and *a priori* without) the corporate structure of a litigant, the claim to privilege may be lost. Murphy J expressed the opinion that there was no doubt this was the case where the dissemination involved the disclosure of the advice to the public or a significant part of it. Where a litigant abandons confidentiality, he can hardly claim privilege. However, more difficult questions arise where the legal advice remains confidential, but records are made or documents created, which contain some reference expressly or by implication to such advice. Murphy J referred to Style and Hollander[50], who suggest:

'A document which merely passes on legal advice within the firm or company is privileged. If the communication goes further, privilege will be lost.'

This would mean that if, for example, the minutes of a board meeting simply summarise the solicitor's advice, it is privileged. But if the board discusses the same, any minutes of their discussion are not privileged. Murphy J did not agree with this approach:

'... I find it difficult to see how one could maintain that precise boundary. The essence of legal professional privilege is that a client should not have to disclose

---

[48]   [1987] NL I 451 at 453 per Slade J.
[49]   *Bula Ltd v Crowley* [1990] ILRM 756.
[50]   *Style and Hollander on Documentary Evidence* (4th edn, 1993, Longman, Sweet & Maxwell) p 103.

the legal advice which he has received. This purpose could be disclosed by a company being forced to disclose minutes of a meeting resolving to take a particular action having regard to but without disclosing the express contents of a legal opinion. For example to advert to the existence of counsel's opinion and to resolve to lodge the full amount of the plaintiff's claim would surely be as revealing as disclosing the contents of the opinion itself. It seems to me that in the present case the documents ... are expressly concerned with and would of necessity disclose to a material extent confidential legal advice given to one or other of the two defendants in pursuit of their common interest. In my view the claim to privilege should be upheld.'

[8.42] The vigour of the judicial defence of this heading of privilege is evident. The *Calcraft v Guest* exception to legal professional privilege does seem, however, somewhat unjust. As Heydon points out, it arose in an age (*Tomkins*), where eavesdropping and interception of communications was difficult, rare and unfavoured. Yet, now there are more efficient mechanical methods of eavesdropping, not so easily guarded against. Therefore it would not be enough for a client to take reasonable precautions. If a client knew of this exception, it might result in a reluctance to speak and thus undermine the rationale of the existence of the privilege.

[8.43] In this regard it is interesting to note the English courts' reluctance to admit such evidence where there has been fraud in the obtaining of information. Rather more important in the context of the Irish courts, is their very different perspective on admissibility. The English courts traditionally have admitted evidence which is relevant no matter how it had been obtained[51]. Indeed this principle is relied on specifically in the *Tomkins* decision. Yet the Irish courts do not start from such a principle, and will refuse to admit evidence because of the manner in which it was obtained when they see fit. The issue arises of how this would affect their treatment of this third exception to the rule on legal professional privilege.

[8.44] In *Breathnach v Ireland (No 3)*[52] a claim of legal professional privilege had been made concerning garda files connected with the investigation of the offence with which the plaintiff had been charged, as well as a report to the DPP for his decision as to whether to initiate a prosecution against the plaintiff. It was submitted that the documents were privileged on the ground (inter alia) that they had come into being in contemplation of litigation. The High Court held that the principle of public policy which protected from discovery communications between lawyer and client made in contemplation of litigation, had no application to documents submitted by an investigating officer to the notice

---

[51] *Kuruma, Son of Kaniu v R* [1955] AC 197.
[52] *Breathnach v Ireland (No 3)* [1993] 2 IR 458.

party (DPP) for the purpose of obtaining his decision as to whether or not a prosecution should be instituted.

[8.45] Legal professional privilege, according to Keane J:[53]

'... enables a client to maintain the confidentiality of two types of communication:

(1)   communications between him and his lawyer made for the purpose of obtaining and giving legal advice; and

(2)   communications between him or his lawyer and third parties (such as potential witnesses and experts) the dominant purpose of which was preparation for contemplated or pending litigation.

With regard to communications in the first category, it has recently been held by the Supreme Court in *Smurfit Paribas Bank Ltd v AAB Export Finance Ltd* [1990] 1 IR 469 that the privilege does not extend to communications made to a lawyer for the purpose of obtaining legal assistance other than advice ...

As has also been frequently pointed out, the privilege is that of the client and may only be waived by him. The position of the Director of Public Prosecutions is, of course, somewhat different: he does not stand in the relationship of "client" to any other lawyer. He is in a sense both lawyer and client, since he formulates the legal opinion on which the institution or non-institution of a prosecution is based and he then becomes one of the parties to the subsequent litigation. However, be that as it may, the public policy which protects from discovery communications in the first category undoubtedly applies equally to communications between the Director of Public Prosecutions and professional officers in his department, solicitors and counsel as to prosecutions by him which are in being or contemplated ...

It was obvious, however, ... that the great bulk of them [the documents] consist of the garda files assembled for the purpose of the investigation of the crime which gave rise to the original criminal proceedings and the report by the investigating gardaí which was forwarded to the Director of Public Prosecutions so that a decision could be taken by him as to whether a prosecution should be initiated against the plaintiff and other persons ... [T]he documents in question in this case could not be equated to the documents which come within the second heading of legal professional privilege, ie communications between a client or his lawyer and third parties the dominant purpose of which is preparation for contemplated or pending litigation.'

Is legal professional privilege merely a rule of evidence?

[8.46] It is sometimes suggested that legal professional privilege is more than just a rule of evidence. Kelly J in *Miley v Flood*[54] states 'Legal professional

---

[53]   *Breathnach v Ireland (No 3)* [1993] 2 IR 458 at 472-474.

[54]   *Miley v Flood* [2001] 2 IR 51 at 65.

privilege is more than a mere rule of evidence. It is a fundamental condition on which the administration of justice as a whole rests.'

In that case, Kelly J reiterates his quotation from Lord Taylor of Gosforth in *R v Derby Magistates Court; Ex p B*[55], previously quoted by Kelly J in *Duncan v Govenor of Mountjoy Prison*[56] ,viz:

> 'The principle which runs through all these cases, and the many other cases which were cited, is that a man must be able to consult his lawyer in confidence, since otherwise he might hold back half the truth. The client must be sure that what he tells his lawyer in confidence will never be revealed without his consent. Legal professional privilege is thus much more than an ordinary rule of evidence, limited in its application to the particular facts of a particular case. It is the fundamental condition on which the administration of justice as a whole rests.'

[8.47] Other jurisdictions, such as Canada, have taken a similar view. In *Solosky v Canada*[57], the Supreme Court of Canada described the right to communicate with a lawyer as a fundamental civil and legal right; while in *Descoteaux v Mierzwinksi*[58], the Supreme Court of Canada took the view that the right to legal confidentiality had developed from a rule of evidence into a substantive right. In *Esso Australia Resources Ltd v Sir Daryl Dawson*[59], the Federal Court of Australia said 'In the case of legal professional privilege, secrecy is defended on the basis that it would promote the administration of justice.'

[8.48] In a similar vein, one could see the commentary in *Hanahoe v Hussey HC*[60] per Kinlen J:

> 'It is essential in our society that lawyers of the highest ability should be available to provide a full and proper defence to persons accused of criminal offences. Unfortunately, public opinion does not always accept that principle and sometimes lawyers are identified with their clients which clearly violates principle 18 of the United Nations basic principles on the role of lawyers. It is a fundamental right in a democratic society that an accused person be fully appraised of all charges made against them and that they have the choice of legal representation. This right is embodied in article 6 of the European Convention on Human Rights. It would undermine our society if that were not so. The courts must protect these standards. Sometimes criminal lawyers are wrongly accused of colluding with their clients and sharing in the profits of crime. These are very serious allegations and should not be accepted until there is proof to establish them. The vast majority of criminal lawyers provide wonderful work to secure

---

[55] *R v Derby Magistates Court; ex p B* [1996] 1 AC 487 at 507.
[56] *Duncan v Govenor of Mountjoy Prison* [1997] 1 IR 558.
[57] *Solosky v Canada* (1980) 105 DLR (3d) 745 at 760.
[58] *Descoteaux v Mierzwinksi* [1982] 1 SCR 860.
[59] *Esso Australia Resources Ltd v Sir Daryl Dawson* [1999] FCA 363 at para 26.
[60] *Hanahoe v Hussey HC* [1998] 3 IR 69 at 106-107.

liberty and to protect our democratic institutions. Sometimes a lawyer might be regarded, because of his success, as an enemy of the State. They are in fact a bulwark to protect justice and the people and are essential in any real democracy.'

'Without prejudice' statements

[8.49] The purpose or the rationale of the privilege attaching to 'without prejudice' statements or communications, is that of reduction of litigation by the encouragement of settlements. If a party makes an offer to settle a matter which is about to be litigated, such might be considered an admission of liability if it could be entered in evidence. However, the rule is that any offer made 'without prejudice' cannot be entered in evidence without the consent of the maker and receiver. This is obviously necessary if any settlement is to be entered into, prior to a court hearing, and any negotiation is to be pursued.

[8.50] Should agreement be reached between the parties to the litigation, as a result of the 'without prejudice' negotiation, the privilege ceases to apply, for the parties' rights have been changed. The 'without prejudice' communication can then be looked at to determine if agreement has in fact been reached, and to determine the terms of that agreement. This is important should a dispute arise as to same[61]. Although the use of 'without prejudice' is a prima facie indication that the communication is in furtherance of a settlement, those words contain no magic properties and are not conclusive. This was held in *O'Flanagan v Ray-Ger Ltd*[62]. It also will not be allowed as a cloak for illegality or impropriety as held in *Greenwood v Fitts*[63], where the defendant told the plaintiff he would perjure himself and/or leave the jurisdiction if they succeeded.

[8.51] A decision of the House of Lords in *Rush & Tomkins Ltd v Greater London Council*[64], however, enters a *caveat* to this principle. The situation was one where proceedings between the plaintiffs and the first named defendant had been settled by the payment of 1.2 million pounds by the first named defendant, which included a sum representing an assessment of the value of the second defendant's claim. The plaintiffs then discontinued their action against the first defendant. The second named defendant applied for discovery of the 'without prejudice' correspondence which had passed between the plaintiffs and the first defendant leading up to the settlement, in order to ascertain the value which had been placed on their claim by the plaintiffs and the first defendant.

---

[61] *Tomlin v Standard Telephones and Cables Ltd* [1969] 3 All ER 201.
[62] *O'Flanagan v Ray-Ger Ltd* (28 April 1983, unreported) HC (Costello J).
[63] *Greenwood v Fitts* (1961) 29 DLR 260.
[64] *Rush & Tomkins Ltd v Greater London Council* [1988] 3 All ER 737.

[8.52] It was held by the House of Lords, however, that the 'without prejudice' correspondence entered into with the object of affecting the compromise of an action, remained privileged after the compromise had been reached, and accordingly, the correspondence was inadmissible in any subsequent litigation connected with the same subject matter, whether between the same or different parties, and furthermore, was also protected from subsequent discovery by other parties to the same litigation.

[8.53] While the discovery by the other parties to the same litigation, might be generally comprehensible, the suggestion that the correspondence remains privileged even as between the same parties, deserves some consideration. Perhaps this refers only to a situation where subsequent litigation is other than that connected with the actual terms of the agreement of the settlement itself? Support for this is to be found in the judgment of Lord Griffiths[65], where he stated: 'Thus the "without prejudice" material will be admissible if the issue is whether or not the negotiations resulted in an agreed settlement ...'. Further, the policy behind the decision is made clear in the final paragraph of Griffith LJ's judgment, where he commented:

> 'I have come to the conclusion that the wiser course is to protect "without prejudice" communications between parties to litigation from production to other parties in the same litigation. In multi-party litigation it is not an infrequent experience that one party takes up an unreasonably intransigent attitude that makes it extremely difficult to settle with him. In such circumstances it would, I think, place a serious pressure on negotiations between other parties if they knew that everything that passed between them would ultimately have to be revealed to the one obdurate litigant. What would in fact happen would be that nothing would be put on paper, but this is in itself a recipe for disaster in difficult negotiations which are far better spelt out with precision in writing'.[66]

[8.54] In *South Shropshire District Council v Amos*[67], the Court of Appeal held that the fact that a document is headed 'without prejudice' does not conclusively or automatically render it privileged. If a claim for such privilege is challenged, the court will look at the document to determine its nature. However, all documents which form part of negotiations between parties are prima facie privileged if marked 'without prejudice', even if the document merely initiates negotiations, and even if the document does not itself contain an offer.

[8.55] In *Ryan v Connolly & Connolly*[68] the facts concerned the circumstances in which a defendant should not be permitted to rely on a defence under the Statute

---

[65] [1988] 3 All ER 737 at 740.

[66] [1988] 3 All ER 737 at 742.

[67] *South Shropshire District Council v Amos* [1987] 1 All ER 340.

[68] *Ryan v Connolly & Connolly* [2001] 1 IR 627.

of Limitations 1957. The plaintiff had been involved in a collision with a car (he was driving a motorbike) on 26 April 1995. He sustained injuries and his motorbike was damaged. On 23 May 1995 his solicitors wrote to the first and second defendants stating that she was at fault and he was claiming damages against her. Her insurers wrote on 11 July 1995 to the plaintiff's solicitors, a letter headed 'without prejudice'. All letters – with one exception – from the insurers were similarly headed. Following a medical report received by the insurers from their doctor on the client, several letters were issued to the solicitors requesting whether they were in a position to discuss settlement. The last of these, on 2 July 1998, was after the limitation period of three years had expired. Two issues arose in the High Court, the first of which was whether, since virtually all letters from the insurance company were headed 'without prejudice', it was privileged and could not be taken into account by the court. Keane CJ noted the rationale of the privilege as follows[69]:

> 'It is clear that this rule has evolved because it is in the public interest that parties should be encouraged, so far as possible, to settle their disputes without resort to litigation …This is how the rule was explained in *Cutts v Head* [1984] 1 Ch 290, and it is clear from that and other authorities that the presence of the heading "without prejudice" does not automatically render the document privileged. In any case where the privilege is claimed but challenged, the court is entitled to look at the document in order to determine whether it is of such a nature as to attract privilege.
>
> The rule, however, although firmly based on considerations of public policy, should not be applied in so inflexible a manner as to produce injustice. Thus where a party invites the court to look at "without prejudice" correspondence, not for the purpose of holding his opponent to admissions made in the course of negotiations, but simply to demonstrate why a particular course had been taken, the public policy considerations may not be relevant. It would be unthinkable that the attachment of the "without prejudice" label to a letter which expressly and unequivocally stated that no point under the Statute of Limitations would be taken if the initiation of proceedings was deferred pending negotiations, would oblige a court to decide, if the issue arose, that no action of the defendant had induced the plaintiff to refrain from issuing proceedings.'

[8.56] Hence the court here was entitled to look at the correspondence, although it did not avail the plaintiff, as Keane CJ could find nothing therein to indicate that they were treating the case as one in which any defence on liability was being abandoned or that they would not raise the Statute of Limitations.[70] Although this judgment may appear to take a narrow view of the privilege, that is probably a factor of the particular facts of the case. The rationale of the

---

[69]   [2001] 1 IR 627 at 631.
[70]   [2001] 1 IR 627 at 634.

privilege in achieving and promoting settlements will probably ensure its future is more aligned with the approach taken by the English Court of Appeal in *Unilever plc v Proctor & Gamble*[71] where Walker LJ stated the privilege has a wide and compelling effect, pointing out that '[o]ne party's advocate should not be able to subject the other party to speculative cross-examination on matters disclosed or discussed in without prejudice negotiations simply because those matters do not amount to admissions.'

Marital privilege

[8.57] The privilege of husband and wife is not to disclose any communications made by the other spouse during the marriage. The privilege originated in the Evidence (Amendment) Act 1853, which provided that all communications between spouses should be privileged. Section 3 provided that:

> 'no husband shall be compellable to disclose any communication made to him by his wife during the marriage, and no wife shall be compellable to disclose any communication made to her by her husband during the marriage.'

This latter section had no application to criminal proceedings, as when it was passed, neither the accused nor the spouse of an accused was ever competent to give evidence in such proceedings. Part V of the Criminal Evidence Act 1992 rendered spouses competent in criminal proceedings as prosecution witnesses, and compellable in a limited number of circumstances. Section 26 of 1992 Act, however, provides that 'nothing in this Part shall affect any right of a spouse or former spouse in respect of marital privacy.'

The privilege against self-incrimination

[8.58] No one is bound to answer any questions which would, in the opinion of the trial judge, have a tendency to expose that witness to any criminal charge, penalty or forfeiture which the judge regards as reasonably likely to be preferred or sued for. This so-called privilege against self-incrimination is based on the rationale that it is repellent for someone to be compelled to give answers exposing him or her to the risk of criminal punishment. In *R v Minahane*[72] it was held that one could not rely on the privilege if the answer were going to incriminate strangers. This decision would have implied that spouses were already covered by the privilege, yet this would not be constitutional in light of Henchy J's dicta in *DPP (Walsh) v Kenneally*[73]. However, the Law Reform

---

[71] *Unilever plc v Proctor & Gamble* [2001] 1 All ER 783 at 793.

[72] *R v Minahane* (1921) 16 Cr App Rep 38.

[73] *DPP (Walsh) v Kenneally* [1985] ILRM.

Commission[74] considered that this privilege should be extended to cover answers tending to incriminate the spouse of a witness. This they proposed in substitution for the existing marital privilege, and is, in that regard, perhaps less obnoxious than the notion of the unity of spouses which grounded the original extension of the privilege against self-incrimination.

[8.59] This privilege protects everyone from having to answer, in a court of law, any question or produce any document or any article if, in the opinion of the judge, it would be liable to expose him to a criminal charge.

[8.60] The question of reasonable foreseeability of the charge or the reality of the witness' fear of incrimination must be addressed. In the decision of the *State (Magee) v O'Rourke*[75], Ó Dálaigh CJ considered that before a person could raise the point that he might be incriminated under foreign law if he were to answer certain questions or produce certain documents, there would have to be a reasonable possibility that the individual in question would be sent to the foreign country in question. In the case of *R v Boyes*[76], the witness concerned invoked the privilege in a situation where that witness had already been given a pardon under the Great Seal. This latter protected that witness from prosecution for the offence before the courts, but he asserted the privilege on the basis that it did not prevent his impeachment by the House of Commons. Yet this latter proceeding was so unlikely an event, that the Court of Queens Bench denied him his right to the privilege. The Court commented:

> 'We think that a merely remote and naked possibility, out of the ordinary course of the law and such as no reasonable man would be affected by, should not be suffered to obstruct the administration of justice.'

[8.61] In a similar vein is the nineteenth century case of the *King of Two Sicilies v Willcox*[77], where it was held that the privilege did not extend to answers that would incriminate a witness under foreign law. This was followed in the decision of *R v Alterton*[78]. However, in the decision of *US v McRae*[79], the United States government filed a writ in London seeking an account of monies which the plaintiff had paid to the defendant during the civil war. The defendant alleged that he was liable to forfeiture of property under United States law if he answered certain questions. It was clear from the pleadings that proceedings had

---

[74] *Report on Competence & Compellability of Spouses as Prosecution Witnesses* (LRC-13, 1985) p 73.

[75] *State (Magee) v O'Rourke* [1971] IR 205.

[76] *R v Boyes* (1861) ,1 B & S 311.

[77] *King of Two Sicilies v Willcox* (1851)1 Sim NS 301.

[78] *R v Alterton* [1912] 2 KB 251.

[79] *US v McRae* (1868) IR 3 Cr App 79.

already started in the United States, so the court allowed such privilege to be claimed.

[8.62] The category of penalties in respect of which such privilege may be claimed has been widened by our accession to the European Communities. Note the decision in *RTZ Corporation v Westinghouse Electric Corporation*[80], where the penalties imposed for breach of terms of the EC Treaty and of Council Regulations were held to qualify.

[8.63] The privilege against self-incrimination applies not only to directly incriminating answers, but also to answers tending indirectly to incriminate the witness. Yet the commentary of Megarry VC in the Court of Appeal in the case of *British Steel Corporation v Granada TV*[81] to the effect that the privilege was not as broad as to allow a witness to determine its ambit, is worth consideration: 'To answer this question might lead to a train of enquiry which if pursued might lead to some evidence which if adduced, might tend to incriminate me'. The court need not accept such a witness's view of potential incrimination and can override it.

[8.64] Some mention should be made in this context of inroads into the privilege against self-incrimination, or the so-called right to silence on the part of an accused in the context of forensic evidence. As has been seen elsewhere, ss 18 and 19 of the Criminal Justice Act 1984 impinge somewhat on the privilege against self-incrimination, to the extent that failure to account for possession of something, or presence in a particular place, on the part of an accused may lead to an inference being made by the court which may amount to corroboration of any evidence against the accused. In similar vein provision under the Criminal Justice (Forensic Evidence) Act 1990, to the effect that the refusal of an accused to consent to the taking of certain samples for the purposes of DNA testing, can lead to such an inference, is also of note in the context of incursion on such a traditional right.

Sacerdotal privilege

[8.65] An additional category has been created by the Irish courts, in attaching a recognised private privilege to the relationship between priest and parishioner. The origins of this particular privilege, which does not have counterparts in other common law jurisdictions, are located in a decision of Gavan-Duffy J in the High Court in the case of *Cook v Carroll*[82].

---

[80] *RTZ Corporation v Westinghouse Electric Corporation* [1978] AC 547.
[81] *British Steel Corporation v Granada TV* [1981] AC 1096.
[82] *Cook v Carroll* [1945] IR 515.

The facts of the case involved a plaintiff's action against the alleged seducer of her daughter, now pregnant. The parish priest who had interviewed the parties, refused to give evidence as a witness. The question of whether he was therefore guilty of contempt of court was reserved for judgment. Gavan-Duffy J adopted Wigmore's 'general principles of privileged communications'[83], to the effect that four fundamental conditions are necessary to establish a privilege against disclosure of communications between persons standing in a given relation:

(1)   the communications must originate in a confidence that they will not be disclosed;

(2)   this element of confidentiality must be essential to the full and satisfactory maintenance of the relation;

(3)   the relation must be one which in the opinion of the community ought to be sedulously fostered;

(4)   the injury which would ensue to the relation by the disclosure of the communication must be greater than the benefit thereby gained for the correct disposal of litigation.

It was held by Gavan-Duffy J that in the present case these four conditions were satisfied, and so a privilege existed.

[8.66] This somewhat surprising recognition of a privilege attaching to communications with a priest, was followed by a decision which to some degree cut down on the potential ambit of the privilege in *Cook v Carroll*. This restriction on the potential of *Cook v Carroll* is perhaps not surprising, in light of both the potential damage to the courts' ability to receive all relevant evidence, which would ensue should the same four principles be applied to other confidential relationships, and the particular reasoning of Gavan Duffy J in the *Cook v Carroll* decision. Gavan-Duffy J, prior to the recognition of the privilege, commented as follows:

'In a State where 9 out of every 10 citizens were Catholic and on a matter closely touching the religious outlook of the people, it would be intolerable that the common law, as expounded after the reformation in a Protestant land, should be taken to bind a nation which persistently repudiated the Reformation as heresy. When as a measure of necessary convenience we allow the common law generally to continue in force, we meant to include all the common law in harmony with the national spirit; we never contemplated the maintenance of any construction of the common law affected by the sectarian background. The Oireachtas is free today to determine how far our courts are to recognise the sacerdotal privilege but I am not concerned with that aspect of the matter. I am

---

[83]   Wigmore *Treatise on the Anglo-American System of Evidence in Trials at Common Law* (3rd edn, 1940) Boston, para 2285.

concerned with the juristic system of evidence surviving to us from an alien policy, and it is unthinkable that we should have imposed on ourselves in this matter the regrettable preconceptions of English judges as having here the binding force of law, when merely re-echoed by pre-treaty judges in Ireland.'

[8.67] In the subsequent decision of *Forristal v Forristal & O'Connor*[84], the facts concerned a letter written by one party to the parish priest of another party, that letter being defamatory of the latter. The priest showed the letter to the defamed party, and allowed him to borrow it for legal advice. In subsequent proceedings the priest claimed privilege of a sacerdotal nature in regard to the letter. Deale J distinguished *Cook v Carroll* on the facts, holding that one of the parties was not a parishioner of the priest in this instance and the communication itself was of dubious confidentiality. Furthermore, the manner of communication (ie a letter through the post) imported a risk that the letter might miscarry and the priest had parted with the letter to the plaintiff's solicitor. Finally, an additional risk was taken by the first defendant by choosing to write on paper. No sacerdotal privilege thus attached to the letter in question.

[8.68] In this regard it can be seen that despite the adoption of Wigmore's principles, the Irish courts have not taken the opportunity to attach private privilege to certain confidential relationships satisfying those criteria. As previously pointed out, this is perhaps preferable in terms of the administration of justice, and although it leaves the anomaly of the recognition of such a privilege in certain circumstances with regard to a Catholic priest, perhaps the mode or route of reform should be the abolition of such a privilege rather than its extension to other analogous personages. In this regard it is interesting to note that the Criminal Law Revision Committee[85] in England considered attaching a privilege to certain analogous relationships – ie that of doctor/patient or psychiatrist/patient and that of a minister of religion and parishioner – yet ultimately concluded that such was not desirable. In relation to the arguments for conferring a privilege for communication to a minister for religion, the committee felt the interests of religion, morality and society generally would dictate that a person who is willing to confide in a minister about his wrong-doing should be encouraged to do so in the confidence that there is no danger the minister will be compelled to reveal that confidence in legal proceedings. With regard to the argument that it is in accordance with the wishes of church leaders that such would be the position, the great majority of the Committee[86], while fully sympathising with the arguments, were opposed to recommending the conferment of a privilege in respect of these communications. Their main

---

[84] *Forristal v Forristal & O'Connor* (1966) 100 ILTR 182.
[85] Criminal Law Revision Committee Eleventh Report Cmnd 4991 (1972) *Evidence*.
[86] CLRC Eleventh Report 1972, paras 273-274.

reason for so doing was that there should be no restriction on the right of a party to criminal proceedings to compel a witness to give any information in his possession which is relevant to the charge, unless there is a compelling reason in policy for the restriction and the arguments for the proposal are not strong enough for this purpose. Additionally the comment was made that:

> '... it might occasionally happen that one of two accused persons had confessed to a minister that he alone, and not his co-accused, committed the offence. Even if any minister of religion felt able to stand by and let a possible innocent person be convicted while a minister was in a position to exculpate him by giving evidence, we should not wish to recommend legislation which would allow this.'

[8.69] In the context of medical practitioners, the Eleventh Report considered a strong proposal from the British Medical Association as to the conferment of such a privilege, particularly to doctors practising in psychiatry, yet again they rejected this contention. They commented as follows:

> 'The argument for this is that the public interest requires that a person should seek medical advice when this is necessary and should be able to speak freely to his doctor even about something embarrassing or discreditable without the danger that the doctor might have to give evidence about this in court. But we think that even if any privilege were given it would be wrong to go as far as this. To do so might exclude information which is important in the interests of justice to have before the court.

> For example it would be a scandal if a criminal who had been injured when blowing a safe or committing a robbery could prevent the doctor who had attended him from revealing what the criminal told him about how he came by his injury. There would be a strong case for giving a narrower privilege according to which a person who had told a doctor practising psychiatry in confidence about an offence ... could object to the doctors giving evidence about this.'

[8.70] However, in the end, the Committee decided by a large majority that for reasons similar to those in relation to ministers of religion in particular, the unlikelihood that any difficulty would arise in practice, they should not recommend that any privilege should be conferred in relation to medical practitioners.

Marriage counsellors

[8.71] An addendum to this particular debate as to the recognition of sacerdotal privilege, concerns the position of marriage counsellors, and in particular situations where marriage counsellors are in fact priests. In a decision in the High Court in *ER v JR*[87], Carroll J considered the question of whether a privilege should attach to a situation where a marriage counsellor who was a priest

---

[87] *ER v JR* [1981] ILRM 125.

counselled a married couple. Carroll J took the decision in *Cook v Carroll* into account, together with the English case of *Pais v Pais*[88]. In considering Wigmore's four principles, as enunciated in *Cook v Carroll*, Carroll J found that the four conditions did indeed apply to the situation of a priest as a marriage counsellor. She stated that the Article, with regard to the special position of the Catholic church in the Constitution, was neither relevant nor essential to this fact. The fact that the marriage counsellor was a priest, did, however, add weight to the relationship. She would include here a minister of religion as well as a priest. She felt that advice given by a minister of religion has an added dimension not present between lay people. Although commenting that courts should be slow to admit new categories of privilege, Carroll J felt that the guarantee of confidentiality was important in building up confidence between a marriage counsellor and the spouses. She considered whether the privilege should attach to all communications, or some communications, and determined that it either existed in relation to all communications or not at all. She noted that in the English case of *Pais,* the privilege had been held to attach to communications made by spouses to a marriage counsellor, and to be that not of the counsellor but of both spouses. In a similar vein, Carroll J determined here that the privilege was that of the spouses, not the priests. She would reserve the question of whether the privilege can arise where the marriage counsellor is not a priest or a minister of religion. Carroll J's judgment differs from that in *Pais v Pais* in so far as, in that case, the privilege attaching to the marriage counselling situation, seemed to be an extension of the marital privilege, rather than having any particular religious dimension. Even though in that specific case the marriage guidance counsellor was also a priest, it was emphasised by the English court that there was no authority for a privilege attaching to the priest himself. What is not clear is the source of Carroll J's privilege, in so far as there seems to be a reliance on the fact that the marriage counsellor was a priest, in so far as the general issue of marriage guidance counselling, and the attachment of a privilege thereto because of the married relationship of the spouses, is not addressed. This is in contrast to the English case, where the privilege attaching to the communications is specifically said to be that of the spouses and accordingly can be said to be part of, or an extension of, the marital privilege itself. Certainly the English authorities make it quite clear that the significant or determinative factor is not the individual's identity as a priest. What precisely is the distinguishing factor in the Irish case is perhaps not so clear, particularly since Carroll J reserves the question of whether the privilege would attach to a non-religious counsellor.

---

[88] *Pais v Pais* [1970] WLR 830.

[8.72] Section 7 of the Judicial Separation and Family Law Reform Act 1989, made provision for the adjournment of proceedings to assist reconciliation or agreements on separation, provided that for such purposes, any oral or written communication between either spouse and any third party (whether or not made in the presence of the other spouse) and any record of such communication caused to be made by such third party, should not be admissible as evidence in any court (s 7(7)). This is now amended by the Family Law (Divorce) Act 1996, which provides for the non-admissibility of evidence of communication relating to reconciliation or separation by the insertion of s 7(A) as follows:

> '7A. – An oral or written communication between either of the spouses concerned and a third party for the purpose of seeking assistance to effect a reconciliation or to reach agreement between them on some or all of the terms of a separation (whether or not made in the presence or with the knowledge of the other spouse), and any record of such a communication, made or caused to be made by either of the spouses concerned or such third party, shall not be admissible as evidence in any court.'

[8.73] A commentary on this somewhat controversial area is offered by the courts in *Johnston v Church of Scientology Mission of Dublin Ltd & Ors*[89]. The plaintiff here was suing the defendants for damages for conspiracy, misrepresentation, breach of constitutional rights, libel and the return of monies paid by her to the first defendant. An order for discovery was made against the defendants, who claimed sacerdotal privilege in respect of certain counselling notes. The notes arose from spiritual practices of 'auditing' and 'training' conducted on a one-to-one basis. The High Court refused to recognise the claim of privilege here, while making the point that it could be waived by the person being counselled, and ordered discovery. The Supreme Court allowed the defendants' appeal in relation to documents held in the United Kingdom, however, on the basis that documents to be discovered must be in the possession, custody or power of a party. Here they were not.

[8.74] In the High Court Geoghegan J points out that *ER v JR* in one sense extended the principle in *Cook v Carroll* in that it went beyond the relationship between parish priest and parishioner, but on the other hand repudiated the idea that the priest counsellor could himself have a privilege he would have to waive.[90] Geoghegan J offered the opinion that the seal of the confessional may be protected even against waiver by the penitent. However, he rejected here the analogy between the practices involved and the seal of the confession:

---

[89] *Johnston v Church of Scientology Mission of Dublin Ltd & Ors* [2001] 1 IR 682.
[90] [2001] 1 IR 682 at 685.

'I think that the absolute unwaivable privilege which probably does attach in Irish common law to the priest penitent relationship in the confessional is *sui generis* and is not capable of development in the manner suggested.'[91]

[8.75] With regard to the privilege which may arise in relation to a priest or minister as counsellor, such as he holds, can always be waived by the person being counselled. He comments further:

'Furthermore, although Carroll J left the question open, I would be inclined to think that in modern times when all kinds of secular counselling is available, and in particular marriage counselling, there may well be a privilege which the courts would uphold in some circumstances, but it would always be capable of waiver unilaterally by the persons being counselled.'[92]

Here the plaintiff waives any privilege and so no claim of sacerdotal privilege is upheld.

Journalistic privilege

[8.76] The issue of whether journalists can claim a privilege with regard to their informants or sources has also been raised in the Irish context. In the case of *Re Kevin O'Kelly*[93], O'Kelly, a journalist, was called as a prosecution witness in proceedings in the Court of Criminal Appeal. O'Kelly refused to answer a particular question, claiming journalistic privilege with regard to sources. The case was referred to the Supreme Court, where Walsh J commented that:

' ... journalists or reporters are not any more constitutionally or legally immune than other citizens from disclosing information received in confidence. The fact that a communication was made under terms of expressed confidence or implied confidence does not create a privilege against disclosure.'

[8.77] The Supreme Court, however, substituted a fine of £250 for the three month imprisonment sentence imposed by the Special Criminal Court. The non-existence of a particular privilege attaching to journalists was confirmed by English authorities in *AG v Mulholland*[94], and *British Steel Corporation v Granada TV Ltd*[95]. In England, however, the situation has been altered by legislation, in so far as s 10 of the Contempt of Court Act 1981 now gives journalists privileges in relation to their sources unless some other overriding public interest requires them to reveal same. There are four such specified public interest headings.

---

[91] [2001] 1 IR 682 at 686.
[92] [2001] 1 IR 682 at 686.
[93] *Re Kevin O'Kelly* (1974) 108 ILTR 97.
[94] *AG v Mulholland* [1963] 2 QB 477.
[95] *British Steel Corporation v Granada TV Ltd* [1981] 1 All ER 417.

[8.78] The Law Reform Commission, in a Consultation Paper on *Contempt of Court,*[96] included proposals with regard to journalistic privilege. In essence, these are to the effect that the law relating to a journalist's obligation to give evidence, and when doing so to answer questions, should not be changed. The Law Reform Commission does not perceive the Court of Criminal Appeal in *Re O'Kelly* as foreclosing the possibility of legislation providing for such a privilege, on the grounds that it is the judiciary alone whose function it is to prescribe what is to constitute evidence (they refer, for instance, to s 16 of the Central Bank Act 1989)[97].

[8.79] The question then resolves itself, according to the Commission, into one concerning possible leeway given to the Oireachtas in prescribing cases where a witness is not obliged to disclose a source:

'We consider that the Constitution permits a legislative exclusion of this nature, provided it serves a rational goal which can be justified or defended on the basis of factors to which the Constitution attaches importance, and which does not infringe against the requirements of natural justice.'

Looking at *Cook v Carroll's* statement of Wigmore's fourfold text, the Commission does not regard the present law as inhibiting the publication of material which should in the public interest be published.

[8.80] In regard to journalistic ethics the Commission commented:

'Every truly democratic system of government rests upon the rule of law, and no system is truly democratic if it does not. If the law of the land is to rule, it follows of necessity, that the courts that administer the law must not be impeded in the performance of the function by any who give their allegiance however sincerely, to the private codes of minorities, however admissible codes may, for other purposes be.'

The Commission stated that it does not wish to minimise the desirability or moral worth of journalistic codes, but it is equally manifest that the claim to follow the prescriptions of a journalistic trade union – or disinterested professional or vocational norms – should in no sense give to a journalist the right to override constitutional or statutory principles as to the admissibility of evidence.

[8.81] The drawbacks to the recognition of journalistic privilege it enumerated as follows:

(1)   An unscrupulous journalist might publish exaggerated or imagined information or allegations.

---

[96] LRC *Contempt of Court* (July 1991).
[97] *Cf Cully v Northern Bank Ltd* [1984] ILRM 683, High Court per O'Hanlon J.

(2)   An unscrupulous informant could whisper exaggerated/false information in a journalist's ear without fear of discovery, eg Anglo-Irish relations in Northern Ireland would become open to manipulation.

(3)   Arguments in favour of privilege based on the public's 'right to know' are self-defeating since allegations cannot be adequately investigated because the source of information is withheld – asserting the public's right to know on one hand; denying it on the other.

[8.82] Finally the Commission commented:

'Moreover as we have already noted, while *O'Kelly's* case is authority for the proposition that journalists enjoy no privilege as such to withhold the sources of their information, this is not to say that the court will never have regard to the confidentiality of the communication. The tests in *Cook v Carroll* were formulated by Gavan-Duffy J in the context of confidences to a spiritual advisor, but that, is not to say that they could not be applied in other contexts. If all the requirements there laid down were established, a court might not consider it proper to order a journalist to disclose his source, even though the evidence was relevant and admissible.'

Once again the issue is relegated to that of judicial discretion operative in the developing field of public privilege.

Police privilege

[8.83] Formerly, if one asked a police officer in the witness box, the source of his information, he would claim a privilege and have such claim accepted on the basis that communications between police and their informants were privileged[98]. (This was followed in *State (Quinn) v Ryan*)[99].

[8.84] In the case of *State (Hanley) v Holley*[100], it was considered whether the basis on which this privilege could be claimed should be varied. In essence, police privilege should be treated in a manner akin to a State privilege as per the decision in *Murphy v Dublin Corporation*[101], ie that a claim of privilege as the general classification to be applied to police communications could not be sustained, so that each privilege should be claimed by the police on individual occasions and be examined by the court when that arises. This approach was confirmed by Keane J and can be said to have relegated police/informant

---

[98]   *People (Attorney General) v Simpson* [1955] IR 105.
[99]   *State (Quinn) v Ryan* [1965] IR 70.
[100]   *State (Hanley) v Holley* (24 June 1983, unreported) HC.
[101]   *Murphy v Dublin Corporation* [1972] IR 215.

communications within that heading of public or State privilege where they possibly more suitably belong.

[8.85] With regard to national security, the decision of Barrington J in *State (Comerford) v Governor Mountjoy Prison*[102], is worth considering. Barrington J allowed a prison governor to claim privilege in relation to information with regard to the threatened kidnap of the prison warder and a breakout from a prison. A privilege was therefore recognised as to a source on the part of a prison governor. Again, this should perhaps be seen as an aspect of public privilege rather than that of private – not one which attaches to a particular relationship either because of the nature of the relationship, or the class of communications involved, but because of an adjudication of the court on the basis of a balancing of the interests involved.

[8.86] In the context of the revelation of the identity of informers and protection of the accused, it is interesting to note the Court of Appeal decision in *R v Agar*[103], where the Court found that the trial judge had paid too much attention to the prohibition on asking a witness to reveal the identity of police informers and too little attention to the interests of the accused who was being tried for possession of drugs with intent to supply.

[8.87] Counsel for the accused here had, in fact, confidentially been informed that X whom the accused alleged had set him up, was a police informer. The judge ruled in chambers that counsel could not cross-examine the police about X's role or reveal the matter to the client. The Court of Appeal quashed the conviction and criticised such practice of going behind the accused's back. Per Lord Mustill:

> 'There was a strong ... overwhelming public interest in keeping secret the source of information, but ... there was an even stronger public interest in allowing a defendant to put forward a tenable case in the best light'.[104]

[8.88] Because these adjudications on the balancing of public interests will inevitably arise in such areas, it is much better to categorise these as cases of public interest immunity, amenable in such manner to judicial discretion or control. Such reclassification, as per Keane J in *Holley,*[105]should commend itself to Irish law and continue.

---

[102] *State (Comerford) v Governor Mountjoy Prison* [1981] ILRM 86.
[103] *R v Agar* [1990] 2 All ER 442.
[104] [1990] 2 All ER 442 at 448.
[105] *State (Hanley) v Holley* (24 June 1983, unreported) HC.

Conclusion

[8.89] In conclusion it can be said that the instances of private privilege remain limited, and the courts have shown some reluctance to extend same. Exceptions have been seen in the case of marriage guidance counsellors, and/or priests, and their relationships with clients. Whether this is a desirable development or not is questionable. Particularly in terms of the overriding public interest in the administration of justice, it is not desirable that there should be an increased incidence of automatic exclusion of relevant evidence from perusal by the courts of trial. To this extent, the recognition of private privilege has far more implications for the interest of the administration of justice than analogous developments in the public sphere of a balancing approach to instances of confidential communications. Perhaps, moreover, it is in that latter realm that confidential relationships should be dealt with, where the courts have an opportunity to adjudge the importance of the relationship concerned, the gravity of the particular incident involved and the quality and import of the communication for litigation, before making a decision. Private privilege leaves that decision to the witness and so is much more powerful, more potentially detrimental to the administration of justice, and more valuable to the relationship.

[8.90] Hence, it is perhaps appropriate that private privilege would be confined to certain situations where there has been perceived to be a need for total frank disclosure without danger of discovery. Legal professional privilege is an instance in case. Marital privilege it is suggested should be abolished as it particularises a relationship which again could be dealt with more effectively elsewhere, and in many situations does not require an automatic attachment of privilege. Similarly journalistic privilege, and priest/parishioner privilege, could be dealt with under the auspices of public privilege, as could doctor/patient relationships. Also, the privilege against self-incrimination, which has proven to be something of a misnomer, should merit re-examination, particularly in light of recent incursions on such privilege on the part of witnesses and/or the accused which have not been considered in that light. Finally, perhaps a legislative formatting of the basis for the privileges and their exceptional loss should be provided for in legislation.

Public privilege

[8.91]

'So when can we quit passing laws and raising taxes? When can we say of our political system, "stick a fork in it, it's done"? When will our officers, officials and magistrates realise their jobs are finished and return, like Cincinnatus to the plough or, as it were to the law practice or the car dealership? The mystery of government is not how Washington works but how to make it stop.'[106]

As was seen in the context of private privilege, certain matters, otherwise relevant, may be excluded and evidence regarding them held inadmissible on the ground that they are privileged. Privilege may arise by reason of public policy, or from the circumstances of the matter itself. When the privilege arises by reason of public policy, it is usually termed State or public privilege.

[8.92] One of the initial issues that arises in this area, is as to the use of the term 'privilege' in this context. At one time, this area was referred to as 'Crown privilege' which gradually became 'State privilege' and then 'public interest' immunity. The reasons for debate or change in the nomenclature, are perhaps best given expression by Lord Simon in *Duncan v Cammell Laird & Co Ltd*[107]:

> 'privilege, in relation to discovery, is for the protection of the litigant and could be waived by him, but the rule that the interest of the State must not be put in jeopardy by producing documents which would injure it is a principle to be observed in administering justice, quite unconnected with the interests or claims of the particular parties in litigation, and indeed is a rule on which the judge should if necessary, insist, even though no objection is taken at all.'

[8.93] In a similar vein is the comment by Lord Simon in *Rogers v Secretary of State for the Home Department*[108], to the effect that privilege is properly applicable only to a claim that could be waived. This was reasserted by Lord Fraser in *Air Canada v Secretary of State for Trade (No 2)*[109] 'public interest immunity is not a privilege which may be waived by the Crown or by any party.' With regard to the waiver of public interest privilege, it is notable that although in England the view is taken that because it involves adjudication of where the public interest lies, waiver has no application here,[110] two decisions of the Irish Supreme Court indicate a different approach.

[8.94] In *McDonald v RTÉ*[111] the plaintiff had brought libel proceedings against RTÉ which he alleged had accused him of membership of the IRA and involvement in the murder of a Co Louth farmer in 1991. The defendant had subpoenaed several gardaí who consulted with the defendant and its legal advisers at its request. The trial was adjourned and the plaintiff sought discovery

---

[106] PJ O'Rourke *Parliament of Whores* Picador 1991, New York, p 14.

[107] *Duncan v Cammell Laird & Co Ltd* [1942] AC 624 at 641.

[108] *Rogers v Secretary of State for the Home Department* [1973] AC 388.

[109] *Air Canada v Secretary of State for Trade (No 2)* [1983] 2 AC 394 at 436.

[110] *Rogers v Secretary of State for the Home Department* [1973] AC 388 at 407; *Air Canada v Secretary of State for Trade* [1983] 2 AC 394 at 436.

[111] *McDonald v. RTÉ* [2001] 1 IR 355.

from the defendant of all documents grounding its defence of justification. Privilege was claimed over two files, on grounds of public interest. This, the plaintiff argued, had been waived because the defendant had had sight and possibily temporary possession of those files.

McGuinness J (with whom the other members of the Court agreed) held such did not amount to waiver, but did not expressly hold it was possible to so waiver public interest privilege. Fennelly J reserved his position.

[8.95] The doubt remaining was resolved by *Hannigan v DPP*[112]. Here the applicant sought inspection of a letter between the DPP and gardaí as to the prosecution of the applicant in the District Court. The respondent claimed public interest privilege, which the applicant alleged had been waived by the disclosure of a confidential portion of the letter on an affidavit filed by the respondent. Hariman J approved of the position in Matthew & Malek on *Discovery*[113]:

'The general rule is that where privileged material is deployed in court in an interlocutory application, privilege in that and any associated materials is waived.'

The decision in *Hannigan* would support the view that when the contents of a document have been disclosed, any subsequent claim of waiver will be ineffective.

[8.96] A second distinction between this area of the law and that of private privilege is that which arises in the context of criminal proceedings, viz, the onus on the court to give overriding force to the interest of the accused in establishing his innocence. If the evidence establishes the latter, it will be disclosed regardless of the disadvantage of disclosure. Hence, this 'privilege' is a rare occurrence in criminal trials as it is liable to be overridden in the interest of protecting the innocent from conviction.

[8.97] This category of evidence is now wider than was originally thought. Lord Hailsham gave expression to this in *D v National Society For Prevention of Cruelty to Children*[114]:

'The categories of public interest are not closed and must alter from time to time whether by restriction or extension as social conditions and social legislation develop.'

It is most useful, perhaps, to sketch the origins of the immunity, and hence indicate its current parameters and the manner of the courts' application of its rubric.

---

[112] *Hannigan v DPP* [2001] 1 IR 378.
[113] Matthew & Malek on *Discovery* (1992) Sweet & Maxwell, London, para 9.15.
[114] *D v National Society For Prevention of Cruelty to Children* [1978] AC 171.

Origins of public privilege

[8.98] One of the early English cases in this area which illustrates the principle and the occasion of its application is *Duncan v Cammell Laird & Co Ltd*[115]. The defendants, in a claim for damages for negligence in relation to the construction of a submarine, were told by the Board of Admiralty to object to the production of documents in their possession in their capacity as government contractors. The structure of the submarines was felt to be a matter that affected national security and ought to be kept secret, particularly when the country was at war. The claim to privilege was thus upheld, and the decision is one which illustrates clearly a situation where disclosure of particular information contained in a document, would have threatened State interest.

[8.99] A claim may also be based, however, not on the particular information contained in the document sought to be discovered, but in the fact that that document belongs to a class of documents which ought to be thus privileged. A recognition of this basis for the claim of public privilege or immunity is found in the statement of Lord Salmon in *Rogers v Secretary of State for the Home Department*[116] that there are:

> 'classes of documents and information which for years have been recognised by the law as entitled in the public interest to be immune from disclosure. In such cases the affidavit or certificate of the Minister is hardly necessary.'

Lord Salmon instanced Cabinet minutes as an example of such documents. Lord Reid recognised the existence of such classes of documents in *Conway v Rimmer*[117], yet queried the basis for same:

> 'I do not doubt that there are certain classes of documents which ought not to be revealed whatever their content may be ... But I do not think that many people would give as the reason that premature disclosure would prevent candour in the Cabinet. To my mind the most important reason is that such disclosure would create an ill-informed or captious public or political criticism.'

[8.100] This issue of inspection by the court of the claim was earlier discussed in *Conway v Rimmer*[118], in the context of disclosure of confidential character reports on a probationary police constable in an action brought by him against a former superintendent claiming damages for malicious prosecution. The House of Lords, in this case, inspected the documents in question, and ordered their production. The House identified the process as one of weighing on balance two public interests: that of the nation, or the public service, in non-disclosure, and

---

[115] *Duncan v Cammell Laird & Co Ltd* [1942] AC 624.
[116] *Rogers v Secretary of State for the Home Department* [1973] AC 388.
[117] *Conway v Rimmer* [1968] AC 910.
[118] *Conway v Rimmer* [1968] AC 910.

that of justice in the production of the documents. If the Minister asserts that to disclose the *contents* of the document should or might do the nation or public service a grave injury, the court will be slow to question that. Unless there is an error of judgment or law on the part of the Minister or a lack of good faith, the court should not even go as far as to inspect the document. In 'class' cases, however, the Minister's certificate is more likely to be open to challenge.

Irish case law on public privilege

[8.101] The case law in Ireland indicates that the Irish courts have diverged also from the principle of *Duncan v Camell Laird,* refusing blanket claims of State privilege. In *AG v Simpson*[119], Davitt P in the High Court stated with regard to a claim of State privilege:

> 'To be a proper claim of privilege ... must be made in pursuance of public policy and based upon the ground that disclosure would be detrimental to the public interest ... the court will not allow (the claim of privilege) unless satisfied that the head of the department of State concerned ... has in fact considered the communication in question, and has in fact formed the opinion that its disclosure would be detrimental to the public interest.'

[8.102] In the subsequent decision in *Murphy v Dublin Corporation and Minister for Local Government,*[120] this matter was given further consideration. The facts involved an inspector's report in relation to a compulsory purchase order, which the plaintiff, Murphy, wished to see. In the High Court, Kenny J dismissed Murphy's application and endorsed the House of Lord's decisions of *Glasgow Corporation v Central Land Board*[121] and *Conway v Rimmer*[122], which laid down that a court should normally endorse a Minister's decision unless (a) it was shown not to have been arrived at in good faith; (b) it is unreasonable; or (c) it is based on a misunderstanding. This principle was subject to two general rules:

(1) certain classes of documents ought not to be produced at any time; and

(2) documents which either in the Minister's view should not in the public interest be published, or belong to a class which as a matter of policy he thinks should not be published, ought to be withheld.

[8.103] The Supreme Court disagreed with Kenny J, thereby establishing a departure from the traditional position of the law in this area of presupposing the validity of the Ministerial claim. Walsh J in the Supreme Court, held that there:

---

[119] *AG v Simpson* [1959] IR 105.
[120] *Murphy v Dublin Corporation and Minister for Local Government* [1972] IR 215.
[121] *Glasgow Corporation v Central Land Board* (1956) SC 1.
[122] *Conway v Rimmer* [1968] AC 910.

'... can be no documents which may be withheld from production simply because they belong to a particular class of documents ... once the court is satisfied that the document is relevant the burden of satisfying the court that a particular document ought not to be produced lies upon the party or the person, who makes such a claim ... It may well be that it would be rare or infrequent for a court after its own examination, to arrive at a different conclusion from that expressed by the Minister, but that is far removed from accepting without question the judgment of the Minister ... The principles of *Duncan v Cammell Laird & Co Ltd* were based on considerations which are inconsistent with the supremacy of the judicial power under the constitution in the administration of justice. Those principles were first formulated when such constitutional supremacy did not exist; they do not now prevail.'

[8.104] It is interesting to note the rationale for this decision and departure from previous subservience to Ministerial claims of privilege in this area: that of the judicial mandate to administer justice and its distinct and superior nature to that of the Ministerial function (that of the government with which this privilege is allied) under the Constitution.

[8.105] Further consideration of the position under Irish law in relation to claims of public privilege or public immunity was given in the decision of *Geraghty v Minister for Local Government*[123]. The plaintiff here appealed to the Minister for Local Government against a decision of the planning authority refusing her planning permission. The Minister again refused permission, which led to the plaintiff going to the High Court, claiming a declaration that the plaintiff's determination was ultra vires the Local Government (Planning & Development) Act 1963 and void. In making discovery of documents, the defendant objected to the production of:

'documents covering normal departmental procedure in dealing with an appeal including arrangements for the oral hearing, departmental minutes between officers of the Minister regarding the appeal, correspondence between the Department and Chief State Solicitor's office regarding the action.'

The ground for such objection was that discovery of documents of that class would be contrary to public policy and detrimental to the public interest.

[8.106] Kenny J, having examined the 22 documents in question, held that:

(i)   the defendant should produce 19 documents;

(ii)   the documents from the legal adviser to the Minister attracted legal professional privilege and should not be produced.

[8.107] The Supreme Court affirming the High Court order except in relation to one document, held inter alia:

---

[123] *Geraghty v Minister for Local Government* [1975] IR 300.

(i) that the party objecting to the production of documents must justify his objection in respect of each individual document and not in respect of the class to which the documents are alleged to belong;

(ii) it is the duty of the High Court to examine each of the documents.

Hence, at an earlier stage than the English courts, the Irish judiciary are seen to have had mitigated the effect of a Ministerial claim of privilege under this head, and asserted their right and duty to examine the documentation in question.

[8.108] It is worthwhile to recall in this regard, the decision of Keane J in the *State (Hanley) v Holley*[124], which concerned an unsuccessful claim of privilege in relation to police informants. Keane J varied the basis on which such was claimed, ie not as a general classification of privilege attaching to police communications, but in a manner similar to State privilege, as delineated in *Murphy v Dublin Corporation*, leading to each claim of privilege being examined by the court when it occurs.

[8.109] The general principles to be applied in this area by the Irish courts are regarded then as having been laid down in *Murphy v Dublin Corporation* and *Geraghty v The Minister for Local Government*. These were subsequently identified and applied in *Folens v The Minister for Education*[125] by Costello J who pointed out the relevant principles as summarised by Walsh J in the *Murphy's* case:

'Where documents come into existence in the course of carrying out of the executive powers of the State, their production may be adverse to the public interest in one sphere of Government in particular circumstances. On the other hand, their non-production may be adverse to the public interest in the administration of justice. As such documents may be anywhere in the range from the trivial to the vitally important, somebody or some authority must decide which course is calculated to do the least injury to the public interest, namely, the production of the document or the possibility of the denial of right in the administration of justice. It is self-evident that this is a matter which fats into the sphere of the judicial power for determination.'

[8.110] Indeed, this latter passage, which neatly summarises the position under Irish law, was again quoted and applied to the facts of the case by Murphy J in *Incorporated Law Society of Ireland v Minister for Justice & Ors*[126].

The plaintiffs here, in pursuance of their action against the defendants brought an application seeking an order allowing them to inspect certain documents in possession of the defendants. The defendants pleaded State privilege for the

---

[124] *State (Hanley) v Holley* [1984] ILRM 149.

[125] *Folens v The Minister for Education* [1981] ILRM 21.

[126] *Incorporated Law Society of Ireland v Minister for Justice & Ors* [1987] ILRM 42 at 43.

documents. In support of such claim, was an affidavit which included the following statement, relevatory of the rationale of the claim:

'I object to producing these documents on the grounds that confidential communications of this nature made between public servants should be protected from disclosure in the interests of the efficient and proper running of the Public Service. I submit that the disclosure ... would tend to hinder the free communication necessary for the proper running of the Public Service.'

[8.111] Murphy J, in accordance with Walsh J's enunciated principles, however, saw it as the function of the court:

'... to determine first whether the production of the documents referred to would be detrimental to the efficiency of the public service and secondly, whether such prejudice outweighs the interest of the plaintiffs in their claim to have justice administered by the court.'

In accordance with precedent, and with the consent of the parties, Murphy J had read the documentation in question. He expressed the view that the possibility that documentation might be open to inspection at a later date in pursuance of discovery could inhibit the transmission and recording of advices within the public service. In addition, the present case concerned correspondence between individual Ministers of Government, necessarily of a sensitive and important nature. However, even bearing that consideration in mind, Murphy J commented that he was satisfied that there was:

'nothing in the documentation for which this particular claim of privilege is made which has any special potential for damage in the proper administration of the public service.'

In fact, given the level of expertise displayed in these documents, Murphy J opined it might rather, enhance same.

[8.112] Murphy J felt that in many such applications it would be difficult to evaluate the benefits which would flow to a plaintiff from disclosure. However, in this case, he did feel that to deny the plaintiff's access:

'would be to impose some measure of injustice on them and in my view that injustice is almost necessarily greater than the potential damage to the public service which I regard as minimal in the present case.'

The comments of Murphy J are interesting in two respects, firstly, the sensitive nature of Ministerial communications, and secondly, the difficulty of determining the value of disclosure to the party seeking it. Here Murphy J felt it could not be assessed until the case was at hearing.

[8.113] English case law in this area has been somewhat controversial. The first of these decisions worthy of note is that of *Secretary of State for Defence v*

Guardian Newspapers Ltd[127]. The document in question, was a secret memorandum from the Ministry of Defence concerning the handling of publicity in relation to the installation of nuclear weapons at an RAF base. The original had gone to the Prime Minister and six copies to senior members of government and the Cabinet Secretary. A photocopy was leaked to the defendants and published. The Crown requested a photostat so that it could attempt to identify the informant from the markings on the documents. The defendant refused, relying on s 10 of the Contempt of Court Act 1981 to the effect that a person is not required to disclose information in a publication for which they are responsible, unless it established to the satisfaction of the court that disclosure is necessary in the interests of justice or national security or for the prevention of crime. The trial judge held the Crown was entitled to discovery of the document, as s 10 did not prevent the enforcement of proprietary rights.

[8.114] The defendants appealed to the Court of Appeal and further to the House of Lords. The House of Lords noted that the prohibition in s 10 of the 1981 Act against the court making an order to disclose was of general application, subject only to four exceptions in that section: interests of natural justice, national security, prevention of disorder or crime. The onus of proof is on the party seeking the order, here, the Crown. The evidence presented was sufficient to discharge the onus of showing disclosure was necessary in the interests of national security. The risk to national security lay not in the publication of the particular document but in the possibility that whoever leaked it might in future leak other classified documents, the disclosure of which would have much more serious consequences on national security.

[8.115] The rationale of the prohibition in s 10 of the 1981 Act, according to Lord Diplock, was that it encourages the purveyors of information; the publishers decide what information to publish and are not confined to that which is in the public interest (cf Denning in the Court of Appeal). In the absence of the prohibition, sources would dry up.

[8.116] In *D v NSPCC*[128], the NSPCC had received a complaint about the treatment of a 14 month-old girl, as a result of which an inspector called at the parents' home. The mother in question brought an action against the Society for damages for personal injuries alleged to have resulted from the Society's negligence. The Society receives and investigates complaints from the public under express pledges of confidentiality. It applied for an order that there be no discovery of any documents which revealed, or might reveal, the identify of the complainant. The Society grounded its application in the proper performance of

---

[127] *Secretary of State for Defence v Guardian Newspapers Ltd* [1984] 3 All ER 601.
[128] *D v NSPCC* [1978] AC 171.

its duties which required that the absolute confidentiality of information be preserved, as if such sources were revealed, they would dry up, and such would be contrary to the public interest.

[8.117] In the House of Lords, Lord Diplock stated that the private promise of confidentiality must yield to the general public interest that in the administration of justice, truth will out, unless by reason of the character of the information or the relationship of the recipient of information to the informant, a more important public interest is served, by protecting the information or the identity of the informant from disclosure in a court of law. The public interest, that the NSPCC relied upon, was analogous to that protected by the well-established rule that the identity of police informers may not be disclosed in a civil action[129]. In relation to police informers, the balance was on the side of non-disclosure, except where upon the trial of a defendant for a criminal offence, disclosure of the identity of the informer could help to establish the defendant's innocence. Lord Diplock noted that information given to a Gaming Board had been protected from disclosure in *R v Lewes Justices ex p SS Home Dept*[130]. It was held there that the justification for such protection was analogous to that of police informers. However, the Court had not accepted the Board's proposition that wherever a party to legal proceedings claims that there is a public interest to be served by withholding documents or information from disclosure in those proceedings, it is the duty of the court to weigh that interest against the countervailing public interest in the administration of justice in the particular case and to refuse disclosure if the balance tilts that way.

In the instant case, Lord Diplock noted that the Court of Appeal had rejected the Society's claim on the basis that Crown privilege was only available where the public interest involved was the effective functioning of departments or other organs of central government. Lord Diplock saw no reason for so confining it. In *Conway v Rimmer*, the public interest to be protected was the effective functioning of a county police force. Here, he noted, it was the effective functioning of an organisation authorised under an Act of Parliament to bring legal proceedings for the welfare of children. The House also noted that there had already been recognition of immunity in relation to the child care investigation records of local authorities in wardship cases. Hence the Law Lords recognised that a public interest was to be protected and deserved recognition in the circumstances. They thus abandoned the restrictive traditional view of the privilege as espoused in the Court of Appeal, but did not go so far as to accept confidentiality, per se, as the basis of such privilege. Indeed, that

---

[129] *Marks v Beyfus* (1890) 25 QBD 494.
[130] *R v Lewes Justices ex parte SS Home Dept* [1973] AC 388.

confidentiality is not a bar to adducing evidence in court was also emphasised in *X Ltd v Morgan-Grampian Ltd*[131].

[8.118] While in *D's* case there is a ready analogy with other informer type situations, sufficient to ground the privilege, there is also evident in the decision the emergence of a general doctrine of public interest. This latter was subsequently further developed in a series of decisions including: *Science Research Council v Nasse*[132], *Neilson v Laugharne*[133] and *Hehir v Metropolitan Police Commissioner*[134].

[8.119] An Irish case concerning an adjudication as to the importance of the recognition of the privilege here, as against the effective pursuance of an action by the plaintiff, is *Gormley v Ireland & Ors*[135]. This case concerned the issue as to whether a claim of executive privilege in relation to a number of documents should be allowed, insofar as the interest of the State based on that claim outweighed the right of the individual litigant to have access to the documents in accordance with the exercise of his constitutional right to assert his legal rights in an appropriate fashion before the courts.

[8.120] The claim related to the plaintiff's right to an appropriate salary in his employment by An Post, having regard to a period of internment spent under the Offences Against the State Act 1940. The defendants denied virtually all of the facts on which this claim was based. Hence, the documents in the possession of the defendants were undoubtedly relevant to the issue. Objection was taken to their production, however, on grounds of national security. Despite the involvement of the Offences Against the State Act, such a claim was not sustained. However, Murphy J recognised that they were unquestionably confidential, sensitive documents, recording for the greater part, submissions and advices by senior civil servants to Ministers and indeed to the Government. It was in the public interest that communications of this nature should be made on the basis that they would not be disclosed in legal proceedings, unless the court is satisfied that the public interest in this regard is outweighed.

[8.121] Of the documents in question, those relating to the detention and subsequent alleged refusal of the plaintiff to give an undertaking with regard to membership of a prescribed organisation, were ordered to be disclosed. Other documentation, which comprised largely of correspondence with the gardaí, was highly confidential material, disclosure of which might be significantly

---

[131] *X Ltd v Morgan-Grampian Ltd* [1990] 2 All ER 1 at 15.
[132] *Science Research Council v Nasse* [1980] AC 1028.
[133] *Neilson v Laugharne* [1981] 1 All ER 829.
[134] *Hehir v Metropolitan Police Commissioner* [1982] 2 All ER 235.
[135] *Gormley v Ireland & Ors* (7 March 1991, unreported) HC (Murphy J).

detrimental to the public interest. While the said documentation might be of some value to the plaintiff, they were not fundamental to his case. They were thus not ordered to be disclosed. Finally, the court stressed the function of discovery as being solely for the proper processing of litigation. Hence, copies were to be made by the solicitor only for counsel briefed, and not to be inspected by other persons.

Tromso Sparebank v Beirne (No 2)

[8.122] The High Court decision in *Tromso Sparebank v Beirne (No 2)*[136], which deals with the issue of legal professional privilege, may indicate in its approach a discontent with the ambit of private privilege which hampers adjudicative scrutiny of evidence, without the alleviation of judicial control. That case concerned proceedings for damages instituted by the plaintiff – a Norwegian savings bank – arising out of the dishonour of two promissory notes for almost £12 million. The Northern Bank Ltd, one of the defendants, sought discovery of a number of documents, including copy documents in relation to which the plaintiff had claimed legal professional privilege. Costello J first considered the claim in relation to copies of documents which were not in themselves privileged but were obtained for the purpose of obtaining legal advice. In support of the claim of privilege was the statement in the *White Book (the Supreme Court Practice)*[137], to the effect that original or copy documents obtained or that were prepared by a party for the purpose of obtaining a solicitor's advice in view of pending or anticipated proceedings, are privileged. This statement was based on *The Palermo*[138] and *Watson v Cammell Laird & Co Ltd.*[139]

[8.123] However, in support of the defendant's submission that this should not be followed as being too wide, was a statement by Denning MR in *Buttes Gas & Oil Co v Hammer (No 3)*[140]: '... if the original is not privileged, neither is a copy made by the solicitor privileged'. Despite an express disapproval of that statement by the court in *R v Board of Inland Revenue ex p Codibert*[141], Costello J concluded as follows:

'I see no reason why legal professional privilege should apply to the copy documents with which this case is concerned. Legal professional privilege exists so that a litigant can have redress to his legal advisers in circumstances which

---

[136] *Tromso Sparebank v Beirne & Ors (No 2)* [1989] ILRM 257.
[137] *White Book (the Supreme Court Practice)* (1988) para 24-5-10.
[138] *The Palermo* (1883) 9 PD 6.
[139] *Watson v Cammell Laird & Co Ltd* [1959] 2 All ER 757.
[140] *Buttes Gas & Oil Co v Hammer (No 3)* [1981] QB 223.
[141] *R v Board of Inland Revenue ex p Codibert* [1988] 3 WLR 522.

enable him to have complete confidence that the communications made to him and from him will be kept secret ... I cannot see that the protection of the interests of a litigant requires the privilege to be extended to copies of documents which came into existence prior to the contemplation of litigation, documents which are themselves not privileged and which the other side could probably inspect as a result of a third party discovery order and which they could have produced at the trial pursuant to a *subpoena duces tecum.* The rules of court are designed to further the rules of justice and they should be construed by the court so that they assist in the achievement of this end. If inspection of the documents cannot conceivably injure the interests of one party and may well assist the other to ascertain the true facts of the case prior to trial I do not think that the court should put a gloss on the rules which would prevent this result ...'[142]

[8.124] Costello J later acknowledged the privilege to attach to letters between the legal advisers of the plaintiff bank, both to one another, and to the bank itself and did not find favour with the suggestion that the privilege had been waived because the plaintiff bank had alleged in its pleadings that it was the holder of the notes in good faith and that as this was now an issue in the proceedings, the steps taken, including the legal advice taken when obtaining the notes, became relevant and the privilege were waived. Costello J acknowledged in so doing that 'it is important ... to maintain the principle of legal professional privilege'.

[8.125] However, that statement and particular vindication of the privilege is at odds with the earlier circumspection, in light of the need to 'further the rules of justice'. The latter is surely more relevant to the sphere of public interest immunity than to the realm of private privilege, where in the context of the limited instances where it applies its invocation at the behest of the parties to the relation is paramount. Costello J seemed to respect this with regard to the waiver of the privilege in the context of the second set of documents considered; yet his construction of the law in relation to copy documents moves an interpretation at odds not only with previous determinations but perspectives on the area. The decision, moreover, would also seem somewhat at odds with that of Murphy J subsequently in *Bula v Crowley*[143].

[8.126] Costello J's decision may be indicative of a broader desire on the part of the judiciary to extend the rubric of judicial discretion to the private privilege area, as part of a corresponding development and enhancement of the public interest immunity sphere. Together with possible greater cohesiveness and fewer anomalies with regard to particularisation of certain relationships (marital, legal, professional, etc), this would have the merit, from a judicial perspective, of an

---

[142] [1989] ILRM 257 at 261-262.
[143] *Bula v Crowley* (25 July 1991, unreported) HC.

enhanced mandate to secure the administration of justice and its reconciliation with competing public interests.

[8.127] That this mandate to balance competing public interests is secured, and founded on judicial sovereignty in the administration of justice, was emphasised in the context of recent challenges to the basic philosophy inherent in *Murphy* and *Geraghty*, viz, under Irish law the concept of Crown privilege or public interest immunity is subservient to judicial and not ministerial discretion.

Bula Ltd v Tara Mines

[8.128] In *Bula Ltd (in receivership) v Tara Mines Ltd, Minister for Energy & Others*, judgment arose out of an affidavit of discovery made on behalf of the Minister for Energy. Some 60 documents were confidential and sensitive to a greater or lesser degree, and in relation to which the Minister was entitled to claim executive privilege. Other documents were furnished to the Court for the purpose of determining whether the interest of the Minister, and the public through him, in maintaining the confidentiality of these communications, was greater than the need of the plaintiffs and the right of the public generally, to ensure that inspection was made of all documentation which would be necessary for the proper exercise of the constitutional right to have access to the courts set up under the Constitution. Per Murphy J:

> 'Virtually all of the documents inspected by me concern advice given at the highest level by senior civil servants to Government Ministers and submissions by Ministers to Cabinet based on such advices. In some cases the documentation contains what might be described as a very frank analysis of the conduct and character of persons engaged in various pursuits. It may appear also that there was not unanimity between all advisers on all topics. Again it is almost inescapable that advices of this nature should contain some reference direct or indirect to views expressed by the Attorney General. It was my anxiety to ascertain how far factors of that nature created a particular concern for the Minister.'

[8.129] Reliance was placed in part on the desirability of not inhibiting civil servants in giving candid advice to the Executive by ordering disclosure in this case. However, Murphy J pointed out that since *Geraghty*[144], all administrators must now be conscious that no absolute privilege attaches to documents containing advice to Ministers, so that any caution or ill-effects induced by that consideration had already occurred. What the hearing did bring to light, per Murphy J, however, is that the Minister's concern that the form in which certain cabinet documents are cast should not be disclosed.

---

[144] *Geraghty* [1975] IR 306.

[8.130] Murphy J found the said form to be similar to that of documents prepared by internal advisers of a substantial company for presentation to its board of directors. Some of the information, per Murphy J, was 'essentially private, confidential, commercial advice'. Some contained reference to legal advice in relation to which the Minister could rely on legal as opposed to executive privilege. Some documents had no bearing on issues in the present case and should not be disclosed. Murphy J concluded that:

> 'In the circumstances it seems to me that the correct balance between the interest of the public in securing an effective public service and the proper administration of justice is to be found by permitting the inspection of all the documents submitted to the court but subject to sealing up or pasting over by any appropriate means so much of the documents as consist or disclose the following:
>
> (1)　Legal advice obtained by the Minister from the Attorney General or any other legal adviser.
>
> (2)　A review of the conduct or affairs of their parties (particularly those engaged in the mining industry) wholly unrelated to any issue arising in the present proceedings.
>
> (3)　The form in which submissions are made to the Government as distinct from the contents of such submissions. In my view it would be appropriate to provide the title of the submission and the date thereof and to obliterate the remainder of the formal submission and the queries raised thereon.'

Ambiorix Ltd v Minister for Environment

[8.131] *Ambiorix Ltd v Minister for Environment*[145] was a Supreme Court decision in a similar vein. The grounds of appeal were against the order of the trial judge granting discovery of documents including memoranda from Government and Cabinet documents, included here the contention that the Supreme Court should reconsider the decision and the principles laid down in *Murphy v Dublin Corporation*[146].

[8.132] Specifically, it was submitted that a class or category of documents, consisting of documents emanating at a level not below that of assistant secretary and for the ultimate consideration of Government Ministers, should be absolutely exempt from production and should not be examined by a judge before privilege was granted to them unless the judge was dissatisfied with the accuracy of the description of the document.

[8.133] There was no contention, as the Chief Justice noted in this case, that the documents were not relevant to the issues arising on the plaintiff's action. The

---

[145] *Ambiorix Ltd v Minister for Environment* (23 July 1991, unreported) SC.
[146] *Murphy v Dublin Corporation* [1972] IR 215.

Chief Justice stated that the flaw in the appellant's submission here was that it ignored the constitutional origin of the *Murphy* decision. The principles set out in that case by Walsh J were as follows:

'(1)   Under the Constitution the administration of justice is committed solely to the judiciary in the exercise of their powers in the courts set up under the Constitution.

(2)   Power to compel the production of evidence (which, of course, includes a power to compel the production of documents) is an inherent part of that judicial power and is part of the ultimate safeguard of justice in the State.

(3)   Where a conflict arises during the exercise of the judicial power between the aspect of public interest involved in the production of evidence and the aspect of public interest involved in the confidentiality or exemption from production of documents pertaining to the exercise of the executive powers of the State, it is the judicial power which will decide which public interest shall prevail.

(4)   The duty of the judicial power to make that decision does not mean that there is any priority or preference for the production of evidence over other public interests, such as the security of the State or the efficient discharge of the functions of the executive organ of the Government.

(5)   It is for the judicial power to choose the evidence upon which it might act in any individual case in order to reach that decision.'

[8.134] The Chief Justice then went on to say that these principles led to certain practical conclusions applicable to a claim of privilege by the Executive of the nature here arising:

'(a)   The Executive cannot prevent the judicial power from examining documents which are relevant to an issue in a civil trial for the purpose of deciding whether they must be produced.

(b)   There is no obligation on the judicial power to examine any particular document before deciding that it is exempt from production, and it can and will in many instances uphold a claim of privilege in respect of a document merely on the basis of a description of its nature and contents which it (the judicial power) accepts.

(c)   There cannot, accordingly, be a generally applicable class or category of documents exempted from production by reason of the rank in the Public Service of the person creating them, or of the position of the individual or body intended to use them.'

The Chief Justice added, however, that he preferred to leave over further consideration of the issue of the safety of the State until it arose for decision in a case.

[8.135] With regard to the issue of a privilege attaching to communications between third parties and Government departments, taking the form of submissions to such departments by citizens, originating in the belief they would be treated in confidence, the Court noted there was no public interest in keeping such communications immune from production. The Chief Justice did point out, however, that a party obtaining documents by discovery, was prohibited from making use of such, other than for the purpose of the action, otherwise a contempt of court would be perpetrated.

[8.136] McCarthy J's view is perhaps the most significant in locating the *Murphy* decision firmly in judicial sovereignty in the administration of justice, discovery of documents being part of the constitutional guarantee of fair procedures.

Breathnach v Ireland (No 3)

[8.137] As a result of these decisions, the courts engaged in an exercise of balancing the public interest in the administration of justice (which obviously requires as much information as possible to be available to the court) and the public interest put forward in favour of non-disclosure. A case which illustrates this process is the decision in *Breathnach v Ireland (No 3)*[147]. In *Breathnach*, in addition to reliance on legal professional privilege to prevent disclosure, the DPP felt that communications made by gardaí to the DPP were in circumstances where they believed they would be confidential, and that it was necessary to maintain the confidentiality of such communications in order to ensure full disclosure by the gardaí (of their suspicions, opinions etc), hence it was in the public interest not to disclose such documents.

[8.138] Keane J emphasised that any claim of privilege by reference to a document belonging to a class of documents had been emphatically rejected by *Murphy, Ambiorix* and his own decision in *DPP (Hanley) v Holly*.[148] The process which he was to engage in was described thus by Keane J:[149]

'[T]he court, as I understand the law, is required to balance the public interest in the proper administration of justice against the public interest reflected in the grounds put forward for non-disclosure in the present case. The public interest in the prevention and prosecution of crime must be put in the scales on the one side. It is only where the first public interest outweighs the second public interest that an inspection should be undertaken or disclosure ordered. In considering the first public interest, it is necessary to determine to what extent, if any, the relevant documents may advance the plaintiff's case or damage the defendant's case or

---

[147] *Breathnach v Ireland (No 3)* [1993] 2 IR 458.
[148] *DPP (Hanley) v Holly* [1984] ILRM 149.
[149] *Breathnach v Ireland (No 3)* [1993] 2 IR 458 at 471.

fairly lead to an enquiry which may have either of those consequences. In the case of the second public interest, the various factors set out by Mr Liddy must be given due weight. Again, as has been pointed out in the earlier decisions, there may be documents the very nature of which is such that inspection is not necessary to determine on which side the scales come down. Thus, information supplied in confidence to the gardaí should not in general be disclosed, or at least not in cases like the present where the innocence of an accused person is not in issue, and authorities to that effect, notably *Marks v Beyfus* (1890) 25 QBD 494, remain unaffected by the more recent decisions, as was made clear by Costello J in *Director of Consumer Affairs v Sugar Distributors Ltd* [1991] 1 IR 225. Again, there may be material the disclosure of which would be of assistance to criminals by revealing methods of detection or combating crime, a consideration of particular importance today when criminal activity tends to be highly organised and professional. There may be cases involving the security of the State, where even disclosure of the existence of the document should not be allowed. None of these factors – and there may, of course, well be others which have not occurred to me – which would remove the necessity of even inspecting the documents is present in this case.'

[8.139] With regard to the specific question of the garda files and whether they attracted privilege here on the grounds of public interest, Keane J concluded[150]:

'It is obvious that in every case where the commission of a crime, whether trivial or serious, is suspected, documentary material will be assembled by the gardaí irrespective of whether a prosecution is ever initiated. The fact that the documents in question may, as in the present case, be submitted by the investigating gardaí to the Director of Public Prosecutions in order to obtain his decision as to whether a prosecution should be instituted could not possibly give that material the same status as, to take an obvious example, a medical report obtained by a plaintiff in a personal injuries action solely for the purpose of his claim. If privilege exists in relation to such documents, it can only be because of the other factors referred to by Mr. Liddy, of which undoubtedly the most important is the desirability of freedom of communication between the gardaí and the Director of Public Prosecutions may subsequently be disclosed in court proceedings is clearly a matter which has to be taken into consideration in determining whether the public interest in the particular case requires its production.

In civil proceedings, the desirability of preserving confidentiality in the case of communications between members of the executive has been significantly eroded as a factor proper to be taken into account by the courts: see in particular the speech of Lord Keith in *Burmah Oil Co Ltd v The Bank of England* [1980] AC 1090 and the observations of McCarthy J in *Ambiorix v Minister for the Environment* [1992] 1 IR 277. However, different considerations would appear to

---

[150] *Breathnach v Ireland (No 3)* [1993] 2 IR 458 at 474-475.

apply to communications between the gardaí and the Director of Public Prosecutions, where the public interest in the prevention and prosecution of crime must be given due weight. It would be clearly unacceptable if in every case where a person was acquitted of a criminal charge, he could, by instituting proceedings for wrongful arrest or malicious prosecution, embark on a fishing expedition through all the files of the gardaí relating to the case. The circumstances of the particular case must determine, in the light of the constitutional principles to which I have referred, whether an inspection should be undertaken by the court and whether, as a result of that inspection, production of any of the documents should be ordered.

The plaintiff's claim includes one for damages for malicious prosecution. If he is to succeed in his claim, he will have to establish as a matter of probability that one or more of the defendants played a part in the institution of the criminal proceedings and, in so doing, acted maliciously and without reasonable and probable cause. It has already been held by the Court of Criminal Appeal that the primary facts found by the Special Criminal Court could only have led to the inference that the interrogation of the plaintiff which culminated in the making of incriminating statements by him did not comply with fair procedures and to the further inference that the statements could not be regarded as voluntary. The factors referred to by the court in reaching that conclusion were, principally, the place and time at which the enquiry was conducted and the unexplained failure to comply with the plaintiff's request that a solicitor be present during the interrogation. I appreciate that, unlike some of the other evidential issues, no question of res judicata arises in relation to those findings. However, in exercising my discretion as to whether particular documents should be produced, I do not think I can disregard the evidential context, as indicated by those findings, in which the issues arising in the present proceedings will ultimately fall to be determined. The material furnished by such of the gardaí as were concerned in the interrogation to the Director of Public Prosecutions might well furnish evidence which would be of significance in establishing a want of reasonable or probable cause for the prosecution. This, of course, is in no sense to pre-judge that issue, which will have to be resolved at the trial of the action. It seems to me that the public interest in the administration of justice outweighs the desirability in general of preserving the confidentiality of such documents.'

Other Irish case law

[8.140] In *Goodman International v Hamilton & Ors*[151], members of the Oireachtas joined as notice parties, had made serious allegations against the applicants before the respondent. They refused to disclose the identities of those persons who had supplied them with the information on which the allegations were made. They argued in the High Court that the relationship between a member of the public and a member of the Oireachtas in such a situation, was a

---

[151] *Goodman International v Hamilton* [1993] 3 IR 320.

relationship within the preconditions of *Cook v Carroll* The Court found it unnecessary to decide this point, but approved of the dictum of Lord Edmond-Davies in *D v NSPCC,* that where a communication was made in the context of a confidential relationship, such that disclosure of the communication would be in breach of some ethical or social value involving the public interest, the court had a discretion to uphold a refusal to give evidence in relation to the communication, provided it was clearly demonstrated that the public interest would be better served by excluding such evidence. The court was also of the view that the extension of the categories giving rise to a private privilege would be contrary to *Murphy, Geraghty* and *Ambiorix*, and emphasised that the exclusion of admissible and relevant evidence was contrary to the public interest in the administration of justice. On the facts, the High Court felt the discretion of the tribunal would be exercised in favour of non-disclosure.

[8.141] In *DPP v Special Criminal Court; Paul Ward*[152] all but 40 statements made by 20 persons had been made available to the defendant's legal advisers, on his trial in the Special Criminal Court for murder. A prosecution witness swore that if the confidential information in relation to organised crime was to become known, they would face a death sentence and it would be impossible to investigate organised crime. The Special Criminal Court felt an injustice might be done if Ward's legal advisers were not allowed to see the statements, so if he was willing to waive his personal rights of inspection and being informed of their contents, they could be produced to his lawyers. On appeal, the High Court (Carney J) held that the Special Criminal court had altered the relationship between lawyer and client and felt the court itself should inspect the documents. The appeal to the Supreme Court was dismissed, but that Court commented that the prosecution task was not just to secure a conviction, but to be 'ministers of justice' in disclosing any evidence that might help the defence. The informer's privilege, they held, was of ancient origin (*Marks v Beyfus*[153]; *People v Reddan*[154]; *Skeffington v Rooney*[155] followed) and was subject only to the 'innocence at stake' exception.

[8.142] In *Johnston v Church of Scientology*[156], the defendants argued that such a degree of confidentiality attached to the counselling notes that the court must weigh up the public interest in the preservation of such confidentiality against the normal public interest in the disclosure of all relevant evidence, and must in

---

[152] *DPP v Special Criminal Court; Paul Ward* [1999] 1 IR 60.

[153] *Marks v Beyfus* (1890) 25 QBD 494.

[154] *People v Reddan* [1995] 3 IR 560.

[155] *Skeffington v Rooney* [1997] 1 IR 22.

[156] *Johnston v Church of Scientology* [2001] 1 IR 682.

all the circumstances come down in favour of preservation of the confidentiality. Geoghegan J in the High Court disagreed:

> '...I reject also the argument that there is a greater public interest in upholding the confidentiality than the public interest in relevant evidence being produced in court for the purposes of the administration of justice.'[157]

[8.143] In *People v Catherine Nevin*[158], the appellant in pursuing an appeal from her murder conviction, sought disclosure from the DPP of certain documents relating to a document drawn up by the anti-racketeering unit of the gardaí in which Jack White's Inn was listed as public house with possible IRA connections. Several weeks after the conviction, the Chief State Solicitor had informed the appellant's solicitor of this document. The significance of it was that the appellant had in her evidence suggested that her late husband was a member of the IRA. The DPP claimed privilege either on the grounds of legal professional privilege (gardaí seeking legal advice), or that the list was furnished in confidence and disclosure would reveal the methodology of gardaí in investigating any potential for disturbance of the public peace. The Court was satisfied the claim of legal professional privilege was well-founded but also the claim of public privilege:

> '...[T]he court would hold that the claim of confidentiality by the Director should be upheld because in the act of balancing the interests of the Director as set out in the affidavit of Deputy Commissioner Conroy on the one hand in non-disclosure and the interests of justice and fair procedures for the appellant on the other the court is quite satisfied that the arguments for non-disclosure outweigh the arguments for disclosure.'[159]

[8.144] Whether or not public privilege ultimately develops to subsume that relating to the heads of private privilege, its future is secure, having been intimately identified with judicial sovereignty and the separation of powers. Undoubtedly, in this jurisdiction at least, it will lead to an enhancement of the role of judicial discretion and scrutiny in an area, the territory of which is gradually being carved out.

---

[157] *Johnston v Church of Scientology* [2001] 1 IR 682 at 687.

[158] *People v Catherine Nevin* (13 December 2001, unreported), CCA (Geoghegan J).

[159] (13 December 2001, unreported), CCA at 7.

Chapter 9

The Rule Against Hearsay

'He had taken my story, with all its – what was it Haslet said? – with all its frills and fancy bits, and pared it down to stark essentials. It was an account of my crime I hardly recognised, and yet I believed it. He had made a murderer of me. I would have signed it there and then, but I had nothing to write with. I even searched my clothing for something sharp, a pin or something, with which to stick myself, and scrawl my signature in blood. But what matter, it did not require my endorsement. Reverently I folded the page in four and placed it under the mattress at the end where my head would be. Then I undressed and lay down naked in the shadows and folded my hands on my breast, like a marble knight on a tomb, and closed my eyes. I was no longer myself. I can't explain it, but it's true. I was no longer myself.'

John Banville *The Book of Evidence* (1989) Minerva, London, p 203.

Introduction

[9.01] Cross describes the rule against hearsay as follows '... a statement other than one made by a person while giving oral evidence in the proceedings is inadmissible as evidence of any fact stated'.[1] The rule operates, therefore, to potentially exclude informal oral remarks, formal written statements, sworn testimony in previous proceedings, as well as gestures, signs, photographs, etc. The reason behind this exclusionary rule affecting otherwise relevant and probative evidence, is that if the maker of the statement does not testify, he is not available for cross-examination (per Wigmore: 'the greatest legal engine ever invented for the discovery of truth'[2]), nor can his demeanour be observed or credibility tested. Moreover, it is desirable that the best evidence be available to the court and that the danger of inaccuracy through repetition be avoided.

[9.02] Hence the rule is located in the faith in the power of cross-examination; distrust of the jury's ability to evaluate hearsay; and a fear that if allowed, the courts would be swamped with hearsay evidence. The rule is one that has developed with the format of the modern trial and is deeply wedded to our process of legal investigation. Correspondingly, it is difficult to overcome, however apparently archaic or undesirable at times, without legislative

---

[1] *Cross on Evidence* (1985 6th edn) Butterworths, p 454.
[2] Wigmore 'A Treatise on the Anglo-American System of Evidence' in *Trials at Common Law* (3rd edn 1940) Boston.

intervention (see the House of Lords decision in *Myers v DPP*)[3]. The definitive statement of the hearsay rule and its ambit and effect in Irish law, is to be found in the judgment of Kingsmill-Moore J in *Cullen v Clarke*[4]:

'... there is no general rule of evidence to the effect that a witness may not testify as to the words spoken by a person who is not produced as a witness. There is a general rule, subject to many exceptions, that evidence of the speaking of such words is inadmissible to prove the truth of the facts which they assert ... This is the rule known as the rule against hearsay. If the fact that the words were spoken rather than their truth is what it is sought to prove, a statement is admissible.'

[9.03] The rule against hearsay, like other rules of evidence, does not automatically apply to administrative tribunals. However, if the circumstances are such that admission of such evidence would result in a breach of natural/ constitutional justice, adherence with same would seem to be required[5].

[9.04] The disadvantages of the rule against hearsay are obvious: the exclusion of evidence of a dead, unavailable or unidentifiable person; the extra cost involved in proving relevant facts; and the exclusion of evidence otherwise thought to be reliable, which may indeed prevent an accused from exonerating himself. There are, however, exceptions to the rule, which in the nature of things – and particularly in the context of the law of evidence – are more important than the rule itself. These exceptions have been carved out by the courts over the years and would now seem to be static[6]. They originate from the fact that the categories concerned involved particularly reliable types of evidence, or are centred on the unavailability of better evidence. In *Myers,* the House of Lords emphasised that further exceptions to the hearsay rule on the basis that evidence was particularly reliable, or the best available, would not now be justified. In Ireland it seems likely the position is similar.

[9.05] Griffiths[7] has commented that the decision in *Myers* is one of particular judicial cowardice. He stated that the case illustrates effectively the absurdity of the continuance in effect of a rule now archaic and out of tune with modern social conditions in its refusal to the courts of the facility/ability to rely on 'business records' (which would be regarded as eminently receivable in the business world on important everyday affairs), simply because of the inability to point to the particular worker who compiled the ledger in question, which was of value in identifying stolen cars.

---

[3]   *Myers v DPP* [1965] AC 1001.
[4]   *Cullen v Clarke* [1963] IR 368 at 378.
[5]   *Kiely v Minister for Social Welfare* [1971] IR 21.
[6]   *Myers v DPP* [1965] AC 100.
[7]   Griffiths *Politics of the Judiciary* (1977).

[9.06] In *People (DPP) v Byrne*[8], facts similar to that in *Myers* arose in the Irish context. The applicant, a car dealer, had been convicted of handling a motor car knowing or believing it to be stolen. Evidence was given by a number of witnesses relating to the importation of the stolen vehicle: from an employee of the National Vehicle Deliveries Ltd who produced a form with his signature relating to the examination and recording of its chassis and engine number at Rosslare; the lorry driver who signed for its delivery to the motor dealership; an employee who inspected the vehicle and signed a form containing its chassis number; an officer of the Revenue, as to the results of his examination of the registered vehicle and the mismatch between identification numbers; and an officer of the Motor Taxation Office who produced original documents relating to the reconstructed vehicle.

On appeal, it was alleged the trial judge erred in admitting evidence which was inadmissible under *Myers*. To come within the remit of the Criminal Evidence Act 1992, it was argued that evidence would have to have been given by persons who compiled the documents, and a certificate pursuant to s 6 of that Act to that effect had not been produced.

The Court of Criminal Appeal held that the prosecution was not obliged to produce a certificate under s 6 of the 1992 Act to render the evidence admissible. Each witness had identified a document s/he had personally filled in or signed. As the situation was distinct from *Myers* (where such employees who had so compiled the documentation could not have been identified), the Criminal Evidence Act did not have to be invoked. In essence, the Court held these individuals were themselves testifying as to knowledge which they had, and hence it was not hearsay. By referring to the documents, they were simply 'refreshing their memories', as is often allowed, for example, to gardaí in consulting their notebooks.[9]

[9.07] The Law Reform Commission, in its *Report on the Rule Against Hearsay*[10] stated that the disadvantages of the hearsay rule are mitigated in practice as the courts freely allow hearsay evidence of probative value when tendered by the defence. In civil cases parties similarly agree to waive the rule, or the trial judge may discourage a pressing argument from counsel on the issue. While, strictly speaking, there is no judicial discretion to excuse or allow breaches of the hearsay rule, should the latter occur, even in a criminal case, no miscarriage of justice can be adjudged to have occurred, in accordance with s 5(1)(a) of the Courts of Justice Act 1928.

---

[8]   *People (DPP) v Byrne* (7 June 2000) CCA.

[9]   See *Northern Banking Company v Carpenter* [1931] IR 268; *Lord Talbot de Malahide v Cusack* (1864) 17 ICLR 213.

[10] LRC *Rule Against Hearsay* working paper (LRC 9-1980) p 11.

[9.08] However, such a solution is undesirable in not providing sufficient certainty for the parties to know where they stand in advance of the case and to facilitate a prediction of the outcome with some degree of accuracy. The Criminal Evidence Act 1992 did make some considerable provision for the admissibility of hearsay evidence in certain circumstances. These relate primarily to the admissibility of certain documentary evidence in criminal proceedings. Outside of such specific exceptional provisions, the strength of the rule prevails. For example, in *DPP v Det Sgt Kelly v McGinley*[11], Keane J, on a bail application, refused to admit hearsay evidence tendered by the gardaí with regard to threats to the victim's family. Objection to its admissibility was upheld on the basis of natural justice.

The distinction between original evidence and hearsay evidence

[9.09] In *Subramaniam v DPP*[12] the accused was charged with the unlawful possession of ammunition. The defence put forward was that one of the accused, having been captured by terrorists, had acted under duress. The question arose as to the admissibility of conversations between the accused and the terrorists for the purpose of establishing the defence. At trial the judge adjudged the statements to constitute hearsay and so be inadmissible. On appeal to the Privy Council it was held that a statement constitutes hearsay and is inadmissible, when the object of the evidence is to establish the truth of what is contained in the statement. It is not hearsay and is admissible when it is proposed to establish by the evidence, not the truth of the statement, but the fact that it was made. Here, statements made by terrorists to the appellant, whether true or not, if they had been believed by the appellant, might reasonably have induced in him a fear of instant death if he did not obey.

Implied assertions

[9.10] The issue has arisen as to whether the rule against hearsay applies not only to express assertions and conduct intended to be assertive (eg nods and gestures), but also to statements or conduct not intended to be assertive, but which rest on an assumption of fact believed by the maker of the statement or actor, which can be inferred by the court.

[9.11] There is a certain amount of difficulty with the case law on this issue, as it is not always apparent if the statement is being admitted because it does not constitute hearsay, or by virtue of an exception to the hearsay rule.

---

[11] *DPP v Det Sgt Kelly v McGinley* (20 May 1998, unreported) SC.
[12] *Subramaniam v DPP* [1956] 1 WLR 965 PC.

[9.12] In *Lloyd v Powell Duffryn Steam Coal Co Ltd*[13], the issue arose as to whether a child was the son of a man who had been killed in the course of his employment with the respondents. There was evidence to the effect that the deceased, knowing the child's mother to be pregnant, promised to marry her; and had told a friend and his landlady that he was going to marry her because of the pregnancy. The Court of Appeal determined the statement to be a declaration against interest and therefore admissible in evidence under an exception to the hearsay rule. The House of Lords, on the other hand, deemed the statement to be admissible, but not as an exception to the hearsay rule, rather because the state of mind of the deceased and his intentions with regard to the child were relevant in their own right. The testimony of the witness was as to the act, ie to the deceased speaking these words, and it was the speaking of the words which was the matter being put in evidence and which possessed evidential value. Thus, the statement was admissible, not constituting hearsay.

[9.13] In *Teper v R*[14] the accused had been convicted of arson, and evidence of a policeman was tendered to the effect that some 26 minutes after the fire had started and about a furlong away, he had heard a woman say, 'Your place is burning and you are going away', and noticed a car with a man in it who resembled the accused.

The Privy Council deemed the evidence inadmissible, not falling within an exception to the hearsay rule, being without the ambit of the doctrine *of res gestae*. (Heydon[15] comments in relation to this decision that the evidence could have been excluded on the basis that it did not constitute hearsay, as the innuendo in the statement was not clear and could be irrelevant as to who caused the fire).

[9.14] Another relevant decision in the area is that of *Ratten v R*[16], where the facts concerned a shooting of the accused's wife with a gun, which he alleged to have been accidental. Evidence was tendered to the effect that around the time of the shooting, a telephonist received a call from the accused's house and heard a woman's voice, evidently hysterical, say, 'Get me the police, please'. The Privy Council determined this did not constitute hearsay. Yet, even if it was considered to be hearsay, it would come within the ambit of the exception constituted by the doctrine of *res gestae*. Lord Wilberforce reasoned that:

> 'The mere fact that evidence of a witness includes evidence as to words spoken by another person who is not called is no objection to its admissibility. Words

---

[13] *Lloyd v Powell Duffryn Steam Coal Co Ltd* [1914] AC 733.
[14] *Teper v R* [1952] 2 All ER 447.
[15] Heydon *Cases and Materials on Evidence* (1984).
[16] *Ratten v R* [1971] 3 All ER 801.

spoken are facts just as much as any other action by a human being. If the speaking of the words is a relevant fact, a witness may give evidence that they were spoken. A question of hearsay only arises when words spoken are relied on "testimonially", ie as establishing some fact narrated by the words.'

Lord Wilberforce's reasoning was to the effect that the words were only facts showing the woman was in a state of fear. (Heydon commented that the evidence was relied on, not only because signs of fear were present, but also because they were justified and sincere).

[9.15] Ultimately, it is not certain how implied assertions are treated by the rule against hearsay: whether the rule against hearsay applies and those statements that are admitted have been rendered admissible by virtue of an exception thereto; or whether the rule does not apply at all to implied assertions; or if those statements that have been admitted, have been admitted only as original evidence. It is evident, however, that to hold that implied assertions do not amount to hearsay, is to distinguish between express and implied assertions. Yet the dangers of inaccurate memory, observation, etc, are just as strong in relation to both, and the safeguard of cross-examination is absent.

Exceptions to the rule against hearsay

[9.16] There are, of course, exceptions to the hearsay rule, which are often more important than the rule itself.

Admissions

[9.17] One party to an action may give evidence of a statement by or on behalf of the other party which is adverse to the latter's case. This can occur in both civil and criminal cases. In criminal cases, where the admission is made by the accused, it is called a confession and particular considerations applied. If the statement is not made to a 'person in authority' in a criminal case, it is termed an admission, as it is in all civil cases.

Confessions

[9.18] One of the more controversial exceptions to the hearsay rule is that concerning confession statements. In relation to the format of a confession, it is noteworthy that a confession statement does not have to take any particular form: it can be oral or in writing; signed or unsigned. These factors and their presence or absence does not affect the admissibility of the confession, but simply its weight or probative value. Moreover, the confession does not have to be in the exact words used by the accused. In *AG v McCabe*[17], Kennedy CJ stated:

---

[17] *AG v McCabe* [1927] IR 129.

'However desirable to have the *ipsissima verba of* a deponent it is not the law that the statement of an accused person must as a matter of law be rejected if it is not in his *ipsissima verba.*'

[9.19] The question has arisen as to whether a distinction should be made in this context between inculpatory and exculpatory statements, in terms of the rules relating to the admissibility of confessions. In *Piche v R*[18], the Supreme Court of Canada rejected the contention that the rules only applied to inculpatory statements, as did the court in *Commissioners of Customs and Excise v Harz*[19].

Voluntariness

[9.20] A mandatory requirement in relation to confessions is that they must be voluntary. Voluntariness is a prerequisite to the admissibility of any confession. The traditional definition of 'voluntariness' is that of Lord Sumner in *Ibrahim v R*[20]:

'a voluntary statement in the sense that it has not been obtained ... either by fear of prejudice or hope of advantage exercised or held out by a person in authority and the onus is on the prosecution tendering that statement to show that it is voluntary in that sense.'

This formula was adopted by Kennedy CJ in *AG v McCabe*.[21]

[9.21] The definition of voluntariness thus expressed contains three elements: that of a 'threat' or 'inducement' and the concept of a 'person in authority'. Each of these elements has been subjected to a measure of interpretation and application by the courts, which varies in accordance with the perceived rationale or function of the rule, put forward as including:

- the reliability principle,
- the protection principle,
- the principle against self-incrimination, and
- the deterrence principle.

Early decisions such as *R v Warickshall*[22], and the development of the doctrine of confirmation by subsequent fact, support the reliability principle as the appropriate rationale for this requirement; yet more recent decisions (as will become evident) seem to take a somewhat broader approach.

---

[18] *Piche v R* (1970) 11 DLR.
[19] *Commissioners of Customs and Excise v Harz* [1967] 1 AC 760.
[20] *Ibrahim v R* [1914] AC 599 at 609, PC.
[21] *AG v McCabe* [1927] IR 129.
[22] *R v Warickshall* (1783) 1 Leach 263.

Historical development

[9.22] Traditionally judges were sceptical of confession evidence for a variety of reasons, including that of the criminal context in which they were being tendered: ie the prisoners came, in the main, from the poorer classes and were not aware of their rights (including the right to silence); criminal punishments were savage (with the death penalty frequently being imposed); little possibility of appeal existed; the accused was incompetent as a witness; and financial difficulties were faced by the accused person in both securing legal representation and the presence of witnesses, in the absence of a legal aid system (see Hailsham LJ in *DPP v Ping Lin*)[23]. Moreover, there was a general distrust of the police, given expression by the sentiments of Cave J in *R v Thompson*[24]:

> '... I always suspect these confessions which are supposed to be the offspring of penitence and remorse, and which nevertheless are repudiated by the prisoner at the trial. It is remarkable that it is of very rare occurrence for evidence of a confession to be given when the proof of the prisoner's guilt is otherwise clear and satisfactory; but when it is not clear and satisfactory, the prisoner is not infrequently alleged to have been seized with the desire ... to supplement it with a confession: a desire which vanishes as soon as he appears in a court of justice.'

[9.23] Moreover, current psychological support seems to underline the need for scepticism in this area, in so far as even in the absence of any improper behaviour on the part of police officers, persons detained and subjected to questioning experience a heightened sense of suggestibility, which may render them likely to confess to crimes which they have not committed[25]. In *Miranda v Arizona*[26] the United States Supreme Court referred to this as the inherently coercive nature of interrogation.

[9.24] Yet judicial opinion has not always been so trenchantly suspicious of confession evidence. At one stage in the nineteenth century, it was felt that the definition of what constituted an inducement was too broad. Baron Parke, in response to an attempt in *R v Baldry*[27] to exclude a confession on the basis that the constable had warned the prisoner that he need not say anything and that if he did it could be used in evidence against him, commented: 'The rule has been extended too far and justice and common sense have too frequently been sacrificed at the shrine of mercy.'

Erie J, in a similar vein, remarked:

---

[23] *DPP v Ping Lin* [1976] AC 574.
[24] *R v Thompson* (1893) 2 QB 12 at 18.
[25] Driver 'Confessions and the Social Psychology of Coercion' (1968) 82 Harv LR 42.
[26] *Miranda v Arizona* (1966) 384 US 436.
[27] *R v Baldry* (1852) 2 Den 430.

'I am of the opinion that when a confession is well proved it is the best evidence that can be produced; and that unless it be clear that there was either a threat or a promise to induce it, it ought not to be excluded.'

[9.25] The question of whether the 'tide of liberalism' should be halted today, given the changed nature of our criminal justice system, has also been more recently raised as per Lord Reid in *Commissioners of Customs and Excise v Harz*[28]:

'... many of the so-called inducements have been so vague that no reasonable man would have been influenced by them, but one must remember that not all accused are reasonable men and women: they may be very ignorant and terrified by the predicament in which they find themselves. So it may have been right to err on the safe side'.

Inducement

[9.26] In *R v Smith*[29], a sergeant major's statement to troops on parade, in the aftermath of a theft, to the effect that none of them would come off parade until he discovered the truth about what happened, was held to constitute an inducement. In *R v Richards*[30], the Court of Appeal deemed that the statement of a police officer to the appellant (who had lied about his movements) – 'I think it would be better if you made a statement and told me exactly what happened' – amounted to an inducement. In *R v Baldry*, the phrase, 'You had better tell the truth', amounted to an inducement; as in *R v Thompson*[31] the phrase 'It will be the right thing to make a clear breast of it', constituted an inducement. In *AG v Cleary*[32], the threat to take the accused to the doctor, in the context where such a medical examination would reveal if the woman had recently given birth, was held to amount to a threat for the purposes of the rule.

[9.27] An inducement obviously covers physical threats, and non-physical threats (eg non-secret trial), but must not be so remote as to have no effect on the accused. The use of tricks or mistakes is not covered, and does not affect admissibility. Some older English cases indicate spiritual threats will not suffice, which seems illogical.

[9.28] If there is a series of confession statements involved, an inducement in relation to an earlier, or initial confession, may not be effective in relation to a later one: for example, because of lapse of time (*R v Smith*, a nine hour interval). An inducement need not relate to the prosecution in order to be effective. The

---

[28] *Commissioners of Customs and Excise v Harz* [1967] 1 AC 760.
[29] *R v Smith* [1959] 2 QB 35.
[30] *R v Richards* [1967] 1 All ER 829.
[31] *R v Thompson* (1892) 2 QB 12.
[32] *AG v Cleary* (1938) 72 ILTR 84.

House of Lords rejected such an argument in *Commissioners of Customs and Excise v Harz.*[33]

Irish case law on confession evidence

[9.29] On examination of the Irish case law in relation to the admissibility of confession evidence, it is interesting to consider the extent to which exclusion is simply a matter of (a) the application of the voluntariness requirement (as traditionally defined, or more recently adorned with the notion of 'oppression') or (b) an expression of a distaste for the concept of arrest for the purpose of investigation through the medium of interrogation, or (c) an aspect of the additional concept of illegally obtained evidence (particularly evidence obtained in a deliberate and conscious breach of constitutional rights), now obviously relevant to the realm of confession evidence as well as to that of 'other' types of 'real' evidence. Connected with the particular basis of the exclusion, is the preferred rationale for same.

[9.30] In *People (AG) v Flynn*[34], Flynn had been convicted of five counts of unlawful carnal knowledge of his niece. As a result of a garda interview with the niece, he had been brought to the garda station for questioning. After two hours, the interviewing garda went for lunch, and the applicant was locked in a cell. Sergeant Mulligan brought a meal to the applicant and a conversation ensued, in the course of which the applicant spoke of his relations with women in England and with his niece – claiming that he had practised 'coitus interuptis' with all of them. As a result, the sergeant advised the applicant it would be 'just as well' for him to 'tell the truth'. When the interviewing garda returned at 2.00 pm, the sergeant told him the applicant was prepared to make a statement, which he did and duly signed. The trial judge admitted the statement, and one of the grounds of appeal to the Court of Appeal centred on whether the statement should have been admitted. Davitt P's reasoning is instructive:

> 'It seems to us that all the circumstantial evidence favours the view that there must have been some inducement used by Sergeant Mulligan to persuade the applicant to agree to make a statement and that it is more than likely that it was to the effect that it would be better for him to do so.
>
> Having regard to the probability and to the undoubted fact that the purpose of arresting the applicant and bringing him to the station was to get a statement from him; that though interviewed for nearly two hours in the morning he persisted in denying all his niece's allegations; that he was kept nearly seven hours in custody, and that he was released only when he had made a statement admitting nearly all

---

[33] *Commissioners of Customs and Excise v Harz* [1967] 1 AC 760.
[34] *People (AG) v Flynn* [1963] IR 255.

her allegations, we consider that notwithstanding the evidence of the garda in question, it is impossible to be sure that the statement was voluntarily made.'

[9.31] *DPP v Pringle McCann & O'Shea*[35] is a decision illustrating a certain lack of judicial consistency on the question of what constitutes an inducement or threat sufficient to eliminate voluntariness, together with indicating a greater judicial tolerance of lengthy interrogations. Pringle had been convicted of capital murder, which occured in the course of a bank robbery. The Court of Appeal stated that although forensic and other evidence had been adduced by the State, Pringle would not have been convicted but for the fact that the court of trial construed certain words spoken after arrest by the accused as an admission of guilt, and held also that those words were admissible in evidence.

[9.32] Pringle had been arrested under s 30 of the Offences Against the State Act 1939, and interviewed on numerous occasions and at considerable length. In the course of one of the last of the interviews, the court of trial found, as a fact, that the accused, speaking to the members of the Garda Síochána who were interviewing him said: 'I know that you know I was involved but on the advice of my solicitor I am saying nothing and you will have to prove it all the way.' The court of trial found the words to be admissible and thus constituted an admission of guilt. An appeal was heard, inter alia, against the latter finding. O'Higgins CJ delivering the judgment of the Court of Criminal Appeal, felt it appropriate to consider the interpretation of the words in the context in which they were spoken.

[9.33] O'Higgins CJ pointed out that during the 43 hours prior to these words being spoken, Pringle had been interviewed for lengthy periods by the gardaí. They had informed him of the evidence against him. He had spoken to his solicitor for approximately two hours following on his arrest at 3 pm on 19 July 1980, and on four subsequent occasions prior to making the admission. His solicitor advised him to say nothing in answer to the questions he was asked and throughout his interviews, when asked to comment on the evidence, he said nothing. He maintained this attitude up to 9.30 am on 21 July. During the said period of questioning (over the weekend) Pringle's girlfriend was also brought to the station and questioned, as was a friend of Pringle's.

[9.34] It is interesting to note the court's use of this context to interpret the statement as an admission of guilt. It is also interesting to note that Pringle's continuing silence, despite lengthy questioning by police – coupled with consultation with his solicitor and advice to stay silent – which were matters mitigating against the voluntariness of the statement made by the accused in the earlier case of *People (AG) v Flynn* and in the later Supreme Court decision in

---

[35] *DPP v Pringle McCann & O'Shea* (22 May 1981, unreported) CCA.

Hoey, here militate in favour of its admission. Per O'Higgins CJ delivering the judgment of the Court of Criminal Appeal:

> 'The Court has no doubt that when viewed in the context in which they were spoken the words used by the accused were an admission by him that he was involved in the raid and the killing of the Gardaí about which he was being questioned and in respect of which the Gardaí had given him detailed evidence which they had persistently claimed implicated him in those crimes. It is to be noted that the accused did not acknowledge that the Gardaí had a suspicion that he was involved in those crimes – such an acknowledgment would not have implied an admission by him of his guilt in the crimes. Nor was he acknowledging that the Gardaí had a belief in his guilt – again, a statement by him that his interrogators believed in his guilt would not convey any admission on his part that their belief was a correct one. What he in fact said amounted to an admission of his appreciation that those who were accusing him of the crimes of murder and armed robbery knew that he had committed them, and this admission was accompanied by a statement that on the advice of his solicitor he was going to say nothing and an observation that the Gardaí were going to have to prove the case themselves.

> It is to be noted that the acknowledgment which he made of the knowledge of the Gardaí was not qualified in any way. It can only be regarded as an admission by him of his involvement in the crimes they were investigating. The Court has not lost sight of the submission made on the accused's behalf that there was no evidence of the intonation in the accused's voice when he spoke the words. But it is of the opinion that such evidence is not necessary to establish beyond a reasonable doubt their meaning and the absence of such evidence had not in any way weakened the prosecution's case.'

[9.35] With regard to the further submission that: firstly, Pringle's questioning was so oppressive and so undermined the will of the accused as to result in the alleged admission not being a voluntary one; secondly, that the admission had been procured by improper inducements and threats which equally vitiated it as admissible evidence; and thirdly, that the Court should hold that the questioning failed to reach the standard of basic fairness which should have been applied during the period of his custody and so the words should not be admitted in evidence, the Court is equally facilitory, in terms of its admission.

[9.36] O'Higgins CJ felt there was no evidence to suggest an irregularity in the custody of the accused or breach of his common law or constitutional rights, and so would only consider the claim of inadmissibility based on oppressive questioning and threats and improper inducements.

O'Higgins CJ noted that the Supreme Court in *DPP v Breathnach*[36] had adopted the description of oppressive questioning given by McDermott LJ in an address to the Bentham Club, and adopted by the Court of Appeal in England in *R v Prager*[37]:

'Questioning which by its nature, duration or other attendant circumstances (including the factor of custody) excites hopes (such as the hope of release) or fears or so affects the mind of the subject that his will crumbles and he speaks when otherwise he would have stayed silent.'

[9.37] The Court further approved the statement of Sachs J in *R v Priestly*[38]:

'if ... to my mind this word in the context of the principles under consideration imports something which tends to sap and has sapped the free will which must exist before a confession is voluntary'.

[9.38] In applying those principles to this case, O'Higgins CJ noted the accused was interviewed over lengthy periods, but it was not continuous and he had five consultations with his solicitor – two in the afternoon and evening of 19 July, two on the morning and evening of 20 July and one in early hours of 21 July. The Court stated:

'The length of the duration of the interviewing of the accused combined with the shortness of the duration of the sleep he obtained do not in themselves establish the validity of the submission now being considered.'

He says it is obvious, as the court of trial pointed out, that:

'what may be oppressive as regards a child, an invalid, or an old man or somebody inexperienced in the ways of the world may turn out not to be oppressive when one finds that the accused person is of tough character and an experienced man of the world.'

The Court continued:

'And so when a court is considering an allegation such as has been made in this case the physical mental and emotional characteristics of the person whose will it is said was undermined must be considered ... It is to be noted that in this case the accused was a man of 42 years of age, in good health, who for some years prior to his arrest had been a fisherman in the Galway area. He was apparently an experienced man of the world not unused to conditions of physical hardship. It was clearly open to the court of trial to hold that the will of such a man would not have been so undermined by the interview he had experienced and by lack of sleep that he spoke the inculpatory words when otherwise he would have remained silent ...

---

[36] *DPP v Breathnach* (16 February 1981, unreported) SC.
[37] *R v Prager* 56 Cr App Rep 151.
[38] *R v Priestly* (1965) 50 Cr App Rep 183.

The accused had had the benefit of five visits from his solicitor prior to the time interviewing recommenced on the morning of July 21, the last having taken place just before he went to bed in the early hours of Monday morning. He was advised by his solicitor that he was entitled to remain silent and that he was not required to answer questions. Those visits and the advice he obtained must have strengthened his resolve and assisted in counteracting any weakness of will which the conditions of his custody and the questioning by the Gardaí may have produced.'

Finally, the Court pointed out, in relation to an allegation that the incriminating words were spoken as a result of inducements and threats having been made, that:

'... although such threats and inducements may have been a motive which brought the accused to admit his involvement in the crimes ... they cannot be regarded as having been oppressive in the sense of having so undermined the will of the accused that he spoke when otherwise he would have remained silent.'

[9.39] Exactly what is meant by this is unclear, unless it is merely to emphasise the distinct and separate effect of 'oppression' and threat/inducement with regard to admissibility. Any threat which may have ensued from the interviewing of Pringle's girlfriend, the court of trial found to be ineffective in so far as its effect was dissipated by subsequent events, including a visit with his solicitor. He had not given this explanation at the 'trial within the trial' or 'voir dire' (hearing before the Special Criminal Court, to determine admissibility of the confession). Moreover, the words of the statement were inconsistent with such a desire to shield a friend. On any possible construction of the events and despite the lengthy interrogation and acknowledgment of possible inducements/threats (if not oppression), the statement went in.

[9.40] An interesting contrast with *Flynn* and *Pringle* is provided by the decision of the Supreme Court in *DPP v Hoey*[39], which contains some evidence of the notion that the purpose of an arrest should not be that of interrogation, and if it is, the result is an inadmissible confession. This is coupled with a modern interpretation of the voluntariness formula.

In that case, as a result of a search carried out under a warrant on 11 August, the gardaí discovered a gun and quantity of ammunition in the premises where Hoey resided. Hoey fled. On 4 November, Hoey presented himself at a garda station with his solicitor, and was interviewed for a period of three hours up until 9.30 pm (in the course of which Hoey spoke to his solicitor at 9.25 pm). At 10.30 pm, until 11.00 pm, the interview resumed, and Hoey made a statement, constituting the only evidence against him. Up until that point, the accused had

---

[39]*DPP v Hoey* (16 December 1987, unreported) SC (McCarthy, Walsh, Henchy JJ).

refused to say anything. His confession occurred in response to a statement to him by a detective to the effect '... it must be someone in the house. Will I have to get members to go up to your family and see if anyone will take responsibility?' The appellant then admitted responsibility, stating 'I am taking responsibility but I am not involving any other person'. At trial, the Special Criminal Court had admitted the statement, on the basis that the detective's statement had been the occasion, but not the cause, of the admission. The Court of Criminal Appeal had determined that it was open to the Special Criminal Court to accept the detective's evidence that it was not intended as a threat, but to draw the appellant's attention to what would happen if he did not take responsibility.

[9.41] The approaches of the three Supreme Court judges on appeal are interesting. McCarthy J felt it to be immaterial what the detective believed. It may well be, he reasoned, that the statement was a correct summary of the facts, yet that is not the point – nor is the purpose of the statement, '... the purpose can hardly have been other than to get the accused to make an admission'. The test, per McCarthy J, is whether or not in the circumstances in which the statement was made following on and occasioned by, the observation of the detective, can be free from any reasonable doubt that it was voluntary. He concluded it cannot.

[9.42] What is interesting about McCarthy J's judgment is the extent to which it reveals an echo of the earlier cases (including *Flynn*), indicating a dissatisfaction with the police practice of using arrest and questioning in the aftermath of same, for the purpose of investigation.

[9.43] Walsh J's judgment, on the other hand, would seem more indicative of a faithful application of the voluntariness test – albeit involving an assessment of the inducement in the particular context (ie conscious of the 'natural concern' of Hoey for his family). Walsh J concluded:

> '... the effect of the words irrespective of what they were intended to mean was that they were calculated to convey that the appellant's family would be left undisturbed and free from further interrogation by the Gardaí, if the appellant admitted responsibility.'

That amounted to an improper inducement, rendering the confession inadmissible.

[9.44] A concern for the apparently 'oppressive' nature of questioning is evident from the judgment of Henchy J, where again emphasising the insignificance attached to the motive of the detective, he referred to the question having 'vitiated the free will' of the appellant, his free will having been 'overborne', and his resolution to remain silent having been broken. Amongst each of the members of the Supreme Court, it is evident that despite agreement on the issue of the fact that *mala fides* is not necessary on the part of the 'person in authority' for the purposes of the rule and the ultimate conclusion that the confession in this instant is inadmissible, there is no consensus but rather divergence with regard to support for any one rationale of the rule (McCarthy J, police misconduct or the deterrence principle; Walsh J, voluntariness/reliability or the trustworthiness rationale; and Henchy J, oppression - the privilege against incrimination or the protectionist principle). Furthermore, in *DPP v Healy*[40] there is an implicit recognition of the 'inherently coercive nature of interrogation' by Finlay CJ:

> 'The undoubted right of reasonable access to a solicitor enjoyed by a person who is in detention must be interpreted as being directed towards the vital function of ensuring that such person is aware of his rights and has the independent advice which would be appropriate in order to permit him to reach a truly free decision as to his attitude to interrogation to the making of any statement, be it exculpatory or inculpatory. The availability of advice from a lawyer must, in my view, be seen as a contribution at least towards some measure of equality in the position of the detained person and his interrogators.'

[9.45] This issue was further addressed in the subsequent Supreme Court decision of *People (DPP) v Kenny*[41], where Finlay CJ, delivering the majority judgment, commented that in their judgments in *Healy*, both he and McCarthy J adopted what he termed 'the absolute protection test for evidence obtained by reason of a breach of a detained person's constitutional right of access to a lawyer.'

Preference for that principle leads to interesting repercussions for the interpretation of the *O'Brien* formula, and in particular, the meaning of deliberate and conscious breach – fraught with obvious importance and relevance for persons subjected to questioning in Garda custody.

'Person in authority'

[9.46] In *Deokinian v R*[42], the accused confessed to a trusted friend while in police custody. The trusted friend had promised to help him recover money he was alleged to have stolen. The argument was put forward that someone regarded as being 'close to the police' (as here), constituted a 'person in authority' for the purpose of the rule. The Privy Council rejected same on the basis that here, the individual was rather a trusted friend. Yet some scepticism with regard to the requirement of 'person in authority' was evident (Viscount Dilhorne):

---

40 *DPP v Healy* [1990] ILRM 313.
41 *People (DPP) v Kenny* [1990] ILRM 569.
42 *Deokinian v R* [1961] 1 AC 20.

'The fact that an inducement is made by a "person in authority" may make it more likely to operate on the accused's mind and lead him to confess. If the ground on which confessions induced by promises held out by persons in authority are held to be inadmissible is that they may not be true, then it may be that there is a similar risk that in some circumstances the confession may not be true if induced by a promise held out a person not in authority, for instance, if such a person offers a bribe in return for a confession. (In this context, it is noteworthy that the Criminal Law Revision Committee in England recommended the abolition of the "person in authority" requirement[43]).'

[9.47] Various categories of persons have been held to satisfy this requirement for the purposes of the rule: a high-ranking officer (sergeant) has been held to be a person in authority with respect to soldiers (*R v Smith*); and a headmistress vis-à-vis schoolgirls (*R v McLintock*)[44]. In *Deokinan,* the implication was that if someone is known by the accused to be close to the police, that person could be considered a person in authority.

[9.48] In *DPP v Ping Lin*[45], the House of Lords took into account the fact that a superintendent's remark, alleged to affect the admissibility of an accused's confession, was made subsequent to, and did not precede the accused's admission. The House of Lords did state that no intention of inducing a confession was necessary, and that it was not necessary to show any improper conduct by the person in authority to render the confession inadmissible.

[9.49] It has also been held, that although the inducement was made by someone not in authority, if it was made in the presence of a person in authority the position is the same as if that person had himself held out the inducement, unless he indicated dissent from it (*R v Cleary*[46]). In *People v Murphy*[47], a garda enlisted the help of a citizen, whose remark to the accused 'Go with the garda, it's for your own good', when followed by a statement from the accused, was treated as that of a person in authority for the purpose of the rule. It has also been held that the confession rule applies, if the inducement takes the form of a suggestion from an accused to police[48].

[9.50] In the Canadian case of *Rothman v The Queen*[49], the Supreme Court of Canada held that the test of whether someone is a 'person in authority' in relation to the accused is a subjective one. What is important, therefore, is

43 Criminal Law Revision Committee *Eleventh Report. Evidence* Cmnd 4991 (1972).
44 *R v McLintock* [1962] Grim LR 549.
45 *DPP v Ping Lin* [1976] AC 574.
46 *R v Cleary* (1963) 48 Cr App Rep 116.
47 *People v Murphy* [1947] IR 236.
48 *R v Zaveckas* [1970] 1 All ER 413.
49 *Rothman v The Queen* (1981) 121 DLR (3d) 578.

whether or not the accused thinks that person is, for example, a police officer. In this case, therefore, the Court admitted statements made by the accused to a police officer in disguise, who was put into the same cell as the accused and whom the accused thought of as a fellow prisoner. With one 'fell-swoop', therefore, the Supreme Court preserved and protected the operation of police undercover officers. Again, this decision, seems out of line with a trustworthiness rationale. Yet if one takes as true the premise that the threat in order to effect the credibility of the confession, must emanate from someone in authority – it is logical to regard the person in question subjectively, from the point of view of the accused, to determine whether or not he is a person in authority; and to regard the effect of the threat objectively if emanating from a person in authority (eg a police officer), yet subjectively if emanating from a person not in authority in relation to the accused.

[9.51] In *The People (DPP) v McCann*[50], McCann had been convicted of the murder of his wife and their foster child who died in a fire at their home. The accused had been arrested under s 30 of the Offences Against the State Act 1939, on suspicion of having committed an offence under s 2 of the Explosive Substances Act 1883, a scheduled offence for the purpose of the Offences Against the State Act 1939. He was brought to Tallaght garda station at 2.07 pm, where he was questioned, but he denied any involvement and refused to answer questions about the explosion. He was visited by his solicitor, Mr Garrett Sheehan, at 3.34 pm, and for the rest of that day maintained that, on the advice of his solicitor, he had nothing to say. The following day he was interviewed extensively and remained generally silent.

[9.52] On the morning of 6 November 1992 he had met with his two brothers and told them he and his wife had a suicide pact. They asked him to repeat that to the gardaí, which he did. At 12 o'clock midday, one of his brothers came into the interview room and said the applicant wanted to make a statement. The applicant told one of the gardaí he wanted him to ask the questions. His brothers and his solicitor, a member of Mr Sheehan's firm, were present. In the course of that interview he admitted starting the fire. At 1.22 pm the member in charge entered the interview room and told the applicant he was released under the provisions of s 30. Nevertheless the applicant returned a couple of minutes later and the interview continued at 1.29 pm with the same parties present.

[9.53] The applicant appealed on the grounds, inter alia, that the trial judge erred in law in holding the inculpatory statements admissible, having regard to:

    (a)   breach of the Judges' Rules;

---

[50] *People (DPP) v McCann* [1998] 4 IR 397.

(b)   the oppressive circumstances of the applicant's detention; and

(c)   the finding that his brothers were not persons in authority vis-à-vis the applicant having regard to the inducements they made to him while in detention in Tallaght garda station.

[9.54] O'Flaherty J delivering the judgment of the Court of Criminal Appeal, noted[51] that the applicant was visited by two solicitors at different times during his detention (five visits in all from 'these very experienced solicitors'), was visited by two doctors, given access to tablets he was taking for stress since the fire, and had an opportunity to sleep and eat. There was no suggestion the Custody Regulations 1987 were breached in any material way.

[9.55] The breach of the Judges' Rules alleged was forbidding the questioning of a suspect. However, the suspect here had asked the detective to lead with questions, these were not then for the purpose of cross-examination but to maintain direction and coherence as per the trial judge. With regard to inducements, O'Flaherty J reasoned[52]:

'It is not suggested that any threats were offered to the applicant and the judge found that there were no inducements. It is true that the gardaí persistently asked the applicant to tell the truth and indicated that they held a certain view of his guilt. As regards the situation of his brothers, Bernard and Michael, the applicant never made the case that Michael attempted to influence him in any way and as regards Bernard, once again, the most he did was to urge him to tell the truth and, on occasion, to protect the reputation of their family.'

[9.56] O'Flaherty J[53] reiterated Walsh J's view in *Shaw*, that a desire to interrogate cannot justify an arrest under s 30. The trial judge had said a section 30 detention was not intended to be a 'genteel encounter'. O'Flaherty J expressed the view that:

'[I]t is clear that the very word "interrogation" means more than some form of gentle questioning and, provided there are no threats or inducements or oppressive circumstances, then the gardaí are always entitled to persist with their questioning of a suspect.'

The trial judge had also laid emphasis on the fact that the applicant had a successful background in business and sport, was highly intelligent ('probably functioning at a higher level than his interrogators'[54]) and was highly manipulative. With regard to what constitutes an inducement, O'Flaherty J adopted the following test:[55]

[51]   [1998] 4 IR 397 at 409.
[52]   [1998] 4 IR 397 at 409.
[53]   [1998] 4 IR 397 at 410.
[54]   [1998] 4 IR 397 at 410.
[55]   [1998] 4 IR 397 at 411.

'... (a) were the words used by the person or persons in authority, objectively viewed, capable of amounting to a threat or promise? (b) Did the accused subjectively understand them as such? (c) Was his confession in fact the result of the threat or promise?'

[9.57] Applying that to the case before him noting that the trial judge had found no such inducement, O'Flaherty J continued:

'It is true that on occasions, in making the admissions he did, the suspect was tearful, distressed and shaking but these symptoms are consistent with the reaction of a person who was recollecting the dreadful deeds that had been done. Further, an argument was advanced before the learned trial judge, and repeated before us, that an unprecedented amount of access had been given to the suspect as regards the visits by his brother. One or other or both brothers had visited him on the three days he was in custody. The Court rejects this submission as quite extraordinary, as did the trial judge.'

[9.58] The trial judge had held that the decision in *Hoey* did not extend:

'... to the pressure emanating from an accused's family, stemming from embarrassment over its dirty linen being washed in public or the consequences for a family member (this was their mother) with a weak heart.'[56]

The trial judge had concluded the brothers were not 'persons in authority'. According to Flaherty J, the question of whether the brothers could be said to be persons in authority '... has always been held to mean someone engaged in the arrest, detention, examination or prosecution of the accused or someone acting on behalf of the prosecution.'[57] Hence this ground was also unsuccessful.

[9.59] *McCann's* case provides an interesting contrast with *Hoey* and is more reminiscent of *Pringle* in its approach to the characteristics of the individual vis-à-vis assessment of 'oppressive circumstances' and its dismissal of pressure, such as visits from family/girlfriend in light of access to solicitors, etc. It is also somewhat prescient of the decision of the Special Criminal Court in *Ward*, where he was referred to as an experienced s 30 detainee, yet not in so far as the family/girlfriend visits were viewed therein.

[9.60] Access to a lawyer is also something that can be seen to be used to mitigate other potentially exclusionary factors. This is questionable given the lawyer's partial role in terms of limited access and not continuous presence during interrogation. The limitations placed on legal access are illustrated in *Lavery v Member in Charge, Carrickmacross Garda Station*[58], where this was considered in the context of an extended detention under ss 30(4) and (4)(A) of

---

[56] [1998] 4 IR 397 at 411.
[57] [1998] 4 IR 397 at 412.
[58] *Lavery v Member in Charge Carrickmacross Garda Station* [1999] 2 IR 390 (SC).

the Offences Against the State Act 1939[59], the latter having been in response to the Omagh bombing, and the allegations put to the accused relating to his having stolen a vehicle subsequently used to plant the bomb in Omagh. In a judgment delivered by O'Flaherty J, the Supreme Court held: 'The solicitor is not entitled to be present at the interviews'.[60]

[9.61] In *C v DPP*[61], admissibility of the accused's statements was challenged on the grounds that at the time when they were made, the accused had had one hour's sleep in a period of 30 hours and had, in the early hours of the morning at the party, consumed a significant quantity of alcohol. Counsel for the accused argued that there was an onus on the State to show beyond reasonable doubt that a statement was voluntary, and that there was no physical or psychological pressure placed on the accused, or excessive questioning. This was not, it was argued, overcome here. It was also contended that the trial judge had a discretion to exclude statements if the manner in which they were obtained fell below acceptable standards of fairness, which it was contended they did in this case because of the accused's lack of sleep and amount of drink he had consumed. Refusing leave to appeal, the Court of Criminal Appeal held that the trial judge found as a matter of fact, that the accused was in a perfectly coherent condition at all times and seemed perfectly normal to the doctor, and that that finding should not be disturbed. The emphasis laid on the doctor's opinion here, however, is questionable in light of the fact that the doctor was there primarily to take samples and did not carry out a full medical examination.

Constitutional dimension

[9.62] Relevant also, in the context of the admissibility of confession statements, is the issue of constitutional rights. The pre-trial period, which covers that entire period between the first encounter with the police, right up until the individual faces a court of law, is one fraught with potential for the abuse of rights. Many of these rights have a constitutional dimension, and indeed the courts have recognised that a necessary corollary of the vindication of the accused's rights in the course of the trial itself, is the recognition of such rights in the pre-trial period, without which the accused would be greatly disadvantaged at trial.

[9.63] Underlying all of this are issues related to powers of arrest, detention, interrogation etc. In so far as they are related to the issue of the admissibility of confession evidence (which by its nature will have been obtained in the course of the pre-trial period), these will be addressed.

---

[59] As inserted by the Offences Against the State (Amendment) Act 1998, s 10.
[60] [1999] 2 IR 390 at 396.
[61] *C v DPP* (31 July 2001, unreported) CCA.

[9.64] Article 40.4.1° of the Constitution enunciates the general principle that 'No citizen shall be deprived of his personal liberty, save in accordance with law.'

Traditionally, the legitimate deprivation of liberty was solely achieved through arrest. In *Dunne v Clinton*[62], Hanna J declared:

> 'In law there can be no half-way house between liberty of the suspect, unfettered by restraint, and an arrest. If a person under suspicion, voluntarily agrees to go to a police station to be questioned, his liberty is not interfered with, as he can change his mind at any time. If, having been examined, he is asked and voluntarily agrees to remain, he is still a free subject and can leave at any time. But a practice has grown up of "detention" as distinct from arrest. It is, in effect, keeping a suspect in custody – without making any definite charge against him and with the intimation in some form of words or gesture, that he is under restraint and will not be allowed to leave. As, in my opinion, there could be no such thing as notional liberty, this so-called detention amounts to arrest and the suspect has in law been arrested and in custody, during the period of his detention.'

The extent to which the above statement continues to represent the law must be questioned in light of developments such as the power of detention consequent on arrest, introduced into the 'normal' criminal justice process by s 4 of the Criminal Justice Act 1984.

[9.65] Along with such modifications have come additional safeguards applying to the pre-trial detention period. Prior to consideration thereof, however, it is useful to note the extent to which common law and constitutional rights have been both recognised and vindicated by the courts in the pre-trial period. The right to know the reason for the arrest, and the charge against one, was recognised in England in *Christie v Leachinsky*[63] and adopted in Ireland in *Re O'Laighleis*[64]. In the latter case, however, the appellant did not satisfy the court that he did not know why he was being arrested. It was held, moreover, that such would not have rendered his detention unlawful. In *People v Raymond Walsh*[65], O'Higgins CJ held that the failure to inform the appellant at the moment of arrest of the reason for same (ostensibly because of the large number of people present in the public house where the arrest took place), did not affect the legality of his subsequent detention. The appellant had not asked the reason for the arrest and shortly thereafter, had been informed of same, at the station.

---

[62] *Dunne v Clinton* [1930] IR 366.
[63] *Christie v Leachinsky* [1947] AC 573.
[64] *Re O'Laighleis* [1960] IR 93.
[65] *People v Raymond Walsh* [1980] IR 294.

[9.66] In *DPP v Michael McCormack*[66], the defendant was charged under s 49(2) of the Road Traffic Act 1961 as inserted by s 10 of the Road Traffic Act 1994. The garda had informed the defendant that she was of the opinion that he had consumed intoxicating liquor, that she required he provide a breath specimen, and of the penalty for non-compliance. The breath specimen proved positive and she arrested him. The District Court judge found as a fact that the garda did not inform the defendant that he was being arrested under s 49(8) of the Road Traffic Act 1961, nor pursuant to any statutory provision, nor in layman's language or otherwise that he was being arrested relating to the consumption of intoxicants, nor that he was being arrested. On a case stated to the High Court, McGuinness J held that, provided an arrested person knew why he had been arrested, the arrest was valid, and this might be communicated to him without the use of technical or precise language, or even implied to him if the circumstances were such he must know of the general nature of the offence for which he was being arrested.

[9.67] The recognition of the right to counsel had been established in the context of a criminal trial in *State (Healy) v Donoghue*[67] (and a consequent right to be informed of same – see Griffin J in the Supreme Court). In the pre-trial period, some doubt lingered as to the constitutional right to counsel, and the corresponding right to be informed of such a right.

[9.68] The Supreme Court decision in *DPP v Paul Healy*[68], however, quelled such doubts, and placed said right on a sound constitutional footing. The right, moreover, can be exercised on the accused's behalf by relatives or friends, and once a solicitor has arrived at the station, the accused has a right of access to him. The argument that the police refused or delayed immediate access by the solicitor, taking the view that it was 'bad manners' to interrupt the interrogation, was not accepted as sufficient.

[9.69] The decision is interesting from a number of perspectives, not least for the purpose of arrest itself. Reliance had been placed by the prosecution on the fact that the probable consequence of permitting the interview to be interrupted by the arrival of a solicitor would be that the accused would change his mind and stop making an incriminating statement.

[9.70] The appellant, on the contrary, contended that the prosecution's reason for postponing access on the basis of permitting the statement to be made without interruption, was unreasonable, having regard to the fact that it violated one of the major objectives of the right of access to a solicitor, viz, that of securing for

---

[66] *DPP v Michael McCormack* [1999] 4 IR 158.
[67] *State (Healy) v Donoghue* [1976] IR 325.
[68] *DPP v Paul Healy* [1990] ILRM 313.

the detainee information and advice with regard to his rights – in particular, the right of avoiding self-incrimination. Significantly, this view was endorsed by members of the Court per Finlay CJ (Walsh and Hedermann JJ concurring):

> 'The undoubted right of reasonable access to a solicitor enjoyed by a person who is in detention must be interpreted as being directed towards the vital function of ensuring that such person is aware of his rights and has the independent advice which would be appropriate in order to permit him to reach a truly free decision as to his attitude to interrogation or to the making of any statement, be it exculpatory or inculpatory.'

Griffin J stated:

> 'The main, if not the sole, purpose of the right of access to a legal adviser is to enable the detained person to obtain advice as to his rights, and in particular advice as to whether, in the circumstances, it would be in his best interests to make a statement or to refuse to make one.'

The Court, as a whole, perceived the right of access to a solicitor as a constitutional right – part of the fundamental requirement of fair procedure which must be adhered to throughout the pre-trial period. It did not, however, address the issue of whether there was a right to be informed of such right.

[9.71] The right to be brought before a court within a reasonable period of time was a logical consequence of the traditional function of arrest itself. In relation to arrests on foot of a warrant, such a right originated from s 15 of the Criminal Justice Act 1951. In relation to arrests made without a warrant, the right has its origins in common law. The issue arose as to what constituted a 'reasonable time'. In *Dunne v Clinton*, it was stated:

> 'no hard and fast rule can be laid down to cover every case. It must depend on many circumstances such as time, the place of the arrest, and the number of the accused, whether a Peace Commissioner is easily available and such other matters as may be relevant.'

[9.72] In *Doherty v Liddane*[69], in an action for damages for false imprisonment, 26 hours was held to be excessive: a court is always available within 24 hours. In *People v Shaw*[70], Costello J adopted the approach of the English courts in *John Lewis and Co Ltd v Timms*[71]:

> 'The question throughout shall be: has the arrester brought the arrested person to a place where his alleged offence can be dealt with as speedily as is reasonably possible? All the circumstances of the case must be taken into consideration in deciding whether this requirement is complied with. A direct route and rapid

---

[69] *Doherty v Liddane* [1940] Ir Jur Rep 58.
[70] *People v Shaw* [1982] IR 1.
[71] *John Lewis and Co Ltd v Timms* [1952] AC 676 per Porter LJ.

progress are no doubt matters for consideration, but they are not the only matters. Those who arrest must be persuaded of the guilt of the accused, they cannot bolster up their assurances or the strength of their case by seeking further evidence and detaining the arrested man in the meantime or taking him to some spot where they may or may not find further evidence. Whether there is evidence that the steps taken were unreasonable or the delay too great is a matter for the judge.'

[9.73] A delay in bringing a person to trial was alleged in *State (O'Connell) v Fawsitt*[72] and *State (Brennan) v DJ Conlon*[73]. In the former case, the principles to be applied were set out by the Chief Justice:

'A person charged with an indictable offence and whose chances of a fair trial have been prejudiced by excessive delay should not be put to the risk of being arraigned and pleading before the jury.'[74]

That principle was relied upon by the applicants in *Hannigan v DJ Clifford & Ors* and *O'Flynn v DJ Clifford & Ors*[75], who argued that to charge them in respect of offences alleged to have been committed 18 months previously, was to subject them to such delay as to seriously prejudice their right to a fair trial. The applicants had been arrested on 3 September 1986 under s 30 of the Offences Against the State Act 1939, released without charge and subsequently charged on 8 February 1988 in relation to offences alleged to have been committed on 7 August 1986.

[9.74] Walsh J in the Supreme Court, approved of the statement of principle in the earlier decisions, but distinguished those cases from the present application in so far as, in the former cases the alleged delay was one in bringing a person to trial after he had been charged. Walsh J acknowledged that:

'... excessive delay may prejudice the chance of a fair trial for a variety of reasons such as a disappearance or death of witnesses, failure of human memory and many other causes.'

The essential difference here, however, per Walsh J, was that there was no suggestion of any delay between the bringing of charges and the progress to trial:

'What is in issue ... is what is claimed to be the unfair delay between the initial arrests under s 30 of the Offences Against the State Act 1939, and the bringing of the charges in February 1988.'

Walsh J stated that while:

---

[72] *State (O'Connell) v Fawsitt* [1986] IR 362.
[73] *State (Brennan) v District Justice Conlon* (17 June 1986, unreported) HC (Hamilton P).
[74] [1986] ILRM 635 at 652.
[75] *Hannigan v DJ Clifford DPP & Ors* and *O'Flynn v DJ Clifford & Ors* [1990] ILRM 65.

'it is quite clear that once a charge has been brought then the matter must be prosecuted without undue delay or otherwise that might prejudice a fair trial.

However with regard to the interval between the forming of suspicion and a decision to charge everything depends upon the circumstances of the case.'

[9.75] While these circumstances may indicate that the charges were not laid until an inexcusable delay had occurred, and so an accused could be hampered for similar reasons to those given in *State (O'Connell) v Fawsitt*, there was per Walsh J:

'... no evidence in the present case that any circumstances existed to indicate that the prosecuting authorities were in a position to institute their prosecution before they did so or that the delay which occurred between the commission of the offences and the bringing of the charges against persons who were already suspected persons for 18 months was such as could lead to the conclusion that a right to a fair trial had been prejudiced.'

[9.76] It would seem that although the same principles apply, therefore, to a delay in charging an accused as those relating to being brought to trial, the presumption that delay will prejudice the accused in the latter context is much stronger than in the former where a case will have to be made on the circumstances.

Development and change of the arrest process

[9.77] In this context, it is useful to comment briefly on the changing nature of the function of arrest, and the extent of the requirement to bring an arrested person before a court within a reasonable period of time.

[9.78] The reason why this is of such importance in the context of hearsay, and in particular confession evidence, is because it is the rules in relation to arrest and detention which, in governing the pre-trial interrogation process, impact upon the admissibility of confession evidence. Although the manner in which the statements were obtained is only one factor pertaining to admissibility (the other factor here being voluntariness), it is a very significant one.

Given that many cases still focus on the admissibility of confessions (eg *Ward*) and that powers of detention have been the subject of considerable augmentation by the legislature (eg Criminal Justice (Drug Trafficking) Act 1996), it might be expected that future case law will focus on exactly these pre-trial considerations in relation to confessions, in much the same way as the laws on search and seizure have become encrusted with constitutional argument.

[9.79] The advent of a practice of 'helping the gardaí with their inquiries' and the practice of interrogation consequent on arrest, grew up in the aftermath of the use of s 30 of the Offences Against the State Act 1939, which provided the gardaí with a power to detain persons for an initial period of 24 hours, followed by a further potential period of 24 hours.

[9.80] Police interrogation skills were thus 'honed' (on the basis per *Stephens* that it is far easier to sit in the shade rubbing hot pepper into some poor devil's eyes, than search about under the hot sun looking for clues[76]). Extension of detention periods under s 30 of the 1939 Act are grounded on the suspicion of the officer that the detainee has committed a scheduled offence. This suspicion has to be expressly proved at the subsequent trial of the accused, to legitimate his detention. It cannot be inferred either from the signing of the formal direction or by hearsay evidence of a verbal direction. Thus in *The People (DPP) v Dermot Byrne*[77], where the Chief Superintendent concerned had died and could therefore not testify as to his state of mind at the time of the extension, at trial an incriminating statement made by the accused during that extended period was deemed inadmissible. Walsh J stated that:

'... the production of the document in question could not be offered as proof of what was the state of mind of Chief Superintendent Joy when he directed an extension of the period of arrest. Apart form the hearsay nature of the evidence, it made it impossible for any examination or cross-examination to be made of the actual state of mind of the Chief Superintendent which is necessary proof of fact in the case.'

[9.81] Hence Walsh J held that as it was well-established that a person who is under arrest, but whose arrest is not in accordance with law, is being held in violation of his constitutional right to liberty, and any evidence obtained during that period is inadmissible, and a confession made during the extended period of detention, should be excluded.

[9.82] There followed a demand for police powers of detention for the purposes of interrogation in relation to 'ordinary' or 'non-subversive' crime. The police were then using s 30 of the 1939 Act in relation to 'ordinary' offences, but this was felt to be a practice of doubtful validity (unnecessarily so, as witness the subsequent Supreme Court decision in *DPP v Quilligan*[78], where the Supreme Court sanctioned the use of s 30 in relation to both 'subversive' and 'non-subversive' crime).

[9.83] The Criminal Justice Act 1984 thus made provision for a period of detention of an initial six hours, followed by a further potential six hour period following an arrest, in relation to offences carrying at least a five-year period of imprisonment. Such a power did not come into force until the introduction,

---

[76] Stephens *A Digest of the Law of Evidence* (1936).
[77] *The People (DPP) v Dermot Byrne* [1989] ILRM 613.
[78] *DPP v Quilligan* [1987] ILRM 600.

however, of a series of regulations regarding the treatment of persons in Garda custody[79] and a Garda Complaints Tribunal.

Provisions regarding the treatment of persons in custody

The Judges' Rules

[9.84] Traditional safeguards regarding the treatment of persons in garda custody following an arrest, consisted of the 'Judges' Rules'. The Judges' Rules were, in essence, a series of administrative directions, originally handed down by the judiciary in England in *R v Voisin*[80], but since updated. The rules, as they apply here are set out by Walsh J in *People (AG) v Cummins*[81].

[9.85] It is important to remember that these rules are purely discretionary in effect, and breach of them does not automatically lead to the exclusion of evidence. They are as follows:

(1)   When a police officer is investigating a crime there is no objection to his putting questions to persons from whom he thinks useful information may be obtained.

(2)   When a police officer has made up his mind to charge someone with a crime, that person should be cautioned before further questioning.

(3)   Persons 'in custody' should not be questioned without the usual caution being administered.

(4)   If the prisoner wishes to volunteer a statement, the usual caution should be administered, ending with the words 'be given in evidence'.

(5)   The caution administered to a formally charged prisoner should be 'do you wish to say anything in answer to the charge? You are not obliged to say anything unless you wish to do so, but whatever you say will be taken down in writing; and may be given in evidence'.

(6)   The absence of a caution before a statement does not automatically exclude that statement, but a caution should be given as soon as possible.

(7)   If a voluntary statement has been made by the prisoner, further questioning should only be as to the details of same.

(8)   In the case of two or more persons charged, the statements of one should be shown to the other, yet should not be meant to invite a reply.

(9)   A statement should, if possible, to taken down in writing and signed.

---

[79] See Appendix A.
[80] *R v Voisin* [1918] 1 KB 531.
[81] *People (AG) v Cummins* [1972] IR 312.

[9.86] It should also be noted that in *Travers v Ryan*[82], Finlay P stated that:

'in relation to a person under 14 years of age it is most desirable in the interests of justice that, unless there are practical impossibilities, if they are suspected of crime they should not be questioned except in the presence of a parent or some person "of an adult kind" in the position of guardian.'

(By implication, these same principles should apply to extensions under s 30 of the Offences Against the State Act 1939).

[9.87] In essence, the weakness of the Judges' Rules is that they are not mandatory in effect, merely granting to the trial judge a discretion as to whether to exclude evidence obtained by reason of their breach or not.

The Custody Regulations 1987

[9.88] The Regulations with Regard to Treatment of Persons in Garda Custody,[83] introduced under the Criminal Justice Act 1984, are of similar effect to the Judges' Rules. Section 7(3) of the 1984 Act provides:

'A failure on the part of any member of the Garda Síochána to observe any provision of the regulations shall not of itself render that person liable to any criminal or civil proceedings or of itself reflect the lawfulness of the custody of the detained person, or the admissibility in evidence of any statement made by him.'

The main thrust of the Custody Regulations is to provide for a monitoring of the accused's treatment in custody by means of a 'custody record' kept by a designed officer in charge; regulated sessions of interrogation; and provision for rest periods etc.

[9.89] In *DPP v Spratt*,[84] O'Hanlon J interpreted s 7(3) of the 1984 Act as follows:

'The phrase "of itself" is obviously an important one in the construction of the statutory provisions, and I interpret the sub-section as meaning that non-observance of the Regulations is not to bring about automatically the exclusion from evidence of all that was done and said while the accused person was in custody. It appears to be left to the court of trial to adjudicate in every case as to the impact the non-compliance with the regulations should have on the case for the prosecution.'

---

[82] *Travers v Ryan* [1985] ILRM 163.
[83] Regulations with Regard to Treatment of Persons in Garda Custody (SI 119/1987) (see Appendix A).
[84] *DPP v Spratt* [1995] 1 IR 585.

[9.90] In *DPP v Devlin*[85], Budd J held that, in addition to adjudicating on whether there had been a breach of the Custody Regulations, the trial judge must assert what impact that had on the case for the prosecution. This was applied in *DPP v Cullen*[86], where the respondent had been charged with drink driving, which was dismissed by the District Justice on the basis of breaches of the Custody Regulations whereby the respondent had not been handed a notice of his rights while in custody, and had not had his rights read to him or explained to him. Ó Caoimh J concluded the District Justice had erred in not having gone on to consider the effect of these breaches on the prosecution case. He indeed expressed a doubt whether, given that it was mandatory for a suspect to give a sample, any failure regarding the Custody Regulations would have a causative link to the evidence justifying its exclusion.

[9.91] With regard to monitoring of the pre-trial period, the *Martin Committee Report*[87], included recommendations of electronic/video recording of interrogation sessions in the garda station. Section 27 of the 1984 Act made provision for the introduction of same. The effectiveness of such presupposes the absence of an increase, in the number of confessions obtained on the way to the station. A pilot scheme introducing electronic recording to police stations in Ireland has led to a commitment to make such facilities widely available but as yet they are limited to certain stations.

[9.92] In *People (DPP) v O'Connell*,[88] the appellant had been questioned in excess of the four-hour period authorised by the Custody Regulations. He had been told he was not obliged to continue but he had declined rests. The Court of Criminal Appeal held that the regulations (art 12(4)) did not allow waiver by an arrested person (this was confirmed in *People (DPP) v Reddan & Hannon*[89]). In *O'Connell* other breaches of the regulations including failure to make entries in the custody record, failure to contact the appellant's solicitor, and the fact that the appellant had no sleep – all contributed to the Court of Criminal Appeal's decision that the inculpatory statement made by the appellant should not have been admitted.

[9.93] In *DPP v Spratt*[90] it was held that where a breach of the Custody Regulations has occurred, it should be determined whether the accused has been thereby prejudiced and whether any information might not have been obtained,

---

[85] *DPP v Devlin* (2 September 1998) HC Budd J.
[86] *DPP v Cullen* (7 February 2001) HC Ó Caoimh J.
[87] *Report of the Committee to Enquire into Certain Aspects of Criminal Procedure* (1990) (Chairman Judge Frank Martin).
[88] *People (DPP) v O'Connell* [1995] 1 IR 244.
[89] *People (DPP) v Reddan & Hannon* [1995] 3 IR 560.
[90] *DPP v Spratt* [1995] 2 ILRM 117.

save for the breach. With regard to the relationship between the Judges' Rules and the Custody Regulations, Keane J in *People (DPP) v Darcy*[91], emphasised that a suspect is entitled to the protection of both.

[9.94] One controversial aspect of the rules is their provision to do with the undesirability of questioning an accused with regard to the charge on foot of which he is arrested. This is, indeed, indicative of the perspective of some of the function of the arrest (ie not as a means of garnering information), but indicative of the culmination of the investigative process. As we have seen, provision for after-arrest detention has to some extent weakened that proposition; yet even prior to that, the police had developed a practice of arresting persons on what was known as a 'holding-charge' – ie, a more minor charge than the original offence – and then questioning the accused with regard to that, usually significantly more important, offence.

[9.95] In *DPP v Quilligan*[92], the Supreme Court addressed that issue, and effectively sanctioned the use of such holding charges (such as the malicious damage arrest in that case, where the accused were then questioned about a murder) as long as there was 'some reality' to the more minor charge – even if it was both submerged in time and overshadowed in importance, by the graver offence.

[9.96] The approach was further endorsed by the decision of the Court of Criminal Appeal in *People (DPP) v Sean Howley*[93], where the court considered an application for leave to appeal against a murder conviction, which related to the trial judge's admission of a statement of an incriminatory nature. The applicant had been arrested under s 30 of the Offences Against the State Act 1939, on suspicion of having committed a scheduled offence (maiming cattle). He was interrogated with regard to the disappearance of the deceased. A further detention period was sanctioned, in the course of which, he made a statement admitting the murder.

[9.97] The applicant contended that to render the statement admissible, the prosecution must establish that the primary or predominant motive for the arrest was the necessity to investigate the maiming of cattle – which they had failed to do. The trial judge had ruled solely on the basis that the arrest was lawful, hence the statement was admissible, also noting, however, that the offence was a real offence.

---

[91] *People (DPP) v Darcy* (29 July 1997, unreported) HC.
[92] *DPP v Quilligan* [1987] ILRM 600.
[93] *People (DPP) v Sean Howley* [1989] ILRM 629 (affirmed by the Supreme Court).

[9.98] Finlay CJ referred in *Howley* to *People (DPP) v Walsh*, where a similar issue arose and Walsh J commented:

'The fact that there was a great disproportion between the nature of the offence in question and that the greater concentration of police effort was on the investigation into the more serious of them, namely the murder charge, is not in itself sufficient to establish as a reasonable probability that the arrest in respect of malicious damage charge was simply a colourable device to hold the accused in custody for an ulterior purpose on an alleged offence in which the Guards had no interest.'

[9.99] Finlay CJ also referred to *Quilligan*[94] which again supports the view that once there was a bona fide suspicion, the fact that the importance of the offence was very slight in relation to the offence of murder being investigated was not significant. Finlay CJ, therefore, rejected the predominant motive test and saw the test as being that:

'the court must ascertain whether the arrest under s 30 is a genuine bona fide arrest carried out on a suspicion actually held of complicity by the applicant in a real schedule offence. If it is, then the arrest is and remains lawful and statements made which otherwise cannot be objected to on grounds of fairness or the form of questioning with regard to any matter must be admissible in evidence. If on the other hand the arrest is made a device to secure the detention of a person who is not really under a bona fide suspicion with regard to the commission of a real scheduled offence but when the Gardaí wish to interview with regard to murder which is not a scheduled offence then the position is different.'

[9.100] McCarthy J in *People (DPP) v Healy*, in commenting with regard to the function and/or purpose of the s 30 power of detention after arrest, endorsed what was stated in *Quilligan's* case:

'The object of the powers given by section 30 is not to permit the arrest of people simply for the purpose of subjecting them to questioning. Rather is it for the purpose of investigating the commission or suspected commission of a crime by the person already arrested and to enable that investigation to be carried on without the possibility of obstruction or other interference which might occur if the suspected person were not under arrest. Section 30 is part of the statute law of the state permanently in force and it does not permit of any departure from normal police procedure save as to the obligation to bring the arrested person before a court as soon as reasonably possible.'

[9.101] Again in *Hannigan v Clifford*[95], Walsh J in the Supreme Court commented that *Quilligan* had laid down the principles governing s 30 arrests

---

[94] *DPP v Quilligan* [1987] ILRM 600.
[95] *Hannigan v Clifford* [1990] ILRM 65.

'... persons cannot be arrested under that section simply for the purpose of enabling evidence to be gathered'.

Despite a suggestion by Griffin J in *People v Shaw,* that the *O'Brien ratio* (see search and seizure; illegally obtained evidence) was confined to instances of real evidence, and did not apply to the question of the admissibility of confession evidence, it seems to now be generally accepted (see the comment of O'Higgins CJ in *People v Lynch*) that the said formula is also applicable to confession statements. Hence, a statement may well be voluntary; and yet not admissible.

[9.102] In *People v Shaw,* Shaw's constitutional right to liberty, was held to be superseded by the constitutional right to life of the victim. Hence, although there was a deliberate and conscious breach of constitutional rights, there were extraordinary excusing circumstances to excuse that breach. Interesting in that decision are two contrasting views as to the function of arrest. Per Walsh J:

'No person may be arrested (with or without warrant) for the purpose of interrogation or the securing of evidence from that person. If there exists a practice of arresting persons for the purpose of "assisting the police with their enquiries" it is unlawful. In such circumstances the phrase is no more than a euphemism for false imprisonment.'

Per Griffin J:

'I do not think it is correct to state without qualification that no person may be arrested with or without a warrant for the purpose of interrogation, or securing evidence from that person'.

Griffin J stated further with regard to the hierarchy of rights:

'Although the right to personal liberty is one of the fundamental rights, if a balance is to be struck between one person's right to personal liberty, for some hours or even days and another person's right to protection against danger to his life, then in any civilised society in my view, the latter right must prevail in circumstances such as those which confronted Superintendent Reynolds.'

[9.103] In *People v Lynch*[96], there was a conflict of evidence with regard to whether the appellant had remained voluntarily in the police station.[97] Due to a failure to resolve same by the jury, the confession was ultimately excluded on the basis that the accused had been subjected to 22 hours interrogation where, per O'Higgins CJ:

'... so obstructive and dominating a feature of this interrogation was its length, that such should not have been ignored or overlooked. The fact that the appellant

---

[96] *People v Lynch* [1982] IR 64.
[97] Cf, the later case of *People (DPP) v Conroy* returned said determination to the realm of judicial activity: *People (DPP) v Conroy* [1986] IR 460.

was subjected for almost 22 hours to sustained questioning, never had the opportunity of communicating with his family and friends and never being permitted to rest or sleep until he made an admission of guilt, all amount to such circumstances of harassment and oppression as to make it unjust and unfair to admit in evidence anything he said.'

[9.104] O'Higgins CJ felt that the trial judge 'in exercising his discretion ignored the features of oppression, harassment and fatigue which should have caused the statements, even if prima facie voluntary, to be excluded'. It is also interesting to note O'Higgins CJ's rejection of Griffin J's suggestion as to a restriction of the *O'Brien* ratio to real evidence:

'Once the Constitution has been violated for the purpose of securing a confession on that ground alone, the fruits of the violation must be excluded from evidence. Nor can it be said that the matter can safely be left to a decision on the fairness or the voluntary nature of a statement. If such confessions were ever admitted in evidence, because it was voluntary or because it was fairly taken or for any other reason, then the courts would, in the words of Warren CJ, "be made party to lawless invasions of the constitutional rights of citizens by permitting unhindered governmental use of the fruits of such invasions".'

The basis on which the statement was excluded in *Lynch* is uncertain. It was not on the basis of the unlawful deprivation of liberty and consequent breach of constitutional rights adhering thereto (due to a factual discrepancy, remaining unresolved), nor it would seem on the basis of the voluntary nature of the statement (despite reference to 'oppression' – see below), but rather on the basis of fairness. Is this a forerunner of the *Healy* decision's reference to a constitutional right to fairness of procedure in the pre-trial process perhaps, which will now operate to subsume the hitherto group of miscellaneous rights in that period?

[9.105] If the latter proposition is correct, the implication is that the 'Judges' Rules' in Ireland have not been alone in having amended or augmented the 'voluntariness' requirement, in so far as a reference to oppression is included.

[9.106] Some expansion of the *Ibrahim*[98] formula did occur in the United Kingdom, when 'oppression' was introduced as part of the principles in the introduction to the Judges' Rules in 1964. This concept was subsequently defined in *R v Priestly*[99] as importing something:

'... which tends to sap, and has sapped that freewill which must exist before a confession is voluntary – whether or not there is oppression in an individual case depends upon many elements. They included such things as the length of time of

---

[98] *Ibrahim v R* [1914] AC 599.
[99] *R v Priestly* (1965) 51 Cr App Rep 1.

any individual period of questioning, the length of time intervening between periods of questioning, whether the accused person has been given proper refreshment or not, and the characteristics of the person who makes the statement. What may be oppressive as regards a child, an individual or an old man or somebody inexperienced in the ways of this world may turn out not to be oppressive when one finds that the accused is of a tough character and an experienced man of the world.'

This was followed in *R v Praeger*[100] and adopted by the Irish Court of Criminal Appeal in *People (DPP) v McNally* and *People (DPP) v Breathnach*, where it would seem that the lack of oppression was regarded as part of the compliance with the voluntariness requirement.

[9.107] In Canada, the concept of oppression is seen not as a separate concept, but one of the factors taken into account in determining whether the accused gave his statement voluntarily within the *Ibrahim* formula. In *Horwath v Queen*[101] a 17-year-old youth, unintentionally but without his consent, was put into a light hypnotic state and made inculpatory statements. The trial judge had described the accused's mental condition at the end of the interview as being one of complete emotional disintegration. The Supreme Court held, in restoring the trial judge's verdict, that the voluntariness test in *Ibrahim* was not exhaustive in relation to the circumstances where a statement was involuntary and therefore inadmissible. Here the statement was not voluntary, because of the way it was induced. In *Ward v Queen*[102] it was held that in the case of an accused giving statements to police after a serious car accident, when the accused was visibly in a state of shock, that the:

'... examination of whether there was any type of advantage or fear of prejudice inducing the statement is simply an investigation of whether the statement was freely and voluntarily made in considering the mental condition of the accused to determine whether or not the statement represented the operating mind of the accused.'

Hence, it would appear that the Canadian courts have developed a somewhat wider notion of voluntariness.

[9.108] In *R v Flynn and Leonard*[103], Lord Lowry CJ invoked the notion of 'oppressive circumstances' to infringe the voluntariness requirement in the context of confessions emanating from the Hollywood Interrogation Centre, a place described by the court as amounting to a virtual 'confession factory', ie

---

[100] *R v Praeger* [1972] 1 All ER 1114.
[101] *Horwath v Queen* [1979] 3 WCB 181.
[102] *Ward v Queen* 44 CCC (2nd ed) 498.
[103] *R v Flynn and Leonard* (24 May 1972, unreported) Belfast City Commission.

physically constructed in such a manner as to encourage or indeed compel a detained person to make a confession of guilt.

[9.109] The voluntariness requirement, it cannot be over-emphasised, is a peremptory requirement – a pre-condition to admission, but not solely a determination of admissibility. Other factors, as seen hitherto, can then operate to influence a trial judge to exercise his discretion to refuse to admit same. A trial judge does not, however, as emphasised by Walsh J in *People (AG) v Cummins*[104], have any discretion to admit a confession which is not voluntary. Whether matters affecting the pre-trial process, therefore, are classified as part of that pre-emptory 'voluntariness' requirement, or the rather more vulnerable 'constitutional right to fairness' in that process, is not without significance.

Detention under the Criminal Justice (Drug Trafficking) Act 1996

[9.110] Section 2(1) of the Criminal Justice (Drug Trafficking) Act 1996 provides that where a member of the Garda Síochána arrests without warrant a person he suspects with reasonable cause of having committed a drug trafficking offence, they may be detained for up to a maximum of 7 days. Initially they can be held for 6 hours on the authorisation of the 'member in charge', which period can be extended up to 18 hours by a Chief Superintendent and subsequently by a further 24 hours by a Chief Superintendent. Any further detention may then be authorised by a District Court judge who may grant an extension of 72 hours, at which time a Chief Superintendent can apply to the District Court judge for a further 48 hours. Such extensions will only be authorised where the person granting the extension is satisfied further detention is necessary for 'the proper investigation of the offence concerned and that the investigation is being conducted diligently and expeditiously'.[105]

[9.111] The judicial intervention here is to comply with the European Court of Human Rights determination in *Brogan v United Kingdom*[106]. In *DPP v DJ Early O'Riordan, Kelly & Maguire*[107], several individuals were arrested under s 2 of the Criminal Justice (Drug Trafficking) Act 1996, but their extension was sanctioned by a District Court judge not so authorised under the legislation, and so they were released. They were rearrested but successfully challenged the arrest on the basis that they could only be rearrested under s 4 of the Criminal Justice (Drug Trafficking) Act 1996, under which new information is required before parties can be rearrested. These proceedings arose by way of judicial

---

[104] *People (AG) v Cummins* [1972] IR 312.
[105] Criminal Justice (Drug Trafficking) Act 1996, s 2(2)(g)(i).
[106] *Brogan v United Kingdom* (1989) 11 EHRR 117.
[107] *DPP v DJ Early O'Riordan Kelly & Maguire* (2 December 1997, unreported) HC (McGuinness J) (at p 12-13).

review. McGuinness J identified the safeguard in s 4 as being one against repeated detention by the gardaí on the same offence without any new information having come to light. She went on to reason:

'However this is different from the situation which can arise where a person has been released from detention under ... section 2 of the 1996 Act and at a later stage a decision is made by the Director of Public Prosecutions or by the gardaí to charge that person with an actual offence...It is essential to distinguish carefully and clearly between arrest for the purposes of detention for investigation and arrest for the purposes of charging the alleged offender, of bringing him or her before the Court and of initiating the procedures ... which eventually will lead to his or her trial.'

This approach reveals the extent to which the arrest process has changed and offers a dual approach to arrest which sanctions and mainstreams that of interrogation.

Confrontation between the police and the citizen

[9.112] Given the desire to vindicate the individual's rights, yet accommodate police investigations, it is interesting to view the judicial perspectives on the status of the inquiry. In *McCarrick v Leavy*[108], Davitt P in the High Court stated that it was never intended by the Judges' Rules that a police officer should caution every person of whom he proposed to ask a question. In the Supreme Court in that case, Walsh J commented:

'A failure to comply with the provisions of the judges rules, gives a discretion to the trial judge to refuse to admit the evidence in question, but the exercise of that discretion is not governed by whether or not the statement is voluntary. A statement obtained in breach of the provisions of the judges rules is admissible provided it is a voluntary one. But the fact that it is a voluntary one does not take away the trial judge's discretion to refuse to admit the evidence if it has been obtained in violation of the judges rules ...'

[9.113] In *People v O'Loughlin*[109], it was held that a suspect could be said to be 'in custody' from the moment the garda had made up his mind to charge him. On the facts, it was held that from the time the gardaí realised that the accused's initial oral explanation had not been substantiated by their enquiries, the accused had been detained deliberately in unlawful custody in contravention of his constitutional rights, and his written statement, made during such unlawful detention, should not have been admitted.

---

[108] *McCarrick v Leavy* [1964] IR 225.
[109] *People v O'Loughlin* [1979] IR 85.

[9.114] One of the difficulties arising, particularly in relation to those detained consequent on arrest, is in respect of the status of the questioning of those persons thus detained. In *People v Madden*[110], the Court of Criminal Appeal held that the obligation of the suspect arrested under s 30, to account for movements under s 52 of the Offences Against the State Act 1939, did not prohibit further questioning of that person by the gardaí. This was confirmed in *People v Kelly*[111] by Finlay P, who commented:

'So to hold would be to create a uniquely anomalous position whereby a person arrested at common law under suspicion of having committed an ordinary offence could be questioned by the Garda Siochana, and provided due procedures and fair treatment were afforded to him, any answers he gave to such questions would be admissible in evidence against him, whereas a person arrested under s 30 – a statute specifically enacted to deal with more serious crimes tending to undermine the stability of the state could not be so questioned.'

[9.115] Arrest, as previously noted, was traditionally a process indicative of the end of the State's investigative process. However, change had occurred as a result of the evolution of powers of detention consequent on arrest – originally invoked under s 30 of the Offences Against the State Act 1939.

[9.116] The judiciary, along with this development, had become watchful of any over-spill from this original 'extraordinary' realm, into the 'ordinary' criminal justice system. Judgments such as that of the Supreme Court in *People v Christopher Lynch*[112], effectively abolished the police tactic of 'inviting someone into the police station to help them with their inquiries'. Note the comment of the then Garda Commissioner McLaughlin[113]:

'... for a while we surmounted this problem of being unable to detain a suspect by inviting him to come voluntarily to the Garda Station to be interviewed. For many years, suspects who had in this fashion come voluntarily to Garda Stations were interviewed unless they expressed a desire to leave the station. This procedure was acceptable and statements made during these interviews were treated as admissible in court provided of course that they were otherwise voluntary and taken in accordance with the Judges Rules.'

[9.117] The comment of Walsh J in *Lynch,* where the accused was held without any lawful arrest for 22 hours and questioned, was to the effect that:

---

[110] *People v Madden* [1977] IR 336.
[111] *People v Kelly* [1983] ILRM 271.
[112] *People v Christopher Lynch* [1981] ILRM 389.
[113] McLaughlin P 'Legal Constraints in Criminal Investigation' (1981) Vol XVI Part 2 Ir Jur (ns) 217.

'If a person is asked to come to a Garda Station and he goes voluntarily, he has been asked to come for some particular purpose, to give assistance in the investigation of a crime or some other purpose. When he is subjected to interrogation of a nature which would suggest he may well be a suspect in the case or questioned or interrogated in circumstances which reasonably would give rise to that inference, he should be informed that he is free to leave at any time unless and until he is arrested.'[114]

[9.118] In *DPP v Eamonn Kelly*[115], the appeal of the accused against his conviction, obtained solely on the basis of a number of written statements and one comprehensive written statement made while in police custody, was based on the fact that while under a s 30 arrest, Kelly was moved in the course of his detention to a number of garda stations in succession.

The point of law of public importance certified by the Court of Criminal Appeal to the Supreme Court, was whether a person arrested under s 30 and detained in a particular garda station and then transferred to another garda station ceased by reason of that transfer, to be in lawful custody.

[9.119] The Supreme Court held that as long as the duration of the detention was within a permitted period, the plurality of places or removals did not contravene the section. The Chief Justice commented:

'... if in any case, the removal of a person detained under section 30, from one Garda Station or other place to another was *mala fides* or was done for the purposes either of harassment or isolating him from assistance or access to that which he could properly be entitled, then that fact itself would clearly render his detention unlawful.'

[9.120] Significant here also is the decision of *Trimbole v Governor of Mountjoy*[116], where Egan J stated that:

'... the only rational explanation for the section 30 arrest on 25 October 1984, was to ensure that the applicant would be available for arrest and detention when Part II of the 1965 Act would apply to the Commonwealth of Australia. There was a gross misuse of s 30 [of the 1939 Act], which amounted to a conscious and deliberate violation of constitutional rights. There were no extraordinary excusing circumstances.'

[9.121] An important determination, in the context of a breach of the accused's constitutional rights, is as to the actual status of the accused's detention. This led to some difficulty in *Lynch*, in so far as there had not been a determination at

---

[114] This was followed in *People v Coffey* (6 March 1981, unreported) and *DPP v Herron* (27 October 1981, unreported).

[115] *DPP v Kelly* [1983] ILRM 271.

[116] *Trimbole v Governor of Mountjoy* [1985] ILRM 465.

trial on the facts, as to whether the accused was in fact free to leave the garda station, and so was there voluntarily. The Supreme Court in *Lynch*, moreover, suggested such determination – as to whether there had been an illegal detention – should be made by the jury. According to O'Higgins CJ stated:

> 'In my view, the jury, either by a specific question, or by an appropriate direction ought to have been asked to decide, as a question of fact, material to the defence, whether the appellant's evidence that he had been held against his wishes was or was not true.'

[9.122] Subsequently, in *People (DPP) v Conroy*[117], the Supreme Court declined to follow that view. Per Henchy J:

> '... a jury informed of the circumstances and contents of inadmissible evidence would be unfit to try the issue of guilt or innocence since it would lack the characteristic of impartiality and the alternative of having separate juries determine the two issues would be inconsistent with the unitary and unbroken trial with a jury guaranteed by the Constitution.'

Such matters were for determination by the trial judge in the absence of the jury.

[9.123] To the extent that the pre-trial process is now encrusted with procedure, one may find a parallel movement (echoing the earlier change in the focus from trial (procedural) to pre-trial) from police station (pre-trial and procedural) to 'on the street' confrontation. The 'status' of the individual (hallmark of procedural monitoring) may then merit increasing attention in that context.

[9.124] The decision in *The People v Paul Ward*[118] gives an interesting insight into the approach of the gardaí to interrogation and judicial attitudes to that pre-trial process behaviour. The beginning of the court's judgment gives the context in which it was decided:

> 'On 26 June 1996 Ms Veronica Guerin, a distinguished brave journalist who specialised in the investigation of crime, was brutally murdered when riddled with bullets as she sat in her car waiting for traffic lights to change at the Naas Road, Boot Road junction, Clondalkin, Dublin.'

[9.125] The case against Ward comprised verbal admissions allegedly made by him in custody under s 30 of the Offences Against the State Act 1939 (the first three of the four pillars of the case against him, according to the State), and the testimony of Charles Bowden, an accomplice. Given the centrality of the admissions to the State's case, the following comment made by the Special Criminal Court is revelatory:

---

[117] *People (DPP) v Conroy* [1986] IR 460.
[118] *People v Paul Ward* (27 November 1998, unreported) SCC (Barr J).

'The accused is an experienced Section 30 detainee having been arrested on that basis on earlier occasions and he stated in evidence that he was well aware of the importance in his own interest of adopting a policy of total silence in the course of interrogation and he alleged that he did so.'

[9.126] In the course of his detention, Ward's girlfriend, Vanessa Meehan, and his mother, Elizabeth Ward, 74 years of age, were taken to visit him. Neither of these visits was requested by Ward. In relation to this treatment, which is reminiscent of that meted to Pringle (an aforementioned miscarriage of justice case)[119] when his girlfriend was also brought in while he was in custody, the Special Criminal Court comments:

'The police were under severe pressure to bring charges in relation to that crime. The coincidence that the accused's capitulation after more than 14 hours of silence during interrogations had occurred immediately after a visit by Ms Meehan is a remarkable volte face which gives rise to unease and raises a series of pertinent questions ... In reality was the visit a deliberate ploy devised by the police to soften up the accused and cause him to incriminate himself as to the murder?'

[9.127] Describing the history of the accused's interrogation as 'very remarkable indeed', the Court concludes with regard to the visit by Ward's mother:

'The court is satisfied beyond all reasonable doubt that the visit from Mrs Ward was a deliberate ploy devised and orchestrated by the police in a final effort to prevail on the accused to disclose what he had done with the gun ... The court is satisfied that the visit was not arranged for any humanitarian purpose but was a cynical ploy which it was hoped might break down the accused ...'

[9.128] The Court's conclusion with regard to the alleged admissions and their admissibility is fairly damning:

'Both meetings amounted to a conscious and deliberate disregard of the accused's basic constitutional right to fair procedures and treatment while in custody. They constituted deliberate gross violations of the fundamental obligation which the interrogators and their superiors had of conducting their dealings with the accused in accordance with the principles of basic fairness and justice ... In all the circumstances the court is satisfied that in the interests of justice and fairness all admissions allegedly made by the accused during the period of his detention at Lucan garda station must be ruled inadmissible.

The Court also has some element of doubt about whether the alleged verbal admissions were in fact made by the accused or where, as he contends, he made no admissions at all during the entire period of his detention.'

---

[119] *DPP v Pringle McCann & O'Shea* (22 May 1981, unreported) CCA.

Of course, in declaring the admissions inadmissible, there remains quiescent in this non-jury court the artificiality of the Court members, being triers of fact, ignoring them.

[9.129] The remaining leg of the prosecution case was the testimony of the accomplice Charles Bowden, alleged by the defence to be similar to that of the supergrass type witness in Northern Ireland, in that he struck a deal with the State and was part of its new Witness Protection Programme. The court did not accept the argument that Bowden was a supergrass, requiring special caution, but declared itself to be 'deeply mindful of the fundamental principle of criminal law that it is unsafe to act upon the evidence of an accomplice which is not corroborated in some material particular implicating the accused.'

[9.130] In relation to Bowden, the Court commented:

> 'The Court accepts without any doubt that Charles Bowden is a self-serving, deeply avaricious and potentially vicious criminal. On his own admission he is a liar and the court readily accepts that he would lie without hesitation and regardless of the consequences for others if he is perceived it to be in his own interest to do so. The Court fully appreciates that assessment of his evidence must be made with great caution and with the foregoing firmly in mind.'

Having so classified the witness, the Special Criminal Court then convicted Ward on the sole basis of Bowden's testimony.

[9.131] Ward's conviction was, of course, subsequently overturned by the Court of Criminal Appeal, largely on the basis of the lack of credibility of the witness who required corroboration. It is worth remembering here, also, that confessions attract a corroboration warning by virtue of s 10 of the Criminal Procedure Act 1993.

The doctrine of *res gestae*

[9.132] Evidence relevant to the 'transaction' and arising contemporaneously with it may be admissible. The doctrine has been rather more critically described by Lord Tomlin in *Holmes v Newman*[120], as 'a phrase adopted to provide a respectable legal cloak for a variety of cases to which no formulae of precision can be applied'. Some idea of the more modern rationale behind this exception to the hearsay rule is to be gleaned from Lord Wilberforce's statement in *Ratten v R*[121]: 'it must be for the judge by preliminary ruling to satisfy himself that the statement was so clearly made in circumstances of spontaneity and involvement in the event, that the possibility of concoction can be disregarded'.

---

[120] *Holmes v Newman* [1931] 2 Ch 112.
[121] *Ratten v R* [1972] AC 378 at 389.

[9.133] The traditional view was that statements coming within this exception, formed part of the event. Hence, the requirement of contemporaneity between the statement and the fact in issue was viewed quite strictly, and any difference in location between the event and the utterance, significant.

[9.134] A classic illustration of the original, very strict, interpretation of the requirement of contemporaneity is to be found in *R v Beddingfield*[122]. Here the deceased's throat had just been cut, and she walked out of the room, where the accused was, and said, 'Oh dear Aunt, see what Beddingfield has done to me'. The statement was excluded, because it was made after the act was completed. The present position is quite different, as seen from the rationale as expanded in modern terms in *Ratten*:

'The possibility of concoction, or fabrication, where it exists, is on the other hand an entirely valid reason for exclusion, and is probably the real test which judges in fact apply. In their Lordships' opinion this should be recognised and applied directly as the relevant test: the test should be not the uncertain one whether the making of the statement was in some sense part of the event or transaction. This may often be difficult to establish such external matters as the time which elapses between the events and the speaking of the words (or vice versa), and differences in location being relevant factors but not, taken by themselves, decisive criteria. As regards statements made after the event it must be for the judge, by preliminary ruling, to satisfy himself that the statement was so clearly made in circumstances of spontaneity or involvement in the event that the possibility of concoction can be disregarded. Conversely, if he considers that the statement was made by way of narrative of a detached prior event so that the speaker was so disengaged from it as to be able to construct or adapt his account, he should exclude it. And the same must in principle be true of statements made before the event. The test should be not the uncertain one whether the making of the statement should be regarded as part of the event or transaction. This may often be difficult to show. But if the drama, leading up to the climax has commenced and assumed such intensity and pressure that the utterance can safely be regarded as a true reflection of what was unrolling or actually happening, it ought to be received. The expression *res gestate* may conveniently sum up these criteria, but the reality of them must always be kept in mind: it is this that lies behind the best reasoned of the judges' rulings.'

[9.135] Lord Wilberforce looked at various authorities and concluded:

'... there is ample support for the principle that hearsay evidence may be admitted in the statement provided it is made in such conditions (always being those of approximate but not exact contemporaneity) of involvement or pressure as to exclude the possibility of concoction or distortion to the advantage of the accused.'

---

[122] *R v Beddingfield* (1879) 14 Cox CC 341.

On the facts, Lord Wilberforce opined that since around the time the accused's wife was shot (allegedly accidentally) the local exchange received a telephone call from the accused's house, where a female voice called hysterically, 'Get the Police', had that been considered hearsay evidence, it was still admissible under the doctrine of '*res gestae*'.

[9.136] Lord Wilberforce felt that there was ample evidence of a close and intimate connection between the statement ascribed to the deceased and the shooting which occurred very shortly afterwards:

> 'The way in which the statement came to be made (in a call for the police) and the tone of the voice used showed intrinsically that the statement was being forced from the deceased by an overwhelming pressure of contemporary event. It carried its own stamp of spontaneity and thus was endorsed by the proved time sequence and the proved proximity of the deceased to the appellant with his gun.'

[9.137] Cross[123] attempted to divide the admissibility of *res gestae* evidence into four categories:

> (1) *Statements accompanying and explaining relevant acts.* In *R v Edwards*[124] the wife of the accused handed a knife to a neighbour saying she would feel safer if it was out of the way. It was held that the statement was admissible as evidence to prove that previous threats had been made by the accused to his wife. The vital prerequisites being satisfied viz, the statement being contemporaneous with the act in question; the statement was made in relation to the act; and it was made by the person performing the act.

> (2) *Spontaneous statements in relation to an event in issue.* In *Davies v Fortior*[125] the statement of the deceased emitted on falling into an acid bath ('I shouldn't have done it') was admitted in a subsequent civil action in relation to the accident.

> (3) *Statements in relation to the maker's contemporaneous state of mind or emotion.* In *R v Vincent, Frost &` Edwards*[126], at a public meeting, where it was alleged that general alarm had been caused, statements were admitted to show fear. (Authorities conflict as to whether the doing of an act can be inferred from a statement of intention to do it: in *R v Wainright*[127] the statement of a murdered girl that she was going to D's place was deemed admissible to show her state of mind and intention, but not admissible as evidence that she had indeed gone to D's place; whereas in *R v Buckley*[128] in the context of the murder of a police

---

[123] *Cross on Evidence* (6th edn, 1985) p 580.
[124] *R v Edwards* (1872) 12 Cox CC 230.
[125] *Davies v Fortior* [1952] 1 All ER 1355.
[126] *R v Vincent, Frost & Edwards* (1840) 9 C & P 275.
[127] *R v Wainright* (1875) 13 Cox CC 171.
[128] *R v Buckley* (1873) 13 Cox CC 293.

officer, who had expressed an intention to go to D's house, the statement was admitted as evidence in relation to the issue of whether he did in fact go there.)

(4) *Statements of physical sensation.* Admissible as evidence of the speaker's contemporaneous sensation, but not as to its possible cause: *R v Nicholas*[129]. *CB Pollack:* 'One can say in evidence that one has indeed got a wound, but not how one got it'.

[9.138] The most recent decision on the issue of *res gestae* is that of the House of Lords in *R v Andrews*[130]. The facts concerned the appellant and another man who knocked on the door to the victim's flat, and when the victim opened it, stabbed him in the stomach and robbed the flat. The victim was discovered minutes later and the police arrived quite soon after. The victim was seriously wounded, and told the police he had been attacked by two men, and gave the name of the appellant and the name and address of the other man. He then became unconscious, was brought to hospital and died two months later. The appellant was tried for murder, and the Crown sought to admit the victim's statement. The accused appealed on the basis that the statement should not have been admitted on the basis of the doctrine of *res gestae*. The House of Lords confirmed the approach to the doctrine of *res gestae* elucidated in *Ratten* and subsequently applied in *R v Blastland*[131], *R v Nye & Loan*[132], *R v Boyle*[133] and *R v O Shea*[134].

[9.139] Hence, the defence counsel's argument that hearsay must form part of the criminal act for which the accused is being tried, as per *Beddingfield*, contending that *Ratten* essentially involved an extension of exceptions to the hearsay rule, was therefore invalid.

[9.140] Lord Ackner stated he did not accept that Lord Wilberforce's principles involved an extension to this exception; and felt that in accordance with same, *R v Beddingfield* would not be so decided today. Indeed, he felt there could hardly be a case where the words uttered carried more clearly the mark of spontaneity and intense involvement. The trial judge therefore, per Lord Ackner, must ask the following questions:

(1)   Can the possibility of concoction or distortion be disregarded?

(2)   Looking at the circumstances in which the statement was made, was the utterance an instinctive reaction, with no possibility of concoction?

---

[129] *R v Nicholas* (1846) 2 Car & Kir 246.
[130] *R v Andrews* [1987] 1 All ER 513.
[131] *R v Blastland* [1985] 2 All ER 1095.
[132] *R v Nye & Loan* (1978) 66 Cr App Rep 252.
[133] *R v Boyle* (6 March 1986, unreported).
[134] *R v O Shea* (27 July 1986, unreported).

(3)   Were there circumstances of spontaneity; was the mind of the declarant still dominated by the event?

(4)   If there are special features in the case (apart from the time factor) the judge must be satisfied that the circumstances were such that, having regard to the special feature of malice, there was no possibility of concoction *or* distortion to the advantage of the accused.

(5)   The possibility of error. Given the fallibility of human recollection, this must affect the weight of the evidence, for example, if there were special features, as here, where the deceased had drink taken, the trial judge must decide if he can exclude the possibility of error.

Declarations against proprietary/pecuniary interests

[9.141] In *Lalor v Lalor*[135], the facts of the case were such that Delaney (since deceased) had purchased certain leaseholds and reassigned them to trustees for his sister Maria. After her death, her husband attempted to upset the trust on the grounds that he was the beneficial owner. He relied on a conversation he had with Delaney, which was alleged to have been contrary to the latter's proprietary interest. Per Fitzgibbon J:

'I am of the opinion that the interest against which the statement appears to be made, must, in order to supply that sanction which, after the death of the party, is accepted as a substitute for an oath, be an interest existing at the time of making the statement.'

[9.142] *Flood v Russell*[136] concerned a statement by a wife (now deceased) to the effect that her husband, who pre-deceased her, had made a will giving her a life interest in certain real estate. It was admitted as being a declaration against pecuniary or proprietary interest for the reason that had there been no will, her share in the intestacy would have been considerably more than the life estate.

Declarations by deceased persons in the course of duty

[9.143] In *Harris v Lambert HC*[137], entries by a deceased solicitor in his diary, were sought to be put in evidence. They were objected to on the grounds of their not having been made in the performance of his duty to this client, but for purposes of recording and later claiming costs. It was held that there was sufficient authority for the proposition that notes can be received if made in discharge of a duty by a solicitor with a view to an ultimate duty to do a specific thing.

---

[135] *Lalor v Lalor* (1879) 4 LR 678.
[136] *Flood v Russell* (1891) 29 LR Ir 91.
[137] *Harris v Lambert HC* [1932] IR 504.

Declarations as to pedigree matters

[9.144] This exception is normally confined to questions strictly of descent of relationship. In *Palmer v Palmer*[138], 'A' devised lands to his son for life and then to his son's sons in order of seniority and in succession. The third of 'B's' sons, in an action to gain possession of the lands, was permitted to prove the death of his two elder brothers by means of family repute under this exception.

Declarations as to public rights

[9.145] In *Giant's Causeway Co Ltd v AG*[139] the original ordinance survey map made in 1832 by an officer of the engineers and produced from the custody of the Ordinance Department, was held admissible in a matter involving questions of public interest. In this case the latter interest was that of a right-of-way.

Post-testamentary declarations by testators as to the contents of their wills

[9.146] In the *Goods of George Ball*[140], on the death of the testator, his will was seen to be a copy, bearing a statement by him that he had substituted the copy for the original. It was held that declarations made by a testator both before and after the execution of his will are, in the event of its loss, admissible as secondary evidence of its contents.

Dying declarations of the deceased on a charge of homicide

[9.147] An oral or written declaration of a deceased person is admissible evidence of the cause of his death at a trial for his murder or manslaughter, provided he was under a settled, hopeless expectation of death when the statement was made, and provided he would have been a competent witness if called to give evidence at that time. The underlying rationale of this rule is the presumption that a person is unlikely to die with a 'lie on his lips'. It is a purely Christian ethic at basis, which assumes the sanction of imminent death to be equivalent to that of the oath. The important elements governing this exception are that the deceased is aware of the danger of *imminent* (though not necessarily immediate) death. Evidence which might be preferred indicating this awareness would include that of anointment. In *The Crown v Mooney*[141], the declaration was held inadmissible, as the deceased had not been told expressly that she was dying, though the doctor had told her she was dangerously ill and the clergyman warned her to prepare for death.

---

[138] *Palmer v Palmer* (1886-7) 18 LR Ir 192.
[139] *Giant's Causeway Co Ltd v AG* (1905) 5 Ir Jur Rep 381.
[140] *In the Goods of George Ball* (1890) 25 LR Ir 556.
[141] *The Crown v Mooney* (1851) 5 Cox cc 318.

[9.148] The form of the declaration was considered in *R v Fitzpatrick*[142], where Palles CB stated that he was quite prepared to decide, neither upon principle or upon authority, if it be held that a dying declaration was inadmissible only because it was cast in narrative form, although it has been given in answer to questions put. But in the second place, he was also of the opinion that the portion of the written document which was relied upon by the prisoner as vitiating the whole declaration, was not part of the dying declaration at all, nor within the rule which treated such dying declarations as being an exceptional class of evidence. He had always regarded it as a settled rule of practice that the fact that a declaration was based on answers to questions went to the weight, but never to the admissibility, of the evidence.

[9.149] Of great importance is the limitation of admissibility to cases of homicide. Hence in *Eliza Smith v Cavan County Council*[143], on a claim for compensation which was a quasi-criminal matter, a dying declaration was held not admissible, as the rule applied only to cases of homicide. Of course, should the witness recover, however miraculously, a charge of homicide will evidently not lie; and on whatever the relevant charge, the witness can, if necessary, be called to testify.

Admission of documentary evidence

[9.150] The Criminal Evidence Act 1992 made major changes to the operation of the rule against hearsay, insofar as it concerns documentary evidence and its admissibility in criminal proceedings. Part II of the 1992 Act provides that information contained in a document shall be admissible as evidence of any fact therein of which direct oral evidence would be admissible, if the information was compiled 'in the ordinary course of business'(not restricted to commercial enterprises, s 1) and supplied by a person who had, or may reasonably be supposed to have had, personal knowledge of the matters dealt with (s 5). Evidence of admissibility (s 6) must be provided by means of a certificate signed by a person who occupies a position in relation to the management of the business in the course of which the information was compiled; and notice given of such documentary evidence under s 7. Section 8(1) further provides that such evidence shall not be admitted if the court is of the opinion that, in 'the interests of justice', such should not be admitted.

---

[142] *R v Fitzpatrick* (1912) 46 ILTR 173.
[143] *Eliza Smith v Cavan County Council* (1927) 58 ILTR 107.

[9.151] In *Company Sergeant Berigan*[144], a complaint was made that documents were admitted without proof that they were originals, emerging from proper custody, identified by those responsible for their creation. In response, the prosecution relied upon s 5 of the Criminal Evidence Act 1992 which provides that information contained in a document is admissible in criminal proceedings as evidence of any fact therein of which direct oral evidence would have been admissible if the information was compiled in the ordinary course of business and supplied by a person who had, or may reasonably supposed to have had, personal knowledge of the matter.

The court rejected the argument that s 5 addressed the difficulty raised by the applicant. The prosecution evidence only identified the documents; there was no evidence that they were compiled in the ordinary course of business or the information supplied by a person who had,, or might reasonably be supposed to have, knowledge of the matters in the documents.

[9.152] Section 8(2) of the 1992 Act provides that, in so considering, the court should have regard to all the circumstances, including: whether the information is reliable (s 8(2)(9)), authentic (s 8(2)(b)), and that its admission or exclusion will result in unfairness to the accused(s 8(2)(c)). The latter, perhaps, is the most interesting, and will require a judicial assessment of the extent to which the rationale of the hearsay rule (itself not confined exclusively to trustworthiness as seen) is rooted in a belief that orality, cross-examination and confrontation are elements or prerequisites to 'fairness' to the accused.

[9.153] Section 8(3) of the 1992 Act provides that in estimating the weight to be attached to information, regard shall be had to the circumstances from which any inference can reasonably be drawn as to its accuracy or otherwise. Evidence as to the credibility of the supplier of information is admissible by virtue of s 9.

Copies of documents

[9.154] Section 30 of the 1992 Act provides that copies of a document may be produced in evidence (whether or not the original is in existence), authenticated in such manner as the Court may approve, and it is immaterial how many removes there are between copy and original or how (including facsimile) the copy was produced. 'Document' here includes film, sound recording and video recording.

[9.155] The extent to which videos or computer-generated information can be interfered with, will undoubtedly become a factor here, as will the question of

---

[144] *Company Sergeant Berigan* (1 November 2001) Courts Martial Appeal Court, *Annual Review of Irish Law 2001*, p 304.

how it can be safeguarded or secured against such interference so as to be admissible.

Further 'exceptional provision' – incremental reform

Proceeds of crime and Criminal Assets Bureau

[9.156] Under the Proceeds of Crime Act 1996, s 6 allows hearsay evidence of a member of the Criminal Assets Bureau as to the possession of property and its connection with the proceeds of crime. This can play a pivotal role in relation to the making of an order under s 3 of the 1996 Act. McGuinness J suggested in *Gilligan*[145] that a court should be slow to make orders under s 3 in the absence of other corroborating evidence. Moriarty J in *M v D*[146] shared that circumspection.

Offences against the State

[9.157] Under the Offences Against the State (Amendment) Act 1998, which was enacted in the aftermath of the Omagh bombing, ss 2–5 of that Act concern changes in the rules of evidence. While, in the main, these relate to inference provisions, s 4 admits what would otherwise be inadmissible hearsay, in so far as its provisions allow for inferences to be drawn with regard to membership, from any statement or conduct by a person accused of membership of an unlawful organisation, which statement or conduct implies or leads to a reasonable inference that he was at the material time a member.

[9.158] Under the Bail Act 1997 it is also not improbable that hearsay evidence will be presented with regard to apprehension of further crimes. Section 2 of the Bail Act 1997 provides that where an application for bail is made by a person charged with a serious offence, a court may refuse the application if satisfied that such refusal is reasonably considered necessary to prevent the commission of a serious offence by that person. In exercising that jurisdiction, the court shall take into account and receive evidence concerning:

'2(2)(a)   the nature and degree of seriousness of the offence with which the accused person is charged and the sentence likely to be imposed on conviction,

(b)   the nature and degree of seriousness of the offence apprehended and the sentence likely to be imposed on conviction,

(c)   the nature and strength of the evidence in support of the charge,

(d)   any conviction of the accused person for an offence committed while he or she was on bail,

---

[145] *Gilligan* (26 June 1997, unreported) HC.
[146] *M v D* [1998] 3 IR 175.

(e)   any previous convictions of the accused person including any conviction the subject of an appeal (which has neither been determined nor withdrawn) to a court,

(f)   any other offence in respect of which the accused person is charged and is awaiting trial,

and, where it has taken account of one or more of the foregoing, it may also take into account the fact that the accused person is addicted to a controlled drug within the meaning of the Misuse of Drugs Act 1977.'

[9.159] Hence it can be seen that specific incursions on the rule against hearsay are being made with regard to exceptional provisions for particular cases. This is a phenomenon which has been seen to be common to many areas of evidentiary law reform. It shares the difficulty with other such moves of a failure to consider the implications for underlying principle of such change.

This incremental mechanism of change, with the particular context in question invoked as justification, risks avoidance of acknowledgement that any real impact on principle occurs, when in fact it does. The 'old chestnut' of the rule against hearsay has proven no more impervious to this phenomenon than other so-called 'obstructionist' rules of evidence.

Chapter 10

Similar Fact Evidence

'How can we know the dancer from the dance?''

Among School Children *Collected Poems of W B Yeats*

(London, Macmillan, 1958).

Introduction

[10.01] In general the three principles governing the admissibility of similar fact evidence can be stated as follows:

(1)   Evidence of past bad behaviour, if offered as evidence that a particular act was done, must be relevant.

(2)   Even if relevant, evidence of past bad behaviour is inadmissible if its only relevance is to show that the actor has a bad disposition.

(3)   Even if (1) and (2) are satisfied, such evidence is inadmissible or can be excluded if its prejudicial effect outweighs its probative value.

[10.02] Lord Herschell enunciated the basic exclusionary premise with regard to evidence as to the accused's past misconduct, in the nineteenth century landmark decision of *Makin v Attorney General for New South Wales*[1]:

'It is undoubtedly not competent for the prosecution to adduce evidence tending to show that the accused has been guilty of criminal acts other than those covered by the indictment, for the purpose of leading to the conclusion that the accused is a person likely from his criminal conduct or character to have committed the offence for which he is being tried.'

That is the general rule. However, the exception to that basic principle, which is largely what concerns us in this chapter, was formulated by Lord Herschell as follows:

'On the other hand the mere fact that the evidence adduced tends to show that commission of other crimes does not render it inadmissible if it be relevant to an issue before the jury, and it may be so relevant if it bears upon the question whether the acts alleged to constitute the crime charged in the indictment were designed or accidental or to rebut a defence which would otherwise be open to the accused.'

---

[1]   *Makin v Attorney General for New South Wales* [1894] AC 57 at 65.

[10.03] The rationale for the general reluctance of the courts to admit or allow the production by the prosecution of so-called 'similar fact evidence' as evidence going to prove the commission of an offence now before the court, is based on fears as to its unduly prejudicial nature. Largely, the fear is that a jury will 'give a dog a bad name and hang him'. It is felt, moreover, that such evidence gives rise to too many collateral issues, and may well lead to differential law enforcement by encouraging the police to look for suspects with records.

[10.04] Generally speaking, similar fact evidence is tendered by the prosecution against the accused. It may also, however, in a rape case, consist of the introduction of evidence by the defence of prior occasions of sexual intercourse between the accused and the complainant, as proof of consent on the occasion in question (*R v Riley*[2]). Conduct in respect of which the accused was acquitted cannot normally be relied upon as similar fact evidence (*Kemp v R*[3]; *G v Coltart*[4]; cf *R v Miles*[5]). While it used to be thought that similar fact evidence could only be admitted to show *mens rea* and not *actus reus*, that perception was ended by the decision in *R v Ball*[6], where such evidence was introduced to establish that acts of incestuous intercourse between the accused brother and sister took place. It is also noteworthy that the prosecution cannot credit an accused with elaborate defences in order to facilitate the introduction of such evidence (*Thompson v R*[7]). Rather, the defence that similar fact evidence is introduced to rebut in such a situation, must have been raised in substance. The prosecution may, however, rebut defences reasonably likely to be run by the accused (*Harris v DPP*[8]).

Rationale for admission

[10.05] Should similar fact evidence be admitted, the courts are said to do so on the basis of the unlikelihood of coincidence. To take the facts of *R v Ball*, as illustrative of this reasoning, is effectively to ask: 'Wouldn't it be odd if a brother and sister, who had committed incest frequently in the past, now lived together as man and wife, sleeping in the same bed, without committing incest?' The dangers of this type of reasoning were given clear expression by Lord Hewart CJ in *R v Bailey*[9]:

---

[2]   *R v Riley* (1887) 18 QBD 481.
[3]   *Kemp v R* (1951) 83 CLR 341.
[4]   *G v Coltart* [1967] 1 QB 432.
[5]   *R v Miles* (1943) 44 SR WSW 198.
[6]   *R v Ball* [1911] AC 47.
[7]   *Thompson v R* [1918] AC 221.
[8]   *Harris v DPP* [1952] AC 694.
[9]   *R v Bailey* [1924] All ER 466.

'It is so easy to derive from a series of unsatisfactory accusations, if there are enough of them, an accusation which at least ... appears satisfactory ... It is so easy to collect from a mass of ingredients, not one of which is sufficient, a totality which will appear to contain what is missing.'

[10.06] In order to minimise the dangers in this context, courts have looked for a high degree of similarity between the evidence preferred, and the incidents now before the courts. *Heydon* explains this approach as follows: 'Similarity narrows the gap between proving the accused was a wrongdoer in general and proving he did this particular wrong.'

[10.07] Because of the difficulties surrounding the establishment or indeed the explanation of when similar fact evidence is admissible, a 'categorical' approach has found some favour in terms of designating the occasions of admission. In large part, the basis for this categorical approach can be found in Lord Herschell's statement in *Makin v Attorney General for New South Wales*, which was subsequently interpreted and used by the court as a definitive framework or formula for admission; rather than being representative of a general approach.

[10.08] Since the 'categories' have had such an important influence on the development of the law in this area, and the treatment of this type of evidence by the court, it is worthwhile delineating each together with some of the case law and the manner in which they have been applied. Initially these categories were regarded as closed (*R v Bond*[10]), but Viscount Simon, in *Harris v DPP*, gave expression to the notion that they were not closed and operated rather as touchstones of admissibility.

The categories

(1) Admissibility of evidence of conduct on other occasions which is of particular relevance in spite of its tendency to show bad disposition

[10.09] *R v Smith*[11] is illustrative of this 'category' of admissibility of evidence of past bad behaviour. Smith was charged with murdering his wife in her bath by drowning her. Two other former wives of Smith had been drowned in the same manner. Each had made a will in Smith's favour. On each occasion, he had bought a suitable bath, placed it in a room which could not be locked from the inside and taken each of the wives the doctor with the suggestion that she suffered from epileptic fits. Each drowning allegedly occurred because of the onset of such a fit while bathing.

---

[10] *R v Bond* [1906] 2 KB 389.
[11] *R v Smith* [1914-15] All ER 262 (CA).

[10.10] In *R v Armstrong*[12], evidence of subsequent behaviour on the part of the accused was introduced to similar effect. The defendant here was charged with the murder of his wife by arsenic poisoning. The defence alleged she had committed suicide. The accused, when found to be in possession of arsenic, claimed it was purchased for the purpose of killing weeds. Evidence to the effect that Armstrong had attempted to poison a man with arsenic eight months after his wife's death was admitted because it suggested the accused was lying when he said he had purchased poison for an innocent purpose.

(2) Admissibility of evidence which forms part of the same transaction to such an extent that the acts are so inextricably bound up that it is impossible to differentiate between them

[10.11] The facts of the decision in *R v Ellis*[13] illustrate the situations covered by this category. The prisoner here was charged with stealing six marked coins. Evidence was presented to the effect that marked coins had been placed in the till and the prosecutrix's son had watched the prisoner withdraw these with money obtained for customers. On his arrest, the accused was found to be in possession of both marked and unmarked coins, amounting in total to the amount missing from the till. Evidence tendered to show he had stolen the unmarked coins was admitted because it went to show the history of the till from the time when the marked money was put into it, up to the time when the money was found in the possession of the prisoner.

[10.12] *O'Leary v R*[14] is another decision illustrating the ambit of this category. Employees of a timber camp had engaged in a drunken orgy over a period of several hours. The following morning, one of their number was found near to death, having been beaten on the head with a bottle, had petrol poured over him and been set alight. The High Court of Australia held that evidence of violent assaults by the accused on other employees, including the deceased, during the orgy, all of which involved brutal blows to the head, was admissible. Dixon J commented:

> 'Without evidence of what, during that time, was done by those men who took any significant part in the matter and especially evidence of the behaviour of the prisoner, the transaction of which the alleged murder formed an integral part could not be truly understood and isolated from it could only be presented as an unreal and not very intelligible event'.

The third and fourth categories are perhaps more conveniently dealt with together.

---

[12] *R v Armstrong* [1922] 2 KB 555.
[13] *R v Ellis* (1826) 6 B & C 145.
[14] *O'Leary v R* (1946) 73 CLR 566.

(3) Admissibility of evidence to show system or (4) to rebut a defence.

[10.13] The first of these two categories perhaps best fits the overall appellation of this type of evidence, as evidence where a very high degree of similarity in the *modus operandi is* required – so-called 'hallmark' cases.

[10.14] The decision in *Makin*[15] is itself illustrative of the type of situation contemplated. *Makin*, sometimes referred to colourfully, if crudely, as the 'babyfarmers' case, involved a husband and wife accused of murdering a baby which they had taken in, in return for a small sum of money from its natural parent. The baby's body was found buried in the Makin's backyard. The accused disclaimed all connection with the mother of the baby and denied all knowledge of the body. Evidence was introduced to the effect that other babies, bodies (which the Malins also denied knowledge of) had been found in the backyards of other houses occupied by the accused, and admitted on the basis that it was 'strikingly similar' and to rebut the accused's suggestion of coincidence and the possible defence that the child's death was accidental.

[10.15] *R v Straffen*[16] is another case in point. The accused here was charged with strangling a young girl. The death had occurred on an occasion when the accused had escaped from Broadmoor (an institution for the criminally insane), where he was incarcerated after being found unfit to plead to charges of having killed two small girls. The accused had commented to the police, 'I did not kill her', at a time when neither the police nor the newspapers had made reference to the death of a girl. Evidence was admitted here of the two previous murders of young girls committed by Straffen, in order to identify him as the perpetrator in this case. The grounds of admission were, firstly, that each of the victims was a young girl; secondly, each of the young girls was killed by manual strangulation; thirdly, no attempt was made at sexual interference nor was there any apparent motive for the crime. Further, there was no evidence of a struggle, and no attempt made to conceal the body.

[10.16] The extent to which these factors may not be perceived as sufficient to warrant admissibility of the evidence of past bad behaviour, is surely now questionable.

[10.17] The case of *People v Dempsey*[17], provides a less controversial Irish example of the admissibility of evidence of past bad behaviour to rebut the defendant's claim of 'chaste-courtship' in a situation where he was charged with unlawful carnal knowledge of a girl between fifteen and seventeen years of age.

---

[15] *Mackin v Attorney General for New South Wales* [1894] AC 57 at 65
[16] *R v Straffen* [1952] 2 QB 911.
[17] *People v Dempsey* [1961] IR 288.

The past behaviour in this case consisted of evidence of earlier occasions of sexual activity between the defendant and the girl in question.

[10.18] Part of the controversy in these cases can be related to the claim of similarity or indeed relevance, which can be controversial and a product not so much of fact, as the inherent attitudes and prejudices of the trial judge. Here, as so often before perceived in the rules of evidence, can be seen the influence of the politics or tenor of the times.

[10.19] *R v Thompson*[18] is a classic case in point, and although now of dubious precedent value, given its subsequent perception by the courts, serves well to illustrate the dangers of the type of reasoning the admissibility of past behaviour on the part of the accused can spawn. In *Thompson*, evidence was admitted to rebut a defence of mistaken identity and to prove the unlikelihood of the identified man having the accused's disposition, as proven by past acts.

[10.20] The facts were that the accused was charged with involvement in acts of gross indecency with two boys on 16 March. A second appointment had been made for 18 March, on which occasion the accused was arrested by the police. The police searched the accused's house and found photographs of naked boys and powder-puffs. These latter were admitted in evidence against the accused. Lord Sumner's reasoning is renowned for the comment which has survived to overshadow the remaining reasoning in that case:

> 'The evidence tends to attach to the accused a peculiarity which, though not purely physical, I think may be recognised as properly bearing that name. Experience tends to show that these offences against nature connote an inversion of normal characteristics which, while demanding punishment as offending against social morality, also partake of the nature of an abnormal physical property. A thief, a cheat, a coiner, or a house-breaker is only a particular specimen of the genus rogue, and, though no doubt each tends to keep to his own line of business, they all alike possess the by no means extraordinary mental characteristic that they propose somehow to get their living dishonestly. So common a characteristic is not a recognisable mark of the individual. Persons, however, who commit the offences now under consideration seek the habitual gratification of a particular perverted lust, which not only takes them out of the class of ordinary men gone wrong, but *stamps them with the hallmark of a specialised and extraordinary class as much as if they carried on their bodies some physical peculiarity.*'

[10.21] The dictum in *Thompson* was subsequently applied in *R v Sims*[19], and in *R v Hall*[20]. In essence the logic applied here in these cases, was that once a

---

[18] *R v Thompson* [1918] AC 221.
[19] *R v Sims* [1946] 1 KB 53.
[20] *R v Hall* [1952] 1 KB 302.

homosexual offence was alleged against an accused, evidence that he had a homosexual propensity was automatically admissible in evidence. It is a logic which had little to commend it, and was subjected to much criticism. In *Boardman v DPP*[21] the question of law as to whether homosexual offences did indeed form a separate category for the purposes of the admissibility of similar fact evidence, was considered by the House of Lords. The House of Lords rejected this contention. In the words of Lord Hailsham:

'There is not a separate category of homosexual cases. The rules of logic and common sense must be the same for all trials where similar fact or other analogous evidence is sought to be introduced.'

[10.22] *DPP v Boardman* is of greater importance as will be seen, however, in terms of forging a new approach to the issue of similar fact evidence, which by this stage was exhibiting the confines, limitations and anomalies of the strict categorical approach.

In *DPP v Boardman* the facts concerned charges of attempted buggery against the defendant headmaster with S, a pupil, and of inciting H, another pupil, to commit buggery. The trial judge in that case held H's evidence admissible on the count regarding S, and vice versa. The House of Lords approved the admissibility of the evidence, deeming the evidence of both pupils to have been strikingly similar in time and methods of advance. The court criticised *Thompson,* and emphasised the necessity of showing striking similarity and not just suggesting same on grounds of coincidence. To this extent, *Thompson* is of doubtful authority.

(5) Admissibility of similar fact evidence to rebut the defence that the acts performed were totally innocent, and involved no guilty intent

[10.23] This category is exemplified by the facts of *R v Bond*[22], which involved a doctor who was charged with using instruments with an intent to procure an abortion. The defence put forward was that of using the same for *bona fide* medical purposes. Evidence was admitted that the doctor had told the woman in question that he had 'put dozens of girls right', alongside the testimony that he had performed an abortion on her also.

[10.24] In summary, then, the categorical approach aside, the essence of the principles or prerequisites for admissibility here are:

(1)   the evidence must be relevant;

---

[21] *Boardman v DPP* [1975] AC 421.
[22] *R v Bond* [1906] 2 KB 389.

(2)   the evidence must be relevant by way of an argument relying at some stage upon an inference drawn from the disposition of the accused; and

(3)   the evidence must be discreditable to the accused in some way.

[10.25] In relation to the third point, which has not been addressed hitherto, it is quite clear that the concept of discredit here, extends further than merely the commission of crimes. In *R v Barrington*[23], the prosecution sought to bolster the evidence of three young complainants of acts of indecency perpetrated by an accused, with evidence from three other girls. The latter's evidence implied that the accused had gone through the same preliminary technique – recruiting them ostensibly for babysitting – and had used similar inducements, including pornographic magazines. Notwithstanding the fact that it was not alleged that any acts of indecency or criminal conduct occurred, the evidence was admitted.

The distinct nature of sexual cases

[10.26] The 'special category' view of certain cases propounded in *Thompson*[24] makes a reappearance, even in the aftermath of *Boardman*[25], and requires further consideration. Lord Sumner's observations were interpreted to the effect that if they involved homosexual behaviour, or were committed against children, sexual offences were so distinctive as to justify the admission of evidence that would not otherwise go in under the rule.

[10.27] In *King*[26], the accused was charged with gross indecency, attempted buggery and assault. In cross-examination he was asked, 'Are you a homosexual?', to which he answered, 'yes'. This was deemed admissible where he denied committing the acts. The Court of Appeal saw the evidence as coming plainly within the principle laid down in *Thompson*.

[10.28] In *Sims*[27], the charges against the accused were those of sodomy and gross indecency with four different men on different occasions. The refusal of an application to try these separately was upheld on the basis that they were relevant and probative in relation to each other. The Court of Appeal was of the view that sodomy was a crime in a special category and hence '... the repetition of the acts is itself a special feature connecting the accused with the crime'.[28] The court would also have applied this logic to offences against children.

---

[23] *R v Barrington* [1981] 1 All ER 1132.

[24] [1918] AC 221.

[25] *Boardman v DPP* (1975) AC 421.

[26] *King* [1967] 2 QB 388.

[27] *Sims* [1946] KB 531.

[28] [1946] KB 531 at 540.

[10.29] In *Boardman*, however, the House of Lords had expressed the view that homosexual cases were not to be placed in a special category. Lord Hailsham explained the distinction as follows:

'In a sex case ... whilst a repeated homosexual act by itself might be quite insufficient to admit the evidence as confirmatory of identity or design, the fact that it was alleged to have been performed wearing the ceremonial head-dress of a Red Indian chief or other eccentric garb might well in appropriate circumstances suffice.'[29]

[10.30] In *Novac*[30], the accused had met boys in places of amusement, offering them money to play gambling machines, and then shelter at his house. He then committed acts of buggery and attempted buggery whilst sharing a bed with them. Bridge LJ expressed the view that this was not committing offences in a strikingly similar manner:

'If a man is going to commit buggery with a boy he picks up, it must surely be a commonplace feature of such an encounter that he will take the boy home with him and commit the offence in bed.'[31]

Bridge J saw the picking up at amusement arcades as as a similarity in the surrounding circumstances, and not a similarity as required in the commission of the crime:

'It is a similarity in the surrounding circumstances and is not, in our judgment, sufficiently proximate to the commission of the crime itself to lead to the conclusion that the repetition of this feature would make the boys' stories inexplicable on the basis of coincidence.'[32]

[10.31] In *Johannsen*[33], by contrast, on similar facts, the court found striking similarity:

'The prosecution's case was that between May and December 1975 he made a practice of accosting boys in amusement arcades and similar places, offering them money or a meal or treating them to a game, taking them to his accommodation or on to the beach, and there committing the offences charged ... We have no hesitation in deciding there were striking similarities...'.[34]

Hence it can be seen that there was some uneven application of the law post *Boardman*.

---

[29] [1975] AC 421 at 454.
[30] *Novac* (1976) 65 Cr App R 107.
[31] (1976) 65 Cr App R 107 at 112.
[32] (1976) 65 Cr App R 107 at 112.
[33] *Johannsen* (1977) 65 Cr App R 101.
[34] (1977) 65 Cr App R 101 at 103.

[10.32] The House of Lords, in *DPP v P*[35], attempted to resolve these divergences. The facts were that the accused was convicted of the offences of rape and incest against his two daughters. The issue before the House was whether or not the evidence of one daughter was properly admitted against the accused in relation to the other. Both daughters gave evidence of a prolonged course of domination by the accused of the whole family, and there was evidence the accused had contributed to the costs of abortions for both. The House of Lords held that the probative force of the evidence is what is required, which is not restricted to 'striking similarity'. The fact that there was no more similarity beyond that of the 'stock in trade' of child abuse, appearing in the majority of cases, did not mean that it was inadmissible.

[10.33] There is a difficulty here regarding the prejudicial nature of such evidence, surely, relative to the limited field within which the accused could lie, and the likely easy satisfaction thereby of 'similarity'. If this is somehow evident in P, it is even more so in H. The facts of *R v H*[36] involved charges against the accused of sexual offences against his adopted daughter and his stepdaughter. The girls had both confided in the accused's wife three years after the commission of the alleged offences, having discussed the matter first between themselves. The adopted daughter had brought the allegations to the attention of her mother at the prompting of her boyfriend. He had moved into the family home shortly after the accused's arrest. The defence alleged the young woman was using the story as an excuse to reject the boyfriend's advances, and that the two young women might have colluded. The question was whether this risk of contamination was a question of admissibility for the trial judge, or a matter of weight for the jury. The House of Lords decided that, save in exceptional cases, the matter was one of weight for the determination of the jury. Doran and Jackson – noting[37] that the laws of evidence have already gone a considerable way to ease the task of prosecution in such cases (corroboration requirements, video link etc and *R v P*[38] making it more feasible to prosecute cases on the basis of more than one witness) – commented:

'At some point, however, the question must arise as to whether the course of change has moved too far in one direction and whether the protection of the accused's interests have been sacrificed to an unacceptable degree in the interest of securing convictions in this highly sensitive class of case.'[39]

---

[35] *DPP v P* [1991] 2 AC 447.

[36] *R v H* [1995] 2 All ER 865.

[37] Dolan and Jackson 'Cross-admissibility of Similar Fact' [1995] All ER, Annual Review, Evidence 224.

[38] *R v P* [1991] 3 All ER 337.

[39] [1995] 2 All ER, Annual Review Evidence 266 at 230.

Instead of showing concern with regard to usurpation of the jury's fact-finding domain, the House of Lords, they argue, '... should perhaps also have turned its mind to the judicial responsibility to ensure that the accused receives a fair trial.[40]'

Relevance in other cases

[10.34] Outside the sphere of sexual cases, the relevance test has been applied more consistently. In *Mansfield*[41], the accused was charged with three counts of arson. Within three weeks they occurred in a hotel where the accused lived, and in two hotels where he worked as kitchen porter. In each case, he had opportunity, lied to police on questioning and his wastepaper bin was found at the third. Each fire was held admissible in relation to the other.

[10.35] In *Rance*[42], charges of corruptly procuring payment to a local councillor were levied against a building company director. R claimed he had been deceived into signing a false certificate describing the councillor as a sub-contractor. Evidence was admitted of similar payments by false certificates to other councillors.

[10.36] With regard to evidence being introduced prior to a particular defence (eg innocent association) being raised by the defence, *Harris v DPP*[43] takes the view that the prosecution are not required to wait until the accused has raised the specific defence. Some cases in the past have suggested that a complete denial by the accused, might mean evidence of a succession of such incidents (which might well be relevant to innocent association) would not go in (*Chandor*[44]; *Flack*[45]). The House of Lords in *Boardman* did not agree, as in both, the accused is saying the accuser is lying.

Burden and standard of proof

[10.37] The prosecution should establish evidence of the extraneous acts beyond reasonable doubt. If there has not been a conviction this means the acts must be proven as if the accused were charged with them. The full criminal standard applies.[46]

---

[40] [1995] 2 All ER, Annual Review Evidence 244 at 230.
[41] *R v Mansfield* [1978] 1 WLR 1102.
[42] *Rance* (1975) 62 Cr App R 118.
[43] *Harris v DPP* [1952] AC 694.
[44] *R v Chandor* [1959] 1 QB 545.
[45] *R v Flack* [1969] 2 All ER 784.
[46] *McGranaghan* [1995] 1 Cr App R 559.

Irish case law

[10.38] While the Irish courts have not forged an identifiable or original jurisprudence in this area, they have generally followed – at least tacitly – the English position with regard to the admissibility of this type of evidence. In general, therefore, an exclusionary approach is adopted unless some reason (not necessarily, but usually, those of the categories of inclusion) persuades the court otherwise.

[10.39] In the case of *AG v McCabe*[47], the facts of which concerned the deaths of six people as a result of a house being set on fire, the accused was charged with the murder of one of their number. The Court of Criminal Appeal held that the evidence of the other deaths had been correctly introduced at trial.

[10.40] In *AG v Joyce and Walsh*[48], the Court of Criminal Appeal held that evidence that on an earlier occasion the accused had put guano into the deceased's milk, was correctly introduced to prove a state of mind and motive on the part of the accused.

[10.41] In a similar vein, the decision of *AG v Fleming*[49] followed *Joyce*, and in the context of an accused charged with the murder of his wife, introduced evidence that he had previously attempted to poison his wife. Both occasions were alleged to be related to his promise to marry a young girl, who on the second occasion, was pregnant with his child. The earlier attempt, according to the court, illustrated the tenor of the relationship between the accused and his wife and his malice toward her.

[10.42] In the decision of *The People (AG) v Kirwan*[50], the Court of Criminal Appeal held that evidence that the accused had previously been in prison was admissible, as was a charge of the accused having murdered his brother, as it came under the rule in *Makin's* case and was relevant to an issue before the jury.

[10.43] The decision of the Court of Criminal Appeal in *The People v Wallace*[51] illustrates the later approach of the Irish courts to such evidence. The facts of the case were as follows. Three brothers were convicted of the larceny of leather jackets and two suits at Thurles, Co Tipperary, on 26 February 1981 and of an attempt to steal clothing at the same premises on 10 March 1981. Two of the brothers appealed the convictions.

---

[47] *The Attorney General v McCabe* [1927] IR 129.
[48] *The Attorney General v Joyce and Walsh* [1929] IR 526.
[49] *The Attorney General v Fleming* [1934] IR 166.
[50] *The Attorney General v Fleming* [1934] IR 166.
[51] *The People v Wallace* (22 November 1982), HC 2 Frewen 1982, 125 (MacWilliam J).

[10.44] On the first occasion, 26 February 1981, the facts established were that two men entered the men's outfitters in question and proceeded to the back of the shop where the suits and jackets were kept, one of them carrying a cardboard box covered with cellotape, which he held against his chest. A third man came into the shop, looking for a white shirt with a peaked collar. When the first two men had left the shop, and the third declared himself not satisfied and departed, a quantity of leather jackets and two suits were found to be missing, although there had been no sales. On 19 March 1981, when the owner and his wife were present in the shop, two men again entered carrying a cardboard box in similar manner to the earlier occasion. A third man entered asking for a shirt with a peaked collar. The owner remained with the first two. After a while they left, followed by the third. None had purchased anything.

[10.45] On appeal it was argued, inter alia, that there should have been separate trials. McWilliam J referred to the decision in *Harris v DPP*[52], where, when there were eight counts of larceny at a market during three successive months – each similarly carried out, but on the first seven occasions there being no further evidence to associate the accused specifically with the thefts – the trial judge ruled there was no good reason for ordering a separate trial on the eighth count, since the charges formed part of a series of offences of the same or a similar character. The House of Lords held that the trial judge had properly exercised his discretion. The House of Lords there also approved of Lord Herschell's general statement of principle in *Makin*[53].

[10.46] On the point of appeal, the Court of Criminal Appeal held in *Wallace* that evidence given of the first incident was relevant on the second count, to show that such a box could be used for the purpose alleged in the second count. Another submission made in *Wallace* was that the trial judge in his charge to the jury, did not direct their attention to the evidence relevant to the identification of the accused on the first count, although he did warn the jury about the dangers when dealing with evidence of visual identification.

[10.47] In *Harris*[54], Viscount Simon had indicated what is necessary in a charge to the jury in a case like this. The trial judge had not warned the jury that the evidence called in support of the earlier counts did not in itself provide confirmation of the charge. Hence, the jury may have been swayed, however illogically, in reaching its verdict on the eighth count by the earlier evidence. Viscount Simon reasoned, therefore, that they should have been warned of this danger.

---

[52] *Harris v DPP* [1952] All ER 1044.
[53] *Makin* (1894) AC 57.
[54] *Harris v DPP* [1952] All ER 1044.

[10.48] In the Irish case, however, McWilliam J concluded that the trial judge had dealt very fully with the dangers of visual identification. However, he had not specifically referred to the evidence which related to the visual identification of the accused in relation to the first count. The trial judge treated the evidence as cumulative, as in *Harris*[55]. Hence, the verdict on the first count per MacWilliam J should be reversed.

[10.49] Regarding the second count, McWilliam J concluded that evidence in relation to the first offence was relevant in order to establish that a box of that sort could be used for the purpose of stealing clothes. The box was prepared and held in such a way as to give the impression that it was closed, whereas it was actually half-open so that articles could be put into it without disturbing the apparent fastening. Hence, the evidence thus designated 'similar fact evidence' or evidence of past misconduct on the part of the accused, was deemed admissible in those circumstances.

[10.50] The Irish courts, for their part, have clung somewhat to the categorical approach. However, a preference for a 'balancing' of the probative worth and prejudicial value of the evidence (whether it be relevant via propensity or not) is apparent in the judgment of Black J in *The People (AG) v Kirwan*[56], and could be used to develop an independent jurisprudence in the area. Firstly, Black J placed the rationale for exclusion firmly in the danger to the guarantee of a fair trial to the accused. (This danger was formerly located in the thought-process of a juror, who was not trained to act judicially: *DPP v MacMahon*)[57].

[10.51] *Kirwan*[58] involved the admissibility of 'similar fact evidence' which revealed that the accused had been in prison for four years before his arrest for his brother's murder. The evidence was as follows. Firstly, the murder victim in question had been dismembered with professional skill: there was evidence tendered that the accused had learned the trade of butcher while in prison. Secondly, the prosecution claimed the accused, in order to avoid detection, had drugged a fellow lodger: there was evidence here that he had luminal tablets in his possession and was, according to the prison doctor's testimony, acquainted with this drug since prison. Finally, there was evidence that after the death the accused had a large amount of money in his possession: unusual in so far as when he had recently left prison he had only a small sum of money. The majority of the Supreme Court admitted the evidence as highly relevant. Black J, entering a reservation, could not see the relevance of revealing that the first witness was a

---

55 Per McWilliam J in *People v Wallace* 2 Frewen 1982, 125 at 128 (HC).
56 *The People (AG) v Kirwan* [1943] IR 279.
57 *DPP v MacMahon* [1984] ILRM 461.
58 *The People (AG) v Kirwan* [1943] IR 279.

prison warden or that the second a prison doctor. In relation to the third factor, however, he felt on the whole it was necessary to reveal the evidence. The approach of Black J was novel, in so far as it indicated an overall balancing approach in favour of the accused, which would operate to exclude such evidence where it was not sufficiently probative to warrant its admission and consequent prejudicial effect.

[10.52] In *People v BK*[59], the applicant was convicted on several counts of attempted buggery and indecent assault against various young males. He appealed on the basis that each of the counts – in so far as they related to a different boy – should have been tried separately. The Court of Criminal Appeal held that the test as to whether the counts should be heard together was whether the evidence of each would be admissible on the other. To be so admissible, the probative value of such evidence must outweigh its prejudicial effect.
The facts and judgment of the court merit attention in so far as they constitute a recent statement by the Irish courts of their approach in this area.

[10.53] Barron J, giving the judgment of the court, notes that count number eight charged attempted buggery on a date unknown between 1 April 1982 and 30 September 1989 with JMD, a male person, and count nine attempted buggery on a date unknown between 1 April 1985 and 30 September 1988 with JH, a male person. Count number one was indecent assault against WMD, a male person, on a date unknown between 1 January 1983 and 31 December 1987, and count number two was buggery on a date unknown between those same dates with WMD.

[10.54] The defendant had been convicted on counts eight and nine. The relevant ground of appeal was that each of the counts, so far as they related to a different boy, should have been tried separately. Counsel submitted that to allow the counts relating to the different boys to be tried together would in effect provide corroboration, where there was none in law. The prosecution argued there was a sufficient similarity between the offences in that they were all alleged to have been committed against young boys in the applicant's care in Trudder House, a residential home for traveller children run by the Eastern Health Board. Holding that the real test as to whether the counts should be heard together, was whether the evidence in respect of each would be admissible on each of the other counts, Barron J comments:

> 'For such evidence to be so admissible, it would be necessary for the probative value of such evidence to outweigh its prejudicial effect. In practice, this test is applied where there is a similarity between the facts relating to the several counts. On the one hand, there is system evidence which is so admissible; and, on the

---

[59] *People v BK* [2000] 2 IR 199.

other hand, there is similar fact evidence, which is inadmissible. In the latter case, the reason is that, just because a person may have acted in a particular way on one occasion does not mean that such person acted in the same way on some other occasion. System evidence on the other hand is admissible because the manner in which a particular act has been done on one occasion suggests that it was also done on another occasion by the same person with the same intent.'[60]

[10.55] The distinction between system and similar fact (although Barron J comments that the latter is sometimes used to refer to the former) was made by applying a test 'to ensure that the effect of the natural prejudice which will arise from similarity of allegation is over borne by the probative effect of the evidence.'[61]

[10.56] Barron J referred to the decision of *AG v Duffy*[62], where the accused was charged with four separate counts of indecent assault and gross indecency against four different male persons on four different occasions. All counts were heard together. A retrial was ordered on the basis that to try the four offences together was to supply corroboration for each of them, when in law there was no such corroboration:

'Human nature, however, is too strong to have allowed the jury to disregard the cumulative effect of evidence given at the same trial in respect of four distinct offences of almost precisely the same character.'[63]

[10.57] Barron J then reviewed the decisions in *Sims, Boardman*, etc. He noted that the decision in *Boardman* seemed to have been regarded as a decision that similar fact evidence was admissible only when there was a striking resemblance between the evidence relating to the several counts. Whether this was necessary was further considered in *P*, where Lord MacKay of Clashfern stated that the essential feature of evidence which was to be admitted was that '... its probative force in support of the allegation that an accused person committed a crime is sufficiently great to make it just to admit the evidence, notwithstanding that it is prejudicial to the accused in tending to show that he was guilty of another crime.'[64]

[10.58] Barron J further interpreted MacKay LJ's judgment as follows:

'Where the identity of the perpetrator is unknown some special feature is necessary before evidence is admissible to establish that it was the same perpetrator in each case. Where, however, the alleged perpetrator in each case is

---

[60] [2000] 2 IR 199 at 203.
[61] [2000] 2 IR 199 at 203.
[62] *AG v Duffy* [1931] IR 144.
[63] [1931] IR 144 at 149 (Kennedy CJ).
[64] MacKay in *DPP v P* [1991] 2 AC 447 at 460.

known, it is not necessary to have that special feature because the issue is no longer was it done by the same person, but was an offence committed on each occasion.

In the former type of case, the issue of admissibility relates to establishing that not only was a crime committed on each occasion, but committed by the same person. In the latter type of case, of which the present is one, the issue of admissibility relates not to whether the same crime has been committed, but to whether offences were committed at all, or, if so, as here, as to their nature.'[65]

[10.59] Barron J pointed out that Budd J considered these cases in *B v DPP*[66] and stated with regard to the reason for admitting evidence of multiple accusations:

'It seems that the underlying principle is that the probative value of multiple accusations may depend on part of their similarity, but also on the unlikelihood that the same person would find himself falsely accused on various occasions by different and independent individuals. The making of multiple accusations is a coincidence in itself, which has to be taken into account in deciding admissibility.'[67]

[10.60] According to Barron J, a number of principles emerge from these cases:

'(1) The rules of evidence should not be allowed to offend common-sense

(2) So, where the probative value of the evidence outweighs its prejudicial effect, it may be admitted.

(3) The categories of cases in which the evidence which can be so admitted, is not closed.

(4) Such evidence is admitted in two main types of cases:–

(i)   to establish that the same person committed each offence because of the particular feature common to each; or

(ii)   where the charges are against one person only, to establish that offences were committed.

In the latter case the evidence is admissible because:-

(a)   there is the inherent improbability of several persons making up exactly similar stories;

(b)   it shows a practice which would rebut accident, innocent explanation or denial.' [68]

---

[65] Per Barron J in *People v BK* [2000] 2 IR 199 at 209-210.
[66] *B v DPP* [1997] 3 IR 140.
[67] Per Budd J in *B v DPP* [1997] 3 IR 140 at 157.
[68] Per Barron J in *People v BK* [2000] 2 IR 199 at 210-211.

[10.61] In *BK*, the court was of opinion that the joinder of counts one and two with eight and nine was incorrect because the evidence went no further than saying, that because the applicant was charged with offences against one boy, he was more likely to have committed the offences alleged against the other boys.

[10.62] The court did find a connection between counts one and two and eight and nine, in so far as they are alleged to have been committed by a carer in Trudder House against inmates of that institution, but concluded that the facts in each case showed a different picture: counts one and two were alleged to have been committed in a dormitory at night, whereas the other two were alleged to have been committed in a caravan to which the applicant and other boys had gone to spend the night. The accused's conduct in relation to one and two was open, whereas in the other two furtive. Barron J concluded:

> 'The evidence in relation to counts number 8 and 9 ... does show the necessary nexus to allow the evidence on the one to be admitted in relation to the other and *vice versa*. They are alleged to have been committed in unusual but identical circumstances, on a visit to the caravan; while the two were sleeping in a double bed; in the same furtive manner; and by broadly similar actions. There were also differences. But overall the similarities were sufficient to make it a jury question as to whether the offence alleged on each count had been committed.'[69]

The court held that the inclusion of counts one and two, therefore, (even though the jury disagreed on those counts), created unfair prejudice, resulting in an unsatisfactory trial.

[10.63] *People v Selliah Ramachchandran*[70] was a case involving a charge of harassment under s 10 of the Non Fatal Offences Against the Person Act 1997. The applicant had been convicted and sentenced to three years as well as restrained with regard to communicating, etc, with the complainant and her family.

[10.64] The facts related to a history of correspondence and events involving the applicant, some of which pre-dated the Act. The prosecution sought to defend the latter on the basis that it was necessary to paint in the background of this particular case. However, the Court of Criminal Appeal held that '...in the circumstances of this case, the opening of this entire correspondence had tended to prejudice the applicant rather than to introduce anything of probative value.'[71]

---

[69] Per Barron J in *People v BK* [2000] 2 IR 199 at 210-211.

[70] *People v Selliah Ramachandran* [2000] 2 IR 307.

[71] [2000] 2 IR 307 at 311, per Barrington J.

Judicial discretion/reform

[10.65] It is important to recall the general discretion a judge has to exclude or limit the admissibility of evidence in this, as in the context of any type of evidence and to exclude evidence of extraneous acts or disposition regarding to the risk of prejudice involved.

Other jurisdictions

[10.66] The High Court of Australia had to consider this area of the law in *Pfennig v R (No 2)*[72]. The facts in this case concerned the murder of a young boy after his abduction for sexual purposes. The abduction was in a white van, his bicycle being taken also and subsequently left in a place suggesting accidental death. The accused was charged with the murder, and it was proposed to adduce in evidence his conviction following a plea of guilty for the abduction of a young boy in a white van for sexual purposes, while leaving his bicycle in a way to suggest accidental death, all of which had occurred a year later. The victim on that occasion had escaped. There was also evidence the accused had told his wife after arrest for the second crime, that he had been contemplating such a crime for a year. On the day before the murder, he had attempted to induce two other young boys to enter his van, and questioned a man about a nude bathing spot which was where the bicycle was found. He had also admitted talking to the deceased boy on the day of the murder. As Tapper notes[73], however, without the evidence of the commission of the other crime (which was much stronger) the accused would not have been convicted, as he was. His conviction was appealed to the High Court, and it is there that some interesting insight was given to this area, particularly in the judgment of McHugh J, which, though agreeing with all the others, was, as Tapper says[74], 'challengingly different' in approach. McHugh J was '... scathing about the idea of balancing two such incommensurable factors as "probative force" and "prejudicial effect". He preferred instead to consider the requirements of a fair trial, and how far the trial would be fair if the propensity evidence were to be admitted ... In each case according to McHugh J the nature of the risk of unfairness requires to be analysed.'[75]

[10.67] It is helpful to recite the dangers or objections to similar fact evidence identified by McHugh J which might profitably be used to guide the courts in cases where the admissibility of such evidence arises:

---

[72] *Pfennig v R (No 2)* [1995] 69 ALJR 147.
[73] CFH Tapper, 'Dissimilar Views of Similar Facts' (1995) Vol III LQR 381 at 382.
[74] CFH Tapper, 'Dissimilar Views of Similar Facts' (1995) Vol III LQR 381 at 383.
[75] CFH Tapper, 'Dissimilar Views of Similar Facts' [1995] Vol III LQR 381 at 384.

1. That it creates undue suspicion against the accused and undermines the presumption of innocence.

2. That tribunals of fact, particularly juries, tend to assume too readily that behavioural patterns are constant and that past behaviour is an accurate guide to contemporary conduct; common assumptions about improbabilities of sequences are often wrong and when the accused is associated with a sequence of events such as deaths/injuries, a jury may too readily assume the association to not be innocent.

3. Other misconduct may cause the jury to be biased against the accused (give a dog a bad name and hang him).

4. Trials would be rendered more lengthy and expensive; police might be encouraged to pursue those with criminal records at the expense of traditional investigation; and rehabilitation might be undermined if the accused's record could be used against him.

[10.68] Very often arguments sustaining change in rules of evidence can be made on a once-off basis. In that light, it is interesting to note that the Violence Against Women Act 1994 amended the Federal Rules of Evidence in the United States by making prior sexual assaults by alleged rapists admissible in trials of rape or sexual assault.[76] Yet, are these not precisely the cases where a jury, on learning of the accused's previous behaviour, will readily assume he has done so again regardless of the strength of the State's case? There is also, of course, the question as to whether we have/should have diminishing confidence in the reliability of such previous convictions.

[10.69] It is also argued that to conceal the record is to deceive the jury. Yet if the decision to allow the convictions in is to affect the jury's scrutiny of the evidence against the accused in this instance, and engage in 'forbidden' reasoning, perhaps that limited deception is justifiable. Once again, the issue is one of fairness and principle here.

[10.70] If one goes back to the underlying premise or rationale of the rule, it is far easier to explain or refashion the structure. To further bolster the validity of this approach, it is interesting to note the recognition of the fundamental issues involved here by representatives of the judicial and academic sides of the debate.

[10.71] See the comment of Lord Hailsham in *Boardman*:

> 'When there is nothing to connect the accused with a particular crime except bad character or similar crimes committed in the past, the probative value of the evidence is nil and the evidence is rejected on that ground. When there is some

---

[76] See critical article by Baker, K 'Once a Rapist? Motivational Evidence and Relevancy in Rape Law' (1997) 110 Harv LR 563.

evidence connecting the accused with the crime, in the eyes of most people, guilt of similar offences in the past might well be considered to have probative value ... Nonetheless, in the absence of a statutory provision to the contrary, the evidence is to be excluded under the first rule in *Makin* because its prejudicial effect may be more powerful than its probative effect, and thus endanger a fair trial because it tends to undermine the integrity of the presumption of innocence and the burden of proof. In other words, it is a rule of English law which has its root in policy, and by which, in Lord du Parcq's phrase, logicians would not be bound'.[77]

[10.72] In like vein, Zuckerman has commented:

'It has been recognised for a long time that the risk attendant on evidence of previous crime, or other morally repugnant conduct, is not so much over estimation of its own probative weight as the distortion of the entire process of adjudication. Similar fact evidence threatens the two central principles or our criminal justice. The first is that in any criminal trial the accused stands to be tried, acquitted or convicted, only in respect of the offence with which he is charged. The second is that conviction must take place only if the jury are persuaded of the accused's guilt beyond all reasonable doubt.'[78]

The Irish judiciary should take the opportunity presented of forging a novel approach to the admissibility of similar fact evidence. To do otherwise may not prove true to our constitutional or jurisprudential rights, and we risk further floundering in the academic quagmire which is the admissibility evidence of the accused's past misconduct in a criminal trial.

---

[77] *Boardman v DPP* [1974] 3 All ER 887 at 904

[78] Zuckerman, AAS, 'Similar Fact Evidence – The Unobservable Rule' (1987) 103 L QR 187.

Chapter 11

Cross-Examination of the Accused

'Someone must have been telling lies about Joseph K, for without having done anything wrong he was arrested one fine morning.'

Franz Kafka *The Trial* (1977) Penguin, p 7.

Introduction

[11.01] In criminal cases if the accused gives evidence, he may not be cross-examined about his other offences, previous convictions or bad character, unless evidence of the previous offences or convictions about which he is asked would have been admissible in-chief, or unless he has thrown his 'shield' away by putting his character in issue, by casting imputations on the character of the prosecutor, or by giving evidence against another person charged in the same proceedings.

[11.02] The Criminal Justice (Evidence) Act 1924 (the equivalent of the Criminal Evidence Act 1898 in England) ensured the competence of an accused at a criminal trial. In order to ensure, however, that the accused was not unduly disadvantaged compared to other witnesses, by virtue of the fact that he could be questioned about his record or past behaviour, and in order to ensure that the prosecution was not stymied by the use of the privilege against self-incrimination by the accused, a compromise position was reached in the Act. The position is one that modifies the privilege against self-incrimination in relation to an accused, while giving the accused what is termed a 'shield' in relation to his past record. The relevant and important provisions for the law of evidence in this regard are s 1(e) and s 1(f) of the 1924 Act. These provisions provide as follows:

'1(e)   A person charged and being a witness in pursuance of this Act may be asked any question in cross-examination notwithstanding that it will tend to incriminate him as to the offence charged.

1(f)   When giving evidence an accused person shall not be asked and if asked shall not be required to answer, any question tending to show that he has committed or been convicted of or been charged with any offence other than that wherewith he is then charged, or is of bad character, unless:

(i)   the proof that he has committed or been convicted of such other offences is admissible evidence to show that he is guilty of the offence wherewith he is then charged; or

(ii) he has personally or by his advocate asked questions of the witnesses for the prosecution with a view to establishing his own good character or has given evidence of his own good character, or the nature or conduct of the defence is such as to involve imputations on the character of the prosecutor or the witnesses for the prosecution; or

(iii) he has given evidence against any other person charged with the same offence.'

[11.03] Section 1(f) of the 1924 Act was enacted when the accused's competence to testify at trial had been assured. It was seen as unfair if an accused were placed in the same position as an ordinary witness, as he could be questioned about past convictions and the jury might understand these as going to his guilt, instead of credibility. However, total protection would leave the accused witness free to smear other witnesses, and thus render him in a better position than that of an ordinary witness. Section 1(f), therefore, is a compromise.

[11.04] An initial question, to be addressed in the context of an examination of these provisions, is that of the relationship between s 1(e) and s 1(f) of the 1924 Act. This very question was discussed by the House of Lords in *Jones v DPP*[1]. The facts of the case concerned an accused who was charged with the murder of a girl guide. The accused set up a false alibi before the trial, alleging that he had spent the night in question with a prostitute and that his wife had been angry because of his late return. This account was strikingly similar to testimony given by the accused at an earlier trial when he had been convicted of the rape of a girl guide. The prosecution got leave to cross-examine the accused to show similarities in the account and that they were so close as to render the defence incredible.

The manner of cross-examination must have created the impression in the jury that the accused had shortly before this murder committed or been charged with some other offence reported in a Sunday newspaper. The accused, in the examination-in-chief, had himself admitted being in trouble with the police before, and a similar admission was contained in a statement of the accused to the police, which was put forward by the accused's counsel. An appeal by the accused against the admission of his record was rejected by the Court of Criminal Appeal and the House of Lords on the grounds that the cross-examination did not tend to show the accused's bad record or character, because 'tending to show' meant to reveal to the jury for the first time, rather than tending to prove.

---

[1] *Jones v DPP* [1962] 1 All ER 569.

[11.05] The House of Lords presented two views of the issue, and two perspectives on the relationship of s 1(e) and s 1(f). The majority position was taken by Lords Reid, Simons, and Morris. The majority view of s 1(e) was a narrow one in that it allowed questions directly incriminating the accused with regard to the offence charged. With regard to their interpretation of s 1(f), their construction of the phrase 'tend to show' was to the effect that 'tends to show' meant 'tends to suggest to the jury'. The crucial point as far as the law is concerned, was whether these questions were to be considered in isolation or in light of what had gone before in the trial. Lord Reid commented:

'... I do not think that the questions ought to be considered in isolation. If the test is the effect the questions would be likely to have on the minds of the jury that necessarily implies that one must have regard to what the jury had already heard. If the jury already knew that the accused had been charged with an offence, a question inferring that he had been charged would add nothing and it would be absurd to prohibit it. If the obvious purpose of this proviso is to protect the accused from possible prejudice, as I think it is, then show must mean reveal because it is only a revelation of something new which could cause such prejudice.'

[11.06] The position taken by Lords Devlin and Denning was somewhat different. With regard to their construction of s 1(f) of the 1924 Act, Lord Denning commented that the questions tended to show that Jones had been charged with an offence, even though he himself had brought out the fact that he had been previously charged in a court of law with another offence. Lord Denning commented as follows:

'It is one thing to confess to having been in trouble before. It is quite another to have it emphasised against you with devastating detail. Before these questions were asked by the Crown all the jury knew was that at some unspecified time in the near or distant past, this man had been in trouble with the police. After the questions were asked, the jury knew in addition, that he had been very recently in trouble for an offence on a Friday night which was of so sensational a character that it featured in a newspaper on the following Sunday ... and that he had been charged in a court of law with that very offence. It seems to me that questions which tend to reveal an offence, thus particularised, are directly within the prohibition in s 1(f) and are not rendered admissible by his own vague disclosure of some other offence.'

[11.07] Thus the conclusions of Lords Devlin and Denning were that the questions were prohibited by the proviso in s 1(f) of the 1924 Act, and the prosecution had not given evidence in order to lay a foundation for its admissibility within the exception in s 1(f). Had the question rested solely on s 1(f), the question would have been deemed to be inadmissible. However, the minority construed s 1(e) of the 1924 Act in such a manner that the questions were seen to be admissible under that proviso. Moreover, the minority felt that this gave a clearer guide to the prosecution on the basis that the criteria of relevance under s 1(e) in terms of incriminating the accused, was a better guide than that put forward by the majority in relation to s 1(f). Lord Devlin stated that:

> 'The difficulty and danger inherent in the approach adopted (by the majority) is that it sets no clear limits to the extent of the cross-examination ... relevance affords a clear guide as to what the limit should be; revelation does not ... I do not think that some vague rule which enables the prosecution to ask what it likes so long as it does not make out the accused's character to be substantially worse than he himself had suggested would be at all a safe guide.'

In summary, therefore, both the majority and minority agreed that the questions were admissible. However, the majority's view was one of a narrow s 1(e) (pro-accused), and a broad s 1(f) (anti-accused). The minority view was one of a broad s 1(e) (anti-accused), and a narrow s 1(f) (proaccused).

[11.08] With regard to the interpretation of the prohibition in s 1(f) of the 1924 Act, and in particular the use of words other than 'convicted of' an offence, the question arises as to the admissibility of, for example, previous acquittals on the part of the accused.

[11.09] In the case of *Maxwell v DPP*[2], the accused was charged with manslaughter alleged to have occurred in the course of procuring an abortion. He gave evidence of his own good character, and was asked in cross-examination about a previous acquittal on the same charge. Viscount Sankey commented that for questions to be permissible under s 1(f)(ii) of the 1924 Act, they must be relevant to the issue of the accused's own good character, and if not, they could not be admissible. He felt that it seemed clear that the mere fact of a charge could not, in general, be evidence of bad character or be regarded otherwise than as a misfortune:

> 'The mere fact that a man has been charged with an offence is no proof that he committed the offence. Such a fact is therefore irrelevant; it neither goes to show that the prisoner did the act for which he is actually being tried nor does it go to his credibility as a witness.
>
> 'It does not result from this conclusion that the word "charged" in proviso (f) is otiose; it is clearly not so as regards the prohibition; and when the exceptions come into play there may still be cases in which a prisoner may be asked about a charge as a step in cross-examination leading to a question whether he was convicted on the charge, or in order to elicit some evidence as to statements made or evidence given by the prisoner in the course of the trial on a charge which

---

[2]   *Maxwell v DPP* [1935] AC 309.

failed, which tend to throw doubt on the evidence which he is actually giving, though cases of this last class must be rare. In general . . . no question should be asked under proviso (f) unless it helps to elucidate the particular issue which the jury is investigating or goes to credibility.'

Loss of the shield: section 1(f)

[11.10] The first exception to the prohibition in s 1(f) of the 1924 Act, relates to a situation where it is permissible to cross-examine the accused about evidence which has already been admitted in-chief. This situation is largely referred to as the 'similar fact evidence' scenario (see chapter 9). Section 1(f)(i) provides that:

The proof that he has committed or been convicted of such other offences is admissible evidence to show that he is guilty of the offence wherewith he is then charged.

This, the admissibility of similar fact evidence, is dealt with in Chapter 10 and so will not be considered further here. Suffice it to say that if such evidence of previous conduct is admissible in-chief by the prosecution, then obviously the accused can be cross-examined with regard to same.

[11.11] Section 1(f)(ii) of the 1924 Act provides that where an accused has:

personally or by his advocate asked questions of the witnesses for the prosecution with a view to establishing his own good character or has given evidence of his own good character ...

This first part of the second exception to the protection in s 1(f) of the 1924 Act, deals with situations where the accused has asserted his own good character. Character, according to the decision in *Selvey v DPP*[3], means reputation and disposition. It has been held that, to attack the character of a person who is not a prosecution witness, is not to assert one's own good character (*R v Lee*[4]). Nor does the exception apply if the defence witness, unasked, praises the defendant's character. The question has arisen in the past of the divisibility of character evidence, but the modern position is taken to be that the accused's character is indivisible. This means that the accused's entire record is admissible, whether it suggests defective credibility, or not.[5]

[11.12] In *Douglas*[6], it was held that the accused put his character in issue when he was cross-examined with a view to showing that he had not drunk alcohol for several years, which had the effect of contrasting him with a co-accused who had been drunk at the time of the relevant accident.

---

[3] *Selvey v DPP* [1970] AC 304.
[4] *R v Lee* [1976] 1 All ER 570.
[5] *Stirland v DPP* [1944] AC 315.
[6] *Douglas* (1989) 89 Crim App R 264.

[11.13] The second limb of s 1(f)(ii) of the 1924 Act provides as follows: '... or the nature or conduct of the defence is such as to involve imputations on the character of the prosecutor or the witness for the prosecution.'

[11.14] It is useful to look at some of the earlier Irish decisions as to the interpretation of the provisions under the 1924 Act.

[11.15] In *The Attorney General v O'Shea*[7] the accused was convicted of murder. Evidence was given against him by a Civic Guard who hid under the bed in the accused's house and testified to incriminating conversations between accused and his sister with regard to the disposal of the clothing used in the crime. It was alleged that the garda was subjected to such rigorous and searching cross-examination, as to result in the loss of the shield by the accused because of imputations cast on the character of prosecution witnesses. This argument was rejected. Per Kennedy CJ:

> '... testing of the truth and accuracy of their testimony by legitimate cross-examination, however severe, is not ... conduct of the defence as to involve imputations ... within s 1(f)(ii).'

[11.16] In *The People (AG) v Coleman*[8], the appellant was convicted of performing a criminal abortion on Judith Bolton (the principal prosecution witness). She had married Mr Mifsud (responsible for the pregnancy) who also testified against Coleman. Cross-examination of both Mifsud and Bolton involved the following imputations:

(1)   that Mr Mifsud had performed the illegal operation of Miss Bolton;

(2)   they conspired to charge Coleman with a crime they knew he was innocent of;

(3)   prior to her marriage, Mrs Mifsud had used contraceptives, contrary to Church teaching;

(4)   they married with the objective of defeating justice.

The trial judge allowed cross-examination and it was upheld on appeal.

[11.17] In *The People (AG) v Bond*[9] the trial judge did not give adequate direction as to the fact that evidence as to previous convictions is admitted only in relation to credit and not as to guilt. A retrial was ordered.

[11.18] In *Selvey v DPP*,[10] the facts concerned an accused charged with buggery on a young man. The prosecution evidence was to the effect that the claimant

---

7   *The Attorney General v O'Shea* [1931] IR 713.
8   *The People (AG) v Coleman* [1945] IR 237.
9   *The People (AG) v Bond* [1966] IR 214.
10   *Selvey v DPP* [1970] AC 304.

had been sexually interfered with, and indecent photographs were found in the accused's room. The accused denied the charge and said that the photographs had been planted, and alleged the complainant had told him he was prepared to go on the bed; he had already done so for £1, and would do so again. The trial judge asked if he were suggesting to the jury that the complainant be disbelieved because he was 'that sort of young man'. To this, the accused answered yes, which led to cross-examination on the accused's prior homosexual offences, but not on his convictions for dishonesty. The accused appealed, and the House of Lords considered the issue and reasoned as follows. The House felt that the words of the statute should be given their ordinary meaning. This implied that when imputations are cast on the character of prosecution witnesses to show their unreliability as witnesses independently of evidence given by them, and also when such imputations are necessary to establish the accused's defence, the section permits cross-examination of the accused on his record. In essence, this interpretation confirmed the earlier approach taken by the Court of Criminal Appeal in *R v Hudson*,[11] where Lord Alverstone CJ stated:

> '... the words ... must receive their ordinary and natural interpretation and it is not legitimate to qualify them by inserting the words "unnecessary" or "unjustifiably" or "for purposes other than that of developing the defence" or other similar words.'

[11.19] In substance, this means that any attack by the accused on prosecution witnesses, even if that is an essential part of and a prerequisite to the running of the accused's defence, will result in the loss of the protection of the shield given by s 1(1) of the 1924 Act.

[11.20] There are, however, three qualifications on this interpretation. Firstly, the rape situation, where an allegation of consent on the part of the complainant will not amount to an imputation, despite a suggestion that the complainant was a dangerous liar and possibly promiscuous (*R v Turner*).[12]

[11.21] The second exceptional situation is that which relates to a denial of allegations. In *R v Rouse*,[13] the accused said in relation to a chief prosecution witness, 'he is a liar'. It was held, however, that that was merely a plea of 'not guilty' put in forcible language, and did not amount to an imputation within the meaning of the section. Thus, an accused can plead not guilty and deny facts alleged by the prosecution without fear of the loss of the shield.

[11.22] Furthermore, to suggest the reason for the prosecution witness's lie, does not amount to an imputation unless that reason itself suggests bad character. For

---

[11] *R v Hudson* [1912] 2 KB 464.
[12] *R v Turner* [1944] KB 463.
[13] *R v Rouse* [1904] 1 KB 185.

example, it has been held that to suggest that the witness lied because he wished the accused no longer to have contact with his wife, is not an imputation as to a bad marriage and is not a sign of bad character (*R v Manley*[14]). The more elaborate the attack, the more likely it is to constitute an imputation. Examples of what have been deemed to be imputations are that someone is a homosexual, as in *Bishop*[15], or where reference was made to a custom's officer asking the accused's mother to 'have a word with him', as in *Courtney*[16].

[11.23] The third qualification on this so-called *Hudson* doctrine relates to the words 'the nature or conduct of the defence'. This exception covers remarks incidental to the defence in question. Examples would include spontaneous remarks, or answers given in cross-examination as a result of the prosecution counsel's attempt to trap the accused. Irrelevant remarks would also be covered.

[11.24] Even as thus qualified by the above three exceptions, the doctrine laid down in *Hudson* makes the position difficult for the accused, where he attempts to do any more in a defence contradicting the prosecution than merely explain away those facts that the prosecution allege.

[11.25] The English Law Commission in their Report 'Evidence of Bad Character in Criminal Proceedings'[17] has recommended the idea that in any given trial there is a central set of facts about which any party should be free to adduce relevant evidence without constraint – even evidence of bad character. 'Evidence falls within this central set of facts if it has to do with the offence charged, or is evidence of misconduct connected with the investigation or prosecution of that offence.'[18]

[11.26] The Commission proposed that the same criteria apply here to defendants and non-defendants – 'Defendants however will have additional protection from the prejudicial impact of such evidence, to reflect the fact that it is their liability to criminal sanction which is at stake.'[19]

[11.27] The Law Commission recommended that leave be given to admit evidence of the bad character of a defendant in four situations:

'(1) To any party if the evidence is of substantial explanatory value, and in addition the interests of justice require it to be admissible even taking account of its potentially prejudicial effect.

---

[14] *R v Manley* (1962) 126 JP 316.
[15] *Bishop* [1975] QB 274.
[16] *Courtney* [1995] Crim LR 63.
[17] Law Com No 273, 9 October 2001.
[18] Law Com No 273, 9 October 2001, summary, para 3.
[19] Law Com No 273, 9 October 2001, summary, para 4.

(2) To the prosecution if the evidence has substantial probative value in relation to a matter in issue of substantial importance and the interests of justice require it to be admissible even taking account of its potentially prejudicial effect.

If it has probative value in showing that the defendant has a propensity to be untruthful leave may not be given unless *in addition*

- the defendant has suggested another person has a propensity to be untruthful and

- in support of that adduces evidence of that person's bad character which falls outside the central set of facts and

- without the evidence of the defendant's bad character the fact finders would get a misleading impression of the defendant's propensity to be untruthful in comparison with that of the other person.

(3) To the prosecution if

- the defendant is responsible for an assertion which creates a false or misleading impression about the defendant

- the evidence has substantial probative value in correcting that impression and

- the interests of justice require it to be admissible even taking account of its potentially prejudicial effect.

(4) To a co-defendant (D2) to adduce evidence of the bad character of a defendant (D1) if the evidence has substantial probative value in relation to a matter in issue between them which is of substantial importance in the context of the case as a whole. If it has probative value only in showing that the D1 has a propensity to be untruthful, leave may not be given unless, *in addition* D1's case is such as to undermine that of D2.'

[11.28] The approach of the Commission is one which encourages a case-by-case approach, recognising that, while often a person's misconduct will have significance in determining the matters in issue, fact finders are susceptible to having their good judgment overborne or distorted by prejudice. The court's function, therefore, is one of 'balancing countervailing consideration'.[20]

[11.29] The above rules, the Commission feels, will ensure, inter alia, that all parties are free to present their case without fear that this will automatically result in previous misconduct being exposed, and that no such evidence is adduced unless it is of substantial value for determination of the case (the enhanced relevance case)[21]. They also see a person's character as not

---

[20] Law Com No 273, 9 October 2001, summary, para 17.
[21] Law Com No 273, 9 October 2001, summary, para 19.

indivisible[22], see the rule as giving greater protection to non-defendants[23] and they see the rule as avoiding directions to juries on 'bizarre and unreal distinctions' between propensity and credibility[24]. This process, as a whole, in departing from the previous common law position will, they suggest, enhance the fairness of criminal trials greatly[25].

Changes to the rules relating to admissibility of past bad behaviour of the accused were recommended by the Auld[26] review in England and followed through in Part II of the Criminal Justice Bill 2002 which at the time of writing proposes to admit such 'bad character' evidence to include not only prior convictions, but any evidence that tends to show that a person has committed an offence or 'has behaved or is disposed to behave in a way that in the opinion of the court, might be viewed with disapproval by a reasonable person'.

[11.30] Much of the controversy with regard to Hudson has been resolved in the Irish context by the Irish Court of Criminal Appeal, in the case of the *Director of Public Prosecutions v McGrail*[27]. The defence allegations in this case had been to the effect that the prosecution witnesses had fabricated evidence of verbal admissions.

[11.31] The facts concerned the entry of detectives to a flat in a house in Dublin, on foot of a search warrant. The accused dropped the keys to the flat and attempted to leave through a window. He was apprehended and the prosecution alleged that, while on the floor, he was asked by the detectives whether there were guns in the flat, to which he replied that there were. A subsequent search found firearms, ammunition, masks, balaclavas, etc. The accused made a number of verbal statements after caution, which were taken down in writing, but which he did not sign. The defence alleged that the accused did not make any verbal admissions, did not point out any hiding place for the guns, and that the gardaí were trying to convict him by inventing verbal statements. Counsel for the prosecution at trial applied for leave to cross-examine the accused as to his own character on grounds that the nature of the defence involved imputations on the character and credibility of garda witnesses.

[11.32] Leave to cross-examine was granted under s 1(f)(ii) of the 1924 Act, and the accused in his direct evidence, stated he had previous convictions which related to cars. On appeal, Hederman J delivering the judgment of the Court,

---

22   Law Com No 273, 9 October 2001, summary, para 19.
23   Law Com No 273, 9 October 2001, summary, para 20.
24   Law Com No 273, 9 October 2001, summary, para 20.
25   Law Com No 273, 9 October 2001, summary, para 22.
26   Right Hon LJ Auld *Review of the Criminal Courts of England and Wales* Sept 2001, http://www.criminal-courts-review.org.uk/auld
27   *Director of Public Prosecutions v McGrail* (18 December 1989, unreported) CCA.

stated that the trial judge erred in principle in ruling that the case made by the defence put the character of the prosecution witnesses in question. He said that every criminal trial involved an imputation as to the character of somebody. If the defence stated that witnesses for the prosecution were not to be believed in their evidence, that was an imputation as to their character. This was inevitable if an accused person was not to be seriously hampered in his defence. A ruling otherwise would have the effect of inhibiting the conduct of the defence, in that an accused person who had a criminal record might be intimidated into abandoning an effort to put the truth of the evidence of a prosecution witness in issue, lest his own character outside the facts of the trial was then put in issue.

[11.33] In this particular instance, the case against the accused was based on confessions which he denied making to the police. The inescapable inference was that the police were lying.

[11.34] It would be intolerable, according to Hederman J if an accused was confined to suggesting a mistake or other innocent explanation to avoid any risk of subjecting his own character to cross-examination. It would be otherwise if the defence case was that this was the usual practice of the police in respect of any person they prosecuted.

[11.35] The view of the Court of Criminal Appeal was to the effect that s 1(f)(ii) of the 1924 Act must be construed as applying only to imputations made on the character of the prosecutor or his witnesses, independent of the facts of the particular case. A distinction should be drawn between questions or suggestions which are reasonably necessary to establish either the prosecution case or the defence case, even if it does involve suggesting a falsehood on the part of a witness. It is otherwise when an imputation of bad character is introduced relating to matters unconnected with the proofs of the material case. Even in the latter case, the trial judge had discretion to refuse leave to cross-examine about previous convictions or bad character because of the danger of unfairness to an accused person who has previous convictions. Hederman J concluded by saying that the principles of fair procedure must apply. A procedure which inhibited the accused from challenging the veracity of the evidence against him, at the risk of having his own previous character put in evidence, was not fair procedure. Recent English decisions to the effect that any challenge to the veracity of the evidence of the prosecution was sufficient to open the way for a cross-examination of the accused as to his character, should not then be followed.

[11.36] This is an interesting departure on the part of the Irish courts from the rigours of the *Hudson* doctrine, and is to be welcomed in so ar as the result of the application of that doctrine was once seen to unduly prejudice certain accused persons, ie those with criminal records. Moreover, yet again the Irish courts are locating their justification for amending the rules in the requirements of fair procedure, seen to underlie so very many of the rules of evidence in Irish law.

[11.37] Section 1(f)(iii) of the 1924 Act provides for the admissibility of an accused's record, where '... he has given evidence against any other person charged with the same offence'.

[11.38] In the case of *Murdoch v Taylor*[28], the facts concerned the joint trial of Murdoch (with a criminal record) and Lynch (no criminal record) for receiving stolen goods. Lynch gave evidence implicating Murdoch. Murdoch gave evidence in cross-examination alleging that Lynch alone had control and possession of the box containing the stolen goods. He was then cross-examined on his record. The Court of Criminal Appeal and the House of Lords dismissed Murdoch's appeal, which had alleged, inter alia, that s 1(f)(iii) of the 1924 Act only applied to evidence given in examination-in-chief, and with hostile intent, and that the trial judge had discretion as to whether to allow said cross-examination on record or not.

Lord Donovan, in relation to the first argument, commented that the effect upon the jury was the same, whether the evidence was given on examination-in-chief or cross-examination. In relation to the second point, he felt that it was the effect of the evidence on the minds of the jury which mattered, not the state of mind of the person who gave it. He felt that one had to look at the evidence in context, and that if the effect of the evidence upon the mind of the jury was to be taken as the test, it cannot be right to regard it in isolation in order to decide if it is evidence against the co-accused. If parliament had meant by s 1(f)(iii) to refer to evidence which was by itself conclusive against the co-accused, it would have been easy for them to say so, he reasoned. Murdoch's evidence was clearly to that effect. In relation to the exercise of a discretion on the part of the trial judge, the court felt that the trial judge had no discretion to prevent a co-accused from cross-examining under s 1(f)(iii). ('So far as the prosecution is concerned the matter should be one for the judge's discretion ... where the co-accused seeks to exercise the right different considerations apply this right can not be fettered in any way'). This approach was confirmed by the Privy Council in the case of *Liu Mei-lin v R*[29].

[11.39] In *Varley*[30], the Court of Appeal added guidance for trial judges to help determine whether an accused is entitled to cross-examine another on his character. The two accused here were jointly charged with robbery. One admitted he and the other had participated in the robbery but claimed he had

---

28 *Murdoch v Taylor* [1965] AC 574.
29 *Liu Mei-lin v R* [1989] 1 All ER 359.
30 *Varley* [1982] 2 All ER 519.

acted under duress from his co-accused. The co-accused, in turn, gave evidence he had taken no part in the robbery and that evidence given that he had was untrue. The latter was cross-examined on his record, on the basis that he had given evidence against the other. The Court of Appeal laid down the following guidelines:

'(1) If it is established that a person jointly charged has given evidence against the co-defendant that defendant has a right to cross-examine the other as to previous convictions and the trial judge has no discretion to refuse an application.

(2) Such evidence may be given during chief or during cross-examination.

(3) It has to be objectively decided whether the evidence either supports the prosecution case in a material respect or undermines the defence of the co-accused. A hostile intent is irrelevant.

(4) If consideration has to be given to the undermining of the other's defence care must be taken to see that the evidence clearly undermines the defence. Inconvenience to or inconsistency with the other's defence is not of itself sufficient.

(5) Mere denial of participation in a joint venture is not of itself sufficient to rank as evidence against the co-defendant. For the proviso to apply, such denial must lead to the conclusion that if the witness did not participate then it must have been the other who did.

(6) Where the one defendant asserts or in due course would assert one view of the joint venture which is directly contradicted by the other, such contradiction may be evidence against the co-defendant.' [31]

[11.40] Hence, if the witness's evidence has the effect of supporting the prosecution case against the co-accused and so undermines the co-accused's case more than it does that of the prosecution, cross-examination is allowed.

[11.41] An example of an instance when it was accepted that the accused's defence did not have such an effect on the co-accused's case so as to allow cross-examination as to record, is *R v Kirkpatrick*[32]. Here, the accused gave evidence that he was asleep during the offence. The co-accused's case, by contrast, was that he had intervened to prevent the commission of the offence. It was held the former had not given evidence against the latter, as he had not supported the prosecution case against him.

[11.42] The distinction may be difficult to perceive in practice, as undoubtedly such would affect the credibility of that accused, which would have undermined his defence, hence strengthening the case against him.

---

[31] [1982] 2 All ER 519 at 522.

[32] *R v Kirkpatrick* [1998] Crim LR 63.

Credibility/guilt distinction: judicial discretion with regard to divisibility of character

[11.43] In *R v Watts*[33], the appellant was of low intelligence and had two previous convictions for sexual offences against children. A young married woman had been indecently assaulted near his home by a man answering his description. He made plain admissions to the police and was charged accordingly. The accused presented an alibi defence at trial and claimed the police had fabricated evidence against him. He was then cross-examined under s 1(f)(ii) of the 1924 Act and convicted. He appealed on the basis that the trial judge had wrongly exercised his discretion by allowing cross-examination with regard to previous convictions.

[11.44] In the Court of Appeal, judgment was delivered by Lord Lane CJ who felt that the nature and conduct of the defence was plainly such here, as to involve imputations on the character of two police officers within s 1(f)(ii) of the 1924 Act. He noted that there was also no doubt, but that the only relevance of the previous convictions admitted by virtue of that sub-section, was as to the credibility of the prisoner, and the jury must not be asked to infer guilt from such convictions. He commented that 'this in many cases requires the jury to perform difficult feats of intellectual acrobatics. In the view of this court the present case is a good example'.

[11.45] Lord Lane CJ continued:

'In any event it seems to us that where the exercise of discretion is concerned, which is the problem here, each case is a case on its own and has to be considered on its own particular facts.

The jury in the present case was charged with deciding the guilt or innocence of a man against whom an allegation of indecent assault on a woman was made. They were told that he had previous convictions for indecent assaults of a more serious kind on young girls. They were warned that such evidence was not to be taken as making it more likely that he was guilty of the offence charged, which it seems it plainly did, but only as affecting his credibility, which it almost certainly did not. The prejudice which the appellant must have suffered in the eyes of the jury when it was disclosed that he had previous convictions for offences against young children could hardly have been greater. The probative value of the convictions on the sole issue on which they were admissible, was at best, slight. The previous offences did not involve dishonesty. Nor were they so similar to the offence which the jury were trying that they could have been admitted as evidence of similar facts on the issue of identity. In short, their prejudicial effect far outweighed their probative value. We would not have allowed this particular man

---

[33] *R v Watts* [1983] 3 All ER 101.

to have been cross-examined about these particular convictions in these particular circumstances.'

[11.46] It is interesting to contrast the decision in *Watts* with a later retraction by Lord Lane CJ in *R v Powell*[34]. Per Lord Lane CJ:

'A defendant with previous convictions for similar offences may indeed have a very great incentive to make false allegations against prosecution witnesses for fear of greater punishment on conviction. It does however require careful direction from the judge to the effect that the previous convictions should not be taken as indications that the accused has committed the offence.

The fact that the defendant's convictions are not for offences of dishonesty, in fact that they are for offences bearing a close resemblance to the offences charged, are matters for the judge to take into consideration when exercising his discretion, but they certainly do not oblige the judge to disallow the proposed cross-examination.'

[11.47] The most fundamental question is what part of an accused's record is admissible, since it goes only to credibility here and not guilt. The danger to be avoided here is that of the 'forbidden reasoning', where jurors take what seems to be very little about creditworthiness (say a conviction for rape), and use it as evidence of predisposition (on a charge of a sexual offence).

[11.48] A related danger is the use by the prosecution of 'previous offences' to demonstrate bad character, when such evidence should not have been introduced as similar fact evidence. In *Barsoum*[35], questioning, which was held to have gone too far, was as to the accused's previous similar convictions, how his defences had been disbelieved therein and as to the details of the offences.

[11.49] In *McLeod*[36], the Court of Appeal offered the following guidance:

'(a)   The mere fact that the previous offences are similar to that charged, or suggest that the accused has the propensity to commit an offence such as that charged does not prevent the prosecution from cross-examining about them, even though their true relevance is confined to the accused's credibility.

(b)   Nonetheless, unless it is contended that the previous offences would anyway be admissible on the issue of guilt (for example as similar fact evidence) there should be no cross-examination prolonged or extensive enough to divert the jury from the real issue in the case, which is whether or not the accused committed the offence charged.

---

[34]   *R v Powell* [1988] 1 All ER 193.
[35]   *Barsoum* [1994] Crim LR 194.
[36]   *McLeod* [1994] 1 WLR 1500.

(c) The fact that the accused had previously offered a similar defence, which a previous jury has rejected, for example a false alibi or the alleged "planting" of evidence, may be a proper subject for cross-examination, because it may reflect on the accused's credibility.

(d) The judge retains a discretion to restrain cross-examination which tends to show particularly bad character, and should take into account both the degree of prejudice likely to be caused to the accused, and the gravity of the attack made on the prosecution in deciding how to exercise his discretion.'

[11.50] The aforementioned English Law Commission Report, subsequent Auld Review (2001) and White Paper 'Justice for All (2002)' followed, by the Criminal Justice Bill 2002,[37] would change the law's position on many of these issues with a greater 'balancing' role for the judge in each instance – including relating to the co-accused. Avoidance of 'forbidden reasoning' might certainly be achieved by the greater ability to direct juries, together with the enhanced powers of leave and notice, and the divisibility of a defendant's character and record. The ultimate touchstone for the Commission was 'to construct a consistent and balanced process under which the conflicting interests of the various parties may best be advanced and protected, and the fairness of criminal trials generally enhanced.'[38] This demonstrates some common territory with how *McGrail*[39] might address very many issues here in terms of 'fair procedure'.

Conclusions

[11.51] Lord Lane CJ's judgment in *Watts* with regard to the exercise of judicial discretion in relation to non-admissibility of an accused's record, when its probative value in terms of credibility is slight, and its prejudicial effect in the eyes of the jury is great, is compulsive in terms of its logic.

[11.52] While the issue is arguably of less import now in Ireland, given the judgment in *McGrail* which eases the burden placed on the judiciary to ameliorate the harshness of the *Hudson* doctrine by the use of judicial discretion to disallow cross-examination on record, it is still an important one in terms of the difficulty of directing the jury as to the relevance of the record lying only to the credibility of the accused. The fundamental issue is raised by Lord Lane CJ in *Watts*, viz, the ability of the jury to engage in the 'intellectual gymnastics'

---

[37] Law Reform Commission Report *Evidence of Bad Character in Criminal Proceedings* Law Com No 273, 9 October 2001; Auld *Review of Criminal Courts of England & Wales* (2001); *Justice for All* Cm 5563 July 2002, HMSO; Criminal Justice Bill 2002, Part 11 c 1 ss 81-97 Evidence of Bad Character.

[38] Law Com No 273 (9 October 2001), summary, para 22.

[39] *DPP v McGrail* (18 December 1989) CCA.

necessitated by the section; or the justification or validity of requiring same. Is such a record of 'character' (undivided) ever relevant to credibility? Can a jury ever be expected to draw such distinctions? And in the light of *McGrail* in the Irish context, can such admission, introduction and direction ever ensure fundamental fairness to an accused?

It is in this light that the issues of character, credibility, divisibility of record and judicial discretion need to be reconsidered in the Irish context. Such a review may result in a *McGrail*-like departure from the English jurisprudence – at least as most recently expressed in *Powell*.

Chapter 12

Estoppel

'Estoppel is a rule of evidence. There are many categories of estoppel – estoppel by deed, common law estoppel (if a person does an act affecting someone else which he is entitled to do only if a certain state of things exists common law estoppel prevents that person from asserting as against that when he did it state of things did not exist), estoppel by representation, estoppel by judgment.'

Finnegan J in *P(D) v Governor of Training Unit* (18 August 2000, unreported) HC at para 8.

Introduction

[12.01] In civil law there is cause of action estoppel, issue estoppel, merger and abuse of process. In criminal law there is issue estoppel, abuse of process, and special pleas of autrefois acquit and autrefois convict.

[12.02] Estoppel is an exclusionary rule of evidence. The party against whom an estoppel is established may not adduce any evidence with regard to the facts covered by the estoppel. Estoppel may only operate if pleaded, and operates without reference to the purpose for which relevance is placed on a particular fact. Estoppel may be by record, by deed, or by conduct.

Estoppel by record

[12.03] The rationale for the rule relating to estoppel by record is one centred on the principle that it is for the common good that there should be an end to litigation, and no one should be sued a second time on the same grounds:

'A judgment is conclusive as against all persons of the existence of the state of things which it actually effects when the existence of that state is in issue or relevant to an issue.'[1]

The conclusiveness of a judgment if it is *in rem is* particularly important. *Halsbury's Law of England*[2], as quoted in Cross[3], defines a judgment *in rem* as:

---

[1] Stephen *Digest of the Law of Evidence* (12th edn) article 41.
[2] Halsbury's Laws of England (Hailsham edn) Vol 13 at 405.
[3] Tapper *Cross on Evidence* (7th edn, 1990), p 75.

'A judgment of a court of competent jurisdiction determining the status of a person or thing or the disposition of a thing (as distinct from a particular interest in it of a party to the litigation).'

Whether a judgment is *in rem* or *in personam,* however, its effect on the parties to the action is much greater than that on others (aside from those claiming through said parties).

Estoppel by record inter partes

[12.04] Parties are estopped from denying not merely the state of affairs established by the judgment but also the grounds on which that judgment was made.

Cause of action estoppel

[12.05] Cause of action estoppel is based on the idea that the cause of action merges in the judgment, which therefore destroys it. If A claims damages from B for a particular assault or breach of contract, and records a specific sum, he cannot sue for more damages for the same cause. However, clearly he would have been entitled to such damages had subsequent events, such as the deterioration of his health in consequences of the assault, been not known at the time of the original claim. A rather harsh extension of the doctrine has developed (see Wigram VC in *Henderson v Henderson*[4]), to the effect that it covers those claims, which though not the subject of formal adjudication, would have been brought forward as part of the cause of action in the proceedings which are alleged to constitute an estoppel, though not if the latter consists of judgment in default.

Issue estoppel

[12.06] Issue estoppel is wider and less technical. It is based on the desirability of achieving finality in the litigation of certain issues between parties. If in June A claims damages for a breach of contract committed by B in January, and B successfully pleads that the contract is void, A would be met by a successful plea of issue estoppel, if in December, he claimed damages for a further breach of the same contract committed in June. The cause of action would have been decided in B's favour in the first litigation.

[12.07] The basic principles of issue estoppel were stated by Lord Diplock in *Mills v Cooper*[5] and the House of Lords in *Hunter v Chief Constable of the West Midlands*[6]. The House of Lords adopted as the rationale for the rule that it

---

4   *Henderson v Henderson* (1843) 3 Hare 100 at 114.
5   *Mills v Cooper* [1967] 2 QB 459 at 468.
6   *Hunter v Chief Constable of the West Midlands* [1982] AC 529 at 541.

amounted to an abuse of process to launch a collateral attack upon a decision of a court of competent jurisdiction, by raising an issue for a second time[7]

However, an earlier judgment may not raise an estoppel if fresh material (either factual material or a change in the interpretation of the law) is available, showing the earlier decision to have been wrong (*Hunter v Chief Constable of the West Midlands*)[8]

[12.08] That consideration apart, however, the prerequisites to raising issue estoppel, as laid down by Lord Brandon in *DSV Silo – und Verwaltungsgesellschaft MbH v Owners of the Sennar*[9], are threefold:

'The first requirement is that the judgment in the earlier action relied on as creating an estoppel must be (a) of a court of competent jurisdiction, (b) final and conclusive and (c) on the merits. The second requirement is that the parties (or privies) in the earlier action relied on as creating an estoppel and those in the later action in which that estoppel is raised as a bar must be the same. The third requirement is that the issue in the later action in which the estoppel is raised as a bar must be the same issue as that decided by the judgment in the earlier action.'

Issue estoppel: Irish case law

[12.09] In *Gilroy v McLoughlin*[10], the question of issue estoppel arose in the context of proceedings arising out of a road traffic accident in 1984. Mr McLoughlin and his brother had initiated Circuit Court proceedings against Mr Gilroy, seeking damages for personal injuries and damage to a motor vehicle. The Circuit Court awarded £3,800 damages to McLoughlin, reduced by 10% by reason of his own negligence. On appeal to the High Court, Lardner J reversed the Circuit Court order and dismissed the action. Gilroy commenced the present proceedings while the Circuit Court proceedings were pending, claiming the collision to have been caused by the defendant McLoughlin's negligence. The defendant here denied any negligence, and pleaded that the collision was caused entirely or alternatively contributed to by the negligence and breach of duty of the plaintiff Gilroy. The plaintiff pleaded that the defendant was estopped by reason of the High Court decision in the previous proceedings, from raising such a defence.

[12.10] The preliminary issue to be determined was whether the defendant was estopped, by virtue of the decision of Lardner J, from alleging that the plaintiff

---

[7] Tapper, *Cross on Evidence* (7th edn, 1990), p 79.

[8] *Hunter v Chief Constable of the West Midlands* [1982] AC 529 at 545.

[9] *DSV Silo – und Verwaltungsgesellschaft Mbh v Owners of the Sennar* [1985] 2 All ER 104 at 110.

[10] *Gilroy v McLoughlin* [1989] ILRM 133.

was negligent or in breach of duty, or was guilty of contributory negligence and breach of duty.

[12.11] Blayney J identified the issue herein raised as being one of issue estoppel rather than action estoppel[11]. He referred to its definition by Lord Gibson in *Shaw v Sloan*[12]:

'It would seem that before estoppel of an issue can arise there must have been a final determination of the same issue in previous proceedings by the court of competent jurisdiction and the parties bound by this earlier decision must have been either the same parties as are sought in the later proceedings to be estopped or their Envies.'

[12.12] Blayney J found the parties to the action to have been parties to the previous proceedings and clearly bound by them. Similarly the decision in the earlier proceedings was clearly a decision of a court of competent jurisdiction. The only issue remaining per Lord Gibson's definition, therefore, was 'whether the issue raised by the plea in the defence is the same issue as was determined in previous proceedings.'

[12.13] Blayney J found that Lardner J dismissed the Circuit Court action, as the defendant had failed to discharge the onus of proving on the balance of probabilities that the plaintiff had been negligent. The only negligence considered was negligence in the sense of a breach of a duty of care owned by the plaintiff to the defendant. The question of contributory negligence on the part of the plaintiff, in the sense that he had failed to take such care as a reasonable man would take for his own safety, did not arise in those proceedings.

[12.14] In the present action, the defendant had raised what amounted to a plea of contributory negligence. Lardner J had not determined the issue of contributory negligence on the part of the plaintiff and the defendant was not estopped by those proceedings from raising it in his defence. A similar failure of the claim of issue estoppel occurred in *McGlinchey v Ireland*[13] where, inter alia, the plaintiff claimed the Extradition Act 1965 (Part III) to be unconstitutional. The State pleaded such issues to be *res judicata*. However, Costello J in the High

---

[11] [1989] ILRM 133 at 136.

[12] *Shaw v Sloan* [1982] N1393 at 398. *Shaw v Sloan* was referred to and applied in *Gilroy v McLoughlin* [1988] IR 44, where the claim of estoppel was made in a situation again arising out of proceedings relating to a motor accident. Blayney J in the High Court held that, as there had not been a final determination by a court of competent jurisdiction of the same issue in earlier proceedings between the same parties, estoppel did not arise. He distinguished the earlier decision of Gannon J in *Donohue v Browne* [1986] IR 90, on the basis that the order of the Circuit Court there included an express finding that the plaintiff had been negligent. In *Donohue v Browne* there had been no such finding.

[13] *McGlinchey v Ireland* [1990] 2 IR 220.

Court noted that, as neither in the previous judgments of the High Court or the Supreme Court in the 1987 *habeas corpus* proceedings had there been any determination made as to the constitutional validity of any section of the 1965 Act, the plaintiff was not now estopped from raising the issues he had raised in this action.

[12.15] In *McCauley v McDermott*[14] and *Bula (In Receivership) v Crowley*[15], the requirement of mutability for issue estoppel was effectively abolished – although as Paul McDermott notes, this was done in each case through use of the doctrine of abuse of process[16]. However, it would seem that these decisions effectively abolished the traditional English rule, under which there is a requirement of identity of parties in issue estoppel.

Pleading

[12.16] Each party who alleges the existence of an estoppel by record must plead the former judgment. If not pleaded it may be treated merely as an item of evidence in favour of that party by the jury (*Vooght v Winch*[17]).

Criminal cases

[12.17] There is no issue estoppel in criminal law (recently confirmed by the House of Lords in *DPP v Humphreys*[18]), but allowance must be made for extensions of the plea of *autrefois acquit* to strengthen the protection of the accused against double jeopardy. Pleas of *autrefois acquit* and *autre fois convict* are the nearest equivalent to cause of action estoppel in criminal cases. They are available whenever the accused is in danger of being convicted of the same offence as one which he has already been acquitted or convicted of, and when he is in danger of being convicted of an offence of which he could have been convicted at a former trial.

[12.18] Relevant in this context is the decision of the Supreme Court in *Hubert Patrick McGrath v Commissioner of An Garda Síochána*[19]. The applicant was charged here, under s 17(2)(d) of the Larceny Act 1916, with embezzling sums of money received by him in the course of his duty. He was tried before a judge and jury and acquitted.

[12.19] Subsequently, a disciplinary enquiry was instituted under the Garda Síochána (Discipline) Regulations 1971 to investigate alleged breaches of

---

14 *McCauley v McDermott* [1997] 2 ILRM 486 (SC).

15 *Bula (In Receivership) v Crowley* (28 April 1997, unreported) HC (Barr J).

16 McDermott, *Res Judicata & Double Jeopardy* (1999), p 91.

17 *Vooght v Winch* (1819) 2 B & Ald 6632.

18 *DPP v Humphreys* [1977] AC 1.

19 *Hubert Patrick McGrath v Commissioner of An Garda Síochána* [1990] ILRM 817.

discipline amounting to corrupt practice. Lynch J granted an order of prohibition in respect of the investigation, on the basis it contradicted the findings of the jury in the criminal trial relating to the same matters. He felt the inquiry could proceed, however, in relation to the allegation of 'improper' and opposed to 'corrupt' practice. The Commissioner agreed. The Supreme Court dismissed the appeal.

[12.20] Finlay CJ (Griffin J concurring) agreed with the judgment of Hederman J that to permit the garda investigation to proceed into a complaint of corrupt practice would amount to an unfair procedure. He went on to note that:

> 'I would emphasise, however, that there cannot, it would appear to me, be any general principle that an acquittal on a criminal charge in respect of an offence, irrespective of the reason for such acquittal, or the basis on which it was achieved could be inevitably an estoppel preventing a disciplinary investigation arising out of the same set of facts.
>
> There was no suggestion contained in this case that the verdict in the criminal trial of the applicant arose through any technicality or any failure of attendance by a particular witness who might be available at a subsequent disciplinary hearing, or other like circumstance. It would appear that the appellant accepted that the verdict was a verdict on the merits of the particular charge on a full and proper hearing.
>
> In those circumstances, it seems to me that a disciplinary hearing now prosecuted, arising out of the identified facts and allegations of corruption would be basically unfair procedure.'[20]

[12.21] Hederman J (Griffin and O'Flaherty JJ concurring) stated:

> 'The object of the criminal proceedings was to establish that the respondent was guilty of dishonest acts which, if established, would have exposed him to punishment. He was acquitted. The object of the disciplinary proceedings is to establish that he was guilty of the same acts as those in respect of which he was acquitted ... Thus he is in effect being retried on issues already determined and he is, once again, exposed to the possibility of punishment. This cannot be done without seeking to set at right the result of the verdict of the jury. I make a distinction between the consequences that might flow from any purely civil action and the disciplinary hearing procedure. The disciplinary hearing is more serious in its consequences than a mere civil action.
>
> For this member of the garda to be tried again before a disciplinary tribunal on identical 'charges' to which he has been acquitted by a jury, having regard to the narrow purview within which the inquiry must be held, would involve a form of unfair and oppressive procedures which calls for the intervention of the Court.'[21]

---

[20]   [1990] ILRM 817 at 818 per Finlay CJ.
[21]   [1990] ILRM 817 at 821 per Hederman J.

[12.22] However, that was sufficient to determine the matter in this case, and Hederman J openly refrained from finding that there was any question of *res judicata*. McCarthy J agreed with Hederman J that to allow the garda investigation to proceed into a complaint of corrupt practice would, in the circumstances of the case, amount to an unfair procedure, as 'the charge of a corrupt failure to account for money received by a member of An Garda Síochána in the course of duty was rejected by the jury in the criminal prosecution.'

He continued:

'Lest it be considered that acquittal on a criminal charge necessarily precludes a disciplinary investigation into the facts arising out of which a criminal charge was brought I reject such a proposition. The argument in support of such a view is one of estoppel. The vital features of issue estoppel are that the fact and the parties in dispute are essentially the same. Where one organ of State has been a contestant in the first trial of the issue, then, in my view, another organ of State has the necessary privity. What is an organ of State? Certainly, the Attorney General, Ireland, the Director of Public Prosecutions, and the Commissioner of the Garda Síochána come within that category. The core question is whether or not the issue was the same. The issue in a criminal trial is the guilt or innocence of the accused; such depends upon a wide variety of circumstances the existence of which has to be proved by the prosecution. As pointed out by Henchy J in *Dublin Corporation v Flynn* [1980] IR 357 for a variety of reasons an accused person may have been prepared to accept a wrong decision in an earlier prosecution to the effect that he had committed an act of assault or had driven a motor car dangerously. In such circumstances, estoppel would be repugnant to the fair administration of justice. In the instant case the claim of estoppel is made by the accused but the legal principle is the same. Acquitting a garda of assault would not preclude a garda investigation into a breach of discipline such as abuse of authority in failing to behave with due courtesy towards a member of the public. In *Kelly v Ireland* [1986] ILRM 318 O'Hanlon J elaborated on this topic including, in his judgement, a consideration of issue estoppel and concluded (page 328):

"In the rare case where a clearly identifiable issue has been raised in the course of a criminal trial and has been decided against a party to those proceedings by means of a judgment explaining how the issue has been decided, I would be prepared to hold that such decision may give rise to issue estoppel in later civil proceedings in which that party is also involved. Such estoppel would arise, not only in relation to the specific issue determined (in this case, whether the statement was made freely and voluntarily) but also to findings which were fundamental to the court's decision on such issue."

He went on to hold that, apart from the applicability of the concept of issue estoppel, the effort to challenge the correctness of decision made by a court of competent jurisdiction against a party in the course of a criminal trial, by means of civil proceedings instituted by such person after that decision has been made, should normally be restrained as an abuse of the process of the court.' [22]

The argument made by the appellant that the latter decision could be distinguished in this case on the basis that there was no judgment giving reasons here, merely the verdict of a jury, was unsuccessful.

[12.23] In England, extensions of *autrefois acquit* have included decisions like *Sambasivam v Malaya Federation Public Prosecutor*[23] and *R v Hay*[24], which accepted that an earlier finding that an accused's statement was untrue, at least partially, must be accepted by the prosecutor in a second trial.

[12.24] Two important distinctions arise here, however, and are noted by *Cross*[25]:

'... The prosecution may not, in case B rely on evidence which is only relevant on the assumption that the accused was guilty of the offence of which he was acquitted in case A.'

However:

'Evidence is no less admissible in the second case because it tends to show that the accused was guilty in the first, provided that, in tendering it, the prosecution is not in effect denying the validity of the acquittal.'

This distinction is somewhat important in the context of similar fact evidence (see chapter 10). The extension of *autrefois acquit* can be seen to give rise to a number of difficulties.

Estoppel by deed in civil cases

[12.25] A party who executes a deed is estopped in a court of law from saying that the facts stated in the deed are not truly stated (*Baker v Dewey*[26]).
The scope of the doctrine is extremely limited. It only applies between parties to the deed (or those claiming through them). The statement must be unambiguous. It can only be raised in an action on the deed. It does not prevent a party from setting up a plea of illegality or fraud or from availing himself of any fact giving rise to a right to rescind the deed.

---

[22] [1990] ILRM 817 at 822-823.
[23] *Sambasivam v Malaya Federation Public Prosecutor* [1950] AC 458.
[24] *R v Hay* [1983] 77 Cr App Rep 70.
[25] Tapper *Cross on Evidence* (7th edn, 1990), p 89.
[26] *Baker v Dewey* (1823) 1 B & C 704 at 707.

Estoppel by conduct

[12.26]

> 'Where one by his words or conduct wilfully causes another to believe in the existence of a certain state of things, and induces him to act on that belief, or to alter his own previous position, the former is precluded from averring against the latter a different state of things as existing at that time.' (*Pickard v Sears*)[27]

The adjudication of 'wilful', in the sense of 'with the intention that the belief which is induced should be acted upon' (*Freeman v Cooke*[28]), is an objective one[29]. Estoppel by conduct embodies, in the main, estoppel by agreement, estoppel by representation, and estoppel by negligence. In the former two, the party in whose favour the estoppel operates, is either the person with whom an agreement is concluded, or someone claiming through that person, *or* else the person to whom a representation is made by the party estopped or someone claiming through such a person. The latter (estoppel by negligence), however, is one in which the party in whose favour it operates is the victim of the fraud of some third person, facilitated by the careless breach of duty of the other party. Cross[30] suggests that the requirements of duty of care and proof of negligence can be dispensed with here, and all that is necessary is proof of intentional words, acts, or conduct, which can reasonably be construed as a representation by the representor to the represented who need not be in direct relationship.

[12.27] Finally, limitations on estoppel by conduct are such that (i) the estoppel must concern an existing state of fact[31]; (ii) it must be unambiguous; and (iii) the result of giving effect to it must not be something that is permitted by law. In *Lynch v Cavan County Council*[32], the defendant's licence to work a quarry involved no obligation to erect a fence, yet he did so. The plaintiff's horse fell into the quarry because the fence was defective. Sheehy J held that the defendants, by having erected and maintained a fence, were estopped from denying liability. In a similar vein, in *Commissioner of Public Works v Mackey*[33], the Supreme Court considered a situation where the Commissioner for Public Works let property to a tenant who was not disputing their title to it. Fitzgibbon J stated:

---

[27] *Pickard v Sears* (1837) 6 Ad & EL 469.
[28] *Freeman v Cooke* (1848) 2 Exch 654.
[29] *Freeman v Cooke* (1848) 2 Exch 654 per Parte B.
[30] Tapper *Cross on Evidence* (7th edn, 1990), p 97.
[31] *Jorden v Money* (1854) 5 HL Gas 185.
[32] *Lynch v Cavan County Council* (1942) 76 ILTR 121.
[33] *Commissioner of Public Works v Mackey* [1941] IR 207.

'A tenant who has accepted possession under a lease and has paid rent to the landlord who gave possession to him, cannot dispute the title of that landlord to recover possession at the expiration of the tenancy.'

[12.28] In *Crawford v Gillmor*[34], Barry J stated that:

'... to create ... estoppel by conduct . . . there must be an alteration in the position of the person in whose favour the estoppel exists, brought about or induced by the person whom the estoppel binds.'

[12.29] An example of an unsuccessful assertion of estoppel by conduct is contained in the decision in *Irene Davitt v The Minister for Education*[35]. The facts in this case concerned the appointment of the applicant to the position of a permanent full-time teacher in June 1987, which appointment was expressly stated to be subject to the approval of the Department of Education. In December 1987 the applicant was notified that the Minister had approved her appointment only as a temporary full-time teacher. The applicant sought judicial review of the Minister's decision on the ground, inter alia, that the conduct of the Minister had given rise to a legitimate expectation in the applicant that she should be appointed as a permanent full-time teacher. The applicant's submission was that the Minister by allowing her to apply for the advertised position of permanent full-time teacher in Commerce and French, and to accept the conditions of service offered, and in September to take up work apparently in a permanent post, and by then only approving of a temporary post, had allowed her to act to her detriment. She claimed legitimate expectation that the position for which she applied existed and that the formal requirements for her appointment had been complied with.

[12.30] Reliance was placed on the decisions in *R v Secretary of State ex parte Kahn*[36] and *R v Secretary of State ex parte Ruddock*[37] and the observations of the Irish Supreme Court in *Webb v Ireland & AG*[38]. In *Webb* Finlay CJ stated that:

'It would appear that the doctrine of "legitimate expectation" sometimes described as "reasonable expectation" has not in these terms been the subject matter of any decision by our courts. However, the doctrine connoted by such expressions is but an aspect of the well-recognised equitable concept of promissory estoppel whereby a promise or representation as to intention may in certain circumstances be binding on the representor and promiser.'

---

[34] *Crawford v Gillmor* (1891) 30 LR Ir 238.
[35] *Davitt v The Minister for Education* [1989] 1 ILRM 639.
[36] *R v Secretary of State ex parte Kahn* [1985] 2 All ER 40.
[37] *R v Secretary of State ex parte Ruddock* [1987] 2 All ER 518.
[38] *Webb v Ireland & AG* [1988] ILRM 565.

[12.31] Finlay CJ adopted Lord Denning's statement of the doctrine in *Amalgamated Investments v Texas Commerce*[39]:

> 'When the parties to a transaction proceed on the basis that an underlying assumption (either of fact or of law and whether due to misrepresentation or mistake makes no difference) on which they have conducted the dealings between them exists, neither of them will be allowed to go back on that assumption when it would be unfair or unjust to allow him to do so.'

[12.32] In *Webb* Finlay CJ had found such an 'unqualified assurance', from which the courts would not allow the defendant renege. Similarly, Lardner J pointed out that in *Kahn* there was a clear statement published by the Secretary of State to the public, setting out the criteria he would apply in admitting children to the United Kingdom for adoption. In *Ruddock,* the case concerned the issue of a warrant by the Secretary of State permitting the interception of the applicant's telephone. The criteria governing the issue of such warrants had been published six times between 1952 and 1982, and expressly adopted by the Secretary of State.

[12.33] By contrast, returning to the facts of *Davitt*, Lardner J found the case to be clearly distinguishable in a number of important circumstances. Firstly, the applicant's relationship and dealings were with the CDVFC, and not with the Minister. There would thus appear to have been no assurance by the Minister of any kind as contended for by the applicant. The proposition made by the applicant that estoppel can operate to prevent the Minister exercising the full scope of her statutory discretion was deemed erroneous (see Henchy J in *Re Greendale Building Co Ltd*)[40]. Applying the criteria to the facts of the case, therefore, Lardner J found no 'unqualified assurance' to the applicant by the Minister in which to ground her claim of legitimate expectation.

[12.34] Similarly unsuccessful was the claim of estoppel by conduct in *Jude Mapp a Minor and Dominic Gilholey*[41]. The appeal here was on the basis, inter alia, that the taking of unsworn evidence from an infant plaintiff in a civil case rendered the trial a nullity.

[12.35] Finlay CJ stated that the relevant principle was that an appellant seeking to rely on the admission of unsworn *viva voce* evidence as constituting a mistrial could only be prevented from so doing inter alia: by estoppel arising from an express or unambiguously implied representation that he was waiving his right to challenge the admission of such evidence, by reason of the absence of an oath

---

[39] *Amalgamated Investments v Texas Commerce* [1982] QB 84.
[40] *Re Greendale Building Co Ltd* [1977] IR 256.
[41] *Jude Mapp a Minor and Dominic Gilholey* (23 April 1991, unreported) SC.

or affirmation, on which the opposing party had acted to his detriment in a manner which would make the finding of a mistrial an injustice.

On balance, the Court found, however, that the defendant here was not estopped by his conduct from relying on the invalidity of the hearing.

[12.36] In *Daly v Minister for the Marine*[42], the applicant relied on the doctrine of legitimate expectations and the equitable doctrine of promissory estoppel, with regard to application for judicial review of the respondent's decision to refuse him the right to use the tonnage of his vessel on de-registration, as replacement capacity to facilitate the entry of another vessel into the fishing fleet. Fennelly J[43] quoted a passage from Barr J in *Cannon v Minister for the Marine*[44] which he says distils the essence of the doctrine which is fairness:

> 'the concept of legitimate expectation, being derived from an equitable doctrine, must be reviewed in the light of equitable principles. The test is whether in all the circumstances it would be unfair or unjust to allow a party to resile from a position created or adopted by him which at that time gave rise to a legitimate expectation in the mind of another that that situation would continue and might be acted upon by him to his advantage.'

In the case in question, Fennelly J pointed out[45] that there is a distinction between the doctrine of legitimate expectations and promissory estoppel:

> 'Legitimate expectation constitutes an accepted part of the principles of administrative law by our courts through the vehicle of judicial review. It is concerned essentially to see that administrative powers are not used unfairly. An expectation may be legitimate and cognisable by the courts even in the absence of the sort of action to the claimant's detriment that forms part of the law of estoppel. On the other hand, I would not accept that the mere fact of an expectation can suffice without some context relevant to fairness in the exercise of legal or administrative powers. These who come within the ambit of an administrative or regulatory regime may be able to establish that it would be unfair, discriminatory or unjust to permit the body exercising a power to change a policy or a set of existing rules, or depart from an undertaking or promise without taking account of the legitimate expectations created by them. However, the very notion of fairness has within it an idea that there is an existing relationship which it would be unfair to alter.'

[12.37] In this case, Fennelly J held the relationship between the applicant and Minister was not altered by correspondence to the disadvantage of the applicant

---

42 *Daly v Minister for the Marine* (4 October 2001, unreported) SC.
43 *Daly v Minister for the Marine* (4 October 2001, unreported) SC at para 28.
44 *Cannon v Minister for the Marine* [1991] 1 IR 82.
45 *Daly v Minister for the Marine* (4 October 2001) per Fennelly J, para 37.

– to the contrary, it was fortuitous. Hence this was not the sort of interest the doctrine is designed to protect.

Fennelly J held that the Supreme Court explained the doctrine of promissory estoppel clearly in *Doran v Thompson*[46] where Griffin J stated:

'Where one party, by his words or conduct, made to the other a clear and unambiguous promise or assurance which was intended to affect the legal relations between then and to be acted on accordingly, and the other party has acted on it by altering his position to his detriment, it is well settled that the one who gave the promise or assurance cannot afterwards be allowed to revert to their previous legal relations as if no such promise or assurance had been made by him, and that he may be restrained in equity from acting inconsistently with such promise or assurance.'

[12.38] Fennelly J[47] pointed out that Kenny J[48] had cited as being correct the statement of the law on promissory estoppel in *Snell's Principles of Equity*[49] which reads:

'Where by his words or conduct one party to a transaction makes to the other an unambiguous promise or assurance which is intended to affect the legal relations between them (whether contractual or otherwise) and the other party acts upon it, altering his position to his detriment, the party making the promise or assurance will not be permitted to act inconsistently with it.'

Here, although the correspondence in question constituted the kind of unambiguous promise or assurance contemplated, Fennelly J held that the applicant has not satisfied the second requirement.

---

[46] *Doran v Thompson* [1978] IR 222 at 230.
[47] Fennelly J in *Daly v Minister for the Marine* (4 October 2001) SC at para 42,43.
[48] *Doran v Thompson* [1978] IR 222 at 233.
[49] *Snell's Principles of Equity* (27th edn, 1973), p 303.

Chapter 13

Discovery

Introduction

[13.01] It is important at the outset to sketch the context in which the process of discovery lies. It is a topic of undoubted and increasing importance, yet of uneasy classification, due both to its relatively recent maturity, if not birth, and its hybrid nature as a creature of procedure and evidence. Zuckerman[1] lays down some fundamentals in this area which are worth stating. In particular he identifies:

> 'one fundamental and uncontroversial principle: that all relevant evidence is not only admissible but is also compellable. It is an axiomatic requirement of justice that litigants must have an opportunity to be heard. This implies not just an opportunity to put forward arguments but also an opportunity to place evidence before the courts. For in factual controversies arguments without facts are just as sterile as arguments without authority in legal controversies. Accordingly, parties to litigation have a right to bring before the court all evidence relevant to their claims. It is a principle of general importance Lord Hailsham explained, that "in all cases before them, the courts should insist on parties and witnesses disclosing the truth, the whole truth and nothing but the truth, where this would assist the decision of the matters in dispute".'[2]

[13.02] Zuckerman[3] continues:

> 'The disclosure of the whole truth is as important to the administration of justice as it is to individual litigants. A judgement, which is known to have been given not on the basis of all the available evidence but on only part thereof, cannot inspire confidence in its correctness. The efficiency of the system of justice is in large measure a function of the confidence that it commands amongst the public at large. Full confidence is bound to be undermined by the knowledge that the courts systematically allow a party to litigation, or a third person who is in possession of relevant information, to withhold evidence from the court. Justice in such situations cannot be seen to be done.'

---

[1] AAS Zuckerman 'Public Interest Immunity – A Matter of Prime Judicial Responsibility'(1994) Vol 57 MLR 703.

[2] *D v NSPCC* [1977] 1 All ER 589 at 600.

[3] AAS Zuckerman 'Public Interest Immunity – A Matter of Prime Judicial Responsibility'(1994) Vol 57 MLR 703.

[13.03] There is therefore both a private interest and a public interest in the disclosure of all relevant evidence. The former is a function of the litigant's entitlement to prosecute his cause. The latter is informed by the public interest in promoting an effective and fair system of justice. In spite of this, however, there is not a duty on courts to seek out all available evidence. Ours is an adversarial system and so parties are left to find their own evidence. Nor is the law of procedure obliged to arm litigants with all possible instruments for unearthing evidence. (For example, there is no right of private litigants to get search warrants to ransack premises.) It is not a requirement of justice that all possible means for disclosing the existence of evidence should be placed at the parties' disposal.

Yet we are entitled to demand courts implement effectively and consistently the law's existing commitment to disclosure of evidence. This commitment may be gauged for the procedures that the common law and rules of courts provide for the disclosure of evidence.

[13.04] In this regard it is only necessary to point to the development of *Anton Pillar* and third party discovery. Zuckerman describes these as 'concrete indications of the importance that the administration of justice attaches to the rendering of judgments on the basis of all available and relevant evidence'.[4] The law is prepared to place the interest in securing evidence above, for example, the convenience of third parties. However, the commitment to full disclosure is not absolute (eg legal professional privilege). Yet, the commitment to securing all evidence relevant to disputes is a powerful and well-entrusted policy.

Historical perspective

[13.05] Wigmore[5] states that the common law rule in general recognised no rule requiring prior notice of intended evidence to be given to the opponent, or the furnishing of legal process to obtain such information. This common law doctrine, however, he acknowledges[6], was open to subsequent modification on one of two grounds, namely either (i) when the overbalancing danger of furnishing an unscrupulous opponent with the opportunity of fraud could be flatly ignored or (ii) when this danger could be found to be of comparatively trifling magnitude.

[13.06] An exception with regard to 'documents, chattels and premises' developed, therefore, because the danger of improper tampering with evidence

---

[4]   Zuckerman (1994) 57 MLR 703 at 704.
[5]   Wigmore 'Treatise on the Anglo-American System of Evidence' in *Trials of Common Law* (3rd edn, 1940) Boston, para 1846.
[6]   Wigmore, para 1847.

by an unscrupulous opponent is of comparatively small probability where the evidence constitutes documents, chattels or provisos in the first party's possession. To allow the opponent, under proper safeguards, to have prior inspection of them and even to take a copy of documents, cannot endanger the integrity of the object. Nor can the warning thus given create any substantial danger of procuring perjured testimony against the execution of the document or the facts. All the justice of assisting an innocent opponent may be attained without any appreciable risk of furnishing the means of fraud to an unprincipled one.

[13.07] The germ of this exception for documentary evidence had already existed in the common law rule of 'profert and oyer', but it represented a significant abandonment of the sportman's theory of litigation. Wigmore again notes that:

> 'The right to use a rule of procedure or evidence precisely as one plays a trump card or draws to three aces or holds back a good horse till the home stretch, is a distinctive result of the common-law moral attitude toward parties in litigation'.[7]

[13.08] This feature of games or sports influenced powerfully the policy of the common law. To require the disclosure to an adversary of the evidence that is to be produced, would be repugnant to all sportsmanlike instincts. Thus, the common law permitted a litigant to reserve his evidential resources (tactics, documents, witnesses) until the final moment, marshalling them at the trial before his surprised and dismayed antagonist. This was rather colourfully put by Pound C in *Ulrich v McConaughey*:

> 'The common law originally was very strict in confining each party to his own means of proof, and as it has been expressed, regarded a trial as a cock fight wherein he won whose advocate was the gamest bird with the longest spurs. But we have come to take a more liberal view, and have done away with most of those features which gave rise to that reproach.'[8]

This sportman's theory of litigation was, however, deliberately abandoned and the use of discovery before trial (on both sides of Atlantic) very much extended.

[13.09] There is a distinction, however, noted by Wigmore[9], between a 'rule of evidence' and a 'rule of procedure and pleading'. The sole question for the law of evidence here is whether, because of surprise or lack of notice, certain evidence will be excluded. If no such effect is given, then the rules of evidence are no longer involved. But the policy of guarding against unfair surprise may lead to other rules, not of evidence. Then rules are of two sorts – the court could

---

[7] Wigmore, para 1846/6.
[8] *Ulrich v McConaughey* 763 Web 10, 20, 88 NW 150, 154 (1901).
[9] Wigmore, para 1848.

grant continuance or postpone the trial, or the claimant's pleadings may be required to state with greater particularity the footing upon which the claim is based.

[13.10] From 1850, in England, professional opinion developed in favour of better methods, broad in scope, for parties seeking inspection of documents in the adversaries' hands. Legislation and rules of court made these change. These provisions were plainly driven by a conviction that the existing principles were defective and that an inroad should be made on the theory that the adversary is entitled to keep his own evidence to himself until the trial. However, the rules applied to relevant documents specifically described and existing in the opponent's possession or control. There was also much issue made of the question of the conclusiveness of the opponent's oath as to the relevance of the document, and the fact of his possession.

Third person's documents

[13.11] A bill of discovery did not historically lie against a third person not a party, either for his testimony or for documents in his possession. But modern pre-trial procedures now provide opportunity for such document discovery. In criminal cases, at common law, no right of inspection of documents before trial was conceded to the accused, and of course the privilege against self-crimination prevented any such concession to the prosecution. But the same considerations of fairness which led to the statutes providing for a list of witnesses to be furnished to the accused, call also for conceding the opportunity of inspection of documents – the danger of an unscrupulous tampering with documents and the possibility of manufacturing a reputation being far less than for witnesses.

General principles

[13.12] Irish law has been characterised by a movement towards further – and arguably better – discovery. The inclusion of Order 31 and 29 in the 1986 Rules of the Superior Courts introduced third party discovery to the legal process. Recent Irish decisions, moreover, have clarified the basis upon which discovery is to be granted. This elucidation of principle and approach may be the most significant development in recent procedural legal history in indicating in which direction future Irish Courts will go. Decisions have not been short on general policy.

[13.13] According to McCarthy J in *Megaleasing UR Ltd v Quantum Data*[10]: 'In principle, the Courts should aid in obtaining all information relevant and necessary to the true determination of facts'.

---

[10]   *Megaleasing UR Ltd v Quantum Data* [1992] 1 IR 219 at 221.

In relation to both discovery by a party to an action (Order 31, rule 12), and discovery by a person not a party to the action (Order 31, rule 29), Finlay CJ in *Allied Irish Banks plc v Ernest & Whinney*[11] stated that:

> '... the basic purpose and reason for the procedure of discovery remains identical in both instances. It is to ensure as far as possible that the full facts concerning any matter in dispute before the Court are capable of being presented to the Court by the parties concerned so that justice on full information, rather than on a limited or partial revelation of the facts arising in a particular action may be done'.

O'Flaherty J[12], in the same case, commented that:

> 'The purpose of discovery is to help to define the issues as sharply as possible in advance so that the actual hearing is allowed to take its course as smoothly as possible. Discovery is but an instrument to advance the cause of justice. It should be availed of to give the parties a proper appraisal of the case and on occasion, at least, to remove same issues from the debate thus saving time and costs.'

On a tactical note, O'Flaherty J does note[13] that there has been the experience in other jurisdictions of discovery being used to swamp the opposing party with masses of material. To engage in such a tactic, he states, is as much an abuse, as to withhold relevant information.

[13.14] To pursue a little, however, the distinction between Order 31, rule 12 and Order 31, rule 29, the Supreme Court in *AIB v Ernest & Whinney*, clarified the distinct approach and criteria applicable to each. Finlay CJ[14] classified the various distinctions as being in regard to (1) the burden of proof, (2) judicial discretion and (3) the form of the order. It is worthwhile quoting from his judgement. Firstly, in regard to 'burden of proof':

> '... comparing the terms of these two rules, a major distinction between them is that in the event of an application for discovery by a party to an action, made pursuant to ord 31, r 12, it would appear that the court should only adjourn or misuse such an application if it is satisfied that it is not necessary, either at all or at the time at which it is made, either for disposing fairly of the cause or matter or for saving costs. The onus of establishing that would appear, prima facie, to lie upon the party against whom discovery is sought and who resists it. In the case of an order or discovery pursuant to r 29 however, where application is made for an order against a person not a party, I am satisfied, as has been held by Costello J in this case, that the onus is on the applicant to establish, firstly, that the party named is likely to have or to have had documents in his possession, custody or

---

[11] *Allied Irish Banks plc v Ernest & Whinney* [1993] 1 IR 375 and 390.
[12] [1993] 1 IR 375 at 396.
[13] [1993] 1 IR 375 at 396 and 397.
[14] [1993] 1 IR 375 at 388.

power and secondly, to establish that they are documents which are relevant to an issue arising or likely to arise out of the cause or matter.'

[13.15] Next, Finlay CJ deals with 'judicial discretion':

'The second significant difference between r 29 and r 12 of Ord 31, is that the proper construction of r 12 dealing with discovery by a party, is that the court's discretion to refuse it is confined to its being satisfied that either in the form of the application itself or in respect of the time at which it is made, it is not necessary either for disposing fairly of the cause or matter, or saving costs. The provisions of r 29, on the other hand, create a situation in which after it has been established to the satisfaction of the court that a person not a party has, or is likely to have, in his possession documents which are relevant to an issue arising, the court still has a further discretion.

This arises from the fact that the rule provides that, upon that being established, the leave of the court to make the order for discovery still is required.

I take the view that the further discretion thus arising must relate, even where documents may be in the custody or procurement of a stranger to the action, and where they may have some relevance to the issues arising in the action, to a consideration of particular oppression or prejudice which will be caused to the person called upon to discover such documents, not capable of being adequately compensated by such payment by the party seeking it of the costs of make such discovery.

I do not, however, consider that r 29 can be construed as imposing upon a party seeking an order for discovery pursuant to it an obligation, not only to establish that the person against whom the order is sought has or is likely to have in his possession or procurement documents which are relevant to an issue arising in the cause or matter, but also to establish specific documents as distinct from categories of documents which prima facie are relevant.'

[13.16] Finally, there is the 'form of the order':

'A third difference appears to me to arise, though not expressly provided for in r 29, between the form of order which a court should make pursuant to that rule when discovery is being granted, as distinct from the order which is made pursuant to Order 31, rule 12. In the case of the discovery by a party, it is sufficient to direct discovery of either a particular category of documents or all documents which are relevant to the issues arising in the case. The person who is obliged under sanction to make full discovery of such documents is a party to the action and knows, essentially, the issues which are arising, deriving such knowledge from the pleadings and notices which are part of the action at the time the discovery is made.

On the other hand, a stranger to an action can have no such knowledge, nor would it appear reasonable that he should be obliged to investigate or, more realistically, to engage a lawyer to investigate pleadings in the action, and to interpret them so as to permit him to conclude what documents are or are not relevant. Orders made pursuant to r 29, therefore should, in my view, in some simple form either by the annexing of pleadings or by a schedule to the order, identify the issues, by reference to the pleadings, to which an alleged relevance occurs.'

[13.17] McCarthy J, for his part noting that Order 31, rule 29, was there to advance to the course of justice, commented: 'It is extending the scope of discovery in a very material and helpful way'[15].

[13.18] Actions in which this procedure is invoked may vary from the simple, where the medical history of an injured person is concerned, to the complex, such as here where the facts concerned the Ministerial regulatory function over Insurance companies. The Minister contended there should be restriction on the form of the order, relying on an argument of hardship or oppression. McCarthy J dismissed this:

'Persons seeking discovery under Order 31 rule 29 must pay the costs of expenses of such discovery irrespective of any result in the action. I am not impressed by the case made in that part of the affidavit which I have quoted. One can well envisage the serious damage that might be done to a small firm of auditors or accountants or the like if they had to take one or two members of staff to devote to an exercise of little direct importance to that firm. Such an objection taken by a Department of State, charged with monitoring the insurance industry should not be sustained.' [16]

[13.19] O'Flaherty J was of a similar view, invoking a reminder of the alternative option of bringing the witnesses and documents together into court to produce:

'I think the case as presented before us does admit to the making of the order sought and that the interests of justice require that it should be made. The Minister's officers will be put to a degree of inconvenience, no doubt, but as between the obligation of the courts and, indeed the State (which is involved in one way or another in a great deal of litigation), to ensure that justice is done in any individual case, there is no doubt which should predominate and that is the interests of justice over the inconvenience of the departmental officers; especially when provision is made for the Minister's costs. The Minister's officers will have the consolation, too, of knowing that compliance with the order for discovery will be far less onerous than the alternative – which would involve attendance with all the documents day in and day out in court in answer to a subpoena duces tecum.' [17]

---

[15] [1993] 1 IR 375 at 393.
[16] [1993] 1 IR 375 at 395-6.
[17] [1993] 1 IR 375 at 397.

[13.20] Finlay CJ[18], commenting on the High Court decision in this case, and the information made available to him, laid down a marker with regard to the proofs in such an action:

'whereas in the submissions before this Court we have been afforded a written schedule linking each of the categories of documents to particular issues raised in the pleadings in one or other, or, in some instances, in both of the actions, such a document does not appear to have been produced in the hearing of the application in the High Court. Such a schedule or some similar document linking categories of documents to specific issues would, in my view, be an essential proof in an action such as this with multiple issues.'

[13.21] Once an order for discovery has been successfully obtained, the format which the affidavit of discovery should take, has been laid down in *Bula Ltd (in receivership) v Laurence Crowley*[19], which involved appeals against orders of discovery made in High Court, seeking further and better discovery of documentation concerned.

[13.22] With regard to the proper manner of identifying documents in respect of which a legal professional privilege is claimed on an affidavit of discovery, Finlay CJ referred to *Bula Ltd v Tara Mines Ltd*[20]. Walsh J therein stated that what was required was an individual listing of the documents, with the general classification of privilege claimed in respect of each document, indicated in such fashion by enumeration, as would convey to a reader of the affidavit the general nature of the document concerned in each individual case, together with the broad heading of privilege being claimed for it. Such is necessary, per Finlay CJ, to comply with the decision in *Smurfit Paribas Bank Ltd v AAB Export Finance Ltd*[21].

[13.23] With regard to the failure to make adequate discovery, Finlay CJ did not quite agree with Murphy J in the High Court[22] that discovery was a matter for the integrity of the parties themselves. Per Finlay CJ[23]:

'I am not satisfied that such an absolute protection of the decision by a deponent with regard to the question of discovery is warranted on principle. I accept that a court should be satisfied, as a matter of probability, that an error has occurred in an omission for an affidavit of discovery of documents on the basis of irrelevancy before making any order for further discovery and that it should not, in particular, permit the opposing party to indulge in exploratory or fishing operations.'

---

[18] [1993] 1 IR 375 at 392.
[19] *Bula Ltd (in receivership) v Laurence Crowley* [1990] ILRM 756.
[20] *Bula Ltd v Tara Mines Ltd* (5 February 1990, unreported) SC.
[21] *Smurfit Paribas Bank Ltd v AAB Export Finance Ltd* [1991] ILRM 588.
[22] (19 December 1989, ex temp).
[23] (5 February 1990, unreported) SC at 10.

[13.24] A similar admonition came from a Northern Irish court as to the limitations of discovery, and specifically the courts' role in restricting those parties who wish to gain access on a 'search' basis to information which might aid their case or indeed establish another: a facilitation which, if allowed, would make a mockery of the concept of 'public privilege', though it would favour the attainment of a modicum of freedom of information (the tension between the two being a constant element here (see public privilege at para **[8.91]**). The decision is that of Carswell J in *In the Matter of an Application by Glor na nGael for Judicial Review*[24]. The applicant sought an order for the production and inspection of certain documents within the possession of the Secretary of State for Northern Ireland. The respondent claimed they should not be disclosed on grounds of public interest immunity. Funding to the West Belfast Committee of Glor na nGael had been provided from November 1985 until August 1990, when the Committee was informed that the Secretary of State had directed that funding should cease where there was a risk such support would assist, directly or indirectly, a paramilitary organisation. Carswell J granted leave to apply for judicial review of that decision. The Association then sought discovery of the documents and an order was made by McCollum J for same. Some 47 items were discovered and inspected. However, objection was taken to the production of certain other documents including memoranda, minutes, and other correspondence, on the grounds it would be injurious to the public interest.

[13.25] The applicant argued that the withholding and editing of documents meant he had no means of ascertaining from essential documentary evidence what was presented to the Secretary of State when he made his decision to withhold funding. Rule 12(1) of the Rules of the Superior Court provided no such order should be made unless the court is of the opinion that the order is necessary either for disposing fairly of the cause or matter, or for saving costs. This, Carswell J said, meant that the party seeking production must show something more than a mere possibility that the documents might be of assistance to his case. His Lordship said there was a distinction to be made between discovery in judicial review and discovery in plenary actions. Judicial review was only concerned with the manner in which a decision was reached, not its merits. Per Carswell J:

> 'In the present case there had been no suggestion that the evidence relied on by the Secretary of State was inaccurate or false, nor had the Association pointed to any respect in which it might be said that he took into account the wrong considerations or omitted to take into account those to which he ought to have had regard. The Association wished to have material from which it could assess

---

[24] *In the Matter of an Application by Glor na nGael for Judicial Review* (1 March 1991, unreported) High Court of Justice of Northern Ireland.

the correctness of the Secretary of State's decision, by probing his reasons and the evidence upon which he formed his judgment. But the Secretary of State's reasons had been set out in affidavit form and were either valid or invalid. It was unnecessary to probe these reasons further. The court had set their face against what was referred to as 'contingent' or 'micawber' discovery, undertaken in the hope of eliciting some impropriety in arriving at the decision and founding a new case ... Discovery should not therefore be permitted to allow the Association to probe further the decision reached in the present case.'

Carswell J felt that discovery was not necessary at all in the Association's application for the purpose of dispensing fairly of the case, although some discovery had been given. This conclusion meant that it was unnecessary for his Lordship to consider the question of weighing or balancing competing public interests. The application was dismissed.

[13.26] The conflict of interest involved in the context of a claim for an order of discovery coupled with a claim of legal privilege, was enunciated by Finlay CJ in *Smurfit Paribas Bank Ltd v AAB Export France Ltd*[25], where such conflict resolved itself in favour of the claim of legal professional privilege (see with regard to legal professional privilege as private privilege below). Finlay CJ stated:

'... the requirement of the superior interest of the common good in the proper conduct of litigation which justified the immunity of communications from discovery insofar as they were made for the purpose of litigation as being the desirability in that good of the correct and efficient trial of actions by the courts.'[26]

[13.27] Significantly, with regard to the purpose of disclosure of documents on an order for discovery, is the comment in the High Court of Murphy J in *Bart Gormley v Ireland, AG, Minister for Communications and An Post*[27], viz, that the function of discovery, is that solely of the proper processing of litigation. Hence, it was emphasised by the court that copies were to be made by the solicitor only for counsel briefed and not to be inspected by any other person.

[13.28] On occasion, the parties themselves may not at trial have 'discovered' or requested relevant evidence in existence at the time of the trial. Such a situation arose in *Donal Murphy v Minister for Defence*[28]. The claim was one of negligence and breach of duty resulting in personal injuries incurred by the plaintiff, and had failed in the High Court. Application was made to adduce

---

[25] *Smurfit Paribas Bank Ltd v AAB Export France Ltd* [1991] ILRM 588.

[26] [1991] ILRM 588 at 598.

[27] *Bart Gormley v Ireland, AG, Minister for Communications and An Post* (7 March 1991, unreported) HC.

[28] *Donal Murphy v Minister for Defence* (19 April 1991, unreported) SC.

fresh evidence. The relevant applicable principles set down in *Lynagh v Mackin*[29] were invoked. Per Finlay CJ:

'(1)   The evidence sought to be adduced must have been in existence at the time of the trial and must have been such that it could not have been obtained with reasonable diligence for use at the trial;

(2)   The evidence must be such that if given it would probably have an important influence on the result of the case, though it need not be decisive;

(3)   The evidence must be such as is presumably to be believed or, in other words, it must be apparently credible, though it need not be incontrovertible.'

On application to the facts of this case, and in particular to the existence of a training and medical circular relevant to the case, these conditions were met. The court was also satisfied that there had not been, as claimed by the respondents, any want of due diligence in having failed to obtain an order of discovery. Given the absence of actual knowledge of the existence of same, O'Flaherty J termed this merely 'a mutual inadvertence to potentially important evidence' on the part of both parties.

[13.29] Given the aforementioned controversy, with regard to the various laws of evidence in the context of an inquiry or occasion of litigation – specifically those of tribunal hearings – it is interesting to note a determination of an issue of discovery in such a tribunal inquiry. The decision is that of *Haussman v Minister for the Marine, Ireland, the Attorney General, Southern Regional Fisheries Board & South Western Regional Fisheries Board*[30]. The facts here were that on 7 July 1990, one of the fourth named defendant's fishery patrol vessels sank, with the loss of the lives of four fishery patrol officers. The Minister for the Marine on 9 July 1990 appointed a person under s 728 of the Merchant Shipping Act 1894 to report on the nature and cause of the accident. That report was prepared by Captain Kirwan and delivered to the Minister. Subsequently, the Minister appointed the same Captain Kirwan to hold a preliminary inquiry under s 465 of the 1894 Act, but this was not proceeded with, a formal inquiry being established under s 466 of the 1894 Act chaired by O'Reilly DJ. The plaintiff, a widow of one of the deceased, sought an order compelling the defendants to produce copies of all documents and reports in their power, possession or procurement, utilised in the course of the inquiry on 9 July 1990. She was furnished with a copy of all witnesses' statements and other evidence the inquiry

---

[29]   *Lynagh v Mackin* [1970] IR 180.
[30]   *Haussman v Minister for the Marine, Ireland, the Attorney General, Southern Regional Fisheries Board & South Western Regional Fisheries Board* [1991] ILRM 387.

had before it when making the report under s 728, but not a copy of the report itself which the Minister refused. Blayney J considered the plaintiff's claim:

'These grounds might be summarised as follows: The plaintiff needs a copy of the report (1) to avail adequately of the inquiry, (2) because it constitutes necessary evidence for her at the inquiry, and (3) because she would be seriously prejudiced if she is unable to have it.

I am not convinced by these reasons. To start with the last, I do not think that the plaintiff will be in any way prejudiced. Her interest is to have the inquiry carry out as thorough an investigation as possible with a view hopefully to being able subsequently to establish that some party is civilly liable for her husband's death. The inquiry will not in an way be impeded in its investigation by not having Captain Kirwan's report before it, and so her interest in having as thorough an investigation as possible earned out will not be prejudiced.

As to the second point, the report is clearly not necessary evidence being no more than the findings of a third party based on evidence which the inquiry will undoubtedly have before it also, and there must be some doubt as to whether it would be admissible evidence since it would be purporting to express views on matters which it is not for the inquiry to decide.

Finally, I do not think that the report is necessary to enable the plaintiff to avail adequately of the inquiry. The copies of the statements and other evidence which have been furnished to her contain all the information she will need in order to take part fully in the inquiry. I am satisfied accordingly that the grounds put forward by the plaintiff cannot be supported and that it has not been shown that she has a right to the production of the report ... Reference was also made to *Holloway v Belenos Publications Ltd*, but in my opinion that cannot assist the plaintiff either. It was concerned with discovery and the court's inherent jurisdiction to make an order for discovery. But this is not a motion for discovery: it is a claim to a personal right, based on natural and constitutional justice, to the production of the report. The *Holloway* case does not support any such right.

In my opinion the plaintiff has not established that she has a right to the production of the report and so the relief sought must be refused.'[31]

Limitations on discovery

[13.30] Limitations are placed on the use of discovery inter partes as well as on third party discovery. In *Galvin v Twomey*[32], O'Flaherty J in the High Court went back to the rationale of the procedure to enunciate such a limitation. He was especially concerned with what might be termed 'fishing' expedition by the parties.

---

[31] [1991] ILRM 387 at 384.
[32] *Galvin v Twomey* [1994] 2 ILRM 315.

'... is it a correct use of the remedy of discovery that is either inter partes discovery or in regard to third party discovery, to allow a party access to documents so that the party can plead a cause of action which has not been pleaded up to date? This has not been shown to be possible on existing authority nor would I consider that it is justified in principle. The point of discovery ... is to aid a party in the process of litigation; it is not to be invoked so as to enable a person to plead a cause of action which he is not otherwise in a position to do.'

'[The plaintiff] ... cannot be permitted to launch his proceedings and then hope by discovery to be able to amend his pleadings and thereby make his case. In my judgement that is not the purpose of discovery and would be a quite wrong use of the procedural remedy of discovery'.[33]

Relevance

[13.31] Relevance, of course, is always a primary criteria and consideration for discovery. In *Burke v Central Independent Television*[34], the issue as to whether the documents in question were of any relevance to the case was raised by O'Flaherty J[35]. Since they appeared to him to be of no relevance, he points out they might properly not have been discovered at all. The main basis on which that case, which concerned a claim for damages in respect of a libel allegedly published by the defendant in a television programme which dealt with the activities of the IRA and its fundraising, had been argued, however, was that if the names of the people who had supplied information to the defendant were revealed, or the documents containing such information were revealed, the lives of the persons who provided the information or who were named in the documents might be put at risk. Murphy J had ordered discovery on the terms that only the lawyers acting for the plaintiffs would have access to the documents. However, on appeal the Supreme Court felt that such was not a procedure which could be adopted by the court, and in any event, would constitute an undesirable breach of the duty which counsel owed to their clients, and a breach of the proper trust between a lawyer and client.

[13.32] Ultimately, discovery was not granted, on the basis that the constitutional right of individual citizens to the protection of their life and of their bodily integrity, must of necessity take significant precedence over even so important a right as the right of citizens to the protection and vindication of their good name.

[13.33] The strictness of the courts' approach in relation to third party discovery is illustrated by the decision in *Angelo Fusco v Edward O'Dea*[36]. Order 31

---

[33] [1994] 2 ILRM 315 at 320.
[34] *Burke v Central Independent Television* [1994] 2 ILRM 161.
[35] [1994] 2 ILRM 161 at 186.
[36] *Angelo Fusco v Edward O'Dea* [1994] ILRM 389.

rule 29, the Supreme Court emphasised, was an unusual provision in that it required a stranger to an action to make discovery, and thus should be construed strictly. The onus was on the applicant to satisfy the court that the documents were in the third parties' possession or power. The court emphasised that whether such an order should be granted was a matter for the courts' discretion and it was not available as of right. This restrictive approach had been given earlier expression by Costello J in *AIB plc v Ernest v Whinney*:

'The onus is on the applicant to satisfy the Court that such documents are in the notice party's power or possession. If it does not do so, the Court has no jurisdiction to make an order'

The Supreme Court emphasised in *Fusco v O'Dea*:

'Ord 31 r 29 is an unusual provision in that it requires a stranger to an action to make discovery.

Accordingly it should be construed strictly ....'

[13.34] In relation to the question which arose in this case as to whether such an order for third party discovery should be made against a sovereign state, it was felt that unless the foreign state had submitted itself to the jurisdiction of the Irish courts, to allow discovery would undermine the principle of immunity of sovereign states. Moreover, Order 11 was exhaustive as to service outside the jurisdiction and since Order 31, rule 29 was silent as to its possible application to third parties outside the jurisdiction, it should not be read as conferring an extra-territorial jurisdiction on the Irish Courts in addition to that conferred by Order 11.

[13.35] Another decision addressing the issue of 'possession or power' of documents by a third party is *Bula Ltd v Tara Mines*[37]. The plaintiffs here sought discovery of certain documents in the possession of advisers retained by the Minister for Energy. An issue arose as to whether Order 31, rule 29, was the appropriate procedure. The High Court felt it was. The plaintiffs claimed not, however, as they would then have to bear the costs of third party discovery. The Minister argued that the documents were not in his 'possession or power' within the meaning of Order 31, rule 12. O'Flaherty J found that documents that would be discoverable inter parses were the final documents, approved (by the adviser) for sight by the Minister. Everything else was preparatory, and therefore personal to the adviser, and therefore not discoverable. Regarding the final documents, the Minister had an enforceable legal right to obtain whoever actually held them, therefore they were in his 'power', and discoverable under Order 31, rule 12.

---

[37]   *Bula Ltd v Tara Mines* [1994] ILRM 111.

[13.36] An issue arose in *O'Brien v Ireland and AG and Minister for Defence*[38] with regard to judicial inspection of documents on a claim of privilege. It was an application for an Order of Discovery of documents relating to a claim of damages in relation to the death of a member of the Irish army while serving with the United Nations (UN) forces in South Lebanon. The defendants made a claim of privilege in relation to three items: the UN UNIFIL Board of Inquiry Report, the UN Contingent Book of Inquiry Report and the Court of Inquiry Report (under the Defence Act 1954). An application to the Minister for further and better discovery having been refused, the plaintiff looked to the High Court for an order directing the defendants to make further and better discovery of the documents in their possession relating to the death, and to specify by enumeration each and every document with the general classification of privilege claimed in respect of each such numbered document. The defendants claimed privilege under the Diplomatic Relations and Immunities Act 1967 in relation to the UN Reports, on grounds of public interest and security. The Defence Acts and regulations thereunder also provided the documents were not admissible.

[13.37] The plaintiff relied on a number of Supreme Court judgments (eg *Murphy v Corporation of Dublin; Ambiorix Ltd v Minister for Environment*[39]), in which the Court maintained that the ultimate decision in relation to the issue of disclosure or non-disclosure of documentation in proceedings before the courts, must lie with the courts themselves.

[13.38] O'Hanlon J looked at these judgments and noted that their statements of law were expressed in absolute terms, as leaving it to the ultimate decision of the courts in all cases to decide what documentary evidence must be produced (if production is sought by appropriate means), and what documentary evidence may be exempted from production, and to decide where necessary between conflicting claims based on the public interest between compelling production of documents and exempting them from production. He continued:

> 'I do not consider, however, that either decision was intended to convey that the power of the legislature to intervene and confer the privilege of exemption from production and specified conferring of documentary or other evidence was curtailed or restricted in any way, save in so far as any legislation enacted must not conflict with the overriding provisions of the Constitution.'

---

[38] *O'Brien v Ireland and AG and Minister for Defence* (26 August 1994, unreported) HC (O'Hanlon J).

[39] *Murphy v Corporation of Dublin* [1972] IR 215; *Ambiorix Ltd v Minister for Environment* [1992] 1 IR 272.

[13.39] O'Hanlon J then refered to *Cully v Northern Bank Finance Corp*[40], where documents of the Central Bank were held to be privileged by reason of the oath of secrecy taken by those employed by the Bank, in conformity with the provisions of the Central Bank Act 1942, s 31 ('statutory privilege'); and the decision in *AG v (Beef) Tribunal*[41], where the Supreme Court considered that privilege from disclosure of contents and details of discussions at meetings of the government, derived of necessity from the Constitution. The effect of these decisions, per O'Hanlon J, appeared to be:

> 'that a complete prohibition on disclosure exists in such a case without the courts being left with any scope to decide where necessary between conflicting claims based on the public interest between compelling production of documents and exempting them from production.'

[13.40] O'Hanlon J then accepted that the description given in each case was intended to comprise all the documentation arising in and derived from the different inquiries referred to therein. He applies the following principle, referred to by Finlay CJ[42] in *Ambiorix,* to uphold the defendant's claim of privilege:

> 'There is no obligation on the judicial power to examine any particular document before deciding that it is exempt from production, and it can and will in many instances uphold a claim of privilege in respect of a document merely on the basis of a description of its nature and contents which it (the judicial power) accepts.'

[13.41] This is perhaps a surprising limitation on the judicial discretion apparently conferred by the decisions in *Murphy* et al. It could be seen as an example, in the Irish context, of perceived judicial condoning of the suppression of evidence in the 'public interest' by their failure to scrutinise ministerial claims. It is also a reminder of ministerial/public interest privilege seen here and in *AG v Beef Tribunal*.[43]

[13.42] Certainly O'Hanlon J's approach here, in the context of such a 'public interest' privilege, is in contrast to that taken by him in *O'Driscoll v DJ Wallace*[44], where the solicitor's request for copies of all statements for the Guards, before deciding to make an election, met with the response that 'it would be illogical to hold such disclosure cannot be applied for – until the

---

[40] *Cully v Northern Bank Finance Corp* [1984] ILRM 683.
[41] *AG v (Beef) Tribunal* [1993] ILRM 82.
[42] *Ambiorix Ltd v Minister for Environment* [1992] 1 IR 277.
[43] *AG v Beef Tribunal* [1993] ILRM 82.
[44] *O'Driscoll v DJ Wallace* (17 August 1994, unreported) HC (O'Hanlon J).

accused made an election' – although this is perhaps explicable on the basis that courts are more lenient on such matters in criminal cases.

[13.43] In *Aquatechnology Ltd v National Standards Authority of Ireland*[45], Murray J delivered the judgment of the Supreme Court, on an appeal from an order of the High Court, refusing the application of the appellant for discovery. The appellant was challenging the failure of the respondents to certify his product (plastic piping), and was seeking access to other third party applications. However, the grounds on which he was challenging the respondent's actions did not contain any allegation of discrimination or unequal treatment. Murray J stated quite clearly the principle that:

'…documents sought on discovery must be relevant, directly or indirectly, to the matters in issue between the parties in the proceedings. Furthermore, an applicant for discovery must show it is reasonable for the Court to suppose that the documents contain information which may enable the applicant to advance his own case or to damage the case of his adversary. An applicant is not entitled to discovery based on mere speculation or on the basis of what has been traditionally characterised as a fishing expedition.'[46]

[13.44] Murray J concluded that the discovery application could not be successful in the context in which it arose:

'Fundamentally, the Appellant has claimed that discovery of these documents concerning the applications made by third parties for a certification of their particular products is appropriate in order to demonstrate that the first-named Respondent treated the application in a discriminatory fashion as compared to its other Irish competitors. In my view the first-named Respondents were correct in relying on the fact that this is not an issue which forms part of the issues in the proceedings since it did not form part of the Statement of Grounds for which leave to apply for judicial review upon by the Appellants in the Statement on which the proceedings are based are not, in my view, in any way open to the construction that they were making the case that the first-named Respondent had exercised bias or discrimination in their evaluation of applications for certification for plastic piping by Irish companies other than the Appellant, by reason of the origin of the product or otherwise.'[47]

---

[45] *Aquatechnology Ltd v National Standards Authority of Ireland* (10 July 2000, unreported) SC.

[46] *Aquatechnology Ltd v National Standards Authority of Ireland* (10 July 2000, unreported) SC at p 6, para 24.

[47] *Aquatechnology Ltd v National Standards Authority of Ireland* (10 July 2000, unreported) SC at p 12, para 26.

Discovery and legal professional privilege

[13.45] Legal professional privilege can, of course, defeat a claim for discovery, and it is interesting to note how recent decisions which have dealt with this heading of private privilege, are indicative of the Irish courts' more general attitude to discovery, private privilege claims and public interest immunity. They may well give some indication of how the law is developing in this area and in accordance with what criteria. A fairly straightforward decision, in terms of the effect of legal professional privilege, is *SPUC v Grogan (No 3)*[48]. Here, the defendants sought to introduce the evidence of P, a senior adviser to the Attorney General (AG), as to the nature and effect in law of the solemn declaration to the protocol of the Maastricht Treaty. It was argued the evidence was (1) irrelevant (since the protocol had not yet come into effect) and (2) privileged.

[13.46] Morris J accepted that any evidence relating to the solemn declaration was indeed irrelevant to the issues before the Court, and that evidence sought in relation to legal advice given by P to the AG was inadmissible in accordance with the principle of legal professional privilege. This constituted a clear recognition of legal professional privilege in the relationship between senior adviser to the AG and the AG.

[13.47] In contrast, is the decision in *Irish Press plc v Ingersoll*[49], not, strictly speaking, a case on legal professional privilege, but involving an order for third party discovery against a firm of solicitors in relation to documents relating to a company in which each of the parties was a 50 per cent shareholder. The case was a section 205 application, alleging the persons appointed to the company by the respondent had acted in his, and not the companies, interests. The petitioner sought discovery of attendances, advices, documents, draft documents and internal memos relating to one of those companies. The solicitors objected to making discovery of documents which were their own property, essential for the daily administration of their office and generated solely for internal private use. Barron J held that discovery of documents did not depend upon the private nature or ownerships of such documents, but on their relevance, that is, what the party seeking discovery might consider to be relevant, and that since the allegation in respect of the respondent's appointee was a serious issue in the proceedings, discovery should be made. The notice party objected that it would not be in a position to determine what is or is not relevant. Barron J felt that was a fair objection but could be met by the form in which the order would be settled.

---

48 *SPUC v Grogan (No 3)* [1992] 2 IR 471.
49 *Irish Press plc v Ingersoll* [1994] 1 IR 209.

[13.48] Barron J did accept that this was a serious matter for any firm of professional advisers:

> 'Matters which come within their own administrative processes are clearly sensitive areas and in most cases would involve an unnecessary interference with their right to run their own affairs as they wish. It must be in only very rare cases that a document coming within [the category of attendance/memo etc] could be identified as being relevant to an issue in litigation to which such advisers are not a party'[50]

The Supreme Court confirmed the order, varying it only insofar as the concession made by the petitioner confined the documents to be discovered to attendances.

[13.49] A 'core' decision on legal professional privilege, illustrating the limitations on the 'cover' provided by legal professional privilege, is *Smurfit Paribas Bank Ltd v AAB Export Finance Ltd*[51]. The case involved a dispute between plaintiff and defendant in relation to the defendant's floating charge. The documents comprised correspondence between defendant and solicitor relating to the charge. The case drew a distinction between legal assistance and legal advice. The Supreme Court commented that for the expansion of legal professional privilege, from cases of actual or contemplated litigation, to cases of legal assistance other than advice, to be justified, the documents should be closely and proximately linked to the conduct of litigation. There was no sufficient public interest or common good to be secured justifying exemption from disclosure of communications to lawyers for the purpose of obtaining legal assistance other than advice, and which did not contain any relationship with the area of potential litigation. This decision was in the context of the assertion of a vigorous judicial discretion in such matters. Per Finlay CJ:

> '... the question as to whether or not a party to litigation will be privileged to refuse to produce particular evidence is a matter within the sole competence of the Courts.'[52]

[13.50] There has always, of course, been recognition that the privilege has limitations. It did not cover 'criminal activities', for example, but in *Murphy v Kirwan*[53], the Supreme Court expanded this somewhat. The case involved a claim by the plaintiffs for specific performance of an agreement, the defendants' motion for dismissal on the grounds of abuse of the court resulting in its dismissal, and the defendants' claim for damages, wherein they sought discovery of legal advices relating to the specific performance action up to the

---

[50] [1994] 1 IR 209 at 210.
[51] *Smurfit Paribas Bank Ltd v AAB Export Finance Ltd* [1990] 1 IR 469.
[52] [1990] 1 IR 469 at 475.
[53] *Murphy v Kirwan* [1993] 3 IR 501.

date of trial. The Supreme Court stated that the reason for the exception to legal professional privilege was that professional privilege could not and must not be applied so as to be injurious to the interests of justice and those in the administration of justice. It thus did not cover those persons who had been guilty of conduct of moral turpitude, even though it might not be fraud.

[13.51] *Bula Ltd v Crowley*[54] clarified this somewhat, however, in stating that exemption from the doctrine of legal professional privilege is restricted to cases where there is an allegation against the person claiming privilege which contains a clear element of moral turpitude, as is contained in allegations of fraud, criminal conduct or conduct constituting a direct interference with the administration of justice (this did not include the commission of a tort.) *Bula* had involved the plaintiff's claim that the defendant was negligent as a receiver, in having obtained legal advice and failing to follow it, resulting in damage to the defendant.

[13.52] In a decision which attempted to 'claw back' the heading of legal professional privilege, Finlay CJ found a judicial discretion to look at the documents in question, in order to decide if they should be available, to be 'quite inconsistent with the principle applicable to legal professional privilege'[55]. He reiterated his view given in *Smurfit Paribas v AAB Export Finance*[56], that the underlying principle of legal professional privilege was as expressed in *Anderson v Bank of British Columbia*[57], where Jessell MR made it clear that a person entitled to and consulting a lawyer, should be able to place unrestricted and unbounded confidence in the professional agent, and that the communication he so made should be kept secret unless with his consent, it was disclosed.

Finlay CJ went further in *Bula*[58], saying it had become clear as stated by Lawrence LJ in *Minter v Priest*[59]:

'that such privilege extended not only to advice sought and obtained in the expectation of or in preparation for actual or pending litigation, but also to such communications with a lawyer as pass as professional communication in a professional capacity.'

[13.53] The contention made in this case, that exception to legal professional privilege should be extended to any case where it was proved that the nature of

---

[54] *Bula Ltd v Crowley* [1994] 1 ILRM 495.
[55] [1994] 1 ILRM 495 at 497.
[56] *Smurfit Paribas v AAB Export Finance* [1990] 1 IR 469.
[57] *Anderson v Bank of British Columbia* (1876) 2 Ch D 644.
[58] *Bula v Crowley* [1994] 1 ILRM 495 at 498.
[59] *Minter v Priest* [1929] 1 KB 655.

the legal advice obtained by a party was clearly relevant to an issue as to the commission of a tort, was unilaterally rejected by Finlay CJ:

'It would be a massive undermining ... of the important confidence in relation to communications between lawyers and their clients which is a fundamental part of our system of justice and is considered in all the authorities to be a major contribution to the proper administration of justice.'[60]

[13.54] With regard to the suggestion that the courts should look at the documents to assess the strength of their relevance to the issue and exercise their discretion accordingly, Finlay CJ dismissed it as being based on a fundamental error:

'Two conditions would exist before any question of a lifting of or exemption from this legal professional privilege could arise. The first is that the legal advice and the communications are probably relevant to one of the issues concerned, and the second is that the situation arising in the case comes within one of the special exemptions which have been identified so as to destroy the privilege. To contend as is contended in this aspect of the case, as well as on the first general principle that the more relevant or important the legal advice may be, the greater is the discretion of the court to lift the privilege is to confuse two separate preconditions to the removal of the privilege.'[61]

[13.55] The newly contended exemption to legal professional privilege was thus here denied. However, it should be remembered that whereas in *Bula v Crowley*[62] the documents concerned legal advice, in *Smurfit* they were merely documents concerning instructions between solicitor and client in relation to a charge taken by the defendant over the assets of a third party.

If *Bula v Crowley* seems a vindication, then, of legal professional privilege, one has to look closer at the earlier decisions in *Murphy v Kirwan* and *Smurfit Paribas v AAB* to see what they now mean. *Murphy v Kirwan*[63] followed in the tradition of the exemption applied in *R v Cox & Railton*[64]. In *Murphy*, Finlay CJ[65] had pointed out that the real reason for the exemption was that 'a professional privilege cannot and must not be applied so as to be injurious to the interests of justice where persons have been guilty of conduct of moral turpitude or of dishonest conduct, even though it may not be fraud', and continued:

---

[60] *Bula v Crowley* [1994] 1 ILRM 495 at 498 per Finlay CJ.
[61] [1994] 1 ILRM 495 at 498-499.
[62] *Bula v Crowley* [1994] 1 ILRM 495.
[63] *Murphy v Kirwan* [1993] 3 IR 501.
[64] *R v Cox & Railton* (1884) 14 QBD 153.
[65] *Murphy v Kirwan* [1993] 3 IR 501 at 511 per Finlay CJ.

'Nothing could be more injurious to the administration of justice nor the interests of justice than that a person should falsely and maliciously bring an action, and should abuse for an ulterior or improper purpose the processes of the court'.[66]

By contrast with his comments in *Bula*, in *Smurfit*, Finlay CJ had stated:

'The existence of a privilege or exemption from disclosure for communications made between a person and his lawyer clearly constitutes a potential restriction and diminution of the full disclosure both prior to and during the course of legal proceedings which in the interests of the common good is desirable for the purpose of ascertaining the truth and rendering justice. Such privilege should, therefore, in my view, only be granted by the courts in instances which have been identified as securing an objective which in the public interest in the proper conduct of the administration of justice can be said to outweigh the disadvantage arising from the restriction of disclosure of all the facts.

It is necessary to bear these general considerations in mind in attempting to ascertain the underlying principle which appears to have led to the expansion of the privilege for communications with a lawyer from cases of actual or contemplated litigation to cases of communications seeking legal advice and/or legal assistance other than advice. The decided cases do not appear to me to provide any satisfactory explanation of this expansion. For the expansion to be justified, having regard to the considerations which I have just set out in this judgment, it would appear necessary that it should be closely and proximately linked to the conduct of litigation and the function of administering justice in the courts.

Where a person seeks or obtains legal advice there are good reasons to believe that he necessarily enters the area of potential litigation. The necessity to obtain legal advice would in broad terms appear to envisage the possibility of a legal challenge or query as to the correctness or effectiveness of some step which a person is contemplating. Whether such query or challenge develops or not, it is clear that a person is then entering the area of possible litigation.

Having regard to those considerations I accept that where it is established that a communication was made between a person and his lawyer acting for him as a lawyer for the purpose of obtaining from such lawyer legal advice, whether at the initiation of the client or the lawyer, that communication made on such an occasion should in general be privileged or exempt from disclosure, except with the consent of the client.

Similar considerations do not, however, it seems to me apply to communications made to a lawyer for the purpose of obtaining his legal assistance other than advice. There are many tasks carried out by a lawyer for his client and properly within the legal sphere, other than the giving of advice, which could not be said to contain any real relationship with the area of potential litigation. For such

---

[66] *Murphy v Kirwan* [1993] 3 IR 501 at 511 per Finlay CJ.

communications there does not appear to me to be any sufficient public interest or feature of the common good to be secured or protected which could justify an exemption from disclosure.

Accepting as I do, therefore, the inferences drawn by the learned trial judge from his perusal of the documents which he was entitled to and indeed bound to carry out, I also find myself in agreement with the principles of law applied by him to the inferences thus raised and accordingly would affirm his decision and dismiss this appeal.

I have summarised in this judgment the arguments as they were presented to this court on behalf of the defendant and the plaintiff. No general challenge to the overall concept of privilege for communications in certain circumstances between persons and their lawyers was raised and no issue arose or was considered concerning the exceptions to such privilege such as where the purpose of seeking legal advice might be the commission of criminal or tortious acts.

This judgment is, therefore, not intended to deal with any aspect of these problems.'[67]

[13.56] McCarthy J's judgment in *Smurfit* was to similar effect:

'I join with the Chief Justice in stating that the question as to whether or not a party to litigation will be privileged to refuse to produce particular evidence is a matter within the sole competence of the courts. It follows that the courts have whatever power is necessary to examine any relevant documents, irrespective of the wishes of the parties and to determine whether any communication, written or otherwise, between a party to litigation and any other person or body is privileged from disclosure.

In the instance case, the fundamental issue arises from the contrasting demands – candour by the client to his solicitor and the public interest in the true resolution of litigation. In my view communication of fact leading to the drafting of legal documents and requests for the preparation of such, albeit made to a solicitor, unless and until the same results in the provision of legal advice, is not privileged from disclosure.'[68]

[13.57] Why, then, this change of heart between *Smurfit* and *Bula*, and how significant is it? How effective is *Bula* in clawing back the territory carved out earlier? Where does it leave the certainty of legal professional privilege?

[13.58] Lest the inroads on legal professional privilege be taken to mark the beginnings of an era of 'openness and disclosure', it is useful to note the relative ease with which the High Court, in *Goodman International v Hamilton (No 3)*[69],

---

[67] *Smurfit Paribas v AAB Export Finance* [1990] 1 IR 469 at 477 per Finlay CJ.

[68] [1990] 1 IR 469 at 480.

[69] *Goodman International v Hamilton (No 3)* [1993] 3 IR 320.

found a privilege for TDs. The notice parties (three members of the Oireachtas) submitted that the relationship between a member of the public and a member of the Oireachtas, in cases where such a member of the public gave information of public interest to such member of the Oireachtas on the understanding that his identify would not be disclosed, was a relationship falling within the conditions identified by Gavan Duffy J in *Cook v Carroll*[70], and to which, accordingly, private privilege attached. The High Court (Geoghegan J) found it unnecessary to decide the issue on that basis and commented that 'any unnecessary extension of privilege by reference to fixed categories of relationships would seem to me to offend the jurisprudence of the Irish Courts'.

[13.59] Geoghegan J found it inappropriate to apply the test in *Cook v Carroll* (Wigmore's criteria) to the privilege here, which he said had '… a direct public interest dimension far beyond the mere private interest in confidentiality.' He then refered to *Murphy*, *Geraghty* and *Ambiorix*:

> 'The common factor in these cases was a rejection of any kind of class or category privilege. Underlining them is the public interest in the administration of justice. The exclusion of admissible and relevant evidence is in general contrary to that public interest. It is for the courts to decide on the merits of a plea of privilege in any particular case. But in no Irish case has it ever been held that there are no circumstances where the general public's interest in the non-exclusion of admissible and relevant evidence cannot be over-ridden by a conflicting public interest in a particular case in favour of non-disclosure.'[71]

Geoghegan J then adopted the House of Lords decision in *D v NSPCC*[72] which he said enunciated the principle that:

> '… confidentiality alone is never a ground for non-disclosure but it may be a relevant factor in determining whether there is a public interest in non-disclosure'.

[13.60] It is worth citing in full Geoghegan J's reference to *D v NSPCC*, as it may well form the cornerstone in future of 'public interest' type approaches to discovery in this area.[73]

> 'Subject to slight modifications necessitated by *Cook v Carroll* [1945] IR 515 and *ER v JR* [1981] ILRM 125, I accept and adopt the summary of the legal rules relating to permitted non-disclosure of information contained in the speech of Lord Edmund-Davies in *D v NSPCC* [1978] AC 171, which, at p 245 of the report, reads as follows:

---

70 *Cook v Carroll* [1945] IR 515.
71 *Goodman International v Hamilton (No 3)* [1993] 3 IR 320 at 325 per Geoghegan J.
72 *D v NSPCC* [1978] AC 171.
73 *Goodman International v Hamilton (No 3)* [1993] 3 IR 320 at 328-330 per Geoghegan J.

"(I)   In civil proceedings a judge has no discretion, simply because what is contemplated is the disclosure of information which has passed between persons in a confidential relationship (other than that of lawyer and client), to direct a party to that relationship that he need not disclose that information even though its disclosure is (a) relevant to and (b) necessary for the attainment of justice in the particular case. If (a) and (b) are established, the doctor or the priest must be directed to answer if, despite the strong dissuasion of the judge, the advocate persists in seeking disclosure.

This is also true of all other confidential relationships in the absence of a special statutory provision...

(II)   But where (i) a confidential relationship exists (other than that of lawyer and client) and (ii) disclosure would be in breach of some ethical or social value involving the public interest, the court has a discretion to uphold a refusal to disclose relevant evidence provided it considers that, on balance, the public interest would be better served by excluding such evidence.

(III) In conducting the necessary balancing operation between competing aspects of public interest, the presence (or absence) or involvement of the central government in the matter of disclosure is not conclusive either way, though in practice it may affect the cogency of the argument against disclosure ...

(IV)   The sole touchstone is the public interest, and not whether the party from whom disclosure is sought was acting under a 'duty' – as opposed to merely exercising "powers". A party who acted under some duty may find it easier to establish that public interest was involved than one merely exercising powers, but that is another matter.

(V)   The mere fact that relevant information was communicated in confidence does not necessarily mean that it need not be disclosed. But where the subject matter is clearly of public interest, the *additional* fact (if such it be) that to break the seal of confidentiality would endanger that interest will in most (if not all) cases probably lead to the conclusion that disclosure should be withheld. And it is difficult to perceive of any judicial discretion to exclude relevant and necessary evidence save in respect of confidential information communicated in a confidential relationship.

(VI)   The disclosure of all evidence to the trial of an issue being at all times a matter of considerable public interest, the question to be determined is whether it is clearly demonstrated that in the particular case the public interest would nevertheless be better served by excluding evidence despite its relevance. If, on balance, the matter is left in doubt, disclosure should be ordered."

Even though some of these rules may not be relevant to the case, I thought it best to set out the suggested rules in full so as to place those which are relevant in context. I should also add that I can see no relevant difference in principle between information given on a confidential basis to the intent that it would not be disclosed and information given with a view to its being publicly aired but on the understanding that the identity of the informant would not be disclosed. The principles on which the confidence is each should be maintained by a court or tribunal are the same.

In my view the combination of the second and sixth principles as enunciated by Lord Edmund-Davies gave the respondent a discretion as to whether he would insist on disclosure. Having regard to all the surrounding circumstances and in particular the fact that the unknown informants could not reasonably have expected that, through an accidental and erroneous understanding of constitutional privilege, the members of the Oireachtas laid themselves open to being forced to disclose and the fact that the respondent has at all times made clear that no hearsay evidence will be admitted to undermine the good names of the applicants, the discretion in my view would have to be exercised in favour of non-disclosure. I have therefore arrived at the same decision as the respondent by a different route. For this reason I do not find it necessary to comment on the forceful arguments of Mr Gleeson and Mr O'Donnell on *Gravel v US* (1972) 408 US 606. With regard to the Canadian case already referred to, I have thought it best not to rely on it. In the first place it was a kind of moot in that the judges were answering academic questions without knowing the facts which led to their being asked and secondly it related to a criminal trial. It has always been acknowledged that many instances of privilege have to give way if the guilt or innocence of an accused is at stake.

For the reasons which I have given I refuse judicial review as sought.'

The question here is whether that decision is indicative of the ever-expanding head of 'public interest' privilege and its subsuming of all 'confidential' private relationships analogous to lawyer/client.

[13.61] Both 'public interest' and legal professional privilege were involved in *Breathnach v Ireland (No 3)*[74]. The plaintiff had brought proceedings against the defendant, claiming damages for assault and battery, false imprisonment, etc. The High Court ordered the DPP to discover 'all records relating to communications between (members of the gardaí) and the DPP'. The DPP claimed privilege on grounds of public interest and contemplation of litigation.

[13.62] Keane J applied the following legal principles, and in so doing, attempted to clarify those principles governing the law in this area:

'A party is entitled to the production and inspection of documents in the possession, custody or power of a person who is not a party to the proceedings where the documents are relevant to an issue arising or likely to arise out of the

---

[74] *Breathnach v Ireland (No 3)* [1993] 2 IR 458.

proceedings. This power was conferred for the first time by Order 31, r 29 of the Rules of the Superior Courts 1986, and it is clear that in deciding whether to make an order the same principles apply as in applications for discovery against parties to the proceedings. The principle was thus stated by Brett LJ in *Compagnie Financiere du Pacifique v The Peruvian Guano Co* (1882) 11 QBD 55 at 63, in a passage which has frequently been cited with approval:

> 'It seems to me that every document relates to the matters in question in the action, which would not only be evidence upon any issue, but also which, it is reasonable to suppose, contains information which may – not which must – either directly or indirectly enable the party requiring the affidavit either to advance his own case or to damage the case of his adversary. I have put in the words 'either directly or indirectly', because, as it seems to me, a document can properly be said to contain information which may enable the party requiring the affidavit either to advance his own case or to damage the case of his adversary, if it is a document which may fairly lead him to a train of inquiry, which may have either of those two consequences ...'"[75]

Keane J went on to point out that it had at one time been the law that there were classes of documents wholly protected by executive privilege and even scrutiny by a court. That had been rejected in a triad of cases. Those, he noted, however, were civil cases, as was the present one. Yet in this case, the documents sought to be discovered related exclusively to criminal proceedings.

[13.63] Walsh J had emphasised in *Murphy v Dublin Corporation* that the court was not concerned with the considerations that might arise in a criminal case 'where the refusal to disclose certain evidence relevant to the trial could result in the condemnation of an innocent accused'. Keane J himself, in *DPP (Hanley) v Holly,* rejected the view in *Attorney General v Simpson (No 2)*[76] that police communications were, as a class, privileged, and rejected any claim to privilege here, also, to the extent that it is based on the documents belonging to a particular class.

[13.64] Keane J pointed out[77] that if he was to accept the claim for privilege here, the DPP 'would be in a position to prevent the courts from inspecting any documents which came into being for the purpose of criminal proceedings by making a claim in similar terms. That would be wholly at odds with the constitutional position of the courts as laid down in the authorities to which I have referred.'

---

[75] [1993] 2 IR 458 at 467.
[76] *Attorney General v Simpson (No 2)* [1959] IR 105.
[77] *Breathnach v Ireland (No 3)* [1993] 2 IR 458 at 469.

[13.65] Public interest at this juncture again enters the question:

'... [T]he court, as I understand the law, is required to balance the public interest in the proper administration of justice against the public interest reflected in the grounds put forward for non-disclosure in the present case. The public interest in the prevention and prosecution of crime must be put in the scales on the one side. It is only where the first public interest outweighs the second public interest that an inspection should be undertaken or disclosure should be ordered. In considering the first public interest, it is necessary to determine to what extent, if any, the relevant documents may advance the plaintiff's case or damage the defendants' case or fairly lead to an enquiry which may have either of those consequences. In the case of the second public interest, the various factors set out by Mr Liddy must be given due weight. Again, as has been pointed out in the earlier decisions, there may be documents the very nature of which is such that inspection is not necessary to determine on which side the scales come down. Thus, information supplied in confidence to the gardaí should not in general be disclosed, or at least not in cases like the present where the innocence of an accused person is not in issue, and authorities to that effect, notably *Marks v Beyfus* (1890) 25 QBD 494, remain unaffected by the more recent decisions, as was made clear by Costello J in *Director of Consumer Affairs v Sugar Distributors Ltd* [1991] 1 IR 225. Again, there may be material the disclosure of which would be of assistance to criminals by revealing methods of detection or combating crime, a consideration of particular importance today when criminal activity tends to be highly organised and professional. There may be cases involving the security of the State, where even disclosure of the existence of the document should not be allowed. None of these factors – and there may, of course, well be others which have not occurred to me – which would remove the necessity of even inspecting the documents is present in this case.'

[13.66] It has been contended that the burden of satisfying the court that the documents should be inspected, rests on the party seeking disclosure. There was English authority to suggest such a view. That approach, however, was not, per Keane J, open to an Irish Court.

[13.67] Keane J felt that, in line with Irish decisions (eg *Murphy*), '... the burden of satisfying the court that it should not proceed with inspection should lie upon the person seeking to withhold the document.'[78]

Finally, Keane J made a comment regarding procedure under Order 31, rule 29:

'I should mention one other matter. In *Holloway v Belenos Publications Ltd* [1987] IR 405, Costello J pointed out that Order 31, r 29 does not provide for the service of a motion such as this on all the parties in the action. He observed that, notwithstanding this omission, the court should know the views of all the parties to the action before the order is made. I was informed at the hearing of this

---

[78] *Breathnach v Ireland (No 3)* [1993] 2 IR 458 at 470.

application that the defendants would not be participating and I inferred, I hope correctly, that they did not consider that any useful purpose would be achieved by their also being parties to the motion.'

[13.68] The straightforward 'public interest' handling of garda communications, and the respect given to same, even to the extent of access to a solicitor, is demonstrated in *Gormley v Ireland*[79]. In this case, the plaintiff, who was employed as a clerical officer by An Post, was interned in 1957 under the Offences Against the State Act 1939, and suspended without pay. He was released in 1958 but his suspension was not lifted until he signed a declaration in 1983. He was seeking a declaration that he was entitled to a salary reflective of his age without deduction for interruption. An order for discovery was made and the defendants swore affidavits of discovery, claiming executive privilege. This led to a plaintiff's motion for further and better discovery. Murphy J commented initially:

'In the light of this wide-ranging and somewhat surprising dispute of fact it is inevitable that many documents in the possession of the defendants would be relevant in relation to the issues and as such discoverable in pursuance of the order made in that behalf. Indeed it might be well to stress the converse: if the defendants found it possible to admit some of the allegations made by the plaintiff many of the documents would become irrelevant and would not require to be discovered by the defendants less still inspected by the plaintiff.'[80]

[13.69] The defendants argued the documents release would be contrary to public policy and national security. Murphy J commented:

'Notwithstanding the claim made by Mr Grant in his affidavit and the undoubted involvement of the Offences Against the State Act 1939, I would not go so far as to say that all the documents in respect of which executive privilege is claimed would involve national security. On the other hand they are unquestionably confidential, sensitive documents recording for the greater part submissions and advices by senior civil servants to Ministers and indeed to the Government. It is in the public interest that communications of this nature should be made on the basis that they would not be disclosed in legal proceedings unless the court is satisfied that the public interest in this regard is outweighed by the conflicting interest of the litigant to have access to such documents as may be necessary to enable him to prosecute fairly and properly his action in the courts set up under the Constitution. In attempting to balance these conflicting claims in the light of the issues raised on the pleadings it seems to me that notwithstanding the executive privilege attaching to all of these documents that those which set out the Government policy in relation to an undertaking being required to be given by a civil servant who has been detained under the Offences Against the State Act

---

[79] *Gormley v Ireland* [1993] 2 IR 75.
[80] [1993] 2 IR 75 at 77.

1939, as a condition of restoration to duty should be disclosed. In addition documentation dealing specifically with the alleged refusal of the plaintiff to give such undertaking should likewise be disclosed.'

[13.70] Murphy J did accept, however, that 'other documentation which comprises largely correspondence with the gardaí would be properly treated as highly confidential material, the disclosure of which might be significantly detrimental to the public interest. The information contained in those documents might be of some value to the plaintiff in the conduct of his case but they are in no sense fundamental to it'.[81] His comment with regard to the use of documents is noteworthy:

'Finally it is important to stress in relation to the documents which are discovered and inspected in pursuance of the order of the court that those documents are made available for the proper processing of the present litigation and not for any other purpose. In the circumstances of the case it seems to me that the documents will be properly made available to the solicitor on behalf of the plaintiff on the undertaking of the solicitor to provide copies of such documents to the counsel briefed by him but not to permit those documents to be inspected by any other person.'[82]

[13.71] *Buckley v Incorporated Law Society*[83] concerned a plaintiff's claim for discovery of documents relating to complaints made to the defendant concerning a solicitor, in relation to whom the plaintiff claimed the defendant was negligent in allowing him to continue to practise. The defendant claimed privilege either as legal professional privilege or in the protection of the public interest being 'executive privilege' or for the prevention and detection of crime.

[13.72] Costello J held legal professional privilege did not apply as the documents did not form part of the conduct of the legal affairs of the complainant or advice given by the solicitor. With regard to executive privilege, it was held to apply in two situations:

(1)   where the proper functioning of the public service requires it, balancing the need to protect the privacy of the public service and the need to avoid a possible injustice to litigants;

(2)   to protect the identity and communications of police informers, as otherwise information to enable the police to deter and detect crime might not be forthcoming.

Here, it was held the defendant was not part of the public service; nor could the second ground be extended to cover complaints made to a professional

---

[81]   [1993] 2 IR 75 at 80.
[82]   [1993] 2 IR 75 at 80.
[83]   *Buckley v Incorporated Law Society* [1994] 2 IR 44.

disciplinary body relating to professional misconduct. To extend the second ground, Costello J held, would be to frustrate the court's duty to ascertain the truth and do justice between the parties. Discovery was ordered.

[13.73] *Skeffington v Rooney*[84] considered the question of the discovery of documents containing statements collected by the Garda Síochána Complaints Board in the course of an investigation following allegations by the plaintiff that the defendants, who were police officers, had assaulted him. The plaintiff sued the defendants for damages and sought discovery of the statements to the Board. The Board claimed privilege on the grounds of public interest in the maintenance of confidentiality of its investigations so as to encourage people to assist, being assured of confidentiality. Barr J, following the principles laid down in *Ambiorix*[85] – that any conflict between the public interest in the production of evidence and the public interest in the confidentiality of documents fell to be decided by the courts – resolved the conflict in favour of the plaintiff. He felt such considerations as were put forward by the Board – ie, the inhibition of potential complainants in the absence of an assurance of confidentiality – did not apply to the present case. Barr J felt that, as the complainant here was the one seeking discovery and all statements were in nature broadly similar to those in the book of evidence in a criminal trial, and there was nothing to suggest they were made on a confidential basis, disclosure should be made.[86]

[13.74] If there is a general trend discernible here, is it towards the diminution of the territory safeguarded by the heads of private privilege? Is this trend towards greater judicial scrutiny, and possible subsuming of the heads of private privilege, equally applicable to what might be termed the original or core ground of public or State privilege? Zuckerman would argue not. He would contend that there is a measure of judicial cowardice detectable in certain English cases – mainly those concerning Ministerial assertions of privilege.[87]

[13.75] Is this detectable in the Irish context? *An Blascaod Mór Teo v Commrs of Public Works*[88] concerned s 4 of An Blascaod Mór National Historic Park Act 1989, which authorised the first defendant to compulsorily acquire any lands on the Great Blasket Island. The plaintiffs were the beneficial owners of most of the lands comprising the Blasket Island and challenged the constitutionality of the

---

[84] *Skeffington v Rooney* [1994] 1 IR 480.
[85] *Ambiorix Ltd v Minister for Environment* [1992] 1 IR 277.
[86] [1994] 1 IR 480 at 486.
[87] AAS Zuckerman 'Public Interest Immunity – A Matter of Prime Judicial Responsibility' (1994) Vol 57 MLR 703.
[88] *An Blascaod Mór Teo v Commissioners of Public Works* [1994] 2 IR 372.

Act. They sought discovery of documents relating to the manner in which the Ministers decision to sponsor the Act of 1989 was reached and to preparations for and drafting of the Act, including materials considered at cabinet meetings. The application was refused on the grounds that any question as to the validity of legislation having regard to the provisions of the Constitution must be determined by references to the Act and not the purpose of the Minister or others who supported it. Therefore, the documents were irrelevant. Moreover, any inquiry by the court into such motives would be impracticable and contrary to the doctrine of separation of powers.

[13.76] Is this not illustrative of Zuckerman's thesis in Ireland? Zuckerman stated:

> 'In this country Carol Harlow and Richard Rawlings write "a wall of silence blocks public access to information. Britain is almost alone in the Western world in possessing neither freedom of information legislation nor a general right to access to data held in official files." (Harrow & Rawlings *Pressure Through Law* (London: Routledge 1992), p 172). On their part the judiciary have shown remarkable willingness to bolster this wall of silence by placing their trust in the ability of Ministers to judge what is in the public interest.'[89]

Decisions since *Conway v Rimmer*, according to Zuckerman, are '... harmful to a healthy administration of justice and inimical to good government in a democratic society.' Zuckerman's contention is that Ministers do not bear a major responsibility for this state of affairs. They have followed well-established practices which have the courts' seal of approval. If Ministers were made the sole culprits, that would ensure the courts would remain free to continue granting licence for suppression of evidence in all but criminal prosecutions. Zuckerman's argument is that the courts should be put on trial also.

[13.77] The contention that England is alone in maintaining its shroud of secrecy is not borne out by the Irish experience. Smyth & Brady[90] comment:

> 'The right of the public to access to information held by the state, whether personal files on the individual citizen, or access to the policy process, is now very clearly established in international law and is the growing practice in western democracies. The Irish system of almost obsessive secrecy is another of the legacies of the British administrative tradition whose philosophy is best summed up in the words of Sir Humphrey Appleby in *Yes Minister:* "Open government is a contradiction in terms. You can have openness, or you can have government". It is a view not shared by all British politicians, however. Lord

---

[89] AAS Zuckerman 'Public Interest Immunity – A Matter of Prime Judicial Responsibility'(1994) Vol 57 MLR 703 at 724.

[90] Smyth and Brady *Democracy Blindfolded: The Case for A Freedom of Information Act in Ireland* (1994) p 1.

Egremont, Harold Macmillan's private secretary, considered all spying and secrets a waste of time and money. "Much better", he said, "if the Russians saw the cabinet minutes twice a week. Prevent all that fucking dangerous guesswork". For Russians read "public".'

[13.78] What is evident from these decisions on discovery is that, though there is an evident readiness on the part of the courts to cut down on 'private' access to privilege (*Smurfit, Buckley, Breathnach*, etc), there is equally evident an absence of scrutiny of government or state activities (*Goodman, An Blascaod Mór*). In terms of the conflicting elements or interests of 'the administration of justice', confidentiality, effective government and full disclosure, it seems that while private interests may not supersede over that of the public, the definition of the latter is such that the State interest in the 'public interest' may be so great as to sacrifice the collective 'private' interests of the public (even if unassailable in terms of 'community' support) constantly and at the altar of the 'private' interest of the State in the public.

Allegation of non-discovery

[13.79] With regard to challenging discovery which has been made by a party, in *Phelan v Goodman*[91], Murphy J on an appeal from the order of the High Court, refusing the application of the plaintiff for further and better discovery, dealt with the issue of allegations of non-discovery of material documents. Mr Phelan could not say with certainty whether any particular document was or had been in the possession of Mr Goodman. What he had contended was that, given the very limited banking documentation discovered by Mr Goodman, there was a very high degree of probability that other relevant documentation existed. The issue was not whether particular documents were relevant or privileged but whether a document or range of documents was or had been in the power or possession of the deponent. Murphy J[92] refered to *Sterling Winthrop Group Limited v Farbenfabriken Bayer AG*[93], where Kenny J considered the issue as to how far the sworn statement of a deponent making an affidavit of discovery was conclusive. He summarised the position as follows:

'*British Association of Glass Bottle Manufacturers v Nettlefold Ltd* [1912] AC 709 is authority for the view that the Court may order a further affidavit when it is satisfied that the party making the first affidavit has not properly understood the issues involved in the action. The speech of Viscount Haldane contains this passage:

---

[91] *Phelan v Goodman* (24 January 2000, unreported) SC.
[92] (24 January 2000, unreported) SC at p 8.
[93] *Sterling Winthrop Group Limited v Farbenfabriken Bayer AG* [1967] IR 97.

"But while it is true that as a general rule you cannot go behind the affidavit in the absence of admissions in that or some other document, the rule is qualified where the basis on which the affidavit of documents has been made turns out to have been wrong. If the party making the affidavit has misconceived his case, so the Court is practically certain that if he had conceived it properly, and had acted upon a proper view of the law, he would have disclosed further documents, then the Court can refuse to recognise an affidavit as conclusive, and order a further affidavit".[94]

Murphy J pointed out[95] that these principles were applied by the Supreme Court in the unreported decision of *Kreglinger and Fernau v Irish National Insurance Company*[96], in which the Court reversed a decision of the High Court which ordered a further affidavit of discovery.

[13.80] In *Bula Limited v Crowley*,[97] Finlay CJ delivering the judgment of the court, dealt with a similar problem in the following terms:

'I accept that a Court should be satisfied, as a matter of probability, that an error has occurred in an omission from an affidavit of discovery of documents on the basis of irrelevancy before making any order for further discovery and that it should not, in particular, permit the opposing party to indulge in an exploratory or fishing expedition.'

Murphy J pointed out[98] that in that case, it was conceded that the deponent did have certain documents in his possession, and the issue was whether his sworn statement that those documents were irrelevant was entirely conclusive. The Supreme Court rejected that proposition but held in relation to the question of relevance that the court must be satisfied on the balance of probabilities that an error has occurred[99]. Murphy J concluded:

'Where a deponent accepts that he does have documents in his power or possession an effective order can be made to compel their discovery. Difficulties obviously arise in directing the discovery of documents or a particular range or class of document which the deponent denies are in his possession. To order Mr Goodman to swear a further affidavit of discovery presumably would result in his repeating the statements made and sworn by him on several occasions, namely, that he has not and never had any documents in addition to those already discovered in his power or possession relating to the matters in issue in the present proceedings. In those circumstances the Court would have to be satisfied on the evidence before it that it was making a meaningful order. Whilst I

---

[94] *Sterling Winthrop Group Limited v Farbenfabriken Bayer AG* [1967] IR 97 at 103.
[95] *Phelan v Goodman* (24 January 2000, unreported) SC at p 10 per Murphy J.
[96] *Kreglinger and Fernau v Irish National Insurance Company* (2 July 1954).
[97] *Bula Limited v Crowley* [1991] 1 IR 220 at 223
[98] (24 January 2000, unreported) SC at p 10.
[99] (24 January 2000, unreported) SC at p 10.

recognise the force of the arguments made by Counsel on behalf of Mr Phelan, it seems to me that the evidence presented to the High Court or to this Court on appeal is insufficient to satisfy the Court that relevant documents are or have been in the possession of Mr Goodman which should have been but have not been discovered by him.'[100]

Cross-examination on affidavits of discovery

[13.81] In *Duncan v Governor of Portlaoise Prison*[101] the applicant sought discovery against the respondent and a number of notice parties (DPP, Minister for Justice) relating to his detention in custody. The Minister for Justice and the DPP claimed both legal professional privilege and executive privilege in relation to a number of documents. Counsel for the applicant sought to cross-examine the deponents on their respective affidavits of discovery. Although not satisfied that in the circumstances of this case cross-examination was either necessary or appropriate, the High Court (Kelly J) held as follows:

'I do not accept that in Irish law an Affidavit of Discovery must be considered as conclusive and can never be the subject of cross-examination.

Just as a certificate concerning the concentration of alcohol in a specimen of blood or a specimen of urine was unacceptable to the Courts as "conclusive evidence" (vide *Maher v Attorney General* [1973] IR 140). It appears to me that the administration of justice, which is vested by the Constitution in the Courts, requires that the Courts have the ability to adjudicate fully upon the adequacy and accuracy of an Affidavit of Discovery. In exceptional cases this may involve the cross-examination of the deponent of such an Affidavit. To hold otherwise would mean that the Court would be deprived from investigating the accuracy or adequacy or an Affidavit of Discovery and would have to accept at face value which is averred therein. It appears to me that the Court must always retain the power and make available the necessary machinery to ensure that it is not so limited in administering justice.

Such observations apply *a fortiori* where the court is engaged upon an inquiry under Article 40 to the Constitution. ...It appears to me that there are circumstances in which it may be permissible to cross-examine on an Affidavit of Discovery. However, I am satisfied that such circumstances are extremely rare. This is so because of the variety of other remedies which are available with a view to testing matter contained in an Affidavit of Discovery. These other remedies include Orders for further and better discovery, the delivery of interogoratories, and the inspection by the Court itself of documents referred to in an Affidavit of Discovery. Furthermore it appears to me to be wholly undesirable that the Court should, save in the most exceptional cases, be called

---

[100] (24 January 2000, unreported) SC at p 10 at 20.
[101] *Duncan v Governor of Portlaoise Prison* [1997] 1 IR 558 at 573.

upon to deal with questions such as the existence or non-existence of a document in circumstances where such a question might impinge to a serious extent on the issues in the action. Clearly at the stage when an issue of discovery of this type is being argued, the Court cannot be au fait with all the issues in the proceedings. I do not in this judgment wish to specify the rare circumstances in which cross-examination on an Affidavit of Discovery may be permitted. But it does appear to me that when permitted at all, it should only arise in circumstances where it is both necessary and where other remedies, such as those already mentioned, prove inadequate.'[102]

Applicability to criminal proceedings

[13.82] Whether discovery procedure under the Rules of Court may be invoked in criminal prosecutions, was considered by the Supreme Court in *People (DPP) v Sweeney*[103]. In this case, Geoghegan J commented that:

'there is nothing in the character of the criminal jurisdiction vested in the present High Court which could lead to any view that the Rules of Court relating to "discovery" were suddenly to apply to it when they had never applied to it predecessors.'[104]

Geoghegan J pointed out that it was well-established that a defendant had a right to see relevant documentation in the hands of the prosecution. This arose, he states '…from the Constitutional obligation on the court to ensure fair procedures. It does not involve the swearing of an affidavit of discovery and it has nothing whatsoever to do with the conventional discovery procedure set out in the Rules of the Superior Courts.'[105] The latter was what was being sought here in an order for non-party discovery against the Rape Crisis Centre, the alleged purpose being the defence of a prosecution for rape.

[13.83] Geoghegan J stated that the learned High Court judge was not entitled to make the order he had made, because such an order could not be made in connection with criminal proceedings. Geoghegan J pointed out[106] that particularly in the case of non-party discovery, the issues in the case are first defined and therefore discovery not made until after the close of pleadings in a civil case. None of this could be done in a criminal case, as only the prosecution must show its hand. With limited statutory exceptions (eg alibi evidence), the defence can spring surprises and is entitled to give no indication as to what issues might be raised. Hence, 'discovery' documents under the Rules of Court

---

[102] At para 40-43.

[103] *People (DPP) v Sweeney* (9 October 2001, unreported) SC.

[104] *People (DPP) v Sweeney* (9 October 2001, unreported) SC at p 5.

[105] *People (DPP) v Sweeney* (9 October 2001, unreported) SC at p 15.

[106] *People (DPP) v Sweeney* (9 October 2001, unreported) SC at p 6.

can never have been intended to apply to criminal proceedings. He also refered to the issue of privilege as supporting this view:

'A general consideration of the issue of privilege would certainly support the view that the machinery of discovery as operated in civil proceedings could not be applied to a criminal prosecution. The wide range of documents and communications created in contemplation of criminal proceedings and which justice would require the prosecution to make available to the defence would almost certainly be privileged from production in civil proceedings.' [107]

McDermott[108] points out that it has long been the understanding of criminal practitioners that discovery was available in criminal as in civil law. There is the additional factor in criminal law of the prosecution duty of full disclosure (ss 4B and 4C of Criminal Procedure Act 1967 as inserted by s 9 Criminal Justice Act 1999, provide, for example, for furnishing of the Book of Evidence). Nonetheless, discovery was an useful additional tool. In Canada, documents in the possession of third parties can be obtained if the defence affidavit established their 'likely relevance'.

[13.84] In *DH v Judge Groarke*[109] the applicant had been charged with offences of sexual assault on the complainant, at various dates from June 1983 to June 1989. The applicant required the presence of two social workers involved at the time, at the preliminary examination. In their depositions, they referred to the notes of their conversations with the complainant. The applicant sought discovery of these notes from the DPP and Health Board. The Circuit Court refused, and the applicant sought judicial review in the High Court, and appealed to the Supreme Court. Counsel for the applicant argued fair procedure mandated discovery orders against Health Boards in cases such as this. Keane CJ, delivering the judgment of the Supreme Court, felt Geoghegan J in *Sweeney,* had referred to the obligation of the prosecution to furnish the defence with any relevant documentation, and drew a distinction between this and the inappropriate use of civil discovery. Keane CJ then gave a strong reaffirmation of the decision in *Sweeney* making it clear that discovery is not available in criminal proceedings:

'The function of discovery in civil proceedings, whether it be inter parties or third party discovery, is to enable both parties to advance their own case or damage their opponent's case. The court in such cases is normally in a position to ascertain from a consideration of the pleadings what the issues are between the parties and accordingly what documents will be relevant to those issues and, specifically, whether, if discovered and inspected, they will enable a party to

---

[107] *People (DPP) v Sweeney* (9 October 2001, unreported) SC, para 14, p 8.
[108] PA McDermott 'Evidence & Procedure Update [2001] 11 Ir Crim LJ 23.
[109] *DH v Judge Groarke* (31 July 2002) SC.

advance his own case or damage that being made by his opponent. In a trial on indictment, such as the present, the issue which the court has to determine is not defined until the accused has been arraigned and had pleaded to the courts laid against him. Even then, he is not required to do more than plead guilty or not guilty. There are some rare statutory exceptions to that, such as the requirement to notify the prosecution in advance of a proposed alibi. But in every other respect, while the prosecution must disclose comprehensively and in detail the case they propose to make against the accused, he in under no such obligation. Discovery, accordingly, in a trial on indictment would be a wholly one-sided process, which was certainly not what was envisaged by the procedure for inter partes and third party discovery provided under the Rules of Court. It is clear, accordingly, that, in the case of the Rules of Court dealing with discovery, to treat the word "cause" as extending to criminal proceedings would be clearly repugnant to the context in which it was being used.

The fact that discovery in the form provided for in the rules for civil litigation is not available in criminal proceedings does not have as a necessary consequence an erosion of the fair procedures to which defendants are entitled. Thus, in the present case, it was open to the solicitor for the applicant to ensure at the deposition state that any relevant records or notes in the possession of the social workers were produced and, to at least a limited extent, that was done. Moreover, the social workers can be required by the applicant to attend the trial and produce any relevant documents by the issue of a *subpoena duces decum*.'

[13.85] Fundamental fairness may play a significant part here, however, in demanding defence access to prosecution material. This was seen in *Murphy v DPP*[110], where a motor car was released by gardaí, following their own forensic examination, notwithstanding an arrangement with the accused's solicitor for access. It was held by the High Court that although nothing might have been found on forensic examination, the accused had been deprived of the reasonable possibility of discovering evidence to rebut the prosecution case. Trial was prohibited.

[13.86] In *Robert Dunne v DPP*[111], the Court considered the unavailability of video tapes from a filling station in Dublin where a robbery had taken place. Unlike the earlier Supreme Court decision in *Braddish v DPP*[112], however, Fennelly J pointed out that in this case it had not been established that the video evidence had actually been in the possession of the gardaí. He commented:

'It does not, ... necessarily follow that, where an accused person is in a position to show that the Gardaí have failed to seek evidence which would have had a potential bearing on the innocence of the accused, that will suffice to meet the

---

[110] *Murphy v DPP* [1989] ILRM 71.
[111] *Robert Dunne v DPP* (25 April 2002, unreported) SC (Fennelly J).
[112] *Braddish v DPP* (18 May 2001, unreported) SC (Hardiman J).

test of a real and serious risk to a fair trial. On such an assumption, a trial will be prohibited, wherever a court can be persuaded that the gardaí have failed to seek out any identifiable evidence which might even possibly tend to exonerate the accused. I cannot agree that our criminal law should go so far. It is difficult to say where the line will be drawn. Giving the increasing prevalence of CCTV in our towns, it is to be anticipated that there will a rash of applications for prohibition wherever video evidence is not produced. Even where it does not cover the crime scene, why should it not be arguable that video recordings of activity in surrounding areas should be obtained. The danger is that there will develop a tendency to shift the focus of criminal prosecution onto the adequacy of the police investigation rather than the guilt or innocence of the accused.'[113]

Hence, the order of prohibition here was refused.

[13.87] It is worthy of note that in *Swaine v DPP*[114], it was held that the extent of the prosecution duty not to hold back material evidence helpful to a defendant may vary in parameter and extent in the case of summary prosecution and more serious prosecutions on indictment.

Tribunals and discovery

[13.88] Discovery, although inapplicable to criminal proceedings, is applicable to tribunal proceedings, which though arguably similar in effect to criminal proceedings, so often avoid the strictures of same.

Flood v Lawlor[115]

[13.89] Flood J initially sought discovery from Mr Lawlor voluntarily. When this was not seen to be forthcoming on the 8 June 2000, the Sole Member made an order of discovery. One of the objections of Mr Lawlor was that the order was too wide both as to its scope and time. In the High Court, Smyth J rejected that submission on the basis that unlike *Haughey v Moriarty*[116], where orders of discovery were first made and Mr Haughey and other plaintiffs then given an opportunity of applying to the Tribunal to vary or discharge the order, here Mr Lawlor was given an opportunity to put his point of view before the order was made (over fifty letters had been written to him since October 1998).

[13.90] Smyth J applied three tests as to whether the demand for documents was excessive or unreasonable (as per Laffoy J in *Dunnes Stores Ireland Company v Maloney*[117]): was the demand made without jurisdiction, and to satisfy this test

---

[113] *Robert Dunne v DPP* (25 April 2002, unreported) SC at 24 (Geoghegan J).

[114] *Swaine v DPP* (26 April 2002, unreported) SC.

[115] *Mr Justice Flood, Sole Member of the Tribunal v William Lawlor* (24 October 2000, unreported) HC (Smyth J).

[116] *Haughey v Moriarty* [1999] 3 IR 1.

one needs to know to what purpose the demand was made; was the demand reasonable in content; and had a reasonable time been given for compliance.

[13.91] Smyth J was satisfied the first test was met. The second was met in so far as the scope of the subject matter was reasonable in content, but he made the point that the scope, as to time or length of period over which discovery was sought, should also be reasonable (he felt the Order ought not extend backwards before 1 October 1964). As to the third test, while 14 days might seem severe, it was not, considering the general background and difficulty the Tribunal had in obtaining information on the matter for over a period of two years; the immediate background to the orders; and that Mr Lawlor had both challenged and sought extensions for compliance with earlier orders.

[13.92] Mr Lawlor's solicitors, in correspondence with the tribunal, had referred to the necessity of compliance with the provisions of Order 31, rule 12 of the Rules of the Superior Courts 1986 as amended by insertion by SI 223/1999. Smyth J pointed out that this indicated a failure to appreciate the following[118]:

'(1)   An inquiry is not *lis inter partes*;

(2)   The Tribunal is not obligated to first seek Orders of the Court for Discovery before ordering Discovery;

(3)   If the Tribunal makes an Order of Discovery, the validity of which has not being challenged and struck down by Court Order, it is prima facie valid and must be complied with;

(4)   That unless so challenged and stuck down, there is no inhibition in law in the Tribunal proceedings to make Production Orders or issuing Orders by way of summons to attend, produce and answer questions in respect of the documents directed to be discovered and produced.

It is clear from Mr Lawlor's solicitors letter of 24 July 2000 that it was considered that the Discovery sought was in the nature of a general trawl through his personal and business affairs and that being called to make a statement in public did not arise.

I reject this submission made on Mr Lawlor's behalf in that the failure by Mr Lawlor to make Discovery within the time stipulated by the Tribunal, the Tribunal were obligated to first invoke Section 4 of the Tribunal of Inquiry (Evidence) (Amendment) Act 1997 before proceeding to make the Orders of 21 September 2000. In the instant case, the Tribunal invited Mr Lawlor by letter dated 28 July 2000 to challenge the validity of its Orders of 8 June 2000 if he thought it was invalid. The invitation was not accepted nor the issue of Discovery

---

[117] *Dunnes Stores Ireland Company v Maloney* [1999] 3 IR 564.
[118] *Flood v Lawlor* 24 October 2000, HC at p 19 para 30.

properly addressed by Mr Lawlor or his solicitors. The Tribunal's letter of 28 July 2000 was not replied to until 9 October 2000.

In the absence of compliance with the Order for Discovery or a challenge to the validity of the Order or a meaningful response to the letter or 28 July, the Sole Member proceeded to issue two summonses pursuant to the provisions of the Tribunals of Inquiry (Evidence) Act 1921-1998 commanding Mr Lawlor to attend before the Tribunal to:

(i) bring and hand over to the Tribunal the documents and records and subject of the Order for Discovery

(ii) to give evidence to the Tribunal in relation to the documents and records the subject of the Order for Discovery. In my judgment, the Tribunal had jurisdiction to issue the summonses, and did so within jurisdiction.'[119]

[13.93] Counsel for Mr Lawlor sought to correct the order in so far as the summons to attend and answer questions should be done in private, not public. The court held that Mr Lawlor himself had first indicated his intention to not attend the Tribunal by press interview, and held the order of discovery valid:

'The Tribunal has an entitlement to sit and take evidence in public. The limitation of the right of the Tribunal to refuse to allow the public or any portion of the public to be present at any of the proceedings is expressly referred to in Section 2 of the 1921 Act and I am not prepared to strike down the Order to give evidence in public and direct the evidence to be heard in private. The Tribunal will be aware of the judgment of the Supreme Court both in *Haughey v Moriarty* and the more recent decision in *Bailey and Ors v Flood* (unrep, 14 April 2000) and I am not disposed to curtailing (for I may not) the discretion of the Tribunal.'[120]

The judgment of the Supreme Court (12 December 2001) approved the approach of Smyth J. That court delivered another judgment properly in support of tribunals and their orders.

[13.94] In *Bailey v Flood*[121], the reliefs sought were based on the argument that the discovery and production orders in respect of the applicants' bank accounts and other documentation in possession of the bank ought not to be given effect having regard to constitutional and legal considerations. The specific arguments put forward were the following:

'(1) That the Respondent acted ultra vires in making the orders otherwise than at a public sitting of the Tribunal, it being argued–

---

[119] *Flood v Lawlor* 24 October 2000, HC at p 18, para 30 per Smyth J.
[120] *Flood v Lawlor* 24 October 2000, HC at p 30, para 47, per Smyth J.
[121] *Bailey v Flood* [1998] IEHC 74 (15 May 1998) HC.

(a) that the Respondent did not make any order reciting that he had formed the opinion that it was expedient in the public interest to make the Discovery Orders in private; and

(b) that at any rate there was no material before the Respondent to support such an opinion.

(2) That Respondent breached the rules of natural and constitutional justice by making Discovery Orders affecting the Applicants without giving prior notice to the Applicants of his intention to make such orders and giving them an opportunity to make representations in respect thereof.

(3) That decisions to make Discovery Orders against the bank were unreasonable, irrational and arbitrary in that there was allegedly no material before the Respondent to indicate that the bank was likely to have or to have had in its possession custody or power of any documents relevant to the proceedings of the Tribunal.

(4) That the Respondent erred in law in failing to give adequate reasons for the decision to issue Orders of Discovery.

(5) That the Respondent acted ultra vires in seeking Orders for Discovery and Production rather than making use of other powers available to him under the Bankers' Books Evidence Acts.

(6) The Discovery and Production Orders served on the bank represented an unjustified interference with the Applicants' constitutional rights both to fail procedures and to privacy and that this was especially so in relation to one of the bank accounts which was a private family account of the first and third named Applicants.

(7) That the terms of the Discovery Orders are excessively wide and therefore ultra vires, the primary argument on this point being that there was no commencement or termination date specified in the Orders.' [122]

[13.95] Geoghegan J also noted, however, that the overriding argument which was made was that, as a matter of law, the High Court practice and procedure in relation to non-party discovery ought to be applied. In essence, that would mean that the tribunal would have to give reasons justifying an order of discovery or production before it confirmed an order.

'Put simplistically, the argument runs that in the case of a Tribunal everybody against whom an order for Discovery is made and everybody affected by an order of Discovery is a non party by definition because there are no "parties" to a Tribunal. The Sole Member is a person conducting an enquiry and not an adjudication of a dispute between two or more persons.'[123]

---

[122] *Bailey v Flood* (15 May 1998) HC at p 1 para 1, per Geoghegan J.
[123] *Bailey v Flood* (15 May 1998) HC at p 2, para 2.

Geoghegan J concluded that this was not the case:

'If a Tribunal of Inquiry under the 1921 Act as amended is confined in its powers of making Discovery Orders to the parameters of Rule 29 of Order 31, this would, I think, considerably curb the Tribunal in its powers of investigation. I have come to the conclusion that the rules relating to Discovery from non parties do not have any application to Tribunals of Inquiry made under the 1921 Act.' [124]

His reasoning is as follows:

'Section 1 of the Tribunals of Inquiry (Evidence) Act 1921 provides that in the case of a Tribunal established in the manner described by the Act, such a Tribunal "shall have all such powers, right and privileges as are vested in the High Court, ... or a Judge of (that) court, on the occasion of an action "in respect of several matters therein set out, one of them being "the compelling the production of documents". The concept of non party discovery and the special limitations and safeguards relating to it were not in existence or known to Parliament at the time that the 1921 Act was enacted. I am satisfied, especially having regard to the reference to "an action" in the section, that Parliament was intending that even though there are no parties to a Tribunal, the Tribunal nevertheless should have the same powers, rights and privileges as though the person against whom Discovery or Production was being sought was in fact a party. What the Act permits, in my view, is ordinary discovery on the assumption that the person against whom discovery is being made is a party rather than on the assumption that he is a non party. Even though strictly speaking the 1921 Act refers only to the compelling of the production of documents and not to an Order for Discovery as such, I think that the reference to "all such powers, rights and privileges as are vested in the High Court" must include the order to make discovery which is a natural preliminary to an order for the production of documents. But if I am wrong in that interpretation, I am satisfied that the Tribunal would have a power to make Orders of Discovery under Section 4 of the Tribunals of Inquiry (Evidence) (Amendment) Act 1979, which confers on the Tribunal power to make such orders as it considers necessary and it is to have in relation to making such orders all powers, rights and privileges as are vested in the High Court. But as of the passing of the 1979 Act also, non party discovery was not provided for in the Superior Court Rules and was not a practice in the High Court. The Sole Member, therefore, in my view, has power to make an Order for Discovery against a person as though that person was a party. He cannot make an Order for Discovery if such an order would not have been procurable in High Court proceedings as against another party, but he is not bound by any of the restrictions imported into the concept of non party discovery.' [125]

---

[124] *Bailey v Flood* (15 May 1998) HC at p 3, para 5.
[125] *Bailey v Flood* (15 May 1998) HC at p 3, para 6.

[13.96] With regard to the remaining grounds, the court was satisfied that they were not sustained. In particular, the court pointed to the fact that any difficulties with regard to having the discovery order varied or discharged, the tribunal was willing to hear same. The court found that the applicant's primary interest was to defeat the order for discovery altogether, on either jurisdictional grounds or grounds that the tribunal had not satisfied the requirement of the High Court in relation to non-party discovery and that they were not interested in confining themselves to so-called 'factual grounds'.[126]

Fair procedures and tribunals

[13.97] In *Haughey v Moriarty*[127], the plaintiffs' appeal was against dismissal by the High Court of their claim for a declaration that the Tribunal of Inquiry (Evidence) Act 1921 is invalid having regard to the Constitution. The Supreme Court reviewed the relevant provisions of the 1921 Act as amended, and summarised, per Hamilton CJ, their effect as follows:[128]

'The effects of the foregoing legislation may be summarised as follows:

1.   The tribunal shall not refuse to allow the public or any portion of the public to be present at any of the proceedings of the tribunal unless in the opinion of the tribunal it is in the public interest so to do for reasons connected with the subject matter of the inquiry or the nature of the evidence to be given.[129]

2.   The tribunal has all the powers, rights and privileges as are vested in the High Court on the occasion of an action in respect of the following matters:

    (a) enforcing the attendance of witnesses and examining them on oath, affirmation or otherwise;

    (b) compelling the production of documents;

    (c) subject to Rules of Court, the issuing of a commission or request to examine witnesses abroad[130].

3. (i)   The tribunal has the power to make such orders as it considers necessary for the purposes of its functions.

    (ii)   In the making of such orders, the tribunal has all such powers, rights and privileges as are vested in the High Court or a judge of that Court in respect of the making of orders[131]. The Tribunal however does not have

---

[126] *Bailey v Flood* (15 May 1998) HC at p 5, para 13.

[127] *Haughey v Moriarty* [1998] IESC 17 (28 July 1998).

[128] *Haughey v Moriarty* [1998] IESC 17 (28 July 1998) para 17, p 5 per Hamilton CJ.

[129] Tribunals of Inquiry (Evidence) Act 1921, s 2(a).

[130] Tribunals of Inquiry (Evidence) Act 1921, s 1(a).

[131] Tribunals of Inquiry (Evidence) (Amendment) Act 1979, s 4.

the powers, rights and privileges vested in the High Court for enforcing compliance with its orders. To secure compliance therewith it must apply to the High Court in accordance with Section 7 of the 1998 Act.

4. The tribunal has the power to award costs.[132]

5. A witness before the tribunal shall be entitled to the same immunities and privileges as if he were a witness before the High Court[133].

6. A statement or admission by a person before a tribunal shall not be admissible as evidence against that person in any criminal proceedings, other than proceedings for an offence under the 1979 Act[134].

7. A person who produces or sends a document to the tribunal in pursuance of an order of that tribunal shall be entitled to the same immunities and privileges as if he or she were a witness before the High Court[135].'

[13.98] With regard to the challenge to the power of the Oireachtas to establish a Tribunal of Enquiry, the Supreme Court held:

'The Court is satisfied that while the 1921 Act (as amended) does not empower the establishment of a Tribunal of Inquiry such as was established in this case, that the Houses of the Oireachtas had and to have the inherent jurisdiction to resolve that it is expedient that a Tribunal be established to inquire into what they consider to be urgent matters of public importance.'[136]

However, the Supreme Court pointed out that that power cannot be abused, exercised for improper motives or in breach of Constitutional rights, including the right to fair procedures[137].

[13.99] With regard to the Tribunal of Inquiry amounting to the 'administration of justice', contrary to Article 34.1 of the Constitution, following the decision in *Goodman Internationa v Hamilton No 1*[138], the Supreme Court, in *Haughey v Moriarty,* felt that '… the conduct of such an inquiry does not amount to the administration of justice. The critical factor is trial and adjudication, not inquiry.'[139] The court held further that it was entitled to assume that a Tribunal of Inquiry would conduct its inquiry, as it is obliged to do, in accordance with the principles of constitutional justice and in particular with regard to fair procedure.'[140]

---

[132] Tribunal of Inquiry (Evidence) (Amendment) Act 1997, s 3.

[133] Tribunals of Inquiry (Evidence) Act 1921, s 1(3).

[134] Tribunals of Inquiry (Evidence) (Amendment) Act 1979, s 5.

[135] Tribunal of Inquiry (Evidence) (Amendment) Act 1997, s 2.

[136] *Haughey v Moriarty* [1998] IESC 17 at para 41.

[137] *Haughey v Moriarty* [1998] IESC 17 at para 43.

[138] *Goodman International v Hamilton No 1* [1992] IR 542.

[139] *Haughey v Moriarty* [1998] IESC 17 at para 77.

[140] [1998] IESC 17 at para 81.

[13.100] With regard to arguments relating to the validity of such tribunal proceedings, the Supreme Court commented on their rationale as follows:

'The underlying policy of the 1921 Act ... is to provide the machinery, wholly independent of the political process, whereby matters of grave public concern may be investigated and the true facts brought to light. Such an inquiry, generally but not necessarily conducted by one or more judges, typically takes the form of an investigation such as the present into circumstances which have raised the possibility of corruption or other impropriety in public life. The terms of the legislation, however, do not restrict the Oireachtas and the Executive to initiating such an inquiry to that area: the *"definite matters"* of *"urgent public importance"* can obviously extend to disasters involving loss of life and serious injury such as were the subject of the *Whiddy Island Disaster Report* [1979] and the *Stardust Fire Report* [1982]'. [141]

[13.101] With regard to the right to fair procedures, the Supreme Court noted that, as per *Re Haughey*[142], there is a constitutionally protected guarantee of basic fairness of procedures, but that both Houses of the Oireachtas and the Taoiseach were entitled to assume the tribunal would conduct its inquiry, and all necessary proceedings in relation thereto in accordance with fair procedures and the principles of constitutional justice. Hence, there was no breach of fair procedures on the part of either the Houses of the Oireachtas or the Taoiseach.[143]

[13.102] In *Haughey v Moriarty,* with regard to the allegations that the tribunal itself was not being conducted in accordance with fair procedures, challenge was made, inter alia, to the discovery orders issued in regard to Mr Haughey's and his family bank accounts. The High Court had determined that the latter ('connected persons') ought to have received prior notice of an intention to make discovery order against the banks, to enable them to make objections. Mr Haughey was in a different position, but due to ambiguities, could not be expected to know the period for which discovery would be sought, and that in the absence of clarification of the terms of reference by the Tribunal, was entitled to an opportunity to object to all discovery orders on his bank. However, the High Court went on to hold that the unfairness that occurred was not sufficiently fundamental to render the proceedings void. With regard to the tribunal carrying on its proceedings in private, the learned judge held that it was inherent that the preliminary work would be done in private – the prohibition on refusing the public to be present relates to the actual hearings.

[13.103] The Supreme Court was satisfied that the tribunal was entitled to conduct its preliminary investigation in private, for the purpose of ascertaining

---

[141] [1998] IESC 17 at para 172.
[142] *Re Haughey* [1971] IR 217.
[143] [1998] IESC 17 at para 207

what evidence was relevant, and to enable the tribunal in due course to serve copies of such evidence on the plaintiffs/appellants in order to enable them to observe their constitutional right to be present at the hearing of the tribunal where witnesses would give evidence on oath and be liable to cross-examination.'[144]

[13.104] With regard to the High Court's decisions as to fair procedures in making the discovery orders, however, the Supreme Court's decision is different in effect:[145]

'Fair procedures require that before making such orders, particularly orders of the nature of the orders made in this case, the person or persons likely to be affected thereby should be given notice by the Tribunal of its intention to make such order, and should have been afforded the opportunity prior to the making of such order, of making representations with regard thereto. Such representations could conceivably involve the submission to the Tribunal that the said orders were not necessary for the purpose of the functions of the Tribunal, that they were too wide and extensive having regard to the terms of reference of the Tribunal and any other relevant matters.

Such procedure was not adopted in this case and the learned trial judge held that in making such orders the Tribunal did not act in accordance with the requirements of fair procedures.

The Court is satisfied that the learned trial judge was correct in his findings that the orders sought to be impugned herein made by the Tribunal were made in contravention of the requirements of constitutional justice and that fair procedures were not adopted by the Tribunal in the making of such orders. ...

There may be exceptional circumstances, such as a legitimate fear of destruction of documents if prior notice was given, where the requirements of fair procedures in this regard may be dispensed with. No such circumstances exist in this case.

Each of the Plaintiffs/Appellants is entitled to the benefit of fair procedures and the Court is satisfied that the learned trial judge erred in differentiating between the rights of the first-named Plaintiff/Appellant and the remaining Plaintiffs/Appellants.

The vindication of such rights requires that the impugned orders of discovery made by the Tribunal other than in accordance with fair procedures be quashed and that the Tribunal be deprived of the benefit of such orders and the Court will so order.

The following statement made by Ó Dálaigh CJ in the course of his judgment in *In re Haughey* [1971] IR 21 7 at page 264 is particularly apt:

---

[144] [1998] IESC 17 at para 294.
[145] [1998] IESC 17 at para 300-311.

"The provisions of Article 38.1 of the Constitution apply only to trials of criminal charges in accordance with Article 8; but in proceedings before any tribunal where a party to the proceedings is in risk of having his good name, or his person or property, or any of his personal rights jeopardised, the proceedings may be correctly classed as proceedings which may affect his rights, and in compliance with the Constitution, the State, either by its enactments or through the Courts must outlaw any procedures which will restrict or prevent the party concerned from vindicating these rights."

The quashing by the Court of the said Orders made by the tribunal does not preclude the Sole Member of the Tribunal from making similar orders in the future should it consider that the making of such orders is necessary for the purposes of its functions, provided that in the making thereof he applies fair procedures as outlined herein.'

Other relevant investigatory powers

[13.105] Section 7 of the Bankers' Books Evidence Act 1879 as amended by s 2 of the Bankers' Books Evidence (Amendment) Act 1959, provides for the inspection of bank book entries by a party to a proceeding, including criminal proceedings. However, the stage at which such a facility is most useful to prosecution authorities is prior to the initiation of proceedings when an investigation is being conducted. In view of this, s 131 of the Central Bank Act 1989 amends the Act of 1879 by inserting s 7(a), which provides:

'If, on an application made by a member of the Garda Síochána not below the rank of superintendent, a court or a judge is satisfied that there are reasonable grounds for believing –

(a)   that an indictable offence has been committed; and

(b)   that there is material in the possession of a bank specified in the application which is likely to be of substantial value (whether by itself or together with other material) to the investigation of the offence; a judge may make an order that the applicant or another member of the Garda Síochána designated by him be at liberty to inspect and take copies of any entries in a bankers' book for the purposes of investigation of the offence'.

(Section 126 of the Building Societies Act 1989, extends the definition of 'bank' in the 1879 Act to include a building society).

[13.106] A defendant can raise the privilege against self-incrimination to resist such an application for inspection, but the simple discovery of assets is not necessarily incriminating. (In *Waterhouse v Barker*[146], the defendant objected to producing her bankers' books under the 1879 Act, on the grounds that such an

---

[146] *Waterhouse v Barker* 40 TLR 805.

action might incriminate her. The majority of the Court of Appeal allowed her claim of privilege).

[13.107] With regard to taxing of costs and discovery orders, in *Bula Ltd v Flynn*[147] a number of matters, in relation to which Bula sought a review of taxation of costs, related to the costs of discovery. Bula argued that under Order 31, rule 25, in the absence of a certificate from the court given at the trial of an action, the costs of discovery cannot be allowed as part of the costs of the parties seeking such discovery.

[13.108] Order 31, rule 25 provides as follows:

'In every cause, or matter, the costs of discovery, by interrogatories, or otherwise, shall unless otherwise ordered by the Court be allowed, as part of the costs of the parties seeking discovery, either as between party and party or solicitor and client, where, and only where, such discovery shall be certified by the Court of the trial or, if there is no trial, shall appear to the Court, or to the Taxing Master, upon special grounds to be certified by such Taxing Master, to have been reasonably asked for.'

McGuinness J noted that it was clear that the aim of this rule was to guard against unnecessary applications for discovery and the resulting unnecessary expenditure in costs. From the evidence given before the Taxing Master, and from the Taxing Master's rulings, it was clear, according to McGuinness J, that discovery in this action played a very large part both in the action itself and in the amount of work that had to be undertaken by both solicitors and Counsel for all sides.

[13.109] Hence, McGuinness J held:

'It seems to me that, in the circumstances of this particular trial, it would be lacking in reality to refuse costs of discovery on account of the absence of a certificate. It is quite clear that ... the discovery process was sparked off by the Plaintiffs and in those circumstances it is form that a cross-order would also be made against the Plaintiffs themselves. The Plaintiffs were well aware from the beginning that discovery on all sides would be necessary and it seems to me that it would be particularly unjust to permit them to rely on the technical absence of a certificate in order to deny costs of discovery to the Defendants. As I have already said the certificate provision in Order 31 is designed to prevent unnecessary discovery: in this action all parties were at one in agreeing that discovery was essential.'[148]

---

[147] *Bula Ltd v Flynn* (7 March 2000, unreported) HC (McGuinness J).
[148] *Bula Ltd v Flynn* (7 March 2000, unreported) HC (McGuinness J) at p 21.

Reform

[13.110] With regard to the general issue of clarity and justification of the application for discovery – something which has been particularly litigated in the tribunal context – the Rules of the Superior Courts have been amended to require this information to be included in such notice of motion which shall specify the precise categories of documents sought, and in the grounding affidavit, verify they are necessary and furnish the reasons why.

[13.111] See Rules of the Superior Courts (No 2) (Discovery) 1999[149] which provides:

1. The following shall be inserted as Order 31, rule 12 of the Rules of the Superior Courts in substitution for the existing Order 31, rule 12:

'(1)   Any party may apply to the Court by way of notice for an order directing any other party to any cause or matter to make discovery on oath of the documents which are or have been in his or her possession or power, relating to any matter in question therein. Every such notice of motion shall specify the precise categories of documents in respect of which discovery is sought and shall be grounded upon the affidavit of the party seeking such an order of discovery which shall:

    (a) verify that the discovery of documents sought is necessary for disposing fairly of the cause or matter or for saving costs;

    (b) furnish the reasons why each category of documents is required to be discovered.

(2)   On the hearing of such application the Court may either refuse or adjourn the same, if satisfied that such discovery is not necessary, or not necessary at that stage of the cause or matter, or by virtue of non-compliance with the provisions of subrule 4(1), or make such order on terms as to security for the costs of discovery or otherwise and either generally or limited to certain classes or documents as may be thought fit.

(3)   An order shall not be made under this rule if and so far as the Court shall be of the opinion that it is not necessary either for disposing fairly of the cause or matter or for saving costs.

(4)(1) An order under sub-rule 1 directing any party or under rule 29 directing any other person to make discovery shall not be made unless:

    (a) the applicant for same shall have previously applied by letter in writing requesting that discovery be made voluntarily, specifying the precise categories of documents in respect of which discovery is sought and furnishing the reasons why each category of documents is required to be discovered; and

---

[149] SI 223/1999.

(b) a reasonable period of time for such discovery has been allowed; and

(c) the party or person requested has failed, refused or neglected to make such discovery or has ignored such request.

Provided that in any case where by reason of the urgency of the matter or consent of the parties, the nature of the case or any other circumstances which to the Court seem appropriate, the Court may make such order as appears proper, without the necessity for such prior application in writing.

(2) Any such discovery sought and agreed between parties or between parties and any other person shall, subject to sub-rule 4 below, be made in like manner and form and have such effect as if directed by order of the Court.

(3) In any case in which discovery has been sought and agreed and has not been made within the time agreed, the party who has sought same may make application pursuant to rule 21 provided that when seeking discovery the party requested was informed that:

(a) such voluntary discovery was being sought pursuant to Order 31 rule 12 sub-rule 4;

(b) agreement to make discovery would require it to be made in like manner and form and would have such effect as if directed by order;

(c) failure to make discovery may result in an application pursuant to rule 21;

and the Court may, if satisfied that it is proper so to do, make such order under rule 12, 19 and 21 as is appropriate or such other order as appears just in the circumstances.

(4) An application for discovery whether under rule 12(1) or (4) shall be made not later than twenty-eight days after the action has been set down or in matters which are not set down, twenty-eight days after it has been listed for trial provided that the Court or the party requested may order or agree, as the case may be, to extend the time for the application for discovery in any case which it appears just and reasonable so to do.

(5) The costs of an application to Court for discovery in any case in which prior written application has not been made or in which application has not been made within the time provided, shall be in the discretion of the Court.'

2. This rule shall be construed together with the Rules of the Superior Courts, 1986 to 1999 and may be cited as the Rules of the Superior Courts (No 2) (Discovery), 1999.

3. This rule shall come into operation on the 3rd day of August, 1999.'

[13.112] The changes in the Rules of the Superior Courts in 1999 were an attempt to resolve difficulties related to the growth in the number of unnecessary court applications for irrelevant documentation.

The Rules of the Superior Courts (No 2) (Discovery) 1999[150] according to Kavanagh[151], were an attempt '…to compel applicants to give greater thought to the drafting of discovery applications and …. to encourage agreement being reached without the need for the intervention of the courts.' The new rules require a party seeking discovery to apply by notice of motion specifying the precise categories of documents sought. The application must be grounded on an affidavit stating, inter alia, the reasons why each category of documents is required to be discovered. Rule 12(4) requires that a party seeking discovery must first write to the respondent requesting that discovery be made voluntarily and specifying the precise categories of documents sought and the reasons why each category is sought. According to r 12(4), an order for discovery shall not be made unless such a letter is sent allowing a reasonable period for voluntary discovery to be made. The new rules force a party seeking discovery to specify precisely what he is looking for and why, and encourage parties to reach agreement in relation to discovery. This limits the amount of documentation required to be discovered and the necessity for applications to the courts.

[13.113] The rules were considered in *Swords v Western Proteins*[152]. The facts in this case concerned personal injury sustained in an accident at work, where the plaintiff's solicitor was seeking voluntary discovery of, inter alia, the accident report book. The defendant's solicitors pointed out that they did not outline the precise nature of the documents or the reason they were required. An application was made to the Master, who adjourned, allowing a supplementary affidavit to be submitted by the plaintiff. The High Court was asked whether the Master could make an order for discovery if Order 31, rule 12(4)(1)(a)–(c), was complied with. Morris P pointed out that 'blanket discovery' was a thing of the past and, in an effect, held that the Master's jurisdiction was dependent on Order 31, rule12(4)(1), being complied with, ie that the letter seeking voluntary disclosure set out the required documents and reasons.

The effect of *Swords* is that it is essential that the voluntary discovery letter specifies precise categories of documents and gives reasons. If it does not, the Master has no jurisdiction.

---

150 SI 223/1999.
151 Kavanagh 'Discovery and the need for Strict Compliance with the 1999 Rules' [2001] 6 Bar Rev 273 at 274.
152 *Swords v Western Proteins* (29 November 2000, unreported) HC (Morris P).

This decision would appear to undermine the role of the Master, and perhaps over-emphasise the role of the letter seeking voluntary disclosure. Nonetheless, it does prove the veracity of the statement by Morris P, that:

> '... discovery before the advent of the photocopying machine, fax, e-mail and word processor would probably involve the discovery of a dozen documents. In recent years, the number of documents discovered can amount to many thousand and the process has become unmanageable'.[153]

[13.114] In *Pier v Aghadoe Developments Ltd & Another*[154] it would seem to have been held that, at least in the Master's Court, only documents necessary to prove the principal fact on which liability might be deduced will be discovered. This would seem to significantly narrow the scope of discovery, and would seem to prejudge issues at a very early stage. This would not seem to have been the aim of the new rules which would have been only to introduce stricter procedural requirements in the face of voluminous discovery.

If there are problems which ensue with regard to parties experiencing difficulties accessing evidence, this can only result in appeals, which will further lengthen the process, undercutting the value of what the reforms were introduced to combat in the first place.

---

[153] *Swords v Western Protein* (29 November 2000, unreported) HC at p 7.

[154]*Pier v Aghadoe Developments Ltd & Another* (19 February 2001), HC McKechnie J.

Appendix A

CRIMINAL JUSTICE ACT, 1984 (TREATMENT OF PERSONS IN CUSTODY IN GARDA SÍOCHÁNA STATIONS) REGULATIONS, 1987

SI No 119/1987

CONTENTS

PRELIMINARY AND GENERAL

PRELIMINARY AND GENERAL

I, GERARD COLLINS, Minister for Justice, in exercise of the powers conferred on me by section 7 of the Criminal Justice Act, 1984 (No. 22 of 1984), hereby make the following Regulations with respect to which, pursuant to that section, a draft has been laid before each House of the Oireachtas and a resolution approving of the draft has been passed by each such House:

1. Title and commencement

(1) These Regulations may be cited as the Criminal Justice Act, 1984 (Treatment of Persons in Custody in Garda Síochána Stations) Regulations, 1987.

(2) These Regulations shall come into operation one month after the date on which they are made.

2. Interpretation

(1) In these Regulations:—

"the Act" means the Criminal Justice Act, 1984 (No. 22 of 1984);

"adult" means a person not below the age of eighteen years and

"adult relative" shall be construed accordingly;

"arrested person" means a person who is taken on arrest to, or

arrested in, a station;

"custody" means custody in a Garda Síochána station;

"custody record" means a record kept under Regulation 6;

"district" means a Garda Síochána district;

"doctor" means a registered medical practitioner;

"member" means a member of the Garda Síochána;

"member in charge" has the meaning assigned to it by Regulation 4(1);

"station" means a Garda Síochána station;

"superintendent" means a superintendent of the Garda Síochána and, in relation to a district, means a superintendent who is in charge of the district and includes an inspector of the Garda Síochána who is in charge of the district in the superintendent's absence.

(2) In these Regulations a reference to a person signing a document shall include, in the case of a person unable to write, a reference to the person making his mark.

(3) In Regulations 12(8) and 18(1) "appropriate adult", in relation to a person in custody, means—

(a) in case the person is married and his spouse is an adult and is readily available, his spouse, and

(b) in any other case, his parent or guardian or, where a parent or guardian is not readily available, an adult relative or some other responsible adult, as may be appropriate, in attendance at the station pursuant to subparagraph (b) or (c) of Regulation 13(2).

(4) If and for so long as the member in charge of a station in which a person is in custody has reasonable grounds for believing that the person is not below the age of seventeen years, the provisions of these Regulations shall apply as if he had attained that age.

(5) In these Regulations a reference to a Regulation is a reference to a regulation of these Regulations and a reference to a paragraph or subparagraph is a reference to the

paragraph or subparagraph of the provision in which the reference occurs, unless it is indicated that reference to some other Regulation or provision, as may be appropriate, is intended.

3. General

(1) In carrying out their functions under these Regulations members shall act with due respect for the personal rights of persons in custody and their dignity as human persons, and shall have regard for the special needs of any of them who may be under a physical or mental disability, while complying with the obligation to prevent escapes from custody and continuing to act with diligence and determination in the investigation of crime and the protection and vindication of the personal rights of other persons.

(2) There shall be no unnecessary delay in dealing with persons in custody.

4. Member in charge

(1) In these Regulations "member in charge" means the member who is in charge of a station at a time when the member in charge of a station is required to do anything or cause anything to be done pursuant to these Regulations.

(2) The superintendent in charge of a district shall issue instructions in writing from time to time, either generally or by reference to particular members or members of particular ranks or to particular circumstances, as to who is to be the member in charge of each station in the district.

(3) As far as practicable, the member in charge shall not be a member who was involved in the arrest of a person for the offence in respect of which he is in custody in the station or in the investigation of that offence.

(4) The superintendent in charge of a district shall ensure that a written record is maintained in each station in his district containing the name and rank of the member in charge at any given time.

5. Duties of member in charge

(1) The member in charge shall be responsible for overseeing the application of these Regulations in relation to persons in custody in the station and for that purpose shall visit them from time to time and make any necessary enquiries.

(2) Paragraph (1) is without prejudice to the responsibilities and duties of any other member in relation to persons in custody.

(3) Where it appears to the member in charge that a direction given or action taken by a member of higher rank is inconsistent with the proper application of these Regulations, he shall inform that member accordingly and, unless the matter is resolved, report it without delay to another member of or above the rank of superintendent.

(4) (a) Where, by reason of the number of persons in custody or other circumstances, the member in charge is unable to carry out adequately the duty imposed on him by paragraph (1) in relation to visiting persons in custody and making any necessary enquiries, he may authorise in writing another member to carry out that duty.

(b) The authorisation shall specify the reasons for giving it and shall terminate when these reasons no longer apply.

(c) In the case of the Bridewell Station, Dublin, the member with particular responsibility for the cell area shall be deemed to have been authorised under subparagraph (a) by the member in charge and subparagraph (b) shall not apply.

6. Custody record

(1) A record (in these Regulations referred to as the custody record) shall be kept in respect of each person in custody.

(2) The member in charge shall record or cause to be recorded in the custody record as soon as practicable such information as is required to be recorded by these Regulations. Each entry in the record shall be signed or initialled by the member making it.

(3) Where a person in custody is transferred to another station, the member in charge of the station from which he is transferred shall send with him the custody record relating to him, or a copy of it, to the member in charge of that other station.

(4) Without prejudice to the responsibility of any other member for the accuracy and completeness of any entry which he has made in a custody record, the member in charge shall be responsible for the accuracy and completeness of all entries made in the custody record while he is the member in charge.

(5) Paragraph (2) does not apply to a record referred to in Regulation 10(5) or paragraph (10) or (11) of Regulation 12.

ARRESTED PERSONS

7. Record of arrest and detention

(1) in relation to an arrested person, a record shall be made of—

(a) the date, time and place of arrest and the identity of the arresting member (or other person effecting the arrest),

(b) the time of arrival at the station,

(c) the nature of the offence or other matter in respect of which he was arrested, and

(d) any relevant particulars relating to his physical or mental condition.

(2) In the case of a person who is being detained in a station pursuant to section 4 of the Act the member in charge at the time of the person's arrival at the station shall, when authorising the detention, enter in the custody record and sign the following statement:

> "I have reasonable grounds for believing that the detention of (*insert here the name of the person detained*) is necessary for the proper investigation of the offence(s) in respect of which he/she has been arrested."

(3) (a) Where a direction has been given by an officer of the Garda Síochána under section 4(3)(b) of the Act that a person be detained for a further period not exceeding six hours, the fact that the direction was given, the date and time when it was given and the name and rank of the officer who gave it shall be recorded.

418

(b) The direction or (if it was given orally) the written record of it shall be signed by the officer giving it and—

    (i) shall state the date and time when it was given and the officer's name and rank and that the officer had reasonable grounds for believing that such further detention was necessary for the proper investigation of the offence concerned, and

    (ii) shall be attached to and form part of the custody record.

(4) Where a direction has been given under section 30 of the Offences against the State Act, 1939 (No. 13 of 1939), that a person be detained for a further period not exceeding twenty-four hours, the fact that the direction was given, the date and time when it was given and the name and rank of the officer who gave it shall be recorded.

8. Information to be given to an arrested person

(1) The member in charge shall without delay inform an arrested person or cause him to be informed—

(a) in ordinary language of the offence or other matter in respect of which he has been arrested,

(b) that he is entitled to consult a solicitor, and

(c) (i) in the case of a person not below the age of seventeen years, that he is entitled to have notification of his being in custody in the station concerned sent to another person reasonably named by him, or

    (ii) in the case of a person under the age of seventeen years, that a parent or guardian (or, if he is married, his spouse) is being given the information required by Regulation 9(1)(a)(i) and is being requested to attend at the station without delay.

The information shall be given orally. The member in charge shall also explain or cause to be explained to the arrested person that, if he does not wish to exercise a right specified in subparagraph (b) or (c)(i) immediately, he will not be precluded thereby from doing so later.

(2) The member in charge shall without delay give the arrested person or cause him to be given a notice containing the information specified in subparagraphs (b) and (c) of paragraph (1) and such other information as the Commissioner of the Garda Síochána, with the approval of the Minister for Justice, may from time to time direct.

(3) Paragraphs (1) and (2) apply only in relation to the member in charge of the station to which an arrested person is taken on arrest or in which he is arrested.

(4) The time of the giving of the information specified in paragraph (1) and the notice specified in paragraph (2) shall be recorded. The member in charge shall ask the arrested person or cause him to be asked to sign the custody record in acknowledgement of receipt of the notice. If he refuses to sign, the refusal shall be recorded.

9. Notification to solicitor or other persons

(1) (a) Where an arrested person is under the age of seventeen years, the member in charge of the station concerned shall as soon as practicable—

    (i) inform or cause to be informed a parent or guardian of the person—

419

(I)   of his being in custody in the station,

(II)   in ordinary language of the offence or other matter in respect of which he has been arrested, and

(III)   of his entitlement to consult a solicitor, and

(ii)   request the parent or guardian to attend at the station without delay.

(b) If the member in charge is unable to communicate with a parent or guardian, he shall inform the arrested person or cause him to be informed without delay of that fact and of his entitlement to have notification of his being in custody in the station concerned sent to another person reasonably named by him.

(c) If the arrested person is married, this paragraph shall have effect with the substitution of references to his spouse for the references to a parent or guardian.

(2) (a) Where an arrested person has asked for a solicitor or has asked that a person reasonably named by him should be notified of his being in custody in the station concerned—

(i)   the member in charge shall notify or cause to be notified the solicitor or that person accordingly as soon as practicable, and

(ii)   if the solicitor or the named person cannot be contacted within a reasonable time or if the solicitor is unable or unwilling to attend at the station, the person shall be given an opportunity to ask for another solicitor or that another person reasonably named by him should be notified as aforesaid and, if the person asks for another solicitor or asks that another person reasonably named by him should be notified as aforesaid, the member in charge shall notify or cause to be notified that other solicitor or person accordingly as soon as practicable.

(b) If the arrested person is under the age of seventeen years, subparagraph (a) shall also apply in relation to a request for a solicitor by a parent of his or his guardian or spouse or by an adult who is present during the questioning of the arrested person in accordance with subparagraph (b) or (c) of Regulation 13(2) with the substitution of references to a parent of his, his guardian or spouse or such an adult for the references to an arrested person.

(3) Where an arrested person is being transferred to another station, the member in charge of the station from which he is being transferred shall inform any person who has been notified or informed under this Regulation, or cause him to be informed, of the transfer as soon as practicable.

(4) Any request made by a person under this Regulation and the time at which it was made and complied with and any action taken by a member under this Regulation and the time at which it was taken shall be recorded.

10. Enquiries

(1) Information as to the station where an arrested person is in custody shall be given—

(a) if the arrested person consents, in response to an enquiry by a solicitor whose presence has not been requested by him;

(b) if the arrested person consents and the member in charge is satisfied that giving the information will not hinder or delay the investigation of crime, in response to an enquiry by any other person.

(2) As soon as practicable after a person is taken on arrest to, or arrested in, a station other than a district headquarters, the member in charge of the station shall notify the district headquarters for the district or cause it to be notified accordingly and shall also, as soon as practicable, notify the district headquarters for the district or cause it to be notified if the person is transferred to another station or ceases to be in the custody of the Garda Síochána.

(3) Where a person is in custody in a district other than that in which he resides, the member in charge shall also, as soon as practicable, notify or cause to be notified the district headquarters for the district in which the person resides.

(4) A notification to a district headquarters under this Regulation and the time of the notification shall be recorded.

(5) A record shall be kept in each district headquarters of persons whose whereabouts have been notified to it under this Regulation and of the times of the notifications.

(6) The Commissioner of the Garda Síochána may from time to time designate a station or stations in the Dublin Metropolitan Area for the purpose of receiving notifications under this Regulation and, if and for so long as a station or stations is or are so designated, then notwithstanding anything in this Regulation, as respects a district in that Area—

(a) the said notifications shall be made to the station, or one of the stations, so designated and, in case the person in custody resides in a district outside that Area, to the district headquarters for that district, and

(b) paragraphs (4) and (5) shall have effect as if the reference in paragraph (4) to a district headquarters were a reference to a station so designated and as if the reference in paragraph (5) to each district headquarters were a reference to the station or, as the case may be, each of the stations so designated.

(7) In this Regulation "district headquarters" means the Garda Síochána headquarters for a district.

11. Visits and communications

(1) An arrested person shall have reasonable access to a solicitor of his choice and be enabled to communicate with him privately.

(2) Where an arrested person has not had access to a solicitor in accordance with paragraph (1) and a solicitor whose presence has not been requested by the arrested person presents himself at the station and informs the member in charge that he wishes to visit that person, the person shall be asked if he wishes to consult the solicitor and, if he does so wish, the said paragraph (1) shall apply accordingly.

(3) A consultation with a solicitor may take place in the sight but out of hearing of a member.

(4) An arrested person may receive a visit from a relative, friend or other person with an interest in his welfare provided that he so wishes and the member in charge is satisfied

that the visit can be adequately supervised and that it will not hinder or delay the investigation of crime.

(5) (a) An arrested person may make a telephone call of reasonable duration free of charge to a person reasonably named by him or send a letter (for which purpose writing materials and, where necessary, postage stamps shall be supplied on request) provided that the member in charge is satisfied that it will not hinder or delay the investigation of crime. A member may listen to any such telephone call and may terminate it if he is not so satisfied and may read any such letter and decline to send it if he is not so satisfied.

   (b) Subparagraph (a) is without prejudice to the provision of paragraph (1).

(6) Before an arrested person has a supervised visit or communicates with a person other than his solicitor, he shall be informed that anything he says during the visit or in the communication may be given in evidence.

12. Interviews (general)

(1) Before an arrested person is interviewed, the member conducting the interview shall identify himself and any other member present by name and rank to the arrested person.

(2) The interview shall be conducted in a fair and humane manner.

(3) Not more than two members shall question the arrested person at any one time and not more than four members shall be present at any one time during the interview.

(4) If an interview has lasted for four hours, it shall be either terminated or adjourned for a reasonable time.

(5) As far as practicable interviews shall take place in rooms set aside for that purpose.

(6) Where an arrested person asks for a solicitor, he shall not be asked to make a written statement in relation to an offence until a reasonable time for the attendance of the solicitor has elapsed.

(7) (a) Except with the authority of the member in charge, an arrested person shall not be questioned between midnight and 8 a.m. in relation to an offence, which authority shall not be given unless—

   (i) he has been taken to the station during that period,

   (ii) in the case of a person detained under section 4 of the Act, he has not consented in writing to the suspension of questioning in accordance with subsection (6) of that section, or

   (iii) the member in charge has reasonable grounds for believing that to delay questioning the person would involve a risk of injury to persons, serious loss of or damage to property, destruction of or interference with evidence or escape of accomplices.

   (b) Subparagraph (a) (i) is subject to the provisions of Regulation 19(2).

(8) (a) Where an arrested person is deaf or there is doubt about his hearing ability, he shall not be questioned in relation to an offence in the absence of an interpreter, if one is reasonably available, without his written consent (and, where he is under the age of seventeen years, the written consent of an appropriate adult) or in the circumstances specified in paragraph (7)(a)(iii).

(b) A consent shall be signed by the arrested person and be recorded in the custody record or a separate document.

(c) Where an arrested person has requested the presence of an interpreter under subparagraph (a) and one is not reasonably available, any questions shall be put to him in writing.

(9) An arrested person who is under the influence of intoxicating liquor or drugs to the extent that he is unable to appreciate the significance of questions put to him or his answers shall not be questioned in relation to an offence while he is in that condition except with the authority of the member in charge, which authority shall not be given except in the circumstances specified in paragraph (7)(a)(iii).

(10) If, while being interviewed, an arrested person makes a complaint to a member in relation to his treatment while in custody, the member shall bring it to the attention of the member in charge, if he is not present at the interview, and record it or cause it to be recorded in the record of the interview.

(11)(a) A record shall be made of each interview either by the member conducting it or by another member who is present. It shall include particulars of the time the interview began and ended, any breaks in it, the place of the interview and the names and ranks of the members present.

(b) Where an interview is not recorded by electronic or other similar means, the record shall—

   (i) be made in the notebook of the member concerned or in a separate document and shall be as complete as practicable,

   (ii) if it is practicable to do so and the member concerned is of opinion that it will not interfere with the conduct of the interview, be made while the interview is in progress or otherwise as soon as practicable afterwards, and

   (iii) be signed by the member making it and include the date and time of signature.

(12)(a) A record shall be made of the times during which an arrested person is interviewed and the members present at each interview.

(b) Where an authority is given pursuant to this Regulation, the fact that it was given, the name and rank of the member giving the authority and the reasons for doing so shall be recorded.

(c) The fact that an arrested person has consented in writing under section 4 (6) of the Act to the suspension of questioning between midnight and 8 a.m. shall be recorded and the consent shall be attached to and form part of the custody record.

(d) The particulars specified in section 4(6)(d) of the Act shall be recorded.

13. Interviews (persons under seventeen years)

(1) Except with the authority of the member in charge, an arrested person who is under the age of seventeen years shall not be questioned in relation to an offence or asked to make a written statement unless a parent or guardian is present, which authority shall not be given unless—

(a) it has not been possible to communicate with a parent or guardian in accordance with Regulation 9(1)(a),

(b) no parent or guardian has attended at the station concerned within a reasonable time of being informed that the person was in custody and of being requested so to attend,

(c) it is not practicable for a parent or guardian to attend within a reasonable time, or

(d) the member in charge has reasonable grounds for believing that to delay questioning the person would involve a risk of injury to persons or serious loss of or damage to property, destruction of or interference with evidence or escape of accomplices:

Provided that a parent or guardian may be excluded from the questioning with the authority of the member in charge which authority shall not be given unless—

(i) the parent or guardian concerned is the victim of, or has been arrested in respect of, the offence being investigated,

(ii) the member in charge has reasonable grounds—

(I) for suspecting him of complicity in the offence, or

(II) for believing that he would, if present during the questioning, be likely to obstruct the course of justice, or

(III) while so present, his conduct has been such as to amount to an obstruction of the course of justice.

(2) Where an arrested person who is under the age of seventeen years is to be questioned in relation to an offence in the absence of a parent or guardian, the member in charge shall, unless it is not practicable to do so, arrange for the presence during the questioning of—

(a) the other parent or another guardian,

(b) if the other parent or another guardian is not readily available or his presence, having regard to the proviso to paragraph (1), is not appropriate, an adult relative, or

(c) if the other parent or another guardian or an adult relative is not readily available or the presence of the other parent or another guardian is, having regard to the said proviso, not appropriate, some other responsible adult other than a member.

(3) Where a request for the attendance of a solicitor is made during the questioning by the parent or guardian, spouse, adult relative or other adult present, Regulation 12(6) shall apply as if the request had been made by the arrested person.

(4) Where an authority is given to a member to question an arrested person in the absence of a parent or guardian, or to exclude a parent, guardian or other person from the questioning pursuant to paragraph (1) or (2), the fact that the authority was given, the name and rank of the member giving it, the reasons for doing so and the action taken in compliance with the said paragraph (2) shall be recorded.

(5) (a) This Regulation is without prejudice to the provisions of Regulation 12.

(b) This Regulation (other than paragraph (3)), in its application to a person under the age of seventeen years who is married to an adult, shall have effect with the substitution of references to the person's spouse for the references (other than those in subparagraphs (a), (b) and (c) of paragraph (2)) to a parent or guardian and as if "a parent or guardian" were substituted for "the other parent or another guardian" in each place where it occurs in those subparagraphs.

14. Foreign nationals

(1) The member in charge shall without delay inform or cause to be informed any arrested person who is a foreign national that he may communicate with his consul and that, if he so wishes, the consul will be notified of his arrest. The member in charge shall, on request, cause the consul to be notified as soon as practicable. Any communication addressed to him shall be forwarded as soon as practicable.

(2) Consular officers shall be entitled to visit one of their nationals, or a national of another State for whom, by formal or informal arrangement, they offer consular assistance, who is an arrested person and to converse and correspond with him and to arrange for his legal representation.

(3) This Regulation is without prejudice to the application to a national of a foreign country of the provisions of a consular convention or arrangement between the State and that country.

(4) If the member in charge has reasonable grounds for believing that an arrested person who is a foreign national is a political refugee or is seeking political asylum, a consular officer shall not be notified of his arrest or given access to or information about him except at the express request of the foreign national.

(5) A record shall be made of the time when a foreign national was informed or notified in accordance with this Regulation, when any request was made, when the request was complied with and when any communication was forwarded to a consul.

(6) In this Regulation "consul" means, in relation to a foreign national, the diplomatic or consular representative of that person's own country either in the State or accredited to the State on a nonresidential basis, or a diplomatic or consular representative of a third country which may formally or informally offer consular assistance to a national of a country which has no resident representative in the State.

15. Charge sheets

(1) Where a person in custody is charged with an offence, a copy of the charge sheet containing particulars of the offence shall be given to him as soon as practicable. Where the person charged is under the age of seventeen years, a copy of the charge sheet shall also be given to the person's parent or guardian or (where the person is married to an adult) to the spouse if present when the person is charged or, if not present, shall be forwarded as soon as practicable.

(2) A record shall be made of the time when the person was charged with an offence. The charge sheet number (or numbers) shall also be recorded. Where a copy of a charge sheet is given to a person in the station, he shall be asked to sign the custody record in acknowledgement of its receipt. If he refuses to sign it, the refusal shall be recorded.

PERSONS OTHER THAN ARRESTED PERSONS

16. Provisions relating to persons other than arrested persons

(1) This Regulation applies to a person in custody other than an arrested person.

(2) Information as to the station where a person to whom this Regulation applies is in custody shall be given in response to an enquiry by—

    (a) his solicitor,

    (b) if the person consents, another solicitor,

    (c) if the person consents and the member in charge is satisfied that giving the information will not prejudice the person's safe custody, any other person.

(3) Regulation 10, except paragraph (1), shall have effect in relation to a person to whom this Regulation applies and who is expected to remain in custody overnight.

    (4) (a) Where a person to whom this Regulation applies has asked for a solicitor, the member in charge shall notify the solicitor or cause him to be notified accordingly.

        (b) If the solicitor cannot be contacted within a reasonable time or if he is unable or unwilling to attend at the station, the person shall be given an opportunity to ask for another solicitor.

    (5) (a) Paragraphs (1) and (2) of Regulation 11 shall have effect in relation to a person to whom this Regulation applies.

        (b) Such a person may receive a visit from a relative, friend or other person with an interest in his welfare provided that he so wishes and the member in charge is satisfied that the visit can be adequately supervised and that it will not be prejudicial to the interests of justice.

(6) Regulation 14, except paragraph (1), shall have effect in relation to a foreign national to whom this Regulation applies.

PROVISIONS APPLICABLE GENERALLY

17. Searches

(1) A member conducting a search of a person in custody shall ensure, so far as practicable, that the person understands the reason for the search and that it is conducted with due respect for the person being searched.

(2) A person in custody shall not be searched by a person (other than a doctor) of the opposite sex.

(3) Where a search of a person in custody involves removal of clothing, other than headgear or a coat, jacket, glove or similar article of clothing, no person of the opposite sex shall be present unless either that person is a doctor or the member in charge considers that the presence of that person is necessary by reason of the violent conduct of the person to be searched.

(4) A search of a person in custody involving removal of underclothing shall, where practicable, be carried out by a doctor.

(5) Where clothing or footwear of a person is retained, replacements of a reasonable standard shall be provided.

(6) A record shall be made of a search of a person in custody including the name of the person conducting the search and the names of those present.

(7) Particulars of any property taken from or handed over by a person in custody shall be recorded. The person shall be asked to sign the record of such property as being correct. If he refuses to do so, the refusal shall be recorded at the time of refusal.

18. Fingerprints, etc

(1) (a) Fingerprints, palm prints or photographs shall not be taken of, or swabs or samples taken from, a person in custody (otherwise than pursuant to a power conferred on a member by law) except with his written consent and, where he is under the age of seventeen years, the written consent of an appropriate adult.

(b) A consent shall be signed and be recorded in the custody record or a separate document.

(2) The fact that fingerprints, palm prints, photographs, swabs or samples have been taken of or from a person in custody shall be recorded.

(3) Where the authority of a member of the Garda Síochána of a specified rank is required for the taking of fingerprints, palm prints or photographs of a person in custody, the name and rank of the member giving the authority shall be recorded.

19. Conditions of custody

(1) A person shall be kept in custody only in a station which has facilities to enable him to be treated in accordance with these Regulations for the period during which he is expected to be in custody in that station.

(2) A person in custody shall be allowed such reasonable time for rest as is necessary.

(3) A person in custody shall be provided with such meals as are necessary and, in any case, at least two light meals and one main meal in any twenty-four hour period. He may have meals supplied at his own expense where it is practicable for the member in charge to arrange this.

(4) Access to toilet facilities shall be provided for a person in custody.

(5) Where it is necessary to place persons in custody in cells, as far as practicable not more than one person shall be kept in each cell. Persons of the opposite sex shall not be placed in a cell together. A violent person shall not be placed in a cell with other persons if this can be avoided.

(6) Where a person is kept in a cell, a member shall visit him at intervals of approximately half an hour. A drunken person or a person under the influence of drugs shall be visited and spoken to and if necessary roused for this purpose at intervals of approximately a quarter of an hour for a period of two hours or longer if his condition warrants it.

(7) A member shall be accompanied when visiting a person in custody of the opposite sex who is alone in a cell.

(8) A person in custody under the age of seventeen years shall not be kept in a cell unless there is no other secure accommodation available and where practicable shall not be placed in a cell with an adult other than an adult relative.

20. Persons in custody not to be illtreated

(1) No member shall subject a person in custody to ill-treatment of any kind or the threat of ill-treatment (whether against the person himself, his family or any other person connected with him) or permit any other person to do so.

(2) No member shall use force against a person in custody except such reasonable force as is necessary—

  (a) in self-defence,

  (b) to secure compliance with lawful directions,

  (c) to prevent his escape, or

  (d) to restrain him from injuring himself or others, damaging property or destroying or interfering with evidence.

(3) If a member uses force which causes injury to a person in custody, he shall, if he is not the member in charge, report the circumstances to that member, who shall report the matter to the superintendent in charge of the district. If the force is used by the member in charge, he shall report the circumstances to that superintendent.

(4) If it comes to the notice of a member that there has been a contravention of paragraph (1), (2) or (3) by another member—

  (a) he shall report the matter to the member in charge or (in case the contravention is by the member in charge) to the superintendent in charge of the district, and

  (b) unless the matter has already been reported to that superintendent, the member in charge shall report it to him.

(5) The action taken in accordance with paragraph (3) or (4) shall be recorded.

(6) On receipt of a report under paragraph (3) or (4) by a superintendent, he shall investigate the matter without delay or cause it to be so investigated.

(7) If a person in custody makes a complaint concerning the conduct of a member (whether before or after his arrest) or, if such a complaint is made on his behalf, the fact that a complaint was made shall be recorded. Particulars of the complaint shall be recorded in a separate document, a copy of which shall be attached to and form part of the custody record. If the complaint alleges physical ill-treatment, the member in charge shall arrange for the person to be medically examined as soon as practicable unless, in a case where the allegation relates to another member, he considers the complaint to be frivolous or vexatious.

21. Medical treatment

(1) If a person in custody—

  (a) is injured,

  (b) is under the influence of intoxicating liquor or drugs and cannot be roused,

  (c) fails to respond normally to questions or conversation (otherwise than owing to the influence of intoxicating liquor alone),

  (d) appears to the member in charge to be suffering from a mental illness, or

  (e) otherwise appears to the member in charge to need medical attention,

The member in charge shall summon a doctor or cause him to be summoned, unless the person's condition appears to the member in charge to be such as to necessitate immediate removal to a hospital or other suitable place. The member in charge shall ensure that any instructions given by a doctor in relation to the medical care of a person in custody are complied with.

(2) Notwithstanding that paragraph (1) may not apply, medical advice shall be sought if the person in custody claims to need medication relating to a heart condition, diabetes, epilepsy or other potentially serious condition or the member in charge considers it necessary because the person has in his possession any such medication.

(3) The removal of a person in custody to a hospital or other suitable place and the time of removal shall be recorded. Any instructions given by a doctor regarding the medical care of a person in custody and the steps taken to comply with them shall also be recorded.

(4) If a person in custody asks to be examined by a doctor of his choice at his own expense, the member in charge shall, if and as soon as practicable, make arrangements accordingly. This shall not preclude his examination by another doctor summoned by the member in charge provided that the person in custody consents to the examination.

(5) A record shall be made of any medical examination sought by the member in charge or person in custody, the time the examination was sought and the time it was carried out. If it is not practicable to accede to a request by a person in custody for medical examination by the doctor of his choice at his own expense, the relevant circumstances shall also be recorded.

(16) Where a person in custody has been removed to a hospital or other suitable place, an immediate relative and any other person required to be notified under Regulation 9 of the person's detention shall be so informed as soon as practicable. The time at which the relative and other person were informed shall be recorded.

22. Mentally handicapped persons

(1) The provisions of these Regulations relating to persons under the age of seventeen years shall apply, in addition to any other applicable provisions, in relation to a person in custody not below that age whom the member in charge suspects or knows to be mentally handicapped.

(2) In the application of Regulation 13(2)(c) to such a person, the responsible adult referred to in that provision shall, where practicable, be a person who has experience in dealing with the mentally handicapped.

23. Other matters to be recorded

Particulars relating to any of the following matters (including the relevant time and the action, if any, taken by a member in relation thereto) shall also be recorded:

    (a)   visits to persons in custody by the member in charge or other members,

    (b)   any other visits to them,

    (c)   telephone and other enquiries concerning them,

    (d)   telephone calls made or letters sent by them,

(e) any requests made by them or by persons attending at the station and seeking to visit them,

(f) meals supplied to them,

(g) the ending of their custody (release, station bail, etc.).

24. Preservation of custody records

(1) Custody records shall be preserved for at least twelve months or, if any proceedings to which a custody record would be relevant are instituted or any complaint is made in respect of the conduct of a member while a person was in custody, until the final determination of the proceedings or complaint, whichever is the later.

(2) When a person ceases to be in custody, he or his legal representative shall, on request made within twelve months thereafter, be supplied as soon as practicable with a copy of the custody record relating to him or of such entries in it as he may specify.

GIVEN under my Official Seal, this 16th day of April, 1987.

GERARD COLLINS,

Minister for Justice.

Explanatory Note

(This note is not part of the instrument and does not purport to be a legal interpretation.)

The regulations contain detailed provisions regarding the treatment of persons in custody in Garda stations.

Appendix B

CRIMINAL EVIDENCE ACT, 1992

No. 12/1992

Note: Only Parts II-IV are reproduced here

PART II ADMISSIBILITY OF DOCUMENTARY EVIDENCE

4. Definition *(Part II)*

In this Part "business" includes any trade, profession or other occupation carried on, for reward or otherwise, either within or outside the State and includes also the performance of functions by or on behalf of—

(a) any person or body remunerated or financed wholly or partly out of moneys provided by the Oireachtas,

(b) any institution of the European Communities,

(c) any national or local authority in a jurisdiction outside the State, or

(d) any international organisation.

5. Admissibility of documentary evidence

(1) Subject to this Part, information contained in a document shall be admissible in any criminal proceedings as evidence of any fact therein of which direct oral evidence would be admissible if the information—

    (a) was compiled in the ordinary course of a business,

    (b) was supplied by a person (whether or not he so compiled it and is identifiable) who had, or may reasonably be supposed to have had, personal knowledge of the matters dealt with, and

    (c) in the case of information in non-legible form that has been reproduced in permanent legible form, was reproduced in the course of the normal operation of the reproduction system concerned.

(2) Subsection (1) shall apply whether the information was supplied directly or indirectly but, if it was supplied indirectly, only if each person (whether or not he is identifiable) through whom it was supplied received it in the ordinary course of a business.

(3) Subsection (1) shall not apply to—

    (a) information that is privileged from disclosure in criminal proceedings,

    (b) information supplied by a person who would not be compellable to give evidence at the instance of the party wishing to give the information in evidence by virtue of this section, or

    (c) subject to subsection (4), information compiled for the purposes or in contemplation of any—

        (i) criminal investigation,

        (ii) investigation or inquiry carried out pursuant to or under any enactment,

        (iii) civil or criminal proceedings, or

        (iv) proceedings of a disciplinary nature.

(4) Subsection (3) (c) shall not apply where—

    (a) (i) the information contained in the document was compiled in the presence of a judge of the District Court and supplied on oath by a person in respect of whom an offence was alleged to have been committed and who is ordinarily resident outside the State,

        (ii) either section 14 (which deals with the taking of a deposition in the presence of such a judge and the accused) of the Criminal Procedure Act, 1967, could not be invoked or it was not practicable to do so, and

        (iii) the person in respect of whom the offence was alleged to have been committed either has died or is outside the State and it is not reasonably practicable to secure his attendance at the criminal proceedings concerned, or

    (b) the document containing the information is—

(i) a map, plan, drawing or photograph (including any explanatory material in or accompanying the document concerned),

(ii) a record of a direction given by a member of the Garda Síochána pursuant to any enactment,

(iii) a record of the receipt, handling, transmission, examination or analysis of any thing by any person acting on behalf of any party to the proceedings, or

(iv) a record by a registered medical practitioner of an examination of a living or dead person.

(5) Without prejudice to subsection (1)—

(a) where a document purports to be a birth certificate issued in pursuance of the Births and Deaths Registration Acts, 1863 to 1987, and

(b) a person is named therein as father or mother of the person to whose birth the certificate relates,

the document shall be admissible in any criminal proceedings as evidence of the relationship indicated therein.

(6) Where information is admissible in evidence by virtue of this section but is expressed in terms that are not intelligible to the average person without explanation, an explanation of the information shall also be admissible in evidence if either—

(a) it is given orally by a person who is competent to do so, or

(b) it is contained in a document and the document purports to be signed by such a person.

6. Evidence of admissibility

(1) In relation to information contained in a document which a party to criminal proceedings wishes to give in evidence by virtue of section 5, a certificate—

(a) stating that the information was compiled in the ordinary course of a specified business,

(b) stating that the information is not of a kind mentioned in paragraph (a) or (b) of section 5 (3),

(c) either stating that the information was not compiled for the purposes or in contemplation of any investigation, inquiry or proceedings referred to in section 5 (3) (c) or, as the case may be, specifying which of the provisions of section 5 (4) applies in relation to the document containing the information,

(d) stating that the information was supplied, either directly or, as the case may be, indirectly through an intermediary or intermediaries (who, or each of whom, received it in the ordinary course of a specified business), by a person who had, or may reasonably be supposed to have had, personal knowledge of the matters dealt with in the information and, where the intermediary, intermediaries or person can be identified, specifying them,

(e) in case the information is information in non-legible form that has been reproduced in permanent legible form, stating that the reproduction was effected in the course of the normal operation of a specified system,

(f) where appropriate, stating that the person who supplied the information cannot reasonably be expected to have any, or any adequate, recollection of the matters dealt with in the information, having regard to the time that has elapsed since he supplied it or to any other specified circumstances,

(g) unless the date on which the information was compiled is already shown on the document, specifying the date (or, if that date is not known, the approximate date) on which it was compiled,

(h) stating any other matter that is relevant to the admissibility in evidence of the information and is required by rules of court to be certified for the purposes of this subsection,

and purporting to be signed by a person who occupies a position in relation to the management of the business in the course of which the information was compiled or who is otherwise in a position to give the certificate shall be evidence of any matter stated or specified therein.

(2) For the purposes of subsection (1) it shall be sufficient for a matter to be stated or specified to the best of the knowledge and belief of the person stating or specifying it.

(3) Notwithstanding that a certificate may have been given pursuant to subsection (1), the court—

(a) shall, where a notice has been served pursuant to section 7 (2) objecting to the admissibility in evidence of the whole or any specified part of the information concerned, and

(b) may, in any other case,

require oral evidence to be given of any matter stated or specified in the certificate.

(4) If any person in a certificate given in evidence in any proceedings by virtue of subsection (1) makes a statement material in those proceedings which he knows to be false or does not believe to be true, he shall be guilty of an offence and shall be liable—

(a) on summary conviction, to a fine not exceeding £500 or imprisonment for a term not exceeding 6 months or both, or

(b) on conviction on indictment, to a fine or imprisonment for a term not exceeding 2 years or both.

7. Notice of documentary evidence

(1) Information in a document shall not, without the leave of the court, be admissible in evidence by virtue of section 5 at a trial unless—

(a) a copy of the document and, where appropriate, of a certificate pursuant to section 6 (1) has been served on the accused pursuant to section 6(1) of the Criminal Procedure Act, 1967, or

(b) not later than 21 days before the commencement of the trial, a notice of intention so to give the information in evidence, together with a copy of the document and, where appropriate, of the certificate, is served by or on behalf of the party proposing to give it in evidence on each of the other parties to the proceedings.

(2) A party to the proceedings on whom a notice has been served pursuant to subsection (1) shall not, without the leave of the court, object to the admissibility in evidence of the whole or any specified part of the information concerned unless, not later than 7 days before the commencement of the trial, a notice objecting to its admissibility is served by or on behalf of that party on each of the other parties to the proceedings.

(3) A document required by this section to be served on any person may, subject to subsection (4), be served—

   (a) by delivering it to him or to his solicitor,

   (b) by addressing it to him and leaving it at his usual or last known residence or place of business or by addressing it to his solicitor and leaving it at the solicitor's office,

   (c) by sending it by registered post to him at his usual or last known residence or place of business or to his solicitor at the solicitor's office, or

   (d) in the case of a body corporate, by delivering it to the secretary or clerk of the body at its registered or principal office or sending it by registered post to the secretary or clerk of that body at that office.

(4) A document required by this section to be served on an accused shall be served personally on him if he is not represented by a solicitor.

8. Admission and weight of documentary evidence

(1) In any criminal proceedings information or any part thereof that is admissible in evidence by virtue of section 5 shall not be admitted if the court is of opinion that in the interests of justice the information or that part ought not to be admitted.

(2) In considering whether in the interests of justice all or any part of such information ought not to be admitted in evidence the court shall have regard to all the circumstances, including—

   (a) whether or not, having regard to the contents and source of the information and the circumstances in which it was compiled, it is a reasonable inference that the information is reliable,

   (b) whether or not, having regard to the nature and source of the document containing the information and to any other circumstances that appear to the court to be relevant, it is a reasonable inference that the document is authentic, and

   (c) any risk, having regard in particular to whether it is likely to be possible to controvert the information where the person who supplied it does not attend to give oral evidence in the proceedings, that its admission or exclusion will result in unfairness to the accused or, if there is more than one, to any of them.

(3) In estimating the weight, if any, to be attached to information given in evidence by virtue of this Part, regard shall be had to all the circumstances from which any inference can reasonably be drawn as to its accuracy or otherwise.

9. Evidence as to credibility of supplier of information

Where information is given in evidence by virtue of this Part—

(a) any evidence which, if the person who originally supplied the information had been called as a witness, would have been admissible as relevant to his credibility as a witness shall be admissible for that purpose,

(b) evidence may, with the leave of the court, be given of any matter which, if that person had been called as a witness, could have been put to him in cross-examination as relevant to his credibility as a witness but of which evidence could not have been adduced by the cross-examining party, and

(c) evidence tending to prove that that person, whether before or after supplying the information, made (whether orally or not) a statement which is inconsistent with it shall, if not already admissible by virtue of section 5, be admissible for the purpose of showing that he has contradicted himself.

10. Amendment of Criminal Procedure Act, 1967

The Criminal Procedure Act, 1967, is hereby amended—

(a) by the substitution, for paragraphs (d) and (e) of section 6 (1) of that Act (which provides for the service of documents on an accused), of the following paragraphs:

"(d) a statement of the evidence that is to be given by each of them,

(e) a copy of any document containing information which it is proposed to give in evidence by virtue of Part II of the Criminal Evidence Act, 1992,

(f) where appropriate, a copy of a certificate pursuant to section 6 (1) of that Act, and

(g) a list of exhibits (if any).", and

(b) by the substitution, for section 11 of that Act (which provides for service of additional documents on an accused after he has been sent forward for trial), of the following section:

11. Additional documents

(1) Where the accused has been sent forward for trial the Director of Public Prosecutions shall cause to be served on him a list of any further witnesses whom he proposes to call at the trial, with a statement of the evidence that is to be given by each of them, a list of any further exhibits, a statement of any further evidence that is to be given by any witness whose name appears on the list of witnesses already supplied, any notice of intention to give information contained in a document in evidence pursuant to section 7(1)(b) of the Criminal Evidence Act, 1992, together with a copy of the document and any certificate pursuant to section 6 (1) of that Act, and copies of any statement recorded under section 7 and any deposition taken under that section or under section 14.

(2) Copies of the documents shall also be furnished to the trial court.".

11. Evidence of resolution of Dáil or Seanad

In any criminal proceedings evidence of the passing of a resolution by either House of the Oireachtas, whether before or after the commencement of this section, may be given by the production of a copy of the Journal of the proceedings of that House relating to the resolution and purporting to have been published by the Stationery Office.

PART III EVIDENCE IN CERTAIN PROCEEDINGS

12. Offences to which Part III applies

This Part applies to—

    (a) a sexual offence,

    (b) an offence involving violence or the threat of violence to a person, or

    (c) an offence consisting of attempting or conspiring to commit, or of aiding, abetting, counselling, procuring or inciting the commission of, an offence mentioned in paragraph (a) or (b).

13. Evidence through television link

(1) In any proceedings for an offence to which this Part applies a person other than the accused may give evidence, whether from within or outside the State, through a live television link—

    (a) if the person is under 17 years of age, unless the court sees good reason to the contrary,

    (b) in any other case, with the leave of the court.

(2) Evidence given under subsection (1) shall be videorecorded.

(3) While evidence is being given through a live television link pursuant to subsection (1) (except through an intermediary pursuant to section 14 (1)), neither the judge, nor the barrister or solicitor concerned in the examination of the witness, shall wear a wig or gown.

14. Evidence through intermediary

(1) Where—

    (a) a person is accused of an offence to which this Part applies, and

    (b) a person under 17 years of age is giving, or is to give, evidence through a live television link,

the court may, on the application of the prosecution or the accused, if satisfied that, having regard to the age or mental condition of the witness, the interests of justice require that any questions to be put to the witness be put through an intermediary, direct that any such questions be so put.

(2) Questions put to a witness through an intermediary under this section shall be either in the words used by the questioner or so as to convey to the witness in a way which is appropriate to his age and mental condition the meaning of the questions being asked.

(3) An intermediary referred to in subsection (1) shall be appointed by the court and shall be a person who, in its opinion, is competent to act as such.

15. Procedure in District Court in relation to certain offences

(1) Where—

    (a) a person is before the District Court charged with an offence to which this Part applies,

    (b) the person in respect of whom the offence is alleged to have been committed is a person under 17 years of age,

(c) the offence is not being tried summarily or is not being dealt with on a plea of guilty, and

(d) it is proposed, pursuant to section 16(1)(b), that a videorecording of a statement made by that person during an interview as mentioned in that provision shall be given in evidence at the trial,

the prosecution shall, in addition to causing the documents mentioned in section 6(1) of the Criminal Procedure Act, 1967, to be served on the accused—

    (i) notify him that it is proposed so to give evidence, and

    (ii) give him an opportunity of seeing the videorecording of the interview in advance of the preliminary examination.

(2) If at a preliminary examination of an offence to which this Part applies the person in respect of whom the offence is alleged to have been committed is available for cross-examination, any statement made by him on a videorecording mentioned in section 16(1)(b) may be considered by the judge of the District Court conducting the preliminary examination.

(3) If the accused consents, an edited version of the videorecording of an interview mentioned in section 16(1)(b) may, with the leave of the court, be shown at the preliminary examination and, in that event, subsection (2) and the said section 16(1)(b) shall apply in relation to that version as it applies to the original videorecording.

(4) The Criminal Justice (Legal Aid) Act, 1962, is hereby amended—

    (a) by the insertion after section 2 of the following section:

"2A. (1) Where—

    (a) a person is before the District Court charged with an offence to which Part III of the Criminal Evidence Act, 1992, applies, and

    (b) it is proposed that at the preliminary examination of the offence evidence will be given through a live television link pursuant to section 13 of that Act, and

    (c) a certificate for free legal aid (in this Act referred to as a legal aid (preliminary examination) certificate') is granted in respect of him by the District Court,

the person shall be entitled to free legal aid at the preliminary examination pursuant to a legal aid (preliminary examination) certificate and to have a solicitor and counsel assigned to him for that purpose in such manner as may be prescribed by regulations under section 10 of this Act.

(2) A legal aid (preliminary examination) certificate shall be granted in respect of a person if (but only if)—

    (a) application is made therefor,

    (b) it appears to the District Court—

        (i) that his means are insufficient to enable him to obtain legal aid, and

        (ii) that, having regard to all the circumstances of the case (including the nature of such defence (if any) as may have been set up), it is essential in the interests of justice that he should have legal aid at the preliminary examination.", and

(b) by the insertion in section 9 (2), after "legal aid (District Court) certificate," of "a legal aid (preliminary examination) certificate,".

16. Videorecording as evidence at trial

(1) Subject to subsection (2)—

(a) a videorecording of any evidence given by a person under 17 years of age through a live television link at the preliminary examination of an offence to which this Part applies, and

(b) a videorecording of any statement made by a person under 14 years of age (being a person in respect of whom such an offence is alleged to have been committed) during an interview with a member of the Garda Síochána or any other person who is competent for the purpose,

shall be admissible at the trial of the offence as evidence of any fact stated therein of which direct oral evidence by him would be admissible:

Provided that, in the case of a videorecording mentioned in paragraph (b), either—

(i) it has been considered in accordance with section 15 (2) by the judge of the District Court conducting the preliminary examination of the offence, or

(ii) the person whose statement was videorecorded is available at the trial for cross-examination.

(2) (a) Any such videorecording or any part thereof shall not be admitted in evidence as aforesaid if the court is of opinion that in the interests of justice the videorecording concerned or that part ought not to be so admitted.

(b) In considering whether in the interests of justice such videorecording or any part thereof ought not to be admitted in evidence, the court shall have regard to all the circumstances, including any risk that its admission will result in unfairness to the accused or, if there is more than one, to any of them.

(3) In estimating the weight, if any, to be attached to any statement contained in such a videorecording regard shall be had to all the circumstances from which any inference can reasonably be drawn as to its accuracy or otherwise.

(4) In this section "statement" includes any representation of fact, whether in words or otherwise.

17. Transfer of proceedings

In any proceedings for an offence to which this Part applies in any circuit or district court district in relation to which any of the provisions of sections 13 to 16 or section 29 is not in operation the court concerned may, if in its opinion it is desirable that evidence be given in the proceedings through a live television link or by means of a videorecording, by order transfer the proceedings to a circuit or district court district in relation to which those provisions are in operation and, where such an order is made, the jurisdiction of the court to which the proceedings have been transferred may be exercised—

(a) in the case of the Circuit Court, by the judge of the circuit concerned, and

(b) in the case of the District Court, by the judge of that court for the time being assigned to the district court district concerned.

18. Identification evidence

Where—

(a) a person is accused of an offence to which this Part applies, and

(b) evidence is given by a person (in this section referred to as "the witness") through a live television link pursuant to section 13 (1), then—

   (i)   in case evidence is given that the accused was known to the witness before the date on which the offence is alleged to have been committed, the witness shall not be required to identify the accused at the trial of the offence, unless the court in the interests of justice directs otherwise, and

   (ii) in any other case, evidence by a person other than the witness that the witness identified the accused at an identification parade as being the offender shall be admissible as evidence that the accused was so indentified.

19. Application of Part III to persons with mental handicap

The references in sections 13(1)(a), 14(1)(b), 15(1)(b) and 16(1)(a) to a person under 17 years of age and the reference in section 16 (1) (b) to a person under 14 years of age shall include references to a person with mental handicap who has reached the age concerned.

PART IV COMPETENCE AND COMPELLABILITY OF SPOUSES AND FORMER SPOUSES TO GIVE EVIDENCE

20. Definitions (Part IV)

In this Part—

"decree of judicial separation" includes a decree of divorce a mensa et thoro or any decree made by a court outside the State and recognised in the State as having the like effect;

"former spouse" includes a person who, in respect of his marriage to an accused—

(a) has been granted a decree of judicial separation, or

(b) has entered into a separation agreement;

"separation agreement" means an agreement in writing which provides for the spouses concerned living separately and apart from each other.

21. Competence of spouses and former spouses to give evidence

In any criminal proceedings the spouse or a former spouse of an accused shall be competent to give evidence at the instance—

(a) subject to section 25, of the prosecution, and

(b) of the accused or any person charged with him in the same proceedings.

22. Compellability to give evidence at instance of prosecution

(1) In any criminal proceedings the spouse of an accused shall, subject to section 25, be compellable to give evidence at the instance of the prosecution only in the case of an offence which—

(a) involves violence, or the threat of violence, to—

   (i)   the spouse,

   (ii)   a child of the spouse or of the accused, or

   (iii)   any person who was at the material time under the age of 17 years,

(b) is a sexual offence alleged to have been committed in relation to a person referred to in subparagraph (ii) or (iii) of paragraph (a), or

(c) consists of attempting or conspiring to commit, or of aiding, abetting, counselling, procuring or inciting the commission of, an offence falling within paragraph (a) or (b).

(2) In any criminal proceedings a former spouse of an accused shall, subject to section 25, be compellable to give evidence at the instance of the prosecution unless—

(a) the offence charged is alleged to have been committed at a time when the marriage was subsisting and no decree of judicial separation or separation agreement was in force, and

(b) it is not an offence mentioned in subsection (1).

(3) The reference in subsection (1) to a child of the spouse or the accused shall include a reference to—

(a) a child who has been adopted by the spouse or the accused under the Adoption Acts, 1952 to 1991, or, in the case of a child whose adoption by the spouse or the accused has been effected outside the State, whose adoption is recognised in the State by virtue of those Acts, and

(b) a person in relation to whom the spouse or the accused is in loco parentis.

23. Compellability to give evidence at instance of accused

Subject to section 25, in any criminal proceedings the spouse or a former spouse of an accused shall be compellable to give evidence at the instance of the accused.

24. Compellability to give evidence at instance of co-accused

(1) Subject to section 25, in any criminal proceedings—

(a) the spouse of an accused shall be compellable to give evidence at the instance of any person charged with the accused in the same proceedings only in the case of an offence mentioned in section 22(1),

(b) a former spouse of an accused shall be compellable to give evidence at the instance of any person charged with the accused in the same proceedings unless—

   (i)   the offence charged is alleged to have been committed at a time when the marriage was subsisting and no decree of judicial separation or separation agreement was in force, and

   (ii)   it is not an offence mentioned in section 22(1).

(2) Subsection (1) is without prejudice to the power of a court to order separate trials of persons charged in the same proceedings if it appears to it to be desirable in the interests of justice to do so.

25. Saving

Where persons (being either a husband and wife or persons who were formerly husband and wife) are charged in the same proceedings, neither shall at the trial be competent by virtue of section 21(a) to give evidence at the instance of the prosecution, or be compellable by virtue of section 22, 23 or 24 to give evidence, unless the person concerned is not, or is no longer, liable to be convicted at the trial as a result of pleading guilty or for any other reason.

26. Right to marital privacy

Nothing in this Part shall affect any right of a spouse or former spouse in respect of marital privacy.

Index

All references are to *paragraph* numbers.